FLAVIUS JOSEPHUS

VOLUME 5

JUDEAN ANTIQUITIES BOOKS 8-10

FLAVIUS JOSEPHUS

TRANSLATION AND COMMENTARY

EDITED BY

STEVE MASON

VOLUME 5

JUDEAN ANTIQUITIES BOOKS 8-10

TRANSLATION AND COMMENTARY

BY

CHRISTOPHER T. BEGG & PAUL SPILSBURY

BRILL
LEIDEN · BOSTON
2005

MT

This book is printed on acid-free paper.

Library of Congress Cataloging-in-Publication Data

Josephus, Flavius.
 [Antiquitates Judaicae. Liber 8-10. English]
 Flavius Josephus ; Judean antiquities books 8-10 / translation and commentary by
Christopher Begg and Paul Spilsbury.
   p. cm.
 Originally published as v. 5 of Flavius Josephus, translation and commentary
(Leiden ; Boston : Brill, 2001)
 Includes bibliographical references and index.
 ISBN 90-04-11786-5 (alk. paper)
  1. Jews—History—1200-953 B.C. 2. Bible. O.T. Joshua—History of Biblical
events—Early works to 1800. 3. Bible. O.T. Judges—History of Biblical events—Early
works to 1800. 4. Bible. O.T. Samuel—History of Biblical events—Early works to 1800. 5.
Josephus, Flavius. Antiquitates Judaicae. Liber 8-10. I. Begg, Christopher. II. Spilsbury,
Paul. III. Title.

DS121.55.J6713 2004
933—dc22

2005042008

ISBN 90 04 11786 5

PRINTED IN THE NETHERLANDS

3/13/08

For

Joseph and Teresa Begg
for their many years of
interest and support

&

Professor William Horbury,
a scholar of excellent spirit (Dan 5:12)

CONTENTS

SERIES PREFACE

THE BRILL JOSEPHUS PROJECT

Titus (?) Flavius Josephus (37–ca. 100 CE) was born Joseph son of Mattathyahu, a priestly aristocrat in Judea. During the early stages of the war against Rome (66-74 CE), he found himself leading a part of the defense in Galilee, but by the spring of 67, his territory overrun, he had surrendered under circumstances that would furnish grounds for endless accusation. Taken to Rome by the Flavian conquerors, he spent the balance of his life writing about the war, Judean history and culture, and his own career. He composed four works in thirty volumes.

If Josephus boasts about the unique importance of his work (*War* 1.1-3; *Ant.* 1.1-4) in the fashion of ancient historians, few of his modern readers could disagree with him. By the accidents of history, his narratives have become the indispensable source for all scholarly study of Judea from about 200 BCE to 75 CE. Our analysis of other texts and of the physical remains unearthed by archaeology must occur in dialogue with Josephus' story, for it is the only comprehensive and connected account of the period.

Although Josephus' name has been known continuously through nearly two millennia, and he has been cited extensively in support of any number of agendas, his writings have not always been valued as compositions. Readers have tended to look beyond them to the underlying historical facts or to Josephus' sources. Concentrated study in the standard academic forms—journals, scholarly seminars, or indeed commentaries devoted to Josephus—were lacking. The past two decades, however, have witnessed the birth and rapid growth of "Josephus studies" in the proper sense. Signs of the new environment include all of the vehicles and tools that were absent before, as well as K. H. Rengstorf's *Complete Concordance* (1983), Louis Feldman's annotated bibliographies, and now a proliferation of Josephus-related dissertations. The time is right, therefore, for the first comprehensive English commentary to Josephus.

The commentary format is ancient, and even in antiquity commentators differed in their aims and methods. Philo's goals were not those of the author of Qumran's *Commentary on Nahum* or of the Church Father Origen. In order to assist the reader of this series, the Brill Project team would like to explain our general aims and principles. Our most basic premise is that we do not intend to provide the last word: an exhaustive exegesis of this rich corpus. Rather, since no commentary yet exists in English, we hope simply to provide a resource that will serve as an invitation to further exploration.

Although we began with the mandate to prepare a commentary alone, we soon realized that a new translation would also be helpful. Keeping another existing translation at hand would have been cumbersome for the reader. And since we must comment on particular Greek words and phrases, we would have been implicitly challenging such existing translations at every turn. Given that we needed to prepare a working translation for the commentary in any case, it seemed wisest to include it with the commentary as an efficient point of reference. A few words about the translation, then, are in order.

Granted that every translation is an interpretation, one can still imagine a spectrum of options. For example, the translator may set out to follow the contours of the original language more expressly or to place greater emphasis on idiomatic phrasing in the target language. There is much to be said for both of these options and for each interim stop in the spectrum. Accuracy is not necessarily a criterion in such choices, for one might gain precision in one respect (e.g., for a single word or form) only at the cost of accuracy elsewhere (e.g., in the sentence). Homer's epic poems provide a famous example of the problem: Does one render them in English dactylic hexameter, in looser verse, or even in prose to better convey the sense? One simply needs to make choices.

In our case, the course was suggested by the constraints of the commentary. If we were preparing a stand-alone translation for independent reading, we might have made other choices. And certainly if Josephus had been an Athenian poet, other considerations might have weighed more heavily. But Greek was his second or third language. His narratives are not great literature, and they vary in quality considerably from one part to another. Since the commentary bases itself upon his particular Greek words and phrases, it seemed necessary in this case that we produce a translation to reflect the patterns of the Greek as closely as possible. We can perhaps tolerate somewhat less clarity in the translation itself, where the Greek is ambiguous, because we intend it to be read with the commentary.

We happily confess our admiration for the Loeb translation, which has been the standard for some time, begun by Henry St. John Thackeray in the 1920s and completed by our colleague on the Brill Project (responsible for *Ant.* 1-4) Louis H. Feldman in 1965. For us to undertake a new translation implies no criticism of the Loeb in its context. The older sections of it are somewhat dated now but it still reads well, often brilliantly.

The chief problem with the Loeb for our purpose is only that it does not suit the needs of the commentator. Like most translations, it makes idiomatic English the highest virtue. It renders terms that Josephus frequently uses by different English equivalents for variety's sake; it often injects explanatory items to enhance the narrative flow; it collapses two or more Greek clauses into a single English clause; it alters the parts of speech with considerable freedom; and it tends to homogenize Josephus' changing style to a single, elevated English level. Since we have undertaken to annotate words and phrases, however, we have required a different sort of foundation. Our goal has been to render individual Greek words with as much consistency as the context will allow, to preserve the parts of speech, letting adjectives be adjectives and participles be participles, to preserve phrases and clauses intact, and thus to reflect something of the particular stylistic level and tone of each section.

Needless to say, even a determined literalness must yield to the ultimate commandment of basic readability in English. Cases in which we have relinquished any effort to represent the Greek precisely include Josephus' preference for serial aorist-participle clauses. Given the frequency of complicated sentences in Josephus, as among most of his contemporaries, we have dealt quite freely with such clauses. We have often broken a series

into separate sentences and also varied the translation of the form, thus: "After X had done Y," "When [or Once] X had occurred," and so on. Again, although in a very few cases Josephus' "historical present" may find a passable parallel in colloquial English, we have generally substituted a past tense. Thus we have not pursued literalness at all costs, but have sought it where it seemed feasible.

In the case of Josephus' personal names, we have used the familiar English equivalent where it is close to his Greek form. Where his version differs significantly from the one familiar to Western readers, or where he varies his form within the same narrative, we have represented his Greek spelling in Roman characters. That is because his unusual forms may be of interest to some readers. In such cases we have supplied the familiar English equivalent in square brackets within the text or in a footnote. Similarly, we keep Josephus' units of measurement and titles, giving modern equivalents in the notes.

We do not pretend that this effort at literalness is always more accurate than an ostensibly freer rendering, since translation is such a complex phenomenon. Further, we have not always been able to realize our aims. Ultimately, the reader who cares deeply about the Greek text will want to study Greek. But we have endeavored to provide a translation that permits us to discuss what is happening in the Greek with all of its problems.

The commentary aims at a balance between what one might, for convenience, call historical and literary issues. "Literary" here would include matters most pertinent to the interpretation of the text itself. "Historical" would cover matters related to the hypothetical reconstruction of a reality outside the text. For example: How Josephus presented the causes of the war against Rome is a literary problem, whereas recovering the actual causes of the war is the task of historical reconstruction. Or, understanding Josephus' Essenes is a matter for the interpreter, whereas reconstructing the real Essenes and their possible relationship to Qumran is for the historian—perhaps the same person, but wearing a different hat. These are not hermetically sealed operations, of course, but some such classification helps us to remain aware of the various interests of our readers.

To assist the reader who is interested in recovering some sense of what Josephus might have expected his first audience to understand, we have tried to observe some ways in which each part of his narrative relates to the whole. We point out apparently charged words and phrases in the narratives, which may also occur in such significant contexts as the prologues, speeches, and editorial asides. We look for parallels in some of the famous texts of the time, whether philosophical, historical, or dramatic, and whether Greco-Roman, Jewish, or Christian. We observe set pieces (*topoi*) and other rhetorical effects. Even apparently mundane but habitual features of Josephus' language and style are noted. Where puzzling language appears, we discuss possible explanations: rhetorical artifice, multiple editions, unassimilated vestiges of sources, the influence of a literary collaborator, and manuscript corruption.

A basic literary problem is the content of the text itself. Although we decided against preparing a new Greek edition as part of the project, we have paid close attention to textual problems in translation and commentary. The translation renders, essentially, Benedictus Niese's *editio maior*, since it remains the standard complete text with apparatus. But we have tried to take note of both the significant variants in Niese's own critical apparatus and other modern reconstructions where they are available. These include: the Loeb Greek text, the Michel-Bauernfeind edition of the *Judean War*, the current Münster project directed by Folker Siegert for Josephus's later works, and the ongoing French project led by Étienne Nodet. Niese's reconstructed text in the *editio maior* is famously conservative, and we have felt no particular loyalty to it where these others have proposed better readings.

Under the "historical" rubric fall a variety of subcategories. Most important perhaps are the impressive archaeological finds of recent decades in places mentioned by Josephus: building sites, coins, pottery, implements, inscriptions, and other items of material culture. Reading his stories of Masada or Herodium or Gamala is greatly enriched by observation of these newly identified sites, while in return, his narrative throws light on the history of those places. The commentary attempts to include systematic reference to the relevant archaeology. Other major historical categories include the problems of Josephus' own biography, his social context in Rome, and the historical reconstruction of persons, places, events, and social conditions mentioned by him. These issues can

only be explored by reference to outside texts and physical evidence. Alongside questions of interpretation, therefore, we routinely discuss such problems as they appear in particular passages.

In preparing a commentary on such a vast corpus, it is a challenge to achieve proportion. Some stretches of narrative naturally call for more comment than others, and yet the aesthetics of publication requires a measure of balance. We have attempted to maintain both flexibility and a broad consistency by aiming at a ratio between 4:1 and 8:1 of commentary to primary text. This commitment to a degree of symmetry (cf. *Ant.* 1.7!) has required us to avoid too-lengthy discussion of famous passages, such as those on Jesus or the Essenes, while giving due attention to easily neglected sections.

A different kind of challenge is posed by the coming together of ten independent scholars for such a collegial enterprise. To balance individual vision with the shared mission, we have employed several mechanisms. First is simply our common mandate: Having joined together to produce a balanced commentary, we must each extend ourselves to consider questions that we might not have pursued in other publishing contexts. Second, each completed assignment is carefully read by two experts who are not part of the core team, but who assist us in maintaining overall compliance with our goals. Third, each assignment is examined by the same general editor, who encourages overall consistency. Finally, for the *War* and *Antiquities* we use a system of double introductions: the general editor introduces each of Josephus' major works, to provide a coherent context for each segment; then each principal contributor also introduces his own assignment, highlighting the particular issues arising in that section. The *Life* and *Against Apion* have only one introduction each, however, because in those cases the individual assignment corresponds to the entire work.

Thus uniformity is not among our goals. Committees do not create good translations or commentaries. We have striven rather for an appropriate balance between overall coherence and individual scholarly insight—the animating principle of humanistic scholarship. The simple Greek word *Ioudaios* affords an example of the diversity among us. Scholars in general differ as to whether the English "Judean" or "Jew" comes closest to what an ancient Greek or Roman heard in this word, and our team members reflect that difference. Some of us have opted for "Judean" as a standard; some use both terms, depending upon the immediate context; and others use "Jew" almost exclusively. For the modern translator, as for Josephus himself, any particular phrase is part of an integrated world of discourse; to coerce agreement on any such point would violate that world. We hope that our readers will benefit from the range of expertise and perspective represented in these volumes.

It remains for the team members to thank some central players in the creation of this work, *amici* in scholarship whose names do not otherwise appear. First, many scholars in Josephan studies and related fields have offered encouragement at every step. Though we cannot name them all, we must express our debt to those who are reading our work in progress, without thereby implicating them in its faults: Honora Howell Chapman, David M. Goldenberg, Erich Gruen, Gohei Hata, Donna Runnalls, and Pieter van der Horst.

Second, we are grateful to the editorial staff at Brill for initiating this project and seeing it through so professionally. In the early years, Elisabeth Erdman, Elisabeth Venekamp, Job Lisman, and Sam Bruinsma provided constant encouragement as the first volumes appeared,

even as we announced unavoidable delays with much of the publishing schedule. More recently, Loes Schouten, Jan-Peter Wissink, Anita Roodnat, and Ivo Romein have absorbed these delays with grace, working with us patiently, flexibly and with unflagging professionalism to ensure the success of this important project.

Finally, in addition to expressing the entire group's thanks to these fine representatives of a distinguished publishing house (not least in Josephus) I am pleased to record my personal gratitude to the various agencies and institutions that have made possible my work as editor and contributor, alongside other demands on my time. These include: York University, for a Faculty of Arts leave fellowship and then successful nomination as Canada Research Chair (from 2003), along with encouragement from various directions; the Social Sciences and Humanities Research Council of Canada (SSHRC) for funding throughout the project; the Killam Foundation of Canada, for a wonderful two-year leave fellowship in 2001-2003; and both All Souls College and Wolfson College for visiting fellowships in Oxford during the Killam leave.

Steve Mason, York University
General Editor, Brill Josephus Project

ACKNOWLEDGEMENTS

The Bible translation used in Christopher Begg's portion of this volume is the Revised Standard Version of the Bible, copyright by the Division of Christian Education of the National Council of the Churches of Christ in the United States of America. Used by permission. All rights reserved.

As I conclude this large and lengthy project, I am conscious of the thanks I owe to so many family members and friends. As representatives of my family, I wish to mention in particular my brother and sisterinlaw, Joseph and Teresa Begg (to whom I dedicate my portion of this volume) and my stepbrother Joseph Fantom, his wife Susan Hanna Fantom, and their beautiful children Hannah and Michael. Among my friends, my gratitude goes especially to three fellow priests, Rev. Msgr. Paul J. Langsfeld, Rev. Michael J. Murray, and Rev. Daniel B. Gallagher.

Christopher Begg

An undertaking such as the present one depends much on the labors of others. Throughout my work on Josephus's reworking of the Book of Daniel, I have relied heavily on Klaus Koch and Martin Rösel's very helpful *Polyglottensynopse zum Buch Daniel* (Neukirchener, 2000). Among previous commentators on this section of the *Judean Antiquities* none has done as much as Louis Feldman, for whose work I am very grateful. I have also leaned heavily on J.J. Collins's *Daniel: A Commentary on the Book of Daniel* (Hermeneia; Fortress, 1993). Many thanks go to John Barclay who very kindly sent me a pre-publication copy of his commentary for the present project on the Berosus material in *Against Apion*. My indebtedness to many other scholars is indicated in the notes and bibliography. The Bible translation used in my portion of this volume is the New Revised Standard Version, copyright by the Division of Christian Education of the National Council of the Churches of Christ in the United States of America. Used by permission. All rights reserved.

My work on this project began in earnest during a year of sabbatical leave provided by Alliance University College, for which I am very grateful indeed. Funding was provided by a research grant from the Social Sciences and Humanities Research Council of Canada (SSHRC). Without their generosity the work could never have been accomplished. I am also very grateful to the Leverhulme Trust (UK) for a fellowship that made it possible for my family and me to spend a wonderful year at the University of Wales in Lampeter. To the Theology and Religious Studies Department in Lampeter I also offer my heartfelt thanks for their generosity and collegial hospitality. Steve Mason's direction and input as editor have been invaluable. I am particularly grateful to him for his personal encouragement, as well as for his expert reading of the work and thoughtful interaction with it at every stage. My wife, Bronwyn, is a constant source of encouragement to me, for which I am deeply thankful. Finally, I wish to dedicate my portion of the present volume to Professor William Horbury of the University of Cambridge. As my doctoral supervisor in the early 90's he was my first guide into the world of Josephus's interpretation of the Bible. I benefited enormously both from his vast learning and from his generosity of spirit at that time, and ever since then he has continued to be a source of encouragement and assistance to me.

Paul Spilsbury

SIGLA

The sigla used for journals and monograph series, etc. are those prescribed in Alexander et al.: 1999. In addition, the following terms and signs are employed: The term "plus" refers to an element that is present in one biblical textual witness (e.g., the MT), but absent in another (e.g., the LXX). The > sign indicates that a particular textual element is absent in a given witness. An asterisk following a siglum (e.g., L*) calls attention to the fact that only some representatives of the textual family designated by that siglum exhibit the reading in question. Finaly, Roman (i.e. "a" and "b") and Greek (i.e. 'alpha' and 'beta') are used to indicate the component sense units and sub-units of biblical verses, e.g., Josh 1:1a'alpha'.

I. *Biblical Sigla*

A	Codex Alexandrinus of the LXX
B	Codex Vaticanus of the LXX
L	The Lucianic Manuscripts of the LXX
LXX	The (original) Greek Translation of the Hebrew Bible
MT	The Massoretic Text of the Hebrew Bible
OL	The Old Latin Translation of the Bible
Tg.	The Targum (Aramaic Translation of the Bible)
Vulg.	The Vulgate (Latin) Translation of the Bible
4QSam^a	A Samuel Manuscript from Qumran, cave 4
Θ	Theodotion's Greek Translation of the Hebrew Bible

II. *Josephan Sigla*

E	Epitome (10th-11th cents.)
Ed. pr.	*Editio princeps* (first printed edition, 1544)
Exc	Excerpta Peiresciana (10th cent.)
Lat	Latin translation (original, 6th cent.)
Lau	Codex Laurentianus (14th cent.)
M	Codex Marcianus (Venetus) (13th cent.)
O	Codex Oxoniensis (15th cent.)
P	Codex Parisinus G 1419 (11th cent.)
R	Codex Regius Parisinus (14th cent.)
S	Codex Vindobonensis (11th cent.)
V	Codex Vaticanus (13th-14th cents.)
Zon	Zonaras' *Chronicon* (12th cent.)

JOSEPHUS, *JUDEAN ANTIQUITIES*

BOOK EIGHT

(1.1) 1 In the volume before this one, then, we have explained about David, about his virtue and his being the cause of many good things for his compatriots: having succeeded in wars and battles, he died in old age.[1] **2** His son Solomon, who was still a youth, assumed the kingship; David had appointed him master of the people according to the will of God while he was still alive. Once he sat upon the throne, the whole mob—as is customary with a king when he begins—expressed the wish that affairs would turn out well for him and that his leadership might reach old age smoothly and happily in every respect.[2]

Solomon's accession

(1.2) 3 Now Adonias, who while his father was still living had attempted to obtain the rule,[3] came to Bersabe [Bathsheba], the mother of the king, and greeted her in a friendly way.[4] When she inquired whether he had come to her on account of some need and directed him to disclose this so that she might show herself well-disposed,[5] he began to say **4** that whereas, as she knew, the kingship was intended to be his, both in virtue of his age and the intention of the crowd, it had been transferred to her son Solomon according to the plan of God.[6] He, for his part, cherished and loved slavery under him and was delighted with the present state of affairs.[7] **5** He asked her, therefore, to be of service to him with his brother and convince him to give him Abisake, who had slept beside their father, in marriage, for, since their father had not approached her due to his age, she still remained a virgin.[8] **6** Bersabe promised that she would be of service enthusiastically and bring about the marriage, both because the king would grant him whatever he desired and because of her earnestly asking.[9] Adonias went away, confident about the marriage,[10] while Solomon's mother imme-

Adonijah asks Bathsheba's intercession with Solomon

---

[1] With this transitional phrase Josephus sums up the content of *Antiquities* Book 7, which is focussed on the career of David from the death of Saul to his own demise.

[2] On David's appointment of Solomon, see *Ant.* 7.357-358.

[3] This cross reference to Adonijah's attempted seizure of power as recounted in *Ant.* 7.345-346 takes the place of the qualification of him as "son of Haggith" in 1 Kgs 2:13.

[4] Josephus' reference to Adonijah's "greeting" the queen mother seems to reflect the plus of LXX BL 1 Kgs 2:13a, where he not only comes to her as in MT, but also "does her homage."

[5] This is Josephus' compressed version of the double opening exchange between Adonijah and Bathsheba of 1 Kgs 2:13b-14, in which the latter asks the former whether he has come "peaceably" and is told that he has. Adonijah then states that he has something to say to Bathsheba, who enjoins him to speak. Josephus' rendition highlights Bathsheba's control of the proceedings—she alone speaks as the conversation begins.

[6] See 1 Kgs 2:15. Josephus supplies the reference to

Adonijah's age as a further reason why the kingship should have been his. Adonijah's acknowledgement about the kingship's transfer to Solomon "according to the plan of God" recalls Josephus' editorial statement that David appointed Solomon his successor "according to will of God" in 8.2.

[7] Josephus appends this statement by Adonijah concerning his own (purported) stance towards Solomon's rule. The statement functions as an (ironic-sounding) *captatio benevolentiae* on Adonijah's part.

[8] See 1 Kgs 2:16-17. Josephus omits mention of Bathsheba's granting (v. 16b) Adonijah' petition (v. 16a) to make a request of her. Conversely, he expands on the latter's reference to "Abishag" with details about her relationship with David derived from *Ant.* 7.344 (= 1 Kgs 1:3-4).

[9] Josephus elaborates on Bathsheba's promise to "speak to" David (1 Kgs 2:18) with a double assertion as to why she is confident that her mission will be successful. He thereby intensifies readers' surprise at Solomon's subsequent, negative reaction.

[10] This added notice, like Bathsheba's preceding assurances (see previous note), serves to make Solomon's ultimate refusal all the more a surprise.

diately rushed to her son to speak to him about those things that she had promised Adonias when he asked her.[11]

Solomon rebufs Bathsheba

7 Her son advanced to meet her and embraced her;[12] then he accompanied her to the building in which the royal throne was situated.[13] He took his seat and directed that another be placed on his right for his mother. Once Bersabe was seated,[14] she said: "grant me, my child, the one favor I request; do not behave stubbornly and disagreeably[15] by refusing."[16]

8 Solomon directed her to issue her order—for whatever it might be, he would award it to his mother.[17] He also added a certain word of reproach because she had not already spoken in the well-founded hope of obtaining that which she was requesting him to do, but was apprehensive of a refusal.[18] She therefore appealed to him to give the virgin Abisake to his brother Adonias in marriage.

(1.3) 9 Made wrathful by her word, the king sent his mother away,[19] saying that Adonias was striving after greater things[20] and that he was surprised that she did not appeal to him to yield also the kingship to him, who was older than himself, when requesting Abisake's marriage to one who had powerful friends in the general Joab

Adonijah executed

and the priest Abiathar.[21] At that, dispatching Banai, who was over the bodyguards, he ordered him to kill his brother Adonias.[22]

Abiathar dismissed

10 Calling the priest Abiathar, he said: "[Although you deserve] death, your having suffered along with my father and borne the ark with him delivers you and yours.[23] This, though, is the punishment I am imposing on you for having sided with Adonias and sympathized with him: you are neither to remain here nor be in my presence at all.[24] Go rather to your ancestral estate[25] and live on among your fields until you die,

---

[11] In this rendering of 1 Kgs 2:19aα Josephus underscores the alacrity of Bathsheba's approach to her son.

[12] In MT 1 Kgs 2:19aβ Solomon "pays homage to" his mother, while in LXX BL he "kisses" her.

[13] Josephus adds the reference to the site of the upcoming exchange between mother and son. The notice presupposes the existence of a royal throne (and of a structure housing this), which, however, will only be constructed subsequently; see 8.140.

[14] See 1 Kgs 2:19b.

[15] Greek: δύσκολος (καὶ) σκυθρωπός. This collocation occurs only here in Josephus.

[16] Josephus elaborates on Bathsheba's opening announcement that she has a request to make (1 Kgs 2:20a) with mention of the negative light in which Solomon would put himself by rejecting it.

[17] See 1 Kgs 2:20b. Josephus underscores Solomon's submissiveness—for the moment—by having him refer to Bathsheba's request as an "order."

[18] With this appended statement by the king, Josephus continues to "set up" both the story's other characters and its readers for the surprise of Solomon's eventual, vehement rejection of Bathsheba's request.

[19] Josephus prefaces his version of Solomon's verbal response (// 1 Kgs 2:22) to his mother's request (2:21) with mention of the king's emotional response to her words and of his dismissal of Bathsheba. He thereby highlights the vehemence of the royal refusal

and the reversal of the expectations he has created about how Solomon would react to Bathsheba's petition.

[20] This initial affirmation takes the place of Solomon's opening question to Bathsheba in 1 Kgs 2:22a: "why do you ask Abishag… for Adonijah?" Compare the characterization of Cataline as one who *nimis alta semper cupiebat* ("he always desired things that were too lofty") in Sallust, *Bel. Cat.* 5.

[21] See 1 Kgs 2:22b. In having Solomon call Joab by his title ("general"), Josephus follows the plus of LXX BL, where he is designated as "commander in chief and friend." In contrast to both MT and LXX, Josephus leaves aside the qualification of Joab as "son of Zeruiah." On Adonijah's 2 main supporters as mentioned by Solomon here, see *Ant.* 7.346.

[22] Josephus transposes into a command by the king the notice of 1 Kgs 2:25 that Benaiah, having been "sent" by Solomon, "struck" Adonijah so that he died. He leaves aside the double oath concerning his intention of executing Adonijah pronounced by Solomon in 2:23-24. He thereby "keeps God out of" the king's bloody initiative.

[23] See 1 Kgs 2:26aβb. Josephus adds Solomon's assurance of safety also for Abiathar's household, while holding over to a later point his initial directive (2:26aα) that the priest retire to his estate.

[24] Josephus appends this sequence to the biblical Solomon's word to Abiathar (1 Kgs 2:26). By means of

as one who has offended and who may no longer justly continue in office."[26]

11 Thus the house of Ithamar was dismissed from the high priestly honor for the above-mentioned cause,[27] as God had predicted to Helei [Eli] the ancestor of Abiathar,[28] while [the high priesthood] was transferred to the family of Phinees with Sadok.[29] **12** Those of the family of Phinees had lived as private persons during the time in which the high priesthood was passed down in the house of Ithamar, of whom Helei [Eli] was the first to assume [the office].[30] These were: Bokias the son of the high priest Iesous,[31] Jotham, the former's son,[32] Maraioth[33] son of Jotham, Arophai[34] son of Maraioth, Achitob,[35] son of Arophai, and Sadok, son of Achitob, who was the first [of his family] to become high priest during David's reign.[36]

The high priest's succession

(1.4) 13 When the general Joab heard of the elimination of Adonias, he became very anxious, for he was rather more a friend of his than of King Solomon.[37] Not unreasonably suspecting that he was in danger from Solomon because of his loyalty to Adonias, he fled for refuge to the altar.[38] He supposed that he would thus procure safety for himself, given the king's piety towards God.[39]

Joab executed

14 But when some persons reported Joab's plan to him, Solomon dispatched Banai, directing him to forcibly remove Joab and bring him as a defendant to the law court.[40] Joab, however, said that he would not leave the sacred site and would

---

it he provides a rationale for the king's opening assertion that the priest is indeed "worthy of death," just as he spells out the negative implications of Abiathar's dismissal that the king is about to impose.

[25] This is Josephus' delayed use of Solomon's initial word to Abiathar in 1 Kgs 2:26aα ("go to Anathoth, to your estate"), from which he omits the site's name.

[26] This conclusion to Solomon's word to Abiathar is an expansion of the king's discourse in 1 Kgs 2:26, offering an additional motivation for the priest's dismissal and a further clarification of its negative implications for Abiathar.

[27] Josephus elaborates on the narrative remark of 1 Kgs 2:27a concerning the dismissal of Abiathar from his priestly position with an allusion to his link with Ithamar (whose line according to *Ant.* 5.361-362 held the high priesthood from Eli down to the time of Solomon) and to the reason for his dismissal (a point already highlighted in Solomon's preceding word to Abiathar).

[28] See 1 Kgs 2:27b, where there is a cross-reference to the divine judgments pronounced against Eli's line in 1 Sam 2:35-36 and 3:12-14 (// *Ant.* 5.350). In making Eli Abiathar's "ancestor" Josephus bases himself on the genealogical data of 1 Sam 14:3 and 22:20.

[29] On Zadok's appurtenance to the line of Phineas, see *Ant.* 7.110, which itself draws on the genealogy given in 1 Chr 5:30-34 (MT; Eng. 6:4-8).

[30] This notice recapitulates Josephus' statement concerning the accession of Eli to the high priesthood in *Ant.* 5.361-362.

[31] Compare *Ant.* 5.362, where "Bokki" (= "Bukki," 1 Chr 5:31 [MT; Eng. 6:5]) is called the son of

"Abiezer" (= "Abishua," 1 Chr 5:30 [MT; Eng. 6:4]). Overall, the names of Zadok's ancestors from Phineas on down given by Josephus in 8.12 differ markedly from those listed both in 1 Chr 5:30-34 (MT; Eng. 6:4-8) and his own *Ant.* 5.362.

[32] Compare *Ant.* 5.362, where the son of "Bokki" is named "Ozis" (= "Uzzi," 1 Chr 5:31 [MT; Eng. 6:5]).

[33] This name reflects the "Meraioth" of 1 Chr 5:32 (MT; Eng. 6:6). Josephus has no equivalent to the name that intervenes between "Uzzi" and "Meraioth" in 5:32 (MT; Eng. 6:6), i.e. "Zerahiah."

[34] The son of "Meraioth" is called "Amariah" in 1 Chr 5:33 (MT; Eng. 6:7).

[35] This name corresponds to that of Zadok's father, i.e. "Ahitub" in 1 Chr 5:34 (MT; Eng. 6:8).

[36] On David's designation of Zadok as high priest along with Abiathar, see *Ant.* 7.110.

[37] See 1 Kgs 2:28a, to which Josephus adds explicit mention of Joab's "anxiety." In speaking of Joab's not having been a (close) friend of *Solomon*, he follows the reading of LXX L as against MT and LXX B, which mention Joab's non-support for *Absalom*.

[38] See 1 Kgs 2:28b. Josephus adds the reference to Joab's "suspicion," while omitting the biblical references to the "tent of the Lord" as the site of the altar to which he flees and to the "horns of the altar" that he grasps.

[39] This reference to Joab's state of mind is a Josephan addition, one reflecting favorably on Solomon, who, already at the outset of his reign, enjoys a reputation for piety.

[40] In 1 Kgs 2:29 Solomon simply instructs Benaiah to go and strike Joab down. Josephus' version presents

die there rather than in another spot.[41] **15** When Banai disclosed his answer to the king, Solomon ordered him to cut off his head there in accord with his wish,[42] exacting this judgment on behalf of the two generals whom Joab had wickedly killed.[43] He was, however, to bury the body so that his offenses would never depart from Joab's family, while he [Solomon] himself and his father would be guiltless of his death.[44] **16** Once he had done as directed,[45] Banai was appointed general of the entire force, just as the king made Sadok the sole high priest in place of Abiathar, whom he had deposed.[46]

Beniah and Sadok appointed

(1.5) 17 [Solomon] now commanded Soumouis[47] to build a house and to remain in Hierosolyma, staying with himself; he was not authorized to cross the Kedron [Kidron] brook. If he disobeyed these [directives], death would be the penalty.[48] Solomon likewise compelled him, by means of a severe threat, to take oaths.[49]

Shimei executed

18 Soumouis stated that he rejoiced over the things Solomon had ordered him and likewise swore that he would do these.[50] He then left his ancestral estate and made his residence in Hierosolyma.[51] But when, after three years had passed, he heard that two of his slaves had run away from him and were in Gitta,[52] he rushed after those domestics.

---

a less arbitrary king who, first of all, thinks of giving Joab a trial. Compare *Ant.* 6.215, where Josephus, in his reworking of 1 Sam 19:11, adds a reference to Saul's intention of having David appear before "the law court" and there be condemned to death.

[41] In 1 Kgs 2:30abα Joab's refusal is preceded by Benaiah's arrival at the "tent of the Lord" and his summons to the fugitive in the king's name that he "come forth."

[42] See 1 Kgs 2:30bβ-31a. In having the king direct his henchman to "behead" Joab, Josephus makes more specific the biblical Solomon's injunction that Benaiah "strike him down."

[43] 1 Kgs 2:32b supplies the names of the 2 figures, i.e. Abner and Amasa (who are named by the dying David in his address to Solomon calling on him to avenge their murders in *Ant.* 7.386// 1 Kgs 2:5). For Josephus' previous condemnations of Joab's murder of the 2 rival commanders, see *Ant.* 7.31-38 (Abner) and 7.284-285 (Amasa). Josephus omits Solomon's preceding declaration (2:32a) that the Lord will bring Joab's "bloody deeds upon his own head" as well as his affirmation that it was without David's knowledge that Joab killed his military rivals.

[44] Having utilized the content of 1 Kgs 2:32 in what precedes (see previous note), Josephus here combines and rearranges elements of Solomon's additional words to Benaiah in 1 Kgs 2:31 and 33, citing these in the following order: vv. 31bα (Joab's burial), 33a (the everlasting guilt of Joab's house), and 31bβ (cf. 33b) (the definitive exculpation of David's line).

[45] This phrase summarizes the notices on the killing of Joab by Benaiah and the former's burial in 1 Kgs 2:34. Josephus leaves aside the biblical detail about Joab's being "buried in his own house in the wilderness."

[46] See 1 Kgs 2:35. Josephus has no equivalent to the long plus (2:35[a-o]), consisting of notices drawn from different portions of the Solomon story of 1 Kings, which follows 2:35 in LXX BL. On Josephus' predominant use of a form of 1 Kings 1-11 more similar to MT than to LXX for his Solomon story in 8.1-211, see Rahlfs 1911: 92-97.

[47] MT 1 Kgs 2:36 שמעי (Eng.: "Shimei"); LXX Σεμεεί; Josephus Σουμούις. In *Ant.* 7.207 David's curser is called "Samouis," in 7.388 "Soumouis" (as here in 8.17). With his admonition to Shimei at this juncture Solomon begins acting on David's directive to him in 7.388 that he find a way of punishing the former for the abuse he had heaped on the king during his flight from Absalom (see 7.207-210).

[48] See 1 Kgs 2:36b-37. Josephus leaves aside the figurative language with which Solomon's speech to Shimei concludes in v. 37: "your blood shall be upon your own head."

[49] Josephus' reference to Solomon's "adjuring" Shimei reflects the plus at the end of LXX BL 1 Kgs 2:37. In MT, Shimei's "swearing" is mentioned for the first time in 2:42, where Solomon, confronting the culprit, reminds him that he had made him "swear by the Lord."

[50] See 1 Kgs 2:38a. Josephus adds the reference to Shimei's "swearing" to do as Solomon had directed him, this corresponding to the latter's compelling him "to take oaths" in what precedes.

[51] The reference to Shimei's move is Josephus' addition to the notice on his extended residence in Jerusalem of 1 Kgs 2:38b.

[52] Compare 1 Kgs 2:39aβ, where Shimei's 2 slaves flee to Achish (MT LXX L; Amesa, LXX B), son of Maacah, king of Gath (LXX BL: Geth).

19 Upon his return with them,[53] the king ascertained that he had despised his commands and, what was worse, had given no thought to his divine oaths. He took this badly[54] and, having called him, said: "Did you not swear not to leave me nor to go out from this city to another?[55] You will then not elude the judgment for perjury.[56] **20** Not only that, but I shall also punish you for those things with which you, in your vileness, outraged my father during his flight,[57] that you may know that evildoers gain nothing by not undergoing judgment right away for their misdeeds. Rather, throughout the entire time when they suppose themselves secure and to have suffered nothing, their punishment increases and becomes worse than it would have been had they immediately undergone it."[58] He then directed Banai to kill Soumouis.[59]

(2.1) 21 With Solomon's kingship now already established and his enemies punished, he married the daughter of Pharaoh, the king of the Egyptians.[60] He constructed the walls of Hierosolyma to [make them] larger and more solid than they were before.[61] For the rest, he conducted affairs in great peace; nor was he impeded by his youth from justice and the observance of the laws and the memory of that which his dying father had commanded him.[62] Instead, he performed everything with much conscientiousness, just like those who are advanced in years and mature in their thinking.[63]

Solomon's marriage and administration

---

[53] Josephus compresses the circumstantial sequence concerning Shimei's initiatives regarding his runaway slaves of 1 Kgs 2:39b-40.

[54] Josephus elaborates on the reference to Solomon's hearing of Shimei's deed in 1 Kgs 2:41 with mention of the king's inner reaction to what he learns. The added reference to Shimei's violation of his "oaths" picks up on the (also added) mention of his being made to swear in 8.17-18.

[55] Josephus compresses Solomon's opening words to Shimei in 1 Kgs 2:42-43, where he 1st (v. 42) reminds the latter of his having been adjured and warned about the consequences of his leaving Jerusalem and of Shimei's assent, and then (v. 43) asks why he has violated his oath to the Lord and the king's commandment.

[56] This statement, underscoring the wrongfulness of Shimei's oath-breaking, lacks an explicit equivalent in Solomon's words to him in 1 Kgs 2:42-45.

[57] Compare 1 Kgs 2:44, where Solomon avers that Shimei knows in his heart all the evil he did to David and states that the Lord will bring this evil upon the miscreant's head. In Josephus' rendering, it is Solomon himself, rather than the Lord, who will effect Shimei's punishment. Josephus describes Shimei's verbal abusing of David in *Ant.* 7.207-210.

[58] This extended reflection on evildoers' not benefitting from the postponement of their punishment has no equivalent in Solomon's words to Shimei of 1 Kgs 2:42-45. It takes the place of Solomon's closing affirmation (1 Kgs 2:45) that he—in contrast to Shimei—will be "blessed," while David's throne will be established forever. Josephus' omission of this statement might reflect the fact that its claims for Solomon

personally and for the house of David overall did not prove true in the long run: Solomon ended up being condemned by God, while David's dynasty was eventually deposed.

[59] Josephus compresses 1 Kgs 2:46a, which mentions not only Solomon's order to Benaiah, but also the latter's actual "striking" of Shimei so that he dies.

[60] See MT 1 Kgs 2:46b-3:1aα. This sequence is lacking in LXX BL, which instead present a long plus (2:46ᵃ⁻ˡ), made up of items found elsewhere in the Solomon story of 1 Kings, to which Josephus has no equivalent. Josephus adds the reference to the punishment of Solomon's enemies, which sums up his foregoing account of the king's moves against Adonijah, Abiathar, Joab, and Shimei in 8.9-20.

[61] Cf. the reference to Solomon's (later) building of the "wall around Jerusalem" in MT 1 Kgs 3:1bβ. Josephus leaves aside the content of 3:1aβbα, i.e. Solomon's placing his Egyptian wife in "the city of David" until he finished building his palace and the temple—constructions that he will relate only subsequently. In speaking of Solomon's enhancing the strength of Jerusalem's already existing wall—rather than simply "building" that wall as in 1 Kgs 3:1bβ— Josephus takes into account his earlier mention (see *Ant.* 7.66) of David's encircling the combined citadel and lower city of Jerusalem with a wall.

[62] David's deathbed instructions to Solomon are recorded by Josephus in *Ant.* 7.383-388 on the basis of 1 Kgs 2:1-9.

[63] This encomium for the youthful Solomon and his precocious maturity elaborates on the mention of the king's "walking in the statutes of David his father" in 1

22 He decided to go to Gibron[64] to offer sacrifice to God[65] on the bronze altar that Moyses had constructed.[66] He offered as holocausts victims, numbering 1,000.[67] In doing this, he seems to have greatly honored God, for the Deity appeared to him in a dream that night[68] and directed him to request, in return for his piety, whatever gifts he might bestow upon him.[69]

23 Solomon, for his part, requested God to bestow those best and greatest things that are most pleasing to God and most advantageous for a person to receive.[70] For he did not ask him to confer on himself gold or silver or other riches as a person or a youth [might do] (these things are, so to speak, supposed by the majority to be the only ones worthy of attention and [of being] God's gifts).[71] He rather said: "Give me, O Master, an upright mind and a good intellect by which, once I have received them, I may judge the people in accordance with truth and what is just."[72]

24 God was pleased at these requests,[73] and promised to give him all those other things he had not mentioned, namely wealth, glory, and victory over his enemies, in addition to his choice, and above all a sagacity and wisdom[74] such as no other

---

Kgs 3:3aβ. As Feldman (1998: 577) points out, Josephus' stress on Solomon's precociousness has a counterpart in his characterization of both Moses and Josiah. Josephus lacks an equivalent to the notices about the people and Solomon himself worshipping on the "high places" of 1 Kgs 3:2 and 3b, respectively. He likewise leaves aside the statement of 1 Kgs 3:3aα ("Solomon loved the Lord").

[64] MT (1 Kgs 3:4) גבעון (Eng.: "Gibeon"); LXX BL Γαβαών; Josephus Γιβρών (Schalit *s.v.* reads Γαβαών here; the codices SP and Lat have "Hebron"). Like 1 Kgs 3:4, Josephus depicts Solomon's going to the site as a private pilgrimage, whereas in 2 Chr 1:2-3a he is accompanied by the entire Israelite leadership. On Josephus' account of Solomon's dream at the site in relation to its biblical parallels, 1 Kgs 3:4-15// 2 Chr 1:2-13, see Begg 1996a: 688-95 and Gnuse 1996: 174-6.

[65] Josephus lacks an equivalent to either of the alternative "motivations" given in the biblical accounts for Solomon's going precisely to "Gibeon" to offer his sacrifice, i.e. "for that was the great high place" (1 Kgs 3:4aβ, MT; compare LXX BL: "for it was high and great") versus "for the tent of meeting which Moses. had made was there" (2 Chr 1:3b).

[66] Josephus draws his mention of the Mosaic bronze altar from 2 Chr 1:5 (no parallel in 1 Kgs 3:4-15), while leaving aside the Chronicler's further details concerning the object (its construction by Bezalel and its having been placed before the "tabernacle"). He does reproduce the specifications for this altar from Exod 27:1-8; 38:1-7 in *Ant.* 3.149.

[67] This figure for Solomon's victims agrees with that given in 1 Kgs 3:4b// 2 Chr 1:6b.

[68] Josephus agrees with 1 Kgs 3:5a in specifying that God manifested himself to Solomon in a "dream by night," as against 2 Chr 1:7a, which lacks this double

specification. The explicit, prefatory statement that the theophany came in response to and as a reward for the king's "honoring" God is Josephus' own.

[69] See 1 Kgs 3:5b// 2 Chr 1:7b. The reference to the king's "piety" as that which prompts the divine offer is Josephus' addition; see previous note on his earlier accentuation of the point.

[70] Josephus adds an evaluation of Solomon's choice to the biblical notices on that choice (see 1 Kgs 3:6-9// 2 Chr 1:8-10). The evaluation takes the place of the king's opening words to the Lord, acknowledging the divine benefits to his father and himself, of 3:6-8// 1:8-9.

[71] This remark about what Solomon did *not* ask of God anticipates the Deity's reply to Solomon in 1 Kgs 3:11// 2 Chr 1:11, in which the Lord enumerates a variety of items (including "wealth") that the king had not requested of him. Josephus supplies the reference to what a "youth" (cf. 8.21) or the majority would likely have chosen.

[72] Compare 1 Kgs 3:9a (where Solomon asks for an "understanding heart to govern thy [God's] people") and 2 Chr 1:10a (where his request is for "wisdom and knowledge to go out and come in before the people"). The wording of Solomon's request in Josephus recalls the historian's earlier statement about David in *Ant.* 7.110: "he was just by nature and looked only to the truth when he made his judgments."

[73] This mention of God's inner reaction to Solomon's request reflects 1 Kgs 3:10 (no parallel in 2 Chr 1:2-13): "it pleased the Lord that Solomon had asked this."

[74] Greek: σύνεσις καὶ σοφία. This same collocation is applied by Josephus to Solomon in 8.49. (These are the only 2 occurrences of the binomial in Josephus' corpus.)

person—whether kings or private citizens—had.[75] He also promised that he would preserve the kingship for his descendants for a very long time, should he continue to be just and obedient to him and mindful of his father in those things in which he [David] was excellent.[76]

25 When he heard these things from God, Solomon immediately leapt up from his bed and paid him homage.[77] He then returned to Hierosolyma, where he offered great sacrifices before the tent and feasted all the Judeans.[78]

(2.2) 26 In those days a difficult case was brought to him, the solution to which would be laborious to find.[79] I have thought it necessary to relate the matter that the [king's] judgment happened to concern, in order that the difficulty of the case might become clear to my readers, so that they might, as it were, receive an image of the king's shrewdness in being able to easily judge about those things that were sought [from him].[80]

Solomon's judgment in case of two mothers

27 Two women, prostitutes[81] by occupation, came to him.[82] Of these, she who appeared to be the one wronged[83] began to speak first: "I live," she said, "O king, with this [woman] in a single room.[84] It happened that we both gave birth to male children several days ago at the same hour.[85] **28** When three days had passed, she

---

[75] Josephus rearranges the sequence of 1 Kgs 3:12-13// 2 Chr 1:12, mentioning the divine promise to give Solomon what he had not requested before God's conferral on him of what he had asked for. Having anticipated God's opening statement about what Solomon had (not) requested of 1 Kgs 3:11// 2 Chr 1:11 in 8.23, Josephus omits the content of that statement from his version of the Deity's reply.

[76] Josephus recasts the concluding divine promise of 1 Kgs 3:14 (no parallel in 2 Chr 1:2-13), i.e. of a long life for Solomon personally should he follow the law-abiding ways of David, as a pledge concerning the duration of the Davidic dynasty. He likewise appends the qualification regarding David's excellence in line with his encomium on that king in *Ant.* 7.391, with its allusion to David's transgression with Uriah's wife.

[77] This reference to Solomon's immediate reaction to God's promises is Josephus' creation; it accentuates the alacrity of the king's response.

[78] Both 1 Kgs 3:15 and 2 Chr 1:13 mention Solomon's going back to Jerusalem, though only the former text adds a reference to his sacrifices and the feast provided by him there. In his reworking of 1 Kgs 3:15 Josephus has Solomon sacrifice "before the tent" (i.e. the one erected by David for the ark, see *Ant.* 7.86; compare "before the ark" [MT 3:15]/ "facing the altar which stood before the ark" [LXX BL 3:15]). He likewise depicts him feasting a much larger group ("the Judeans" in general; compare "all his [Solomon's] servants," 3:15) than does his biblical counterpart (this last point presupposes the correctness of the reading "the Judeans" [Greek: τοὺς Ἰουδαίους] of RO adopted by Niese; compare, however, the alternative reading, more in line with the biblical one, namely τοὺς ἰδίους

["his [Solomon's] own [household]") of the other codices, which Marcus follows, and Lat, which leaves unspecified whom Solomon feasted).

[79] Josephus supplies this heading-transition to the famous story of the "judgment of Solomon" (1 Kgs 3:16-28). In the segment (8.26-49) that now follows, Josephus employs the material of 1 Kgs 3:16-5:14 (MT; Eng. 3:16-4:34), to which the Solomon story of 2 Chronicles 1-9 has no equivalent, as his source.

[80] This prefatory statement concerning Josephus' intent in reproducing the story of Solomon's judgment is the historian's addition. It underscores the significance of the following story and highlights Solomon's wisdom as its dominant theme.

[81] Greek: ἑταῖραι. Elsewhere in Josephus' writings this noun occurs only as a variant reading in *War* 7.399, 404.

[82] See 1 Kgs 3:16. Josephus omits the biblical detail about the pair's "standing before" the king.

[83] This characterization of the 1st speaker lacks a counterpart in 1 Kgs 3:17, where she is simply called "the one woman." By means of it Josephus intimates from the start that the 1st speaker is the one who is to be believed.

[84] In 1 Kgs 3:17 the 1st speaker refers to her living "in the same house" as the other.

[85] Josephus' notice that the 2 sons were born "at the same hour" replaces the 1st speaker's statement in 1 Kgs 3:18a according to which their births took place 3 days apart. Josephus, at this point, leaves aside the 1st speaker's emphatic affirmation that she and the other woman were the only ones living in the house (3:18b); see, however, next note.

lay upon her own child while she slept and killed it.[86] She removed my child from my knees and carried it over to where she herself was, placing the dead [child] in my arms as I was sleeping.[87] **29** In the early morning when I wished to nurse my child, I did not find it; instead, I saw that it was hers that was lying dead beside me, as I realized by careful examination.[88] Having requested my son but not getting him back [from her], I have turned to you, O master, for help. For since we were alone, in her arrogant confidence that she [need not] fear anyone who can convict her, she stubbornly persists in denying it."[89]

30 When she had said this, the king asked the other woman what she had to say in reply.[90] She denied having done it, saying that the living child was hers, while it was her legal opponent's that was dead.[91] No one could resolve the case; rather all were, as if by a riddle, mentally blinded concerning its solution; the king alone thought things out as follows.[92]

31 He directed that both the living and the dead child be brought.[93] Then, summoning one of his bodyguards, he directed him to draw his sword,[94] and to cut both children in half, so that each woman might receive a half, both of the living one and of the one who had died.[95]

32 At this, the whole people secretly jeered at the king as a mere boy.[96] But then the one who had asked [for her child back]—whose true mother she was—cried out not do this, but to hand over the child to the other woman as though it were hers, for she was satisfied with his being alive and simply seeing him, even if he should be regarded as another's.[97] The other woman, for her part, was ready to see the child

---

[86] See 1 Kgs 3:19. Josephus reapplies the 3-day period cited in 1 Kgs 3:18a as the interlude between the boys' births (see previous note) to the interval between the other woman's delivery and her accidental killing of her child. In 1 Kgs 3:19 the child's death is said to have occurred "in the night."

[87] See 1 Kgs 3:20, where the speaker avers that both babies were laid in the mothers' "bosoms." In having the speaker state that she was "asleep" during the other woman's "exchange," Josephus follows the plus of MT, lacking in LXX BL. He has no equivalent to the detail, common to both MT and LXX, that the other woman took her initiative "at midnight."

[88] See 1 Kgs 3:21, where the 1st speaker refers to the child she found beside her as "not the one I had borne." Her statement about her not "finding" her own child is Josephus' addition.

[89] Josephus supplies this conclusion to the 1st woman's discourse, which, e.g., explains her reason for bringing the matter before the king, while also highlighting the other woman's intransigence. The reference to the pair's being "alone" is a delayed reminiscence of the 1st woman's words to that effect in 1 Kgs 3:18b.

[90] In having the king ask the 2nd woman for her response, Josephus evidences a concern with proper protocol. Compare 1 Kgs 3:22a, where she takes the initiative in responding.

[91] See 1 Kgs 3:22a. Josephus omits 3:22b, where,

after the 1st woman speaks once again and asserts the opposite of what the 2nd has alleged, their exchange terminates with the summary notice "thus they spoke before the king."

[92] This editorial notice, contrasting the king's insight with the befuddlement of everyone else, replaces the king's (rather obvious) summation of what the 2 women have just said in 1 Kgs 3:23.

[93] This directive has no counterpart in the biblical account where, following the women's dispute (1 Kgs 3:16-22) Solomon simply reiterates what has already been said by them (3:23). Josephus' addition of the directive prepares the king's subsequent order concerning the bodies of the 2 infants.

[94] Compare 1 Kgs 3:24, where Solomon commands that a sword be brought and this is done. With his mention of the "bodyguard" Josephus supplies a subject for the king's subsequent order (// 3:25 LXX BL) about the cutting up of the infants' bodies.

[95] Josephus' version of the king's order here agrees with LXX BL 1 Kgs 3:25, where the bodies of both infants are to be divided and distributed to the mothers. MT mentions only a division of the living infant.

[96] This reaction on the part of the crowd lacks a biblical counterpart. It picks up on the reference to Solomon's precocity in 8.21, just as it serves to highlight the surprising vindication of the king's wisdom in what follows.

[97] See 1 Kgs 3:26a. Josephus omits the biblical no-

divided and likewise requested that she herself be interrogated under torture.[98]

33 The king realized the truth from the utterances of each.[99] He assigned the child to the one who had cried out, for she truly was the mother.[100] But he condemned the vileness of the other one, who, having killed her own child, was quite ready to countenance the loss of her friend as well.[101]

34 The crowd supposed this to be a great proof and token[102] of the king's intelligence and wisdom;[103] from that day on they regarded him as one having divine understanding.[104]

(2.3) 35 These now were his generals and the leaders of the entire country:[105] Ures[106] was over the inheritance of Ephraim;[107] Diokler[108] was over the toparchy of Bithiemes.[109] Abinadab,[110] who was married to Solomon's daughter,[111] had under him Dor and the coastal region.[112] **36** The great plain was under Banai,[113] the son of

Solomon's officials

---

tice on the woman's "yearning for her son," while elaborating on her words to the king there, i.e. "... give her [the other woman] the living child, and by no means slay it."

[98] See 1 Kgs 3:26b. Josephus adds the remark about the other woman's readiness to undergo torture, thereby underscoring her brazen confidence in her ability to sustain her deception—see the appended characterization of her that he places in the mouth of the 1st woman at the end of her initial speech in 8.29.

[99] Josephus adds this remark on Solomon's reasoning process.

[100] Josephus' qualification of the mother as "the one who had cried out" corresponds to the plus of LXX BL 1 Kgs 3:27 ("to the one who said 'give it to her'") that it appends to Solomon's mention of her as "the first woman" in MT. The terminology used of the woman to whom Solomon awards the child here is reminiscent of that used of her in 8.32, where she, as "the true mother," "cries out" at the prospect of having her living son cut in half.

[101] This "condemnation" has no parallel in the biblical account, where Solomon only issues a judgment (1 Kgs 3:27) in favor of "the 1st woman." Josephus' reference to the condemned woman's being a "friend" of the actual mother has no biblical basis; the addition highlights the reprehensibility of the former's dealings with the latter.

[102] Greek: δεῖγμα καὶ τεκμήριον. This collocation occurs only here in Josephus.

[103] Greek: φρόνησις καὶ σοφία. Josephus applies this same collocation twice subsequently to Solomon; see 8.42 and 8.171 (reverse order). He also uses it of Joseph in *Ant.* 2.87.

[104] See 1 Kgs 3:28, where the reference is to all Israel's recognition that the "wisdom of God" was in Solomon. Josephus' equivalent phrase, "divine understanding" (Greek: θεία διανοία), occurs only here in his writings.

[105] 1 Kgs 4:7 specifies the number of these figures as 12 and assigns them the duty of provisioning Solomon's court. In following his account of Solomon's judgment (8.26-34// 1 Kgs 3:16-28) directly with his enumeration of the king's provincial governors (8.35-37// 1 Kgs 4:7-19), Josephus passes over the intervening list (4:1-6) of the chief royal officials stationed in Jerusalem itself. As Rahlfs (1911: 93, 95) points out, the Josephan names of the provincial governors and the sequence of those names stands closer to the MT than to the LXX listing. At the same time, Josephus also differs from the MT listing in several respects: he has no equivalent to the form בֶן ("son of") prefaced in MT to 4 of the names he does cite, just as he has only 10 names, as compared to MT's 12.

[106] MT (1 Kgs 4:8) בֶן־חוּר (Eng.: "Ben-hur"); LXX Βαιώρ; Josephus Οὔρης (this form corresponds to the MT name, minus its opening element בֶן).

[107] 1 Kgs 4:8 speaks of the "hill country of Ephraim" as Ben-hur's area of jurisdiction.

[108] MT (1 Kgs 4:9) בֶן־דֶקֶר (Eng.: "Ben-deker"); LXX B υἱὸς Ῥήχας; LXX L υἱὸς Ῥήχαβ; Josephus Διόκληρος.

[109] This is Josephus' equivalent to the 3rd (MT: Beth-shemesh) of the 4 sites under Ben-deker's jurisdiction according to 1 Kgs 4:9.

[110] MT (1 Kgs 4:11) בֶן־אֲבִינָדָב (Eng.: "Ben-abinadab"); LXX B ἀνὰ Δὰν καὶ ἀνὰ Βαθεί; LXX L Ἀναδὰβ καὶ Βαθνάη; Josephus Ἀβινάδαβος. Josephus has no equivalent to the 3rd of MT's 12 provincial governors as cited in 4:10, i.e. "Ben-hesed in Arubboth."

[111] Josephus omits her name, cited as "Taphath" in MT 1 Kgs 4:11b.

[112] According to MT 1 Kgs 4:11a, Ben-abinadab's domain was "all Naphath-dor."

[113] MT (1 Kgs 4:12) בַּעֲנָא (Eng.: "Baana"); LXX B Βακχά; LXX L Εἰσβαχά; Josephus Βαναίας. The "great plain" is the "Valley of Megiddo"/ "Plain of Jezreel."

Achil;[114] he also governed everything up to the Jordan.[115] Gabar[116] had under him Galaditis and Gaulanitis as far as Mount Liban and sixty great and very solidly fortified cities.[117] Achinadab[118] administered all Galilee as far as Sidon;[119] he too was married to a daughter of Solomon, whose name was Basima.[120] **37** Banakat[121] had the coastal region around Ake.[122] Saphat[123] was assigned Mount Itabyrion[124] and Mount Karmel and the lower Galilee, as well as all the country as far as the river Jordan.[125] Soumouis[126] was entrusted with the inheritance of Benjamin,[127] while Gabar[128] had the country beyond the Jordan.[129] In addition to these, one further ruler[130] was appointed.

Israelites'
prosperity

38 The people of the Hebrews and the tribe of Iouda made remarkable progress by devoting themselves to agriculture and the care of the soil.[131] For enjoying peace, and not being preoccupied with enemies or troubles, and likewise making full use of their longed-for freedom,[132] each was able to enlarge his own house and make this of greater worth.[133]

---

[114] MT (1 Kgs 4:12) אחילוד (Eng.: "Ahilud"); LXX B ᾿Αχειμάχ; LXX L ᾿Αχιάβ; Josephus ῎Αχιλος.

[115] 1 Kgs 4:12 states that Baana's district encompassed "Tanaach, Megiddo, and all Beth-shean...."

[116] MT (1 Kgs 4:13) בן־גבר (Eng.: "Ben-geber"); LXX BL υἱὸς Γάβερ; Josephus Γαβάρης.

[117] Josephus simplifies the indications of 1 Kgs 4:13 concerning the territory of "Ben-geber."

[118] MT (1 Kgs 4:14) אחינדב (Eng.: "Ahinadab"); LXX B ᾿Αχειναάβ; LXX L ᾿Αχιναδάβ; Josephus ᾿Αχιναδάβος. Josephus omits the name of his father, i.e. "Iddo" (MT).

[119] 1 Kgs 4:14 places "Ahinadab" in "Mahanaim."

[120] MT (1 Kgs 4:15) בחמת (Eng.: "Basemath"); LXX BL Βασσεμάθ; Josephus Βασίμα. According to 1 Kgs 4:15, "Basemath" was the wife, not of "Ahinadab" (4:14), but of his colleague "Ahimaaz" in Naphtali; Josephus conflates the 2 governors.

[121] MT (1 Kgs 4:16) בענא (Eng.: "Baana"); LXX B Βαανά; LXX L Βαναίας; Josephus Βανακάτες. Josephus omits the name of his father, i.e. "Hushai" (MT).

[122] 1 Kgs 4:16 assigns "Baana" the region of "Asher and Bealoth."

[123] MT (1 Kgs 4:17) יהושפט (Eng.: "Jehoshaphat"); LXX BL ᾿Ιωσαφάτ; Josephus Σαφάτης. In mentioning this figure 3rd from last in his list of provincial governors, Josephus assigns him the same position he has in the MT enumeration. By contrast, in LXX BL he appears as the last of the 12 governors. Josephus omits the name of his father ("Paruah," MT).

[124] On this site (= Mount Tabor), see the note to "Mount Itabyrion" at *Ant.* 5.84.

[125] In 1 Kgs 4:17 Jehoshaphat's area of jurisdiction is "Issachar."

[126] MT (1 Kgs 4:18) שמעי (Eng.: "Shimei"); LXX B υἱὸς ᾿Ηλα; LXX L Σαμαά; Josephus Σουμούις. Josephus omits the name of the governor's father, i.e. "Ela" (MT; compare LXX B, which does not name the

governor in question, referring to him only as "son of Ela").

[127] This is the area assigned to Shimei in 1 Kgs 4:18.

[128] MT (1 Kgs 4:19a) גבר (Eng.: "Geber"); LXX B υἱὸς ᾿Αδαί; LXX L υἱὸς ᾿Αδδαί; Josephus Γαβαρής. Josephus leaves aside the name of his father, "Uri" (MT), whereas LXX BL omit the governor's own name, calling him simply "son of Ad(d)ai."

[129] 1 Kgs 4:19a assigns "Geber" to "Gilead," identifying this with the former territories of Kings Sihon and Og.

[130] With this term (Greek: ἄρχων) Josephus "translates" the Hebrew word נציב (RSV: "officer") of MT 1 Kgs 4:19b, which LXX B (νασέφ) and LXX L (Νασείβ) transliterate, apparently taking it as a proper name. Josephus leaves aside the biblical specification that this figure was "in the land of Judah."

[131] This reference to the agricultural pursuits of Solomon's subjects seems inspired by the mention of their "sitting under their vines and fig trees" in 1 Kgs 5:5 (MT; RSV 4:25). It also recalls Josephus' (pejorative) allusions to the people's focus on agricultural activity in the time of the Judges in *Ant.* 5.129, 132, 173. The passage has further parallels in Josephus' description of the Essenes in *Ant.* 18.19 and of the Judeans as a whole in *Apion* 2.294, descriptions which are perhaps intended to play on Roman nostalgia for the bucolic life. I owe this suggestion to Prof. Steve Mason.

[132] Cf. the references to the all-sided "peace" and "safety" of Solomon's time in 1 Kgs 5:4b-5a (MT; RSV 4:24b-25a).

[133] This sequence, highlighting the "home improvements" undertaken by Solomon's subjects in their state of peace and freedom, has no counterpart in the biblical record. In fact, it stands in some contrast to the Bible's emphasis on the people's leisure and self-indulgence in 1 Kgs 4:20; 5:5b (MT; RSV 4:25b).

(2.4) 39 There were also leaders who were companions to the king. These had
command of the land of the Syrians and of the foreign tribes that extended from the
Euphrates river as far as that of the Egyptians; they collected taxes for him from
these nations.[134] **40** They[135] also provided daily for the king's table and dinner thirty
cors of wheat-flour and sixty of wheat-meal, plus ten fattened cattle and twenty
pasture-fed cattle, along with one hundred fattened lambs.[136] All these, I say, were
in addition to the wild deer, antelopes, birds, and fish that were brought to the king
each day by aliens.[137]

Solomon's supplies

41 The number of Solomon's chariots was so great that he had 40,000 stalls for
the horses that were harnessed in front of these.[138] In addition he had 12,000 horsemen.[139] Of these, half were in attendance on the king in Hierosolyma, while the remainder were dispersed, being stationed in the royal towns.[140] The same leader who
had been entrusted with the royal expenditures himself also supplied the needs of
the horses, conveying these to the place where the king resided.[141]

(2.5) 42 The intelligence and wisdom that God bestowed on Solomon[142] was so
great that he surpassed the ancients,[143] and even the Egyptians, who are said to be
superior to all in prudence, when compared with him proved to be not merely a little
deficient, but completely unequal to the king's intelligence.[144]

Solomon's wisdom

43 He likewise exceeded and was superior in wisdom to those of his own time
who had a reputation for cleverness among the Hebrews, whose names I shall not
pass over.[145] They were Athan,[146] and Haiman,[147] Chalke[148] and Dardan,[149] the sons

---

[134] See 1 Kgs 5:1 (MT; RSV 4:21), where there is
reference to the borders of Solomon's empire and the
tribute brought him by its component kingdoms. Here
in 8.39 Josephus introduces a further, distinct category
of royal officials, i.e. in addition to the provincial governors cited by him in 8.35-37, who have jurisdiction
over these outlying territories.

[135] According to 1 Kgs 4:7 and 5:7 (MT; RSV
4:27), it was the 12 provincial governors of 4:8-19a
who were responsible for provisioning Solomon's
court. Josephus assigns the task rather to the governors
of the outlying territories introduced by him just previously in 8.39.

[136] These figures correspond to those given for the
agricultural commodities delivered to Solomon in 1
Kgs 5:2-3a (MT; RSV 4:22-23a).

[137] The list of wild game supplied to Solomon in 1
Kgs 5:3b (MT; RSV 4:23b) does not mention "fish,"
nor does it specify that "aliens" were the source of this
game.

[138] Josephus' figure for the "facilities" provided for
his chariot horses accords with that cited in MT 1 Kgs
5:6a (MT; RSV 4:26a). LXX BL (and 2 Chr 9:25) mention 4,000 stalls, while 2 Chr 1:14 speaks of 1,400
chariots.

[139] This figure agrees with that given in both 1 Kgs
5:6b (MT; RSV 4:26b) and 2 Chr 1:14= 9:25.

[140] Josephus derives this specification—lacking in
1 Kgs 5:6 (MT; RSV 4:26)—concerning the distribution of Solomon's horsemen from 2 Chr 1:14= 9:25.

[141] See 1 Kgs 5:8 (MT; RSV 4:28), where it is the
provincial governors collectively (see 5:7// 4:27) who
supply "barley and straw for the horses."

[142] See 1 Kgs 5:9 (MT; RSV 4:29), where the image
"like the sand on the shore" is used of Solomon's God-
given "largeness of mind." Josephus typically avoids or
recasts such figurative language.

[143] In 1 Kgs 5:10 (RSV 4:30) MT uses a Hebrew
expression (בני־קדם), which could be rendered either
"the people of the east" (so RSV) or "the people of old"
(so the LXX). Josephus' rendition follows the line of
the LXX.

[144] Josephus embellishes the allusion of 1 Kgs 5:10
(MT; RSV 4:30) to Solomon's surpassing "all the wisdom of Egypt." Given the Egyptians' reputation for
pre-eminent wisdom, Solomon's superiority to them
appears all the more remarkable. Josephus' acknowledgement of the Egyptians' wise reputation here contrasts with the negative remarks about them one finds
elsewhere in his writings (see *Ant.* 2.201; *Apion* 2.70)
and in Greco-Roman literature generally; see BJP 3
(Feldman) 187-8, n. 563. On the other hand, it does
have a counterpart in *Apion* 1.14, where Josephus refers
to the general agreement that the first Greek cosmolo-
gists learned from the Egyptians (and Chaldeans), who
in turn, according to *Ant.* 1.167-168, gained their
knowledge of arithmetic and astronomy from Abraham.

[145] In 1 Kgs 5:11 (MT; RSV 4:31) the figures in
question are not qualified as Solomon's contemporaries; nor are they said to have enjoyed their intellectual

of Hemaon.[150] **44** He also composed 1,005 books of odes and songs,[151] as well as 3,000 books of parables and allegories.[152] For he spoke a parable about each kind of tree, from the hyssop to the cedar.[153] In the same way he spoke of all the animals, those on the earth, those that swim, and those in the air.[154] For there was nothing in nature of which he was ignorant or which he left unexamined. Rather, he investigated everything methodically and evidenced a remarkable knowledge of the peculiarities of things.[155]

Solomon the exorcist

45 God also enabled him to learn the technique against demons for the benefit and healing of humans.[156] He composed incantations by which illnesses are relieved, and left behind exorcistic[157] practices with which those binding demons expel them so that they return no more.[158]

Eleazar's exorcism

46 And this same form of healing remains quite strong among us until today.[159] For I became acquainted with a certain Eleazar of my own people, who, in the presence of Vespasian and his sons,[160] along with their tribunes and a crowd of soldiers,[161] delivered those possessed by demons. The method of healing is as follows:

---

reputation "among the Hebrews" in particular.

[146] MT (1 Kgs 5:11 [RSV 4:31]) אֵיתָן (Eng.: "Ethan"); LXX B Γαιθάν; LXX L Αἰθάμ; Josephus Ἄθανος. Josephus omits his biblical gentilic, i.e. "the Ezrahite."

[147] MT (1 Kgs 5:11 [RSV 4:31]) הֵימָן (Eng.: "Heman"); LXX B Αἰνάν; LXX L Αἰμάν; Josephus Αἴμανός.

[148] MT (1 Kgs 5:11 [RSV 4:31]) כַּלְכֹּל (Eng.: "Calcol"); LXX B Χαλκάδ; LXX L Χαλκάχ; Josephus Χάλκεος.

[149] MT (1 Kgs 5:11 [RSV 4:31]) דַּרְדַּע (Eng.: "Darda"); LXX B Δαραλά; LXX L Δαρδαέ; Josephus Δάρδανας. Josephus may have modified the name of this biblical figure so as to assimilate him to the famous Hellenistic magician "Dardanos," on whom see Torijano 2002: 98, n. 31.

[150] MT (1 Kgs 5:11 [RSV 4:31]) מָחוֹל (Eng.: "Mahol"); LXX B Μάλ; LXX L Μααλά; Josephus Ἡμάων (Schalit *s.v.* sees this form as due to a corruption under the influence of the 2nd name on Josephus' list, i.e. Αἴμανός).

[151] 1 Kgs 5:12b (MT; RSV 4:32b) attributes 1,005 "songs" to Solomon, whereas Josephus makes him the author of that number of song "books."

[152] 1 Kgs 5:12a (MT; RSV 4:32a) refers to 3,000 "proverbs"; once again (see previous note), Josephus uses the biblical figure to refer, not to individual compositions, but to entire "books."

[153] Josephus reverses the order of the 2 plants according to 1 Kgs 5:13a (MT; RSV 4:33a), where the "cedar" is further qualified as "in Lebanon" and the "hyssop" as "growing out of the wall."

[154] 1 Kgs 5:13b (MT; RSV 4:33b) enumerates "beasts, birds, reptiles, and fish."

[155] This summarizing comment concerning the extent of Solomon's knowledge of nature takes the place of the notice of 1 Kgs 5:14 (MT; RSV 4:34) about rep-

resentatives of "all peoples" and all the earth's "kings" coming to hear Solomon's wisdom. Josephus will deal with a special case of such a visit, i.e. that of the "queen of Sheba" subsequently; see 8.165-175.

[156] With this statement Josephus begins a segment (8.45-49) concerning Solomon's medical, in particular exorcistic, abilities that has no parallel in either Kings or Chronicles, but which does pick up on a widespread tradition associating Solomon with magical practices. On the segment, see Deines 2003: 372-92. According to Torijano (2002: 93-105), that tradition was so well-known in Josephus' time that he felt compelled to make reference to it, notwithstanding his general tendency to diminish the miraculous and the mysterious in his re-telling of the biblical account. In any case, here at the outset, Josephus makes clear that also Solomon's medical/magical prowess was given him by God.

[157] The noun ἐξόρκωσις (literally: "exorcism") occurs only here in Josephus.

[158] Compare Luke 11:24-26// Matt 12:43-45, where Jesus refers to an unclean spirit "returning" to the person from whom it had earlier departed.

[159] With this transitional notice Josephus begins connecting the story of the ancient King Solomon with his own present; thereby, he gets the opportunity of interjecting himself into the narrative. For a detailed analysis of the following episode, see Torijano 2002: 101-5; Deines 2003: 385-90.

[160] With this reference Josephus gives his Flavian patrons, i.e. Vespasian and his sons Titus and Domitian, a place in his biblical history. This reference is of particular interest because, as Josephus and his Roman audience knew, Vespasian himself had been credited with the gift of healing and exorcism (see Tacitus, *Hist.* 4.81; Suetonius, *Vesp.* 7). I owe these references to Prof. Steve Mason.

[161] With his mention of these figures alongside the Flavians as witnesses to Eleazar's exorcism, Josephus

47 Bringing up to the nose of the demonized person a ring that had under its seal a root from among those prescribed by Solomon, he [Eleazar] would then draw out the demonic [presence] through the nostrils, as the man sniffed. Upon the man's immediately falling down, he adjured the demonic [presence] not to return to him again, making mention of Solomon and likewise reciting the incantations he had composed.[162] **48** Eleazar, wishing to persuade and convince those present that he had this power, first placed a cup or foot-basin filled with water a short distance away and ordered the demonic [presence], which was now outside the person, to knock these over, and so cause the spectators to realize that it had left the person.[163] **49** When this happened, the sagacity and wisdom of Solomon became evident through this. We felt bound to speak of these matters so that all might know the greatness of his nature and his closeness to God,[164] and so that the king's preeminence in every sort of virtue should not hidden from any of those beneath the sun.[165]

(2.6) 50 When Heirom,[166] the king of the Tyrians, heard that Solomon had succeeded to his father's kingship, he rejoiced exceedingly, for he had been a friend of David.[167] Sending to him, he greeted him and congratulated him on the good things that were now his.[168] Solomon, for his part, sent him a letter[169] reading as follows:

Hiram (Heirom)– Solomon correspondence

51 "King Solomon to King Heirom.[170] Know that my father, although he wished to construct a sanctuary for God, was prevented by wars and continuous campaigns.[171] For he did not cease subjugating his enemies until he had made them all

---

highlights the credibility of his report: Eleazar's deed was done very publicly, in the presence of many non-Jews.

[162] Compare Mark 9:25, where Jesus "commands" the evil spirit to come out of the boy and "never enter him again." In contrast to Eleazar, Jesus in the NT effects his exorcisms without use of incantations or mention of Solomon.

[163] In the Gospels Jesus does not offer such proofs of the reality of his exorcisms. Compare, however, Philostratus, *Vit. Apoll.* 4.20, where, having ejected a demon from a young man, Apollonius of Tyana provides a "visible sign" that the demon has indeed left the young man by commanding the ejected demon to overturn a nearby statue and the demon does so.

[164] Josephus applies this same expression (Greek: τὸ θεοφιλές) to David in *Ant.* 6.280.

[165] With this formula Josephus marks the end of his extended extra-biblical excursus concerning Solomon the exorcist, 8.45-49. The phrase "beneath the sun" is prominent in the Book of Qoheleth; see, e.g., 1:9, 14; 2:11, 17.

[166] MT (1 Kgs 5:15 [RSV 5:1]) חירם (Eng.: "Hiram"); LXX BL Χειράμ; MT (2 Chr 2:3 [RSV 2:2]) חורם (Eng.: "Huram"); LXX BL Χειράμ; Josephus Εἴρωμος. This king was earlier mentioned by Josephus in *Ant.* 7.66 (// 2 Sam 5:11-12// 1 Chr 14:1-2) in connection with the assistance he gave David with his building projects. Josephus' account of the exchange between Solomon and Hiram stands much closer to the

version found in 1 Kgs 5:15-27 (MT; RSV 5:1-12) than to its counterpart in 2 Chr 2:2-15 (MT; RSV 2:3-16).

[167] See 1 Kgs 5:15 (MT; RSV 5:1), which speaks of Hiram's hearing of Solomon's "anointing" and of his having "always loved David." Josephus adds the reference to the Tyrian king's "rejoicing exceedingly," anticipating the notice of 5:21 (5:7), where Hiram responds in this way upon hearing Solomon's message to him.

[168] Josephus elaborates on the mention of Hiram's "sending his servants" to Solomon in 1 Kgs 5:15a (MT; RSV 5:1a), spelling out the content of the former's message to the latter.

[169] In 1 Kgs 5:16 (MT; RSV 5:2)// 2 Chr 2:2 (MT; RSV 2:3) Solomon "sends to Hiram saying." Josephus' explicit reference to the dispatch of a "letter" has in view his subsequent statement (see 8.55) that copies of the Solomon-Hiram correspondence may still be seen in the Tyrian archives.

[170] His use of this standard ancient epistolary salutation, unparalleled in either of the biblical accounts, reflects Josephus' previous added reference to Solomon's "letter" to Hiram.

[171] See 1 Kgs 5:17a (MT; RSV 5:3a); Josephus adds the mention of David's desiring to build the temple. His wording here recalls that used by him in his account of David's temple project in *Ant.* 7.90-95; see 7.90 (his wish to build a temple for God) and 7.92 (the king's wars that God cites in forbidding him to carry out his plan personally).

payers of tribute.[172] **52** I know that I have God to thank for the present peace, because of which I am free to build the house for God as I wish.[173] For God announced to my father that this would happen under me.[174] I therefore appeal to you to dispatch certain men along with my people to Mount Liban in order to cut timber, since the Sidonians are more proficient in felling trees than we are. I shall pay your woodworkers the wage you set."[175]

(2.7) 53 When he read the communication, Heirom was pleased with its requests.[176] He wrote back to Solomon:

"King Heirom to King Solomon.[177] God is indeed worthy of praise, because he has entrusted your father's leadership to you, a wise man, having every virtue.[178] For these [reasons] I shall willingly be of service in regard to all your requests.[179] **54** Once many large cedar and cypress logs have been cut down by my men, I shall send them down to the sea. I shall also direct my men to assemble a raft and deliver this, sailing it to the place in your own country that you wish.[180] Then your men will convey it to Hierosolyma.[181] For your part, see to it that, in return for these things, you provide us with the wheat we need because we live on an island."[182]

Correspondence preserved

(2.8) 55 Copies of these letters have endured until today, having been preserved not only in our records, but also in those of the Tyrians. Thus, if anyone should wish to learn about their reliability, upon his asking the keeper of the Tyrian archives

---

[172] MT and LXX L 1 Kgs 5:17b (RSV 5:3b) have Solomon refer to the Lord's putting David's enemies "under the soles of his feet."

Josephus agrees with the original text of LXX B 1 Kgs 5:17 in not mentioning the Deity's role in the subjugation of the enemies. At the same time, he also spells out what that subjugation involved, i.e. the paying of tribute.

[173] See 1 Kgs 5:18-19a (MT; RSV 5:4-5a), where Solomon states that, given the all-sided "rest" God has awarded him, he now has in mind to build the temple.

[174] See 1 Kgs 5:19b (MT; RSV 5:5b). The reference is to Nathan's announcement to David in *Ant.* 7.93 (where Josephus goes beyond 2 Sam 7:13a// 1 Chr 17:12a in having Nathan mention Solomon by name as the future temple-builder).

[175] See 1 Kgs 5:20 (MT; RSV 5:6), where Solomon attributes to Hiram himself the "knowledge" that the Sidonians are more skilled in cutting timber than the Israelites.

[176] 1 Kgs 5:21a (MT; RSV 5:7a) speaks of Hiram's "rejoicing greatly" over Solomon's words. Josephus incorporates into Hiram's message itself (a version of) his "blessing" God for having given David a worthy successor that in 5:21b (MT; RSV 5:7b) precedes the king's sending to Solomon. He likewise delays his rendering of this blessing until after the formalized greeting (see 8.53) with which Hiram's letter begins.

[177] Compare the similar salutation supplied by Josephus in 8.51. Here, as there, Josephus turns what in the Bible appears to be a verbal message between the 2 kings into an explicitly written one.

[178] This is Josephus' "delayed" (see note to "Heirom was pleased with its requests" at 8.53) version of Hiram's "blessing of the Lord" for having given David so wise a son as his successor that Hiram pronounces prior to sending his message to Solomon in 1 Kgs 5:21b (MT; RSV 5:7b).

[179] See 1 Kgs 5:22 (MT; RSV 5:8), where Hiram states more specifically that it is Solomon's desires regarding "cedar and cypress timber" that he is ready to satisfy. Josephus supplies a motivation for Hiram's willingness, i.e. Solomon's status as David's God-designated, wise successor as affirmed by him in what precedes.

[180] See 1 Kgs 5:23a (MT; RSV 5:9a). Josephus adds the reference to the "cutting" of the trees as a preliminary to the following measures mentioned by Hiram.

[181] 1 Kgs 5:23bα (MT; RSV 5:9bα) speaks of the breaking up of the log rafts by Hiram's men and Solomon's "reception" of the delivery without mention of Jerusalem as its ultimate destination. Cf., however, 2 Chr 2:15 (MT; RSV 2:16), where Hiram refers to Solomon's taking to Jerusalem the timber that he (Hiram) will deliver to Joppa.

[182] Compare 1 Kgs 5:23bβ (MT; RSV 5:9bβ), where Hiram speaks more generally of Solomon's supplying "food for his household." Josephus appends the reference to Tyre's island location, which explains its need for imported foodstuffs. His statement that Hiram asked for "wheat" in particular anticipates 1 Kgs 5:26 (MT; RSV 5:11), where this is mentioned first among the items that Solomon supplies to Hiram.

he will find that what we have said agrees with what is in these.[183] **56** I have gone through these things in detail, then, wishing readers to know that we are speaking nothing but the truth. Nor are we trying to avoid research, or asking to be trusted immediately, by interlarding the history with persuasive and seductive items [with a view] to deception and delight; nor yet to remain unpunished, indulged, if we are violating what is appropriate to the work. Rather, we appeal for no other accolade than that we are capable of setting forth the truth by means of demonstration and compelling proofs.[184]

Josephus' claims as a historian

(2.9) 57 When King Solomon was brought the letter from the Tyrian king, he commended the latter's eagerness and loyalty.[185] He likewise set up an exchange for those items he had requested. He sent him annually 20,000 cors of wheat[186] and as many *batoi* of oil (the *batos* is equivalent to seventy-two *xestas*);[187] he also provided the same amount of wine.[188] **58** The friendship between Heirom and Solomon thus increased still more as a result of these things, and they swore that it would last for all time.[189]

Preparatory measures for temple building

The king imposed a levy of 30,000 workers on all his people,[190] for whom he made the work not overly taxing by dividing this up sagaciously.[191] For he made 10,000 chop [wood] for one month on Mount Liban; going to their homes, these then rested for two months until the [other] 20,000 had completed the work in their

---

[183] Josephus incorporates this reference (8.55-56) to the "Tyrian archives" into his reproduction of the biblical accounts concerning the Hiram-Solomon exchange. By means of the addition he calls readers' attention to the existence and public availability of ancient, external confirmation of his Bible-based narrative. He mentions the Tyrian "archives" again in *Ant.* 8.144; 9.283, 287; cf. *Apion* 1.111, which asserts that many of the letters Hiram and Solomon exchanged are "preserved in Tyre" until this day. On these (purported) documents, see Garbini 1980. Eupolemus ("Fragment 2," in the citation of Alexander Polyhistor preserved by Eusebius, *Praep. ev.* 9.32-34.1) cites (alleged) correspondence between Solomon and "Souron" king of Tyre, Sidon, and Phoenicia, while in 9.31 he quotes a letter by Solomon to King Vaphres of Egypt.

[184] To his mention of the Tyrian archives in 8.55, Josephus appends this *apologia* for his own credibility as a historian, exemplified in the fact that he can point to extant non-biblical support for what he relates concerning the Solomon-Hiram exchange.

[185] Josephus' reference to Solomon's "commendation" of Hiram takes the place of the notice of 1 Kgs 5:24 (MT; RSV 5:10) that the latter did in fact supply the former with all the timber desired by him. The combination "eagerness and loyalty" (Greek: προθυμία καὶ εὐνοία) occurs, in reverse order, also in *Ant.* 6.82; 15.201; 17.195.

[186] This figure corresponds to that found in LXX BL 1 Kgs 5:25 (RSV 5:11) as well as in 2 Chr 2:9 (MT; RSV 2:10); MT 1 Kgs 5:25 reads "20 cors." Josephus has no equivalent to the additional reference to 20,000

cors of barley found in 2 Chr 2:9. The biblical "cor" is equivalent to *ca.* 360 liters; see Powell (1992: 6: 907).

[187] Josephus' figure for the oil given Hiram by Solomon has a counterpart in both 1 Kgs 5:25 (MT; RSV 5:11) and 2 Chr 2:9 (MT; RSV 2:10). Having transliterated the Hebrew liquid measurement term "bath" of the biblical accounts, he appends a notice on its Greek equivalent, i.e. the ξέστης (which itself corresponds to the Latin *sextarius*). The "bath" equals *ca.* 24 liters; see Powell (1992: 6: 905).

[188] For this item Josephus draws on the plus of 2 Chr 2:9 (MT; RSV 2:10), lacking in the parallel text 1 Kgs 5:25 (MT; RSV 5:11), according to which Solomon supplied Hiram with 20,000 *baths* of wine. Eupolemus ("Fragment 2," in the citation of Alexander Polyhistor cited by Eusebius, *Praep. ev.* 9.33) states that Solomon promised to supply the Tyrian king with 10,000 cors of both grain and wine *each month* (rather than annually as in Josephus and the Bible), as well as unspecified amounts of oil and beef.

[189] Compare 1 Kgs 5:26b (MT; RSV 5:12b), which refers to the "peace" existing between the 2 kings and their making a "covenant"; as usual, Josephus employs a substitute for the latter term. He leaves aside the seemingly extraneous reference (1 Kgs 5:26a [MT; RSV 5:12a]) to God's giving Solomon wisdom, as he had promised.

[190] See 1 Kgs 5:27 (MT; RSV 5:13).

[191] This remark about Solomon's concern not to overburden his Israelite work force and the intellectual acumen evidenced by his provisions is a Josephan addition.

prescribed time.[192] **59** Thus it happened that the original 10,000 had to report back to work in the fourth month.[193] Adoram[194] was the overseer of this levy.

Of the aliens living in the land whom David had left alive, 70,000 were carriers of stone and other material;[195] 80,000 were stone-masons,[196] and 3,300 were their foremen.[197] **60** He ordered them to cut great stones for the foundation of the sanctuary.[198] They were first to join and carefully fit these together on the mountain and bring them down thus to the city.[199] These things were not done solely by native builders; Heirom also sent craftsmen.[200]

Temple building started

(3.1) 61 Solomon began the building of the sanctuary when he was already in the fourth year of his reign, in the second month,[201] the one that the Macedonians call *Artemision* and the Hebrews *Iar*.[202] This was 592 years after the Exodus of the Israelites from Egypt,[203] 1,020 years after the arrival of Abram in Chananaia from Mesopotamia,[204] and 1,440 years after the Flood.[205] **62** From Adam, the first human to have existed, until Solomon built the sanctuary, there elapsed 3,102 years in all.[206]

---

[192] See 1 Kgs 5:28a (MT; RSV 5:14a). Josephus appends the reference to the activity of the other 2 divisions and supplies the detail about the workers' "chopping wood" on Mount Lebanon.

[193] Josephus deduces this datum about the date on which the original 10,000 return to work from the procedure as described in 1 Kgs 5:28a (MT; RSV 5:14a).

[194] MT (1 Kgs 5:28b [RSV 5:14b]) אדנירם (Eng.: "Adoniram"); LXX BL Ἀδωνειράμ; Josephus Ἀδώραμος. This figure has already been mentioned as the overseer of the levy in the time of David in *Ant.* 7.293.

[195] See 1 Kgs 5:29a (MT; RSV 5:15a), which speaks of 70,000 "burden bearers," whose ethnic origins it leaves unspecified. Josephus derives his indication concerning their non-Israelite status from 2 Chr 2:16-17a (MT; RSV 2:17-18a). Via his appended reference to David's "leaving them alive" he alludes back to his notice in *Ant.* 7.335 (// 1 Chr 22:7) about the king's assigning burden-bearing responsibilities to those of the 180,000 aliens counted by him, apart from the 80,000 stone-cutters and the 3,500 overseers.

[196] This figure for Solomon's stone-masons agrees with that cited in 1 Kgs 5:29b (MT; RSV 5:15b) and 2 Chr 2:17 (MT; RSV 2:18).

[197] Josephus' total for Solomon's foremen agrees with that of MT/1 Kgs 5:30 (RSV 5:16); LXX B (and 2 Chr 2:17 [MT; RSV 2:18]) read 3,600, LXX L 3,700.

[198] See 1 Kgs 5:31 (MT; RSV 5:17). Like LXX B, Josephus does not qualify the foundation stones as "costly," as do MT and LXX L.

[199] This further directive by Solomon concerning the stones is Josephus' addition to 1 Kgs 5:31 (MT; RSV 5:17). The "mountain" in question is the "Mount Liban" mentioned in 8.58.

[200] See 1 Kgs 5:32 (MT; RSV 5:18). Josephus does not mention the 3rd group involved in the stone-work according to MT, i.e. "the men of Gebal" (compare LXX

BL: "and they threw this").

[201] Josephus' dating the beginning of the temple's construction to the 2nd month of Solomon's 4th regnal year agrees with 1 Kgs 6:1a and 2 Chr 3:1. Eupolemus ("Fragment 2," preserved in Alexander Polyhistor's *On the Jews* as cited by Eusebius, *Praep. ev.* 9.34.2) dates it rather to Solomon's 13th year.

[202] See 1 Kgs 6:1b, where MT calls the 2nd month (i.e. of a year beginning in the spring) in which the temple construction began by its earlier Hebrew name, i.e. "Ziv" (LXX BL lack this identification). Josephus adds the Macedonian equivalent. The month in question corresponds to April-May.

[203] MT and LXX L 1 Kgs 6:1 date the beginning of the temple's construction *480* years after the Exodus, LXX BA rather *440* years. Josephus' date here in 8.61 differs from that given by him in *Apion* 2.19 and *Ant.* 20.230, i.e. *612* years.

[204] According to *Ant.* 2.318, the Exodus occurred 430 years after Abram's coming to Canaan. If one combines this figure with that for the interval between the Exodus and the start of the temple's construction given in 8.61, one arrives at a total of 1,022 years for the period between Abram's coming to Canaan and Solomon's initiative, i.e. 2 years more than the time cited by Josephus here in 8.61.

[205] As Marcus (*ad loc.*) points out, Josephus' figures here indicate a total of 420 years between the Flood (1440 years before the start of Solomon's temple) and Abram's coming to Canaan (1020 years prior to the temple's initiation). However, the figures given by him in *Ant.* 1.148 (Abram is born 992 years after the flood) and 1.154 (Abram goes to Canaan at age 75) add up to a notably lower total for the interval between the flood and Abram's arrival in Canaan, i.e. 1,067 years.

[206] As Marcus (*ad loc.*) notes, this total for the span between Adam and the start of work on the temple di-

When the sanctuary began to be built, it was already the eleventh year of Heirom's reign in the kingdom of Tyre.[207] From the inception [of that kingdom] until the building of the sanctuary 240 years elapsed.[208]

(3.2) 63 Now then the king laid the foundations for the sanctuary extremely deep in the ground, the stone material being strong and capable of resisting [the passage of] time. These stones, fitted closely together in the ground, were intended as the base and support for the structure that was to be built. On account of their underlying strength, they would effortlessly bear the burden of what was placed upon them and the costly decorations, the weight of which was not to be inferior to that of the other [parts] that were designed for height and breadth of beauty and a graceful magnificence.[209]

Temple foundations laid

64 So he raised it [the structure], which had been made of white stone,[210] as far as the roof. Thus the height [of the structure] was sixty cubits,[211] as was also its length,[212] while the width was twenty.[213] On top of this was raised up another [building] of equal dimensions, so that the total height of the sanctuary was 120 cubits; it was oriented towards the east.[214]

Temple dimensions

65 They set up its [the sanctuary's] vestibule in front, [this being] twenty cubits in length; it extended the width of the building.[215] Its breadth was ten cubits[216] and it was erected to a height of 120 cubits.[217]

He encircled the sanctuary with thirty low-lying buildings.[218] These, surrounding

Temple out-buildings

---

verges notably from that which results from combining the figure given for the period between Adam and the Flood in *Ant.* 1.82 (2,262 years) and the interval between the latter event and the temple's beginning according to 8.61 (1,400 years), namely 3,792 years.

[207] In *Apion* 1.126 the start of the temple is dated to Hiram's *12th* regnal year.

[208] Josephus cites no source for his double synchronism of the start of Solomon's temple with events of Tyrian history. He may have drawn the datings from his authorities for the history of Phoenicia, e.g., Dios and Menander of Ephesus, whom he quotes at length in *Apion* 1.113-115 and 1.117-125, respectively concerning the succession of Tyrian kings.

[209] These remarks on the temple's foundation stones have no biblical parallel. They pick up on Solomon's directives about the preparation of these stones in 1 Kgs 5:31 (MT; RSV 5:17)// 8.60.

[210] Josephus adds the specification about the color of the temple stones to the mention of them in 1 Kgs 5:31 (MT; RSV 5:17).

[211] MT 1 Kgs 6:2 gives the temple's height as 30 cubits, LXX BL rather as 25. Neither 2 Chr 3:3 nor Eupolemus provides a height indication.

[212] Josephus' figure for the temple's length agrees with that given in MT 1 Kgs 6:2// 2 Chr 3:3 (and Eupolemus ["Fragment 2," the citation of which by Alexander Polyhistor is preserved in Eusebius, *Praep. ev.* 34.2]); LXX BL 1 Kgs 6:2 read 40.

[213] Josephus' figure for the temple's width agrees

with that cited in 1 Kgs 6:2// 2 Chr 3:3, while Eupolemus ("Fragment 2," in a quotation from Alexander Polyhistor preserved by Eusebius, *Praep. ev.* 34.2) gives the figure as 60 cubits.

[214] Marcus (*ad loc.*) sees Josephus' notice on this structure superimposed on the sanctuary itself as reflecting "a confused understanding" of the references in 1 Kgs 6:3// 2 Chr 3:4a to the "vestibule in front of the nave of the house," which stood 120 cubits high according to 3:4a. The confusion is compounded by the fact that in what follows (see 8.65) Josephus will make separate mention of the "vestibule." His allusion to the sanctuary's eastward orientation lacks a counterpart in Kings and Chronicles, but does have a parallel in visionary blueprint for the new temple in Ezek 47:1.

[215] Josephus' notice on the length of the temple's "vestibule/porch" and its running the width of the sanctuary itself (see 8.64) agrees with the data given in 1 Kgs 6:3// 2 Chr 3:4a.

[216] 1 Kgs 6:3// 2 Chr 3:4a state that the "vestibule" was "equal to the width" (i.e. 20 cubits, see 6:2// 3:3) of the temple itself.

[217] Josephus' figure for the height of the vestibule agrees with that given in 2 Chr 3:4a. 1 Kgs 6:3 does not mention the height of this structure, but rather its depth, i.e. 10 cubits.

[218] The word translated "buildings" above is literally "houses" (Greek: οἶκοι). Josephus here alludes to the 3 tiers/ stories of the "side chambers," built around the temple edifice according to 1 Kgs 6:5b. The Book

it from outside, were to hold the whole together by their close joining and number.[219] He also constructed entrances for these from one through the other.[220] **66** Each of these buildings was five cubits wide, the same in length, and twenty cubits high. On top of these were built other buildings and then still others that were equal in their dimensions and number to these[221] so that their total height was equivalent to that of the lower building[222] (for the upper [building] was not built all the way round).[223]

67 A roof of cedar wood was laid on top of them. Each of the buildings had its own roof, rather than being joined to the adjacent one. There was a common roof for the remainder [of the edifice]; this was fashioned with very long beams that passed through and extended over all of it, so that the middle walls were held together by the same timbers and stabilized in this way.[224]

Guilding of temple

68 Beneath the beams he laid a ceiling made of the same timber, the whole of it being divided up into panels and plated with gold.[225] He adorned the walls with cypress planks embossed with gold.[226] As a result, the entire sanctuary gleamed and dazzled the eyes of those who entered it with the radiance of gold that struck one from all sides.[227]

Temple stonework and woodwork

69 The entire edifice of the sanctuary was made with the greatest skill, of smooth-surfaced stones that fit together so exactly and snugly that it disclosed no trace of a hammer or any other building tool to those inspecting the work.[228] Without any use of these [tools], all the wood-work joined up so precisely that the fit seemed spontaneous, rather than something forcibly achieved by [the use] of tools.[229]

Doors and partitions

70 The king constructed a suitable ascent to the upper building through the thickness of the wall. For this did not have one large door, facing east the way the lower building did; instead, there were entrances on the sides through much smaller doors.[230] He divided up the sanctuary, both inside and out, by means of cedar beams

---

of Kings does not specify how many of these chambers there were; Josephus likely derived his figure (30) for them from Ezekiel's plan of the new temple in Ezek 40:17 (cf. also the phrase "to the 30" read by MT and LXX at the end of 1 Kgs 6:8, which is generally emended, in line with the reading of a few Hebrew MSS, "to the 3rd").

[219] Josephus adds this remark about the intended purpose of the structures surrounding the temple itself.

[220] Cf. the reference to the "entrance" of the lowest story of the temple's side chambers in 1 Kgs 6:8.

[221] According to 1 Kgs 6:6, the 3 "stories" making up the side chambers were of unequal width, the lowest being 5 cubits, the middle one 6 cubits, and the topmost one 7 cubits. 1 Kgs 6:10 states that each story was 5 cubits high, as opposed to Josephus' 20. Kings does not provide a figure for the length of the stories.

[222] With each "story" being 20 cubits high according to Josephus, their combined height would come to 60 cubits, i.e. the height of the sanctuary itself as given in 8.64. By contrast, the indication of 1 Kgs 6:10 that each of the 3 surrounding stories was 5 cubits high gives them a total height of 15 cubits.

[223] This indication concerning the topmost story lacks a biblical equivalent.

[224] Josephus expatiates on the summary notice of 1 Kgs 6:9b: Solomon "made the ceiling of the house of beams and planks of cedar."

[225] Josephus here seems to combine 1 Kgs 6:15 (the cedar boards extending from the floor of the house to the rafters of the ceiling) and 2 Chr 3:9 (the upper chambers are overlaid with gold).

[226] Josephus draws this notice from 2 Chr 3:5a, where Solomon lines the nave of the temple with cypress [planks] that he then covers with "fine gold."

[227] Josephus spells out the effect on visitors of the gold with which Solomon overlaid the inside of the temple as reported in 1 Kgs 6:21a (MT; LXX BL lack the indication)// 2 Chr 3:7.

[228] Josephus embellishes the reference in 1 Kgs 6:7b (MT; LXX BL lack the indication) to "neither hammer, nor axe, nor any tool of iron" being used in the construction of the temple, emphasizing the stones' perfect fit.

[229] This remark, further expatiating on Josephus' preceding statement concerning the stones' perfect fit, has no biblical counterpart.

[230] Josephus elaborates on the summary reference to the type of access for each of the 3 "stories" given in 1 Kgs 6:8. His allusion to the eastward-facing door of the

that were held together by thick chains, so as to provide support and reinforce-ment.[231]

(3.3) 71 Dividing the inner sanctuary in two, he made an *adytum*[232] of twenty   *The* adytum
cubits,[233] while allotting forty cubits to the holy sanctuary.[234] He cut through the
middle wall and installed doors of cedar,[235] to which had been affixed many gold
and multi-colored carvings.[236] **72** In front of these he hung brightly colored curtains
made, not only of hyacinth, purple and scarlet [materials], but also of the most lu-
minous and softest linen.[237]

In the *adytum* he erected two cherubim of pure gold,[238] whose width and length   *The cherubim*
was twenty cubits;[239] both of them were five cubits high.[240] Each had two wings,
with an extension of five cubits.[241] **73** He set them up not far from each other, in
order that one of their wings might touch the wall on the south of the *adytum* and
the other that on the north.[242] He placed the ark in between their other wings that
joined each other, so that they might be a guard for it.[243] No one can say of what
sort the cherubim were or draw analogies [with them].[244]

74 He also covered the pavement of the sanctuary with golden plates.[245] He like-   *Doors, gates,*
wise placed doors at the gate of the sanctuary—these having a height proportionate   *guilding*
to that of the wall and a width of twenty cubits—and covered them with gold.[246]

---

lower sanctuary picks up on the statement that the
sanctuary was "oriented towards the east" in 8.64.

[231] 1 Kgs 6:15 speaks of the use of cedar boards to
line the walls of the house and to cover its floor, while
6:16 mentions Solomon's "building 20 cubits of the
rear of the house with boards of cedar from the floor to
the rafters." Finally, 1 Kgs 6:21b refers to the gilded
"chains" that were extended in front of the inner sanctuary.

[232] This Greek term is Josephus' rendering of the
reference to "the inner sanctuary (Hebrew: דביר), the
most holy place (Hebrew: קדש־הקדשים)" in 1 Kgs 6:16b.

[233] See 1 Kgs 6:16a. 1 Kgs 6:20a// 2 Chr 3:8a
specify that all 3 dimensions of the Holy of Holies
measured 20 cubits.

[234] This figure agrees with given for the length of
the temple's "nave" (Hebrew: היכל; LXX: ὁ ναός) in 1
Kgs 6:17.

[235] According to 1 Kgs 6:31a, the doors separating
the nave from the Holy of Holies were made of
"olivewood."

[236] 1 Kgs 6:32a (MT LXX L, > LXX B) specifies that
the doors to the inner sanctuary had carvings of "cherubim, palm trees, and open flowers."

[237] Josephus derives his mention of the "curtain(s)"
before the Holy of Holies and the materials used for this
from 2 Chr 3:14, while omitting the biblical reference
to the "cherubim" portrayed on this curtain. In speaking of both doors and curtains at the entrance to the
adytum in 8.71-72, Josephus combines the indications
of 1 Kgs 6:31a and 2 Chr 3:14, the former verse mentioning doors, the latter a curtain.

[238] According to 1 Kgs 6:23, 28// 2 Chr 3:10, the

cherubim were of (olive-) wood and overlaid with gold.
Josephus accentuates the value of these objects by having them made of "pure gold."

[239] The biblical accounts do not specify either the
length or width of the cherubim.

[240] 1 Kgs 6:23 and 26 (MT LXX L; LXX B and 2
Chr 3:10 lack the indication) state that the cherubim
were 10 cubits high.

[241] According to 1 Kgs 6:24-25a// 2 Chr 3:11-13,
each cherub had a wingspan of 10 cubits, for a total extension of 20 cubits. Here again (see previous note),
Josephus reduces the size of the biblical cherubim.

[242] Josephus derives these indications about the
outstretched wings of the cherubim from 1 Kgs 6:27// 2
Chr 3:11-12.

[243] Josephus anticipates this remark on the wings of
the cherubim covering the ark from 1 Kgs 8:7// 2 Chr
5:8.

[244] This (extra-biblical) remark concerning the cherubim as beings *sui generis* is Josephus' way of countering the impression that Solomon's construction of
them violated the scriptural prohibition of making images of any creature; see Feldman 1998: 601 and n. 39.
Feldman further notes that Josephus' formulation here
recalls that used by him regarding the cherubim of the
Mosaic sanctuary in *Ant.* 3.137: "they are winged creatures, quite similar in form to nothing of those seen by
men."

[245] See 1 Kgs 6:30, where Solomon "overlays the
floor of the house with gold."

[246] On the doors leading into the nave of the temple,
see 1 Kgs 6:33-35, which does not mention their dimensions, but does describe them as double folding

Hiram (Heirom), the temple craftsman

The temple columns

75 In a word, no part of the sanctuary, whether inside or out, was left ungilded.[247] He likewise suspended curtains before these doors, similar to those suspended in front of the inner ones.[248] The gate of the vestibule did not have these, however.[249]

(3.4) 76 Solomon summoned[250] from Tyre, from Heirom, a craftsman named Cheirom,[251] whose mother was a Naphthalite by race (for she was of that tribe),[252] while his father, Ourias,[253] was of the Israelite race.[254] He was knowledgeable about every work, being particularly proficient in working with gold, silver, and bronze;[255] everything for the sanctuary was produced by him in accordance with the king's wishes.[256]

77 This Cheirom also constructed two bronze pillars[257] with an interior thickness of four fingers.[258] These columns were eighteen cubits in height, with a circumference of twelve cubits.[259] He set a decorative lily made out of cast metal on the top of each of these, the height of which was five cubits.[260] This was surrounded by an interlaced lattice-work of bronze that covered the columns.[261] **78** From this hung

---

doors carved with "cherubim, palm trees, and open flowers."

[247] See 1 Kgs 6:22a // 2 Chr 3:7a. This notice recalls Josephus' earlier statement about the gilding of the sanctuary in 8.68.

[248] The description of the outer temple doors leading into the nave in 1 Kgs 6:33-35 does not mention such curtains. Josephus' wording here alludes to his account of the curtains placed in front of the doors before the Holy of Holies in 8.68.

[249] This remark concerning the gate leading into the temple's outermost component, the "vestibule" (see 8.65) has no biblical counterpart.

[250] Josephus agrees with 1 Kgs 7:13, where Solomon himself calls "Hiram" from Tyre, as opposed to 2 Chr 2:12 (MT; RSV 2:13), where King "Huram" speaks of his having sent "Huram-abi" to Solomon.

[251] MT (1 Kgs 7:13) חירם (Eng.: "Hiram"); LXX BL Χειράμ; MT (2 Chr 2:12 [RSV 2:13]) חורם־אבי (Eng.: "Huram-abi"); LXX BL Χειράμ; Josephus Χείρωμος.

[252] 1 Kgs 7:13 calls her "a widow of Naphtali," while 2 Chr 2:13 (MT; RSV 2:14) designates her "a woman of the daughters of Dan."

[253] Neither 1 Kgs 7:13 nor 2 Chr 2:13 (MT; RSV 2:14) names the father of Hiram/Huram-abi. Marcus *ad loc.*) mentions 2 possible sources of inspiration for Josephus' form of this figure's name (Greek: Οὐρίας): it might represent either a corruption of the LXX form Τύριος ("Tyrian") of 7:13 or reflect a confusion with the father (called Οὐρείας in LXX) of the maker, Bezalel, of the Mosaic bronze altar according to Exod 31:1.

[254] According to both 1 Kgs 7:13 and 2 Chr 2:13 (MT; RSV 2:14), the (nameless; see previous note) father of Hiram/Huram-abi was "a man of Tyre." Josephus may have felt it inappropriate to have a "half-Gentile"—as Hiram/Huram-abi is in the biblical accounts—

be the maker of the temple furnishings, and so assigned the craftsman's father Israelite status.

[255] Josephus derives his listing of the 3 metals used by "Cheirom" from 2 Chr 2:13b (MT; RSV 2:14b), while leaving aside the additional materials mentioned there. 1 Kgs 7:14 presents Hiram simply as a "worker in bronze."

[256] Cf. 1 Kgs 7:14bβ, which states that Hiram "came to Solomon and did all his work."

[257] On these objects, see 1 Kgs 7:15-22// 2 Chr 3:15-17.

[258] Josephus derives this figure from 1 Kgs 7:15. In making Hiram, rather than Solomon, the subject of the pillar-making, Josephus agrees with 1 Kgs 7:15 against 2 Chr 3:15. By contrast, in attaching his account of the making of the pillars, etc. directly to his narrative of the construction of the temple itself, Josephus follows the sequence of 2 Chronicles 3-4, whereas Kings' treatment of the construction of the temple edifice (1 Kings 6) and of its pillars, etc. (7:13ff.) is separated by a segment dealing with Solomon's secular edifices (7:1-12). Like the Chronicler, Josephus portrays a more pious Solomon, who completes all building projects relating to the temple before embarking on constructions meant for his own use.

[259] Josephus' figures for the pillars' height and width agree with those of MT 1 Kgs 7:15. LXX BL lists their circumference as 14 cubits, while 2 Chr 3:15 makes them 35 cubits high and does not mention their circumference.

[260] Josephus here combines data from 1 Kgs 7:20 (the "lily work" of the capitals surmounting the pillars) and 7:16 (// 2 Chr 3:15: the height, i.e. 5 cubits, of the capitals).

[261] Compare 1 Kgs 7:17// 2 Chr 3:16, which speak of "chains" suspended from the capitals.

down 200 pomegranates in two rows.[262] He erected one of these columns at the right, by the doorpost of the vestibule, and called it *Iachein*,[263] while the other, on the left, he named *Abaiz*.[264]

(3.5) 79 He also cast a bronze sea[265] having the shape of a hemisphere; this bronze item was called the "sea" because of its size.[266] For the wash-basin was ten cubits in diameter,[267] and was cast from molten metal to the thickness of a handbreadth.[268] At its center it rested on a base that curved around an arch on ten spiral-shaped volutes.[269] 80 The diameter of this [base] was a cubit.[270] Around [the sea] stood twelve calves;[271] of these, three each were facing in the direction of the four winds; their backsides were so arranged that the hemisphere rested upon them, while on all sides they inclined inward.[272] The sea held 3,000 baths.[273]

The "Sea"

(3.6) 81 He also made ten square bronze bases for lavers.[274] The length of each base was five cubits, the breadth four, and the height six cubits.[275] The construction, which was engraved overall, was joined together in this way: there were four small standing columns that were squared-off at the corners, each of which had the sides of the base fitting into them.[276] 82 These [sides] were divided into three parts; in each segment a border reaching to the base below was constructed.[277] In the segments were engraved the likeness of a lion, a bull, and an eagle.[278] The little columns too were carved in relief, in a way similar to the sides [of the base].[279] 83 The

The lavers and their stands

---

[262] Josephus' figure for the pomegranates agrees with given in 1 Kgs 7:20, whereas 2 Chr 3:16 speaks of 100. He draws the specification concerning the pomegranates being "in 2 rows" from LXX BL 1 Kgs 7:18.

[263] MT (1 Kgs 7:21// 2 Chr 3:17) יכין (Eng.: "Jachin"); LXX BL Ἰαχούμ; LXX BL 2 Chr 3:17, translating the Hebrew designation, Κατόφθωσιος; Josephus Ἰαχείν. Both biblical accounts specify that this pillar was "on the south side" of the temple.

[264] MT (1 Kgs 7:21// 2 Chr 3:17) בעז (Eng: "Boaz"); LXX B 1 Kgs 7:21 Βάλαζ; LXX L 1 Kgs 7:21 Βάαζ; LXX BL 2 Chr 3:17, translating the Hebrew designation, Ἰσχύς; Josephus Ἀβαίζ. Both biblical accounts specify that the 2nd pillar was "on the north side" of the temple.

[265] On this object, see 1 Kgs 7:23-26// 2 Chr 4:2-5.

[266] Josephus adds this explanation of the odd name, i.e. "sea," for the large washbasin of the temple court.

[267] This figure corresponds to that given in 1 Kgs 7:23// 2 Chr 4:2.

[268] See 1 Kgs 7:26// 2 Chr 4:5.

[269] 1 Kgs 7:24// 2 Chr 4:3 speak of 2 "gourds" beneath the brim of the sea that were "cast when it was cast."

[270] According to 1 Kgs 7:24// Chr 4:3, the "gourds" beneath the brim of the "sea" extended for 10 cubits.

[271] Josephus' designation for these objects (Greek: μόσχοι) corresponds to that used in LXX BL 2 Chr 4:4, whereas MT LXX BL 1 Kgs 7:25 and MT 2 Chr 4:4 call them "oxen." Josephus will, however, employ the word "oxen" in his subsequent mention of these objects (see 8.195), where he criticizes Solomon's making of them

as a violation of Mosaic law.

[272] On the 12 bovine figures beneath the sea, see 1 Kgs 7:25// 2 Chr 4:4 (which enumerate each of the 4 compass points).

[273] This datum corresponds to 2 Chr 4:5b, whereas MT and LXX L* 1 Kgs 7:26b specify 2,000 baths, and LXX B does not supply a figure. On the "bath," see the note to the word *bathos* at 8.57.

[274] On the 10 lavers and their stands, see 1 Kgs 7:27-39 and the much abridged account concerning these in 2 Chr 4:6. Josephus' version in 8.81-86 reflects the more expansive treatment of Kings, even while also reducing this.

[275] Josephus' dimensions for the "bases" of the lavers agree with those cited in LXX BL 1 Kgs 7:27, whereas MT gives their length and width as both 4 cubits, and their height as 3 cubits.

[276] Josephus derives this detail from 1 Kgs 7:34, which refers to the 4 "supports" at the 4 corners of each stand, "which were of one piece with the stands."

[277] The account of the "stands" in 1 Kgs 7:27-37 does not clearly distinguish their 3 component segments, nor mention a lower base.

[278] 1 Kgs 7:29 mentions carved "lions, oxen, and cherubim" on the frames of the laver stands. Josephus' substitution of an "eagle" for the biblical "cherubim," perhaps stands under the influence of Ezekiel's description of the living creatures in Ezek 1:10, whose 4 faces are those of a lion, ox, and eagle (plus a man) respectively; see Feldman 1998: 601.

[279] Cf. 1 Kgs 7:36, which mentions the "cherubim, lions, and palm trees" carved on the surfaces of the

entire object stood suspended on four wheels.[280] These [wheels] were cast, having hubs and rims a cubit and a half in diameter.[281] Anyone who looked at the fellies of the wheels, which were likewise carved in relief and joined to the sides of the bases, would have been astonished that they fitted smoothly into the rims. And yet, so they did.[282] **84** Shoulder-like projections of extended hands joined the corners above; on these was set a rounded molding that was placed around the bottom of the laver. The laver itself rested upon the hands of the eagle and the lion, which were fitted so closely together that they seemed to those who saw them to have grown together. In between them were palm trees carved in relief.[283] Such was the construction of the ten bases.[284]

85 He [Cheirom] likewise produced ten large buckets, round bronze lavers, each of which held forty *choeis*.[285] These had a height of four cubits,[286] while their rims had this same diameter.[287] He placed these lavers on the ten bases that were called *Mechonoth*.[288] **86** He set five lavers on the left side of the sanctuary that was oriented towards the north and the same number on the right, facing south-east.[289] He placed the sea in the same place as well.[290]

Purpose of "sea" and lavers

87 Filling the sea with water, he set it aside for the priests who entered the sanctuary so that they might wash their hands and feet in it when they were about to ascend the altar.[291] The lavers were for cleaning the innards of animals that were offered as whole sacrifices, as well as their feet.[292]

Bronze altar and vessels

(3.7) 88 He also constructed a bronze altar.[293] Its length and breadth were twenty

---

stands' "stays" as well as on their panels.

[280] See 1 Kgs 7:30a, which also mentions the wheels' "axles."

[281] According to 1 Kgs 7:32, it is the height of the wheels that measured 1.5 cubits.

[282] Cf. 1 Kgs 7:32, which states that the axles of the wheels "were of one piece with the stands." Josephus underscores the remarkable smoothness of the fit, just as he did that of the temple's foundation stones in 8.69. On the word translated "fellies" (Greek: ἀψίς) above, see Marcus (*ad loc*), who renders it rather as "drums."

[283] Josephus here alludes to the "stays [RSV; literally: hands] on the top of the stands" cited in 1 Kgs 7:35. The biblical account does not identify the "hands" in question as those of the "cherubim" (here replaced by Josephus with an "eagle," as in 8.82) and "lions" that were engraved on the "stays/hands" along with "palm trees" according to 1 Kgs 7:36. Here again (see 8.83), Josephus highlights the smooth fit of the component parts.

[284] This summary remark, concluding Josephus' description of the bases/stands for the lavers (8.81-84// 1 Kgs 7:27-37), has a counterpart in 7:37.

[285] See 1 Kgs 7:38aβ, where the lavers are said to hold 40 *baths* each. The *chous* is a Greek liquid measure equivalent to 3/4 of a gallon, whereas the Hebrew *bath* equals *ca*. 9 gallons; see Marcus *ad loc*.

[286] This figure corresponds to that given in MT 1 Kgs 7:38bα, but absent in LXX BL.

[287] This specification has no equivalent in the description of the lavers in 1 Kgs 7:38.

[288] See 1 Kgs 7:38bβ. Like LXX BL, Josephus here transliterates the Hebrew word (מכנות) for the "stands/bases," on which the lavers are placed.

[289] See 1 Kgs 7:39a// 2 Chr 4:6a, which speak first of the lavers set on the South side, then of those on the North. Josephus' mention of a "south-east" orientation for half the lavers might be inspired by the wording of 1 Kgs 7:39b// 2 Chr 4:10, where the sea is situated on "the southeast corner of the house."

[290] See 1 Kgs 7:39b// 2 Chr 4:10, which specify that the sea was placed "on the southeast corner of the house."

[291] For this item, Josephus draws on, while also elaborating the notice, unparalleled in 1 Kings 7, of 2 Chr 4:6bβ concerning the function of the sea, i.e. "for the priests to wash in."

[292] For this notice Josephus draws on 2 Chr 4:6bα (no parallel in 1 Kings 7), which states that the lavers were "to rinse off what was used for the burnt offering," rendering its formulation more precise.

[293] The account of the temple furnishings in 1 Kings 7 does not mention this altar. Josephus derives his notice on it from 2 Chr 4:1. At the same time he reverses the sequence of 2 Chronicles 4, where the bronze altar is dealt with (v. 1), prior to the sea and the lavers (vv. 2-6).

cubits and its height ten cubits;[294] it was for the whole sacrifices.[295] For it he likewise made all the bronze vessels, tripod-like altar utensils, and shovels. In addition to these things, Cheirom fashioned basins, hooks, and every [kind of] vessel from [that] bronze, which in its brilliance and beauty is similar to gold.[296]

89 The king set up a number of tables,[297] together with a large one of gold. It was on this [table] they set out the loaves of God;[298] [he also set up] countless other [tables] that were quite similar to this one, though of a different style.[299] On them were placed the vessels and the bowls, along with 2,000 golden and 4,000 silver libation-vessels.[300]

The tables

90 He made as well countless lamps, according to the order of Moyses.[301] Of these, he erected one in the sanctuary in order that it might give light during the day in accordance with the Law.[302] [He likewise erected] the table on which the breads were placed on the north side of the sanctuary, over against the lamp (for he had stood this on the south side),[303] while the golden altar[304] was situated between them.[305] The forty-cubit building[306] contained all these things in front of the curtain

The lamps. the showbread table, the golden altar

---

[294] These dimensions for the bronze altar correspond to those cited in 2 Chr 4:1.

[295] Josephus adds this specification concerning the function of the bronze altar to the brief mention of it in 2 Chr 4:1.

[296] For this notice, see 1 Kgs 7:40a, 45// 2 Chr 4:11a, 16. Josephus expands the biblical lists with mention of "tripods" and "hooks," as also with the indication concerning the luster of the bronze used for these objects. His reference to the exceptional quality of the bronze used regards recalls his notice in *Ant.* 7.160 about Solomon's future use of the extraordinary bronze captured by David to make the "sea" and the lavers. He leaves aside the details about the place where the bronze vessels were cast and the countless quantity of bronze used cited in 1 Kgs 7:46-47// 2 Chr 4:17-18.

[297] 2 Chr 4:8a specifies 10 such tables and mentions their placement within the temple, 5 on the south side and 5 on the north.

[298] See 1 Kgs 7:48// 2 Chr 4:19, which speak of the "bread of the [divine] Presence" (literally: face). Josephus describes both the table and its bread in more detail in his account of the Mosaic sanctuary in *Ant.* 3.139-142.

[299] Josephus appends this remark about the other tables as compared with the golden one.

[300] See 2 Chr 4:8b, which mentions the making of 100 "basins of gold"; cf. 1 Kgs 7:50a// 2 Chr 4:22a, which enumerate a series of objects crafted for use in the cult out of "pure gold," but without providing figures for these. Josephus supplies (very high) numbers for the vessels made, likewise introducing the distinction between those of silver and gold, and specifying that these were placed on the (other) tables. On

Solomon's precious-metal cultic vessels, see further 8.91.

[301] 1 Kgs 7:49// 2 Chr 4:7 mentions a total of *10* golden lampstands; once again, Josephus embellishes the biblical figures. The Mosaic directive concerning the lampstands alluded to here does not have an explicit counterpart in Josephus' account of the desert sanctuary, where (see *Ant.* 4.144-148// Exod 25:31-40) there is mention only of a single, 7-branched candelabrum that God instructs Moses to have made.

[302] The reference is to the 7-branched candelabrum described by Josephus in *Ant.* 4.144-148 (// Exod 25:31-40).

[303] This indication—unparalleled in either 1 Kings 7 or 2 Chronicles 4—corresponds to Josephus' statement in *Ant.* 4.144 that the candelabrum "stood in front of the table near the wall towards the south."

[304] The golden (incense) altar has not previously been mentioned by Josephus in his account of Solomon's temple; he draws his mention of it here from 1 Kgs 7:48// 2 Chr 4:19. Compare *Ant.* 3.147, where Josephus mentions the "wooden incense-altar," encircled by "a solid plate of metal" of the Mosaic sanctuary.

[305] Josephus' statement concerning the placement of the 3 cultic objects just outside the Holy of Holies here is proleptic, referring to their intended location, since it is only in 8.96 that these objects will actually be installed in the temple.

[306] Josephus here refers to the 40-cubit "holy sanctuary" (the biblical "nave") of the temple mentioned by him in 8.71. The various objects cited in 8.90 were located at the back of this chamber, just outside the *adytum*.

of the *adytum*, in which the ark was about to be situated.[307]

Temple vessels   **(3.8) 91** The king constructed 80,000 wine-jugs and 100,000 bowls of gold, plus twice as many of silver. He made as well 80,000 flat dishes for carrying the finest mixed wheat-flour to the altar, and twice as many of silver. He also made 60,000 gold mixing-jugs, in which the wheat flour was mixed with oil, along with twice this number of silver.[308]

Scales and censers   **92** He also made scales[309] which were very similar to the Mosaic ones that were called *hin* and *assaron*[310]—20,000 of gold and twice as many of silver.[311] He further constructed 20,000 golden censers, in which the incense was brought into the sanctuary.[312] Similarly, there were 50,000 other censers, in which they brought the fire from the great to the small altar.[313]

Priestly garments   **93** He also made priestly garments for the high priests:[314] an upper garment reaching to the feet, robes extending from the shoulders, the oracle, and the 1,000 [precious] stones. The crown, however, on which Moyses wrote [the name of] God, was a single one and has survived down till today.[315] He fashioned 10,000 [ordinary] priestly garments out of fine linen, with purple sashes for each.[316]

Musical instruments   **94** [He made] as well 200,000 trumpets according to the command of Moyses,[317] as also 200,000 robes of fine linen for the Levitical singers.[318] In addition, he fashioned out of amber 4,000 musical instruments, invented for the singing of hymns, that are called *nablai* and *kinyrai*.[319]

---

[307] This summarizing notice on the 3 objects situated before the curtain of the inner sanctuary is Josephus' addition to the biblical accounts. On the ark's designated place within the Holy of Holies, see 8.73.

[308] Josephus here returns to the subject of Solomon's precious-metal cultic vessels, mentioned initially in 8.89. As in his similar catalogue of the Mosaic liturgical vessels in *Ant.* 3.150, so also here, he supplies very large, "un-biblical" figures for these vessels, likewise distinguishing between those of gold and those of silver. The effect is to accentuate the piety of Solomon, who provides the temple with such an abundance of costly vessels.

[309] The lists of Solomon's cultic equipment in 1 Kings 7// 2 Chronicles 4 do not mention such "scales." Josephus may have been familiar with them as part of the fabric of the temple of his own time.

[310] In *Ant.* 3.197, 234 Josephus states that the *hin* is the Hebrew equivalent of two Attic *chous* (on which see 8.85). He mentions the *assaron* (= Hebrew עשרנים, "a tenth [part]," see Lev 24:5) as a unit of measure for the manna in *Ant.* 3.29 and for the "showbread" in 3.142.

[311] Here again (see 8.91), Josephus accentuates Solomon's piety by crediting him with the making of such huge numbers of cultic scales.

[312] Golden "dishes for incense" are mentioned in 1 Kgs 7:50a// 2 Chr 4:22a, but no figures for these are given.

[313] The references to the incense dishes in 1 Kgs 7:50a// 2 Chr 4:22a do not distinguish 2 different uses for these items, as does Josephus here. The "great altar"

is the (bronze) altar of sacrifice situated outside the temple building proper (see 8.88), while the "small altar" is the golden one used for burning incense and located before the Holy of Holies (see 8.90).

[314] The accounts of 1 Kings 7// 2 Chronicles 4 do not mention the making of high priestly garments. Cf. Josephus' more detailed description of Moses' making these items in *Ant.* 3.159-170.

[315] Josephus mentions Moses' inscribing the "name of God" on the high priest's crown in *Ant.* 3.176 (// Exod 28:36; 39:30). Here in 8.93, he adds, likely from his personal knowledge as a priest, that such a crown had survived down to his own time.

[316] Josephus now briefly touches on the garments of the other priests; these are described in more detail in *Ant.* 3.151-158 in his account of the Mosaic cultic system. His added reference to the (high) priestly garments made by Solomon here in 8.93 accentuates the parallelism between Moses' cultic arrangements and those of the king.

[317] This item no has parallel in 1 Kings 7// 2 Chronicles 4. In *Ant.* 3.291 (cf. Num 10:1-2), Josephus credits Moses with inventing "a kind of trumpet."

[318] With this (neutral) mention of Solomon's making the Levitical singers "fine linen robes," compare Josephus' denunciation of these same singers for getting themselves permission to wear "linen robes just like the priests" shortly before the Jewish revolt in *Ant.* 20.116.

[319] Josephus' added notice on Solomon's making of various kinds of musical instruments recalls his men-

(3.9) 95 Solomon fashioned all these things richly and magnificently for the honor of God. Holding nothing back, he expended all his ambition on the beautification of the sanctuary[320] and deposited the [above objects] in the treasuries of God.[321]

Completion of temple structure

He encircled the sanctuary with a parapet—called *geison* in our ancestral tongue, but *thrinkos* by the Greeks—the height of which rose three cubits.[322] This blocked entry into the sacred precinct for the majority, signifying that it was only open to the priests.[323]

Temple courts

96 Outside of this he built [another] sacred precinct[324] in the shape of a quadrangle, also erecting large, broad porticos that were accessible by lofty gates. Each of these was oriented towards one of the four winds and were closed off by means of golden doors.[325] **97** It was into this [precinct] that all those who had submitted to purification and the Law's requirements entered.[326]

The sacred precinct that was outside these was marvelous and surpassed anything that could be told or seen. For he raised the great, filled-in ravines to the height of 400 cubits (on account of their immeasurable depth, one could not comfortably bend over to look at these),[327] making these equal in height to the summit of the mountain on which the sanctuary was built. As a result, the open-air, outermost sacred precinct was level with the sanctuary. **98** He surrounded it [the outermost sacred precinct] with a double portico; this was supported by tall columns of natural stone and its roofs were of polished cypress panels.[328] All the gates he erected for this sacred precinct were of silver.[329]

---

tion of David's doing the same thing in *Ant.* 7.305b-306 (where a 3rd instrument, i.e. the *kymbala*, is cited as well).

[320] Josephus embellishes the notices on the completion of Solomon's temple works of 1 Kgs 7:51a// 2 Chr 5:1a, underscoring the king's enthusiasm for the project.

[321] Josephus omits the specification of 1 Kgs 7:51b // 2 Chr 5:1b that what Solomon deposited in the treasuries were "the things which David his father had dedicated." He thereby keeps the focus on Solomon's own contributions; see Feldman 1998: 596.

[322] The biblical accounts (1 Kings 6-7// 2 Chronicles 3-4) do not speak of such a "parapet" in connection with Solomon's temple. As Marcus (*ad loc.*) suggests, Josephus' description of the constructions surrounding the temple building in 8.95-98 reflects his familiarity with the Herodian temple complex. Thus, in *War* 5.193 (cf. *Ant.* 15.417) he refers to the stone "balustrade," three cubits in height, which surrounded the 2nd court of Herod's temple, while in *War* 5.226 he mentions a "parapet" (Greek: γεῖσιον), approximately a cubit in height, which encompassed both the sanctuary and the altar and served to separate the people from the priests.

[323] Cf. the reference to the "parapet" of Herod's temple, separating the people from the priests, in *War* 5.226 mentioned in the previous note. This (innermost) sacred precinct, immediately surrounding the temple edifice, corresponds to the "Court of the Priests" of the

Herodian temple-complex.

[324] This 2nd "sacred precinct" of the Solomonic temple situated beyond the one immediately surrounding the temple edifice in Josephus' account corresponds to the "Court of the Israelites" of Herod's temple-complex, as mentioned in *War* 5.193 and *Ant.* 15.417.

[325] Compare Josephus' more expansive descriptions of the 2nd court (the "Court of the Israelites") and its multiple gateways in *War* 5.193-206 and *Ant.* 15.417-420.

[326] Compare *Ant.* 15.418, where Josephus speaks of the "great gateway" leading into the 2nd court through which "those of us who were ritually clean used to pass with our wives." In his description of the Solomonic temple complex here in 8.96-97 Josephus does not distinguish between the "Court of the Israelites" (reserved to males) and a "Court of Women" (into which both sexes could enter) as he does in his account of the Herodian temple; see *Ant.* 15.419; *War* 5.198-199.

[327] Compare *Ant.* 15.414, where Josephus mentions the "ravine" surrounding the Herodian temple complex and the more detailed account in *War* 5.184-189 of the gradual filling in the area surrounding the temple hill, a process initiated by Solomon according to 5.184.

[328] Compare Josephus' more detailed description of the portico and its columns of the Herodian temple complex in *War* 5.190-192 and *Ant.* 15.413-416.

[329] On Solomon as the builder of the 1st temple's exterior portico, see *Ant.* 20.221. Josephus' other descriptions of the temple do not mention such silver

Completed temple to be dedicated

(4.1) 99 Now King Solomon fully completed these great and beautiful building works and dedicatory offerings for the sanctuary within seven years.[330] He thus evidenced his wealth and eagerness, so that what any onlooker would suppose could hardly be constructed over the span of all time was finished in a short [period], relative to the size of the sanctuary.[331] He then wrote to the leaders and elders of the Hebrews and directed the entire people to assemble in Hierosolyma in order to see the sanctuary and accompany the ark of God into it.[332]

100 The order about everyone coming to Hierosolyma was proclaimed everywhere; it was only, however, in the seventh month that, with difficulty, they assembled (this month is called *Athurei*[333] by the natives, *Hyberbertai* by the Macedonians).[334] At this same time the season of Tabernacles, a feast that is very sacred and important to the Hebrews, likewise took place.[335]

Ark conveyed to temple

101 Carrying then the ark and the tent that Moyses had erected as well as all the vessels for the sacrificial service of God, they accompanied these to the sanctuary.[336] The king himself led the way with sacrifices,[337] while the whole people and the Levites sprinkled the road with libations and the blood of many victims.[338] They burned such an limitless amount of incense **102** that all the surrounding air was filled with it and wafted its sweetness to all those who were very far away.[339] [This caused them] to realize that God was present and, in accordance with human opinion, was taking up residence in the place that had been just built and consecrated

---

gates of the outermost court.

[330] This figure for the duration of Solomon's temple-building project corresponds to that of MT 1 Kgs 7:38b (LXX BL and 2 Chronicles lack the indication). Josephus has no counterpart to the notice of 7:38a that the construction of the temple commenced in Solomon's 4th year and concluded in his 11th.

[331] This remark picks up on the notice about work on the temple being completed in 7 years at the opening of 8.99. Josephus makes a similar observation concerning the work done on Herod's temple-complex in *War* 5.189.

[332] See 1 Kgs 8:1 // 2 Chr 5:2, where it is only the leaders of the people who are summoned to Jerusalem; Josephus' modification in this regard has in view the notice in 8:2a (MT, > LXX BL)// 5:3a), where it is "all the men of Israel" who assemble before Solomon. Josephus adds the reference to their "seeing the sanctuary" as a motivation for Solomon's summoning the people.

[333] Greek: Ἀθύρει; this is the reading of RO, which Niese follows. Marcus adopts the conjecture of J. Hudson, itself inspired by Lat's *thes(e)ri*, namely Θισρί.

[334] 1 Kgs 8:2// 2 Chr 5:3 date the assembly of all Israel to "the feast in the seventh month"; 1 Kgs 8:2 further names the month as "Ethanim" (MT; LXX BL Ἀθανείν). Josephus supplies his own version of the Hebrew month name, along with its "Macedonian" equivalent (cf. the 2 equivalent month names cited in 8.61).

[335] Josephus here identifies the "feast in the 7th month" that is left unnamed in 1 Kgs 8:2// 2 Chr 5:3. On the celebration of Tabernacles in the 7th month, see Lev 23:34. On Josephus' treatment of this feast generally, see Colautti 2002.

[336] See 1 Kgs 8:3-4// 2 Chr 5:4-5. Josephus leaves the identity of the ark's "carriers" unspecified; compare 1 Kgs 8:3 (the priests)// 2 Chr 5:4 (the Levites); 1 Kgs 8:4 (MT, > LXX BL)// 2 Chr 5:5 (the priests and Levites); see, however, 8.103. Eupolemus ("Fragment Two," preserved in Eusebius' quotation [*Praep. ev.* 34.9] of Alexander Polyhistor) mentions the Mosaic "altar of sacrifice" being brought into the temple on this occasion as well.

[337] See 1 Kgs 8:5// 2 Chr 5:6, which speak of the innumerable sheep and oxen sacrificed during the procession to the temple.

[338] This is Josephus' embellishment of the biblical notices on the accompanying sacrifices (see previous note). His mention of the Levites alone and not (also) the priests here is noteworthy, given his tendency to downplay the role of the former in favor of the latter, as well as the consistent scriptural stipulation (see Lev 3:5, 8, 13) that it is only the priests who are to handle the sacrificial blood. On Josephus' overall treatment of the Levites, see Glessmer 1994.

[339] Neither 1 Kings 8 nor 2 Chronicles 5 speaks of a use of incense during the ark's procession to the temple. Josephus' addition of the item heightens the solemnity and opulence of the occasion.

for him.[340] For they did not stop singing hymns and dancing until they came to the sanctuary.[341]

103 Thus it was that they conveyed the ark. When it had to be brought into the *adytum*, the rest of the crowd departed;[342] it was the priests alone who carried it in and set it down between the two cherubim.[343] Their wings intercrossed, for thus they had been constructed by the craftsman, the ark being completely covered, as it were, by a kind of tent and vaulted roof.[344] **104** The ark contained nothing except the two stone tablets that preserved the ten words spoken by God to Moyses on Mount Sinai that were engraved upon them.[345] They [the priests] set the lampstand, the table, and the golden altar in the sanctuary in front of the *adytum*,[346] in the same positions they had occupied when they were situated in the tent,[347] and offered the daily sacrifices.[348]

105 They set the bronze altar in front of the sanctuary, opposite the door, so that when the door was opened, the altar would be facing one and the sacred rites and the costliness of the sacrifices would be seen.[349] All the remaining vessels he carried together into the interior of the sanctuary and deposited them.[350]

(4.2) 106 Then when the priests had set everything in order around the ark and gone out, suddenly a dense cloud arose. Being neither dark nor filled with rain as in the winter season, but rather diffused and mild, this [cloud] made its way into the sanctuary.[351] It so blinded the eyes of the priests that they did not recognize one

Appearance of cloud

---

[340] With this editorial remark Josephus anticipates Solomon's acknowledgement, as voiced by him in 1 Kgs 8:27// 2 Chr 6:18, that God cannot actually be contained by any human-made house. He will return to the question of God's "location" several times in his account of the temple's dedication; see 8.106.

[341] Josephus' reference to the singing and dancing by the participants in the procession to the temple lacks a counterpart in 1 Kings 8// 2 Chronicles 5. His addition of the reference serves to associate the procession of the ark under Solomon with its transport to Jerusalem in David's time; see *Ant.* 7.81, 85, 87 (cf. 2 Sam 6:5, 14-16// 1 Chr 13:8; 15:27-29).

[342] Josephus' mention of the people's "departure" at this point in the proceedings has no biblical counterpart.

[343] Here, in contrast to 8.101, Josephus follows 1 Kgs 8:6// 2 Chr 5:7 in specifying that it was the priests who bore the ark to its final destination.

[344] Josephus expatiates on the notice of 1 Kgs 8:7 // 2 Chr 5:8 concerning the wings of the cherubim, alluding, e.g., to his account of the placement of these figures in 8.72b-73. The "craftsman" referred to here in 8.104 would seem to be the Tyrian "Cheirom" (who, however, is only introduced by Josephus in 8.76, subsequent to his account of the erection of the cherubim in 8.72b-73).

[345] See 1 Kgs 8:8// 2 Chr 5:9 (whose reference to Mount Horeb Josephus, in accord with his regular practice, replaces with mention of Mount Sinai). Josephus'

language concerning the content of the ark here in 8.104 recalls that used by him in *Ant.* 3.138.

[346] Cf. Josephus' earlier (proleptic) notice on Solomon's placement of these 3 objects in 8.90.

[347] The "tent" here is the Mosaic tabernacle that has just been brought to the new temple; see 8.101. On the 3, just-mentioned cultic objects and their placement within the Mosaic tabernacle, see *Ant.* 3.139-148.

[348] Neither 1 Kings 8 nor 2 Chronicles 5 mentions such a placement of the 3 cultic objects by the priests or their offering the prescribed daily sacrifices subsequent to bringing the ark into the Holy of Holies.

[349] This notice on the setting up of the altar of sacrifice (on which see 8.88) and the reason for its being placed where it is has no direct counterpart in the biblical accounts. Cf., however, the allusion to the bronze altar's being insufficient for the number of Solomon's sacrifices in 1 Kgs 8:64// 2 Chr 7:7, which does presuppose the previous erection of that altar.

[350] This notice, in which the singular verb forms have Solomon as their apparent subject, lacks a biblical basis. On the cultic vessels, see 8.88, 91-92.

[351] See 1 Kgs 8:10// 2 Chr 5:11, 13b; like Kings, Josephus has no equivalent to the Chronicler's intervening reference (5:12-13a) to the activities of the Levitical musicians. He supplies the allusions to the suddenness of the cloud's arrival and its appearance. His description here recalls that given by him of the cloud that manifested itself at the Mosaic sanctuary in *Ant.* 3.203; compare Exod 40:34-35.

another.[352] At the same time, it conveyed to the minds of all the impression and opinion[353] that God was descending into the sacred precinct and was willing to dwell in it.[354]

Solomon's opening prayer

107 While they were all thinking this thought, King Solomon arose—for had been sitting[355]—and spoke to God words he supposed appropriate to the divine nature[356] and suitable to say to him.[357] "We know," he said, "O Master, that you have an everlasting house, in those things you have devised for yourself,[358] namely the heaven, the air, the earth, and the sea; you are spread throughout all these things, but are not encompassed by them.[359] **108** I, however, have constructed this dedicated sanctuary for you, so that from it we may send up our prayers into the air, sacrificing and singing hymns[360] and we may constantly be convinced that you are present and not far distant. For just as you look down upon everything and hear everything, you do not, even as you dwell here—as is possible for you to do—cease to be near to everyone. Rather, to each one who consults you, you are present night and day as a helper.[361]

Solomon addresses people

109 When he had made these prayers to God, he directed his words to the crowd, making clear the power and providence[362] of God for them,[363] in that, of all the things he had disclosed to David his father about the future, many had already come about, while the rest would do so.[364] **110** [He further spoke] of how [God] had con-

---

[352] Compare 1 Kgs 8:11// 2 Chr 5:14, which state that the priests were unable to "stand to minister because of the cloud; for the glory of the Lord filled the house of the Lord" (1 Kgs 8:11; 2 Chr 5:14 has "of God").

[353] Greek: φαντασία καὶ δόξα. This collocation occurs only here in Josephus.

[354] This appended notice recalls the wording used by Josephus in 8.102, where he speaks of the "human opinion" that God was taking up residence in the temple complex.

[355] Cf. the reference to Solomon's "standing" before the altar of the Lord in 1 Kgs 8:22// 2 Chr 6:12 as he begins his address to the Deity. Josephus appends the allusion to the king's previous "sitting." Like Kings, he has no equivalent to the mention of the "bronze platform" on which Solomon first stands and then kneels in 2 Chr 6:13.

[356] Greek: θεία φύσις. This phrase occurs only here in Josephus' writings. It appears also in 2 Pet 1:4, which speaks of Christians becoming "partakers of the divine nature."

[357] Josephus supplies this characterization of the words Solomon is about to pronounce.

[358] This statement about God's self-made cosmic residence takes the place of Solomon's citation of the Lord's own affirmation in 1 Kgs 8:12a// 2 Chr 6:1: "The Lord has set the sun in the heavens, but [the words "has set the sun in the heavens, but" are found in LXX BL 1 Kgs 8:12, but are absent in MT 1 Kgs 8:12 and 2 Chr 6:1] has said that he would dwell in thick darkness." Josephus has no equivalent to the "source no-

tice" found at the end of LXX BL 8:12 ("is it [the preceding divine saying] not written in the Book of the Upright One?").

[359] On the Stoic coloration of this characterization of God by the Josephan Solomon, see Feldman 1998: 619-20.

[360] Josephus conflates Solomon's separate affirmations about his having built the Lord a house in 1 Kgs 8:13// 2 Chr 6:2 (here the "house" is called a "place for thee [God] to dwell in forever") and 8:20b// 6:10b (Solomon has built the house "for the name of the Lord").

[361] This component of Solomon's prayer, with its universalistic thrust, seems inspired by the king's petition that God hear the prayers of foreigners who come to the temple from afar in 1 Kgs 8:41-43// 2 Chr 6:32-33. Josephus' Solomon will return to this topic in 8.116.

[362] Greek: δύναμις καὶ πρόνοια. This collocation occurs only here in Josephus.

[363] Compare 1 Kgs 8:14// 2 Chr 6:3, where Solomon's address to the people is introduced with a mention of his "blessing" them. Josephus avoids attributing such a blessing to the king, who is not a priest, Israel's designated "blesser" according to Num 6:22-27.

[364] Josephus summarizes Solomon's expansive reference to the Lord's fulfillment of his promises to David in 1 Kgs 8:15, 20// 2 Chr 6:4, 10, which mention in particular the realization of 2 such promises, i.e. Solomon's succession and his building of the temple. Josephus appends the reference to additional divine promises that still await their (assured) fulfillment.

ferred his name on him even before he was born and foretold what he was to be called[365] and that this king would build the sanctuary for him after the death of his father.[366] He then requested that they, who saw that it had turned out in accordance with his prophecy, praise God[367] and believe, on the basis of what they had already seen, that he would leave nothing undone in the future of what he had promised for their well-being.[368]

(4.2) **111** Having said these things to the mob, the king again faced the sanctuary.[369] He raised his right hand to the mob[370] and said: "It is not possible for humans by their works to do God a favor, for the sake of the good things they have experienced. For the Deity requires nothing at all and is superior to any sort of recompense.[371] But with that [capacity][372] by which we have been made by you superior to all other living beings, O Master, it is necessary for us to praise your majesty and thank you for your benefits to our house and the people of the Hebrews.[373] **112** For with what else is it more appropriate for us to propitiate you when you are angry[374] and displeased, and to render you well-disposed, than by the voice that we have from the air and that we know ascends through this [element] again?[375] By means of this [voice] I therefore declare my thanks to you, first regarding my father, whom you advanced from obscurity to so great a glory,[376] **113** and then for your having done everything on my behalf that you foretold until the present

Solomon's concluding prayer

---

[365] Cf. *Ant.* 7.93, where in his version of Nathan's oracle to David of 2 Sam 7:13// 1 Chr 17:12, Josephus has the prophet mention the name, i.e. Solomon, of the son of David who will build the temple long prior to the former's birth.

[366] Josephus compresses the biblical Solomon's citation of God's words to David in 1 Kgs 8:16-19// 2 Chr 6:5-9, confining himself to the key point, i.e. the divine announcement that David's son would build a house for "my name" (8:19// 6:9).

[367] Neither 1 Kings 8 nor 2 Chronicles 6 mentions such a call to "praise God" addressed by Solomon to the assembly; in 1 Kgs 8:15// 2 Chr 6:4 the king himself "blesses" God for the fulfillment of his promises to David.

[368] This (added) reference to the divine promises still awaiting their assured fulfillment recalls Solomon's affirmation about the "rest [of God's promises] coming about" in 8.109.

[369] Compare 1 Kgs 8:21// 2 Chr 6:12, where, Solomon, after his address to the people (8:14-20// 6:3-11), "stands before the altar of the Lord" in the presence of the assembly. Josephus' addition of the term "again" refers back to 8.107, where Solomon "stands" when speaking to God.

[370] Greek: εἰς τὸν ὄχλον; this is the reading of the codices, followed by Niese. In light of 1 Kgs 8:22, Marcus (*ad loc.*) suggests the emendation εἰς τὸν οὐρανόν ("towards heaven"). The parallel text, 2 Chr 6:12, simply has Solomon "spreading forth his hands."

[371] Greek: ἀπροδεής. Josephus' one other use of this term is in *Ant.* 3.45, where it is applied to the Hebrew

army. On the term as a Stoic designation for God see Feldman 1998: 620-1 and n. 71. Compare also Paul's characterization of God in his address to the Athenians in Acts 17:25 as one who is "not served by human hands, as though he needed [προσδεόμονος] anything...." In 1 Kgs 8:23a// 2 Chr 6:14a Solomon affirms "there is no God like thee, in heaven above or on earth beneath...."

[372] As Marcus' elucidatory, context-based addition to his translation ("with that *gift of speech*") indicates, Josephus here alludes to the human capacity of speech that differentiates humans from animals and that is to be used in praise of God.

[373] Compare Solomon's acknowledgement of what God has done for his faithful servants in general and for David in particular in 1 Kgs 8:23b-24// 2 Chr 6:14b-15. The term "praise" (Greek: εὐλογέω) picks up on the same term used in Solomon's call to the assembly to "praise God" in 8.110.

[374] Greek: μηνίω. Josephus uses this verb with God as subject also in *Ant.* 15.299 and with a human subject in *War* 2.69.

[375] Josephus supplies this mention of the "human voice" as the means by which people may propitiate God. Its wording recalls 8.108, where Solomon alludes to prayers' being sent up "into the air."

[376] Solomon's allusion to God's "advancement" of David here recalls David's own acknowledgement of the Deity's "having already promoted him from the lowly state of being a shepherd and advanced him to so great a position of leadership and glory" in *Ant.* 7.95.

day.[377] As for the future, I ask you to grant whatever the power of God [gives] to those who have been honored by you.[378] [I also ask you] to prosper our house in everything, so that, as you promised to David, my father, both while he lived and at his death, the kingship will remain with us and that his family will retain it for countless descendants.[379] Therefore, confer these things on me and award to all who are mine that virtue in which you rejoice.[380]

114 In addition to these things, I beg that you send forth a certain portion of your spirit[381] to the sanctuary and cause it to dwell there, so that you may appear to be with us on earth.[382] Now for you, of course, to whom the whole vault of heaven and everything that is beneath it is but a meager dwelling, this is no extraordinary sanctuary.[383] Nevertheless, I appeal to you to preserve it undevastated by enemies as your own for all time and to care for[384] it as a house that is your property.[385]

115 And if, when the people offend and then [are afflicted] with a certain evil[386] blow from you on account of their offense, with fruitlessness of the soil, fatal pestilence,[387] or any of those sufferings with which you bring retribution on those who transgress anything that is holy, they all flee for refuge and assemble at the sanctuary and beg and ask you to be saved, be attentive to them as if you were inside,[388] acting mercifully to them and delivering them from their misfortunes.[389]

---

[377] See 1 Kgs 8:24// 2 Chr 6:15, where Solomon—in terms recalling those used in 8:15// 6:4—acknowledges God's fulfillment of his promises to David on "this day." The king's words of thanks to God here in 8.113 likewise recall his statements to the people about God's having fulfilled the promises made by him to David regarding Solomon himself in 8.109-111.

[378] Compare 1 Kgs 8:25a// 2 Chr 6:16a, where Solomon asks God to "keep" for David what he had spoken to him. The reference to "the power of God" here recalls the phrase in 8.109, where Solomon undertakes to make clear to the people "the power and providence of God."

[379] 1 Kgs See 8:25b// 2 Chr 6:16, where Solomon quotes the (opening of) God's promise to David (see 2 Sam 7:12-13// 1 Chr 17:12b-14; cf. *Ant.* 7.93) that his posterity will never be cut off from sitting on the throne of Israel. Josephus leaves aside the continuation of the biblical Solomon's citation of the divine announcement to his father in which the foregoing promise is made contingent on the Davidic dynasty's ongoing commitment to the Law. He thereby brings Solomon's quotation of the promise into line with the unconditional formulation of the original promise itself.

[380] This double appeal (both for himself personally and for the members of his family) takes the place of Solomon's (reiteration of his) request that God "confirm" his word to David of 1 Kgs 8:26// 2 Chr 6:17; cf. 8:25a// 6:16a.

[381] Greek: μοῖρα. . . τοῦ σοῦ πνεύματος. With this expression compare that used by Josephus in his address to the defenders of Jotapata in *War* 3.372, where he qualifies the "soul" (Greek: ψηχή) as a θεοῦ μοῖρα

("portion of God").

[382] This petition spells out the content of Solomon's request in 1 Kgs 8:28// 2 Chr 6:19 that God heed the prayer he is now making. Its mention of God's "spirit" (Greek: πνεῦμα) is exceptional in Josephus, who tends to avoid biblical mentions of the divine "spirit," whereas the reference to God's "appearing" to be "with us on earth" recalls 8.102 with its reference to "human opinion" about God's dwelling in the temple.

[383] Josephus now has Solomon return to his acknowledgement of the inadequacy of the temple for God that was already articulated by him in 8.107 on the basis of 1 Kgs 8:27// 2 Chr 6:18.

[384] Greek: προνοέω. This verb recalls Solomon's statement of his intention to make clear "the power and providence (Greek: πρόνοια) of God" for the people in 8.109.

[385] Cf. 1 Kgs 8:29a// 2 Chr 6:20a, where Solomon prays that God's "eyes" will be open towards the house about which he [God] has stated "my name shall be there." Josephus avoids the biblical anthropomorphism (and "name theology").

[386] Greek: κακῷ, the reading of the codices, which Niese follows. Marcus (*ad loc.*) adopts the conjecture of Thackeray, i.e. κακῶται ("is smitten").

[387] Solomon's mention of first 2 potential divine "blows" recalls *Ant.* 7.93, where God, via Nathan, threatens the offending descendant of David with "disease and infertility of the soil."

[388] Solomon's "as-if" formulation here recall the previous references (see 8.102, 114) to God's (only) "appearing" to be in the temple.

[389] Josephus compresses the long biblical segment

116 I do not, however, ask for this help from you for the Hebrews alone when they go astray. Rather, even if some should come from the ends of the inhabited world and from any country and turn to God in prayer and earnestly beseech that they obtain some good, be attentive and give [this] to them.[390] **117** For thus all will learn that it was by your wish that this house was built by us for you and that we are not inhuman[391] by nature nor ill-disposed to those who are not compatriots.[392] Rather, we wish that your help and the benefit of good things[393] be common to all.[394]

(4.4) **118** Having said these things[395] and thrown himself on the ground and paid homage until a late hour,[396] Solomon arose and offered sacrifices to God, covering [the altar] with unblemished victims.[397] He then found out very clearly that God willingly accepted the sacrifice.[398] For fire, falling down from the air upon the altar in the sight of all, snatched away and consumed[399] the entire sacrifice.[400] **119** When this manifestation[401] occurred, the people concluded that this disclosed that God's residence was to be in the sanctuary;[402] they gladly paid homage, falling on the ground.[403]

God accepts sacrifices

(1 Kgs 8:33-40// 2 Chr 6:24-41) in which Solomon evokes a range of calamities (defeat by enemies, drought, plague, other agricultural disasters) that might befall the people because of their sins and asks that God hear the prayers they make him on such occasions. He likewise leaves aside the case cited by Solomon in 1 Kgs 8:31-32// 2 Chr 6:22-23 of a person in legal difficulties, who comes to the temple seeking vindication from the Lord.

[390] See 1 Kgs 8:41-43a// 2 Chr 6:32-33a, where Solomon asks that the Lord answer the petition of "the foreigner" who, having heard of the Lord's "great name," prays "towards this house." Josephus' Solomon has already broached the topic of God's universal solicitude in 8.108.

[391] Greek: ἀπάνθωποι. Josephus' 2 remaining uses of this adjective are in *Ant.* 6.298 and 16.42.

[392] Greek: οὐχ ὁμοφύλους. This is the conjecture of J. Cocceius, which Niese and Marcus follow. Among the extant witnesses to 8.117, only M and Lat have a negative particle here; the remainder read "who are compatriots."

[393] Greek: ἡ τῶν ἀγαθῶν ὄνησις. Josephus' one other use of this phrase is in *Ant.* 2.48.

[394] In 1 Kgs 8:43b// 2 Chr 6:33 Solomon asks God to hear the foreigner's prayer in order that the nations might learn "to fear you [the Lord]." The Josephan Solomon's alternative motivation serves, on the one hand, to dispose of Roman sensitivities about Jewish prosletyzing—Jews are not looking to make converts out of gentiles—and, on the other, to counter charges about Jewish hostility/indifference towards other peoples; see Feldman 1998: 614-5.

[395] In Josephus Solomon's prayer on behalf of foreigners (8.116-117) stands as the final, climactic petition made by him. In order to give it this status, he leaves aside the series of further prayers—focussed

once again on Israel—that follow the king's appeal for foreigners (1 Kgs 8:41-43// 2 Chr 6:32-33) in 8:44-53 // 6:34-42.

[396] Josephus offers a more dramatic, intense depiction of Solomon's piety here than does 1 Kgs 8:54, which simply has him, once his prayer is finished, rising from his kneeling position before the Lord's altar. Compare 2 Chr 7:1a, which does not mention a change of posture by Solomon following his prayer.

[397] In 1 Kgs 8:62// 2 Chr 7:4 the people join the king in offering sacrifices. Josephus keeps attention focussed on Solomon himself and his piety. By mentioning the offering of sacrifices at this point, he obviates the problematic sequence of 2 Chr 7:1-4, in which the consumption of the sacrifices on the altar by fire from heaven (v. 1) is referred to prior to Solomon's offering of sacrifice (v. 4).

[398] This notice, spelling out the significance of the consumption of the victims by fire from heaven spoken of in 2 Chr 7:1aβbα, takes the place of the reference to the "glory of the Lord filling the house" in 7:1bβ.

[399] Greek: καταδαίνυμαι. This verb is *hapax* in Josephus.

[400] See 2 Chr 7:1aβbα, 2a (no parallel in 1 Kings 8).

[401] Greek: ἐπιφάνεια. On this noun and its cognates, see Spicq 1978 (1): 284-7.

[402] Josephus adds this remark, paralleling his previous insertion (see 8.118) on Solomon's personal realization about the fire from heaven, concerning the inference drawn by the people as a whole from the fiery "manifestation." The reference to God's "residence" in the temple recalls the language of 8.102.

[403] See 2 Chr 7:3aβbα (no parallel in 1 Kings 8). The people's prostration here recalls that of the king himself in 8.118. Josephus omits the quotation of Ps 136:1 attributed to the worshipping people in 7:3bβ.

Solomon exhorts people

The king began to praise [God] and encouraged the crowd to do the same,[404] seeing that they already had proofs of God's benevolence[405] towards them.[406] **120** [He also encouraged them to] pray[407] that what [came] from him [God] would always turn out in the same way and that their minds would be preserved pure of all evil in justice and devotion[408] and that they would continue to keep the commandments God had given them through Moyses.[409] For thus the nation of the Hebrews would be happy and more blessed than the whole human race.[410] **121** He appealed to them to remember that it was by the same [deeds] that they had obtained the present good things that they would get these confirmed and obtain greater and additional ones. For they should not only realize that they had received these things on account of their piety and justice,[411] but also that they would preserve them in the same way. For it is not so great [a thing] for humans to obtain what they do not possess as to save what they have acquired and not offend to their own hurt.[412]

People dismissed after sacrifices and feasting

(4.5) 122 When he had said these things to the crowd, the king dismissed the assembly,[413] after offering sacrifices for himself and all the Hebrews, sacrificing about 12,000 calves[414] and 120,000 sheep.[415] **123** For the sanctuary then for the first time received its allotment of sacrificial animals,[416] while all the Hebrews, along with their wives and children, were feasted in it.[417] In addition, the festival called Taber-

---

[404] See 8.110, where earlier in the proceedings, Solomon "requests" the assembled people "to praise God."

[405] Greek: δείγματα... τῆς... εὐμείνας. This phrase is comparable to the expression δείγματα τῆς εὐνοίας ("proofs of loyalty") of *Ant.* 6.317 (where Saul uses it of David's fidelity towards himself).

[406] Having utilized the Chronicler's special material (2 Chr 7:1-3) in 8.118-119, Josephus now switches to the presentation of the other biblical account, i.e. 1 Kgs 8:55-61, where Solomon utters a final prayer. This begins (v. 56) "blessed be the Lord...." and continues with mention of God's having fulfilled all his promises as announced by Moses.

[407] In 1 Kgs 8:55-61 Solomon prays on behalf of the people, rather than urging them to join in his own prayer.

[408] This petition has no direct counterpart in Solomon's prayer in 1 Kgs 8:55-61. It takes the place of the king's appeal that the Lord "not leave or forsake us" of 8:57. Josephus' one other use of the collocation "justice and devotion" (Greek: διακαιωσύνη καὶ θρησκεία) is in *Ant.* 6.18, where it is applied to "Aminadab," the keeper of the ark.

[409] This petition corresponds to Solomon's request that God cause the people to "keep his commandments. which he commanded our fathers" in 1 Kgs 8:58.

[410] In place of the appeal that all peoples of the earth might recognize the sole deity of the Lord (1 Kgs 8:60) with its prosletyzing overtones, Josephus has Solomon pray—in language recalling that used by him in 8.110—for the preeminent welfare of the Hebrews themselves.

[411] Greek: εὐσέβεια καὶ δικαιωσύνη. This colloca-

tion recalls the binomial δικαιοωσύνη καὶ θρησκεία ("justice and devotion") of 8.120.

[412] Compare Solomon's concluding, direct-address exhortation in 1 Kgs 8:61: "Let your [the people's] heart therefore be wholly true to the Lord our God, walking in his statutes and keeping his commandments, as at this day."

[413] Josephus anticipates this notice on Solomon's dismissal of the people from 1 Kgs 8:66// 2 Chr 7:10.

[414] 1 Kgs 8:63// 2 Chr 7:5 read 22,000 as the number of bovine sacrifices. Uncharacteristically, Josephus has a lower figure than the biblical one.

[415] This figure agrees with that given in MT and LXX L 1 Kgs 8:63 and MT 2 Chr 7:5. LXX B 1 Kgs 8:63 and LXX BL 2 Chr 7:5 do not mention a sacrifice of sheep by Solomon on this occasion.

[416] This notice takes the place of 1 Kgs 8:64 // 2 Chr 7:7, which speak of Solomon's consecrating the "middle court" by means of sacrifices he offered there, rather than on the bronze altar since this was too small to receive the abundance of sacrifices. Like 1 Kings 8, Josephus lacks mention of the musical accompaniment of the sacrifices cited in 2 Chr 7:6.

[417] The biblical accounts do not mention such a "feasting" of the people. Josephus' addition on the point serves to answer the question of how the enormous number of sacrificial remains were disposed of; see Feldman 1998: 601-2. The addition likewise highlights the parallelism between Solomon's initiative with the ark and that of David who, *Ant.* 7.86 (// 2 Sam 6:19// 1 Chr 16:3) reports, "feasted" the Israelite men, women and children on the occasion of his bringing the ark to Jerusalem.

nacles[418] was splendidly and magnificently[419] celebrated in front of the sanctuary. The king spent fourteen days feasting with the entire people.[420]

(4.6) 124 Then, when they had enough of these things and nothing was left undone of piety towards God,[421] having been dismissed by the king they each went off to their homes,[422] thanking the king for his care[423] of them and for the actions he had displayed. They prayed too that God would award them Solomon as their king for a long time to come.[424] They made their journey with joy and glad amusements, singing hymns to God, so that in their enjoyment they all effortlessly covered the distance to their homes.[425] **125** Those also who had brought the ark into the sanctuary and become acquainted with its size and beauty and participated in the great sacrifices and the feasting in it returned to their individual cities.[426]

People return home

Then a dream[427] appeared to the king as he slept and signified to him that God had been attentive to his prayer[428] **126** and would preserve the sanctuary and remain in it for all time,[429] if his descendants and he[430] and the whole crowd would do what was just. He also said that he would, first of all, abide by his promises to his father. He would further lead him to a limitless summit and greatness of well-being, while those of his family would always reign as kings over the country and the tribe of Iouda.[431]

Solomon's post-dedication dream

---

[418] The references to Solomon's 7-day feast in 1 Kgs 8:65// 2 Chr 7:8 do not identify it with "Tabernacles." Josephus has already associated the dedication of the temple with this feast in 8.100.

[419] Greek: λαμπρῶς καὶ μεγαλοπρεῶς. The adjectival equivalent of this adverbial collocation occurs in *Ant.* 7.378, where the civil and religious leaders, following David's example, make "splendid and magnificent" contributions to the temple-building fund.

[420] This figure for the duration of the festivities surrounding the dedication of the temple appears explicitly in MT 1 Kgs 8:66 (LXX BL read 7 days) and is implicit in 2 Chr 7:9.

[421] This notice on the people's satiation takes the place of the divergent indications concerning the day on which Solomon dismissed the people in 1 Kgs 8:66 (the 8th day)/ 2 Chr 7:10 (the 23rd day), neither of which agrees with Josephus' previous reference to a 14-day festival in 8.123.

[422] See 1 Kgs 8:66// 2 Chr 7:10. Josephus made proleptic reference to the people's dismissal by the king in 8.122.

[423] Greek: πρόνοια. This same term is used by Solomon of God's "providence" for the people in his address to them in 8.109. Divine "providence" is mediated to the Israelites through the king's "care" for them.

[424] Josephus expatiates on, while also modifying, the mention of the departing people's "blessing" the king in 1 Kgs 8:66 (no equivalent in 2 Chr 7:10).

[425] Josephus modifies (and embellishes) the concluding words of 1 Kgs 8:66// 2 Chr 7:10, which speak of the people's going home "joyful and glad of heart," given the Lord's goodness to both David and Israel.

[426] This separate mention of the activities of the

priests, the bearers of the ark into the Holy of Holies (see 8.103), has no biblical parallel. It reflects the priest Josephus' interest in highlighting the role of his fellow-priests on this momentous occasion.

[427] Neither 1 Kgs 9:2 nor 2 Chr 7:12a mentions a "dream" explicitly. The former text speaks of the Lord's appearing to Solomon "a 2nd time, as he had appeared to him at Gibeon," while the latter refers to the Lord's manifesting himself to the king "in the night." Josephus' identification of the happening as a "dream" recalls his use of the same term in connection with Solomon's Gibeon experience in 8.22 (// 1 Kgs 3:5). On Josephus' version of Solomon's 2nd exchange with God (= 1 Kgs 9:1-9// 2 Chr 7:11-21) in 8.125b-129, see Begg 1996a: 695-700 and Gnuse 1996: 176-7.

[428] This initial divine announcement to Solomon parallels those with which the Deity's message to the king begin in 1 Kgs 9:3a// 2 Chr 7:12b.

[429] This is Josephus' compressed version of the Deity's promised commitment to the temple in 1 Kgs 9:3// 2 Chr 7:15-16, from which he eliminates the anthropomorphic references to God's "eyes and heart" (9:3// 7:16) and "eyes and ears" (7:15). Like 1 Kings 9, he has no equivalent to God's preceding promise of forgiveness for the penitent people of 2 Chr 7:13-14.

[430] Greek: καὶ αὐτοῦ. This reference to Solomon himself is found only in E; it is read by Niese, but not by Marcus.

[431] See 1 Kgs 9:4-5// 2 Chr 7:17-18, which speak only of Solomon's own abiding by the law as the condition for God's maintaining the Davidic dynasty, and which also cite the earlier divine word to David, i.e. "there shall not fail you a man upon the throne of Israel" (cf. 2 Sam 7:12-13// 1 Chr 17:12, 14).

127 If, however, he[432] should forsake the prescribed disciplines, forgetting these, and switch to worshiping foreign gods, he would cut him down root and branch and leave no trace of their family.[433] Nor would he let the Israelite people off unharmed, but would annihilate them both by wars and by countless calamities, just as, having tossed them out of the land he had given to their ancestors, he would settle them as foreigners in a land not their own.[434] **128** He would likewise hand over the sanctuary that had just now been built to their enemies to be burnt down and plundered.[435] He would also raze the city by the hands of their enemies,[436] and make their calamities suitable for legends and unbelief, due to the excess of their surpassing magnitude.[437] **129** As a result, when the surrounding nations[438] should hear of their misfortune, they would marvel and wish to know the reason why the Hebrews, who earlier had been led to glory and wealth by him [God],[439] had thus become hateful to God.[440] They would hear the survivors confessing their offenses and transgressions of the ancestral laws.[441] It has been recorded that God said these things to him in a dream.[442]

Solomon's palace complex

(5.1) 130 After the sanctuary had been constructed in seven years, as we mentioned above,[443] and the foundations of the palace edifice laid, the latter was hardly finished within thirteen years.[444] For it was not the object of the same solicitude as

---

[432] In 1 Kgs 9:6// 2 Chr 7:19, the subject of the divine warning is a plural "you" (9:6 MT; LXX BL add "or your children"), i.e. the entire people. Josephus focusses attention on the apostasy of Solomon himself that will subsequently occur.

[433] Having made Solomon personally the potential subject of the defection from God's ways (see previous note), Josephus prefaces the divine warnings, drawn from 1 Kgs 9:7-9// 2 Chr 7:20-22, about the future fate of people and land, with this reference to the implications of Solomon's apostasy for his dynasty.

[434] To the biblical Deity's warning about the Israelites being removed from their land (1 Kgs 9:7a// 2 Chr 7:20a), Josephus, with the later history of both Israel and Judah in view, appends a mention of the people's resettlement in a foreign land.

[435] Compare the metaphorical, anthropomorphic language of 1 Kgs 9:7bα// 2 Chr 7:20bα, which speak of the Lord's "casting" the temple "out of his sight." Josephus' formulation reflects the actual fate of the temple as he will describe this in *Ant.* 10.145-146, where the edifice is plundered and burnt. Cf. also the references to the burning of the Herodian temple and of Jerusalem as a whole in *War* 6.281 and 6.407, respectively.

[436] This threat has no counterpart in the divine warnings of 1 Kgs 9:7// 2 Chr 7:20 concerning the fate of people and temple. It has in view Josephus' description of the Babylonian measures subsequent to the fall of Jerusalem; see *Ant.* 10.146 (Nebuzaradan "demolished the city"), making these as well something that God had predicted long previously.

[437] In 1 Kgs 9:7bβ// 2 Chr 7:20bβ God threatens to

make Israel "a proverb and byword among all peoples." Josephus underscores the magnitude of the threatened disaster.

[438] 1 Kgs 9:8b// 2 Chr 7:21 have "every passerby" raise the question about the temple's destruction.

[439] Josephus adds this reference to God's earlier prospering of the people; he thereby underscores the reversal involved in their (threatened) divine overthrow.

[440] 1 Kgs 9:8b// 2 Chr 7:21 have the passersby ask why the Lord "has done thus to this land and to this house." On Josephus' references to God's "hating" (Greek: μισέω) persons and things, see the note to "hated" at *Ant.* 6.138.

[441] Compare 1 Kgs 9:9// 2 Chr 7:22, where an unspecified "they" (the passersby? the surviving Israelites?) attribute the Lord's having brought evil upon the Israelites to their forsaking him and worshipping other gods.

[442] This concluding notice has no biblical counterpart. Its use of the term "dream" forms an inclusion with the occurrence of the same term in 8.125.

[443] This transitional phrase recalls Josephus' notice on the duration of Solomon's temple-building project in 8.99.

[444] Josephus draws this figure from 1 Kgs 7:1 (which does not explicitly mention the laying of the palace foundation). Whereas the account of Solomon's secular buildings in 1 Kgs 7:1-12 (no parallel in Chronicles) "disrupts" the presentation of his temple building project (1 Kgs 6:1-38; 7:13-8:66), Josephus reserves his version of the former passage until after he has related the completion and dedication of the temple. He

BOOK EIGHT   37

was the sacred precinct; the latter [complex], even though it was great and of a workmanship that was marvelous and extraordinary beyond belief, was, nevertheless, with the cooperation of God for whom it was made, completed within the above-mentioned years.[445] **131** The palace was much inferior to the sanctuary in value; its material was not readied at the same time as was the latter's, nor was the same eagerness applied. Since it was to be a residence for the king, rather than for God, the work was carried out more slowly.[446]

132 And yet it is worthy of mention and was built in accordance with the well-being[447] both of the Hebrews' country and of the king.[448] Therefore it is necessary to speak of its overall arrangement and plan so that from this, those who are to encounter this writing might be able to surmise and perceive its magnitude.[449] **(5.2)** **133** The building[450] was great and beautiful, held up by many pillars.[451] He [Solomon] constructed it to provide space for a number of court cases and judicial inquiries about affairs, as well as to accommodate a mass of people assembled for trials.[452] Its length was a hundred cubits, its breadth fifty, and its height thirty.[453] [The building] was supported by square pillars, all of cedar wood.[454] It was roofed in Corinthian fashion,[455] being likewise secured and adorned with pilasters that were of equal size[456] and triple-grooved door-leaves.[457]

134 A second building[458] was in the middle;[459] it was situated along the entire

---

thereby accentuates the piety of the king who, first of all, devotes all his energy to the temple project.

[445] With this appended statement Josephus continues to highlight the piety of Solomon, who invests more energy in building the temple than his own residence. The statement also provides an explanation—acknowledging both the human and divine factors involved—as to how so grand an edifice as the temple could have been completed in so short a time. Its wording recalls that used in Josephus' notice on the (relative) speed with which the temple complex was built in 8.99.

[446] This notice rounds off Josephus' appended segment (8.130b-131) comparing the building of the temple and the palace and highlighting the greater attention given the former. The addition serves to explain—as the Bible itself does not—why Solomon's palace should have taken almost twice as long to build as the temple.

[447] Greek: εὐδαιμονία. This term echoes the Deity's promise of an "limitless summit and greatness of well-being [εὐδαιμονία]" for Solomon in 8.126. The king's ability to construct his palace-complex evidences the fulfillment of that promise.

[448] By way of this added comment Josephus qualifies his preceding down-playing of the palace vis-à-vis the temple, in order that the former edifice not appear altogether unworthy of a great, wealthy king like Solomon and so reflect negatively on its builder.

[449] This statement of the purpose behind the following description of the palace structure is, like the entire segment 8.130b-132, Josephus' addition.

[450] 1 Kgs 7:2 calls the structure in question "the

house of the forest of Lebanon."

[451] According to 1 Kgs 7:2 the "house of the forest of Lebanon" was built upon "4 [MT; LXX BL: 3] rows of cedar pillars."

[452] 1 Kgs 7:2-5 provides no indication as to the intended use of the "house of the forest of Lebanon." Josephus appears to derive his statements on the matter from what is said concerning the function of another, biblically distinct structure, i.e. the "hall of the throne/ hall of judgment" in 7:7.

[453] These figures for the biblical "house of the forest of Lebanon" agree with those cited in MT 1 Kgs 7:2. LXX BL do not mention the height of the structure.

[454] 1 Kgs 7:2 specifies that there were 4 (MT; LXX BL: 3) rows of cedar pillars, while 7:3 mentions a total of 45 pillars, 15 (MT, > LXX BL) in each row.

[455] The use of this term (Greek: Κορίνθιος) in reference to Solomon's construction is an obvious anachronism; the term also figures in Josephus' accounts of the Herodian temple-complex; see *War* 5.201, 205; *Ant.* 15.414.

[456] MT 1 Kgs 7:3 speaks of the cedar above the chambers resting upon 45 pillars, 15 per row.

[457] 1 Kgs 7:4-5 speaks of 3 tiers of facing windows and window frames, while 7:5 also mentions "doorways."

[458] Josephus' account of this edifice in 8.134a seems to conflate the structures (which some exegetes, in fact, do regard as one and the same) cited in 1 Kgs 7:6 (the "hall of pillars") and 7:7 (the "hall of the throne/ hall of judgment").

[459] Josephus adds this indication concerning the

breadth [of the first building],[460] while its width was thirty cubits.[461] It was positioned opposite the sanctuary and supported by thick pillars.[462] In it was a splendid hall, in which the king sat when he gave judgment.[463] To it was joined another building that had been built for the queen[464] and additional edifices for residence and recreation after the discharge of business.[465] All these were floored with planks hewn from cedar.[466] **135** He built some of these [buildings] with stones [measuring] ten cubits.[467] He covered the walls with another sort of hewn, costly [stone][468] that is mined for the beautification of sacred precincts and the decoration of palaces in an area famous for the places that produce it.[469]

136 The beauty of this stone was displayed in a triple course.[470] The fourth course caused one to marvel at the knowledge of the sculptors. Trees and plants of every sort that gave shade with their branches were made by them, as were leaves that hung down so that one imagined them shaking, due to their exceeding delicacy. The stonework was covered over by these.[471] **137** The remainder [of the wall] up to the roof was painted and tinted with colors and hues. In addition to these, he built edifices for pleasure and very extended porticos that were situated in a beautiful part of the palace. In these porticos was a most splendid structure for banquets and symposia[472] that was crammed with gold. Moreover, the other vessels that were needed for the service of banquet guests were all made of gold.[473]

---

location of the 2nd palace structure, placing it between the temple and the 1st royal edifice described in 8.133.

[460] This indication lacks a counterpart in 1 Kings 7.

[461] This figure agrees with that given in MT and LXX L 1 Kgs 7:6, whereas LXX B specifies 50. Josephus has no equivalent to the biblical indication concerning the structure's length, i.e. 50 cubits.

[462] 1 Kgs 7:6 does not localize the "house of pillars" in relation to the temple. Josephus' reference to the "pillars" supporting the (unnamed) structure reflects the biblical designation for it.

[463] 1 Kgs 7:6b mentions a pillared "porch" (MT אולם; LXX BL αἰλάμ; compare Josephus ἐξέδρα) at the front of the "house of pillars" (as well as a "canopy" [RSV] situated before the pillars of the porch). Josephus' reference to the function of the "hall" draws on the mention of Solomon's constructing the "hall of the throne" as the place where he was "to pronounce judgment" in 7:7 and presupposes his conflation of the "hall of pillars" (7:6) and the "hall of the throne/ hall of judgment" (7:7); see the note to "a second building" at 8.134.

[464] See 1 Kgs 7:8b, which mentions the house made by Solomon for "Pharaoh's daughter whom he [Solomon] had taken in marriage." The pair's marriage is recorded in 1 Kgs 3:1 (// 8.21).

[465] See 1 Kgs 7:8a, which mentions Solomon's "own house" and locates this "in the other court back of the hall" (i.e. the "hall of the throne/ hall of judgment" of 7:7).

[466] For this item Josephus combines the notices of

7:7 (the "hall of the throne/hall of judgment" was finished with cedar "from *floor* to floor" [MT; LXX BL: to the rafters]) and 7:8 (both Solomon's "own house" and that of Pharaoh's daughter were "like the hall").

[467] According to 1 Kgs 7:10 the "foundation stones" of the various palace structures were "of 8 and 10 cubits."

[468] Josephus here alludes to the description of the stones used in constructing the various edifices in 1 Kgs 7:9.

[469] Josephus appends this remark about the (unnamed) "source" of the stone used. The reference is apparently to "Mount Liban," the source of the stones used in the construction of the temple according to 8.58-59.

[470] See 1 Kgs 7:12, which speaks of the "3 courses of hewn stone" surrounding the "great court."

[471] Josephus embellishes the mention of the cedar beams surmounting the 3 courses of stone in 1 Kgs 7:12, with his reference to the life-like carved woodwork that covered them.

[472] Josephus' reference to this Greek institution in Solomon's time is another anachronism; compare his mention of roofing in the "Corinthian fashion" in 8.133.

[473] Josephus derives his notice concerning these palace vessels from 1 Kgs 10:21a// 2 Chr 9:20a (where the "vessels of the "house of the forest of Lebanon" are singled out). He reserves the notice of 10:21b// 9:20b on the non-use and disregard of silver in Solomon's time for a later point in his presentation; see 8.181.

138 It is difficult, however, to describe the size and colorful variety of the palace: how many large edifices there were in it, how many smaller ones, and how many that were completely underground and invisible, the beauty of those that were exposed to the air, and the groves that [offered] a delightful view and were a refuge and a protection for the body against the summer heat. **139** In summary: he made the entire structure out of white stone, cedar, gold, and silver, decorating the roofs and walls with stones set in gold, in the same fashion as he had beautified the sanctuary of God with these things.[474]

140 He also crafted a very large throne out of ivory;[475] this was in the shape of a platform with six steps.[476] Two lions were placed on each of these [steps] on either side; above these stood two other ones.[477] The seat of the throne had arms to receive the king.[478] He used to recline against the head of a calf, that faced backward;[479] the whole [throne] was mounted in gold.[480]

Solomon's throne

(5.4) 141 Solomon constructed these things over a period of twenty years,[481] since Heirom, the king of the Tyrians, had collected much gold and still more silver for him for their building, as well as cedar and pine timbers.[482] He himself gave Heirom great gifts in return; he yearly sent him wheat, along with wine and oil, of which things he was especially in need, due to his living on an island—as we said before.[483] **142** In addition to these things, he also conferred on him cities of Galilee, twenty in number, that were situated not far from Tyre.[484] When, however, Heirom came to these and inspected them, he was dissatisfied with the gift.[485] Sending to Solomon, he said that he had no need of the cities.[486] Therefore they were called the

Solomon's trade with Hiram

---

[474] The bulk of the above 3-paragraph sequence (8.137-139) concerning the palace-complex has no counterpart in the account of 1 Kgs 7:1-12. The whole segment underscores the opulence of Solomon's reign, even while it strongly relativizes Josephus' earlier remarks about the modesty of the palace-complex in comparison with the temple (see 8.130-132).

[475] In 1 Kgs 10:18-20 (// 2 Chr 9:17-19) the account of Solomon's throne occurs separately from the description of the structure in which that throne stood, i.e. "the hall of the throne" (see 7:7). Josephus brings the 2 related items together in a continuous sequence.

[476] 1 Kgs 10:18// 2 Chr 9:18 mention the throne's 6 steps, but not its platform-like shape.

[477] See 1 Kgs 10:19bβ-20a// 2 Chr 9:18b-19a. Reversing the biblical order, Josephus first mentions the lions placed on the throne's 6 steps and then the pair immediately adjacent to the throne. Whereas here in 8.140 he speaks of these objects without criticism, in 8.195 he will refer to their construction as a violation of Mosaic law. He has no equivalent to the appended statement of 10:20b// 9:19b about Solomon's throne being unparalleled elsewhere.

[478] See 1 Kgs 10:19bα// 2 Chr 9:18bα.

[479] Josephus' reference to a "calf's head" corresponds to the (more original) LXX reading in 1 Kgs 10:19aβ (the MT pointing of the equivalent Hebrew phrase, ראש־עגל, turns this into a "rounded top" so as to

disassociate Solomon from the sin of calf-making). 2 Chr 9:18aβ (MT, > LXX BL) substitutes a reference to the "footstool" of the throne.

[480] In 1 Kgs 10:18b// 2 Chr 9:17b Solomon "covers" the throne "with pure gold."

[481] Josephus draws this figure for the total duration of Solomon's building projects from 1 Kgs 9:10// 2 Chr 8:1; cf. the separate figures for the building of the temple (7 years) and the palace-complex (13 years) he gives in 8.130.

[482] The list of Hiram's contributions in 1 Kgs 9:11a cites "cypress" rather than "pine" and does not mention "silver."

[483] Josephus' notice on Solomon's own contributions, corresponding to those of Hiram to him (see 1 Kgs 9:11a), has no parallel in the context of the account of their dealings in 9:11-14; he derives the indication from 5:25 (MT; RSV 5:10). The appended cross reference is to 8.54, where Hiram himself alludes to Tyre's island location and its resultant need for grain.

[484] See 1 Kgs 9:11b; Josephus supplies the specification about the location of the Galilean cities. In 2 Chr 8:2 it is Hiram who cedes cities to Solomon that the latter then rebuilds and populates with Israelites.

[485] See 1 Kgs 9:12. Neither Josephus nor the Bible specifies what it was that Hiram found unsatisfactory about the cities.

[486] Josephus turns into a straightforward statement

land of *Chabalon*,[487] for *Chabalon* in the Phoenician language has the meaning "not pleasing."[488]

Solomon and Hiram exchange riddles

143 The king of the Tyrians also dispatched subtle questions and enigmas to Solomon and appealed to him to elucidate these for him and resolve the difficulty of the questions [posed] in them.[489] None of them stumped the ingenious and sagacious[490] Solomon; rather, he succeeded in explicating them all by use of reason and by learning their meaning.[491]

144 Menander, who translated the Tyrian archives from the Phoenician language into Greek,[492] also mentions these two kings. He says this:[493]

"When Abibal died, his son Heirom received the kingship from him; he lived fifty-three years and reigned for thirty-four. **145** He laid down the *Eruchor*,[494] and erected the golden column in [the temple] of Zeus. In addition, he went off and cut down timbers from the mountain called Liban for the roofs of the sacred precincts. **146** He demolished the old sacred precincts and built new ones for Heracles and for Astarte; he erected that of Heracles[495] first, in the month of Peritius.[496] He undertook a campaign against the Itukaoi,[497] who were not paying their tribute; having subjugated them once again, he returned home. During his reign there lived Abdemon, a young lad, who always solved the problems posed by Solomon, the king of Hierosolyma."

147 Dios[498] also mentions him [Heirom] in this fashion:[499]

Hiram's oblique question to Solomon in 1 Kgs 9:13a: "what kind of cities are these that you have given me, my brother?"

[487] MT (1 Kgs 9:13b) כבול (Eng.: "Cabul"); LXX BL, rendering a Hebrew גבול ("border"), has ὅριον; Josephus Χαβαλών. In *Apion* 1.110 Josephus mentions Solomon's giving Hiram "a present of land in Galilee in the district called Chabulon (Χαβουλών)." There, however, he does not cite the latter's negative reaction to the gift, which, in turn, gives rise to the site's pejorative name, as he does here in 8.142// 1 Kgs 9:13b.

[488] Josephus supplies both the (purported) language and the meaning of the name given the site; commentators identify the term כבול used in MT 1 Kgs 9:13b rather as a Hebrew word meaning "like nothing." Josephus here in 8.142 omits the attached statement of 9:14 about Hiram's having given Solomon 120 talents of gold; he does, however, reproduce that notice in *Apion* 1.110.

[489] Josephus here begins an extended segment (8.143-149) without biblical counterpart whose purpose is to underscore both Solomon's intelligence and his friendly (intellectual) relations with a foreign king, as also to highlight the existence of extra-biblical evidence for the person and attainments of Solomon. Compare his related addition in 8.55-56 on the contemporary availability of copies of the Hiram-Solomon correspondence in the Tyrian archives, as well as the parallel passage in *Apion* 1.111-120.

[490] Greek: δεινός καὶ συνετός. This collocation occurs only here in Josephus.

[491] Josephus' subsequent citation of non-biblical authors will serve to qualify this general assertion about Solomon's prowess.

[492] In *Apion* 1.116 Josephus calls him "Menander of Ephesus" and mentions the account of both Hellenic and non-Hellenic kingships that he drew from "the national records." In *Ant.* 8.324 he cites Menander's notice on the drought that occurred during the time of Ahab's contemporary, King Ithobal of Tyre.

[493] Josephus reproduces the following citation from Menander in largely identical terms in *Apion* 1.117b-120.

[494] Greek: Εὐρύχωρον. The word, meaning "broad place," designated a part of the city of Tyre.

[495] This is the understanding of Menander's phrase (Greek: τοῦ Ἡρακλέους ἔγερσιν ἐποιήσατο) adopted by Thackeray in his translation of *Apion* 1.119. Marcus (*ad loc.*) proposes an alternative understanding of the same phrase here in 8.146, i.e. "(he [Heirom] was the first) to celebrate the awakening of Heracles...," seeing it as an allusion to a fertility cult initiated by the Tyrian king.

[496] This is the Macedonian name for the 4th month of the year, roughly equivalent to January; see Thackeray 1926: 211, n. c.

[497] The term denotes the inhabitants of the city of Utica, a Phoenician colony in North Africa.

[498] In *Apion* 1.112 Josephus mentions that "Dios" is "regarded as an accurate historian of Phoenicia."

[499] The following quotation (8.147-149) from Dios reappears, virtually verbatim, in *Apion* 1.113-115.

"When Abibal died, his son Heirom reigned as king. He made the eastern parts of the city [Tyre] higher and enlarged the town. By filling in the intervening space, he joined the sacred precinct of Olympian Zeus to the city[500] and beautified it with votive offerings of gold. Going up to Liban, he chopped down trees for the building of sacred precincts. **148** It is said that Solomon, the tyrant[501] of Hierosolyma, sent riddles to Heirom and requested that he receive these from him. The one who was unable to solve them would make a payment to the one who could. **149** Heirom admitted that he could not solve the riddles and paid out large sums as a penalty. Then Abdemon,[502] a certain Tyrian man, not only solved the riddles that had been proposed, but suggested other ones for which Solomon, being unable to solve them, paid large sums to Heirom."[503] Dios spoke in this manner.

(6.1) 150 The king then saw that the walls of Hierosolyma were in need of towers *Solomon the* and other fortifications for their security, For, thinking that also the surrounding *city-builder* walls should be in keeping with the city's prestige, he renovated the walls and raised them even higher by means of great towers.[504] **151** He also built cities. Of these, the most important were reckoned to be Asor and Magedo.[505] The third was Gazara; this belonged to the country of the Palestinoi.[506] Pharaoh, the king of the Egyptians, after campaigning against it and besieging it, took it by storm. He killed all the inhabitants and razed it; then he gave it as a gift to his daughter, who had been married to Solomon.[507] **152** The king [Solomon] therefore rebuilt it, [the site] being solid by nature and one that could be useful in war and the vicissitudes of the times.[508] Not far from it he built two other cities; one bore the name Betchora,[509] the other was called Beleth.[510]

153 In addition to these [cities], he constructed still others; these were suitable for recreation and pleasure, given their mild climate and fruitfulness, as well as their

---

[500] Josephus' quotation of Dios in *Apion* 1.113 further notes that the temple of Zeus had previously been "isolated on an island."

[501] Josephus' quotation from Menander in 8.146 gives Solomon his biblical title of "king" of Jerusalem.

[502] This is the same form of the name given in Josephus' citation of Menander in 8.146. Compare *Apion* 1.115, where, quoting Dios, Josephus gives his name as "Abdemoun." There is no mention of this figure in the biblical accounts of Solomon and his interactions with Hiram.

[503] In quoting this (and the related statement of Menander in 8.146), Josephus seems to allow his desire to provide extra-biblical attestation for Solomon to outweigh his concern to portray the king as far superior to all his contemporaries in wisdom (compare 8.42).

[504] Josephus embellishes the passing mention of Solomon's "building the wall of Jerusalem" in 1 Kgs 9:15. His reference to Solomon's "renovating" the city's walls has in view his statement in *Ant.* 7.66 (// 2 Sam 5:9) that David had already enclosed Jerusalem with a wall; cf. also his notice that Solomon "constructed the walls of Hierosolyma [to be] larger and more solid than they were before" in 8.21. From 9:15

Josephus omits the allusion to Solomon's building "the Millo," just as he leaves aside the mention of that site in his version of 2 Sam 5:9 in 7.66.

[505] These names are Josephus' versions of the first 2 extra-Jerusalemite cities cited in 1 Kgs 9:15, i.e. "Hazor" and "Megiddo."

[506] 1 Kgs 9:16 speaks of the "Canaanites" who lived in "Gaza." Josephus' designation of the site as a "Philistine" town reflects other biblical texts (e.g., 1 Sam 6:17) that make it one of the 5 Philistine cities.

[507] See 1 Kgs 9:16, where Pharaoh "destroys Gaza with fire." On the marriage of Pharaoh's daughter to Solomon, see 8.21.

[508] See 1 Kgs 9:17a. Josephus supplies the motivation for Solomon's rebuilding of the demolished city.

[509] MT 1 Kgs 9:17b "Lower Beth-horon"; LXX BL "Beth-horon the Upper"; MT LXX L 2 Chr 8:5 "Beth-horon the Upper [> LXX B] and Beth-horon the Lower"; Josephus Βητχώρα (Schalit *s.v.* reads Βαιθώρων).

[510] MT (1 Kgs 9:18// 2 Chr 8:5) בעלת (Eng.: "Balath," > LXX BL 9:18); LXX B 2 Chr 8:5 Βαλάα; LXX L 2 Chr 8:5 Βαλάαθ; Josephus Βελέθ (this is the reading of RO that Niese follows; Marcus reads Βαλέθ with the remaining codices).

being supplied with springs of water.[511] Advancing into the upper desert of Syria and occupying it, he founded there a great city, two days' journey distant from upper Syria and one from the Euphrates, while [its distance] from the great Babylon was six days.[512] **154** The reason for his establishing this city thus, away from the inhabited parts of Syria was that, whereas lower down there was no water anywhere in the land, it was only in that place that wells and cisterns were found.[513] After building the city and surrounding it with very solid walls,[514] he named it Thadamor,[515] and it is still called this by the Syrians, while the Greeks designate it as Palmyra.[516]

The name "Pharaoh"

(6.2) **155** Solomon the king therefore continued doing these things at that time. I have thought it necessary, however, to speak to those who raise a question[517] [about the fact] that all the kings of Egypt, from Minaias, who built Memphis,[518] and lived many years prior to our ancestor Abram, down to Solomon—the intervening span being more than 1,300 years—were called *Pharaoths* taking the name from King *Pharaoth* who first ruled, in the intervening period. I have done this in order to dispel their ignorance and clarify the reason for the name, namely, that *Pharaoh* means "king" in Egyptian. **156** I surmise that, although they did have other names as children, as soon as they became king they exchanged these names for the one that in their ancestral language signifies their authority.[519] For likewise the kings of Alexandria were called other names earlier, but upon assuming the kingship, they were called the *Ptolemies*, after the first king.[520] **157** Moreover, the Roman emperors,[521] although from birth they have other names, are called *Caesars*, a name [deriving from] the leadership and honor that is conferred upon them, whereas they do not continue to be called [by the names given them] by their parents.

I suppose therefore that when Herodotus of Halicarnassus says that after Minaias who built Memphis, there were 330 kings of Egypt,[522] he does not disclose their names, due to the fact that they were called *Pharaoths* as their common name. **158** For he further states that, following the death of these kings, a woman ruled, whom he calls Nikaule.[523] Thus, while the male kings could have the same name, a woman

---

[511] This transitional notice on Solomon's "pleasure cities," leading into Josephus' account of the building of one such city, i.e. "Tadmor," has no equivalent in the biblical Solomon accounts.

[512] These indications concerning the localization of "Tadmor" (1 Kgs 9:18b// 2 Chr 8:4a) are Josephus' own.

[513] Josephus supplies this motivation for Solomon's establishing Tadmor at the particular place where he does in the Syrian desert.

[514] The biblical accounts (1 Kgs 9:18b// 2 Chr 8:4a) do not mention Solomon's building walls for Tadmor.

[515] Josephus' name for the city (Greek: Θαδάμορα) agrees with that found in some MSS of MT 1 Kgs 9:18b, the *qere*, LXX L, Vulg., and 2 Chr 8:4a. Other MSS of MT 1 Kgs 9:18b read תמר (Eng.: "Tamar"), LXX B Ἰεθερμάθ.

[516] Josephus appends this notice on the contemporary names of Solomon's foundation.

[517] With this phrase Josephus introduces an extended excursus (8.155-159) very loosely appended to his reference to the "Pharaoh" in 8.151 and inspired by

a notice of Herodotus to which he will allude in 8.157-158. The excursus gives him the opportunity of displaying his knowledge of Egyptian, Greek, and Roman history.

[518] Josephus draws the name of the Egyptian king and his status as builder of Memphis from Herodotus, whom he will cite in 8.157-158.

[519] I.e. the name "Pharaoh" that eventually came to mean "king" in Egyptian (see 8.155), the original meaning being something like "great house, palace."

[520] A series of 11 kings, all named "Ptolemy," ruled Egypt in the period 323-80 BCE.

[521] Greek: αὐτοκράτωρ. Here, as, e.g., in *Life* 363, 416 Josephus uses the term as an equivalent for Latin *imperator*, "emperor."

[522] Josephus here alludes to Herodotus' overview of Egyptian history in 2.99ff.; see Marcus *ad loc*. On Josephus' (critical) use of Herodotus, see Bowley 1994: 211-2.

[523] Marcus (*ad loc*.) notes that in the extant text of Herodotus (see 2.100) the queen's name is rather "Nitocris."

could not share this, and therefore he [Herodotus] mentions the name that was hers by nature.[524] **159** I likewise have found in our native books[525] that, after the *Pharaoh* who was the father-in-law of Solomon, no king of the Egyptians was any longer called by this name.[526] [I further find] that the above-mentioned woman later came to Solomon after having ruled over Egypt and Ethiopia.[527] About her we shall have something to say shortly afterwards.[528] I have, however, mentioned these things in order to show that our books and those of the Egyptians agree in many points.[529]

(6.3) 160 Now King Solomon made subject and imposed tribute on those of the Chananaians who had not yet been subjugated, namely those who dwelt on Mount Liban and as far as the city of Amathe.[530] He made a yearly selection of them to work as his servants and to engage in domestic tasks and farming.[531]

Different tasks for Canaanites and Israelites

161 For he enslaved none of the Hebrews.[532] Nor would that have been justified, since God had made many nations subject to them. It was from these that their body of servants ought to be drawn rather than they themselves being reduced to this status.[533] These [the Hebrews], for their part, were all under arms; they spent their time on chariots and horses, campaigning rather than serving as slaves.[534]

---

[524] Twice in 8.157-158 Josephus offers a personal surmise concerning Herodotus' treatment of the Egyptian rulers, i.e. his not citing the name ("Pharaoh") of the male kings, given that this was common to all of them following their accession, while naming the one reigning queen, since she did not assume that (male) title.

[525] Here, after the excursus of 8.155-158, based, *inter alia*, on the non-biblical testimony of Herodotus, Josephus returns to his biblical source (1 Kgs 9:16) and its mention of Pharaoh's giving of captured Gaza as a dowry to his daughter, the wife of Solomon, to which he previously alluded in 8.151.

[526] Josephus alludes here to the use of proper names for post-Solomonic kings of Egypt in the biblical record, see, e.g., "Shishak" who seized Jerusalem in the reign of Solomon's son Rehoboam (1 Kgs 14:25// 2 Chr 12:6), in contrast to the Bible's preceding use of the generic title "Pharaoh" for earlier Egyptian kings (see, e.g., Exod 1:11; 2:15; 5:1). In fact, however, the Bible does employ the title of some Egyptian kings after Solomon; see, e.g., 2 Kgs 18:19, where the Rabshakeh alludes to the (nameless) "Pharaoh" of the time of Hezekiah.

[527] The reference is to the Egyptian queen "Nikaule" whose name Josephus draws from Herodotus in 8.158, and whom he now proceeds to identify with the anonymous "Queen of Sheba" of 1 Kgs 10:1-13// 2 Chr 9:1-12.

[528] Josephus resumes his presentation of this figure in 8.165-175.

[529] Having earlier called attention to "Phoenician" evidence corroborating the Bible's account of Solomon (see 8.55-56, 143-149), Josephus in 8.155-159 adduces comparable Egyptian evidence (or more exactly that of

the Greek historian Herodotus concerning Egypt). The reader is thereby left with an impression of a wide-ranging extra-biblical support for the biblical Solomon-story (as also of Josephus' impressive knowledge of the former material).

[530] The 2 localities cited by Josephus as marking the limits of the territories upon whose subjected inhabitants Solomon imposed tribute take the place of the list of 5 pre-Israelite peoples—among whom the "Canaanites" do not appear—who are mentioned as subject to the royal *corvée* in 1 Kgs 9:20// 2 Chr 8:7. "Amatheh" is Josephus' equivalent for the biblical "Hamath."

[531] Josephus goes beyond 1 Kgs 9:15-21// 2 Chr 8:5-8, which speak only of the subjugated peoples' working on the king's building projects, in mentioning also the agricultural tasks assigned to them.

[532] See 1 Kgs 9:22a// 2 Chr 8:9a, which call Solomon's own people "the Israelites." Apparently, Josephus perceived no contradiction between the above, unqualified statement and his earlier account (8.58-60), based on 1 Kgs 5:12-17 (MT; RSV 5:27-31), of the forced labor that Solomon imposed on the Israelites, i.e. quarrying stones for the temple. Perhaps, he viewed the Israelites' forced labor on the temple-project as merely a temporary imposition, in contrast to the permanent *corvée* imposed on the Canaanites.

[533] Josephus adds these remarks about the legitimacy of Solomon's varying treatment of his own people and the earlier inhabitants.

[534] See 1 Kgs 9:22// 2 Chr 8:9b, which represent the exempt Israelites as Solomon's soldiers and officers in command of his chariots and cavalry. Josephus' remarks in 8.161 on the contrast between the Israelites and the Canaanites are perhaps intended to evoke memories of the Spartan polity, in which the upper classes ("the

*Solomon's
maritime
venture*

(6.4) 162 Over the Chananaians whom he reduced to his domestic service he appointed rulers, 550 in number.[535] These were under the supervision of the king in order that he might teach them the works and enterprises he wanted from them.[536]

163 The king built many boats in the Gulf of Egypt of the Red Sea,[537] at a certain place called Gasion-Gabel,[538] not far from the city of Ilan[539] that is now called Berenike (for this area previously belonged to the Jews).[540] He also received a present that was suitable for his ships from Heirom, the king of the Tyrians. **164** For he sent to him men who were competent as pilots and those experienced in nautical matters.[541] Solomon directed these[542] to sail along with his own stewards to the ancient Sopheir[543] that is now called the "land of gold" (it is a part of India)[544] in order to bring him gold. Having collected about 400 talents,[545] they again returned to the king.

*Visit of "Queen
of Sheba"*

(6.4) 165 The woman who then ruled over Egypt and Ethiopia[546] was an eager student of wisdom.[547] She heard of the marvelous virtue and intelligence[548] of Solomon.[549] It was her desire to see him, based on what was said day after day of

---

Spartans") devoted themselves to military pursuits, while the helots performed menial tasks. On Spartan class structure and the relevant ancient references, see Mitchell 1952: 35-92.

[535] This figure agrees with that given in MT 1 Kgs 9:23 for Solomon's overseers; elsewhere, their numbers are cited as 3,600 (LXX BL 1 Kgs 2:35[h]); 250 (MT 2 Chr 8:10); and 520 (LXX BL 2 Chr 8:10).

[536] This reference to Solomon's personal supervisory role is Josephus' own. It highlights the king's active involvement in the projects initiated by him, while taking the place of the notices on Pharaoh's daughter going to her palace and Solomon's sacrifices in 1 Kgs 9:24-25// 2 Chr 8:11-12(13-15).

[537] The reference is to the Gulf of Aqaba, the eastern arm of the Red Sea. 1 Kgs 9:26 (MT) speaks of "the Sea of Reeds"; compare "the last sea" (LXX BL 1 Kgs 9:26), "on the shore of the sea" (2 Chr 8:17). Josephus has no equivalent to the biblical notices that "the land of Edom" bordered on the sea in question.

[538] MT (1 Kgs 9:26// 2 Chr 8:17) עֶצְיוֹן־גֶּבֶר (Eng.: "Ezion-geber"); LXX B 1 Kgs 9:26 Ἐμασειὼν Γάβερ; LXX L 1 Kgs 9:26 Γεσείων Γάβερ; LXX B 2 Chr 8:17 Γασιὼν Γάβερ; LXX L 2 Chr 8:17 Γεσιὼν Γάβερ; Josephus Γασιὼν Γάβελος.

[539] MT (1 Kgs 9:26) אֵלוֹת (Eng.: "Eloth"); LXX BL Αἰλάθ; MT (2 Chr 8:17) אֵילוֹת (Eng.: "Eloth"); LXX B Αἰλάμ; LXX L Αἰλάθ; Josephus Ἴλανις (Marcus *ad loc.* reads Αἰλανή, Schalit *s.v.* Ἡλαθούς).

[540] Josephus appends these notices on the site's contemporary Greek name and the Jews' earlier possession of it. Compare his added remark on the Greek name for "Thadamor" in 8.154.

[541] See 1 Kgs 9:27a// 2 Chr 8:18aα. Josephus adds the reference to "pilots."

[542] Josephus highlights the stature of Solomon by having him give orders to the seamen sent him by Hiram; in 1 Kgs 9:28// 2 Chr 8:18 Solomon and Hiram's sailors simply go to Ophir, no preceding command by Solomon being mentioned.

[543] MT (1 Kgs 9:28// 2 Chr 8:18) אוֹפִירָה (Eng.: "Ophir"); LXX B 1 Kgs 9:28 Σωφηρά; LXX L 1 Kgs 9:28 // LXX BL 2 Chr 8:18 and Josephus Σωφειρά.

[544] Josephus appends these indications concerning the current name and location of "Sopheir." Various identifications for the region "Ophir" mentioned in MT 1 Kgs 9:28// 2 Chr 8:18 are proposed by modern scholars, e.g., Arabia, Somalia, as well as Josephus' India.

[545] Josephus' figure agrees with that of the Syriac in 2 Chr 8:18. Compare 420 (MT 1 Kgs 9:28); 120 (LXX BL 1 Kgs 9:28); 450 (MT and LXX BL 2 Chr 8:18).

[546] This designation for the biblical "Queen of Sheba" (LXX Σαβά) picks up on Josephus' earlier mention of Solomon's future royal visitor in 8.159, who in turn he identifies with the Egyptian queen "Nikaule" mentioned by Herodotus; see 8.158.

[547] This characterization of the woman is Josephus' own.

[548] Greek: ἀρετὴ καὶ φρόνησις. This collocation occurs only here in Josephus. It recalls the triple use of the phrase "intelligence and wisdom" for Solomon in 8.34, 42, 171. The word φρόνησις ("intelligence") is a *Leitwort* of Josephus' account of the visit of the foreign queen (8.165-175), being twice further applied to the king there; see 8.169, 171.

[549] Cf. 1 Kgs 10:1a// 2 Chr 9:1, where the queen simply hears of Solomon's "fame" (10:1a adds "concerning the name of the Lord"). Josephus spells out the nature of Solomon's "fame" that reaches the queen.

matters there, that brought her to him.[550] **166** For, wishing to be convinced by experience rather than by hearsay (which tends to give its assent to false appearances and then again to convince one of something else, for it is entirely dependent on those making the report),[551] she decided to come to him, desiring above all to test his wisdom for herself by propounding questions and asking him to resolve the mental confusion.[552] She came then to Hierosolyma with much glory and costly pomp. **167** For she brought camels laden with gold, as well as various perfumes and precious stones.[553]

When she arrived, the king received her gladly and was solicitous for her in all respects.[554] By means of his sagacity, he readily apprehended the riddles that were proposed to him and solved these more quickly than anyone expected.[555] **168** She was filled with amazement at the wisdom of Solomon,[556] that it was so outstanding, and when she realized that it was greater, when put to the test, than she had heard.[557] She especially marvelled at the palace, at its beauty and size no less than the arrangement of its edifices, for in this she perceived the king's great intelligence.[558] **169** But it was the building called the "Forest of Liban"[559] and the costliness of the daily banquets that astonished her immeasurably, as did his furnishings and his body of servants, the clothing of his retainers, and their decorum coupled with skill.[560] Most of all, though, it was the sacrifices that were offered daily to God and the priests and Levites' attentiveness to these.[561]

170 Seeing these things each day, she greatly marveled, and, unable to restrain her amazement at what she saw, she made clear her sense of wonderment. For she was led to speak to the king by the things she was shown, her mind being completely overwhelmed by what we have mentioned.[562] **171** "For indeed all those things," she said, "O king, that come to one's knowledge by way of hearsay meet with disbelief.[563] Nonetheless, the report that reached us concerning the good things

---

[550] Josephus supplies this motivation for the queen's eventual visit to Solomon.

[551] Josephus appends this reflection about the difference between first- and secondhand knowledge.

[552] See 1 Kgs 10:1b// 2 Chr 9:1aβ, where the queen comes to "test" Solomon "with riddles."

[553] 1 Kgs 10:2a// 2 Chr 9:1bα list "spices," along with gold and precious stones, as the items brought by the queen.

[554] Josephus adds this notice on Solomon's reception of his visitor, highlighting the king's hospitality.

[555] See 1 Kgs 10:3// 2 Chr 9:2. Josephus underscores, not only Solomon's ability to solve the problems presented to him, but also the speed with which he does so.

[556] Josephus combines the opening words of 1 Kgs 10:4// 2 Chr 9:3 (the queen sees Solomon's wisdom) and 10:5bβ// 9:4bβ ("there was no more spirit in her").

[557] Josephus transposes into an editorial remark the queen's direct address "confession" (1 Kgs 10:6-7// 2 Chr 9:5-6)—which he will cite subsequently, see 8.171-173—about her not having been told "the half" of what she now sees of Solomon's establishment. The remark recalls Josephus' previous observation about the supe-

riority of personal "experience" over mere hearing about things from others in 8.166.

[558] Josephus elaborates on the summary allusion to the queen's seeing the "house" that Solomon had built in 1 Kgs 10:4// 2 Chr 9:3.

[559] This structure is not mentioned in the list of what the queen sees in 1 Kgs 10:4-5// 2 Chr 9:3-4. Josephus uses this name for the edifice for the first time here in 8.169; in 8.133, in his version of the account concerning the "House of the Forest of Lebanon" of 1 Kgs 7:2-5, he speaks simply of "the building."

[560] See 1 Kgs 10:5a// 2 Chr 9:4a (the queen sees Solomon's fare and his attendants).

[561] Josephus elaborates on the passing allusion in 1 Kgs 10:5aβ (and LXX 2 Chr 9:4aβ) to the queen's seeing the sacrifices that Solomon brought to the temple, highlighting the clergy's devotion to their sacrificial duties.

[562] This notice of the effect of what she has seen upon the queen picks up on Josephus' earlier comment about her reaction to this in 8.168 (cf. 1 Kgs 10:5bβ// 2 Chr 9:4bβ).

[563] See 1 Kgs 10:7// 2 Chr 9:6, where the queen admits that she had "not believed" the reports brought

you have within yourself—I speak of your wisdom and intelligence[564]—as also concerning the things that kingship gives you, was no lie.[565] But although true, it [the report] indicated a well-being on your part that is much inferior to what I now see when present. **172** For the reports were only trying to persuade, but did not make evident the status of your affairs, the way the actual sight of them and being present to them brings home. For whereas I did not actually believe my informants, due to the quantity and magnitude of the things I was finding out, I have experienced much more than these.[566] **173** And I judge the Hebrew people to be a blessed[567] one, as also your slaves and friends, who daily enjoy the sight of you and continue to hear your wisdom.[568] Let each one praise God,[569] who so loved this country and those living in it, that he made you king."[570]

(6.6) 174 Having shown by these words how much the king had impressed her,[571] she made her state of mind clear by her gifts. For she gave him twenty talents of gold,[572] plus countless quantities of perfumes and precious stones.[573] For they say that we also have the root of the balsam bush—which our country still produces—as a gift from this woman.[574] **175** Solomon, for his part, gifted her with many good things in return, especially those she selected in accordance with her desire. For there was nothing that she asked to receive that he did not award her. Rather, he displayed his magnanimity by giving up more readily what she requested to obtain than by presenting her things in accordance with his own choice.[575] And the queen of the

---

her about Solomon. The queen's mention of "hearsay" here recalls Josephus' reflection on "hearsay" vs. "experience" in 8.166. Josephus reverses the order of 1 Kgs 10:6-7// 2 Chr 9:5-6, where the queen confesses her previous "unbelief" only after affirming her present realization of the truth of what she had been told.

[564] Greek: σοφία καὶ φρόνησις. Josephus has twice earlier applied this collocation—though with reversal of the component terms—to Solomon; see 8.34, 42. Compare the binomial "virtue and intelligence" in 8.165.

[565] See 1 Kgs 10:6// 2 Chr 9:5, where the queen admits that what had been told her about Solomon, his "wisdom" in particular, is indeed "true."

[566] Josephus' queen expatiates on the words of her biblical counterpart in 1 Kgs 10:7// 2 Chr 9:6, where she admits that whereas she had not believed what was told her, this itself turned out to be not even the half of what she actually saw upon her arrival. Compare Josephus' anticipation of the queen's words here in his editorial comment of 8.168.

[567] Greek: μακάριος. The queen's declaration here recalls Solomon's statement that, if they kept the laws of Moses, "the nation of the Hebrews would be happy and more blessed [Greek: μακαριώτερος] than the whole human race" in 8.120.

[568] See 1 Kgs 10:8// 2 Chr 9:7, where the queen calls Solomon's "men [MT; LXX BL: wives] and servants" happy. Josephus adds the reference to the "Hebrew people" as a whole.

[569] In 1 Kgs 10:9a// 2 Chr 9:8a the pagan queen

herself pronounces the Lord blessed; Josephus has her urge others to praise him. His exhortation to such praise by the people recalls Solomon's own urging the people to praise God in 8.110, 119.

[570] Like 1 Kgs 10:9b// 2 Chr 9:8b, Josephus has the queen associate God's "love" for Israel with his making Solomon its king. He leaves aside the reference to Solomon's royal task ("to execute justice and righteousness") with which the queen's words end in both biblical verses.

[571] Josephus adds this transitional phrase that underscores Solomon's effect upon the queen.

[572] Both 1 Kgs 10:10 and 2 Chr 9:9 cite a much higher figure, read also by E in 8.174, i.e. 120 talents.

[573] Josephus' 3-item catalogue of the queen's gifts corresponds to the listing in 1 Kgs 10:10a// 2 Chr 9:9a, just as it recalls his own earlier listing of the gifts with which she came in 8.167 (cf. 1 Kgs 10:2// 2 Chr 9:1).

[574] For this notice, Josephus draws on his personal knowledge of contemporary Palestine and its traditions; cf. his references to the "balsam" produced at various Palestinian sites in his own time in *War* 1.138, 361; 4.469; *Ant.* 9.8; 14.54; 15.96. The notice takes the place of the indications in 1 Kgs 10:10b (so large an amount of spices/balsam as that brought by the queen never again entered Israel) and 2 Chr 9:9b (the incomparability of the spices/ balsam brought by her).

[575] Josephus anticipates and elaborates upon the notice of 1 Kgs 10:13a// 2 Chr 9:12a about Solomon's giving the queen whatever she asked of him. In so doing, he accentuates the king's generosity by having

Egyptians and Ethiopia, of whom we spoke previously,[576] having obtained both a portion from the king and given him a share of what was hers, returned to her own country.[577]

(7.1) 176 Around the same time precious stones and pine timbers were brought to the king from the land called the land of gold.[578] He employed the timbers as supports for the sanctuary and the palace as well as for the construction of musical instruments, namely *kinyrai* and *nablai*,[579] so that the Levites might sing hymns to God.[580]

Solomon's imports and their uses

[The wood] that was conveyed to him on that day surpassed in size and beauty all that was brought previously.[581] **177** Let no one suppose that those pine trees[582] resembled those that are now so called, being given that name by sellers so as to dazzle buyers. For the former are like fig-trees in appearance, though more gleaming white than these. **178** We have mentioned this so that there will not be anyone who does not recognize the distinctiveness or the nature of the true pine. Since we have mentioned the use of this [pine] by the king, we thought it both opportune and humane to disclose [the matter].[583]

(7.2) 179 Now the weight of the gold that was brought to him was 666 talents,[584] not counting what was bought by the merchants nor the gifts that the *toparchs* and kings of Arabia sent to him.[585] He cast the gold for the construction of 200 long, rectangular shields,[586] each weighing 600[587] shekels. **180** He also made 300 small, round shields, each weighing three *minas* of gold.[588] He dedicated these, carrying

---

him allow the queen to choose herself what she is to be given.

[576] See 8.159, 169 for this designation of the biblical "Queen of Sheba."

[577] See 1 Kgs 10:13b// 2 Chr 9:12b, which also mention the queen's retinue returning with her.

[578] This is Josephus' "delayed" use of the parenthetical notice—inserted within their respective stories concerning the queen's visit—of 1 Kgs 10:11// 2 Chr 9:10. From the biblical lists of products brought to Solomon from "Ophir" (MT)/ "Sopheir," etc. (LXX) (on Josephus' notice concerning "the land of gold" as the contemporary name of biblical "Sopheir," see 8.164), he omits mention of "gold." In his version, the timber received by the king is "pine" rather than "almug wood," while he agrees with MT 10:11// 9:10 in speaking of "precious stones" rather than "hewn" (LXX B 10:11)/ "unhewn" (LXX L 10:11) stone. Finally, Josephus leaves aside the biblical specifications concerning the "bringers" of the treasurers, i.e. "the fleet of Hiram" (10:11)/ "the servants of Huram and the servants of Solomon" (9:10).

[579] Like LXX, Josephus transliterates the Hebrew names for the 2 types of instruments, while also reversing the order of their occurrence in 1 Kgs 10:12// 2 Chr 9:11. Cf. 8.94, where Solomon is said to have made 4,000 *nablai* and *kinyrai*.

[580] Josephus expatiates on the reference to the "singers" in 1 Kgs 10:12a// 2 Chr 9:11a, identifying these as "Levites," and specifying that they

sang "to God."

[581] Compare 1 Kgs 10:12b// 2 Chr 9:11b, where the "almug wood" brought to Solomon is said to be of a sort that was never seen before or since.

[582] Josephus here begins his embellishment of the notice on the uniqueness of the (almug) wood brought to Solomon in 1 Kgs 10:12b// 2 Chr 9:11b. As in 8.176, he identifies the wood in question as "pine."

[583] Josephus appends this rationale for his extended excursus concerning the types of "pine." Compare his similar formulations explaining the reason for his excursus on the title "Pharaoh" in 8.155, 159.

[584] This figure for the gold brought to Solomon agrees with that given in 1 Kgs 10:14// 2 Chr 9:13, which specify that the amount was delivered annually.

[585] See 1 Kgs 10:15// 2 Chr 9:14. Josephus substitutes the Hellenistic title *toparch* (literally, "ruler of a place") for the biblical mention of "the governors of the lands."

[586] Josephus' figure for the number of these shields matches that given in MT 1 Kgs 10:16 and MT LXX BL 2 Chr 9:15. LXX BL 10:16 read 300 *spears*.

[587] Josephus' figure for the weight of the shields agrees with that cited in MT 1 Kgs 10:16 and MT LXX 2 Chr 9:15. LXX BL 10:16 speak of *spears* (see previous note), weighing *300* shekels apiece.

[588] Josephus' figures for the number and weight of the 2nd type of Solomonic shield correspond to those given in 1 Kgs 10:17a// 2 Chr 9:16a. The "mina" (Hebrew: מנה) corresponds to 50 shekels.

them into the building called the "Forest of Liban."[589] He likewise constructed drinking vessels of gold and [precious] stones for feasting with special artistry, and crafted an abundance of other vessels completely out of gold. **181** For no one either sold or brought anything [made] of silver.[590]

Solomon's maritime trade

Now there were many ships that the king stationed in the sea called the *Tarsikdean*[591] and ordered to carry merchandise of every sort into the most interior parts of the nations.[592] Having sold this at a profit, they brought the king silver and gold, along with much Ethiopian ivory, as well as apes.[593] Three years elapsed between the ships' putting out to sea and their return.[594]

Royal gifts for Solomon

(7.3) 182 A splendid report circulated throughout the whole surrounding country, exalting the virtue and wisdom[595] of Solomon,[596] so that from every side kings came, desiring to see him, not believing what was told them due to its excess.[597] **183** They further evidenced their attachment to him by their great gifts, for they kept sending him gold and silver vessels and deep-purple garments[598] and many types of fragrant spices,[599] along with horses and chariots.[600] They selected as well burden-bearing mules that, in virtue of both their vigor and beauty, would be fit to be seen by the king.[601] Thus when the chariots and horses that he had previously were joined to those that were sent to him, he expanded the number of his chariots by 400 (for

Solomon's horses

---

[589] See 1 Kgs 10:17b// 2 Chr 9:16b; cf. Josephus' previous mention of the "Forest of Liban" edifice in 8.169. In the biblical accounts, mention of Solomon's "shields" (1 Kgs 10:16-17// 2 Chr 9:15-16) is followed immediately by the account of his throne (10:18-20// 9:17-19). Josephus has already spoken of the king's throne (see 8.140) as an appendix to his description of the palace structures (8.130-139). Accordingly, he now proceeds directly to his description of Solomon's golden drinking vessels (= 1 Kgs 10:21// 2 Chr 9:20).

[590] See 1 Kgs 10:21// 2 Chr 9:20, which speak of the vessels as those of "the House of the Forest of Lebanon" and state that silver "was not considered as anything in the days of Solomon." With Josephus' statement here, compare his reference to Solomon's increasing the silver supply in Jerusalem in 8.188.

[591] This is Josephus' adaptation of the phrase "ships of Tarshish" of 1 Kgs 10:22// 2 Chr 9:21. On Josephus' (varying) localizations of biblical "Tarshish," see BJP 3 (Feldman): 46, nn. 344-5.

[592] Josephus accentuates Solomon's direction of the proceedings in comparison with 1 Kgs 10:22a// 2 Chr 9:21a, which do not mention such a role for the king with regard to the fleet. He has no equivalent to the appended biblical references to Solomon's nautical enterprise being undertaken in conjunction with the ships of Hiram/Huram.

[593] Josephus has no equivalent to the (varying) final item in the biblical lists, i.e. "peacocks"(?)/"baboons"(?) (MT 1 Kgs 10:22// MT LXX BL 2 Chr 9:21) vs. "carved and (un)hewn stones" (LXX BL 1 Kgs 10:22). He adds the specification about the "ivory"

being "Ethiopian."

[594] Josephus' figure for the duration of the voyage agrees with that cited in 1 Kgs 10:22b// 2 Chr 9:21b.

[595] Greek: ἀρετή καὶ σοφία. This collocation occurs only here in Josephus. Compare the binomial ἀρετή καὶ φρόνησις ("virtue and intelligence") used of Solomon in 8.165.

[596] Josephus substitutes mention of Solomon's "virtue" for the "riches" as that in which, in addition to his "wisdom," he excelled all other kings according to 1 Kgs 10:23// 2 Chr 9:22.

[597] Josephus modifies the wording of the biblical accounts, where it is "all the earth" (1 Kgs 10:24)/ "all the kings of the earth" (2 Chr 9:23) that come(s) to hear Solomon's God-given wisdom. His formulation here in 8.182 recalls the statements he attributes to the visiting queen, who admits not "believing" the reports she had heard about Solomon due to their "quantity and magnitude" in 8.171-172.

[598] Josephus adds this specification concerning the color of the "garments" spoken of in the list of royal gifts in 1 Kgs 10:25// 2 Chr 9:24.

[599] Compare "myrrh [or weapons, Hebrew: נשׁק] and spices" (MT 1 Kgs 10:25// 2 Chr 9:24)/ "oil and perfume" (LXX BL 1 Kgs 10:25// 2 Chr 9:24).

[600] Neither 1 Kgs 10:25 nor 2 Chr 9:24 mentions "chariots," coupling the horses given Solomon rather with "mules" (which Josephus will mention in what follows).

[601] Josephus here elaborates on the mention of "mules" as the last in the series of gifts given Solomon in 1 Kgs 10:25// 2 Chr 9:24.

previously he had 1,000),[602] and the number of horses by 2,000 (for he [already] had 20,000 horses).[603] **184** These were trained for both good looks and speed such that there were none more handsome or swift to compare with them. Rather, they appeared to be the most beautiful of all and were unrivaled in speed.[604]

185 Their riders also complemented their [the horses'] appearance. These, being in the bloom of youth, were most delightful; they were also of remarkable height and much superior to others. They let their hair hang down extremely long and wore tunics of Tyrian purple. They put gold dust on their hair each day, so that their heads shone when the radiance of the gold was reflected by the sun. **186** The king had these men around him, armed and equipped with bows. He himself had the habit of getting into his chariot, wearing a white garment, and taking a ride. There was a certain spot two *skoinoi*[605] from Hierosolyma, called *Etan*,[606] which was delightful for, and rich in, parks and springs, which flowed into it. He used to go on excursions there, riding in his chariot.[607]

Solomon's entourage and excursions

(7.4) 187 In all matters he displayed a divine attention and solicitude.[608] As a great lover of the beautiful,[609] he did not neglect the roads either. Rather, he paved those leading to Hierosolyma, the royal [city], with black stone, both for the ease of travelers and to display the state of his wealth and leadership.[610] **188** He divided up and organized his chariots, so that the number of them in each city was fixed. Keeping a few [chariots] around himself, he called these [cities] the "chariot cities."[611]

Solomon's road-building

The chariot cities

The king made the supply of silver in Hierosolyma as great as that of its stones,[612] just as he made cedar wood—which had not been there before—as plentiful as the sycamore trees, in which the plains of Judea are abundant.[613]

Additional imports

---

[602] Without mentioning their (separate) origins, MT 1 Kgs 10:26 and 2 Chr 1:14 assign Solomon a total of 1,400 chariots, this matching Josephus' combined figure. MT 2 Chr 9:25 speaks rather of 4,000 "stalls for horses and chariots," while LXX BL 1 Kgs 10:26 and 2 Chr 9:25 mention 4,000 "female horses for chariots (+ for breeding, L 10:26)." In 8.41 Josephus cites Solomon's 40,000 stalls for his horses and 12,000 horsemen.

[603] 1 Kgs 10:26// 2 Chr 9:25; and 2 Chr 1:14 all cite a markedly lower total figure for Solomon's horses, i.e. 12,000.

[604] These notices on the qualities of Solomon's horses have no biblical basis. They recall Josephus' (likewise added) remarks concerning the qualities of the mules given the king in 8.183.

[605] This distance corresponds to *ca.* 8-10 miles; see Marcus *ad loc.*

[606] Marcus (*ad loc.*) suggests that this site is to be identified with the "Etame" mentioned in 8.246 (= "Etam" in 2 Chr 11:6) as one of the fortified cities constructed by Rehoboam.

[607] The above sequence (8.185-186) concerning Solomon's entourage and the king's movements is Josephus' invention. It highlights the opulence and glamour of his reign.

[608] Greek ἐπίνοια καὶ σπουδή. This collocation is *hapax* in Josephus.

[609] Greek: φιλόκαλος. Josephus' 2 other uses of this word are in *Ant.* 12.12, 59 (both times of King Ptolemy II).

[610] This whole paragraph is a Josephan creation, designed to highlight those features of Solomon's reign he is especially concerned to accentuate, i.e. the king's wisdom, wealth, and self-display. Its mention of Solomon's attention to the roads is a touch Roman readers would appreciate, given the Romans' reputation as road-builders.

[611] Josephus now finally rejoins—after the 4-paragraph interlude of 8.184-187—the sequence of the biblical accounts, i.e. 1 Kgs 10:26b// 2 Chr 9:25 (and 1:14), for his mention of the distribution of Solomon's chariots.

[612] See 1 Kgs 10:27a// 2 Chr 9:27a (and 2 Chr 1:15a). Like MT 1 Kgs 10:27// 2 Chr 9:27, Josephus lacks an equivalent to the plus of LXX BL 10:27// 9:27 (and 2 Chr 1:15) according to which Solomon made not only "silver" but also "gold" as plentiful as stones in Jerusalem. Earlier (see 8.181), Josephus, following 1 Kgs 10:21// 2 Chr 9:20, stated that nothing made of silver was bought or sold during Solomon's reign.

[613] MT 1 Kgs 10:27b// 2 Chr 9:27b (and 2 Chr 1:15a) all refer to "the Shephelah," which LXX translates as "the plain." Josephus adds the specification "of Judea" to this translation, just as he supplies the refer-

Solomon's bad end

189 He ordered the Egyptian merchants to bring and sell him chariots, along with their two horses, for 600 drachmas of silver.[614] He himself then dispatched these to the kings of Syria and those beyond the Euphrates.[615]

(7.5) 190 Although he was the most famous of kings and close to God,[616] just as he surpassed in intelligence and wealth[617] those who exercised rule over the Hebrews before him,[618] he nevertheless did not persevere in these things until his death. Rather, due to his abandoning the observance of the ancestral customs, he ended up in a way that was unlike what we have told previously.[619]

Solomon's foreign wives

191 Becoming crazy[620] about women and in his weakness for sexual pleasure,[621] he was not satisfied with native [women] alone[622] but also married many foreigners, Sidonians, Tyrians, Ammanites, and Idumeans.[623] [In doing this], he transgressed against the laws of Moyses, who prohibited cohabitating with non-compatriots.[624] **192** He began to worship their gods, indulging these women and his passion for them.[625] This was the very thing the legislator[626] had suspected would happen when

---

ence to the previous non-availability of cedar wood, thereby accentuating the magnitude of Solomon's achievement.

[614] In specifying 600 drachmas as the price for both a chariot and its team, Josephus conflates the indications of 1 Kgs 10:29// 2 Chr 1:17, which list separate prices for chariot (600 drachmas, MT; vs. 100, LXX BL 2 Chr 1:17) and horse (150 drachmas, MT vs. 50, LXX BL 2 Chr 1:17). He omits the mention of the mysterious "Kue" cited alongside Egypt in 1 Kgs 10:28// 2 Chr 1:16 as another place from which Solomon imported horses.

[615] In 1 Kgs 10:29b// 2 Chr 1:17b the horses and chariots are exported to "all the kings of the Hittites and the kings of Syria." 2 Chr 9:28 lacks a corresponding indication.

[616] Josephus has already used this term (Greek: θεοφιλής) of Solomon in 8.49.

[617] Greek: φρόνησις καὶ πλοῦτος. Josephus' only other use of this collocation is in his concluding evaluation of Solomon in 8.211 (where it is combined with a 3rd term, i.e. εὐδαιμονία ["well-being"]).

[618] Josephus' reference here to Solomon's excelling his predecessors in wealth stands in seeming tension with his notice that David left behind more wealth than did any other king, whether of the Hebrews or the Gentiles, in *Ant.* 7.391.

[619] Josephus adds this statement, which both looks back to his earlier notices about Solomon's endowments (see, e.g., 8.24, 49) and forward to the king's coming defection. He thereby provides a smoother transition between the initial, good period of Solomon's reign and his later, bad period than does 1 Kings (the Chronicler passes over this latter period entirely), which, after citing the king's wealth-generating initiatives in 10:26-29, abruptly shifts (11:1) to the subject of the royal love life and its disastrous consequences.

[620] Greek: ἐκμαίνω. Josephus' only other use of this

verb is in *War* 1.443.

[621] Greek: ἀφροδίσιος. Josephus' one remaining use of this term is in *Ant.* 7.344, where the aged David is said to be too infirm for "sexual pleasure."

[622] Josephus embellishes the biblical reference to Solomon's "loving" foreign women (1 Kgs 11:1), underscoring the intensity of the king's passion, just as he heightens the erotic element in his retelling of biblical episodes often elsewhere; see Moehring 1957; Feldman 1998: 565. On Josephus' version of the story of Solomon's foreign wives (1 Kgs 11:1-13) in 8.190-199a, see Begg 1997.

[623] Josephus' 4-element list of the peoples/countries from which Solomon's foreign wives came is shorter than the 6-member list of MT 1 Kgs 11:1 (the daughter of Pharaoh, Moabites, Ammonites, Edomites, Sidonians, and Hittites) and the 7-item enumeration of LXX BL (this lacks MT's Sidonians, but adds Syrians and Amorites). On the other hand, he does introduce one group not cited by either MT or LXX, i.e. the Tyrians; elsewhere too Josephus adds a reference to Tyre/the Tyrians, where the Bible speaks only of Sidon/the Sidonians; see Begg 1997: 297, n. 21.

[624] Josephus turns into a generalized editorial comment the "quotation" of the Mosaic prohibition of intermarriage (Deut 7:3-4) given in 1 Kgs 11:2 (to which he will make more specific reference in 8.192).

[625] Josephus here synthesizes a series of biblical notices on Solomon's defection, i.e. his heart being turned away "after other gods" by his wives (1 Kgs 11:4a), his "going after" various foreign deities (Ashtoreth, Milcom: 11:5), and building "high places" for other such divinities (Chemosh, Molech: 11:7) that his wives used in their worship of them (11:8). Such generalizing of biblical cultic particulars is a recurrent feature of Josephus' rewriting of the Bible; he thereby aims to spare Greco-Roman readers the details of Jewish and other, equally unfamiliar, religious systems.

he told [the Israelites] in advance not to marry those of other countries.[627] [He did this] in order that they not become entangled in foreign ways of life and leave the ancestral ones aside, and while worshipping those gods, fail to honor their own.[628]

193 Solomon, however, disregarded these things, incited by irrational pleasure.[629] He married 700 women, the daughters of rulers and nobles;[630] he also had 300 concubines,[631] and in addition the daughter of the king of the Egyptians.[632] He was immediately overcome by them, so that he imitated their ways. He was compelled to provide them proof of his loyalty and tenderness[633] by living in their ancestral manner.[634] **194** When he became old and his reason was too weakened by time[635] to oppose [this tendency] with the memory of his native customs, he showed still greater contempt for his own God, while he continued to honor those of his alien wives. **195** Even prior to them, however, it happened that he offended and went astray in his keeping of the laws.[636] [He did this] when he constructed likenesses of bronze oxen beneath the "sea" as a votive offering[637] and of lions around his own throne.[638] For in producing these things, he did what was not holy.

196 He had a most beautiful and proximate example of virtue[639] in his father and the glory that he left behind on account of his piety towards God. Nevertheless, he failed to imitate either him[640] or those things in which God, who had twice appeared to him in a dream, urged him to imitate his father,[641] and so he died ignominiously.[642]

Aged Solomon's defection from God

---

[626] On this characteristic Josephan title (Greek: νομοθέτης) for Moses, see Feldman 1998: 399.

[627] Greek: ἀλλοτριόχωρος. Josephus' one other use of this adjective is in *Ant.* 3.281.

[628] Josephus here alludes more specifically to the intermarriage prohibition of Deut 7:3-4 as cited in 1 Kgs 11:2a, after his generalized reference to the "laws of Moyses" that Solomon transgressed in 8.191.

[629] Compare 1 Kgs 11:2b: Solomon "clung to these [his foreign wives] in love." With Josephus' qualification of Solomon's pleasure-seeking as "irrational," compare *Exod. Rab.* 6.1, where the penitent Solomon acknowledges that his earlier thinking himself wiser than the Torah has proved to be "madness and folly." The phrase "irrational pleasure" (Greek: ἡδονὴ ἀλόγιστος) occurs only here in Josephus.

[630] In 1 Kgs 11:3a Solomon's 700 wives are (all) "princesses." Josephus' indication that some of the 700 were drawn from the daughters of (mere) "nobles" might be intended to counteract reader skepticism as to whether Solomon could have found 700 actual princesses to marry.

[631] This figure corresponds to that given in 1 Kgs 11:3a. Josephus uses the same Greek word (παλλακαί) for Solomon's "concubines" as do LXX BL 1 Kgs 11:3a.

[632] Josephus' reference to this woman here represents his delayed utilization of the mention of her in the listing of Solomon's foreign wives in 1 Kgs 11:1.

[633] Greek: εὐνοία καὶ φιλοστοργία. This collocation recurs in *Ant.* 15.68 and 16.21 (both times in reference to the attachments of King Herod).

[634] Here again (see 8.192), Josephus generalizes the more specific indications concerning the cultic initiatives undertaken by Solomon on behalf of his foreign wives cited in 1 Kgs 11:5, 7-8.

[635] Josephus elaborates the reference to Solomon's being "old" in 1 Kgs 11:4a with mention of the effect of the king's advanced age upon his intellect. The term "reason" (Greek: λογισμός) here echoes the word "irrational" (Greek: ἀλόγιστος) in the phrase "irrational pleasure" of 8.193.

[636] This transitional phrase, added by Josephus as a lead-in to the specific cultic charges he is about to make against Solomon, recalls his reference to the king's "transgressing against the laws of Moyses" in 8.191.

[637] Earlier (see 8.80, where, however, he calls them "calves"), Josephus—following the biblical accounts—had mentioned these objects without criticism. Here, he represents them as a violation of the biblical prohibition against image-making.

[638] As in the case of the oxen (see previous note), Josephus earlier (see 8.140) spoke of the lions that were part of Solomon's throne complex without any such criticism of them.

[639] Greek: παράδειγμα τῆς ἀρετῆς. This expression recurs in *Ant.* 17.313; cf. 17.60.

[640] Josephus conflates and embellishes the double reference to Solomon's not living up to the standard set by David in 1 Kgs 11:4b, 6.

[641] Josephus anticipates his allusion to the Lord's 2 previous appearances to Solomon (on these, see 8.22, 125) from 1 Kgs 11:9b-10, which cites as the content

God condemns Solomon

197 Therefore the prophet, who had been sent by God, came immediately, saying[643] that his lawless acts were not concealed from him [God],[644] and threatening that he [Solomon] would not long rejoice in what he had done.[645] Although the kingship would not be taken away while he was still living, since the Deity had promised his father David to make him his successor,[646] **198** when he died, he [God] would bring these things upon his son,[647] although he would not cause the entire people to revolt against him.[648] He would, though, hand over ten tribes to his slave and leave only two[649] for the grandson of David, for the latter's sake, because he loved God,[650] and for the sake of the city of Hierosolyma in which he wished to have a sanctuary.[651]

(7.6) 199 When Solomon heard this, he was grieved and greatly distressed [because] virtually all the good things for which he was envied were undergoing a vile change.[652]

Revolt of Hadad (Ader)

Not much time elapsed from when the prophet announced to him the things that were to happen;[653] rather, God immediately raised up an adversary[654] against him, named Ader,[655] whose hostility had the following cause. **200** This lad was an

---

of the previous divine communications the warning that Solomon not go after other gods (as he is said to do in 11:5). Josephus' alternative wording of the Deity's prior message(s) highlights the exemplary status of David.

[642] This appended phrase recalls Josephus' reference to Solomon's death being unlike his previous life in 8.190.

[643] In 1 Kgs 11:11 the Lord speaks to Solomon directly. Josephus' introducing the figure of a prophet between God and the transgressor king has a counterpart in *S. ʿOlam Rab.* 20.9, where the prophet in question is identified as Ahijah of Shiloh. Josephus will make delayed use of the reference to the Lord's being "angry with Solomon" of 1 Kgs 11:9a in 8.203.

[644] In 1 Kgs 11:11bα the Lord accuses Solomon in more specific terms of having failed to keep "my covenant [MT; LXX BL: commandments] and my statutes." Once again, Josephus avoids the biblical term "covenant."

[645] The Deity's announcement in 1 Kgs 11:11bβ is more specific, i.e. he intends to "tear the kingdom" from Solomon and give it to "his servant."

[646] Josephus adds this reference to God's promise to David concerning Solomon himself; see *Ant.* 7.93. He thereby accentuates Solomon's ingratitude towards God who, for his part, has fulfilled his pledge to David.

[647] See 1 Kgs 11:12b, where the Lord speaks more vividly of his intended "tearing the kingdom out of the hand of your [Solomon's] son."

[648] Josephus adds this reference to a "revolt" by a portion of the people against Solomon's son. He thereby makes the prophet's announcement a more precise prediction of the actual course of events—see the reference to the "remainder of the people revolting from the sons of David" in 8.221.

[649] In 1 Kgs 11:13a God mentions explicitly only the "one" tribe that he will leave for Solomon's son. Josephus' distinction between the 10 rebel tribes and the 2 that will remain faithful to the Davidids is inspired by Ahijah's subsequent word to Jeroboam in 1 Kgs 11:31-32, 35-36, where LXX BL makes this same 10/2 distinction, while, there as well, MT leaves one tribe unaccounted for in its distinction between 10 versus *one* tribe(s).

[650] In 1 Kgs 11:13bα the Lord qualifies David as "my servant," a title which Josephus does not use with nearly the same frequency as does the Bible itself; see Schlatter 1932: 49-50. On Josephus' use of the verb "love" (Greek: ἀγαπάω) with God/divine things as object, see ibid., 154.

[651] Compare 1 Kgs 11:13bβ, where the Lord characterizes Jerusalem as (the city) "which I have chosen."

[652] With this notice Josephus fills a lacuna in the presentation of 1 Kings 11, where there is no mention of Solomon's reaction to God's ominous words to him (11:11-13).

[653] This transitional phrase, with its allusion to the "prophet" mentioned in 8.197, underscores the rapidity with which the divine judgment upon Solomon begins to be realized. 1 Kings 11 leaves the chronological relation between God's announcement (vv. 11-13) and its fulfillment (vv. 14-40) indeterminate.

[654] Greek: πολέμιος. With this term Josephus translates the Hebrew word שָׂטָן ("satan") used in MT 1 Kgs 11:14 to qualify "Hadad" as Solomon's "adversary" (LXX BL transliterate the term). On Josephus' account of Solomon's 2 (foreign) opponents, i.e. Hadad (1 Kgs 11:14-22) and Rezin (1 Kgs 11:23-25), see Begg 1996.

[655] MT (1 Kgs 11:14) הֲדַד (Eng.: "Hadad") LXX BL Ἀδέρ; Josephus Ἄδερος.

Idumean by race, of the royal line.[656] When Joab, David's general, subjugated Idumea and, over the course of six months, destroyed all those in the prime of life and capable of bearing arms,[657] he fled and went to Pharaoh, king of the Egyptians.[658] **201** He received him kindly and gave him a house and land for his sustenance;[659] he loved him so greatly that when he grew up[660] he gave him in marriage the sister of his own wife, whose name was Thaphine.[661] By her he had a son,[662] who was brought up with the king's children.[663]

202 When therefore he [Ader] heard in Egypt of the death of David and Joab, he approached Pharaoh and asked him to allow him to go to his ancestral country.[664] When the king in response inquired what he lacked or what he was suffering that he should be anxious to leave him, he pressed him many times; though he kept appealing to him, he was not permitted to go at that time.[665] **203** Afterwards, however, when things were already beginning to go badly for Solomon due to his above-mentioned transgressions and God's wrath at these,[666] Ader, with Pharaoh's permission, went to Idumea.[667] He was unable to get it to revolt against Solomon, for it was occupied by many garrisons and because of these, revolt was neither a free [option] nor without risk.

Setting out from there, he went to Syria.[668] **204** There he met a certain Raz,[669] who had run away from his master Adraazar,[670] the king of Sophene,[671] and was making

Rezon (Raz) and Hadad (Ader) join forces

---

[656] See 1 Kgs 11:14b. Josephus agrees with LXX BL in calling "Ader" an "Idumean" rather than an "Edomite" (so MT).

[657] See 1 Kgs 11:15, which Josephus here follows in attributing the devastation of Edom/Idumea to *Joab*. In *Ant.* 7.119, by contrast, basing himself on 1 Chr 18:12, he makes Abishai, brother of Joab, the ravager of Edom (in the parallel text, 2 Sam 8:13, David himself ravages Aram [MT; LXX BL: Idumea]).

[658] See 1 Kgs 11:17, from which Josephus omits mention of the entourage that accompanied Hadad as well as the fact of his being a "little child" at the moment of his flight. He likewise leaves aside the details concerning the escape route cited in 11:18a.

[659] 1 Kgs 11:18b mentions Pharaoh's gift of "food" as well as a house and land to Hadad.

[660] This reference to Hadad's "growing up" in Egypt lacks a biblical counterpart; it might, however, reflect the reference to his being "a little child" at the time of his flight there (11:17), a detail previously passed over by Josephus.

[661] MT (1 Kgs 11:19) תחפנים (Eng.: "Tahpenes"); LXX B Θεκεμείνας; LXX L Θεχεμείνας; Josephus Θαφίνη. In the Bible the woman named is the queen herself, rather than her sister, the wife of Hadad.

[662] Josephus omits the biblical name of this son, i.e. MT (1 Kgs 11:20) גנבת (Eng.: "Genubath"); LXX BL Γανηβάθ.

[663] 1 Kgs 11:20 further notes that Hadad's son was "weaned in Pharaoh's house."

[664] See 1 Kgs 11:21.

[665] Josephus embellishes the exchange between Pharaoh and Hadad as related in 1 Kgs 11:22, noting both the latter's repeated requests of the former, and Pharaoh's on-going rebuff of those requests.

[666] This phrase reflects the statement—previously passed over by Josephus—that the Lord "was angry with Solomon" of 1 Kgs 11:9a.

[667] For this sequence Josephus draws on, while also expanding, the LXX BL plus in 1 Kgs 11:22: "and he [Pharaoh] sent Ader to his own country." Subsequently too, he will make use of the alternative presentation of LXX BL in tracing the later career of "Ader"; see 8.205.

[668] These notices on Ader's (Hadad's) career after his leaving Egypt lack a biblical foundation. The added mention of the failure of Ader's effort to wrest Idumea from Solomon motivates the rebel's resultant move to Syria. The latter notice, in turn, prepares Josephus' subsequent reference to Ader's becoming king of Syria in 8.204.

[669] MT (1 Kgs 11:23) רזון (Eng.: "Rezon"); Josephus Ῥάζος (this figure appears together with "Ader" in LXX BL 1 Kgs 11:14 under the name of Ἐσρών). Josephus omits Rezon's patronymic, i.e. "Eliada" (MT). He likewise has no equivalent to the reference to the Lord's "raising Rezon up against" Solomon of 1 Kgs 11:23, whereas he does reproduce the similar notice concerning Hadad of 1 Kgs 11:14 in 8.199.

[670] MT (1 Kgs 11:23) הדדעזר (Eng.: "Hadadezer"); LXX B (11:14) Ἀδράζαρ; LXX L (11:14) Ἀδρααζαρ; Josephus Ἀδραάζαρος.

the country unsafe by his banditry. He [Ader] attached himself in friendship to him;[672] having a gang of bandits around him,[673] he went up and, settling there in Syria, was appointed its king.[674] Making raids against the land of the Israelites, he caused harm and plundered it while Solomon was still alive. These were the things that the Hebrews were destined to suffer from Ader.[675]

Jeroboam (Hieroboam) introduced

(7.7) 205 And one of his compatriots, a certain Hieroboam[676] [Jeroboam] the son of Nabatai,[677] also attacked Solomon in accordance with a prophecy given him long before that aroused his hopes regarding public affairs.[678] For he was left [orphaned] by his father while still a boy and was brought up by his mother.[679] When Solomon saw that he was [a man] of brave and bold[680] intellect, he appointed him overseer of the wall-building when he surrounded Hierosolyma with a city-wall.[681]

Jeroboam-Ahijah (Achias) exchange

206 He took care of the work in such a way that the king approved of him and gave him the honor of a generalship over the tribe of Joseph.[682] When Hieroboam was leaving Hierosolyma at that time, a prophet from the city of Silo named Achias[683] met him. He greeted Hieroboam[684] and led him away a little way off the

---

[671] MT (1 Kgs 11:23) צובה (Eng.: "Zobah"); LXX BL (1 Kgs 11:14) Σουβά; Josephus Σωφήνη. Josephus mentions "Adrazar, king of Sophene" as one of those defeated by David in *Ant.* 7.98 (// 2 Sam 8:3).

[672] 1 Kings 11 does not explicitly mention such a coalition of "Hadad" and "Rezon" (note, however, the paralleling of the 2 figures' "trouble-making" in 11:25). Josephus prepared his notice on the pair's relationship with his reference to Ader's going to Syria in 8.203.

[673] Cf. 1 Kgs 11:24a, which speaks of Rezon's "becoming leader of a marauding band." Josephus makes "Ader" (Hadad) the head of the marauders and omits the further biblical specification that this happened "after the slaughter by David," the referent of which is unclear.

[674] Josephus' reference to Ader's move to Syria here picks up his earlier, initial mention of this move in 8.203. In MT 1 Kgs 11:24b it is rather Rezon who settles "in Damascus" and becomes king there; compare LXX BL, which has "Ader" ruling over "Idumea."

[675] For the above sequence, with its focus on "Ader," Josephus is clearly basing himself on, while also modifying, the alternative presentation of LXX BL as opposed to the Rezon-centered account in MT 1 Kgs 11:24b-25 (here it is Rezon who becomes king over Damascus/Syria and is Israel's "enemy" throughout Solomon's reign). This alternative LXX presentation (1 Kgs 11:25b) reads: "This was the evil which *Ader* did: he oppressed Israel and reigned in the land of Idumea."

[676] MT (1 Kgs 11:26) ירבעם (Eng.: "Jeroboam"); LXX BL Ἱεροβοάμ; Josephus Ἱεροβόμος. On Josephus' version of the introduction of Jeroboam in 1 Kgs 11:26-40, see Begg 1996-1997 and on the Josephan Jeroboam overall, Feldman 1998a: 230-43.

[677] MT (1 Kgs 11:26) נבט (Eng.: "Nebat"); LXX B Ναβάθ; LXX L Ναβάτ; Josephus Ναβαταῖος. Josephus omits the further datum of 11:26, i.e. Jeroboam's being an "Ephraimite of Zeredah."

[678] Josephus here foreshadows the prediction made to Jeroboam by the prophet Ahijah in 1 Kgs 11:29-39 that he will reproduce in 8.206b-208. In so doing he provides, already at this point, a motivation for Jeroboam's revolt against Solomon that is mentioned in 1 Kgs 11:26 without any such motivation being cited.

[679] Josephus omits the name of Jeroboam's widowed mother (MT: "Zeruah") from 1 Kgs 11:27. The plus of LXX BL 1 Kgs 12:24ᵃ calls her a "harlot" (Greek: πόρνη).

[680] Greek: γενναῖος καὶ τολμηρός. Josephus applies this same collocation (in reverse order) to Nimrud in *Ant.* 1.113.

[681] Josephus rearranges and conflates the data of 1 Kgs 11:27b (Solomon builds the Millo and "closes up the breach of the city of David") and 11:28a (Solomon recognizes Jeroboam's ability). In so doing, he ascribes an active role to Jeroboam in the wall-building project that the Bible itself does not mention. The reference to Solomon's "walling" of Jerusalem recalls the notices on this initiative by the king in 8.21, 150.

[682] See 1 Kgs 11:28b, which has Solomon appointing Jeroboam "over all the forced labor of the house of Joseph." Josephus' reformulation avoids a "contradiction" with his earlier statement in 8.161, according to which Solomon "enslaved none of the Hebrews."

[683] MT (1 Kgs 11:29) אחיה (Eng.: "Ahijah"); LXX B Ἀχείας; LXX L Ἀχεία; Josephus Ἀχίας. The Bible calls him a "Shilonite."

[684] This "greeting" is not mentioned in 1 Kings 11; it takes the place of the notice in 11:29bα on Ahijah's

road, diverting him to a certain spot where no one else was present.[685]

207 Tearing the garment that he was wearing into twelve pieces, he directed Hieroboam to take ten,[686] announcing that God willed this.[687] God was [he said] tearing the rule of Solomon from his son,[688] to whom, however, on account of the promise he had made to David, he was giving one tribe and the one adjoining this.[689] "To you, however, [he is giving] ten of the tribes[690] of Solomon, who had offended against him and surrendered himself to his wives and their gods.[691] **208** Since then you know the reason why God has changed his plans regarding Solomon,[692] strive to be just and to observe the laws; a prize is waiting for you, the greatest of all [rewards] for piety and the honoring of God, namely you will become as great as you know David was."[693]

(7.8) 209 Being thus aroused by the words of the prophet, Hieroboam, who was a passionate youth by nature and intent on great matters, did not remain idle. Rather, as one who held a generalship and mindful of what Achias had disclosed,[694] he immediately tried to induce the people to revolt against Solomon, take up arms, and transfer the leadership to himself.[695]

Jeroboam's revolt and flight

210 When Solomon learned of his intention and plot,[696] he sought to arrest and do away with him. Coming to know this in advance,[697] Hieroboam fled to Isak,[698] the king of Egypt, and remained there until the death of Solomon; in this way, he

---

having previously donned "a new garment."

[685] Josephus' formulation explains how it was that the 2 men came to be alone together as they are said to be in 1 Kgs 11:29bβ.

[686] See 1 Kgs 11:30-31a.

[687] Josephus appends this legitimation of Ahijah's order to Jeroboam as cited in 1 Kgs 11:31a.

[688] See 1 Kgs 11:35a (compare 11:32, where the kingdom is to be "torn" from the hand of Solomon himself). In opting to reproduce the announcement of 11:35a (Solomon's son will be deprived of the kingship) rather than 11:32 (Solomon himself is to lose the kingship), Josephus takes care to harmonize Ahijah's statement to Jeroboam here with the earlier message he has "the prophet" deliver to Solomon in 8.197-198.

[689] Josephus agrees with LXX B (cf. L) 1 Kgs 11:32, 36 (and his own 8.198) against MT in having the Davidids promised future rule over 2, rather than merely one tribe. The Josephan Ahijah's reference to "the promise made to David," for its part, seems inspired by the double statement concerning the purpose of the Lord's leaving Solomon's son one (MT; LXX: 2) tribe(s) in 11:32 ("for the sake of my servant David...") and 11:36b ("that David... may always have a lamp before me in Jerusalem...").

[690] In 1 Kings 11, Ahijah delivers this message twice; see vv. 31bβ and 35b.

[691] In this rendition of Ahijah's accusation against Solomon of 1 Kgs 11:33, Josephus generalizes its catalogue of foreign deities, just as he does those of 1 Kgs 11:5, 7 in 8.192, 194. He adds the allusion to Solo-

mon's falling under the influence of his wives, this recalling his statements on the matter in 8.191, 193.

[692] Josephus adds this transition to Ahijah's following exhortation to Jeroboam (cf. 1 Kgs 11:38a).

[693] This is Josephus' expanded version of Ahijah's conditional promise to Jeroboam in 1 Kgs 11:38, in which the latter is informed that if he imitates David in his obedience to the Lord's commandments, the Lord in turn will build him the same "sure house" he did for David and give Israel to him. Like LXX B, Josephus lacks an equivalent to the appended announcement of MT and LXX L 11:39 that the Lord will "afflict" David's descendants, but "not for ever."

[694] Josephus supplies this transitional notice on Jeroboam's character and the impact of Ahijah's words upon him as a motivation for the former's revolt—a matter to which he already made a preliminary allusion in 8.205 (cf. 1 Kgs 11:26-27a).

[695] Josephus elaborates and renders more specific the double, figurative mention of Jeroboam's "lifting up his hand against Solomon" in 1 Kgs 11:26-27a (cf. 8.205, where he speaks of Jeroboam's "attacking" Solomon).

[696] Josephus adds this transitional phrase, motivating Solomon's move against Jeroboam as cited in 1 Kgs 11:41aα.

[697] This transitional phrase is a Josephan addition.

[698] MT (1 Kgs 11:40) שׁישׁק (Eng.: "Shishak"); LXX BL Σουσακείμ; Josephus Ἴσακος (Schalit *s.v.* reads Σούσακος, the form of the king's name found in *Ant.* 7.105, with E).

Closing notices for Solomon

avoided suffering anything at his hands and was preserved for the kingship.[699]

211 Solomon died,[700] already an old man, having reigned as king for eighty years[701] and lived for ninety-four.[702] He was buried in Hierosolyma.[703] He surpassed all who reigned as kings in well-being, wealth, and intelligence,[704] except that in his old age he was led astray by his wives and acted lawlessly.[705] Concerning these things and the calamities that happened to the Hebrews because of them, we shall have to report at a more appropriate moment.[706]

Rehoboam-people exchange at Shechem

(8.1) 212 After the death of Solomon, Roboam,[707] the son who was born to him by his Ammanite wife named Nooma,[708] assumed the kingship.[709] The rulers of the mobs immediately sent to Egypt and called Hieroboam [Jeroboam].[710] He came to them at the city of Sikima[711] and Roboam arrived there as well, since it was there

---

[699] To the biblical notice (1 Kgs 11:40bβ) about Jeroboam's remaining in Egypt until Solomon's death, Josephus appends a statement about the advantages that accrued to him from staying there.

[700] See 1 Kgs 11:43aα// 2 Chr 9:31aα, whose figurative language ("Solomon slept with his fathers") Josephus converts into its prosaic equivalent. In line with his standard practice, Josephus omits the "source notice" for Solomon's reign of 1 Kgs 11:41// 2 Chr 9:29.

[701] Josephus doubles the biblical figure for Solomon's length of reign, i.e. 40 years given in 1 Kgs 11:42// 2 Chr 9:30. He has no parallel to the long plus, (partially) equivalent to MT 1 Kgs 12:2, that follows the mention of his Solomon's length of reign in 11:42 in LXX BL, i.e. "and Solomon slept with his fathers and they buried him in the city of David his father [= 11:43a, MT]. And when Jeroboam the son of Nebat, who was still in Egypt whither he had fled from the face of Solomon and dwelt in Egypt, heard that Solomon was dead, he straightaway came to his city to Sarira on Mount Ephraim."

[702] The biblical accounts provide no indication concerning Solomon's age at death. Josephus' figure makes Solomon 14 at his accession, a datum that would accord with the portrayal of him as a precocious youth in 8.21. Eupolemus ("fragment 3," in the extract of Alexander Polyhistor preserved in Eusebius, *Praep. ev.* 34.20) states that Solomon lived 52 years, of which he reigned for 40, this making him 12 at the moment of his accession.

[703] See MT 1 Kgs 11:43aβ// 2 Chr 9:31aβ, which have Solomon buried "in the city of David." In LXX BL 1 Kings 11 reference to Solomon's burial is incoporated into the long plus that follows 11:42 (see note to "years" at 8.211), and the king's burial is not mentioned in BL's version of 11:43.

[704] Josephus' appended eulogy for Solomon recalls God's promise to him in 8.24, while its mention of the king's "wealth and intelligence" uses the same binomial applied to him in 8.190 (there in reverse order).

[705] This qualification to his preceding positive appreciation of Solomon recalls Josephus' comments on the aged king in 8.191.

[706] Marcus (*ad loc.*) suggests that Josephus is here making an anticipatory allusion to his subsequent account of Pharaoh Shishak's invasion of Judah under Solomon's successor, Rehoboam in 8.253-262.

[707] MT רחבעם (Eng.: "Rehoboam"); LXX Ῥοβόαμ; Josephus Ῥοβόαμος. On Josephus' account of the division of the kingdom that occurred under Rehoboam in 8.212-224 (// 1 Kgs 12:1-24// 2 Chr 10:1-11:4), see Begg 1993: 7-29. On the Josephan Rehoboam in general, see Feldman 1998a: 244-62.

[708] MT (1 Kgs 14:21, 31// 2 Chr 12:13) נעמה (Eng.: "Naamah"); LXX B 1 Kgs 14:21 Μααχάμ; LXX L 1 Kgs 14:21 (and LXX L 2 Chr 12:13) Ναανά; LXX B 2 Chr 12:13 Νοομμά; Josephus Νοομά (Schlatter *s.v.* and Schalit *s.v.* read Νααμά on the basis of Lat "Naama"). Josephus anticipates his mention of her from the conclusion of the biblical accounts of Rehoboam. In so doing, he situates the naming of the royal mother at its normal position in both Kings and Chronicles.

[709] See 1 Kgs 11:43b// 2 Chr 9:31b.

[710] See 1 Kgs 12:3a (MT; LXX BL have no equivalent to MT's 12:2-3aα)// 2 Chr 10:3a. Josephus specifies the identity of those who summon Jeroboam (in LXX B 2 Chr 10:3a an indeterminate "he" does this). Josephus has no equivalent to the notices of MT 1 Kgs 12:2// 2 Chr 10:2 on Jeroboam's hearing of the Shechem assembly in Egypt to which he had fled from Solomon and where he now either remains (so 12:2) or returns from (so 10:2; cf. the plus of LXX BL 1 Kgs 11:42, which has Jeroboam hearing of the death of Solomon while in Egypt and returning, on his own volition, to "his city Sarira on Mount Ephraim").

[711] In thus specifying Jeroboam's destination, Josephus draws on 1 Kgs 12:1// 2 Chr 10:1, where "Shechem" is twice mentioned as the site of the following happening. Compare the plus of LXX BL 1 Kgs 11:42 (see previous note), where Jeroboam returns to

that the Israelites had decided to assemble to appoint him king.[712]

213 The rulers of the people, together with Hieroboam,[713] therefore approached him and appealed to him to somewhat lighten their slavery and to be kinder than his father. For it was a heavy yoke that had been imposed on them by him.[714] They would be more well-disposed to him and would better love their slavery in response to gentleness rather than to fear.[715]

214 When he told them that he would give them an answer to the things they requested after three days,[716] they immediately became suspicious, seeing that he did not right away agree to what they wanted, for they thought kindness and humanity[717] an easy thing, especially for a young man. At the same time, given his willingness not to deny them immediately, it seemed to them that they had a good hope.[718]

(8.2) 215 Assembling his father's friends, Roboam discussed with them what sort of answer he ought to give to the crowd.[719] They, being benevolent and knowing the nature of mobs,[720] urged him to converse with the people in a friendly and more popular vein rather than one in keeping with the royal dignity.[721] For thus he would secure their loyalty,[722] since by nature subjects love affability and a virtual equality in their kings.[723]

Rehoboam rejects advice of older counselors

---

his home town of "Sarira" upon hearing of Solomon's death.

[712] See 1 Kgs 12:1// 2 Chr 10:1, where the reference is to "all Israel" coming to Shechem.

[713] In citing Jeroboam by name as among those who approach Rehoboam, Josephus agrees with MT 1 Kgs 12:3b// 2 Chr 10:3b against LXX BL 1 Kgs 12:3b, where Jeroboam—who in the LXX plus of 1 Kgs 11:42 is said to have gone to "Sarira" (see the note to "Sikima" at 8.212)—is not mentioned. Josephus' reference to "the rulers" recalls his mention of these figures as those who summon Jeroboam in 8.212. Compare "all the assembly of Israel" (MT 1 Kgs 12:3b and LXX BL 2 Chr 10:3b)/ "all Israel" (MT 2 Chr 10:3b).

[714] See 1 Kgs 12:4abα// 2 Chr 10:4abα. Josephus amplifies the speakers' appeal with the request that Rehoboam show himself "kinder" than his father.

[715] Josephus expatiates on the speakers' laconic assertion in 1 Kgs 12:4bβ// 2 Chr 10:4bβ: "and we will serve you [Rehoboam]." On kingship leading to "slavery," see Samuel's words to the people as reported in *Ant.* 6.40-41. The speakers' claim about their "loving slavery" (Greek: ἀγαπᾶν τὴν δουλείαν) under Rehoboam recalls Adonijah's assertion that he "loved slavery" to Solomon in 8.4.

[716] See 1 Kgs 12:5a// 2 Chr 10:5a. Josephus amplifies Rehoboam's dismissal of the speakers, having him commit himself to reply to them once they return.

[717] Greek: τὸ χρηστὸν καὶ φιλάνθρωπον. Josephus uses the noun equivalents of this pair of nominalized adjectives of Gedaliah in *Ant.* 10.164. Compare the phrase "the goodness and loving kindness [Greek: ἡ χρηστότης καὶ ἡ φιλανθρωπία) of God our Savior..." in Tit 3:4 and see Spicq 1958: 176, n. 1.

[718] Josephus adds this whole sequence concerning the conflicting emotions engendered by Rehoboam's initial response to his interlocutors. It replaces the notice of 1 Kgs 12:5b// 2 Chr 10:5b that the people did "depart" following Rehoboam's (preliminary) response to them.

[719] See 1 Kgs 12:6// 2 Chr 10:6. In line with his frequent practice, Josephus substitutes a reference to Solomon's "friends" for the biblical phrase "the old men who stood before Solomon." On the Hellenistic-Roman category of royal "friends," see Spicq 1978 (II): 940-43.

[720] Josephus adds this characterization of Solomon's "friends." He thereby intimates his positive evaluation of their subsequent advice.

[721] Josephus' version of the advice given Rehoboam by Solomon's "friends" with its call for a "popular" (Greek: δημοτικός) response seems to conflate 1 Kgs 12:7a (where the advisers begin by urging him to be a "servant to this people and serve them") and 2 Chr 10:7a (where Rehoboam is initially advised to be "kind to this people"). The advice given to Rehoboam in Josephus has a counterpart in Dionysius of Halicarnassus, *Ant. rom.* 7.54.4, where Marcius is urged to "descend... to a more democratic behavior"; see Begg 1993: 16, n. 59.

[722] See 1 Kgs 12:7b// 2 Chr 10:7b, where the elders assure Rehoboam that if he follows their advice "they [the people] will be your servants for ever."

[723] Josephus appends this conclusion to the older advisors' words to Rehoboam as reported in 1 Kgs 12:7 // 2 Chr 10:7. It picks up on his—likewise added—reference to their "knowing the nature of mobs" earlier in 8.215.

216 But this plan about what the king ought to do—which was good and advantageous, if not equally for all times, at least for that one, when he was about to become king[724]—Roboam rejected, being made, I suppose, by God to repudiate what was advantageous to himself.[725]

Rehoboam adopts advice of younger friends

He called together the young men who had grown up with him, told them the advice the elders had given him,[726] and directed them to say what they thought he should do.[727] **217** They, for their part, whom neither their youth nor God permitted to perceive something better,[728] urged him to answer the people that his little finger was thicker than his father's loins,[729] and if they had experienced him [Solomon] as very severe, they would have a much more unpleasant experience with himself.[730] If he [Solomon] had disciplined them with whips, they should expect that he would to do the same with scorpions.[731]

Rehoboam answers people

218 The king was pleased with these words, thinking them an answer in accordance with the dignity of his rule.[732] When the crowd assembled to hear on the third day,[733] the whole people was in suspense, looking forward to hear what the king would say, whether this would be something humane.[734] Leaving aside the counsel

---

[724] Josephus' addition of this (qualifiedly) positive evaluation of the older friends' advice picks up on his earlier favorable characterization of the friends themselves in 8.215. With the course suggested by the older advisors here in 8.215-216, compare that adopted by Archelaus in expectation of his being appointed king after Herod's death as reported by Josephus in *War* 2.1-9.

[725] See 1 Kgs 12:8a// 2 Chr 10:8a. Josephus' appended "theological" explanation of Rehoboam's rejection of the elders' counsel is an anticipation of the editorial comment of 1 Kgs 12:15b// 2 Chr 10:15b, concerning Rehoboam's answering the people in accordance with the advice of his own contemporaries.

[726] See 1 Kgs 12:8b// 2 Chr 10:8b. Rehoboam's telling his contemporaries what the elders had said is Josephus' addition. Having already rejected the elders' advice himself, Rehoboam now wants to provoke his fellows to offer him contrary advice by informing them of the elders' words.

[727] See 1 Kgs 12:9// 2 Chr 10:9. Josephus avoids the largely verbatim citation of the people's words of 12:4a// 10:4a present in the biblical Rehoboam's address to the younger men.

[728] Josephus prefaces the younger men's words with this double explanation of how they came to proffer such foolish advice. The theological component of this explanation recalls that adduced for Rehoboam's own rejection of the elders' advice in 8.216. The "youthful hothead" is a *topos* of classical literature; see, e.g., the characterization of the young Cataline in Sallust, *Bel. Cat.* 5 and the more general remarks of Cicero, *Cael.* 18.42.

[729] See 1 Kgs 12:10// 2 Chr 10:10, from which Josephus omits the younger men's "citation" of the

people's words of 12:4// 10:4. Josephus' explicit mention of Rehoboam's "little *finger*" has a parallel in LXX BL 2 Chr 10:10, whereas MT and LXX BL 12:10 and MT 10:10 read "my littleness." This is Josephus' only use of the word ὀσφύς ("loin"), a term found mainly in Greek biological and medical writings. It seems an obvious euphemism for τὸ αἰδοῖον ("penis"), which Josephus reserves for vivid, quasi-medical contexts (see *War* 1.656; *Ant.* 17.169; *Apion* 2.143), rather different from the vulgar braggadocio of the young friends' response (I owe these terminological observations to Prof. Steve Mason). See further Begg 1993: 18, n. 77.

[730] Josephus transposes into a prosaic statement the "yoke-imagery" language used by the younger men in 1 Kgs 12:11a// 2 Chr 10:11a, which itself echoes that of 12:4, 10a// 10:4, 10a.

[731] See 1 Kgs 12:11b// 2 Chr 10:11b, whose figurative reference to "scorpions" Josephus, rather exceptionally, retains.

[732] Josephus adds this notice on the emotional effect of the younger men's advice upon Rehoboam. Note the contrast with 8.215, where the older friends (unavailingly) urge Rehoboam to "speak in a friendly and more popular vein rather than one in keeping with the royal dignity."

[733] See 1 Kgs 12:12// 2 Chr 10:12. Like LXX BL in both biblical verses, Josephus does not mention Jeroboam by name as among those returning to Rehoboam at this point. Compare 8.213, where—unlike LXX BL 1 Kgs 12:3—he does cite Jeroboam approaching Rehoboam along with "the rulers of the people."

[734] Josephus appends this notice on the people's mindset that recalls his mention of their reaction to Rehoboam's putting them off in 8.214. The addition

of the older [men], he answered with that of his younger friends.[735] This was done in accordance with the will of God, in order that what Achias had prophesied might be fulfilled.[736]

(8.3) 219 The people, stricken by his words and hurt as though they were experiencing what he said, became indignant;[737] they all cried out that from that day on they would no longer have any kinship with David and his descendants.[738] Saying that they would award him only the sanctuary that his grandfather had constructed,[739] they threatened to abandon him.[740] **220** They were so embittered and felt such wrath that,[741] when Roboam sent Adoram, who was in charge of the levy,[742] to pacify and soothe them into pardoning what he had said, should there be anything rash and unpleasant[743] in this,[744] they did not stand [for this] but killed him by throwing stones at him.[745]

221 Seeing this and supposing that the stones with which the crowd killed his minister had been thrown at himself, Roboam, fearing that he might actually suffer the same terrible [fate], immediately mounted his chariot and fled to Hierosolyma.[746] While the tribe of Iouda and the Benjamite one designated him king,[747] the rest of

People's reaction

Adoram's death and Rehoboam's flight

---

here in 8.218 underscores the irony of the situation, since the reader—unlike the suspense-filled people—already knows how Rehoboam intends to answer them. The adjective "humane" (Greek: φιλάνθρωπον) here echoes the use of the same term in 8.214 [where it is rendered "humanity"] and combined with the word "kindness".

[735] See 1 Kgs 12:13-14// 2 Chr 10:13-14. Josephus leaves aside Rehoboam's "quotation" (12:14b// 10:14b) of the younger men's words to him about the use of "scorpions" in place of his father's "whips" from 12:11b// 10:11b// 8.217.

[736] See 1 Kgs 12:15// 2 Chr 10:15. Josephus has already alluded to the fulfillment of Ahijah's prophecy (on this, see 8.207-208) in his appended remark concerning Rehoboam's rejection of the older friends' advice in 8.216.

[737] Here again (see 8.214, 218) Josephus adds a reference to the people's emotional state.

[738] See 1 Kgs 12:16a// 2 Chr 10:16a, where the people assert that they "have no portion or inheritance in David/the son of Jesse."

[739] Compare 1 Kgs 12:16bα// 2 Chr 10:16bα, where "David" (i.e., his grandson Rehoboam) is called on to "look to his own house [dynasty]." Josephus takes the biblical term "house" in the sense of "sanctuary." That sanctuary had of course actually been built by Solomon, but the plan and the gathering of the materials were due to David, such that its construction might be attributed to him, as Josephus has the Israelites doing here. Compare *Ant.* 1.227, where Josephus refers to the site of Abraham's sacrifice of Isaac as the mountain upon which "David later built the temple." He leaves aside the people's cry, "to your tents, O Israel," that precedes their reference to David's house in the above

biblical texts.

[740] In 1 Kgs 12:16bβ// 2 Chr 10:16bβ the Israelites actually do "disperse to their tents," following their preceding verbal response to Rehoboam. Josephus omits the appended notice of 1 Kgs 12:17// 2 Chr 10:17 about those Israelites who dwelt in the cities of Judah remaining faithful to Rehoboam, which appears extraneous in its context.

[741] Josephus supplies this allusion to the people's emotional state as an explanation of the treatment they will subsequently mete out to Rehoboam's envoy in 1 Kgs 12:18a// 2 Chr 10:18a.

[742] Josephus has mentioned this figure and his office previously in *Ant.* 7.259; 8.59.

[743] Greek: προπετὲς καὶ δύσκολον. This is Josephus' only use of this collocation.

[744] Josephus goes beyond 1 Kgs 12:18aα// 2 Chr 10:18aα in spelling out the purpose of Adoram's mission. In so doing, he gives a more favorable depiction of Rehoboam, who immediately acknowledges the mistake he has made and seeks to make amends for this; see Feldman 1998a: 258.

[745] See 1 Kgs 12:18aβ// 2 Chr 10:18aβ.

[746] See 1 Kgs 12:18b// 2 Chr 10:18b. Josephus prefaces his mention of Rehoboam's flight with an allusion to the king's emotional state that prompts this.

[747] Josephus derives the identity of the 2 tribes that acknowledge Rehoboam's rule from 1 Kgs 12:21// 2 Chr 11:1, where he musters these against the Israelites. In having these 2 tribes actually confer the kingship on Rehoboam, he establishes a parallelism between him and Jeroboam, whose appointment by the Israelites is cited in 1 Kgs 12:20a. Josephus leaves aside the statement of 12:20b that only Judah followed the house of David, which stands in tension with the following ref-

the crowd revolted against the descendants of David from that day[748] and appointed Hieroboam lord of their affairs.[749]

Rehoboam calls off expedition

222 Roboam, the son of Solomon, assembled the two tribes whom he had subject to him. From them he took an army of 180,000 picked men and set out against Hieroboam and his people in order to compel them to be slaves to him by making war on them.[750] **223** He was, however, prevented by God, via a prophet,[751] from undertaking the campaign; for he said that it was not just to wage war on one's compatriots[752] and that these things, namely the revolt of the crowd, were in accord with God's intent.[753] At that, [Roboam] no longer set out.[754]

Josephus' intended procedure

224 I shall now first relate what Hieroboam, the king of the Israelites, did and then disclose what happened under Roboam, the king of the two tribes. For thus the right order will be preserved throughout my entire history.[755]

Jeroboam's planned alternative to temple

(8.4) 225 Hieroboam then,[756] having built a palace in the city of Sikima,[757] made his residence there; he constructed one in the city called Phanouel[758] as well. Not long afterwards, when the Feast of Tabernacles was about to celebrated,[759] he reasoned that if he allowed the crowd to go to pay homage to God in Hierosolyma and

---

erence (12:21) to Benjamin's being under Rehoboam's command as well.

[748] According to 1 Kgs 12:19// 2 Chr 10:19 the Israelites' rebellion has persisted "to this day." Josephus' modification reflects the fact that both the Israelite and Davidic kingdoms had long since ceased to exist.

[749] See 1 Kgs 12:20a (no equivalent in the Judah-centered presentation of Chronicles).

[750] See 1 Kgs 12:21// 2 Chr 11:1.

[751] Compare 1 Kgs 12:22// 2 Chr 11:2, where the figure is named "Shemaiah" (Weill *ad loc.*, on the basis of its appearance in Zon and Lat, holds that the name originally stood in Josephus' text as well) and called "the man of God" (Josephus' substitution of "prophet" for this title is paralleled in the targumic renderings of both biblical passages). Josephus leaves aside the "commissioning formula" ("say to Rehoboam....") which introduces Shemaiah's discourse of 1 Kgs 12:24// 2 Chr 11:4 in 12:23// 11:3.

[752] In 1 Kgs 12:24aα// 2 Chr 11:4aα Rehoboam and his forces are told by Shemaiah not to proceed against the Israelites, but rather to return to their homes. Josephus' version recasts the prophet's commands as a statement about the wrongfulness of the proposed attack, this reflecting the historian's preoccupation with the horrors of intra-Jewish conflict; see Feldman 1998a: 253-4.

[753] Compare Shemaiah's closing word in 1 Kgs 12:24a// 2 Chr 11:4a, i.e. "this thing is from me [God]."

[754] In 1 Kgs 12:24b// 2 Chr 11:4b it is Rehoboam's whole force that, in obedience to the divine word, "turns back." Josephus' formulation highlights Rehoboam personally and his readiness to comply with God's directive. In this connection, Feldman (1998a: 259) points out the contrast between the Kings

Rehoboam and Archelaus, son of Herod (see *War* 2.4-13// *Ant.* 17.204-218) in Josephus' presentation. Like the former, Archelaus is asked at the start of his reign to lighten the burdens imposed by his father. Later his envoy to the people is stoned by them as well. In contrast to Rehoboam, however, Archelaus ends up leading his army against the recalcitrant people and massacring them. The contrast serves to highlight the stature of Rehoboam, who acknowledges the wrongfulness of shedding Jewish blood.

[755] With this added remark Josephus gives readers advance notice of the sequence in which he intends to treat the 2 rulers, rather than leaving them to discover this for themselves, as does the author of Kings. Such "hints to the reader" are a recurrent feature of Josephus' rewriting of the Bible. Josephus has no equivalent to the long "miscellany" of items drawn from other contexts in Kings that follows MT 1 Kgs 12:24 as 12:24[a-z] in LXX BL.

[756] On Josephus' version of 1 Kgs 12:25-31 (no equivalent in 2 Chronicles), the account of Jeroboam's initial religio-political measures in 8.225-229, see Begg 1993: 30-40.

[757] See 1 Kgs 12:25a, which speaks of Jeroboam's "building Shechem." Josephus' rewording of this notice reflects the fact that Shechem was an already existing city at this point (see 12:1).

[758] MT (1 Kgs 12:25b) פְּנוּאֵל (Eng.: "Penuel"); LXX and Josephus Φανουήλ.

[759] Josephus derives this dating indication from 1 Kgs 12:32, which refers to Jeroboam's instituting "a feast on the 15th day of the 8th month like the feast that was in Judah." This feast was intended both to parallel and rival the existing autumn feast of Tabernacles that began on the 15th day of the 7th month (see, e.g.,

celebrate the feast there, they might perhaps change their minds and, captivated by the sanctuary and the worship of the God within it, would abandon him and go over to their first king, while, if this happened, he would be in danger of losing his life.[760] He therefore contrived the following [scheme]:[761]

226 He made two golden heifers[762] and built small shrines for these,[763] one in the city of Bethel and the other in Dan (which is near the sources of the Little Jordan).[764] He placed the calves in each of the small shrines in the just-mentioned cities.[765] Having assembled the ten tribes over which he ruled, he addressed them in these words:[766]

Jeroboam's golden calves

Jeroboam addresses people

227 "Compatriots, I suppose you know that every place has God [in it], and that there is no single designated spot at which he is present. Rather, he everywhere hears and sees those who worship him.[767] Therefore I am not disposed to allow you to go on so long a journey to Hierosolyma, the city of our enemies, to pay homage.[768] **228** For a human being constructed the sanctuary,[769] and I too have made two golden heifers dedicated to God[770] and I have set up one in the city of Bethel and the other in Dan so that those of you who live near these cities might go to them and pay homage to God.[771] I shall also appoint some from among yourselves as priests and Levites for you, so that you will have no need of the Levitical tribe and of the sons of Aaron.[772] Rather, whoever of you wishes to be a priest, let him

---

Lev 23:34). See further 8.230.

[760] See Jeroboam's self-reflection as cited in 1 Kgs 12:26-27, to which Josephus adds the reference to the Israelite pilgrims' being "captivated" by the Jerusalem sanctuary and its cult.

[761] In 1 Kgs 12:28aα Jeroboam "takes counsel" before proceeding with his deviant initiatives. Josephus attributes the following reprobate measures to the king alone.

[762] Like LXX BL 1 Kgs 12:28aβ, Josephus uses a feminine form (δαμάλ(ε)ις, "heifers") for Jeroboam's creations, whereas MT refers to them as "(male) calves."

[763] 1 Kings 12 does not mention these new constructions at sites, i.e. Bethel and Dan, that were already established cultic centers.

[764] This added reference to the localization of Dan has a counterpart in *Ant.* 5.178 and *War* 4.3. See Begg 1993: 33, n. 172.

[765] See 1 Kgs 12:29, where Jeroboam's placement of the calves follows his address to the people (12:28b) concerning them. Josephus has the king set the heifers in place before beginning his discourse.

[766] See 1 Kgs 12:28bα; Josephus adds mention of Jeroboam's prior act of assembling the people. The royal discourse that follows in 8.227-228 represents a large-scale embellishment of the king's compressed statement in 1 Kgs 12:28bβγ.

[767] Jeroboam's opening word here recalls the affirmation concerning God's "ubiquity" as formulated by Solomon at the dedication of the temple; see 8.107-108. Jeroboam thus makes ironic use of the words of Solomon, the founder of the Jerusalem temple, to sup-

port his contention that Solomon's temple is not the only legitimate place of worship. For similar statements about God's omnipresence in Josephus' writings, see *War* 1.630; *Ant.* 2.24; 6.263, and cf. Begg 1993: 35, n. 180.

[768] Compare Jeroboam's opening word to the people in 1 Kgs 12:28bβ: "you have gone up to Jerusalem long enough." Josephus' added references to the length of the journey and Jerusalem's status as an "enemy city" provide an implicit motivation as to why the Israelites should not be "allowed" by him to go there.

[769] As in 8.227, the Josephan Jeroboam echoes Solomon's words at the dedication of the temple (see 8.108, where the latter avers "I have built this sanctuary to your [God's] name...") in support of his assertion that he (Jeroboam) has done something quite analogous (and equally legitimate) in constructing shrines for the heifers.

[770] In 1 Kgs 12:28bγ Jeroboam identifies the calves themselves as "god(s)." Josephus' king takes care to make them rather objects "dedicated to God."

[771] Having informed the audience of his initiative as cited in 8.226, Jeroboam now provides a motivation for his action, i.e. to provide a convenient place of worship for all his subjects as compared with the distant (see 8.227) Jerusalem.

[772] Josephus makes a part of Jeroboam's speech to the people the additional reprobate action attributed to him in 1 Kgs 12:31b, i.e. "appointing priests from among the people who were not Levites." At the same time, he also introduces the distinction—drawn from the Priestly and Chronistic strata of the Bible—between

offer a calf and a ram to God, as Aaron, the first priest, is said to have done."[773]

Jeroboam's move evaluated

229 In saying these things he misled the people and caused them, by their turning away from their ancestral worship, to transgress against the laws.[774] This was the beginning of calamities for the Hebrews, who, having been defeated in war by other peoples, fell into captivity. But we shall disclose these things in their proper place.[775]

Festival at Bethel

230 The feast of the seventh month[776] was now at hand. Wishing to celebrate this himself at Bethel, just as the two tribes were likewise observing it in Hierosolyma,[777] [Hieroboam] built an altar before the calf, and having made himself high priest,[778] ascended the altar with his own priests.[779]

Jadon's intervention

231 When he was about to offer the sacrifices and the whole offerings in the presence of all the people,[780] there came to him a prophet sent by God from Hierosolyma[781] whose name was Jadon.[782] He stood in the midst of the crowd in the hearing of the king and spoke to the altar in these words:[783]

232 "God announces that there will be someone from the family of David, Josiah[784] by name, who will burn upon you the false priests[785] who will be at that

---

2 groups of cultic officers, i.e. priests and Levites, both of whom Jeroboam intends to dispossess. Josephus leaves aside the further charge made against Jeroboam in 12:31a, i.e. he "made houses on the high places."

[773] This exhortation by Jeroboam has no counterpart in the account of 1 Kgs 12:25-31. Marcus (*ad loc.*) points out that the pair of victims prescribed by Jeroboam as an "induction sacrifice" for his cultic officials corresponds to that enjoined for the high priest's entry into the inner sanctuary on the Day of Atonement; see Lev 16:3. See Begg (1993: 37, n. 193) on further possible biblical inspirations for Josephus' formulation here.

[774] This is Josephus' elaboration of the summary evaluative remark concerning Jeroboam's initiatives in 1 Kgs 12:30 ("this thing became a sin, for the people went to the one [calf image] in Bethel and to the other as far as Dan"), highlighting Jeroboam's responsibility for the people's cultic deviations.

[775] With this notice on the consequences of Jeroboam's misleading the people Josephus looks ahead to the ultimate demise of the northern kingdom that he will relate in *Ant.* 9.277-291. Compare the similar foreshadowing remark with which Josephus concludes his account of Solomon at the end of 8.211.

[776] This is the Feast of Tabernacles mentioned in 8.225.

[777] Compare 1 Kgs 12:32 (and cf. 12:33), where Jeroboam institutes a feast on the 15th day of the *8th* month "like the feast that was in Jerusalem." In Josephus Jeroboam more closely mimics the Jerusalem Feast of Tabernacles by celebrating his own festival in the same 7th month as this.

[778] Josephus supplies these 2 preliminaries (building the altar, assuming [high] priestly rank) to Jero-

boam's initiative of "mounting" the Bethel altar that is mentioned in 1 Kgs 12:33aα.

[779] 1 Kgs 12:32-33 does not explicitly refer to Jeroboam's being accompanied by "other priests" as he ascends the Bethel altar and offers sacrifice. Josephus may, however, have found inspiration for his mention of such accompanying priests in the notice of 1 Kgs 12:32b that Jeroboam "placed in Bethel the priests of the high places he had made."

[780] Compare 1 Kgs 13:1, where Jeroboam is "standing by the altar to burn incense" as the confrontation between him and the man of God from Judah begins. On Josephus' version of that confrontation (1 Kgs 12:32-13:34) in 8.231-245, see Begg 1993: 41-63.

[781] 1 Kgs 13:1 calls Jeroboam's antagonist "a man of God out of Judah." Josephus substitutes an alternative title in line with his usual practice, just as he makes the figure arrive specifically "from Hierosolyma," i.e. Bethel's Judean equivalent and rival.

[782] The Judean "man of God" in 1 Kgs 13:1 is nameless. Josephus' name for him has a counterpart in *y. Sanh.* 89; *t. Sanh.* 14.10. Both he and rabbinic tradition likely drew the name from 2 Chr 9:29, which refers to the "visions of Iddo (MT; LXX Ἰωήλ) the seer" against Jeroboam. See further Begg (1993: 44, n. 214) for alternative proposals concerning the origin of Josephus' name for the figure.

[783] See 1 Kgs 13:2a. Josephus adds the explicit mention of the "crowd" and to Jeroboam himself as witnesses to the proceedings.

[784] MT (1 Kgs 13:2) יאשׁיהו (Eng.: "Josiah"); LXX BL Ἰωσείας; Josephus Ἰωσίας.

[785] Greek: ψευδιερεῖς. Josephus' only other use of this term is in *Ant.* 9.133, where it denotes the Baal clergy exterminated by Jehu. The language of "truth"

time[786] and will incinerate upon you the bones of these misleaders of the people,[787] deceivers, and impious persons.[788] That these [people] however, may believe that thus it will happen,[789] I predict to them a sign that is to be:[790] the altar will immediately be torn down and all the fat of the victims that is upon it will be poured out on the ground."[791]

233 When the prophet said these things, Hieroboam was enraged.[792] He stretched out his hand, directing that he be arrested.[793] However, his outstretched hand immediately withered up. He no longer had the strength to bring it back to himself, but held it hanging down, numbed and dead.[794] Likewise the altar was thrown down and everything on it was poured out, as the prophet had predicted.[795]

Jeroboam's hand crippled

Altar overthrown

234 Having learned that the person [Jadon] was truthful and possessed divine foreknowledge,[796] Hieroboam appealed to him to ask God to restore his right hand to him,[797] and he did intercede with God to grant this to him. Once his hand had been restored to its natural condition,[798] [Hieroboam] rejoiced[799] and appealed to the prophet to have supper with him.[800]

Jeroboam's hand restored

Jeroboam's invitation declined

(8.5) 235 Jadon said, however, that[801] he was not permitted to enter his house nor to taste bread and water in that city; for God had forbidden this to him. [God had likewise said] that he was not to make his return by the way on which he had come, but by another.[802] The king marvelled at him for his self-control,[803] but also feared a change in his [own] affairs, suspecting from what had previously been said that it would not be a good one.[804]

---

and "falsity" permeates—often with an ironic twist—Josephus' version of the Bethel incident.

[786] Compare 1 Kgs 13:2bα: "the priests of the high places who burn incense upon you [i.e. the altar, which the Judean is addressing]."

[787] Greek: λαοπλάνος. This word is *hapax* in Josephus.

[788] Josephus pejoratively embellishes the Judean's concluding announcement to the altar in 1 Kgs 13:2, i.e. "men's bones shall be burned upon you."

[789] Josephus adds this rationale for the "sign" the Judean will announce in 1 Kgs 13:3.

[790] See 1 Kgs 13:3a, where the Judean "gives" the sign. On Josephus' use of "sign terminology," see Remus 1982: 543-4.

[791] Compare 1 Kgs 13:3b, where the Judean predicts that the altar's "ashes" will be "poured out."

[792] Josephus supplies this reference to the emotional effect of the Judean's words upon the king.

[793] See 1 Kgs 13:4a.

[794] Josephus embellishes the notice on the incapacitating of Jeroboam's hand of 1 Kgs 13:4b.

[795] See 1 Kgs 13:5 (which, like 13:3, refers to the "pouring out" of the altar's "ashes").

[796] Greek: θεία πρόγνωσις; Josephus supplies this allusion to the effect of the paralyzing of his hand upon Jeroboam (compare his "becoming enraged" at the Judean's words in 8.233). He uses a similar phrase of the Essene Manaemus in *Ant.* 15.373, i.e. "having foreknowledge from God."

[797] See 1 Kgs 13:6a. Josephus specifies that it was Jeroboam's "right" hand that was in need of healing. Like Tg., Josephus reformulates the anthropomorphic phrase "entreat now the face of the Lord your God" found in MT and LXX L 1 Kgs 13:6a (but absent in LXX B).

[798] See 1 Kgs 13:6b.

[799] Josephus supplies this reference to the king's emotional state; compare his (also interjected) reference to Jeroboam's being "enraged" in 8.233.

[800] This single royal invitation takes the place of the king's triple proposition to the man of God as cited in 1 Kgs 13:7, i.e. "Come home with me, and refresh yourself, and I will give you a reward."

[801] Josephus omits the Judean's opening asseveration in 1 Kgs 13:8, i.e. "if you [Jeroboam] give me half your house...," which alludes to the king's previous promise—also omitted by him—of a "reward" in 13:7.

[802] See 1 Kgs 13:8-9. In accordance with his standard practice, Josephus reformulates the biblical reference to "the word of the Lord" of v.9. He likewise appends, under the influence of 13:10a ("so he went another way"), mention of God's positive directive for the Judean.

[803] Greek: ἐγκράτεια. On this term, see Spicq 1978 (I): 61-63 and Begg 1993: 49, n. 266.

[804] Josephus adds this sequence concerning the inner effect of the Judean's words upon the king. Its reference to Jeroboam's "suspicion" given what he has just heard has a close equivalent in *Ant.* 17.346, where the

Bethel false prophet deceives Jadon

(9.1) 236 Now there was in the city a certain vile old man, a false prophet, whom Hieroboam held in honor, being deceived by his telling him what pleased him.[805] He was at that time bed-ridden on account of illness [resulting] from old age.[806] When his sons[807] disclosed to him the matters concerning the prophet coming from Hierosolyma and the signs that had occurred, **237** and how, when Hieroboam's right hand was withered up, it was restored to life by the prophet's prayer,[808] he feared that the stranger might get ahead of him with the king and enjoy greater honor.[809] He ordered his sons to immediately saddle his donkey and prepare it for his departure. **238** After they hastened to do what he ordered, he mounted[810] and pursued after the prophet, whom he overtook resting beneath a tree that was as leafy and shady as a mammoth oak.[811] He first greeted him[812] and then reproached him for not entering his house and sharing his hospitality.[813] **239** The prophet said, however, that he had been prevented by God from tasting [anything] in the house of anyone in that city.[814] "But," said he, "the Deity has by no means forbidden you to have a table set for you in my house.[815] For I too am a prophet and share with you in his worship; I am here now, having been sent by him to bring you to my house and entertain you."[816]

Jadon killed by God-sent lion

240 Convinced by his lying,[817] he returned. While they were still dining and conversing in a friendly way,[818] God appeared to Jadon[819] and said that he, having trans-

---

Essene Simon's elucidation of the dream of King Archelaus is formulated in quite similar terms.

[805] Josephus pejoratively embellishes the "neutral" introduction of the story's new character in 1 Kgs 13:11a, i.e. "now there dwelt an old prophet in Bethel." Josephus' explicit qualification of him as a "false prophet" (Greek: ψευδοπροφήτης)—a term used by him a total of 16 times—has a counterpart in the Tg. and various Latin witnesses to 13:11, as well as in the Qumran document 4Q339, where he appears in a list of 8 "false prophets [Aramaic: נביאי שקרא] who arose in Israel." See further Reiling 1971 and Begg 1993: 50, n. 270.

[806] With this addition, Josephus suggests an explanation as to why the Bethel prophet was not on hand to witness the confrontation between Jeroboam and the Judean for himself and has to be informed of this by his son(s) (see 1 Kgs 13:11b).

[807] Josephus' use of the plural "sons" corresponds to the reading of LXX BL 1 Kgs 13:11b as against the singular "son" of MT (which, however, switches to the plural in the continuation of its account).

[808] Josephus expatiates on the sons' report (1 Kgs 13:11b), having them make explicit mention of the disabling and restoration of Jeroboam's hand (see 8.233-234).

[809] Josephus adds this reference—which picks up on his earlier (see 8.236) allusion to the "honor" in which Jeroboam held him—to the Bethel prophet's state of mind that prompts his subsequent initiatives. The notice takes the place of the exchange between father and son(s) concerning the Judean's return route

in 1 Kgs 13:12.

[810] See 1 Kgs 13:13.

[811] Josephus embellishes the simple mention of the "oak" under which the Judean is "sitting" according to 1 Kgs 13:14a.

[812] Compare 1 Kgs 13:14b, where the Bethel prophet first asks his counterpart whether he is the "man of God from Judah" and receives a positive answer.

[813] In 1 Kgs 13:15 there is no such "reproach," but simply an invitation to the Judean by the Bethel prophet to accompany him to his home and eat there.

[814] Josephus compresses the Judean's lengthy, almost verbatim reiteration (1 Kgs 13:16-17) of the directives given him by God as cited in his earlier reply to Jeroboam in 13:8-9.

[815] This initial assertion by the Bethelite about his being the exception to the apparently absolute divine prohibition just invoked by the Judean has no counterpart in the former's reply as cited in 1 Kgs 13:18a.

[816] In 1 Kgs 13:18aβ the Bethelite ascribes the command he purports to have received rather to "an angel" who spoke to him "by the word of the Lord." Elsewhere too, Josephus replaces biblical mentions of angels with alternative formulations; see the note to "phantasm" at *Ant.* 5.213.

[817] 1 Kgs 13:18bβ simply states "but he [the Bethelite] lied to him [the Judean]." Josephus' version notes also the (efficacious) effect of the former's deception upon the latter.

[818] See 1 Kgs 13:19-20a. Josephus adds the reference to the cordial interaction between the 2 figures.

[819] This reference to a theophany to the Judean

gressed his commands,[820] would suffer punishment; he likewise disclosed what this would be. For he stated that a lion would meet him as he was going off on his way; he would be destroyed by this [lion] and would have no share in the grave of his ancestors.[821]

241 These things happened, I suppose, in accordance with the will of God in order that Hieroboam should not attend to the words of Jadon, who had been shown to be a liar.[822] As Jadon therefore was going again to Hierosolyma,[823] a lion met him, tore him off his beast, and killed him, though to the donkey he did no harm at all. Rather, sitting down beside them, it kept guard over both [the donkey] and the body of the prophet.[824]

242 It (the lion) did this until some of the passersby saw it and, coming to the city to the false prophet, reported it.[825] Sending his sons, he brought the body into the city[826] and honored it with a costly burial.[827] He also commanded his sons to bury him with that one when he died,[828] saying that everything that he had prophesied against that city, the altar, the priests, and the false prophets[829] was true. He himself would, however, suffer no outrage since, due to his being buried with him, their bones could not be told apart.[830]

Jadon buried in future grave of false prophet

---

takes the place of the notice on "the word of the Lord coming" to "the prophet who had brought him back." Josephus' formulation thus denies a divine communication to the Bethelite, whom he has characterized so negatively in 8.236. Contrast *b. Sanh.* 104b, which affirms that, in recognition of his having shown hospitality to the Judean, the Shekinah rested upon the Bethelite even though he was a "prophet of Baal." On Josephus' tendency to introduce, as he does here, mention of divine "appearances," where the Bible lacks this, see Begg 1993: 53-54, n. 300.

[820] Josephus drastically shortens the accusation against the Judean of 1 Kgs 13:21-22bα (where it is placed on the lips of the Bethelite prophet) with its repetition of the wording of the divine prohibitions twice earlier cited by the former, i.e. in 13:8-9 and 16-17.

[821] Josephus expands on the summary announcement of punishment for the Judean voiced by his Bethel colleague in 1 Kgs 13:22bβ, i.e. "your body shall not come to the tomb of your fathers." In particular, drawing on the subsequent biblical account (see 13:24), he has the Deity also announce the circumstances of his death.

[822] This added editorial reflection serves to prepare for Josephus'—also added—account of the subsequent exchange (8.243-245a) between Jeroboam and the Bethelite, in which the latter successfully discredits the Judean to the former.

[823] Josephus supplies this indication concerning Jadon's destination on the basis of his earlier (see 8.231) qualification of him as "a prophet.... from Hierosolyma." 1 Kgs 13:24 speaks simply of the Judean's meeting his death as "he goes away." Josephus leaves aside the preceding reference (13:23) to the Bethelite's saddling the Judean's donkey following their shared repast.

[824] Josephus elaborates on the account of the Judean's end in 1 Kgs 13:24, specifying, e.g., that his donkey suffered no harm from the lion. He likewise has the lion "sit" rather than "stand" beside the Judean's body.

[825] See 1 Kgs 13:25.

[826] In the line of LXX BL* (which lack an equivalent to MT's 1 Kgs 13:26bβ-27), Josephus' account of the recovery of the prophet's body is much more concise than is the circumstantial narrative of MT 1 Kgs 13:26-29, where the Bethelite himself retrieves the body of his colleague. Given the former's age and physical state (see 8.236), Josephus has him act through his sons.

[827] See 1 Kgs 13:30a, which specifies that the Bethelite buried the Judean "in his own grave." Josephus highlights the pomp accorded Jadon's corpse, while leaving aside the mourning cry raised by the Bethelite and his sons, i.e. "Alas, my brother," in 13:30b.

[828] See 1 Kgs 13:31.

[829] The Bethelite's reference to these figures echoes Jadon's own words about those whose bones will be burned on the Bethel altar in 8.232, just as it picks up on the designation of the Bethelite himself as a "false prophet" in 8.236. The formulation is Josephus' replacement for the biblical Bethelite's reference (1 Kgs 13:32) to the Judean's having spoken also "against all the houses of the high places which are in the cities which are in Samaria," an indication that has no equivalent in the Judean's actual words as cited in 1 Kgs 13:2 // 8.232.

[830] With this addendum to the Bethelite's directives to his sons as cited in 1 Kgs 13:31-32, Josephus has him spell out the rationale for his command that he be bur-

False prophet
misleads
Jeroboam

243 Having then buried the prophet and commanded these things to his sons, he, being a vile and impious[831] man,[832] went in before Hieroboam[833] and said: "Why, O master, were you thrown into consternation by the words of that foolish [man]?"[834] When the king recounted to him the matter of the altar and his own hand and called him [Jadon] a truly divine[835] and best prophet,[836] he began [cunningly][837] to shake this opinion of his and, by using plausible words about what had happened, to impugn its truth.[838] **244** For he undertook to convince him that his hand had been numbed by the exertion of carrying the sacrifices; then, once it relaxed, it returned again to its natural state.[839] The altar, for its part, was new, and having received many large sacrifices, was thrown down and fell, due to the weight of what had been placed on it.[840] He also disclosed to him the death of the one who had predicted these signs, namely, his having been slain by a lion.[841] "Thus, he had nothing of a prophet either in who he was or what he said."[842]

245 By saying this, he persuaded the king; he completely turned his mind away from God and holy and just[843] deeds and induced him into impious practices.[844]

---

ied with the Judean, i.e. to insure the future inviolability of his own remains.

[831] Greek: πονηρὸς καὶ ἀσεβής. Josephus uses this collocation elsewhere in *Ant.* 8.299 (Baasha); 9.1 (Ahab, reverse order); 12.252 (apostate Jews, reverse order); 12.385 (the high priest Menelaus); and 13.34 (Jewish renegades).

[832] This (added) qualification of the Bethelite recalls Josephus' initial presentation of him as a "vile old man" in 8.236.

[833] 1 Kings 13 does not mention any such meeting of the king and the Bethelite. The purpose of Josephus' extended insertion on the matter (8.243-245a) is to account for the fact that, notwithstanding all that he had experienced during his encounter with the Judean, Jeroboam subsequently persisted (see 1 Kgs 13:33-34) in his earlier cultic misdeeds (see 1 Kgs 12:31-32), as though nothing had happened.

[834] The Bethelite "takes charge" of the proceedings with this provocative opening question, whose negative characterization of the Judean as "foolish" (Greek: ἀνόητος) he will subsequently substantiate.

[835] On Josephus' other uses of the term "divine" (Greek: θεῖος) in reference to human beings and the Hellenistic background of this usage, see Begg 1993: 59, n. 334.

[836] This is Josephus' only use of the phrase "best [Greek: ἄριστος] prophet"; compare, however, his designation of Balaam as the "best [Greek: ἄριστος] seer [Greek: μάντις]" in *Ant.* 4.104. Jeroboam's characterization of Jadon here recalls Josephus' own remark about the king's having learned that he "was truthful and possessed divine foreknowledge" in 8.234.

[837] Greek: κακουργῶν. This word is absent in Lat and bracketed by Niese (though not by Marcus).

[838] In what follows Josephus' Bethelite will address

in turn those features of Jeroboam's recent experience that had convinced the king of Jadon's veracity, endeavoring to expose their lack of credibility. Josephus' comment here reflects a recurrent theme in his writings, i.e. the use of rhetoric to disguise the truth; see e.g., *War* 1.16; *Life* 40.

[839] With this statement, the Bethelite, contradicting Josephus' own presentation of the facts (see 8.233-234), asserts that neither the disabling nor the revival of the king's hand had been brought about by Jadon himself.

[840] The Bethelite here offers a "naturalistic" explanation of the altar's collapse designed to undermine Jeroboam's belief that this came about due to the prophetic word pronounced against it by Jadon. Once again (see previous note), the Bethelite's claims are clearly at variance with Josephus' own presentation of the relevant events; see 8.232, 233b.

[841] The Bethelite at this point presents Jeroboam with new information that serves to clinch his case against Jadon's credibility, i.e. the latter's unexpected, violent death. In so doing, he naturally makes no reference to his own role in precipating Jadon's demise.

[842] This affirmation sums up the Bethelite's case against Jadon in words which run directly counter to those used of Jeroboam's own previous view of him, i.e. as one who "was truthful and possessed divine foreknowledge" (8.234) and was a "truly divine and best prophet" (8.243).

[843] Greek: ὅσιος καὶ δίκαιος. This collocation occurs also in *Ant.* 6.87; 8.285 (reverse order); 9.35; 15.138; cf. 19.323.

[844] With this notice on the (successful) effect of the Bethelite's arguments on the king, Josephus, rounding off the extended insertion of 8.243-245a, makes the transition to the source mention (1 Kgs 13:33-34) of Jeroboam's persistence in his reprobate behavior, not-

Thus he so outraged the Deity[845] and acted lawlessly that he daily sought nothing else than to perform something new and more obnoxious than those things he had already dared [to do].[846] Let this suffice for the present as an account concerning Hieroboam.[847]

(10.1) 246 Roboam,[848] son of Solomon, king, as we said before, of the two tribes, built many great fortified cities:[849] Bethleem,[850] Etame,[851] Thekoe,[852] Bethsour,[853] Socho,[854] Odollam,[855] Eipa,[856] Marisa,[857] Zipha,[858] Adoraim,[859] Lacheis,[860] Azeka,[861] Saram,[862] Elom,[863] and Chebron.[864] 247 These he built first in the tribe [and inheritance][865] of Iouda; he also constructed other great cities in the inheritance of Benjamin.[866] Having provided them with walls, he appointed leaders over all of them.[867] He also stored up much grain, wine, oil and other things needed for sustenance in each of the cities in abundance.[868] In addition, he placed there small shields[869] and

Rehoboam's military preparations

withstanding the impression the Judean had earlier made upon him.

[845] On Josephus' uses of (variants of) this phrase (Greek: ἐξύβρισεν εἰς τὸ θεῖον) elsewhere in his work, see Begg 1993: 61, n. 355.

[846] The above formulation is Josephus' version of 1 Kgs 13:33-34, where Jeroboam is first charged generally with not "turning from his evil way" (v. 33a), and then, more specifically, with making "priests for the high places" (v. 33b), with the result that his dynasty suffers eventual destruction (v. 34).

[847] This notice harks back to Josephus' announcement in 8.224 that he will first treat Jeroboam and serves to frame his initial account of that king (to whom he will return in 8.265) in 8.225-245a.

[848] In shifting from Jeroboam to Rehoboam at this point, Josephus departs from the sequence of Kings, which completes its account of the former (1 Kgs 12:25-14:20) before turning to its presentation of the latter (1 Kgs 14:21-31). In so doing, he likewise bases himself on the more expansive treatment of Rehoboam's reign given in 2 Chr 11:5-12:16, as compared with the summary narrative of 1 Kgs 14:21-31. On Josephus' account of Rehoboam in 8.246-264, see Begg 1993: 64-85.

[849] Josephus now, exceptionally, reproduces the full list of Rehoboam's 15 fortress cities given in 2 Chr 11:5b-10a.

[850] MT (2 Chr 11:6) בית־לחם (Eng.: "Bethlehem"); LXX B Βαιθσέεμ; LXX L and Josephus Βηθλεέμ.

[851] MT (2 Chr 11:6) עיטם (Eng.: "Etam"); LXX B Ἀπάν; LXX L Αἰτάμ; Josephus Ἠταμέ.

[852] MT (2 Chr 11:6) תקוע (Eng.: "Tekoa"); LXX B Θεκῶε; LXX L Θεκοῦε; Josephus Θεκωέ.

[853] MT (2 Chr 11:7) בית־צור (Eng.: "Beth-zur"); LXX B Βαιθσουρά; LXX L Βαιθσούρ; Josephus Βηθσούρ.

[854] MT (2 Chr 11:7) שׂוכו (Eng.: "Soco"); LXX B Σοκχώθ; LXX L Σοκχώ; Josephus Σωχώ.

[855] MT (2 Chr 11:7) עדלם (Eng.: "Adullam"); LXX B Ὀδολάμ; LXX L and Josephus Ὀδολλάμ.

[856] MT (2 Chr 11:8) גת (Eng.: "Gath"); LXX BL Γέθ; Josephus Εἰπά. Josephus' version of the place name, as read by Niese, differs markedly from that of the biblical witnesses. Marcus (ad loc.) and Schalit (s.v.) suggest that it is a corrupt doublet of the form Ἠταμέ, which stands 2nd in Josephus' list. Schlatter (s.v.), by contrast, sees it as a miswriting of an original Γιττάν, while Naber (ad loc.) and Weill (ad loc.) hold that it is a scribal error for Ἰπάν (cf. Lat hippam).

[857] MT (2 Chr 11:8) מרשה (Eng.: "Mareshah"); LXX B Μαρεισά; LXX L Μαρησά; Josephus Μάρισα.

[858] MT (2 Chr 11:8) זיף (Eng.: "Ziph"); LXX B Ζείβ; LXX L Ζίφ; Josephus Ζιφά.

[859] MT (2 Chr 11:9) אדורים (Eng.: "Adoraim"); LXX B Ἀδωραί; LXX L Ἀδωράμ; Josephus Ἀδωραίμ.

[860] MT (2 Chr 11:9) לכיש (Eng.: "Lachish"); LXX BL Λαχείς; Josephus Λάχεις.

[861] MT (2 Chr 11:9) עזקה (Eng.: "Azekah"); LXX BL and Josephus Ἀζηκά.

[862] MT (2 Chr 11:10) צרעה (Eng.: "Zorah"); LXX BL Σαραά; Josephus Σαράμ.

[863] MT (2 Chr 11:10) אילון (Eng.: "Aijalon"); LXX B Ἀλδών; LXX L Αἰλώμ; Josephus Ἠλώμ.

[864] MT (2 Chr 11:10) חברון (Eng.: "Hebron"); LXX BL Χεβρών; Josephus Χεβρῶν.

[865] Greek: καὶ κληροιχία. These words are bracketed by Niese.

[866] Whereas Josephus refers to additional Benjamite cities constructed by Rehoboam in addition to the 15 Judean ones built by him, 2 Chr 11:10b speaks rather of the 15 cities cited in 11:6-10a as situated in "Judah and Benjamin" (compare 11:5b, which seems to place them all in Judah).

[867] See 2 Chr 11:11a. Josephus specifies the biblical reference to Rehoboam's "making the fortresses strong" with mention of his endowing the cities with walls.

[868] See 2 Chr 11:11b, which speaks of the "stores of food, oil and wine" with which Rehoboam stocked his cities.

barbed lances, numbering many ten thousands.[870]

Israelites come to Judah

248 There assembled to him in Hierosolyma priests from all the Israelites, and Levites, and certain others of the crowd, who were good and just.[871] They abandoned their cities in order to worship God in Hierosolyma, for they were not pleased at being compelled to pay homage to the calves that Hieroboam had constructed.[872] These augmented the kingdom of Roboam for three years.[873]

Rehoboam's family

249 He married a certain relative[874] and had three children by her.[875] Later, he also married the daughter of Apsalom's daughter Thamar,[876] whose name was Machane;[877] she too was a relative. A male child was born to him by her, whom he named Abias.[878] He had other children by many other wives,[879] but cherished Machane more than all of them.[880] **250** He had eighteen wives whom he married according to law[881] and thirty[882] concubines; twenty-eight sons and sixty daughters were born to him.[883] As his successor to the kingship he appointed Abias, his son by Machane,[884] and entrusted his treasuries and the solidly fortified cities to him.[885]

---

[869] Josephus' word for these objects (Greek: θυρεός) is the same as that used in LXX BL 2 Chr 11:12a.

[870] 2 Chr 11:12a refers to "spears," without mention of their number. Josephus lacks an equivalent to the references to Rehoboam's "making the cities very strong" and "holding Judah and Benjamin" with which 11:12 concludes.

[871] Josephus adds mention of a 3rd party to the notice of 2 Chr 11:13 on the Israelite priests and Levites who joined Rehoboam, characterizing its members in highly positive terms. The addition is likely inspired by the reference to "all those who set their hearts to seek the Lord coming after them" (i.e. the priests and Levites, 11:13) in 11:16.

[872] Josephus modifies and compresses 2 Chr 11:14-15, where it is the Levites in particular who come to Jerusalem in response to Jeroboam's deposing them from the priesthood (11:14) and replacing them with his own priests "for the high places, for the satyrs, and for the calves which he had made" (11:15). In his presentation all 3 of the previously mentioned groups leave Israel, prompted by Jeroboam's making of the calves (see 8.226).

[873] Cf. 2 Chr 11:17, which concludes with the notice that during the 3 years "they [the Israelite arrivals] walked in the way of David and Solomon."

[874] 2 Chr 11:18 calls her "Mahalath," daughter of Jerimoth, son of David, and of Abihail, daughter of Eliab, son of Jesse.

[875] 2 Chr 11:19 names the 3 sons of Rehoboam and Mahalath as Jeush, Shemariah, and Zaham.

[876] Josephus has previously mentioned this figure in *Ant.* 7.243 (// 2 Sam 14:27).

[877] MT (2 Chr 11:20) מעכה (Eng.: "Maacah"); LXX BL Μααχά; Josephus Μαχάνη. In designating "Machane" as the *grand-daughter* of "Apsalmon" (Absalom) and daughter of "Thamar," Josephus differs from both 2 Chr 11:20-21, where she is called Absalom's "daughter" and 2 Chr 13:2, which makes her daughter of "Uriel of Gibeah" (in 1 Kgs 15:2 the father of "Maacah" is named "Abishalom"). His indication on the point likewise is at variance with his own statement in *Ant.* 7.190, drawn from the LXX plus in 2 Sam 14:27, according to which it was Absalom's daughter—rather than his grand-daughter (so 8.249)—who was to become the wife of Rehoboam and mother of "Abias" (Abijah). For further discussion, see Begg 1993: 68, n. 386.

[878] MT (2 Chr 11:20) אביה (Eng.: "Abijah"); LXX BL Ἀβιά; Josephus Ἀβίας.

[879] This general notice takes the place of the names of the 3 other children of Rehoboam by Maacah, i.e. Attai, Ziza, and Shelomith (MT 2 Chr 11:20b). It has in view the statistics for Rehoboam's wives and children that Josephus will supply in 8.250 (// 11:21b).

[880] See 2 Chr 11:21a.

[881] Josephus' figure for Rehoboam's "wives" agrees with that cited in 2 Chr 11:21bα (MT and LXX BL).

[882] Josephus' figure for this category of women corresponds to that given in LXX B (and OL) 2 Chr 11:21bα. MT (and most LXX MSS) read "60."

[883] Josephus' figures for Rehoboam's children agree with those cited in 2 Chr 11:21bβ (MT and LXX BL).

[884] In 2 Chr 11:22 Rehoboam makes Abijah "chief prince among his brothers, for he intended to make him king."

[885] Compare 2 Chr 11:23, which mentions Rehoboam's benefactions to his other sons as well (placing them in the various fortress cities, giving them provisions, and finding them wives). Josephus underscores Rehoboam's attachment to the son of his most loved wife by having him confer these additional benefits rather on Abijah himself.

(10.2) 251 A frequent cause, I think,[886] of calamities and lawlessness for persons is the greatness of their affairs and the turn for the better.[887] For seeing his kingdom augmented in this way, Roboam was misled into unjust and impious practices[888] and despised the worship of God[889] so that also the people under him became imitators of his lawless deeds.[890] **252** For the morals of subjects are corrupted together with the character of their leaders; giving up their own prudence as a reproach to the licentiousness of the latter, they follow them in their wrongdoing, as though it were a virtue. For it is not possible to seem to approve of the deeds of kings without doing the same things [as they do].[891]

Rehoboam and people defect

253 This then is also what happened to those under Roboam's orders;[892] when he became impious and lawless, they were solicitous not to offend the king by wishing to be just. As the avenger of his [Roboam's] outrages[893] against him, God sent Isok,[894] the king of the Egyptians,[895] about whom Herodotus is in error when he attributes his exploits to Sesostris.[896] **254** For this Isok, in the fifth year of Roboam's kingship,[897] launched a campaign against him with many ten thousands.[898] For he

Shishak (Isok) invades Judah

---

[886] Josephus pauses at this juncture to introduce an extended reflection (8.251-253) on what 2 Chr 12:1 simply reports as a fact, i.e. Rehoboam, once his kingdom was firmly established, forsook the Lord's Law along with "all Israel." On this editorial addition as an attempt to mitigate Rehoboam's personal culpability, see Feldman 1998a: 254, 260.

[887] With this remark Josephus alludes to the starting point of a sequence in which success leads to arrogance, which in turn provokes calamity, that he highlights often in his account and which figures prominently in Greek literature as well; see, e.g., Herodotus 1.207 and cf. Feldman 1998: 180-1.

[888] With his reference to Rehoboam's being misled into "impious practices" (Greek: ἀσεβεῖς πράξεις), Josephus assimilates the Judean king in the later part of his reign to the reprobate Jeroboam, whom the Bethelite false prophet "induced into impious practices" of his own according to 8.245.

[889] Greek: τῆς τοῦ θεοῦ θρησκείας καταφρονεῖν; this is Josephus' only use of this phrase. Compare "he [Rehoboam] forsook the law of the Lord" (2 Chr 12:1b).

[890] Greek: ἀνομημάτα; Josephus uses this term twice elsewhere: 8.289 and 14.309. In contrast to 2 Chr 12:1b, where "all Israel" simply joins Rehoboam in defecting from the Law, Josephus, with an eye to the continuation of his reflection in 8.252, underscores Rehoboam's personal responsibility for the people's following his wrongful lead. Compare 1 Kgs 14:22-24, where it is the collective sin of Judah that is highlighted and Rehoboam's own defection is not explicitly mentioned.

[891] To the notice of 2 Chr 12:1b about "all Israel's" joining Rehoboam in his forsaking of the Law Josephus appends this generalizing reflection on the psychology of subjects, in particular their readiness to follow the misbehavior initiated by their rulers and the reason for this.

[892] Josephus now applies the foregoing general reflection to the specific case of Rehoboam's people and their response to his defection from the "worship of God" (8.251).

[893] The use of this noun (Greek: ὕβρις) generates another (see the note to "impious practices" at 8.251) verbal link between Rehoboam and Jeroboam, who in 8.245 is said to "outrage [Greek: ἐξυβρίζω] the Deity."

[894] MT (2 Chr 12:2) שׁישׁק (Eng.: "Shishak"); LXX BL Σουσακείμ; Josephus Ἴσακος (MSPE read Σούσακος here, as do Naber and Weill). Josephus made previous mention of this king in *Ant.* 7.105 and 8.210. In the context of his address to the defenders of Jerusalem in *War* 6.436, Josephus refers to the king under the name of "Asochaeus" (Greek Ἀσωχαῖος) as the 1st in a series of conquerors of the city.

[895] Josephus agrees with 2 Chr 12:2 in explicitly representing Shishak's advance as a divinely-initiated retribution for Rehoboam's defection, whereas in 1 Kgs 14:22-25 God's retributive role in Shishak's attack (14:25) is left implicit (as is the connection between this attack and Judah's sinfulness as described in 14:22-24).

[896] The reference is to *Histories* 2.102ff. (to which Josephus will return in 8.260-262). Also elsewhere Josephus criticizes Herodotus' historical inaccuracies; see *Ant.* 10.19; *Apion* 1.63, 73, and cf. Begg 1993: 71, n. 421; and Bowley 1994: 210-11 (who notes that Josephus is not alone among Greek historians in such criticism of the "Father of History").

[897] This dating for Shishak's invasion agrees with that given in 1 Kgs 14:25 and 2 Chr 12:2.

[898] This initial, indeterminate figure corresponds to the reference in 2 Chr 12:3b to "the people without

had following him 1,200 chariots, 60,000 horsemen, and 400,000 foot soldiers.[899] The majority of those he brought with him were Libyans and Ethiopians.[900]

God rejects people's appeal

255 Advancing then against the country of the Hebrews, he captured the most solidly fortified cities of Roboam's kingdom without a fight. Having secured these, he finally marched against Hierosolyma.[901] **(10.3)** Roboam and the crowd, who were shut up in it as a result of Isok's campaign, begged God to give them victory and safety.[902] **256** They did not, however, persuade God to take their side.[903] Rather, the prophet Samaias[904] told them that God was threatening to abandon them, just as they themselves had forsaken his worship.[905] When they heard this, their souls immediately sank and, no longer seeing any hope of safety,[906] they all hastened to confess that God was justly ignoring[907] them, who had been impious towards him and violated his prescriptions.[908]

God relents

257 When God saw them in this state of mind and acknowledging their offenses, he said to the prophet that he would not make an end of them.[909] He would, however, make them subject to the Egyptians, in order that they might learn which was easier: to be a slave to a human being or to God.[910]

Shishak plunders Jerusalem

258 Isok got possession of the city without a fight, Roboam having admitted him out of fear.[911] He [Isok] did not, however, stick to the agreements he had made.[912]

---

number," who followed Shishak from Egypt; see following note.

[899] Josephus' figures for Shishak's chariots and horsemen agree with those given in 2 Chr 12:3a. In place of the Chronicler's vague additional allusion to the "people without number" who accompanied the king from Egypt, already utilized by him in what precedes (see previous note), Josephus supplies a precise figure for the Egyptian "infantry." 1 Kgs 14:25 offers no indication concerning the size of Shishak's forces.

[900] 2 Chr 12:3b cites a 3rd, obscure component of Shishak's force, i.e. the "Sukkim" (MT LXX L; LXX B: "Troglodites").

[901] See 2 Chr 12:4. Josephus adds the specification, inspired by the wording of Herodotus' account of the Egyptian's exploits (see 8.260), that the cities fell to Shishak "without a fight." He thereby underscores the cowardice of Rehoboam and his people—a point that will be picked up in his subsequent account; see 8.258, 260, 261.

[902] This initial appeal to God by king and people has no counterpart in 2 Chronicles 12. The appeal functions to call forth the divine response brought by the prophet Shemaiah (// 2 Chr 12:5) in what follows.

[903] This added editorial comment serves to prepare readers for the negative answer that the king and people are about to receive to their appeal.

[904] MT (2 Chr 12:5) שמעיה (Eng.: "Shemaiah"); LXX B Σαμμαίας; LXX L and Josephus Σαμαίας. The intervention of this prophet is not mentioned in the parallel text of 1 Kings 14. According to 1 Kgs 12:22 // 2 Chr 11:2 it was "Shemaiah" who earlier restrained Rehoboam from advancing against the rebel northerners; in Josephus' version of that event the prophet is

nameless; see the note to "a prophet" at 8.223.

[905] See 2 Chr 12:5. Josephus omits the "messenger formula" with which Shemaiah's oracle begins there, as well as the specification that the prophet addressed himself to "Rehoboam and the princes of Judah." The phrase "forsake his [God's] worship" (Greek: τὴν θρησκείαν καταλειπεῖν) recurs in *Ant.* 8.270; 11.182; 12.384. The phrase recalls Josephus's statement that Rehoboam "despised the worship of God" in 8.251.

[906] Josephus adds this notice on the effect of Shemaiah's words upon his hearers.

[907] Greek: ὑπεροράω; Josephus uses this verb with the Deity as subject also in *Ant.* 6.307; 12.281.

[908] Josephus elaborates on the reference to the king's and princes' "humbling themselves" and confessing that "the Lord is righteous" of 2 Chr 12:6.

[909] See 2 Chr 12:7a. Josephus substitutes the reference to God's "telling the prophet" for the biblical phrase "the word of the Lord came to Shemaiah." He omits the additional divine assurances of 12:7b, i.e. God will grant the people "some deliverance" and not "pour out his wrath upon Jerusalem" through the agency of Shishak.

[910] According to 2 Chr 12:8, the purpose of God's announced subjection of the Judeans to Shishak is that they may know "my service *and* the service of the kingdoms of the countries." Josephus' formulation introduces a contrast between the 2 kinds of service.

[911] Josephus adds this explicit mention of Shishak's occupation of Jerusalem and the explanation of how it happened. Here too (see note on "against Hierosolyma" at 8.255), he underscores the cowardice of the city's defenders, Rehoboam in particular.

Rather, he plundered the sacred precinct and emptied the treasuries of God and those of the kings; he carried off countless quantities of gold and silver and left nothing whatever behind.[913] **259** He likewise took away the golden small shields and the large shields that King Solomon had constructed.[914] Nor did he leave untouched the golden quivers that David had dedicated to God after taking them from the king of Sophene.[915] Having done this, he returned to his own country.[916]

260 Herodotus of Halicarnassus[917] also mentions this campaign, about which he is in error only concerning the king's name[918] and about his marching against many other nations and enslaving Palestine-Syria, taking its inhabitants without a fight.[919] **261** It is obvious, however, that it is our nation that he means to represent as subjugated by the Egyptian.[920] For he relates that, in the [territory] of those who surrendered themselves to him without a fight, he [Sesostris] left pillars inscribed with women's private parts.[921] But now, it was our king Roboam who handed the city over to him without a fight.[922] **262** He also says that the Ethiopians have learned the circumcision of their private parts from the Egyptians.[923] "For the Phoenicians and

Critique of Herodotus

---

[912] This allusion to Shishak's perfidy is a Josephan addition.

[913] See 2 Chr 12:9a// 1 Kgs 14:26a. Josephus expands the biblical catalogues of Shishak's depredations with mention of the mass of precious metals removed by him, thereby underscoring Jerusalem's previous wealth.

[914] 1 Kgs 14:26b// 2 Chr 12:9b mention only a single kind of "shield." Josephus' distinction between the 2 types recalls 8.179, where, following 2 Chr 9:15b // 1 Kgs 10:16, he cites Solomon's making both sorts.

[915] Josephus' mention of this final act of despoliation by Shishak has a parallel in the plus at the end of LXX BL 1 Kgs 14:26 (no equivalent in either MT 1 Kgs 14:26 or 2 Chr 12:9) according to which the Egyptian removed the golden "spears" (Josephus: quivers) that David had earlier taken from the servants of King Adraazar of Souba. By means of the notice here, Josephus makes good on his promise, given in connection with his parallel to the LXX BL plus of 2 Sam 8:7 in *Ant.* 7.104-105, concerning the items (quivers and suits of armor) seized by David from the retinue of King Adad, that he intends to relate the eventual loss of these objects to the Egyptian king at a later point. See further Begg 1993: 76-78 for more on the divergences in detail between 7.104-105 and 8.259 (and their respective LXX equivalents).

[916] Shishak's "return" is not explicitly mentioned in either 1 Kings 14 or 2 Chronicles 12.

[917] Josephus now returns to the subject of Herodotus' (purportedly confused) account of Shishak's campaign, which he had introduced in 8.253.

[918] I.e. in calling him "Sesostris" (see 8.253) rather than "Isok."

[919] Having previously (see 8.253) averred that Herodotus erred only in the name he gives the invader

king, Josephus now proceeds to call attention to an additional (alleged) mistake on the historian's part, i.e. his statement (2.102ff.) that the Egyptian's campaign extended to "many other nations." The phrase "without a fight," twice earlier inserted by Josephus (8.255, 258), was drawn by him from the passage of Herodotus that he (selectively) quotes here in 8.260.

[920] Josephus here spells out the nature of Herodotus' additional mistake: the Egyptian's campaign involved, not "many other nations" and all "Palestine-Syria," but only Rehoboam's territory.

[921] Josephus here reverts to his "quotation" of Herodotus' text (2.102ff.), whose "mistake" regarding the extent of Shishak's campaign he will then proceed to expose.

[922] Josephus finally "clinches"—at least to his own satisfaction—his demonstration of Herodotus' error: the latter had affirmed that the Egyptian king expressed his contempt for the cowardice of the many nations who yielded to him "without a fight," but, in fact, the only people for whose cowardly surrender to him any (earlier) evidence exists is precisely the Judeans of Rehoboam's time. It should, however, be noted here that Josephus' whole demonstration rests on a literary "sleight of hand": he reworks the biblical accounts (which nowhere explicitly mention the Judeans' surrendering to Shishak "without a fight") under the influence of Herodotus' presentation in order then to use this reworking to discredit Herodotus' statements about whom it was that Shishak subjugated.

[923] Josephus here summarizes the content of a further statement by Herodotus (2.104) that he will then "quote" and critique. In so doing, however, Josephus notably misrepresents Herodotus' own affirmation at the start of 2.104: "as to the Egyptians and the Ethiopians themselves, I cannot say which nation learned it

the Syrians in Palestine acknowledge that they have learned it from the Egyptians."⁹²⁴   Now then it is clear that there are no others who practice circumcision in Palestine-Syria except ourselves alone.⁹²⁵ But about these matters let each speak as seems good to him.⁹²⁶

End of Rehoboam's reign

(10.4) 263 Once Isok returned home,⁹²⁷ King Roboam made the same [number] in bronze of the golden small shields and the large shields, and handed these over to the palace guards.⁹²⁸ Instead of distinguishing himself by brilliant generalship and splendid statesmanship, he ruled as king with much quiet and fear,⁹²⁹ being all the time an enemy of Hieroboam.⁹³⁰ **264** He died after living fifty-seven years⁹³¹ and reigning as king for seventeen.⁹³² He was a man of boastful⁹³³ and foolish⁹³⁴ manner, who, on account of his not paying attention to his father's friends, lost his rule.⁹³⁵ He was buried in Hierosolyma in the graves of the kings.⁹³⁶ His son Abias⁹³⁷

[the practice of circumcision] from the other." Oddly, in *Apion* 1.170, Josephus does correctly reproduce Herodotus' words on the matter.

⁹²⁴ Josephus quotes this portion of *Histories* 2.104 almost verbatim (in contrast to his distorted rendering of its preceding part; see previous note). The same passage (along with its continuation) is also cited by him in *Apion* 1.169-170. The inspiration for Josephus' attaching this further citation of Herodotus to that adduced by him in 8.261 is that both texts speak of "private parts" and of "Palestine-Syria" (2.102)/ "Palestine of the Syrians" (2.104).

⁹²⁵ Having cited Herodotus' claim about the general practice of circumcision among the "Syrians in Palestine," Josephus now exposes its inexactitude: the only group that actually observes the practice in the region in question is his own people. He makes the same affirmation in *Apion* 1.171, further asserting that Herodotus "must therefore have known this, and his allusion is to them."

⁹²⁶ Having exposed no less than 3 historical errors of the great Herodotus in what precedes, Josephus, by means of this formula, now tolerantly leaves it to readers to decide for themselves on the points at issue between himself and Herodotus. He appends similar formulations to his accounts of biblical miracles in a whole series of instances; see Begg 1993: 82, n. 483 for references.

⁹²⁷ With this phrase, Josephus resumes his main story line at the point (see 8.259) where he paused in order to incorporate the "Herodotus digression" of 8.260-262.

⁹²⁸ This is Josephus' delayed equivalent to 1 Kgs 14:27// 2 Chr 12:10. As he did with the golden "shields" taken by Shishak (see the note to "shields ... constructed" at 8.259), Josephus introduces a distinction concerning the 2 types of bronze replacements Rehoboam makes for these. He leaves aside the notice of 14:28// 12:11 concerning the guards' carrying the bronze shields before the king when he entered the

temple and thereafter returning them to the guardroom.

⁹²⁹ This characterization of Rehoboam's latter reign might reflect the statement of 2 Chr 12:12b about "conditions being good" in Judah following Shishak's incursion. In any case, Josephus focusses attention not on the nation as a whole, but rather on Rehoboam and the nature of his rule in this period.

⁹³⁰ Josephus draws this item from 2 Chr 12:15b// 1 Kgs 14:30; cf. 1 Kgs 15:6. The biblical passages speak of "warfare" between the 2 kings. Josephus' alternative reference to Rehoboam's being a constant "enemy" of Jeroboam suggests that his hostility did not lead to actual conflict between them—something that would have violated the prophetic prohibition of such civil war and Rehoboam's submission to this in 8.222-223.

⁹³¹ Josephus obtains this figure for Rehoboam's span of life by combining the notices on his age at accession (41) and length of reign (17) found in 1 Kgs 14:21aβα// 2 Chr 12:13aβα, which, however, yield a total (i.e. 58) that is higher by 1 year.

⁹³² This figure for Rehoboam's length of reign corresponds to that given in 1 Kgs 14:21bα// 2 Chr 12:13bα. Josephus lacks an equivalent to the biblical verses' specification that Rehoboam reigned "in Jerusalem, the city that the Lord had chosen out of all the tribes of Israel to put his name there."

⁹³³ Greek: ἀλαζών. Josephus' 2 remaining uses of this term are in *War* 6.172 (the Judean Jonathan) and 6.395 (the Judean rebels). On the term, see Spicq 1978 (I): 64-66.

⁹³⁴ This term (Greek: ἀνόητος) recalls the Bethelite prophet's characterization of "Jadon" as "that foolish man" (Greek: ἀνόητος) in 8.243.

⁹³⁵ This closing assessment of Rehoboam, with its allusion back to the disastrous beginning of his reign that resulted from the king's character flaws, contrasts with the more theological evaluation of him offered in 2 Chr 12:14 ("he did evil, for he did not set his heart to seek the Lord."). Josephus leaves aside both the "source notices" of 1 Kgs 14:29// 2 Chr 12:15 and the

assumed the kingship when Hieroboam was already in the eighteenth year of his ruling as king over the ten tribes.[938]

265 This then is the outcome of these matters. We now, however, have to relate the things that happened subsequently concerning Hieroboam and how he finished his life.[939] For he did not cease or desist from outraging God; rather, he daily continued to erect altars on the high mountains and appoint priests from among the crowd.[940]

(11.1) 266 Within a short time, however, the Deity, however, was about to bring these impieties and the judgment for them upon his head and that of each member of his family.[941] His son, whom they called Obime,[942] fell sick at that time. [Hieroboam] ordered his wife to put off her robe and, assuming the dress of a commoner, to go to Achias the prophet.[943] **267** He was a man who was remarkable for his predicting of the future,[944] for he had disclosed the matter of his kingship to himself.[945] He directed her to go inquire, as though [she were] a stranger, about the child, whether he would come through his illness.[946] Disguising herself as her husband had ordered her, she went to the city of Silo, for it was there that Achias resided.[947]

268 When she was on the point of entering his house and with Achias' eyes being blinded as a result of old age,[948] God appeared to him and informed him both

---

reference to Rehoboam's mother of 14:31bβ// 12:14bβ, the latter item having already been anticipated by him in 8.212.

[936] 1 Kgs 14:31aβ// 2 Chr 12:16aβ have Rehoboam buried "in the city of David."

[937] MT (1 Kgs 14:31) אבים (Eng.: "Abijam")/ (2 Chr 12:16) אביה (Eng.: "Abijah"); LXX B 14:31 Ἀβιού; LXX L 14:31// LXX BL 12:16 Ἀβιά; Josephus Ἀβίας. This figure was introduced in 8.249-250 as Rehoboam's favorite son.

[938] Josephus combines the notice on the accession of "Abijah" of 1 Kgs 14:31bβ// 2 Chr 12:16b and the synchronization of this with Jeroboam's year of reign of 1 Kgs 15:1// 2 Chr 13:1a.

[939] This added transitional notice serves to redirect attention to Jeroboam, whom Josephus temporarily put aside (see 8.245) in order to focus on Rehoboam (8.246-264).

[940] Josephus here picks up on his negative evaluation of Jeroboam as a persistent "outrager" of God from 8.245, just as his allusion to the king's (non-Levitical) priestly appointments recalls his account of that initiative in 8.228.

[941] With this statement, Josephus prepares the following story of the first divine initiative against Jeroboam's house, i.e. the death of his son Abijah. In placing his version of this episode (1 Kgs 14:1-20, MT) after his account of Rehoboam's reign (1 Kgs 14:21-31) Josephus reverses the sequence of 1 Kings 14 (MT). The LXX witnesses BL* lack a counterpart to the narra-

tive of Abijah's death (1 Kgs 14:1-20) in its MT position (various elements of this narrative are, however, incorporated into these witnesses' earlier plus, 1 Kgs 12:24ᵃ⁻ᶻ); such a counterpart does occur in, e.g., the Hexaplaric LXX witness Codex A. On Josephus' rendition of 1 Kgs 14:1-20 in 8.265-273, see Begg 1993: 86-96.

[942] MT (1 Kgs 14:1) אביה (Eng.: "Abijah"); LXX BL* (1 Kgs 12:24c) Ἀβιά; Josephus Ὀβίμης.

[943] Compare 1 Kgs 14:2, where Jeroboam instructs the queen to "disguise herself" so as not to be recognized as his wife.

[944] Josephus adds this characterization of Ahijah to the words about the prophet attributed to Jeroboam in 1 Kgs 14:2.

[945] In 1 Kgs 14:2bβ Jeroboam recalls that Ahijah had told him that he would be "king over this people."

[946] In 1 Kgs 14:3b Jeroboam simply informs his wife that Ahijah "will tell you what shall happen to the child," rather than instructing her to inquire about this. Josephus lacks an equivalent to the catalogue of items (10 loaves, some cakes, and a jar of honey), which the queen is instructed to bring to Ahijah in 14:3a of which nothing further is said in the continuation of the episode.

[947] Josephus combines Jeroboam's command that his wife go to Shiloh, where Ahijah is currently living (1 Kgs 14:2bα), with the notice of her doing this (14:4a).

[948] Josephus derives the detail about Ahijah's im-

that the wife of Hieroboam was coming to him and what he should answer concerning the matter about which she was coming.[949]

Ahijah's words to queen

269 When the woman came into the house, as though a commoner and a stranger,[950] he cried out: "Enter, wife of Hieroboam. Why are you hiding yourself? For you are not concealed from God, who has appeared to me and disclosed your coming and ordered me to use these words.[951] Go off then to your husband and tell him that [God] is saying this:[952] **270** Just as, from being little and nothing, I [God] made you [Hieroboam] great,[953] and tore the kingship from the family of David and gave it to you[954]—while you disregarded these things and forsook my worship,[955] constructing gods of cast metal and honored these[956]—so I shall bring you down once again and exterminate your entire family and cause them to become food for dogs and birds.[957] **271** For a certain king of the entire people will be raised up by me who will not leave anyone of Hieroboam's family [alive].[958] The rabble too will share in this punishment;[959] they will be driven off the good land[960] and scattered to places beyond the Euphrates, because they followed the impieties of the king[961] and are paying homage to the gods made by him[962] after leaving off sacrifice to me. **272** But you, woman, hurry to announce these things to your husband.[963] You will en-

---

paired sight and its cause from 1 Kgs 14:4b.

[949] 1 Kgs 14:5a does not mention such a divine "appearance" to Ahijah; Josephus' addition of the item recalls his (likewise added) reference to God's appearing to Jadon in 8.240. He has no equivalent to the portion of God's word to Ahijah in 14:5bα, informing him of Abijah's sickness.

[950] 1 Kgs 14:5c speaks of the queen's "pretending to be another woman." Josephus' reference to her as a (purported) "commoner and a stranger" recalls the wording of Jeroboam's instructions to his wife in 8.266.

[951] See 1 Kgs 14:6, from which Josephus omits the mention of Ahijah's hearing "the sound of [the queen's] feet at the door." Conversely, he adds the allusion by Ahijah to the divine communication he has just received (see 8.268).

[952] Compare the "messenger formula" ("thus says the Lord, the God of Israel"), with which Ahijah introduces his words in 1 Kgs 14:7a.

[953] Cf. 1 Kgs 14:7b, where God mentions his "exalting" Jeroboam "from among the people."

[954] See 1 Kgs 14:8a.

[955] Greek: τὴν ἐμὴν θρησκείαν καταλιπεῖν. This is the same phrase applied by Shemaiah to Rehoboam and the Judeans in 8.256.

[956] Of the list of charges made against Jeroboam by Ahijah in 1 Kgs 14:8b-9, Josephus lacks an equivalent to the graphic image with which v. 9 ends, i.e. "you have cast me [God] behind your back." Similarly, Tg. tones down this formulation in its rendition: "you [Jeroboam] have put my service far from opposite your eyes." Josephus likewise has no counterpart to Ahijah's statement about Jeroboam's not being like the righteous David of 14:8b.

[957] Josephus compresses Ahijah's announcement of punishment for Jeroboam's house of 1 Kgs 14:10-11, eliminating, e.g., its vulgar allusions to "every one pissing against the wall" and the house of Jeroboam being consumed the way "a man burns up dung until it is all gone" of 14:10. He likewise leaves aside the distinction between the dogs eating "those in the city," the birds "those who die in the open country" of 14:11 (subsequently, however, he will make use of this distinction; see 8.289). Conversely, he adds an announcement concerning God's coming punishment of Jeroboam himself, i.e. his reducing him to his original, lowly state.

[958] See 1 Kgs 14:14. Josephus makes this announcement precede that of the death of prince Abijah (14:12-13), whereas in 1 Kings 14 it follows this.

[959] This prosaic formulation replaces the vivid image of 1 Kgs 14:15aα: "the Lord will smite Israel as a reed is shaken in the water."

[960] From Ahijah's word in 1 Kgs 14:15aβ Josephus omits the characterization of the "good land" as one "which he [God] gave to their fathers."

[961] Ahijah's words against Israel in 1 Kgs 14:15-16 do not mention the nation's imitating the impious Jeroboam. Josephus' addition of the reference recalls his previous emphasis (see 8.251-253) on the Judeans' imitation of Rehoboam's offenses and the consequences of this for them.

[962] Ahijah's word in 1 Kgs 14:15bβ refers rather to "the Asherim which they [the people] made, provoking the Lord to anger." Josephus' rendering recalls Ahijah's charge about Jeroboam's "constructing gods of cast metal" in 8.270.

[963] Josephus makes Ahijah's instructions to the

counter your son dead, for upon your entering the city, life will leave him.[964] He
will be buried, lamented by the whole rabble and honored by their common mourning.[965] For he alone of the family of Hieroboam was good."[966]

273 Upon his prophesying these things, the woman rushed out, upset and distressed at the predicted death of the child. She wept on the way, and beat her breast
over the boy's imminent end. Pitiable in her suffering, she was driven on by un-
speakable calamities and made a haste that was bad luck for her son—for the sooner
she came to him, the sooner she would see him dead—, but which was necessary
for her husband's sake.[967] When she arrived, she did find him [her son] expired[968]
as the prophet had said, and told her husband everything.[969]

Queen returns to find son dead

(11.2) 274 Hieroboam, however, gave no thought to these things.[970] Collecting[971]
a large army, he set out to make war on Abias, the son of Roboam, who had assumed his father's kingship,[972] for he despised him, given his age.[973] When he heard
of Hieroboam's advance against [his kingdom], Abias was not dismayed, for with
his intellect, he was superior to his [own] youthfulness and the hopes of the enemy.[974] Selecting an army from the two tribes, he met Hieroboam at a certain place
called Mount Samaron.[975] Pitching camp near him, he made preparations for battle.[976]
275 His force consisted of 400,000 men, while Hieroboam's army had twice as
many.[977] When the armies had been arrayed against each other for action and its

Jeroboam advances against Abijah of Judah

queen regarding her son and husband (// 1 Kgs 14:12-13) the climax of the prophet's word to her, whereas in the Bible these are followed by additional announce-ments concerning Jeroboam's replacement (14:14) and the punishment of the entire people (14:15-16).

[964] See 1 Kgs 14:12.

[965] See 1 Kgs 14:13a. Josephus reverses the biblical order, where the "mourning" for the prince is mentioned prior to the announcement of his burial.

[966] Neither Josephus nor the Bible (1 Kgs 14:13b) identifies the "something good" that Abijah possessed. *B. Mo'ed Qat.* 28b offers divergent Rabbinic views on the point: Abijah went on pilgrimage himself to Jerusa-lem or, alternatively, removed the guards blocking the Israelites' route to the city so that they might make such pilgrimages.

[967] Josephus greatly embellishes the summary no-tice of 1 Kgs 14:17a on the woman's response to Ahijah's word to her ("then Jeroboam's wife arose, and departed"), highlighting the pathos of her situation and her emotional reaction to this.

[968] 1 Kgs 14:17aβb specifies that she arrived in "Tirzah" and that her son died "as she came to the threshold of the house."

[969] Josephus appends these indications to the death notice of 1 Kgs 14:17, noting both the fulfillment of Ahijah's prediction of Abijah's demise and the queen's carrying out of her commission to inform her husband of the prophet's message (see 8.272).

[970] This notice on Jeroboam's disregard of his wife's report replaces the account of the mourning for Abijah in fulfillment of Ahijah's announcement in 14:13a (//

8.272) of 1 Kgs 14:18.

[971] At this point, Josephus reverts to Chronicles as his source, reproducing its story—unparalleled in Kings—of the combat between Jeroboam and Abijah of Judah (2 Chronicles 13) in 8.274-286; on this segment see Begg 1993: 97-112. In so doing, he delays his ver-sion of the closing notices for Jeroboam of 1 Kgs 14:19-20 (// 8.287) until after he has related this addi-tional episode concerning him.

[972] See 8.264.

[973] In 2 Chr 13:3 it is the Judean Abijah, who ini-tiates the hostilities, thereby violating the prophetic prohibition of such a move delivered to his father Rehoboam according to 1 Kgs 12:24a// 2 Chr 11:4// *Ant.* 8.223. Josephus makes the reprobate Jeroboam the aggressor, who, having just lost his son, can think of nothing else but to commence a civil war with Judah. He further supplies a motivation for his venturing to at-tack Judah precisely at this point, i.e. his contempt for Abijah's youth.

[974] Josephus supplies this notice on the state of mind with which Abijah meets Jeroboam's advance and the intellectual endowment that underlies his unper-turbed response. Abijah's precocity recalls that of the Josephan Solomon; see 8.21.

[975] MT (2 Chr 13:4) צמרים (Eng.: "Zemaraim"); LXX BL Σομορών; Josephus Σαμαρών. 2 Chr 13:4a adds that the mountain was situated "in the hill coun-try of Ephraim."

[976] 2 Chronicles 13 does not mention either Abijah's "camping" or his preparations for battle.

[977] Josephus' figures for the 2 armies correspond to

Abijah addresses Israelites

dangers and they were about to engage,[978] Abias took his stand on a certain elevated place.[979] Motioning with his hand, he requested the crowd and Hieroboam to first hear him quietly.[980] **276** Once there was silence, he began to speak:[981]

"That God entrusted the leadership to David and his descendants for all time, not even you are unaware.[982] I wonder, nevertheless, how it is that, revolting against my father, you went over to his slave Hieroboam.[983] Together with him you are now present, about to make war on those who have been designated by God to rule as kings and to despoil them of the rule that was conferred on them and that Hieroboam has been unjustly holding until now.[984]

277 But he will not, I think, enjoy it for a longer time. Rather, having paid to God the penalty for what is past, he will desist from the lawlessness and outrages with which he has not ceased to outrage him and has induced you [the Israelites] to do the same.[985] You[986] were done no injustice by my father, but because he did not respond as you wished when present at your assembly, you, persuaded by the counsel of vile persons, abandoned him out of anger,[987] as it seemed, whereas in truth you were separating yourselves from God and his laws.[988] **278** And yet, it would have been a good thing for you not only to pardon the unpleasant words of a young man and one inexperienced in governing people,[989] but also whatever unpleasantness into which his youth and ignorance of public affairs led him[990] for the sake of

---

those cited in 2 Chr 13:3 (which specifies that Jeroboam's force numbered 800,000).

[978] Cf. 2 Chr 13:3b, which mentions Jeroboam's drawing up his line of battle, consisting of 800,000 men, against Abijah.

[979] 2 Chr 13:4a states that this was on Mt. Zemaraim (see 8.274) itself.

[980] See 2 Chr 13:4b (where Abijah appeals for a hearing to "Jeroboam and all Israel"). Josephus adds the detail about the Judean king's accompanying hand motion.

[981] Josephus supplies this transitional notice on the success of Abijah's appeal for a hearing by the enemy. In what follows Josephus treats Abijah's biblical discourse (2 Chr 13:5-12) with considerable freedom, rearranging, omitting, and above all amplifying its components.

[982] Josephus turns Abijah's rhetorical question as to whether Israel "ought not to know" of God's abiding grant of kingship over Israel to the Davidids of 2 Chr 13:5 into an affirmation that his hearers are indeed not "unaware" of this. In line with his standard practice, he omits Abijah's further assertion that the grant was made "by a covenant of salt."

[983] Cf. 2 Chr 13:6-7, whose wording Josephus modifies in several ways: the people as a whole—rather than Jeroboam alone—are accused of "revolting" against Rehoboam, while the pejorative qualification of Jeroboam's supporters as "worthless scoundrels" is held over for a later point in Abijah's discourse (see 8.277).

[984] Compare 2 Chr 13:8a, where Abijah says to the Israelites: "now you think to withstand the kingdom of the Lord in the hand of the sons of David...."

[985] This statement concerning the fate awaiting Jeroboam for his crimes has no explicit counterpart in the biblical Abijah's speech. It does, however, recall Josephus' earlier remarks concerning the king in 8.228, 245, 265-266.

[986] After the preceding digression (8.277a) focussed on the person of Jeroboam, Abijah now redirects himself to the Israelites as a whole.

[987] Josephus, expatiating on 2 Chr 13:7, now has Abijah recall the confrontation between Rehoboam and the Israelites at Shechem as described in 8.212-224. Abijah's claim that the people were "never done an injustice" by Rehoboam seems an exaggeration/distortion of his father's actual dealings with the Israelites on that occasion.

[988] This affirmation corresponds to Abijah's charge against the Israelites at the end of 2 Chr 13:11: "... but you have forsaken him [God]."

[989] Greek: δημαγωγία. This is Josephus' only use of the term.

[990] Josephus elaborates on the biblical Abijah's reference (see 2 Chr 13:7b) to Rehoboam as "young and irresolute and unable to withstand them [Jeroboam and his supporters]," drawing from this characterization the conclusion that the Israelites ought to have dealt indulgently with his father. At the same time, Abijah here implicitly qualifies his earlier claim (8.277) that Rehoboam had done the Israelites "no injustice."

his father Solomon and his benefits.[991] For the merits of ancestors[992] ought to be an expiation for the offenses of their descendants.[993]

279 You, however, gave no thought to this, either then or now. Instead, you yourselves have brought so great an army against us.[994] In what have you put your trust of victory?[995] Is it in the golden heifers and the altars on the mountains—which are proofs of your impiety[996] rather than of your devotion?[997] Or is it your numbers, which are superior to those of our army, that make you hopeful?[998] **280** There is, however, no strength in an army of ten thousands that fights unjustly. For it is solely in justice and piety[999] towards God that well-founded hope of conquering opponents has been destined to lie.[1000] Such is the case with us who, from the beginning, have kept the ordinances and adored our own God,[1001] whom no hands have made from transitory matter[1002] nor did the scheme of a vile king construct [him] for the deception of the mobs.[1003] He [Judah's God] is rather his own work[1004] and the beginning and end of all things.[1005] **281** I advise you therefore even now to change your minds, and taking thought for what is better, to cease from making war and acknowledge

---

[991] Josephus' Abijah supplies an additional reason why the Israelites ought to have overlooked Rehoboam's irascibility, i.e. the good things Solomon had conferred upon them.

[992] This expression (Greek: αἱ τῶν πατέρων εὐποιίαι) occurs only here in Josephus, although it does have a counterpart in Nehemiah's invocation of the "memory of our fathers" and their justice that prompts God not to cease his care for the Jews in *Ant.* 11.169. On the concept of "the merits of the fathers" in Jewish tradition, see Marmorstein 1968: 147-71.

[993] This is the general truth that ought, according to the Josephan Abijah, to have prevailed in the case of Solomon's son Rehoboam and the Israelites' stance towards him.

[994] Josephus has Abijah again allude to the presence of the hostile Israelite force to which he had already referred in 8.276 (// 2 Chr 13:8a).

[995] Josephus turns Abijah's statement (2 Chr 13:8b) about those things which the Israelites (wrongfully) suppose to be their assurance of victory (their large numbers and the presence of the golden calves) into this pointed question.

[996] Greek: δείγματα τῆς ἀσεβείας. This phrase occurs only here in Josephus.

[997] Josephus appends to Abijah's mention of the golden calves from 2 Chr 13:8b a reference to another cultic item, i.e. the mountain-top altars (on these see 8.265), likewise adding the derogatory qualification of both objects. Conversely, he leaves aside Abijah's further charge (13:9) about the Israelites' having expelled their legitimate clergy and replaced these with priests of their own making.

[998] Josephus' king elaborates on the initial (false) "ground" for the Israelites' confidence adduced by

Abijah in 2 Chr 13:8b: "... because you are a great multitude."

[999] Greek: τὸ δίκαιον καὶ τὸ εὐσεβές. On the key wordpair "justice and piety" in Josephus see Mason 1991: 85-89, 142-52.

[1000] These reflections on the only true ground for an army's confidence lack a biblical counterpart. They serve to set up the contrast that Josephus' Abijah will, on the basis of 2 Chr 13:10-11, make between the Israelite and Judean forces in this regard.

[1001] With this general affirmation Josephus encompasses the more particular claims about the legitimacy of Judah's worship in all its dimensions that Abijah makes in 2 Chr 13:10-11.

[1002] Greek: ἐξ ὕλης φθαρτῆς. This phrase (with its nominal and adjectival elements transposed) occurs in reference to the human body in the context of Josephus' discourse on suicide in *War* 3.372.

[1003] This statement about the kind of God whom Judah does *not* worship lacks a biblical counterpart. Its allusion to the king's "deception of the mobs" recalls Josephus' denunciation of Jeroboam in 8.229 as one who "misled the people."

[1004] Greek: ὃς ἔργον... αὐτοῦ. Montgomery (1920-1921: 285) calls this formulation "a step in theosophy." See further Schlatter 1913: 17; 1932: 5, 6, n. 1. Contrast *Ant.* 6.61, where Samuel avers that the human race is οὐχ... ἴδιον [the human king's] ἔργον.

[1005] Greek: ἀρχὴ καὶ τέλος τῶν ἁπάντων. This double qualification of God has a counterpart in *Apion* 2.190, as also in Rev 21:6; 22:13; see van Unnik 1976. The foregoing negative and positive statements concerning the nature of Judah's God take the place of Abijah's affirmation (2 Chr 13:12a) about God and the trumpeter priests being with the Judean army.

the ancestral [ways] and him who has brought you to such greatness of well-being."[1006]

(11.2) 282 Abias addressed these things to the crowd.[1007] While he was still speaking, however, Hieroboam secretly sent some of his soldiers to encircle Abias from certain parts of the camp that were not visible.[1008] Once he [Abias] was surrounded in the midst of the enemy, his army grew fearful and their souls sank.[1009] Abias, however, encouraged them and appealed to them to have hope in God, for *he* was not encircled by the enemy.[1010]

283 All together they invoked their alliance with God[1011] while the priests sounded the trumpet;[1012] raising the battle cry, they advanced against the enemy.[1013] God impaired their [the Israelites'] minds and weakened their prowess. At the same time, he made Abias' army victorious,[1014] **284** for so great a slaughter has never yet been recorded as having happened, whether in the wars of the Greeks or the barbarians.[1015] Killing so many of Hieroboam's force, they were allowed by God to obtain a marvelous and outstanding[1016] victory. For they massacred 500,000 of the enemy[1017] and plundered their most solidly fortified cities, which they took by storm, namely Bethel and its toparchy[1018] and Isana[1019] and its toparchy.

285 After this defeat Hieroboam was no longer powerful during the time in which Abias held the upper hand.[1020] The latter died, surviving his victory for a short time

---

[1006] This conclusion to Abijah's discourse represents Josephus' version of the king's final appeal in 2 Chr 13:12b: "O sons of Israel, do not fight against the Lord... for you cannot succeed." His rendition adds a positive alternative to the prohibition enunciated by the biblical Abijah. The phrase "greatness of well-being" (Greek: μέγεθος εὐδαιμονίας) recalls God's promise to Solomon in 8.126, where the same expression occurs.

[1007] Josephus supplies this closing formula for Abijah's discourse (8.276-281).

[1008] Cf. 2 Chr 13:13a, where Jeroboam positions the ambush to attack Abijah "from behind." Josephus underscores the former's utter heedlessness—compare his similar reaction to his wife's earlier report to him in 8.274—, noting that he prepared his ambush even as Abijah is making his urgent appeal to the Israelites.

[1009] Josephus interprets the biblical reference to the Judeans' "crying to the Lord" upon discovering themselves surrounded (2 Chr 13:14a) in a negative sense, i.e. of their losing courage. He delays the associated notice on the priests' blowing the trumpets (13:14b) to a later point; see 8.283.

[1010] Josephus supplies this notice on Abijah's intervention, which allays the fears of his men. In 2 Chr 13:14-15 the Judeans appear to rally from their fears on their own.

[1011] This appeal to God's "alliance" (Greek: συμμαχία) with them as the king's and people's first act has no counterpart in 2 Chronicles 13. On Josephus' use terms of the συμμαχ-stem in relation to God, see the note to "loyal and an ally" at *Ant.* 5.98.

[1012] This is Josephus' delayed used of the notice of 2 Chr 13:14b, where the priests' blowing of trumpets is associated with the Judean army's initial response to finding itself surrounded, i.e. their "crying to the Lord."

[1013] 2 Chr 13:15a mentions the raising of the battle cry by the Judeans, but not their advance against the Israelites.

[1014] Josephus combines the separate notices on God's role in Judah's triumph of 2 Chr 13:15b (God "defeated Jeroboam and all Israel") and 16b ("God gave them [the Israelites] into their [the Judeans'] hand").

[1015] Josephus uses similar formulas, citing both "Greeks" and "barbarians," to highlight the unprecedented character of events related by him also elsewhere (see, e.g., *War* 1.1-2; 6.199; *Ant.* 4.12; 11.299), as does Dionysius of Halicarnassus (see, e.g., *Ant. rom.* 2.63.2; 5.79.2; 7.3.2, 12.4). Cf. Begg 1993: 107, n. 673.

[1016] This same adjectival combination (Greek: θαυμαστῆς καὶ διαβόητος) is used of the victory won by David's hero Eleazar over the Philistines in *Ant.* 7.309.

[1017] See 2 Chr 13:17. Josephus lacks an equivalent to the appended note of 13:18 that the Judeans' triumph was due to their trust in the Lord.

[1018] 2 Chr 13:19 cites Abijah's capture of "Bethel and its villages [literally: daughters]."

[1019] MT (2 Chr 13:19) ישנה (Eng.: "Jeshanah"); LXX B Κανά; LXX L Ἰεσσηνά (etc.); Josephus Ἰσανά (the site is mentioned by him also in *War* 1.334 and its parallel *Ant.* 14.458). 2 Chr 13:19 lists a 3rd site seized by Abijah, i.e. "Ephron/Ephrain" that Josephus leaves unmentioned.

[1020] See 2 Chr 13:20-21a.

and having reigned as king three years.[1021] He was buried in Hierosolyma, in the tombs of his ancestors.[1022] He left behind twenty-two sons and sixteen daughters, all of whom he fathered with his fourteen wives.[1023]

286 His son Asan[1024] assumed the kingship; the mother of this youth was named Machaia.[1025] With him in power, the country of the Israelites enjoyed peace for ten years.[1026] **(11.4) 287** These are the things we have received concerning Abias, the son of Roboam, son of Solomon.[1027]

Asa (Asan) succeeds

Hieroboam, the king of ten tribes, also died, having ruled as king for twenty-two years.[1028] His son Nabad[1029] succeeded him when Asan was already in the second year of exercising his kingship. Now the son of Hieroboam ruled for two years;[1030] he was similar to his father in impiety and vileness.[1031]

Nadab (Nabad) succeeds Jeroboam

288 During these two years he campaigned against Gabathon,[1032] a city of the Palestinoi, where he settled down in order to take it by siege.[1033] He died there, after being conspired against by a certain friend of his named Basanes,[1034] the son of Seidos.[1035] He, taking possession of the kingship after [Nabad's] death,[1036] destroyed

Baasha (Basanes) exterminates Jeroboam's line

[1021] Josephus derives his figure for the duration of Abijah's reign from 1 Kgs 15:2a// 2 Chr 13:2a. He goes beyond 2 Chronicles 13 itself in specifying that Abijah's demise came shortly after his victory over Jeroboam.

[1022] 2 Kgs 15:8a// 2 Chr 13:23aβ (Eng. 14:1aβ) have Abijah buried "in the city of David."

[1023] Josephus draws these statistics from 2 Chr 13:21b. In line with his regular practice, he omits the "source notice" for Abijah of 2 Chr 13:22// 1 Kgs 15:7.

[1024] MT (1 Kgs 15:8b// 2 Chr 13:23bα [Eng. 14:1bα]) אסא (Eng.: "Asa"); LXX BL Ἀσά; Josephus Ἄσανος. 1 Kgs 15:9 specifies that Asa acceded in Jeroboam's 20th (MT; LXX BL*: 24th; LXX L MS 127: 21st) year. On the Josephan Asa, see Feldman 1998a: 263-72.

[1025] MT (1 Kgs 15:10b) מעכה (Eng.: "Maacah"); LXX BL Ἀνά; Josephus Μαχαία. 1 Kgs 15:10 adds that she was "the daughter of Abishalom." On the confusion—eliminated in Josephus' own presentation—concerning the mothers of Abijah and Asa in the biblical documentation, see Begg 1993: 109-10, n. 689.

[1026] See 2 Chr 13:23bβ (Eng. 14:1bβ). As Marcus (*ad loc.*) points out, Josephus' reference to "the land of the Israelites" having peace under Asa—who was king rather of Judah—seems a "slip" on his part. In MT (and some LXX L manuscripts) the reference is simply to "the land," while LXX BL* correctly qualify the land in question as that "of Judah."

[1027] Josephus supplies this closing formula for his presentation of Abijah and his victory over Jeroboam (8.274-286).

[1028] Josephus here makes delayed use of the indications on Jeroboam's death and length of reign from 1 Kgs 14:20. He leaves aside the source notice for this king of 14:19.

[1029] MT (1 Kgs 14:20b; 15:25) נדב (Eng.: "Nadab"); LXX B (15:25) Ναβάθ; LXX L (15:25) Ναβάτ, etc.; Josephus Νάβαδος (this form involves a reversal of the 2nd and 3rd consonants of the MT one). On Nadab and his overthrow by Baasha in Josephus' presentation (8.287-289), see Begg 1993: 113-6.

[1030] Josephus derives these chronological indications for Nadab's reign from 1 Kgs 15:25 (where the LXX L manuscript 127 has him acceding in Asa's 3rd year). In proceeding immediately from the accession of Nadab (// 1 Kgs 14:20b) to the continuation of his reign (// 1 Kgs 15:25-32), Josephus departs from the sequence of 1 Kings 14-15, in which the account of the first 3 Judean kings (1 Kgs 14:21-15:24) supervenes between these 2 elements.

[1031] Compare 1 Kgs 15:26, which accuses Nadab of "walking in the way of his father, and in his sin which he made Israel to sin."

[1032] MT (1 Kgs 15:27) גבתון (Eng.: "Gibbethon"); LXX BL Γαβαθών; Josephus Γαβαθῶν.

[1033] See 1 Kgs 15:27b.

[1034] MT (1 Kgs 15:27) בעשא (Eng.: "Baasha"); LXX BL Βαασά; Josephus Βασάνης. Josephus heightens the pathos of Nadab's death by making his killer a "friend" of the king.

[1035] Josephus anticipates the name of Baasha's father from 1 Kgs 15:33, where MT calls him אחיה (Eng.: "Ahijah"), LXX BL Ἀχειά. The form Σειδοῦ read by Niese (and Marcus) is that of RO. Schlatter (*s.v.*) sees this form as a corruption of that found in the *Ed. pr.*, i.e. Μαχείλου, while Schalit (*s.v.*) maintains that Josephus himself wrote ὄνομα Ἀχειάς (see LXX).

[1036] 1 Kgs 15:28 (and 15:33a) specifies that Baasha acceded in the 3rd year of Asa (the L MSS 19 108 127 read "4th" in 15:28 and "5th" in 15:33a).

the whole family of Hieroboam.[1037] **289** Thus it happened, in accordance with the prophecy of God,[1038] that the relatives of Hieroboam who died in the city were torn and consumed by dogs, those in the country by birds.[1039] The house of Hieroboam therefore suffered due punishment for his impiety and lawless deeds.[1040]

Asa's religious and military initiatives

(12.1) 290 Asan, the king of Hierosolyma,[1041] by contrast, was of excellent character. He was oriented to the Deity, and neither did nor thought anything that was not directed towards piety and the observance of the ordinances.[1042] He ruled his own kingdom beneficially, rooting out whatever vileness there was in it and cleansing it of every blemish.[1043] **291** He had an army of picked men; of these, 300,000, armed with short shields and spears, were from the tribe of Iouda.[1044] Of the Benjamites, there were 250,000[1045] who carried long shields and bows.

Ethiopian invasion

292 He had already been reigning as king ten years[1046] when Zarai,[1047] the king of Ethiopia, campaigned against him with a great force of 900,000 infantry, 100,000 horsemen,[1048] and 300 chariots.[1049]

Asa appeals to God

293 When he had marched as far as the city of Maresa[1050] (this is located in the tribe of Iouda),[1051] Asan met him with his own force. He drew up his army opposite

---

[1037] See 1 Kgs 15:29a.

[1038] See 1 Kgs 15:29b, which states that Baasha acted "according to the word of the Lord which he spoke by his servant Ahijah the Shilonite," i.e. the one recorded in 14:10-11 (// 8.271). Josephus uses the phrase "according to the prophecy of God" (Greek: κατὰ τὴν τοῦ θεοῦ προφητείαν) also in *Ant.* 6.136; 9.129.

[1039] Josephus adds this reminiscence of his version of Ahijah's announcement to the wife of Jeroboam concerning the fate of Jeroboam's line in 8.270 (// 1 Kgs 14:11). In so doing, he now introduces the distinction between the respective ends of the city and country dwellers among Jeroboam's progeny from 1 Kgs 14:11, which he did not utilize in formulating 8.270 itself; see note on "food for dogs and birds" there.

[1040] Cf. 1 Kgs 15:30, which motivates the annihilation of Jeroboam's house (15:29) in terms of the king's sins and his provocation of the Lord's anger. The mention of Jeroboam's "impiety" (Greek: ἀσέβεια) recalls 8.288, where Nadab is said to be like his father in his "impiety," while the reference to the king's "lawless deeds" (Greek: ἀνομημάτα) echoes the ascription of these to Rehoboam in 8.251.

[1041] Compare the reference to "the country of the Israelites" as Asa's kingdom in 8.286.

[1042] Compare the general positive evaluation of Asa in 1 Kgs 15:11// 2 Chr 14:1 (MT; Eng. 14:2) as one who "did what was right in the eyes of the Lord" (15:11 adds "as David his father had done"). The wording of Josephus' evaluation seems inspired by the subsequent notice of 2 Chr 14:3(4): "he [Asa] commanded Judah to seek the Lord... and to keep the law and the commandment."

[1043] Josephus generalizes the catalogue of specific cultic deviations eliminated by Asa according to 1 Kgs 15:12 (male cult prostitutes and idols) and 2 Chr 14:2,

4 (MT; Eng. 14:3, 5) (altars, high places, pillars, Asherim, incense altars). Such generalizations of biblical "cultic particulars" are frequent in Josephus' rewriting of the Bible and seem designed to keep gentile readers from feeling overwhelmed by the details of an alien religious system.

[1044] Josephus' figure for the Judeans and the equipment he assigns them agrees with 2 Chr 14:7(8)a. He passes over the king's military preparedness measures cited in 14:5, 6aαb(6, 7aαb), i.e. building fortified cities and providing these with walls, towers, gates, and bars. He likewise omits Asa's intervening statement of confidence in the Lord of 14:6(7)aβ.

[1045] This same figure for the Benjamite forces is cited in LXX B 2 Chr 14:7(8)bα, whereas MT and LXX L have 280,000.

[1046] With this dating indication, Josephus alludes to his earlier mention (8.286// 2 Chr 13:23bβ [MT; Eng. 14:1bβ] of the peace the land enjoyed for 10 years under Asa. On Josephus' version of Asa's Ethiopian triumph and its sequel (MT 2 Chr 14:9-15:19), to which Kings has no equivalent, see Begg 1993: 117-28.

[1047] MT (2 Chr 14:8[9]) זרח (Eng.: Zerah); LXX BL Ζαρέ; Josephus Ζαραῖος.

[1048] 2 Chr 14:8(9)a simply assigns Zerah 1,000,000 men; Josephus divides these up among infantry and cavalry.

[1049] Josephus' figure for Zerah's chariots agrees with that given in 2 Chr 14:8(9)a.

[1050] MT (2 Chr 14:8[9]b) מרשה (Eng.: "Mareshah"); LXX B Μαρισήλ; LXX L Μαρησά; Josephus Μάρησα.

[1051] Josephus adds this localization of the site (which he had mentioned, under the name of "Marisa," as one of the 15 cities of Judah fortified by Rehoboam in 8.246// 2 Chr 11:8).

him in a certain valley called Sabatha,[1052] not far from the city. Despising the crowd of Ethiopians and raising a cry,[1053] he asked for victory from God and to do away with many ten thousands of the enemy.[1054] For he said that in going to meet Zarai in battle he put his confidence in nothing else but help from him who was able to make the few prevail over the many, and the weak over those superior to them.[1055]

(12.2) 294 When Asan had said these things, God signified that he would be victorious.[1056] Joyfully engaging, he killed many of the Ethiopians, as had previously been announced by God;[1057] he pursued those who turned to flee as far as the country of Gerar.[1058] They desisted from slaughtering and proceeded to plunder the cities—for they had captured Gerar[1059]—and their camp.[1060] The result was that they carried off a great deal of gold and silver.[1061] They likewise took away camels, beasts of burden,[1062] and flocks of sheep.

Asa's victory

295 After thus attaining so great a victory and profit[1063] from God,[1064] Asan and the army with him returned to Hierosolyma. A prophet named Azarias[1065] met them coming along the way.[1066] He directed them to halt their march,[1067] and began to say to them that they had duly obtained this victory from God, because they showed themselves just and holy[1068] and had done everything according to the will of God.[1069] 296 He therefore stated that if they persevered, God would grant them to always defeat their enemies and live in well-being.[1070] If, on the contrary, they turned

Azariah (Azarias) addresses victorious Judeans

[1052] MT (2 Chr 14:9[10]) צְפָתָה (Eng: "Zephathah"); LXX BL, seemingly reading Hebrew צָפֹנָה, translate with κατὰ βορρᾶν ("towards the north"); Josephus Σαβαθά (this is the reading of RO adopted by Niese; Marcus reads Σαφαθά with MLat).

[1053] Josephus prefaces Asa's "cry to the Lord" (2 Chr 14:10[11a]) with mention of his contempt for the Ethiopians' numerical superiority.

[1054] Josephus renders the content of Asa's appeal ("help us... let not man prevail against thee [God]") of 2 Chr 14:10[11]b more definite.

[1055] This is Josephus' rendering of the biblical Asa's statement of confidence that serves to motivate his appeals to the Lord in 2 Chr 14:10(11)b.

[1056] Josephus transposes into a divine assurance the statement of 2 Chr 14:11(12)a: "so the Lord defeated the Ethiopians before Asa and before Judah." The wording of the assurance picks up on the king's request for "victory" in 8.293.

[1057] In 2 Chr 14:12(13)aβ the Ethiopians are slain to a man; Josephus' version recalls his added reference to God's response to Asa's appeal at the start of 8.294.

[1058] See MT LXX L 2 Chr 14:12(13)aα, where the pursuit of the fleeing Ethiopians (14:11[12]b) extends "as far as Gerar" (LXX B: "until Gedor").

[1059] In MT LXX L 2 Chr 14:12b-13(13b-14) the Judeans smite and plunder "all the cities around Gerar (LXX B: Gedor)."

[1060] This reference to the Ethiopians' "camp" seems to have in view the notice on the Judeans' plundering "the tents" of the enemy livestock owners in 2 Chr 14:14(15)a.

[1061] Josephus adds these precious metals to the list of livestock seized by the Judeans of 2 Chr 14:14(15)a.

[1062] These are an addition to the list of captured livestock, i.e. sheep and camels, cited in 2 Chr 14:14(15)a.

[1063] Greek: νίκη καὶ ὠφέλεια. This collocation occurs only here in Josephus.

[1064] Josephus prefaces the mention of Asa's return of 2 Chr 14:14(15)b with this transitional notice, echoing the "victory language" of 8.293, 294. The formulation likewise recalls that used of Abijah's defeat of Jeroboam in 8.284, where the Judean army is "allowed by God to obtain a marvelous and outstanding victory."

[1065] MT (2 Chr 15:1) עֲזַרְיָהוּ (Eng.: "Azariah"); LXX BL and Josephus Ἀζαρίας.

[1066] See 2 Chr 15:2aα. Josephus, in line with his frequent practice, omits the preceding notice of 15:1 about the "Spirit of God" coming upon Asa's interlocutor.

[1067] Compare Azariah's opening, direct discourse words in 2 Chr 15:2aβ: "Hear me, Asa, and all Judah and Benjamin."

[1068] Greek: δίκαιοι καὶ ὅσιοι. This collocation recurs in reverse order in 8.245, where the Bethel prophet turns Jeroboam away from "holy and just deeds."

[1069] This statement, with its explicit allusion to the preceding battle episode and the moral to be drawn from it, has no counterpart in the words of Azariah as cited in 2 Chr 15:2-7.

[1070] This general affirmation corresponds to Azariah's conditional promise in 2 Chr 15:2bα, i.e. the Lord will be with the Judeans and be found by them if

away from his worship, the opposite of these things would happen.[1071] A time would come[1072] "when no truthful prophet will be found among your mob,[1073] nor a priest giving instruction about what is just.[1074] **297** The cities likewise would be desolate;[1075] the nation would be scattered over the entire earth and live a wandering and vagrant[1076] life."[1077] He advised them, however, while they had time, to be good and not forfeit God's benevolence towards themselves.[1078]

Judeans' response

When he heard this, the king and people rejoiced and took much care, both all in common and as individuals, for what was just.[1079] The king also sent round the country those who were to have oversight of the ordinances.[1080]

Deprivity of Baasha

(12.3) 298 This was the state of affairs under Asan, the king of the two tribes.[1081] I return now to the crowd of the Israelites and their king Basanes who, having killed Nadab, the son of Hieroboam, took hold of the rule.[1082] **299** Living in the city of Tharsale[1083] that he had made his residence, he reigned as king for twenty-four years.[1084] He was even more vile and impious[1085] than Hieroboam and his son; he inflicted many calamities on the people and outraged God.[1086]

---

they themselves are with him and seek him.

[1071] Compare Azariah's warning in 2 Chr 15:2bβ: "... but if you forsake him [God], he will forsake you."

[1072] Josephus understands the middle portion of Azariah's discourse (2 Chr 15:3-6) as speaking of *future* developments, whereas the words of his biblical counterpart are generally taken (see, e.g., the RSV rendering) to refer to Israel's *past*.

[1073] This warning concerning the future lack of a "truthful prophet" substitutes for Azariah's statement that Israel had for a long time been "without the true God" of 2 Chr 15:3a. Josephus uses the same expression "truthful prophet" (Greek: ἀληθής προφήτης) of Elijah in *Ant.* 9.23; cf. 8.234, where Jeroboam recognizes that "the man [Jadon] is truthful [Greek: ἀληθής]."

[1074] Josephus conflates Azariah's reference to Israel's (past) lack of both "a teaching priest" and "law" in 2 Chr 15:3b. He has no equivalent to the prophet's statement of 15:4 that when Israel sought the Lord in its distress he was found by them.

[1075] With this warning Josephus' Azariah turns into threats for the future the God-sent afflictions that had already befallen the inhabitants of the land(s) according to the prophet's words in 2 Chr 15:5-6.

[1076] Greek: ἀλήτης. Josephus' one other use of this term is in *Ant.* 3.87.

[1077] This announcement of a coming exile has no direct counterpart in Azariah's catalogue of Israel's (past) afflictions in 2 Chr 15:5-6. It does, however, recall Ahijah's prediction of Israel's coming dispersion in 8.271 (// 1 Kgs 14:15).

[1078] In 2 Chr 15:7 Azariah concludes his discourse to the Judean army with the exhortation "but you, take courage! Do not let your hands be weak, for your work shall be rewarded."

[1079] This generalized notice on the response of king

and people takes the place of the enumeration of Asa's specific cultic measures (removal of idols, repair of the altar) of 2 Chr 15:8. Compare Josephus' similar handling of the "cultic particulars" of 2 Chr 14:2, 4(3, 5) in 8.290.

[1080] This remark takes the place of the extended account of Asa's "gathering" both the southern and northern tribes for purposes of covenant-making in 2 Chr 15:9-15. Josephus has no equivalent to the appended complex of notices in 15:16-19 (Asa's deposing his mother Maacah from her position, destruction of her Asherah, continued toleration of the high places, dedication of votive gifts, and the absence of war until Asa's 35th regnal year).

[1081] Josephus supplies this closing notice for his (markedly abridged) account of Asa's early reign in 8.290-297 (// 2 Chr 14:1[2]-15:19). He will refocus on Asa in 8.304, after the northern-centered interlude in 8.298-303.

[1082] This notice resumes Josephus' initial mention of Baasha from 8.288-289, after the "Asa interlude" of 8.290-297. On Josephus' account of Baasha (8.298-302// 1 Kgs 15:33-16:4) and his conflict with Asa (8.303-306// 1 Kgs 15:16-22// 2 Chr 16:1-6), see Begg 1993: 129-39.

[1083] MT (1 Kg 15:33) תִּרְצָה (Eng.: "Tirzah"); LXX BL Θερσά; Josephus Θαρσάλη (This is the reading of the codices that Niese adopts; Marcus *ad loc.*, Schlatter *s.v.*, and Schalit *s.v.*, following the emendation of J. Hudson, read Θάρση).

[1084] This figure for Baasha's length of reign corresponds to that cited in 1 Kgs 15:33.

[1085] Greek: πονηρὸς καὶ ἀσεβής. Josephus applies this same collocation to the Bethel prophet in 8.243.

[1086] Josephus embellishes the judgment notice of 1 Kgs 15:34 on Baasha that simply makes him an imita-

God sent to him the prophet Jeous[1087] to predict that he would destroy and exterminate his entire family by means of the same calamities he had inflicted on the house of Hieroboam.[1088] **300** [He would do this] because, having been made king by him,[1089] he had given no thought to his benefits by governing the crowd justly and piously[1090]—as would have been good first for them and then pleasing to God as well.[1091] Instead, he imitated the most wicked[1092] Hieroboam and, though that one's soul was gone, showed his vileness to be alive.[1093] Jeous said that, since he [Basanes] was similar to him [Hieroboam], he would therefore experience the same sort of misfortune as he had.[1094]

Jehu (Jeous) denounces Baasha

301 Knowing in advance the calamities that were to happen to him, along with his whole family, because of the things he had dared to do, Basanes did not keep quiet for the future so as not to appear still more vile and die, or, by changing his mind subsequently with regard to what had occurred, obtain pardon[1095] [from God[1096]]. **302** Like athletes to whom a prize is extended, who, in their solicitude for this, do not discontinue exerting themselves for it, so too Basanes, after the prophet had told him in advance what was to be, thought the worse of calamities, namely, the destruction of his family and the loss of his house, the best of things. Each day, like an athlete of evil-doing,[1097] he increased his efforts in this respect.[1098]

Baasha ignores warning

303 Finally, again taking his army,[1099] he went out against a certain, not unimpor-

Baasha

---

tor—rather than a "surpasser"—of Jeroboam.

[1087] MT (1 Kgs 16:1) יֵהוּא (Eng.: "Jehu"); LXX B Εἰού; LXX L ᾿Ιού; Josephus ᾿Ιηοῦς. Josephus omits the name of his father ("Hanani," MT 16:1), while adding the title "prophet" to his name, perhaps under the influence of its occurrence in 16:7.

[1088] Josephus compresses and generalizes the wording of Jehu's announcement of punishment for Baasha's line of 1 Kgs 16:3-4 with its verbatim re-application (16:4) of "the dogs and birds prediction" used for the house of Jeroboam in 1 Kgs 15:11; cf. 8.289.

[1089] Jehu's word in 1 Kgs 16:2a has God recall his "exalting Baasha out of the dust" in order to make him Israel's "leader."

[1090] Greek: δικαίως καὶ εὐσεβῶς. The (nominalized) adjectival form of this collocation is used by King Abijah in his address to the Israelites in 8.280.

[1091] This initial charge about Baasha's failing to repay God's initiatives on his behalf, notwithstanding the benefits this would have brought him, lacks a counterpart in the biblical Jehu's word of 1 Kgs 16:2-4.

[1092] Greek: κάκιστος. Josephus applies this superlative adjectival form to Joseph's brothers in *Ant.* 2.128, 136, to the Transjordanian tribes in *Ant.* 4.167, to the murderers of Ishbosheth in *Ant.* 7.50, to Haman in *Ant.* 11.257, 265, and to Pheroras in *Ant.* 16.209, 212.

[1093] See 1 Kgs 16:2b, where Baasha is accused, in stereotyped terms, of walking in the way of Jeroboam and leading Israel into the sin that provokes the Lord's anger. The formulation of the charge he ascribes to Jehu here echoes Josephus' earlier editorial comment con-

cerning Baasha in 8.299.

[1094] This closing formula for Jehu's address picks up on its initial announcement of punishment for Baasha's line in 8.299, the double announcement on the matter framing the intervening accusations against the king in 8.300a.

[1095] Greek: συγγνώμη. On this term and its word-field in Greek literature generally, see Metzler 1991.

[1096] Greek: παρὰ τοῦ θεοῦ. These words are absent in RO and omitted by Niese. Marcus reads them with MSPLat.

[1097] Greek: ἀθλητὴς κακίας. Philo (*Somn.* 1.126) uses a similar—though positive—expression for Jacob, whom he calls "the athlete of noble pursuits" (Greek: ὁ ἀθλητὴς τῶν καλῶν).

[1098] This whole sequence (8.301-302) concerning Baasha's response to Jehu's words has no biblical counterpart. It does, however, have a certain parallel in Josephus' (also added) mention of Jeroboam's heedlessness in the face of the warning words of Jadon (8.245) and Ahijah (8.274). Also in this respect, then, Baasha appears as an imitator/surpasser of Jeroboam, as affirmed in 8.299-300.

[1099] This preliminary detail lacks a counterpart in 1 Kgs 15:17// 2 Chr 16:1. Its addition by Josephus serves to reinforce the parallelism between his portrayals of Jeroboam and Baasha: both men express their disregard for a prophetic warning by launching an attack on their respective Judean counterparts, i.e. Abijah (see 8.274) and Asa (see 8.303). Like 1 Kgs 15:17, Josephus has no equivalent to the specification of 2 Chr 16:1 that

captures Ramah (Aramathon)

tant, city named Aramathon,[1100] forty *stadia* distant from Hierosolyma.[1101] Having captured it, he fortified it, leaving behind in it the force he had previously decided on, so that from there they might set out to devastate the kingdom of Asan.[1102]

Asa asks for Syrian help

(12.4) 304 Fearing the advance of the enemy and calculating that the army left behind in Aramathon would inflict many calamities on everything over which he reigned as king,[1103] Asan sent envoys to the king of the Damascenes, along with gold and silver.[1104] He appealed to him to make an alliance,[1105] recalling that also their fathers' friendship was a [bond] between them.[1106] **305** The Syrian king will-

Syrian attack forces Baasha to withdraw

ingly accepted the sum of money. Making an alliance with him, he dissolved his friendship with Basanes.[1107] He sent the commanders of his own army against the cities over which he [Basanes] reigned as king and directed them to devastate these.[1108] They went and set fire to some of these, while they plundered others, namely Joan,[1109] Dan[1110] and Abelane,[1111] as well as many others.[1112] **306** When he heard this, the king of the Israelites ceased to build and fortify Aramathon[1113] Rather, he returned in haste to help his own devastated countrymen.[1114] Asan, for his part,

---

Baasha's move took place in Asa's 36th (MT; LXX BL 38th) regnal year.

[1100] MT (1 Kgs 15:17// 2 Chr 16:1) הרמה (Eng.: "Ramah"); LXX B (1 Kgs 15:17) Ῥααμά; LXX L (1 Kgs 15:17) and LXX BL (2 Chr 16:1) Ῥαμά; Josephus Ἀραμαθῶν.

[1101] Josephus supplies the indications concerning the city's status and distance from Jerusalem.

[1102] Josephus modifies and embellishes the notice of 1 Kgs 15:17// 2 Chr 16:1, in which Baasha simply "builds" Ramah with a view to blocking access to Asa.

[1103] Josephus supplies this statement concerning Asa's state of mind in the face of Baasha's assault that prompts his subsequent turning to the king of Syria.

[1104] From 1 Kgs 15:18// 2 Chr 16:2 Josephus omits the source of Asa's tribute (the temple and palace treasuries) as well as the name of the recipient, i.e. King Ben-hadad. He likewise provides an alternative title for this figure, whom the Bible calls "the king of Aram [Syria], who dwelt in Damascus."

[1105] Greek: συμμαχεῖν. This is the conjecture of Niese, followed by Marcus, for the nominal form συμμαχίαν of the codices.

[1106] Josephus reproduces only the opening portion of Asa's message to Ben-hadad as recorded in 1 Kgs 15:19// 2 Chr 16:3, i.e. his appeal for a "covenant" (LXX διαθήκη, which Josephus replaces with the verbal form συμμαχεῖν; see previous note), such as their fathers had maintained. He leaves aside Asa's (self-evident) reference to the gold and silver he has sent, as well as his request that the Syrian king dissolve his covenant with Baasha so that Baasha would withdraw from him (he will, however, make use of this request when recounting the Syrian king's response; see 8.305).

[1107] Josephus elaborates on the reference to Ben-hadad's "listening" to Asa at the start of 1 Kgs 15:20//

2 Chr 16:4, spelling out what this entailed on the basis of Asa's appeal, previously passed over by him, of 1 Kgs 15:19// 2 Chr 16:3 that the Syrian "break" his covenant with Baasha.

[1108] See 1 Kgs 15:20aβ// 2 Chr 16:4aβ. Josephus appends the indication concerning the purpose of the Syrian king's dispatching his officers against the Israelite cities. The term "devastate" (Greek: κακόω) here picks up on the same term as used of Baasha's own intentions regarding Asa's kingdom in 8.303.

[1109] MT (1 Kgs 15:20// 2 Chr 16:4) עיון (Eng.: "Ijon"); LXX BL 1 Kgs 15:20 Ἀίν; LXX B (2 Chr 16:4) Ἰώ; LXX L (2 Chr 16:4) Αἰδών; Josephus Ἰωάνου (this is the genitival form read by Niese; Naber and Marcus follow the conjecture of J. Hudson, i.e. Ἀϊών, while Schlatter [*s.v.*] and Schalit [*s.v.*] hold for an original Ἰώνη).

[1110] MT (1 Kgs 15:20// 2 Chr 16:4) דן (Eng.: "Dan"); LXX BL 1 Kgs 15:20// LXX L 2 Chr 16:4 (and Josephus) Δάν; LXX B 2 Chr 16:4 Δανώ.

[1111] MT (1 Kgs 15:20) אבל בית־מעכה (Eng.: "Abel-bethmaacah") / (2 Chr 16:4) אבל מים (Eng.: "Abel-maim"); LXX B 1 Kgs 15:20 Ἀδελμάθ; LXX L 1 Kgs 15:20 Ἀβελμαά; LXX B 2 Chr 16:4 Ἀβελμάν; LXX L 2 Chr 16:4 Ἀβελαίμ; Josephus Ἀβελάνη.

[1112] With this phrase Josephus alludes to the remaining, varying place names of 1 Kgs 15:20 (all Chinneroth, with all the land of Naphtali) and 2 Chr 16:4 (all the store-cities of Naphtali).

[1113] See 1 Kgs 15:21a// 2 Chr 16:5.

[1114] Compare 1 Kgs 15:21b (no parallel in 2 Chr 16:5): "he [Baasha] dwelt in [MT; LXX BL returned to] Tirzah." Josephus supplies the motivation for Baasha's return; its reference to his "devastated" countrymen recalls Ben-hadad's directive to his generals to "devastate" the Israelite cities in 8.305.

with the material he [Basanes] had prepared for building, erected two strong cities in the same place, one called Gabaa,[1115] the other Mastapha.[1116] **307** After this Basanes did not have the opportunity of campaigning against Asan.[1117] For he was overtaken by fate[1118] and buried in the city of Tharse,[1119] while his son Elan[1120] assumed the rule.[1121] The latter died after ruling two years,[1122] being murdered in a plot by Zambri,[1123] the cavalry commander of half his contingent.[1124] **308** For while he was enjoying hospitality in the house of his steward[1125] named Osa,[1126] Zambri, having persuaded some of the calvary who were under him to make an assault upon him,[1127] through them killed him,[1128] who had been left alone by his troops and their leaders, for all these were at the siege of Gabathon of the Palestinoi.[1129]

*Asa's
fortification*

*Ela (Elan)
succeeds
Baasha*

*Ela
assassinated by
Zimri (Zambri)*

[1115] MT (1 Kgs 15:22// 2 Chr 16:6) גבע (Eng.: "Geba"); LXX B 2 Chr 16:6 Γάβαε; LXX L 2 Chr 16:6 (and Josephus) Γαβαά; LXX BL 1 Kgs 15:22 (πᾶν βουνόν) "translate" the Hebrew place name. Like 2 Chr 16:6, Josephus has no equivalent to the specification of 1 Kgs 15:21 that the site pertained to Benjamin.

[1116] MT (1 Kgs 15:22// 2 Chr 16:6) המצפה (Eng.: "Mizpah"); LXX BL 2 Chr 16:6 Μασφά; Josephus Μασταφάς (so Niese; Naber and Marcus follow the conjecture of J. Hudson, based on Lat's Masphas, i.e. Μασφά, while Schalit *s.v.* proposes Μασφαθή). LXX BL 1 Kgs 15:22 translate the Hebrew place name with ἡ σκοπία ("the lookout").

Like 1 Kings, Josephus has no equivalent to the appended sequence of 2 Chr 16:7-10 on Asa's mistreatment of the seer Hanani for the latter's denunciation of his reliance on the king of Syria rather than the Lord as related in 16:1-6. His non-use of the Chronicles passage furthers his overall portrayal of Asa as an unblemished king.

[1117] Josephus supplies this transitional phrase connecting Baasha's ill-fated venture (// 1 Kgs 15:17-22// 2 Chr 16:1-6) with his demise (// 1 Kgs 16:6a). The addition sets up a final parallel between Jeroboam and Baasha, both of whom are reduced to military impotence for the remainder of their reigns after having unsuccessfully attacked their Judean counterparts; see 8.285 (Jeroboam) and 8.307 (Baasha). In accord with his regular practice, Josephus passes over the source notice for Baasha of 1 Kgs 16:5.

[1118] Greek: ἐφθάσθη ὑπὸ τοῦ χρεῶν. This circumlocution for "die" occurs only here in Josephus' writings.

[1119] Greek: Θαρσῆ; this is the emendation of J. Hudson, which is adopted by Niese, etc.; compare Ἀρσῆ (RO); Ἀρσάνη (MSP); Thersa (Lat). 1 Kgs 16:6a has Baasha "sleeping with his fathers" and being "buried in Tirzah."

[1120] MT (1 Kgs 16:6b) אלה (Eng.: "Elah"); LXX B Ἠλαάν; LXX L Ἠλα; Josephus Ἤλανος.

[1121] See 1 Kgs 16:6b. Josephus has no equivalent as this point (but see 8.309) to the appended allusion to Jehu's prophecy against Baasha and his house of

16:7, which itself duplicates Jehu's earlier word as cited in 16:1-4 (// 8.299-300).

[1122] Josephus leaves aside the synchronism for Elah's accession found at the opening of MT 1 Kgs 16:8, i.e. Asa's 26th regnal year (in LXX BL the corresponding notice occurs in 1 Kgs 16:6b, where the date given is Asa's 20th [the LXX L manuscript 127 has 29th] year of reign). Josephus also omits the specification of 1 Kgs 16:8b that Elah's 2-year reign took place "in Tirzah." On the contrast between Israel's political anarchy and Judah's internal stability developed by Josephus in 8.307-315, see Begg 1993: 140-50.

[1123] MT (1 Kgs 16:9) זמרי (Eng.: "Zimri"); LXX BL Ζαμβρεί; Josephus Ζαμβρίας.

[1124] Josephus' title for Zimri corresponds to that of LXX B 1 Kgs 16:9a, whereas according to MT and LXX L the general commanded half the royal "chariots."

[1125] Josephus uses the same title (Greek: οἰκονόμος) for Elah's host as do LXX BL 1 Kgs 16:9b; the corresponding MT phrase translates literally as "he who was over the house." Josephus leaves aside the source specification that the official's house was "in Tirzah."

[1126] MT (1 Kgs 16:9b) ארצא (Eng.: "Arsa"); LXX BL Ὠσά; Josephus Ὠσά (so Niese and Marcus; Naber and Weill read Ὀλσᾶ with SPE; Hudson conjectures Ὀρσᾶ, while Schlatter [*s.v*] and Schalit [*s.v.*] propose Ὀρσά).

[1127] In 1 Kgs 16:10a Zimri appears to act alone in murdering Elah, no confederates being mentioned. Josephus, more realistically, represents him having the cooperation of others.

[1128] Like LXX B 1 Kgs 16:10, 15, Josephus lacks an equivalent to the MT synchronic notice in these 2 verses, dating Elah's assassination to Asa's 27th year (LXX L has no counterpart to this indication in 16:10, while in 16:15 its manuscripts 19, 109, 93 read the 22nd, manuscript 127 the 21st year).

[1129] Josephus anticipates this indication concerning the whereabouts of Elah's forces—whose absence serves to explain the ease with which the king could be assassinated—from 1 Kgs 16:15b where, appended to the notice on Zimri's accession (16:15a), one finds the no-

Zimri's 7-day reign

(12.5) 309 Once he had murdered Elan, Zambri, the cavalry commander, himself ruled as king and destroyed the entire family of Basanes, in accordance with the prophecy of Jeous. For it happened that his line was annihilated root and branch[1130] on account of his impiety, in the same way as was that of Hieroboam, as we have written.[1131] **310** When, however, the army besieging Gabathon found out about the matter of the king and that Zambri, who had killed him, held the kingship, it appointed its leader Amarin[1132] king.[1133] Bringing up the army from Gabathon to Tharse, he arrived at the palace; attacking the city, he captured it by storm.[1134] **311** When Zambri saw the city captured, he fled to the innermost part of the palace.[1135]

Omri (Amarin) secures rule

He set fire to this and burned himself up along with it,[1136] having ruled as king for seven days.[1137] Immediately, the people of the Israelites was divided; some of them wished Thamanai[1138] to rule as king, others rather Amarin.[1139] Those who desired the latter to rule were victorious and killed Thamanai; Amarin then reigned as king over the whole mob.[1140]

Reign of Omri

312 [Acceding] in the thirtieth year of Asan,[1141] Amarin ruled twelve years: six of these in the city of Tharse, the rest[1142] in the city named Somareon,[1143] which is called Samareia by the Greeks.[1144] Amarin named it thus[1145] after Somar,[1146] the one

---

tice "now the troops were encamped against Gibbethon, which belonged to the Philistines." Josephus has made previous reference to this site and an earlier Israelite siege of it under Nadab in 8.288.

[1130] Greek: πρόρριζον ἀπολέσθαι. This same construction recurs in 8.314 (subject: the Deity) and 11.213. The adjective πρόρριζος occurs in other constructions also in *Ant.* 7.376; 8.127; 9.109.

[1131] See 1 Kgs 16:11-13, whose wording Josephus compresses. On his account of the extermination of Jeroboam's line, see 8.288-289 (// 1 Kgs 15:29-30). Josephus leaves aside the source notice for Elah of 1 Kgs 16:14.

[1132] MT (1 Kgs 16:16b) עמרי (Eng.: "Omri"); LXX B Ζαμβρεί; LXX L Ἀμβρεί; Josephus Ἀμαρῖνος.

[1133] See 1 Kgs 16:15b-16. Josephus has no equivalent at this point to the notice of 1 Kgs 16:15a about Zimri's reigning 7 days in Tirzah during the 27th year of Asa (so MT; LXX B lacks the synchronization with Asa's reign and its original version gives Zimri a 7-*year* rule, while LXX L* dates Zimri's accession to the Judean's 22nd [MS 127 33rd] year). Josephus will reproduce the datum about Zimri's length of reign in 8.311.

[1134] 1 Kgs 16:17 only mentions Omri's "besieging" Tirzah. Josephus bases his further statement about his "capturing it by storm" on the allusion in 16:18 to Zimri's "seeing that the city was taken."

[1135] See 1 Kgs 16:18a, which refers to "the citadel (MT; LXX BL: cave) of the king's house." Josephus' allusion to the "innermost part" of the palace corresponds to Tg.'s rendering.

[1136] See 1 Kgs 16:18b.

[1137] Josephus derives this figure from 1 Kgs 16:15a

(MT LXX L), earlier passed over by him, while omitting the preceding synchronic notice that places Zimri's reign in the 27th (so MT) year of Asa. Likely in view of the extreme brevity of Zimri's reign, Josephus passes over the (negative) judgment notice concerning him of 16:19, just as he does the source notice of 16:20.

[1138] MT (1 Kgs 16:21) תבני (Eng.: "Tibni"); LXX B Θαμνεί; LXX L Θαβεννεί; Josephus Θαμαναῖος. Josephus omits the name of the pretender's father, i.e. "Ginath" (MT).

[1139] See 1 Kgs 16:21, where (as in 16:16) the MT name for the other, ultimately victorious claimant is "Omri."

[1140] Compare 1 Kgs 16:22, which states that "Tibni died," without specifying whether this happened violently or not. Like MT, Josephus has no equivalent to the phrase "and Jotam [B; L Joram] his brother after him" that LXX BL 1 Kgs 16:22 append to their mention of Tibni's death. He likewise lacks a counterpart to these witnesses' odd concluding indication that Omri ruled "with [the already dead] Thameni/Thabennei."

[1141] 1 Kgs 16:23 dates Omri's accession to Asa's *31st* year

[1142] 1 Kgs 16:23 does not specify where Omri spent the 2nd half of his reign. Josephus' indication on the point is based on the mention of Omri's purchase of the "hill of Samaria" in 16:24.

[1143] MT (1 Kgs 16:24) שמרון (Eng.: "Samaria"); LXX B Σεμερών; LXX L Σομορῶν; Josephus Σωμαρεών.

[1144] Josephus appends this contemporary Greek equivalent to the city's biblical Hebrew name.

who sold him[1147] the mountain on which he constructed the city.[1148]

313 He was in no way different from those who ruled as kings before him, except in being worse than they.[1149] For they all kept seeking how they might turn the people away from God by their daily impieties. It was because of this that God caused them to do away with one another and to leave none of their families alive.[1150] He too died in Samareia[1151] and his son Achab[1152] succeeded him.

(12.6) 314 From these things one may learn that the Deity has very close oversight of human affairs and how he loves the good,[1153] but hates[1154] and annihilates root and branch[1155] those who are vile. For many kings of the Israelites, one after the other, were, within a short time, designated to be calamitously destroyed, along with their families, on account of their lawlessness and injustice.[1156]

Theological reflection on Israel's history

Asan, the king of Hierosolyma and the two tribes, on the other hand, given his piety and justice, was led by God to a long and happy old age.[1157] He died felicitously,[1158] after ruling forty-one years.[1159] **315** Upon his death his son Josaphat[1160] assumed the leadership; he was born to a wife of Asan named Abidas.[1161] From his deeds all have recognized that he was indeed an imitator of his ancestor David in

Jehoshaphat (Josaphat) succeeds Asa

[1145] The above rendition presupposes the emendation of Marcus *ad loc.*, followed by Schalit *s.v.*, i.e. οὕτως Ἀμαρῖνος.

[1146] MT (1 Kgs 16:24) שמר (Eng.: "Shemer"); LXX B Σεμηρ; LXX L Σέμμηρ; Josephus Σώμαρος.

[1147] Josephus omits the biblical purchase price, i.e. "2 talents of silver" (1 Kgs 16:24).

[1148] 1 Kgs 16:24 has Omri "fortifying the hill."

[1149] 1 Kgs 16:25b accuses Omri of "doing more evil than all who were before him." Josephus omits the stereotyped reference to Omri's persisting in the "way of Jeroboam" of 16:26, just as he does the source notice for Omri of 16:27.

[1150] With this appended notice Josephus sums up his history of the northern kingdom thus far, highlighting its violent instability as a divinely-initiated punishment for the impiety of its kings.

[1151] Josephus omits the biblical mention of Omri's being buried "in Samaria" (1 Kgs 16:28aβ), having him rather die there (cf. 16:28aα).

[1152] MT (1 Kgs 16:28b) אחאב (Eng.: "Ahab"); LXX BL Ἀχαάβ; Josephus Ἄχαβος. On Josephus' portrayal of Ahab and its many positive retouchings of the biblical presentation of him, see Feldman 1998a: 273-90.

[1153] Compare 8.173, where the Queen of Sheba praises God, who "loves" the country and people of Israel.

[1154] This formulation recalls 8.129, where God predicts that other peoples will marvel over his "hating" the unfaithful Israelites.

[1155] Greek: προρρίζους ἀπολέσθαι. This is the same construction used in 8.309 in connection with the annihilation of Baasha's family.

[1156] Greek: παρανομία καὶ ἀδικία. This collocation

occurs only here in Josephus. The reflection on the history of the Northern Kingdom presented by him in 8.314 draws a moral from Josephus' previous remarks on the subject in 8.313. Its wording recalls that used in such other reflective passages as *Ant.* 1.14 and 10.277-281.

[1157] In the interest of maintaining a sharp contrast between the fates of the impious northern kings and that of the pious Judean Asa, Josephus conveniently passes over both the summary reference of 1 Kgs 15:23b to the foot disease that befell the latter, as well as the elaboration of this item in 2 Chr 16:12, with its allusion to the afflicted Asa's "seeking" not the Lord, but his physicians. Compare Josephus' earlier omission of the equally unedifying episode of Asa's confrontation with the seer Hanani of 2 Chr 16:7-10 concerning his recourse to Syrian help; see the note on "Mastapha" at 8.306.

[1158] Greek: εὐμοίρως. This adverb is *hapax* in Josephus.

[1159] Josephus' figure for the length of Asa's reign corresponds to that given in 1 Kgs 15:10a and 2 Chr 16:13. He leaves aside both the mention of Asa's burial (15:24aβ// 16:14 [which adds a reference to the "great fire" made in Asa's honor]) and the source notice for the king of 15:23a// 16:11.

[1160] MT (1 Kgs 15:24b// 2 Chr 17:1) יהושפט (Eng.: "Jehoshaphat"); LXX B 1 Kgs 15:24b Ἰωσαφάθ; LXX L 1 Kgs 15:24b// LXX BL 2 Chr 17:1a Ἰωσαφάτ; Josephus Ἰωσαφάτης.

[1161] MT (1 Kgs 22:42b) עזובה (Eng.: "Azubah"); LXX B 1 Kgs 22:42b// 2 Chr 20:31 Ἀζουβά; LXX L (1 Kgs 16:28a) Γαζουβά; Josephus Ἀβιδάς. Josephus leaves aside the name of her father, i.e. "Shilhi" (MT).

his courage and piety.[1162] But there is no necessity to speak about this king at
present.[1163]

Ahab (Achab) introduced

(13.1) 316 Achab, the king of the Israelites, for his part, resided in Samareia; he
exercised his rule for twenty-two years.[1164] He was in no way different from the
kings before him, except in his contriving still worse [things] in accordance with his
excessive vileness.[1165] For he imitated all their evil deeds and outraging of the Deity, zealously emulating[1166] Hieroboam's lawlessness, in particular.[1167] 317 For he
paid homage to the heifers constructed by that one,[1168] and built other strange objects as well.[1169]

Jezebel's (Jezabele's) innovations

He married the daughter of Eithobal,[1170] king of the Tyrians and Sidonians,[1171]
whose name was Jezabele;[1172] from her he learned to pay homage to her own
gods.[1173] 318 She was an energetic[1174] and bold[1175] little woman;[1176] she plunged into
such great licentiousness[1177] and madness[1178] that she built a sanctuary to the Tyrian

---

[1162] Like Weill *ad loc.*, I take the reference here to
be to Jehoshaphat, who has just been introduced by
Josephus; so understood, the notice corresponds to the
(qualifiedly) positive evaluation of him in 1 Kgs 22:43
// 2 Chr 20:32-33. Marcus (*ad loc.*), on the contrary,
sees it as a final allusion to Asa.

[1163] Josephus supplies this (provisional) closing
notice for Jehoshaphat (see previous note), to whom he
will return in 8.393, following a long segment (8.316-
392) dealing with events in the Northern Kingdom.

[1164] See 1 Kgs 16:29. Josephus omits the synchronic notice of MT 16:29 dating Ahab's accession to
Asa's 38th year (LXX BL: the 2nd year of Jehoshaphat).
On Josephus' initial presentation of Ahab in 8.316-318
(// 1 Kgs 16:29-34), see Begg 1993: 151-5.

[1165] Compare 1 Kgs 16:30, where Ahab is accused
of "doing evil in the sight of the Lord more than all that
were before him."

[1166] Greek: ζηλόω. Josephus uses this verb 4 times
elsewhere, i.e. *Ant.* 6.343; 14.116, 154; 20.41 (the 2
uses in *Antiquities* 14 are citations from Greek sources).
His relatively infrequent use of the term likely has to
do with its being a cognate of the noun ζηλωτής, the
self-designation of the "Zealots," of whom he so vehe-
mently disapproved.

[1167] 1 Kgs 16:31a speaks in stereotyped terms of
Ahab's "walking in the sins of Jeroboam...."

[1168] Josephus adds this reference to *the* sin of Jeroboam, this recalling his account of that king's idolatrous initiative in 8.226.

[1169] This notice seems to allude to the 2 specific
idolatrous items whose construction is attributed to
Ahab in 1 Kgs 16:32b-33a, i.e. "an altar for Baal in the
house of Baal in Samaria" and an "Asherah." In 8.318
Josephus will ascribe the making of these objects rather
to Ahab's wife Jezebel.

[1170] MT (1 Kgs 16:31a) אתבעל (Eng.: "Ethbaal");
LXX B Ἰεθεβάαλ; LXX L Ἰεθβάαλ; Josephus Εἰθώβαλος

(thus Niese; Marcus *ad loc.* and Schalit *s.v.* read
Ἰθώβαλος with MSP).

[1171] 1 Kgs 16:31b calls Ethbaal simply "king of the
Sidonians." Josephus' addition of the "Tyrians" has in
view his subsequent quotation (see 8.324) of Menander, who calls Ethbaal "king of the Tyrians."

[1172] MT (1 Kgs 16:31) איזבל (Eng.: "Jezebel"); LXX
BL Ἰεζάβελ; Josephus Ἰεζαβέλη.

[1173] 1 Kgs 16:31b, after mentioning Ahab's marrying of Jezebel, goes on to state "he went and served
Baal, and worshiped him." Josephus spells out the connection between Ahab's 2 initiatives, while also generalizing the biblical reference to a single, named foreign
deity, i.e. Baal.

[1174] Josephus employs this adjective (Greek: δραστήριος) with negative connotations as here also in *War*
2.590 (John of Gischala); 4.312 (John of Gischala); and
Ant. 9.27 (King Joram of Israel). See Begg 1993: 153,
n. 991.

[1175] Josephus uses this adjective (Greek: τολμηρός)
with clearly negative connotations as here also in *War*
1.529 (Diophantus); 2.116 (Glaphyra); 4.343 (2 Zealots); *Ant.* 1.113 (Nimrud); 4.248 (the false accuser of a
virgin); 6.178 (David, in Eliab's reproach to him);
8.358 (Naboth's [false] accusers); and 17.32 (Antipater).
See Begg 1993: 153, n. 992.

[1176] Greek: γύναιον. This diminutive occurs 36
times in Josephus. As Schlatter notes (1932: 148), its
frequent use does not speak for Josephus' high appreciation of women.

[1177] This term (Greek: ἀσέλγεια) recalls 8.252, where
it appears in Josephus' reflection concerning subjects
who do not allow their own self-control to stand as a
"reproach to the licentiousness" of their rulers.

[1178] This is Josephus' only collocation of the terms
"licentiousness" (Greek: ἀσέλγεια) and "madness"
(Greek: μανία).

god,[1179] whom they call Belias[1180] and planted a grove of all kinds of trees.[1181] She [also] installed priests and false prophets for this god; the king himself had many such persons around him,[1182] exceeding in senselessness and vileness[1183] all those who preceded him.[1184]

(13.2) 319 A certain prophet[1185] of the greatest God[1186] from the city of Thessebone[1187] in the Galaadite country[1188] approached Achab and said that God had announced to him that he would send down neither rain nor dew upon the country in those years, apart from his [the prophet's] appearing.[1189] Having sworn to these things,[1190] he withdrew[1191] to the southern regions,[1192] making his residence beside a

Elijah's appearance and withdrawal

[1179] Josephus supplies this specification concerning "Belias" (biblical Baal); compare his added qualification of Ethbaal as king "of the Tyrians" in 8.317.

[1180] MT (1 Kgs 16:32) בעל (Eng.: "Baal"); LXX BL Βάαλ; Josephus Βελίας (Niese; Schalit *s.v.* reads Βάαλ, the LXX form). 1 Kgs 16:32 attributes the erection of the Baal altar "in the house of Baal in Samaria" to Ahab himself.

[1181] MT 1 Kgs 16:33a speaks of Ahab himself making an "Asherah." In agreement with LXX BL, Josephus renders this term with the word "grove" (Greek: ἄλσος); see Begg 1993: 153, n. 998. In contrast to both MT and LXX, he attributes the initiative to Jezebel rather than to Ahab.

[1182] The catalogue of Ahab and Jezebel's misdeeds in 1 Kgs 16:30-34 does not refer to these figures. Josephus' mention of the couple's patronage of such groups here is inspired by (and serves to prepare for) subsequent biblical references to them; see 1 Kgs 18:19; 2 Kgs 10:19.

[1183] This collocation (Greek: ἄνοια καὶ πονηρία) occurs only here in Josephus. The reference to Ahab's "exceeding in vileness" recalls the phrase "excessive vileness" used of him in 8.316.

[1184] Compare 1 Kgs 16:33b, which avers that Ahab "did more to provoke the Lord to anger than all the kings of Israel who were before him."

Josephus has no equivalent to the notice of 1 Kgs 16:34 (MT LXX B; LXX L lacks the verse) about the Bethelite Hiel rebuilding Jericho in Ahab's time, paying for his doing so with the lives of his eldest and youngest sons, in accordance with the curse pronounced by Joshua in Josh 6:26 against anyone who would rebuild Jericho. The absence of such an equivalent is all the more remarkable given the fact that, in his version of Josh 6:26 in *Ant.* 5.31, Josephus explicitly states that he will subsequently relate the fulfillment of Joshua's curse. Various (complementary) explanations of this phenomenon can be suggested. It might, e.g., reflect Josephus' dependence on a text like that of LXX L, which lacks 1 Kgs 16:34. Alternatively, it might be due to Josephus' (belated) realization that the text of 1 Kgs 16:34, with its seeming suggestion of

human sacrifice, could well prove off-putting to gentile readers. Still another possibility is that, given the extended length of time it took him to compose *Antiquities*, Josephus simply forgot his announcement back in 5.31 when he came to write 8.318. See Begg 1993: 154.

[1185] Josephus uses this title in place of the proper name "Elijah" (which he will cite for the first time only in 8.329) of MT LXX L 1 Kgs 17:1 (LXX B has both the title and the name). On Josephus' presentation of Elijah's initial activities in 8.317-327 (// 1 Kings 17), see Begg 1993: 156-65 and on his overall treatment of Elijah, see Feldman 1998a: 291-306.

[1186] Greek: προφήτης τοῦ μεγιστοῦ (thus Marcus; Niese reads μεγάλου with RO) Θεοῦ. Josephus uses this same designation for Jonah in *Ant.* 9.211.

[1187] MT (1 Kgs 17:1) מתשבי (RSV: "from Tishbe" [this rendering is based on the LXX readings, whereas the vocalized Hebrew form has the meaning "from the settlers"]); LXX B Θεσβών; LXX L Θεσσεβών; Josephus Θεσσεβώνη (this is the reading of RO, which Niese follows; Schalit [*s.v.*] reads Θεσβώνης with MSPE). Josephus omits the related epithet "the Tishbite" used of Elijah in 17:1.

[1188] MT 1 Kgs 17:1 calls the region "Gilead," LXX BL "Galaad."

[1189] Josephus characteristically substitutes this closing "condition" for the conclusion of Elijah's announcement in 1 Kgs 17:1b, i.e. "except by my word." The formulation looks ahead to Elijah's subsequent appearance before Ahab and the resultant rain; see 8.328, 346.

[1190] Compare Elijah's opening "oath formula" in 1 Kgs 17:1b: "as the Lord... lives, before whom I stand."

[1191] Josephus compresses the account of 1 Kgs 17:2-5, where Elijah's "withdrawal" (17:5) comes in response to a divine command/assurance (17:2-4). In his presentation—which eliminates the biblical reference to the Lord's "word" (see 17:2)—Elijah acts on his own initiative in this instance.

[1192] In 1 Kgs 17:2-5 Elijah, at God's direction, heads "east" across the Jordan. Josephus' modification may have been prompted by the consideration that the area east of the Jordan was also part of Ahab's kingdom,

certain stream,[1193] from which he also had his drink;[1194] for ravens brought him food daily.[1195]

320 When the river dried up because of the drought,[1196] he went at God's direction[1197] to the city of Sariphtha[1198] (it is not far from Sidon and Tyre—it lies between them),[1199] for he would find there a widow-woman who would provide food for him.[1200]

321 When he was not far from the gate, he saw a woman, a day-laborer, gathering wood.[1201] When God disclosed to him that this was the one who would supply him with food,[1202] he, after approaching and greeting her, appealed to her to bring him water so that he might drink.[1203] As she went off, he called her back and directed her to bring bread as well.[1204]

322 She, however, swore that she had nothing except a handful of meal and a little oil;[1205] she was going to collect wood so that she might knead this and make bread for herself and her child.[1206] After that, she would die, she said, consumed by the famine, there being nothing left any longer.[1207] He, however, said: "Be of good cheer, depart, expecting better things;[1208] but first make a little something for me and bring it.[1209] For I announce to you[1210] that neither that vessel of meal nor the jar of oil will fail until God sends rain."[1211] **323** Upon the prophet's saying this, she went

---

and so would not have afforded Elijah as secure a refuge as he would find in the "south," i.e. in Judah (compare 1 Kgs 19:3, where, fleeing Jezebel, Elijah heads south, to Beersheba of Judah).

[1193] 1 Kgs 17:3, 5 identify the stream as "Cherith."

[1194] See 1 Kgs 17:6b.

[1195] 1 Kgs 17:6a specifies that the ravens brought Elijah "bread and meat" both in the morning and the evening.

[1196] See 1 Kgs 17:7. In 8.319 Josephus called Elijah's source of water a "stream" (in line with the consistent terminology of 1 Kgs 17:2-7); his designation of it now as an actual "river" underscores the severity of the drought—this dried up even a river.

[1197] In contrast to his handling of the biblical presentation of Elijah's initial move (see 8.319 in comparison with 1 Kgs 17:2-5), Josephus does follow 17:8-9 in ascribing Elijah's 2nd move to a divine prompting. At the same time, he eliminates the reference to the "word of God" coming to the prophet of 17:8.

[1198] MT (1 Kgs 17:8) צרפתה (Eng.: "Zarephath"); LXX BL Σαρεπτά; Josephus Σαριφθά (this is the reading of RO followed by Niese; Marcus reads Σαρεφθά with MSPLat).

[1199] Josephus elaborates on the datum of 1 Kgs 17:9, which qualifies Zarephath as "belonging to Sidon." Compare his addition (8.317) "of the Tyrians" to the mention of Ethbaal as "king of the Sidonians" in 1 Kgs 16:31.

[1200] In 1 Kgs 17:9 God informs Elijah that he has already "commanded" the widow to feed him.

[1201] See 1 Kgs 17:10a. Josephus adds the characterization of her as a "day laborer" (Greek: χερνῆτις), the

same term he uses for the Endor medium in *Ant.* 6.339.

[1202] With this added phrase, Josephus accounts for Elijah's knowing which particular woman in the foreign city he is to approach.

[1203] See 1 Kgs 17:10b. Josephus adds the preliminary details about Elijah's approaching and greeting the woman.

[1204] In 1 Kgs 17:11b Elijah asks for a "morsel of bread."

[1205] See 1 Kgs 17:12a. As usual, Josephus leaves aside the wording ("as the Lord your God lives") of the woman's oath.

[1206] See 1 Kgs 17:12b. Josephus' use of the singular "child" agrees with MT, whereas LXX BL read the plural "sons."

[1207] Josephus elaborates on the woman's closing word in 1 Kgs 17:12 ("that we [she and her son] may eat it, and die"), supplying the woman with a reason (i.e. the current famine) why she is expecting imminent death.

[1208] This opening word of assurance is Josephus' version of the exhortation "fear not" with which Elijah's reply to the woman begins in 1 Kgs 17:13.

[1209] In 1 Kgs 17:13bα Elijah asks more specifically for a "little cake." Josephus omits the prophet's further statement (17:13bβ), i.e. once she has provided for him, the woman may prepare something for herself and her son.

[1210] Compare the "messenger formula" ("for thus says the Lord the God of Israel") with which Elijah begins his announcement/promise of 1 Kgs 17:14.

[1211] See 1 Kgs 17:14.

to her home and did what had been said and had food available for herself, her child, and the prophet.[1212] For none of these things failed them until the drought ceased.[1213]

324 Menander[1214] too mentions this drought, saying this about events under King Ithobal of the Tyrians:[1215]

Heneander's testimony on drought

"In his time there was a shortage of water from the month Hyperberetai[1216] until the Hyperberetai of the following year. When he made intercession, severe thunderstorms struck. He founded the city of Botrus in Phoinike and Auza in Libye."

In disclosing these things, Menander was recording the drought in the time of Achab, for it was in his time that Ithobal ruled the Tyrians.[1217]

(13.3) 325 Now when the son[1218] of the woman of whom we spoke previously, who fed the prophet,[1219] fell so sick that his soul left him and he seemed dead,[1220] she cried out, injuring herself with her own hands, and emitted sounds that expressed her suffering.[1221] She laid the blame on the presence in her house of the prophet,[1222] as one who had come to punish her offenses; it was because of this that the boy had died.[1223]

Elijah resuscitates woman's son

326 He appealed to her, however, to be of good cheer and to hand her son over to him, for he would give him back alive.[1224] When she therefore handed him over, he carried him into the room in which he resided. Putting him down on the bed,[1225] he cried out to God that he was not honorably compensating the one who had received and fed him, by snatching away her son.[1226] He asked him to send his soul into the boy again and grant him life.[1227]

327 God, for his part, taking compassion on the mother, while also wishing to do

---

[1212] See 1 Kgs 17:15. Josephus supplies the title "prophet" for Elijah (see 8.319).

[1213] This concluding statement takes the place of the notice (1 Kgs 17:16) about matters proceeding "according to the word of the Lord" as spoken by Elijah (see 1 Kgs 17:13-14).

[1214] On Menander and Josephus' previous citation of him in connection with the exchange between Solomon and King Hiram, see 8.144-146.

[1215] Josephus' reference to Ithobal as "king of the Tyrians" here (compare 8.317, where he is called "king of the Tyrians and Sidonians") draws on Menander's mention of Ithobal's "ruling the Tyrians" in the passage Josephus is about to cite.

[1216] This Greek month-name corresponds to late October; see Schalit *s.v.*

[1217] Having cited Menander's testimony, Josephus here correlates this with the biblical record (see 1 Kgs 16:31; 17:1). Compare his linking the witness of Herodotus and the Bible's account of the invasion of Judah by Shishak in 8.253, 261.

[1218] In 1 Kgs 17:17-24 the woman's son remains nameless, as he does throughout Josephus' version (8.325-327). In, e.g., *y. Sukkah* 5.55a and *Gen.Rab.* 98.11 he is identified with the future prophet Jonah.

[1219] Josephus here re-introduces Elijah's hostess from 8.323, after the "Menander interlude" of 8.324.

[1220] See 1 Kgs 17:17, where the reference is to there being "no breath in him." Josephus adds the notice on

his "seeming to be dead," thus accentuating the gravity of the situation (and so also the stature of Elijah who proves capable of resolving it). On Josephus' re-telling of Elijah's resuscitation (1 Kgs 17:17-24) in 8.325-327, see Hogan 1992: 216-7.

[1221] Josephus supplies this description of the woman's distress. Compare his similar, likewise added, portrayal of the afflicted mother of the deathly sick prince Abijah in 8.273.

[1222] In 1 Kgs 17:18 the woman addresses Elijah as "man of God." Josephus' alternative title is paralleled in Tg.

[1223] See 1 Kgs 17:18, where the woman accuses Elijah of coming to "bring my sin to remembrance." Josephus' formulation spells out the meaning of that charge.

[1224] Josephus expatiates on Elijah's command in 1 Kgs 17:19aα, underscoring the prophet's assurance that he will indeed be able to resuscitate the boy.

[1225] See 1 Kgs 17:19aβb, which specifies that Elijah lodged in "the upper chamber."

[1226] Josephus recasts Elijah's urgent question about whether God has "slain" the woman's son (1 Kgs 17:20) into a pointed statement by the prophet.

[1227] See 1 Kgs 17:21b. Josephus omits the intervening notice (17:21a) on Elijah's stretching himself upon the boy's body 3 times, the purpose of which remains unclear.

the prophet the favor that his having come to her house should not seem a calamity,[1228] contrary to all expectation, revived [him].[1229] She thanked the prophet,[1230] and then said that she had clearly learned that the Deity was conversing with him.[1231]

Ahab-Obadiah (Obedias) exchange

(13.4) 328 A short time having passed,[1232] he went to King Achab in accordance with the will of God,[1233] in order to disclose to him that there would be rain.[1234] A famine was then ravaging the entire country, and there was a so great a lack of the necessities of life that not only were humans destitute of these,[1235] but also the ground was not yielding any suitable forage for the horses and other beasts on account of the drought.[1236]

329 The king therefore called Obedias,[1237] the overseer of his livestock,[1238] and said to him that he wanted him to go off to the springs of water and the streams so that, should grass be found anywhere in these [places], they might mow it and have it as food for the beasts.[1239] [He further said that], though he had sent [men] throughout the entire world to seek the prophet Elias,[1240] he had not been found.[1241] Then he directed [Obedias] to accompany him.[1242]

Obadiah meets Elijah

330 They therefore decided to set out; dividing up the roads, Obedias and the king each went off by a different road.[1243] (It happened at the time when Queen Jezabele killed the prophets that the former hid a hundred prophets in caves[1244] beneath

---

[1228] Josephus supplies this notice on God's double motivation for acting as he does.

[1229] Cf. 1 Kgs 17:22. Josephus omits the following details (17:23) concerning Elijah's descent to the mother, to whom he restores her son with the words "see, your son lives."

[1230] Compare 1 Kgs 17:24a, where the woman begins by declaring "now I know that you [Elijah] are a man of God." Tg. substitutes "prophet of the Lord."

[1231] Compare the woman's closing statement to Elijah in 1 Kgs 17:24b: "(I know) that the word of the Lord in your mouth is truth."

[1232] Josephus' chronological indication here differs from the double notice of 1 Kgs 18:1, i.e. "after many days... in the third year." Perhaps, Josephus' divergent rendering has in view the statement of Menander quoted by him in 8.324, according to which the drought in the reign of "Ithobal" (and Ahab) lasted a single year, a year, which, after the events described in 8.319-327, would certainly be drawing to a close at this point. On Josephus' version of 1 Kings 18 in 8.328-346, see Begg 1993: 166-88.

[1233] This formulation is Josephus' replacement for the reference in 1 Kgs 18:1a to the "word of the Lord" coming to Elijah and "saying."

[1234] In 1 Kgs 18:1bβ Elijah is to tell Ahab in God's name "I [God] will send rain upon the earth." Josephus lacks an equivalent to the notice that Elijah actually did go to Ahab of 18:2a.

[1235] Greek: αὐτῶν. This is the reading of SP, which Niese follows. Marcus (*ad loc.*) reads ἄρτων ("bread[s]") with ROM.

[1236] Josephus expatiates on the summary notice on

the famine being "severe" in Samaria in 1 Kgs 18:2b in light of Ahab's subsequent words about the state of the livestock in 18:5.

[1237] MT (1 Kgs 18:3) עבדיהו (Eng.: "Obadiah"); LXX BL Ἀβδειού; Josephus Ὠβεδίας.

[1238] MT 1 Kgs 18:3 calls Obadiah "he who was over the house," LXX BL "the steward." Josephus' alternative title may have been suggested by the directives Ahab gives Obadiah concerning the livestock in 18:5.

[1239] In proceeding directly from Ahab's summoning of Obadiah (// 1 Kgs 18:3) to the king's directives to him (// 18:5), Josephus passes over—for the moment (but see 8.330)—the parenthetical notices concerning Obadiah's rescue of the prophets in 18:4.

[1240] MT אליהו (Eng.: "Elijah"); LXX B Ἠλειού; LXX L and Josephus Ἠλίας. This is Josephus' first use of the prophet's name; see note to "prophet" at 8.319.

[1241] Josephus adds this statement by Ahab on the basis of 1 Kgs 18:10, where Obadiah informs Elijah that "there is no kingdom or nation whither my lord [Ahab] has not sent to seek you," and that Ahab has required the nations to swear "that they have not found you."

[1242] This command by Ahab to Obadiah is a Josephan addition to the former's words in 1 Kgs 18:5.

[1243] See 1 Kgs 18:6. Josephus' reference to the pair's dividing up "the roads" corresponds more closely to LXX BL 1 Kgs 18:6, where they divide "the road" between them; in MT it is "the land" that they divide.

[1244] The parenthetical notice of 1 Kgs 18:4 speaks of a single "cave" and specifies that the 100 prophets were concealed "by 50s."

Garis[1245] and fed them, supplying them solely with bread and water.)[1246] **331** The prophet Elias met Obedias, who was separated from the king.[1247] Upon his inquiring of him who he was and learning this, he paid him homage.[1248] Elias directed him to go to the king and say that he was coming to him.[1249]

332 He, however, asked what evil had been done by him that he was sending him to one who was seeking to kill him[1250] and was searching the whole earth for him.[1251] Or was he [Elias] ignorant that [the king] had left no place to which he had not sent [men] to lead him off—should he be taken—to death?[1252] **333** For he said that he was in fear of him [Achab],[1253] that, if God were to appear to him [Elias] again and he went off to another place,[1254] then he [Obedias] would fail the king who sent him, being unable to find wherever on earth he [Elias] might be, and thus would be put to death.[1255] **334** He therefore appealed to him to have care for his safety,[1256] telling him of his solicitude for his colleagues,[1257] that he had kept a hundred prophets safe when Jezabele had done away with all the others and how they had been kept hidden and fed by him.[1258] Elias, however, directed him to fear nothing and go to the king,[1259] giving him sworn pledges that he would indeed appear to Achab that day.[1260]

(13.4) 335 Once Obedias reported to the king, Achab went to meet Elias.[1261] In his wrath[1262] the king asked whether he was the one who was bringing calamity upon the Hebrew people and had been the cause of the [land's] infertility.[1263] Elias, how-

Elijah (Elias) rebukes Ahab

[1245] Greek: ὑπὸ Γάρις. This is the reading of R, which Niese prints. Naber, Weill, and Marcus all emend to ὑπογείοις ("underground [caves]"). 1 Kgs 18:4a speaks simply of "a cave" in which Obadiah hides the prophets.

[1246] In stating that the prophets' nourishment was "solely" bread and water Josephus goes beyond 1 Kgs 18:4b, where this restriction is absent. The indication reflects Josephus' earlier accentuation of the severity of the famine in 8.328 (compare 1 Kgs 18:2b).

[1247] See 1 Kgs 18:7aα.

[1248] Josephus recasts the sequence of 1 Kgs 18:7aββ-8a (where, having "recognized" Elijah, Obadiah falls on his face before him; thereupon, he asks if the other man is Elijah and is told that he is) into a more logical order.

[1249] See 1 Kgs 18:8b.

[1250] See 1 Kgs 18:9.

[1251] See 1 Kgs 18:10a, whose opening oath formula Josephus omits. Josephus has prepared Obadiah's statement here with his addition (8.329) to Ahab's words to Obadiah of 18:5, in which the king informs the latter about his search initiative; see note to "found" at 8.329.

[1252] This question—which spells out the purpose of Ahab's world-wide "dispatch"—takes the place of the reference to the king's "adjuring" (so MT; LXX BL "burning") those localities that claimed that Elijah was not present among them in 1 Kgs 18:10b. Josephus omits Obadiah's perplexed repetition of Elijah's initial directive to him (18:8b) in 18:11.

[1253] Josephus supplies this reference by Obadiah to his present emotional state.

[1254] This reference to a divine appearance to Elijah and the latter's going off elsewhere is Josephus' characteristic substitute for Obadiah's mention (1 Kgs 18:12a) of "the Spirit of the Lord carrying Elijah whither I know not."

[1255] Josephus modifies the wording of 1 Kgs 18:12b, where Obadiah points out that if he were to report his inability to find Elijah to Ahab, the latter would kill him, notwithstanding his (Obadiah's) lifelong fear of the Lord.

[1256] Josephus supplies this appeal by Obadiah.

[1257] Greek: ὁμότεχνος, literally "fellow craftsmen." The term ὁμότεχνος is *hapax* in Josephus.

[1258] Josephus rewords as a statement in indirect discourse Obadiah's direct-address question ("has it not been told...?") of 1 Kgs 18:13 about his maintenance of the 100 prophets. As he did in his handling of 18:11 in 8.332, he leaves aside Obadiah's renewed repetition of Elijah's opening directive to him in 18:14; see note to "to death" at 8.332.

[1259] Josephus supplies this re-assuring command by Elijah.

[1260] See 1 Kgs 18:15. Josephus omits the wording of Elijah's "oath" to Obadiah.

[1261] See 1 Kgs 18:16.

[1262] Josephus adds this reference to Ahab's emotional state.

[1263] Josephus elaborates on Ahab's derogatory allu-

ever, not flattering him at all,[1264] said that he and his family had done every terrible thing by introducing foreign gods into the country and adoring these, while they abandoned their own [God]—who was the only true one—and no longer gave him any care.[1265]

Preparations for contest of Mount Carmel

336 Now, however, he directed him to go up[1266] and gather all the people to him to Mount Karmel,[1267] along with his prophets and those of his wife, mentioning their number,[1268] as well as the prophets of the groves, who amounted to about 400.[1269]

337 When all had run together at the above-mentioned mountain in accordance with Achab's dispatch,[1270] the prophet Elias stood in the middle of them[1271] and asked how long they would live thus, divided in mind and opinions.[1272] For if they thought their native God[1273] to be the true and only one,[1274] he urged them to follow him and his commandments.[1275] If, however, they thought nothing of him, and supposed that the foreign gods were the ones they ought to worship, he advised them to follow after these.[1276]

338 When, however, the crowd answered nothing to these things,[1277] Elias requested that there be a test of the strength of the foreign gods and of his own,[1278] he being the only prophet of the latter, while the former had 400.[1279] He[1280] would take

---

sion to Elijah as "the troubler of Israel" in 1 Kgs 18:17.

[1264] Josephus' editorial remark on Elijah's defiant stance towards the king takes the place of the prophet's opening denial (1 Kgs 18:18) that he is the "troubler of Israel" Ahab has just accused him of being. The verb ὑποθωπεύω ("to flatter") is *hapax* in Josephus.

[1265] Josephus both elaborates and generalizes the 2nd half of Elijah's 2-part accusation against Ahab and his house in 1 Kgs 18:18, i.e. they had "followed the Baals." In so doing, he agrees with LXX BL's formulation of Elijah's preceding charge, i.e. Ahab has "forsaken the Lord" himself, whereas in MT the king is accused of having forsaken the Lord's "commandments."

[1266] Greek: ἀνελθόντα. This is the reading of R, which Niese follows. Marcus reads ἀπελθόντα ("going off") with SP.

[1267] MT (1 Kgs 18:19) כרמל (Eng.: "Carmel"); LXX BL and Josephus Καρμήλιον.

[1268] 1 Kgs 18:19 specifies that the 1st group of prophets, i.e. those "of Baal" (MT; LXX BL: "of shame" [Greek: τῆς αἰσχύνης]) numbered 450.

[1269] Josephus agrees with LXX BL 1 Kgs 18:19 in their reference to the 400 "prophets of the groves," whereas MT speaks of "prophets of Asherah"; compare the similar case cited in the note to "a grove of all kinds of trees" at 8.318. He omits the concluding biblical detail about these prophets "eating at Jezebel's table."

[1270] Cf. 1 Kgs 18:20.

[1271] In 1 Kgs 18:21a Elijah "comes near to all the people." Compare Josephus' reference to the prophet Jadon's "standing in the middle of the crowd" in 8.231.

[1272] Josephus transposes Elijah's figurative ques-

tion in 1 Kgs 18:21aα (literally: "how long will you hobble on two crutches?") into a prosaic, indirect discourse query.

[1273] Josephus' only other use of this expression (Greek: ὁ ἐγχώριος θεός) is in *Ant.* 18.198, where it appears in the plural. He employs a related formula in 9.99.

[1274] Greek: ἀληθής καὶ μόνος. Josephus applies this same collocation to God in *Ant.* 8.343; 10.263; cf. *War* 7.323; *Ant.* 6.148. He already had Elijah refer to the "only [Greek: μόνος] God" in his word to Ahab in 8.335.

[1275] To Elijah's exhortation in 1 Kgs 18:21aβ ("If the Lord is God, follow him") Josephus adds the call to adhere to God's commandments as well.

[1276] Josephus expands and generalizes the 2nd alternative Elijah puts before the people in 1 Kgs 18:21bα, i.e. "but if Baal, follow him."

[1277] See 1 Kgs 18:21bβ.

[1278] Josephus prefaces his reproduction of Elijah's words from 1 Kgs 18:22-25a with this proposal of a "test." The opposition between "foreign gods" and "his own God" here recalls that introduced by the Josephan Elijah in his words to Ahab in 8.335.

[1279] The Josephan Elijah's reference to the 400 prophets opposing him corresponds to the LXX BL plus in 18:22b. Josephus leaves aside the "450 prophets of Baal" cited by both MT and LXX BL there.

[1280] Josephus reverses the order of Elijah's words in 1 Kgs 18:23, where he first speaks of what the rival prophets are to do, and then of his own corresponding action. He leaves aside the opening element of Elijah's proposal, i.e. "let two bulls be given to us...."

a cow, slaughter it,[1281] and place it on the wood, but without lighting a fire.[1282] They, having done the same,[1283] would call upon their own gods to set fire to the wood.[1284] For if this were done, they would learn the true nature of God.[1285]

339 Once his plan was approved,[1286] Elias directed the prophets to choose their cow first, slaughter it, and call upon their own gods.[1287] Then,[1288] when nothing happened as a result of the prayer and invocation of the prophets who had sacrificed,[1289] Elias, mocking [them], directed them to call on their gods in a loud voice,[1290] for they were either on a journey or were sleeping.[1291] **340** This they did from the early morning until the middle of the day;[1292] they likewise cut themselves with swords and lances, according to their ancestral custom.[1293] When Elias was about to offer his sacrifice, he directed them [the 400 prophets] to withdraw, while he [ordered] those who had approached nearby to keep [an eye on] him, in order that he not secretly apply fire to the wood.[1294] **341** When the crowd approached,[1295]

Rival prophets receive no response

Elijah obtains fire from heaven

[1281] Josephus uses a feminine demonstrative adjective (Greek: ταυτῆς) for the bovine that is to be used; Marcus (*ad loc.*) renders "ox," Weill *ad loc.* rather "heifer" (*génisse*).

[1282] See 1 Kgs 18:23b.

[1283] Josephus summarizes the series of steps to be taken by the rival prophets according to Elijah's proposal in 1 Kgs 18:23a, having just previously (// 18:23b) had Elijah enumerate the measures he himself intends to take.

[1284] Josephus supplies this content for the "appeal" that the other prophets are to make according to Elijah's proposal in 1 Kgs 18:24aα. He has no equivalent to Elijah's corresponding statement (18:24aβ) that he himself will "call on the name of the Lord."

[1285] Compare 1 Kgs 18:24bα: ". . . the God who answers by fire, he is God." Elsewhere, Josephus uses the phrase "nature of God" (Greek: φύσις τοῦ θεοῦ) in *Ant.* 1.15, 19; 2.146; 4.269; 10.42; *Apion* 1.224; 2.168 (*bis*), 180, 248, 250; cf. *Ant.* 8.107; *Apion* 1.232. Compare the expression "divine nature" (Greek: θεία φύσις) of 8.107.

[1286] 1 Kgs 18:24bβ cites the words of the people's response to Elijah's proposal: "it is well spoken."

[1287] From Elijah's injunctions to the prophets in 1 Kgs 18:25 Josephus omits his parenthetical reference to their being "many," as well as his closing reminder that they are not to set fire to the wood. Like LXX L, he has Elijah refer to the "gods" of the other prophets, whereas LXX B reads a singular, and MT's form might be understood as either plural or singular (so RSV).

[1288] Josephus compresses and rearranges the sequence of 1 Kgs 18:26, which first speaks of the prophets' initiatives (including their appeal "O Baal, answer us!"), then of the lack of response to their endeavors, and finally of the prophets' "limping about the altar they had made."

[1289] Compare 1 Kgs 18:26bα: "there was no voice, and no one answered." Josephus omits the reference to

the prophets "limping about" their altar in 18:26bβ.

[1290] Josephus reformulates Elijah's (ironic) confession "he [Baal] is a god," attached as a motivation ("for") to his urging the prophets to "cry aloud" in 1 Kgs 18:27aβ. He thereby frees Elijah from any suspicion of acknowledging the existence of other gods. He reserves for a later point the chronological indication ("at noon") with which 18:27 begins; see 8.340.

[1291] Josephus omits the first 2 of the 4 possible activities in which, Elijah suggests, the prophets' god(s) may currently be engaged, i.e. "musing" and "going aside" (this last is often understood as a euphemism for defecation) in 1 Kgs 18:27 (MT; LXX BL—in contrast to Josephus—lack the 3rd of these items, i.e. the gods' being "on a journey"). He likewise leaves aside the phrase attached to the mention of the gods' "sleeping," i.e. "and must be awakened."

[1292] Josephus here makes delayed use of the chronological indication "until noon" of 1 Kgs 18:26 (cf. "at noon," 18:27).

[1293] From the description of the prophets' self-laceration in 1 Kgs 18:28 Josephus omits the gory detail about their doing this "until the blood gushed out upon them." He further leaves aside the summary notice on the prophets' unavailing activity of 18:29, with its repetition of previous narrative elements (compare 18:26b).

[1294] The Josephan Elijah's command to the prophets that they withdraw has a (more expansive) counterpart in the plus appended at the end of LXX BL* 1 Kgs 18:29. His further directive that the onlookers keep watch lest he violate the conditions of the "test" (see 8.338) serves to underscore both the prophet's credibility and the magnitude of the following miracle as one that cannot be attributed to some secret trick on his part.

[1295] See 1 Kgs 18:30bα. Josephus lacks an equivalent to the appended reference in MT 1 Kgs 18:30bβ MT (LXX BL gives its version of this notice in 18:32a) to Elijah's "repairing the altar that had been thrown

he took twelve stones according to the tribe(s) of the Hebrew people[1296] and from these erected an altar,[1297] around which he dug a very deep ditch.[1298] Having arranged the logs on the altar and placed the pieces of the victim on these,[1299] he directed that four jars of water from the fountain be poured on the altar,[1300] with the result that it overflowed, and the entire ditch was filled with water, as though it were a gushing spring.[1301]

342 When he had done these things,[1302] he began to pray to God[1303] and appeal to him to make his power clear to the people, who had been in error for a long time already.[1304] As he said this,[1305] fire from heaven[1306] suddenly fell on the altar in the sight of the people,[1307] and consumed the sacrifice so that even the water was vaporized and the place became dry.[1308]

God acclaimed   **(13.4) 343** When the Israelites saw this, they fell on the ground and paid homage to the one God,[1309] calling him the greatest[1310] and the only true[1311] one, whereas the

---

down," an event not previously mentioned in the Bible (or by Josephus himself). In addition, the MT notice in 1 Kgs 18:30bβ seems to duplicate the mention, which Josephus will reproduce in the continuation of 8.341, of Elijah's building an altar—apparently "from scratch" in 18:32a.

[1296] Compare 1 Kgs 18:31, where the tribes are those "of the sons of Jacob to whom the word of the Lord came, saying, 'Israel shall be your name'."

[1297] In making explicit mention of Elijah's using the stones to erect "an altar," Josephus agrees with MT 1 Kgs 18:32a (although he omits MT's qualification of this altar as one built "in the name of the Lord"). By contrast, LXX BL have Elijah simply "building the stones (in the name of the Lord)"; these witnesses then continue with their version of 18:30bβ (Elijah's repair of "the altar that had been thrown down," to which they lack an equivalent in its MT position (see note to "approached" at 8.341). Josephus thus differs from both MT and LXX in nowhere mentioning Elijah's repair of a previously overthrown altar.

[1298] Josephus substitutes a more general indication ("very deep") for the specification of MT LXX L 1 Kgs 18:32b that Elijah's "trench" (LXX B calls it a "sea") was "as great as would contain 2 measures of seed."

[1299] From Elijah's measures as recounted in 1 Kgs 18:33a Josephus omits the gory mention of his "cutting the bull in pieces."

[1300] In 1 Kgs 18:33b the water is to be poured on "the burnt offering and the wood." Josephus adds the indication concerning the "source" of the water.

[1301] Josephus compresses the biblical presentation (1 Kgs 18:33b-35), in which there is a 3-fold pouring of water, this resulting in the filling of the trench. He adds the reference to the ditch taking on the appearance of a "gushing spring."

[1302] This transitional notice takes the place of the chronological indication ("and the time of the offering of the oblation"), with which MT LXX L (> LXX B) 1

Kgs 18:36 introduce Elijah's appeal.

[1303] In 1 Kgs 18:36a Elijah addresses himself to the "the Lord, God of Abraham, Isaac, and Jacob."

[1304] Josephus' rendering of Elijah's prayer with its single petition represents a significantly compressed version of the much longer one in MT 1 Kgs 18:36b-37. In this regard, Josephus goes still further than LXX BL, which lacks an equivalent to MT's 18:37a. Conceivably, Josephus' formulation, with its reference to the people's having been "in error," represents his (negative) interpretation of the MT phrase of 18:37b, i.e. "... thou [the Lord] hast turned their [the people's] heart back (LXX: the heart of this people after you [the Lord])," as referring to the people's heart turning away from the Lord. Compare Tg., where Elijah's prayer of 18:37 ends with the assertion "they [the people] gave you [the Lord] a divided heart." See further Begg 1993: 181, n. 1191.

[1305] This added transitional phrase underscores the immediacy with which Elijah's prayer is answered.

[1306] Compare the designations used in MT 1 Kgs 18:38aα ("fire from the Lord") and LXX BL ("fire from the Lord from heaven"). In contrast to both witnesses, Josephus avoids explicitly associating the Deity and the fire.

[1307] This added phrase underscores the public character and credibility of the fulfillment of Elijah's previous appeal.

[1308] 1 Kgs 18:38aβb mentions also the "consumption" of the wood, the stones, and the dust.—Josephus adds the reference to the site's being made dry.

[1309] In 1 Kgs 18:39b the prostrate people twice proclaim "the Lord, he is God."

[1310] This is the same term (Greek: μέγιστος) used in 8.319, where Elijah is introduced as "prophet of the greatest God."

[1311] The reference to God as the "only true" (Greek: ἀληθῆς μόνος) here has a counterpart in the LXX BL plus in 1 Kgs 18:39b, where the Israelites declare "*truly*

others [were but names], made by false and foolish[1312] opinion.[1313] At Elias' urging, *Prophets killed* they seized the prophets and killed them.[1314] He also told the king to go to his meal without any further thought,[1315] for in a little while he would see God sending rain.[1316]

344 Achab was relieved,[1317] while Elias ascended to the top of Mount Carmel and *Coming of rain* sat on the ground, resting his head upon his knees.[1318] He directed his attendant to go up to a certain lookout point and look out to sea, and tell him if he saw a cloud rising from there, for until then the sky happened to be clear.[1319]

345 He ascended and, several times, stated that he saw nothing.[1320] After the seventh time,[1321] he said that he had seen a certain blackened [part] of the sky, no larger than a human footprint.[1322] When Elias heard this, he sent to Achab, directing him to depart for the city before the rain-water should pour down in torrents.[1323] **346** He [Achab], for his part, went to the city of Jerezela;[1324] not long afterwards, the sky became dark and covered with clouds. A violent wind arose and [there was] much rain-water.[1325] The prophet, becoming divinely possessed,[1326] ran alongside the king's chariot as far as the city of Jerezela.[1327]

[Greek: ἀληθῶς, > MT] the Lord is God." It likewise recalls the phrase "true and only" (Greek: ἀληθῆς καὶ μόνος) used of God by Elijah in his words to the people in 8.337.

[1312] Greek: φαύλος καὶ ἀνόητος. This collocation occurs only here in Josephus.

[1313] Josephus expands the people's positive recognition of the one true God (// 1 Kgs 18:39b) with this denigration of all other deities. Its use of the term "opinion" (Greek: δόξα) recalls 8.337, where Elijah alludes to the people's being "divided in mind and opinions."

[1314] In 1 Kgs 18:40 Elijah himself kills the prophets "at the brook Kishon." Subsequently, however, Josephus will (see 8.347, 348, 350) attribute the massacre to Elijah personally; on the point, see Begg 1993: 183-4, n. 1209.

[1315] Josephus appends the reference to the king's having no need to give matters further thought to Elijah's instructing Ahab to "go up and eat and drink" in 1 Kgs 18:41a.

[1316] Josephus supplies an explicit mention of God's role in his version of Elijah's announcement about hearing "a sound of the rushing of rain" of 1 Kgs 18:41b.

[1317] Josephus substitutes this mention of Ahab's emotional state for the notice of 1 Kgs 18:42a about the king's "going up to eat and drink" in accordance with Elijah's instructions in 18:41a.

[1318] See 1 Kgs 18:42b.

[1319] In 1 Kgs 18:43a, the servant is merely told "go up now, look toward the sea." Josephus has Elijah issue him more precise instructions.

[1320] Compare 1 Kgs 18:43bβ, where, after carrying out his command and reporting that he has seen nothing (18:43bα), the servant is told "go again 7 times"

(MT; LXX B adds "and return 7 times," while LXX BL conclude with the plus "and the lad returned 7 times").

[1321] In 1 Kgs 18:44a the servant makes his positive report "at the 7th time."

[1322] The Greek word ἴχνος rendered "footprint" here—the same term read by LXX BL 1 Kgs 18:44a—may also denote the palm of the hand, as does its Hebrew equivalent, i.e. כף.

[1323] In 1 Kgs 18:44b Elijah simply instructs Ahab to "go down." Josephus has him also indicate a destination for the king. Conversely, he has no equivalent here to the words "your [Achab's] chariot," which BL* append to Elijah's MT directive that the king "prepare"; subsequently, however, he will make use of this LXX plus, see 8.346.

[1324] MT (1 Kgs 18:45b) יזרעאל (Eng.: "Jezreel"); LXX B Ἰσραήλ; LXX L Ἰεζραήλ; Josephus Ἱερέζηλα (so Niese; Marcus reads Ἰεζάρελα, a form that will appear subsequently in Josephus' text; see 8.355).

[1325] See 1 Kgs 18:45a. Josephus reverses the biblical sequence, where Ahab's trip to Jezreel (18:45b) is mentioned after the storm's advent (18:45a).

[1326] Josephus substitutes this phrase (Greek: ἔνθεος γενόμενος) for the anthropomorphic reference to the "hand of the Lord being upon" Elijah in 1 Kgs 18:46aα; on the phrase, see note to "becoming possessed" at *Ant.* 6.56. He omits the reference to Elijah's "girding up his loins" of 18:46aβ.

[1327] 1 Kgs 18:46b depicts Elijah "running before Ahab." Josephus derives his reference to the king's "chariot" from the LXX plus in 1 Kgs 18:44b (previously passed over by him; see note on "in torrents" at 8.345), where LXX adds the specification "your chariot" to Elijah's MT instruction that Ahab "prepare."

Elijah's flight

(13.7) 347 When Jezabele, the wife of Achab, learned of the signs done by Elias and that he had killed their prophets,[1328] she, in her wrath, dispatched messengers to him, threatening through them to kill him, just as he had executed her prophets.[1329]

348 In fear[1330] Elias fled to the city called Bersoubee[1331] (this is the last [city] of the country of the tribe of Iouda, bordering on the land of the Idumeans).[1332] There, he left his attendant[1333] and withdrew into the desert,[1334] praying that he might die. For he was no better than his ancestors that he should long to live when they had perished.[1335]

Elijah reaches Sinai

349 When he had lain down under a certain tree,[1336] someone[1337] roused him.[1338] When he got up, he found food and water set out for him.[1339] Having eaten and gained force from that food, he went[1340] to the mountain called Sinai,[1341] where Moyses is said to have received the laws from God.[1342]

God–Elijah exchange

350 On it he found a certain hollow cave, which he entered and where he remained, making his dwelling in this.[1343] A certain unseen voice[1344] asked him why he had come there, after leaving the city.[1345] He said that it was because he had

---

[1328] 1 Kgs 19:1a states that Ahab informed his wife of what Elijah had done. Here Josephus follows the biblical wording (see 19:1b) in attributing the prophets' killing to Elijah personally, whereas in 8.343 he represents the Israelites slaying them at Elijah's urging; see note on "and killed them" at 8.343. On Josephus' version of 1 Kings 19 in *Ant.* 8.347-354, see Begg 1993: 189-98.

[1329] See 1 Kgs 19:2. Josephus' reference to Jezebel's "messengers" corresponds to MT's specification that she sent "a messenger" to him, whereas LXX BL have her simply "sending to" the prophet. As usual, Josephus omits the queen's opening oath formula ("so may the gods do to me and more also, if....").

[1330] Josephus' reference to Elijah's "fear" agrees with the initial verb of 1 Kgs 19:3 in its MT vocalization. Reading another possible vocalization, LXX BL have rather "he [Elijah] saw."

[1331] MT (1 Kgs 19:3) באר שבע (Eng.: "Beersheba"); LXX BL Βηρσάβεε; Josephus Βερσουβεέ.

[1332] Compare the qualification of Beersheba in 1 Kgs 19:3bα: "which belongs to Judah."

[1333] See 1 Kgs 19:3bβ.

[1334] Josephus omits the further details given in 1 Kgs 19:4a, i.e. Elijah journeyed for a day and "sat down under a broom tree" (this latter item is duplicated in 19:5a, which Josephus does reproduce; see 8.349).

[1335] See Elijah's prayer for death as cited in 1 Kgs 19:4b. Josephus has Elijah draw a conclusion from the biblical prophet's affirmation about his being no better than his ancestors, i.e. given his status he ought not wish to live any longer.

[1336] 1 Kgs 19:5a specifies a "broom tree."

[1337] Josephus' vague designation for Elijah's "waker" parallels BL 1 Kgs 19:5bα, whereas MT identifies the figure as "an angel/messenger."

[1338] Josephus omits the waker's directive "arise and

eat" of 1 Kgs 19:5bβ.

[1339] Josephus compresses the wording of 1 Kgs 19:6a, which mentions Elijah finding "at his head a cake baked on hot stones and a jar of water."

[1340] In MT LXX BL* there is a double mention of Elijah's "consuming" the provisions made available to him (1 Kgs 19:6bα and 8a) with a sequence (19:6bβ-7) concerning Elijah's lying down again and a 2nd angelic intervention supervening. In the line of the LXX L MSS 82, 93, 127 (which lack an equivalent to MT etc. 19:6bβ-8a), Josephus directly links his single mention of Elijah's eating (// 19:6bα) with his notice (// 19:8a) on the prophet's resuming his journey, strengthened by the food he has eaten. He has no counterpart to the specification of 19:8b that Elijah's journey to Horeb took him "40 days and 40 nights."

[1341] This is Josephus' substitution for the "Horeb" of 1 Kgs 19:8b, a name never employed by him.

[1342] With this qualification of the mountain—which takes the place of the phrase "the mount of God" used of it in MT (but not LXX BL) 19:8b—Josephus reminds readers of his earlier references to the site and the events that transpired there. He appends similar qualifications to his mentions of "Sinai" in *Ant.* 3.286; 8.104.

[1343] See 1 Kgs 19:9a. Josephus adds the specification that the cave was "hollow."

[1344] In 1 Kgs 19:9bα the "word of the Lord" addresses Elijah. Josephus' vague designation of the prophet's interlocutor ("an unseen voice") recalls his equally vague designation ("someone") for Elijah's "waker" in 8.349.

[1345] In 1 Kgs 19:9bβ Elijah is asked "what are you doing here, Elijah?" Josephus adds the reference to the prophet's having "left the city" (Jezreel [8.346]?, Beersheba [8.348]?).

killed the prophets of the foreign gods[1346] and convinced the people that only God is the existent one,[1347] whom they had served from the beginning.[1348] For it was on account of this that he was being sought for punishment by the king's wife.[1349]

351 Again he heard that he was to go out into the open air on the following day,[1350] for thus he would find out what he should do.[1351] He went out of the cave the next day,[1352] and heard an earthquake[1353] and saw a brilliant flash of fire.[1354]

352 When it became quiet,[1355] a divine voice[1356] appealed to him not to be disturbed at what was happening, for none of his enemies would prevail.[1357] It ordered him to return to his own [country][1358] and appoint Jeous,[1359] son of Nemesai,[1360] king

Three leaders to be appointed

[1346] This affirmation has no equivalent in Elijah's response as cited in 1 Kgs 19:10 (where the reference is rather to the Israelites' slaying of "thy [God's] prophets"). It corresponds to Josephus' notice on Jezebel's hearing that Elijah had "killed their [her and Ahab's] prophets" in 8.348, whereas in 8.343 the people kill the royal prophets at Elijah's urging.

[1347] Greek: ὁ ὤν. This phrase, which takes the place of the qualification of the Lord as "the God of hosts" in 1 Kgs 19:10, is absent in MSPE Lat. Marcus (*ad loc.*) notes that Josephus' phrase corresponds to the LXX rendering of the words "I am who I am" of MT Exod 3:14 (in his version of this passage in *Ant.* 2.276 Josephus avers that he is "not to permitted to speak" of the divine name). In the NT the phrase is used, in conjunction with other designations, of God in Rev 1:4, 8; 4:8; 11:17; 16:5. Philo uses both the masculine ὁ ὤν and the neuter τὸ ὄν of the Deity with considerable frequency; for the former formula see, e.g., *Abr.* 121; *Deus* 69,109; *Ebr.* 107; *Somn.* 1.182 and for the latter, e.g., *Deus* 11; *Post.* 27, 168; *Migr.* 182; *Plant.* 86. See further Begg 1993: 192, n. 1271.

[1348] Josephus' version of Elijah's reply supplies a content for the prophet's opening claim in 1 Kgs 19:10aα about his being "jealous/zealous" for the Lord—a claim which, with its "Zealot" overtones, he refrains from reproducing; see Begg 1993: 192, n. 1268. He leaves aside the continuation of Elijah's words in 19:10aβbα, in which he denounces the Israelites' wrongdoing and asserts that he is the only one of the Lord's prophets left. The prophet's allusion to his "convincing the people" about the uniqueness of the Deity here recalls 8.343, where the Israelites acclaim Elijah's God as "the only true one."

[1349] In 1 Kgs 19:10bβ Elijah avers "they seek my life." Josephus' more specific formulation has in view Jezebel's threat as cited in 8.347 (// 19:2).

[1350] This indication concerning when Elijah is to "come forth" has a parallel in the LXX BL plus in 1 Kgs 19:11a.

[1351] Josephus appends this word of explanation to the instructions given Elijah in 1 Kgs 19:11a.

[1352] Josephus supplies this notice of Elijah's com-

pliance with the instructions given him in 1 Kgs 19:11a.

[1353] In 1 Kgs 19:11b the earthquake is mentioned in 2nd place, after the mighty wind. Josephus omits the latter phenomenon completely, while substituting a notice on Elijah's "hearing" the earthquake for the biblical reference to the Lord's not (so MT LXX L; the original text of LXX B lacked the negation) being in the earthquake.

[1354] As he did with the earthquake (see previous note), Josephus substitutes an allusion to Elijah's perceiving the fire for the notice of 1 Kgs 19:12a (MT LXX L) that the Lord was not "in" that fire.

[1355] Compare 1 Kgs 19:12b: "and after the fire a still small voice." Josephus omits the appended notice of 19:13, where Elijah responds to his hearing of the voice by wrapping his face in his mantle and standing at the entrance of the cave (in his presentation Elijah's exiting the cave has already been mentioned, prior to the onset of the various phenomena, in 8.351).

[1356] Greek: φωνὴ θεία; Josephus uses this same phrase in *Ant.* 1.185, cf. 2.283 ("the voices of God"). In 1 Kgs 19:14bα it is simply "a voice" that comes to Elijah; Josephus' characterization of the voice as "divine" would seem to be based on 19:15aα, where "the Lord" is introduced as the speaker of the words that follow in 19:15aβ-18. Josephus omits the question and answer sequence (19:13bβ-14) between the voice and the prophet, which largely reproduces that already cited in 19:10.

[1357] This word of assurance has no equivalent in the Lord's communication to Elijah in 1 Kgs 19:15aβ-18, which opens with the directive "go, return on your way."

[1358] In 1 Kgs 19:15aβb Elijah is instructed to go to the "wilderness of Damascus," where he is to anoint Hazael king of Syria. Josephus' modification of Elijah's initial prescribed destination is due to the fact that he will mention the appointment of the Israelite "Jehu" in first place.

[1359] MT (1 Kgs 19:16) יהוא (Eng.: "Jehu"); LXX B (τὸν υἱὸν) Εἰού; LXX L 'Ιού; Josephus 'Ιηοῦς. Josephus substitutes the more general term "appoint" for the

of the crowd[1361] and Azael[1362] king of Damascus of the Syrians.[1363] In his own place Elissai,[1364] from the city of Abela,[1365] was to be made prophet by him.[1366] Of the impious mob,[1367] Azael would destroy some, Jeous others.[1368]

Call of Elisha (Elissai)

353 Having heard these things, Elias returned to the country of the Hebrews.[1369] He came upon Elissai, the son of Saphat,[1370] who was ploughing; with him were some others, who were driving twelve teams.[1371] Approaching him, he threw his own garment over him.[1372] **354** Elissai, for his part, immediately began to prophesy;[1373] leaving the oxen, he followed Elias. He asked that he permit him to greet his parents.[1374] When he directed him to do this, he said goodby to them;[1375] he then went with Elias as long as he lived, as his disciple[1376] and minister.[1377] Such was the situation with this prophet.[1378]

---

word "anoint" used in 19:16 for what Elijah is do regarding Jehu.

[1360] MT (1 Kgs 19:16) נמשי (Eng.: "Nimshi"); LXX B Ναμεσθεί; LXX L Ναμεσσεί; Josephus Νεμεσαιος.

[1361] 1 Kgs 19:16a specifies "king of Israel."

[1362] MT (1 Kgs 19:15b) חזאל (Eng.: "Hazael"); LXX BL Ἀζαήλ; Josephus Ἀζάηλος.

[1363] Hazael is to be anointed "king over Syria" according to 1 Kgs 19:15b. Josephus may have drawn his reference to Damascus from the phrase "the wilderness of Damascus" that designates Elijah's destination in 19:15a.

[1364] MT (1 Kgs 19:16b) אלישע (Eng.: "Elisha"); LXX BL Ἐλεισσαῖε; Josephus Ἐλισσαῖος. Josephus here omits the name of Elisha's father, i.e. "Shapat" (MT); he will, however, supply the name in 8.353.

[1365] MT (1 Kgs 19:16b) אבל מחולה (Eng.: "Abelmeholah"); LXX B Ἐβελμαουλά; LXX L Ἀβελμεούλ; Josephus Ἄβελα.

[1366] In 1 Kgs 19:16b the Lord instructs Elijah to "anoint" Elisha prophet is his place. Josephus' re-formulation disposes of the difficulty that in the subsequent biblical account (see 1 Kgs 19:19-21) Elijah does not in fact "anoint" his successor.

[1367] In 1 Kgs 19:17 the Lord does not specify the identity of those to be slain by the trio that Elijah will anoint. Josephus' clarification on the point ("the impious mob") serves to legitimate the divinely-ordered execution of these persons.

[1368] According to 1 Kgs 19:17 also Elisha is to have a personal role in the prescribed killings—one which, however, unlike Hazael and Jehu, he is not shown exercising in what follows. Josephus omits the Lord's statement of 19:18 about his intended sparing of 7,000 persons, who have not defected to Baal, nothing having been said about such a group in the preceding biblical account.

[1369] Josephus specifies Elijah's destination in accord with the divine order given him in 8.352; 1 Kgs 19:19aα merely states "he departed from there."

[1370] MT (1 Kgs 19:19) שפט (Eng.: "Shaphat"); LXX BL Σαφάτ; Josephus Σαφάτης.

[1371] Josephus varies the account of 1 Kgs 19:19aβ,

where Elisha is ploughing with the last of 12 yoke of oxen.

[1372] See 1 Kgs 19:19b.

[1373] Josephus' addition of this reference parallels his (likewise added) notice on David's "prophesying" in response to Samuel's anointing of him in *Ant.* 6.166. In both instances, the addition evidences Josephus' tendency to highlight the "prophetic factor" in his rewriting of the Bible.

[1374] See 1 Kgs 19:20. In having Elisha mention his "parents," Josephus agrees with the MT (and LXX L*) reading, where Elisha asks permission "to kiss my father and my mother," as against LXX B (and the LXX L MS 93), where he speaks only of his father. Josephus omits Elisha's appended declaration "and then I will follow you."

[1375] This sequence is Josephus' replacement for Elijah's obscure reply to Elisha's request (1 Kgs 19:20aβ) in 1 Kgs 19:20b: "And he said to him, 'Go back again, for what have I done to you'?" Whereas the biblical Elijah seems to take offense at Elisha's request, the Josephan prophet readily endorses this. Josephus' modification here perhaps reflects his concern that the prophet Elijah not appear to be denigrating the central (Jewish and gentile) value of piety towards parents. Josephus likewise omits the further details of Elisha's preparations for joining Elijah as recounted in 19:22abα: slaying the oxen, boiling their flesh, using the yokes for this purpose, and distributing the meat to the people, who then eat it.

[1376] On Josephus' use of this term (Greek: μαθητής), see note to "disciple" at *Ant.* 6.84.

[1377] Greek: διάκονος. On Josephus' use of this term, see note to "minister" at *Ant.* 6.52. With Josephus' double designation ("disciple and minister") for Elisha in relation to Elijah, compare the notice of 1 Kgs 19:22bβ "then he [Elisha] arose and went after Elijah and ministered to him." Josephus underscores the fact that the service undertaken by Elisha at this moment lasted for the remainder of Elijah's life.

[1378] This appended formula rounds off Josephus' version of the story of Elijah's Sinai experience and its

355 Now a certain Naboth,[1379] from the city of Jezarela,[1380] was a rural neighbor of the king.[1381] The latter appealed to him to sell him, at whatever price he wished,[1382] his field[1383] that adjoined [the king's] own [fields], so that, by joining [them] he might make a single property.[1384] If he did not wish to take money, he would allow him to select any of his own fields.[1385] [Naboth], however, said that he would not do this; rather, he would enjoy the produce of his own land that he had inherited from his father.[1386]

Naboth rebuffs Ahab's proposal

356 The king grieved, as though at an outrage, over his not receiving the other's property, and took neither bath nor food.[1387] When his wife Jezabele inquired why he was grieving and was neither bathing nor having breakfast or supper set before him,[1388] he related Naboth's rude behavior[1389] to her, and how, although he used gentle words with him that were lacking in kingly authority, he had been outraged in not obtaining what he asked for.[1390] **357** She, however,[1391] appealed to him not to be depressed[1392] at these things, to cease from grief, and to turn to his customary care for his body,[1393] for she would see to the punishment of Naboth.[1394]

Ahab–Jezebel exchange

358 She immediately sent letters to the leading men of the Jezarelites[1395] in

Naboth

---

sequel (8.347-354// 1 Kings 19).

[1379] MT (1 Kgs 21:1) נבות (Eng.: "Naboth"); LXX BL Ναβουθαί; Josephus Νάβωθης (this is the reading of RO, which Niese follows; Marcus reads Νάβωθος). Josephus agrees with LXX BL in placing his version of the "Naboth episode" (MT 1 Kings 21) immediately after Elijah's "mountain experience" (MT 1 Kings 19), whereas in MT the account of Ahab's Aramean wars (MT 1 Kings 20) supervenes. On Josephus' retelling of the Naboth episode in 8.355-362, see Begg 1993: 199-210.

[1380] 1 Kgs 21:1 calls Naboth a "Jezreelite" (MT LXX L; LXX B: "Israelite").

[1381] Greek: ἀγρογείτων, a Josephan *hapax*. This qualification of Naboth takes the place of the reference to his "having a vineyard in Jezreel (> LXX BL) beside the palace of Ahab" in 1 Kgs 21:1.

[1382] In 1 Kgs 21:2b such monetary compensation is the 2nd, rather than the 1st of the 2 alternatives offered Naboth by Ahab, whereas Josephus has the king begin by offering Naboth money for his property.

[1383] 1 Kgs 21:1-2 calls Naboth's property a "vineyard," a term which Josephus will use for it subsequently; see 8.359-360.

[1384] Compare 1 Kgs 21:2αβ, where Ahab asks Naboth to give him his vineyard so that he might turn this into a "vegetable garden," given its proximity to his own house.

[1385] Compare 1 Kgs 21:2bα, where Ahab's 1st offer to Naboth is of "a better vineyard"; see note to "at whatever priced he wished" at 8.355.

[1386] 1 Kgs 21:3 cites Naboth's oath formula "The Lord forbid that I should give you [Ahab] the inheritance of my fathers."

[1387] Josephus' reference to Ahab's not "bathing" replaces the notice of 1 Kgs 21:4bα concerning his "laying down on his bed and turning away his face." In supplying an explicit motive for Ahab's irritation, Josephus parallels the plus of MT 1 Kgs 21:4a (and LXX L 1 Kgs 20:4a), absent in LXX B 1 Kgs 20:4a.

[1388] See 1 Kgs 21:5. Here too (see previous note), Josephus adds the allusion to Ahab's not "bathing," and elaborates on the biblical Jezebel's general reference to his not "eating."

[1389] Greek: σκαιότης; the term is *hapax* in Josephus.

[1390] Josephus' version of Ahab's "objective" report of the exchange between himself and Naboth from 1 Kgs 21:6 turns this into an emotionally-charged contrast between their respective behaviors.

[1391] Josephus omits the contemptuous question ("Do you now govern Israel?") with which Jezebel begins her response to Ahab in 1 Kgs 21:7.

[1392] Greek: μικροψυχέω; this verb is *hapax* in Josephus.

[1393] Josephus reformulates, in negative terms, Jezebel's positive exhortation to Ahab, "let your heart be cheerful," just as he generalizes her directive that the king "eat bread" of 1 Kgs 21:7αββα.

[1394] In 1 Kgs 21:7 Jezebel concludes her response to Ahab with the promise "I will give you the vineyard of Naboth the Jezreelite." Josephus' alternative language has in view the immediate continuation of the story, which will feature the "punishment" of Naboth.

[1395] Greek: Ἰεζαρηλιτῶν; this is a conjecture, ultimately going back to J. Hudson, for the reading of the codices, i.e. Ἰσραηλιτῶν ("Israelites"). The conjecture is adopted by both Niese and Marcus. In 1 Kgs 21:8b Jezebel sends her letter(s) "to the elders and nobles who dwelt with Naboth in his city" (MT; LXX BL 20:8b lack the phrase "in his city").

executed at Jezebel's direction

Achab's name.[1396] She directed them to hold a fast, and, having convened an assembly, to make Naboth preside over this, for he was of a distinguished family.[1397] They were to have in readiness three[1398] daring[1399] men to bear false witness against[1400] him that he had defamed both God and the king.[1401] He was to be stoned and in this way put to death.[1402]

359 Now Naboth, as the queen had written,[1403] was thus falsely witnessed against about having defamed God and Achab. He died, after being pelted [with stones] by the crowd.[1404] When Jezabele heard this, she went in to the king and directed him to inherit the vineyard of Naboth at no cost[1405]

Elijah denounces Ahab

360 Achab was pleased at what had happened;[1406] leaping up from his bed,[1407] he went to see the vineyard of Naboth. God, however, being indignant,[1408] sent the prophet Elias[1409] to Naboth's small holding to confront Achab[1410] and to ask, regard-

---

[1396] See 1 Kgs 21:8. Josephus' plural form, "letter*s*," corresponds to that of MT, whereas LXX BL (20:8) read the singular. Josephus omits the source detail about Jezebel's "sealing the letter(s) with his [Ahab's] seal."

[1397] This reference to Naboth's social status as the reason for his being given the presiding role at the assembly lacks a basis in 1 Kgs 21:9, where Jezebel simply enjoins that he is to "be set on high among the people." It is, however, paralleled in Rabbinic tradition; see *b. Sanh.* 48b; *t. Sanh.* 4.6.

[1398] In 1 Kgs 21:10 Jezebel specifies the number of "witnesses" that are to be employed as 2. Josephus' increasing this to 3 reflects his version of the law of Deut 19:15 (where 2 or 3 witnesses are required to prove a charge) in *Ant.* 4.219 ("...let there be three, or, at the very least, two..."). See further BJP 3 (Feldman) 411, n. 671 and Begg 1993: 203, n. 1344.

[1399] Greek: τολμηροί. This same adjective is used of Jezebel herself in 8.318. Words of the τολμ-stem are featured in Josephus' version of the Naboth story of 1 Kings 21(MT); see 8.361, 362.

[1400] Greek: καταμαρτυρέω. Josephus' 2 other uses of this verb are in *Ant.* 4.219; 8.359. In having Jezebel direct that a false accusation be made against Naboth, Josephus represents her as still more brazen than her counterpart in 1 Kgs 21:10, who does not explicitly qualify the charge she wants made as "false."

[1401] See 1 Kgs 21:10aβ. Josephus replaces the euphemism, common to both MT and LXX (Naboth is to be charged with having "blessed" God and king) with a term ("defame," Greek: βλασφημέω) that clearly expresses the intended meaning. His substitute language is paralleled in both the Tg. and the Vulg. In *Ant.* 4.202 (// Lev 24:16) Josephus cites Moses' prescribing the penalty of death by stoning—the one that Naboth will undergo (see 8.359)—for the "defamer."

[1402] Jezebel's concluding directive in 1 Kgs 21:10b specifies that Naboth is to be "stoned to death."

[1403] This phrase corresponds to the plus of MT 1 Kgs 21:11b (and LXX B 20:11b), absent in

LXX L 20:11b.

[1404] Josephus drastically abridges the extended account of the execution of Jezebel's order (1 Kgs 21:9-10) this using much of the same wording employed in that order itself, of 21:11-13. In 21:13 an indeterminate "they" stones Naboth; Josephus specifies that "the crowd" did this. He omits the report made to Jezebel about the fulfillment of her orders by the "they" in 21:14.

[1405] See 1 Kgs 21:15. Having earlier designated Naboth's property as a "field" (see 8.355), Josephus, in reproducing Jezebel's words to Ahab here, does employ the biblical term, i.e. "vineyard." In his citation of the queen's words, he leaves aside Jezebel's closing announcement that Naboth is dead. In place thereof, he has Jezebel inform Ahab that Naboth's plot is now his "for free."

[1406] Josephus supplies this reference to Ahab's emotional state. The reference stands in marked contrast to the king's reaction to Jezebel's words as portrayed in the LXX BL plus in 1 Kgs 20:16 (MT 21:16), i.e. "Ahab rent his garments and donned sackcloth, and it came to pass...."

[1407] With this vivid phrase, Josephus highlights Ahab's eagerness to take possession of his ill-gotten property; in 1 Kgs 21:16 he simply "arises." Josephus' phrase might be inspired by the notice—not previously reproduced by him—of 1 Kgs 21:4, where the rebuffed Ahab "lays down on his bed."

[1408] Josephus adds this reference to God's emotional reaction to what has happened, which, in turn, prompts his dispatch of Elijah.

[1409] In having God himself dispatch Elijah here, Josephus aligns himself with the reading of LXX BL 1 Kgs 20:17 ("and the Lord said...") against MT 21:17's "then the word of the Lord came to...." He substitutes the title "the prophet" for the biblical qualification of Elijah as "the Tishbite."

[1410] Josephus omits the initial (geographically problematic) indication of 1 Kgs 21:18 about Ahab's being

ing what had occurred, whether, after killing the true master of the small holding, he was going to unjustly inherit it.[1411]

361 When he came to him, the king said that he should proclaim to him as God's will[1412] whatever he wished (for he was ashamed and had been taken in his offense by him [Elias]).[1413] Elias said that at the very place where the corpse of Naboth happened to be consumed by dogs, his blood[1414] and that of his wife would be shed[1415] and his entire family would be exterminated[1416] because he had dared to act so impiously[1417] and, contrary to the ancestral laws, had unjustly done away with a citizen.[1418]

362 Grief and regret at what had occurred came upon Achab;[1419] he put on sackcloth[1420] and went about barefoot.[1421] He touched no food and confessed his of-

Ahab's
repentance and

"in Samaria" at this juncture, whereas the preceding story appears to be set in Jezreel. In so doing he limits himself to the Bible's subsequent mention of the king's presence "in the vineyard of Naboth."

[1411] From the divine message confided to Elijah in 1 Kgs 21:19, Josephus omits its opening "messenger formula," while adding reference to Ahab's "killing" and his "unjustly" inheriting the victim's property.

[1412] Greek: χράω. Josephus' other uses of this verb are in *Ant.* 4.77; 5.182, 349.

[1413] Josephus modifies Ahab's opening, sarcastic question to Elijah in 1 Kgs 21:20a: "Have you found me, O my enemy?," turning the question into an admission by Ahab about his "shame" and his having been "taken" by Elijah "in his offense." In mentioning an (initial) repentance by Ahab already at this point, prior to the dire threats Elijah will make against him, Josephus aligns himself with the presentation of LXX 1 Kgs 20:16, where (see note to "Achab was pleased at what had happened" at 8.360) the king's repentance likewise precedes Elijah's judgment speech against him. By contrast his repentance in MT comes only after the prophet's threats; see 1 Kgs 21:27. Josephus' recasting of Ahab's question about having been "found" by his enemy (21:20a), likewise causes him to dispense with Elijah's corresponding reply in 21:20b: ("I have found you, because you have sold yourself to do what is evil in the sight of the Lord"), which picks up on this.

[1414] Josephus derives the content of this announcement of punishment for Ahab personally from the message God instructs Elijah to convey to the king in 1 Kgs 21:19b (LXX BL 20:19b add mention of "swine" having consumed Naboth's blood and the prediction that prostitutes will bath in the king's blood [see 1 Kgs 22:38]. In so doing, he places the announcement on the lips of Elijah (rather than of God speaking to Elijah, as in 21:19b) and turns it into a response made by the prophet to Ahab's opening word to him (rather than something that precedes the whole king-prophet exchange, as it does in 1 Kings 21).

[1415] Josephus combines into one the biblical an-

nouncements of doom for Ahab and Jezebel, whereas these appear separately in 1 Kgs 21:19b and 21:23, respectively.

[1416] With this summary threat against Ahab's line, Josephus compresses the more expansive wording of 1 Kgs 21:21-22a, 24, with its reminiscence of earlier biblical prophecies against the dynasties of Jeroboam and Baasha.

[1417] With this accusation Josephus sums up the more specific (cultic/religious) charges, e.g., of idolatry, made against Ahab by Elijah in 1 Kgs 21:22b, 25-26.

[1418] This charge recalls the message earlier entrusted to Elijah by God (8.360// 1 Kgs 21:19) with its reference to Ahab's having "killed the true master of the small holding." Its use of the term "citizen" (Greek: πολίτης) for Naboth is an obvious Hellenization. On the term and its cognates, see Spicq (1978) II: 710-20.

[1419] This reference to Ahab's emotional state at this point parallels the opening plus of LXX BL 1 Kgs 20:27 (= MT 21:27): "because of the word [of Elijah] Ahab was pierced with sorrow before the Lord and went about weeping." The reference has a later counterpart in the description of Ahab "going about dejectedly" at the end of MT 21:27 (LXX B 20:27 lacks the word "dejectedly," while the entire phrase is absent in LXX L). Like LXX BL 1 Kings 20, but in contrast to MT 1 Kings 21, Josephus mentions a double repentance by Ahab, one before, the other after Elijah's threatening words to him; see note to "taken in his offense by him [Elias]" at 8.361.

[1420] 1 Kgs 21:27 makes double mention of Ahab's use of sackcloth; Josephus has no equivalent to the Bible's preceding reference to his "rending his clothes."

[1421] This element of Josephus' description of the penitent Ahab corresponds to Tg.'s rendering of the Hebrew word אט (no equivalent in LXX BL 1 Kgs 20:27) at the end of MT 1 Kgs 21:27 (RSV: "dejectedly"). See further Begg 1993: 207, n. 1374.

God's relenting   fenses,[1422] gratifying God in this way.[1423] God told the prophet[1424] that, as long as he
[Achab] lived, since he had changed his mind about the things he had dared [to
do],[1425] the punishment of his family would be delayed; the threat would be realized
upon Achab's son.[1426] And the prophet disclosed these things to the king.[1427]

Samaria   **(14.1) 363** At the same time these things [were going on] around Achab,[1428] the
(Samareia)   son of Adad,[1429] who was ruling as king over the Syrians and Damascus,[1430] as-
besieged   sembled an army from his entire country, made allies of thirty-two kings beyond
the Euphrates, and campaigned against Achab.[1431] **364** Achab, whose army was not
equal to his, did not draw up for battle. Rather, he shut up everything in his country
in the most solidly fortified cities, while he himself remained in Samareia, for it was
surrounded by a very strong wall and otherwise seemed impregnable.[1432] The Syrian, bringing up his force, came to Samareia; placing his army around it, he besieged
it.[1433]

Negotiations   **365** Sending a herald to Achab, he requested that he receive messengers from
fail   himself, through whom he would disclose to him what he wished.[1434] Once the king
of the Israelites permitted him to send [them],[1435] the messengers came and said that,
by the king's command, Achab's wealth, his children, and his wives belonged to
Adad.[1436] If he acknowledged this and allowed him to take what he wished of these

---

[1422] 1 Kgs 21:27 mentions Ahab's "fasting," but not
a (verbal) confession by him. Josephus' depiction of
the king "confessing his offenses" recalls his portrayal
of the penitent Judeans in the face of Shishak's invasion in 8.257.

[1423] Josephus appends this indication concerning
the effect of Ahab's penitential initiatives as related in
1 Kgs 21:27 upon the Deity. His other uses of the
phrase "gratify God" (Greek: τὸν θεὸν ἐξευμενίζω) are in
Ant. 11.115; 12.113.

[1424] Josephus has God communicate directly with
Elijah rather than via his "word" as in 1 Kgs 21:28. He
omits the opening divine question to Elijah in 21:29aα
("have you seen how Ahab has humbled himself before
me?").

[1425] This motivation for the delay of Ahab's punishment corresponds to the MT plus in 1 Kgs 21:29aβ
("because he [Ahab] has humbled himself before me
[God]...") absent in LXX BL 1 Kgs 20:29.

[1426] See 1 Kgs 21:29b.

[1427] The account of 1 Kings 21 does not explicitly
mention Elijah's delivery of the divine word of v. 29 to
the king.

[1428] Josephus adds this transitional phrase, linking
his version of 1 Kings 20 with his rendering of 1 Kings
21 (which, like LXX BL, he gives in reverse order to
the MT sequence; see note to "Naboth" at 8.355). On
Josephus' retelling of 1 Kings 20 in 8.363-392, see
Begg 1993: 211-35.

[1429] MT (1 Kgs 20:1) בֶּן־הֲדַד (Eng.: "Ben-hadad");
LXX BL υἱὸς Ἀδέρ; Josephus ὁ τοῦ Ἀδάδου. Subsequently, he will call the Syrian king both "Adad[os]"
(see, e.g., 8.365) and also "Ader" (see 8.401)

[1430] MT 1 Kgs 20:1 calls Ben-hadad "king of
Aram," LXX L (21:1) "king of Syria." LXX B (21:1)
lacks a corresponding title.

[1431] Josephus' reference to the origin of the 32
kings has no equivalent in 1 Kgs 20:1. Wacholder
(1962: 151 and n. 40) suggests that he may have derived this (and other of his embellishments of 1 Kings
20) from the Herodian historian Nicolaus of Damascus.
Conversely, Josephus omits mention of the "horses and
chariots" that accompany Ben-hadad according to 1
Kgs 20:1, just as he "delays" that verse's mention of
Samaria as the Syrian's specific target. Josephus has
made an earlier, foreshadowing reference to "Adad" and
his future attack on Ahab in *Ant.* 7.101-103a.

[1432] Josephus adds this sequence in order to explain
how it came to a siege of Samaria (see 1 Kgs 20:1bβ),
deep within Israelite territory, without any prior resistance being offered. His insertion further offers more a
positive perspective on Ahab's response to Ben-hadad's
assault: Ahab acted, not out of panicked cowardice, but
with a clear awareness of the balance of power between
the 2 armies and deliberately choosing the best possible
spot to make a stand.

[1433] See 1 Kgs 20:1bβ.

[1434] Josephus prefaces the biblical account of the
negotiations between Ben-hadad and Ahab (1 Kgs 20:2-
12) with mention of this preliminary initiative by the
former.

[1435] Like Ben-hadad's initial request itself (see previous note), this mention of Ahab's response to it is a
Josephan addition.

[1436] Josephus' explicit mention of Ben-hadad's
"messengers" agrees with MT 1 Kgs 20:2 against LXX

things, he would lead his army away and cease besieging him.[1437] **366** Achab directed the messengers to go and say to their king that he and all who were his were his possessions.[1438]

367 When they announced this [to him], the Syrian sent to him again,[1439] requesting him, who had acknowledged everything to be his, to receive the slaves sent by him on the following day.[1440] To them, whom he [Adad] had directed to search out the palace and the houses of his [Achab's] friends and relatives,[1441] he [Achab] was to give the best of everything that they should find in these. "They will, however, leave behind for you what does not please them."[1442]

368 Taken aback[1443] by this second embassy from the Syrian king,[1444] Achab assembled the crowd[1445] and said that he was ready, for the sake of their safety and peace,[1446] to turn over his own wives and children to the enemy and yield all his possessions, for it was these things that the Syrian had sought when he sent his first embassy.[1447] **369** "Now, however, he has requested to send his slaves to search out the houses of everyone and to leave behind none of the best of their possessions in them, wishing to obtain a pretext for war.[1448] Knowing that for your sake I would not spare what is my own, he is devising a grounds for going to war via this unpleasantness[1449] of his towards you. I shall, nonetheless, do what seems good to you."[1450]

BL 1 Kgs 21:2. Conversely, like LXX BL, he lacks an equivalent to MT's qualification of Ahab's wives whom the messengers are claiming for their master as his "fairest" ones.

[1437] Josephus appends this (conditional) promise to the messengers' demand of 1 Kgs 20:3, thereby giving Ahab more of a reason to submit to that demand.

[1438] See 1 Kgs 20:4.

[1439] Josephus adds this transitional sequence in order to fill in gaps in the biblical account, where following Ahab's reply (1 Kgs 20:4), the messengers immediately "come again" (20:5), without anything being said either of their reporting back to Ben-hadad or of the latter's further instructions to them.

[1440] The Josephan Ben-hadad's new request that his envoys be "received" by Ahab takes the place of the Syrian's largely verbatim citation of his earlier word to Ahab (see 1 Kgs 20:3) as quoted by his messengers in 20:5.

[1441] Mention of these 2 groups replaces the general term used in 1 Kgs 20:6, i.e. "your [Ahab's] servants," for those who houses are to be plundered along with the king's palace.

[1442] This appended "promise" recalls that attached to Ben-hadad's initial demand in 8.365.

[1443] Greek: ἄγαμαι. This is Josephus' only use of this verb in the above meaning. Elsewhere (see *War* 6.187; *Ant.* 10.200; 12.219, 281, 307; 15.25; 19.136).

[1444] This reference to the emotional effect of Ben-hadad's new demands upon Ahab is Josephus' addition.

[1445] MT 1 Kgs 20:7aα designates Ahab's audience as "all the elders of the land" (LXX B [21:7aα] lacks "of the land," while LXX L [21:7aα] qualifies them as

"of Israel"). Josephus' "enlarging" of the audience serves to resolve the seeming discrepancy between 20:7 (Ahab addresses himself [only] to the elders) and 20:8 ("all the elders and all the people" respond to him).

[1446] Greek: σωτερία καὶ εἰρήνη. This collocation occurs only here in Josephus.

[1447] In his reproduction of Ahab's report (1 Kgs 20:7aβb) concerning his initial interaction with the Syrians (see 20:3-4) Josephus has the king make mention of his magnanimous motivation in acceding to Ben-hadad's demands, i.e. "for the sake of their [the people's] safety and peace." He holds for a later point in Ahab's address the king's reference (20:7aβ) to the bellicose intentions behind Ben-hadad's diplomatic initiatives. Like MT 20:7bα (and LXX L 1 Kgs 21:7βα), he does not explicitly mention, as does the original text of LXX B 1 Kgs 21:7bα, Ahab's "daughters" among those whom the king reports were claimed by Ben-hadad's embassy.

[1448] Josephus prefaces his version of the biblical Ahab's initial statement "mark, now, and see how this man [Ben-hadad] is seeking trouble" (1 Kgs 20:7aβ) with an allusion to the demands of his 2nd embassy; see 8.367.

[1449] Greek: ἀηδοῦς. This is the reading adopted by Niese and Marcus. RO read αἰδοῦς ("shame").

[1450] Josephus appends this conclusion to Ahab's discourse (// 1 Kgs 20:7). In it the king reiterates his solicitude for his subjects' welfare (see 8.368) and his claims about Ben-hadad's intentions (see 8.369a), while also displaying a democratic impulse in leaving the decision as to what he should do up to the people.

370 The crowd, however, said that he ought not to listen to [what was being said] to him, but should despise this and be ready for war.[1451] He [Achab], therefore, answered the messengers that they were to go away and say that what he [Adad] had first requested he would even now agree to for the sake of the citizens' security, but he would not obey his second request.[1452] He then dismissed them.[1453]

Siege intensified

(14.2) 371 Adad, hearing this and being displeased,[1454] sent messengers a third time to Achab,[1455] threatening to raise earthworks higher than the walls in which he [Achab] put such confidence by having [each man in] his army take a handful of earth,[1456] thus making clear to him the size of his force and terrifying [him].[1457]

372 Achab, however, answered that it was not the one putting on his armor who ought to boast, but rather he who proved superior in battle.[1458] [Achab's] messengers came and, encountering the king dining with the thirty-two kings, his allies, disclosed [Achab's] answer to him.[1459] He immediately ordered that [his men] invest the city with entrenchments and throw up earthworks and forgo no siege practice.[1460]

Prophet's words to Ahab

373 Achab, as these things were being done, was in terrible agony[1461] along with all the people. He regained his courage, however, and was relieved of his fears,[1462] when a certain prophet approached him and said to him that God promised that he would subjugate these so many ten thousands of the enemy.[1463] **374** When Achab

---

[1451] In 1 Kgs 20:8 "all the elders and all the people" respond to Ahab, even though in 20:7 the king addresses himself only to the former (see note to "the crowd" at 8.368). Josephus disposes of the difficulty by having Ahab both address and be answered by "the crowd." He likewise expands the audience's response of 20:8 about what Ahab ought not do with by having the crowd also suggest a positive course of action ("be ready for war") to the king.

[1452] See Ahab's instructions to the Syrian messengers as cited in 1 Kgs 20:9abα, where, responding to Ben-hadad's 2nd set of demands (20:5-6), Ahab avers "this thing I cannot do." Once again (see 8.368-369), Josephus has Ahab affirm his solicitude for his people's welfare.

[1453] Josephus' notice on Ahab's "dismissal" of the messengers takes the place of the reference to their departing and bringing back word to Ben-hadad of 1 Kgs 20:9bβ.

[1454] Josephus supplies this reference to Ben-hadad's emotional reaction to Ahab's response.

[1455] Josephus omits Ben-hadad's opening oath formula ("the god[s] do so to me and more also, if...") of 1 Kgs 20:10a.

[1456] Josephus clarifies Ben-hadad's obscurely laconic words in 1 Kgs 20:10: "... if the dust of Samaria will suffice for handfuls [MT and LXX L 1 Kgs 21:10b; LXX B 21:10b: for foxes] for the people who are at my feet": the Syrian's soldiers will use the handfuls (of earth) they pick up to construct earthworks higher than Samaria's own walls. Josephus' wording here recalls his notice on Ahab's "remaining in Samareia, for it was

surrounded by a very strong wall and otherwise seemed impregnable" in 8.364.

[1457] Josephus appends this elucidation of Ben-hadad's threat in 1 Kgs 20:10b (see previous note): the fact that the handfuls of earth collected by the Syrian soldiers will allow for the building of such high earthworks is meant to show Ahab just how large the enemy army is.

[1458] Josephus clarifies Ahab's reply in 1 Kgs 20:11 ("let not him that girds on his armor boast as he that puts it off"), taking the phrase "put off armor" as a reference to the victor in battle.

[1459] Compare 1 Kgs 20:12a, where Ben-hadad is informed of Ahab's final response as he is "drinking" with his fellow kings "in booths." Josephus repeats the number of the allied kings from 8.364// 1 Kgs 20:1.

[1460] Niese and Marcus suggest that something is missing in the Greek text of the above sentence. With it Josephus elaborates on LXX BL 1 Kgs 21:12bα, where Ben-hadad commands his servants "build a defensive wall" (in MT 1 Kgs 20:12bα his order is "take up your positions"). He leaves aside the notice on the Syrians' carrying out the king's command of 20:12bβ.

[1461] Greek: ἀγωνία δεινή. Josephus uses this expression of Saul and his associates in *Ant.* 6.107 and of Sennacherib in 10.22.

[1462] Josephus supplies the reference to Ahab's emotional state and its subsequent reversal as a preface to the prophetic intervention mentioned in 1 Kgs 20:13.

[1463] Josephus shortens the words of the biblical prophet cited in 1 Kgs 20:13, omitting both his opening question to Ahab ("have you seen all this great

inquired through whom the victory would come about, he said "through the sons of the leaders, with you leading them because of their inexperience."[1464] When [Achab] then called the leaders' sons, they were found to number about 232.[1465] Upon learning that the Syrian had turned to feasting and relaxation, he opened the gates and sent the boys out.[1466] **375** When the lookouts disclosed this to Adad,[1467] he sent *Syrians routed* some men to meet them, commanding that, if they were advancing as if to battle, they should bind them and bring them to him, while if they were coming in peace, they should do the same thing.[1468] (For his part, Achab also had another army in readiness inside the walls).[1469] When the rulers' sons engaged the [Syrian] guards, they killed many of them and pursued the others back to the camp.[1470] Seeing them victorious, the king of the Israelites released his whole other army.[1471]

376 Falling suddenly upon the Syrians, they conquered them, for they were not expecting them to come out against them, and so they were assaulting men who were unarmed and drunk.[1472] **377** The result was that, fleeing their camp, they left their armor behind,[1473] while the king barely escaped, making his flight on horseback.[1474] **378** Pursuing the Syrians, Achab covered a long stretch of road; after do-

---

multitude?") and his closing statement concerning the intended purpose of God's promised handing over of the Syrians into Ahab's power ("and you shall know that I am the Lord").

[1464] According to the prophet's response to Ahab in 1 Kgs 20:14aβ it is "the servants of the governors of the districts" who will serve as God's instruments. Josephus' appended reference to Ahab's functioning as their leader incorporates into the prophet's reply to Ahab's 1st query (20:14aα) the pair's 2nd exchange in 20:14b: "Then he [Ahab] said, 'who shall begin the battle?' He [the prophet] answered 'you'."

[1465] Josephus' figure agrees with that given in MT 20:15a and LXX L 1 Kgs 21:15a, as against the 230 of LXX B 1 Kgs 21:15a. At this point Josephus omits the appended notice of 20(21):15b, where the witnesses give widely varying numbers for "the people of Israel" whom Ahab also musters at this point, i.e. 7,000 (MT), 60 (LXX B), 60,000 (LXX L). Subsequently, however, he will draw on this notice; see 8.375.

[1466] Josephus compresses and clarifies the (confusing) sequence of 1 Kgs 20:16-17a, where an indeterminate "they" goes forth at noon, even as Ben-hadad and his fellow kings are drinking in booths, whereupon the group, i.e. "the servants of the governors of the districts," designated by the prophet in 20:14, on its own volition, goes out "first." Josephus' version underscores Ahab's control of the proceedings, in accordance with the prophet's statement about his leadership role in 8.374a.

[1467] Like LXX BL 1 Kgs 21:17b, Josephus lacks an equivalent to the mention in MT 1 Kgs 20:17b of Ben-hadad's initial "sending out scouts," who then report to him about the Israelite advance.

[1468] Josephus reverses the sequence of Ben-hadad's instructions in 1 Kgs 20:18, which speaks 1st of what

is to be done with the Israelites should they be coming in peace and then of how they are to be dealt if their intentions are bellicose. Josephus has the king mention the latter, more likely of the 2 possibilities, in 1st place.

[1469] This parenthetical notice seems based on the mention of Ahab's mustering "all the people of Israel" in 1 Kgs 20:15b, which Josephus previously passed over; see note to "about 232" at 8.374.

[1470] In 1 Kgs 20:19-20a the rout of the Syrians is effected, not only by the "servants of the governors of the districts," but also by "the army which followed them." Josephus ascribes the initial defeat of the Syrians solely to (his equivalent of) the former group. He further specifies the direction of the Syrians' flight (20:20a) at this juncture, i.e. towards their camp.

[1471] This is the force, which, earlier in 8.375, Ahab is said to hold in readiness inside the walls. Here too highlighting the king's leadership role, Josephus depicts him as dispatching this group only after he has witnessed the initial success of the first contingent.

[1472] This notice on the (separate) success achieved by the "second wave" of the Israelite forces and the reason for its success has no explicit equivalent in the biblical account, where the 232 and the army that follows them cooperate in routing the Syrians; see 1 Kgs 20:19-20a. The wording of this notice is reminiscent of Josephus' description of Abraham's victory over the Assyrians in *Ant.* 1.177 and of David's overthrow of the Amalekites in *Ant.* 6.362, as well as of Herodotus' account (1.211) of a military triumph won by Cyrus the Persian. See Begg 1993: 221, n. 1448.

[1473] This added reference to the Syrians' flight picks up on the allusion to their being driven back to "their camp" in 8.375.

[1474] See 1 Kgs 20:20b, which also mentions the "horsemen" who accompany the fugitive Ben-hadad.

ing away with them, he plundered what was in the camp[1475]—this was no little wealth, but a mass of gold and silver. Taking the chariots and horses of Adad as well, he returned to the city.[1476] The prophet told him to remain prepared and to keep his force in readiness, since in the following year the Syrian would once again campaign against him.[1477] And Achab did these things.[1478]

Prophet warns Ahab

New Syrian tactics

(14.3) 379 Having escaped from the battle with as much of his army as he could,[1479] Adad consulted with his friends as to how he should campaign against the Israelites.[1480] They suggested that they not engage them in the mountains, for their God was powerful in such places,[1481] and therefore they had been defeated by them just now. They said, however, that they would conquer if they joined battle in the plain.[1482] **380** In addition to this, they advised that he dismiss the kings, whom he had summoned as his allies, to their homes, but retain their army, designating satraps instead of them.[1483] [To replace] the ranks of those who had been lost, he should levy a force from their country, along with horses and chariots.[1484] Thinking these things well said, he [Adad] outfitted the force in this way.[1485]

Preparations for battle

(14.4) 381 At the beginning of the year, bringing up his army, he came against the Hebrews.[1486] When at a certain city, which they call Aphek,[1487] he pitched camp in a great plain.[1488] Achab, going to meet him with his force, pitched camp opposite him.[1489] His army, however, was much the smaller in comparison with that of the enemy.[1490]

[1475] Josephus modifies the notice on Ahab's activities of 1 Kgs 20:21 in several respects. He replaces its opening reference to the king's "going out" with mention of the extent of his pursuit. He likewise reverses the sequence of 20:21a, where Ahab's "capturing" (so LXX BL 1 Kgs 21:21aβ; MT smiting) "horses and chariots" is cited prior to his "killing" the Syrians. He thereby presents Ahab's initiatives in a militarily more logical order: the enemy troops are first eliminated, and only then is their camp plundered.

[1476] Josephus elaborates on the "capture notice" of LXX BL 1 Kgs 21:21aβ (see previous note), which mentions only the "horses and chariots" seized by Ahab. He likewise supplies the reference to the king's return to Samaria.

[1477] See 1 Kgs 20:22, where the upcoming Syrian advance is predicted by the prophet for "the spring" (literally: the turn of the year).

[1478] Josephus appends this notice on the king's compliance with the directives given him by the prophet in 1 Kgs 20:22.

[1479] This added transitional phrase picks up on the notice of Ben-hadad's flight in 8.377.

[1480] According to 1 Kgs 20:23a, it is Ben-hadad's "servants" who take the lead in presenting their plan to him. Josephus' rendition assigns the initiative to the king himself.

[1481] Compare the opening words of Ben-hadad's counsellors in 1 Kgs 20:23bα: "their god(s) are god(s) of the hills [LXX BL 1 Kgs 21:23bα add: and not a god of the valleys], and so they were stronger than we."

Josephus has the speakers draw a conclusion about what the Syrians should *not* do on the basis of this recognition, i.e. fight the Israelites in the mountains.

[1482] See 1 Kgs 20:23bβ.

[1483] See 1 Kgs 20:24. Josephus adds the advisors' proposal that the kings' armies be retained. His word for the replacement leaders, i.e. "satraps" (Greek: σατράπαι) is the same as that used in LXX BL 1 Kgs 21:24.

[1484] See 1 Kgs 20:25aα. Josephus prefaces the advisors' final proposal with an indication concerning the purpose of the suggested muster. He leaves aside the counsellors' concluding affirmation of certain victory should they fight this time in the plain (20:25aβ), which recapitulates their claim in 20:23bβ.

[1485] See 1 Kgs 20:25bβ. Josephus adds the reference to the king's approval of the advisors' proposals.

[1486] See 1 Kgs 20:26a, where Ben-hadad's new campaign occurs "in the spring" (literally: at the turn of the year), as announced by the prophet in 20:22.

[1487] MT (1 Kgs 20:26) אֲפֵק (Eng.: "Aphek"); LXX BL 1 Kgs 21:26 and Josephus Ἀφέκα.

[1488] Josephus adds the reference to Ben-hadad's encamping.

[1489] Compare 1 Kgs 20:27aα, which does not mention Ahab by name in its account of Israel's countermove. Once again, Josephus highlights the leadership role assumed by the king.

[1490] Josephus' notice on the disparity between the Israelite and Syrian forces eliminates the figurative characterization of the former as being "like 2 little

382 But the prophet,[1491] approaching him again,[1492] stated that God was giving him the victory, so that he might show that his own strength was present, not only in the mountains, but also in the plains—something which did not seem [to be the case] to the Syrians.[1493] For seven days they remained quiet, encamped opposite one another.[1494] On the last of these days, at dawn, the enemy approached from their camp and drew up for battle, while Achab likewise led out his own force against them.

383 Once they engaged, a fierce battle ensued.[1495] [Achab] put the enemy to flight and followed them in pursuit. They, however, were also exterminated by their own chariots and by each other, though a few of them managed to escape into the city of Aphek.[1496] **384** Those upon whom the walls collapsed also died; [they amounted to] 27,000,[1497] in addition to the 100,000 destroyed in the battle.[1498] Adad, the king of the Syrians, fleeing with some of his most trusted domestics[1499] into an underground chamber, hid himself there.[1500]

Syrians routed again

385 When these [Adad's domestics] stated that the Israelite kings were humane and merciful[1501] and they would be able to obtain safety for him from Achab[1502] by using the customary manner of intercession, should he [Adad] give them permission to go off to him,[1503] Adad did permit them.[1504] They put on sackcloth and placed ropes around their heads, for thus the Syrians of old made intercession.[1505] They

Syrians appeal to Ahab

---

flocks of goats" of 1 Kgs 20:27aβ.

[1491] This designation for Ahab's interlocutor is paralleled in Tg. 1 Kgs 20:28, whereas MT and LXX BL 1 Kgs 21:28 designate the figure as "(a) man of God."

[1492] Josephus' use of the term "again" here serves to identify "the prophet" in question with the one who earlier addressed Ahab (see 8.378). By contrast, MT 1 Kgs 20:28 and LXX BL 1 Kgs 21:28 leave it unclear whether the "man of God" they mention is the same figure as "the prophet" who advises Ahab in 20(21):22.

[1493] Josephus reproduces the substance of 1 Kgs 20:28, where the man of God first "quotes" the Syrians' earlier words (see 20:23) and then proceeds to announce that, in response to those words ("because") the Lord is giving them into Ahab's hand in order that "you [pl., MT; sg., LXX BL 1 Kgs 21:28] will know that I am the Lord."

[1494] See 1 Kgs 20:29aα.

[1495] Josephus elaborates on the summary biblical reference (1 Kgs 20:29aβ) to "battle being joined on the 7th day."

[1496] Josephus here both anticipates and elaborates upon the allusion to the surviving Syrians' retreat into Aphek of 1 Kgs 20:30aα, with, e.g., mention of their causing one another's death in their headlong flight.

[1497] This figure for those killed by the falling wall corresponds to that cited in 1 Kgs 20:30aβ.

[1498] This is Josephus' delayed use of the Syrian battlefield casualty figure cited in MT 1 Kgs 20:29b and LXX B 1 Kgs 21:29b (LXX L 1 Kgs 21:29b has 120,000).

[1499] Josephus adds mention of the king's servants

accompanying the fugitive Ben-hadad (see 1 Kgs 20:30b) in view of their subsequent role in the narrative.

[1500] Josephus' word for "chamber" here (Greek: οἶκος, literally: "house") is the same as that used by LXX BL 1 Kgs 21:30bβ. Also like LXX BL, Josephus lacks an equivalent to the localization of this chamber "in the city" given in MT 1 Kgs 20:30bβ.

[1501] Compare 1 Kgs 20:31, where Ben-hadad's servants affirm "we have heard [MT; LXX BL 1 Kgs 21:31: know] that the kings of the house of Israel are merciful kings." The adjective collocation "humane and merciful" (Greek: φιλάνθρωπός καὶ ἐλεήμων) recurs in *Ant.* 10.41 (which is Josephus' only other use of the term ἐλεήμων).

[1502] Josephus' servants express themselves more confidently about the outcome of their proposed mission than do their biblical counterparts in 1 Kgs 20:31, who merely declare: "perhaps he [Ahab] will [LXX B 1 Kgs 21:31 adds again] spare your life."

[1503] In their word to Ben-hadad in 1 Kgs 20:31 the servants spell out which supplicatory gestures they have in mind. Josephus reserves his mention of these gestures for his notice on the servants' subsequent approach to Ahab.

[1504] Josephus appends this notice about the servants' getting the permission they have asked for from Ben-hadad (see 1 Kgs 20:31), prior to their setting out to Ahab (20:32). He thereby highlights the Syrian king's continuing control of the proceedings.

[1505] See 1 Kgs 20:32a, which specifies that the sackcloth was placed on the servants' "loins." Josephus

came to Achab and said that they were asking him to grant safety to Adad, who would be his slave forever in response to his kindness.[1506]

Ahab and Benhadad (Adad) make peace

386 [Achab] told them to congratulate him on having survived and suffered no [injury] in the battle, and promised him the honor and loyalty one might confer on a brother.[1507] Having obtained his [Achab's] oaths that he would not do him [Adad] any wrong,[1508] they went and brought him out into the open from the chamber in which he had been hidden and brought him to Achab, who was sitting in his chariot and to whom he paid homage.[1509] **387** At that, Achab, giving him his right hand, lifted him up into the chariot.[1510] Embracing him, he directed him to be of good cheer and to expect no harm.[1511] Adad, for his part, thanked him and affirmed that, for his entire lifetime he would be mindful of his beneficence.[1512] He promised that he would give back the Israelite cities that the kings before him had taken away and would make Damascus accessible, so that they might travel there, just as his [own] ancestors had done the same with Samareia.[1513] **388** Oaths and agreements having been made,[1514] Achab sent him [Adad] back to his own kingdom, after giving him many gifts.[1515] Such was the end of the campaign of Adad, the king of the Syrians, against Achab and the Israelites.[1516]

Prophet

(14.5) 389 However, a certain prophet named Michaias,[1517] approaching one of

---

appends the reference to the antiquity of the practices in question.

[1506] Compare 1 Kgs 20:32aβ, where the servants quote the words of "your servant Ben-hadad" to Ahab, i.e. "pray, let me live." Josephus has them add mention of the Israelite's (hoped-for) "kindness," which, the Syrians claim, will lead to Ben-hadad's becoming Ahab's lifelong "slave."

[1507] Josephus embellishes Ahab's laconic response as cited in 1 Kgs 20:32b: "Does he [Ben-hadad] still live? He is my brother." In so doing, he highlights Ahab's chivalrous stance towards his suppliant foe, thereby validating the Syrian retainers' earlier statement (8.385) about the "humane and merciful" character of Israel's kings.

[1508] This is Josephus' clarifying rendition of the obscure 1 Kgs 20:33abα, which RSV renders: "Now the men were watching for an omen, and they quickly took it up from him, and said, 'Yes, your brother Ben-hadad.' Then he said, 'Go, and bring him'." He may have understood the "omen" the biblical Syrians are said to be looking for as a guarantee ("oath") that Ahab would not harm their master.

[1509] Josephus elaborates on the summary notice of 1 Kgs 20:33bβ about Ben-hadad's being brought before Ahab with mention of the latter's sitting in his chariot and the former's act of self-humbling. The 1st of these additions has in view the reference to Ahab's taking Ben-hadad into his chariot, with which 20:33 concludes.

[1510] The concluding words of 1 Kgs 20:33 simply have Ahab "causing Ben-hadad to come up [LXX BL 1 Kgs 21:33 add to him] into the chariot." Josephus sup-

plies the reference to the hand gesture by which Ahab assists Ben-hadad in his "ascent."

[1511] With this addition Josephus continues highlighting the gracious reception given Ben-hadad by Ahab, vis-à-vis 1 Kgs 20:34, where Ben-hadad initiates the exchange between them without any such prior encouragement by Ahab.

[1512] This opening, generalized statement of enduring appreciation by Ben-hadad has no parallel in the Syrian king's words as cited in 1 Kgs 20:34a.

[1513] In his declaration of 1 Kgs 20:34a Ben-hadad speaks more specifically of what his "father" had done, and states that he will permit Ahab to "establish bazaars in Damascus."

[1514] This formulation replaces the notice of 1 Kgs 20:34bβ: "so he [Ahab] made a covenant with him [Ben-hadad]." It seems to reflect Ahab's (RSV supplies his name as subject here) preceding statement in 20:34bα: "I will let you [Ben-hadad] go on these conditions."

[1515] Josephus adds the mention of Ahab's parting gifts to Ben-hadad to the notice on the former's dismissal of the latter at the very end of 1 Kgs 20:34.

[1516] Josephus appends this closing formula to his extended account (8.363-388) of the Syro-Israelite conflict.

[1517] In 1 Kgs 20:35 the reference is to a (nameless) "certain man of the sons of the prophets" (who in 20:38 will be called simply "the prophet"). Josephus' identification of this figure with the prophetic protagonist of 1 Kings 22 ("Micaiah") has Rabbinic parallels; see *S. 'Olam Rab.* 20.16; *b. Sanh.* 89b; *t. Sanh.* 14.15b.

the Israelites, directed him to strike him [the prophet] on the head, for his doing this would be in accord with God's will.[1518] When the other was not persuaded, he announced to him, who had disobeyed God's orders, that he would run into a lion, which would destroy him.[1519] When this happened to the man, the prophet once again went up to a different one, ordering him [to do] the same.[1520]

390 When that one struck and wounded him on the skull, he wrapped up his head[1521] and approached the king.[1522] He said to him that he had been on the campaign with him and had been set as a guard over a certain prisoner by his officer.[1523] But now that he [the prisoner] had fled,[1524] he was in danger of dying at the hands of the one who had entrusted him [the prisoner] to him,[1525] for he had threatened that, if the prisoner escaped, he would be killed.[1526] **391** When Achab stated that his death would be just,[1527] he uncovered his head and was recognized by him [Achab] as the prophet Michaias.[1528] **392** He had used this trick on him to [introduce] his following words:[1529] For God would, he said, execute vengeance on him for having allowed Adad, who had defamed him [God], to escape punishment,[1530] and would cause him to die in his place, and his people in place of [the Syrian's] army.[1531] Enraged at the prophet,[1532] Achab directed that he be locked under guard,[1533] while he himself, disturbed by Michaias' words, returned home.[1534]

Micaiah (Michaias) prepares to confront Ahab

Micaiah's word of doom for Ahab

[1518] Josephus goes beyond 1 Kgs 20:35a in having the prophetic figure specify where he wishes to be "struck."

[1519] See 1 Kgs 20:35b-36a, where it is "the voice of the Lord" that the other man is said not to have obeyed.

[1520] See 1 Kgs 20:36b-37a, where (v.37a) the prophetic figure repeats the words of his "striking command" from v. 35a.

[1521] Josephus combines the indications of 1 Kgs 20:37b (the wounding of the "prophet," to which Josephus adds the specification that this was "on the skull," cf. 8.389) and 38b (the prophet "disguises himself with a bandage over his eyes"). He will make use of the intervening v. 38a in the immediate continuation of his account.

[1522] According to the sequence of 1 Kgs 20:38a, 39aα, the prophet "waits for the king by the way" and then speaks to him as he passes by.

[1523] In 1 Kgs 20:39aβbα the prophet identifies himself to the king as one who had "gone out in the midst of the battle," and designates the one who entrusted the prisoner to him as a "soldier." Josephus "delays" for the moment his (partial) "quotation" of the alternative threats the one handing over the prisoner makes as cited in 20:39bβ.

[1524] Josephus omits the prophet's opening phrase of 1 Kgs 20:40 "and as your servant was busy here and there," which itself serves to explain (and justify) the escape of the (fictive) prisoner that he will proceed to relate.

[1525] This statement, underscoring the danger facing him, has no counterpart in the prophet's report to the king in 1 Kgs 20:39-40a.

[1526] Here, Josephus makes (delayed) use of the 1st of the 2 threats (supposedly) made to the solider by his counterpart in 1 Kgs 20:39bβ: "if by any means he [the prisoner] be missing, your life shall go for his life." On the other hand, Josephus leaves aside the alternative penalty cited by the other at the end of v. 39, i.e. "… or else you shall pay a talent of silver," to which there is no further reference in what follows.

[1527] Compare Ahab's response to his interlocutor in 1 Kgs 20:40b: "so shall your judgment be; you yourself have decided it."

[1528] In 1 Kgs 20:41 Ahab recognizes his interlocutor simply as "one of the prophets." Josephus' specification on the matter reflects his earlier naming (8.389) of the prophetic figure of 20:35 as "Michaias."

[1529] Josephus supplies this transitional phrase.

[1530] Compare 1 Kgs 20:42a, where the prophet refers to Ahab's "letting go out of your hand the man I [God] had devoted to destruction." The "defamation" of God to which Michaias alludes here is the claim by Ben-hadad's servants—which the king himself endorses as "well said"—that the power of the Israelite God is limited to the mountains; see 8.379, cf. 8.382.

[1531] See 1 Kgs 20:42b.

[1532] Josephus supplies this reference to Ahab's emotional state.

[1533] In adding this directive by Ahab concerning "Michaias" at the conclusion of their (initial) confrontation, Josephus likely found his inspiration in 1 Kgs 22:27b, where, after a similar confrontation between them, Ahab commands that Micaiah be "put in prison."

[1534] 1 Kgs 20:43 characterizes Ahab as "resentful and sullen," following his confrontation with the "man of God." Josephus omits the biblical specification that the king's "return home" took him "to Samaria."

*Start of
Jehoshaphat's
reign*

(15.1) 393 This was the state of affairs for Achab. I now revert to Josaphat, the king of Hierosolyma,[1535] who augmented his kingship and posted forces in the cities of the country subject to him.[1536] He likewise stationed garrisons in those [cities] of the inheritance of Ephraim that his grandfather Abias had captured at the time when Hieroboam ruled as king over the ten tribes.[1537] **394** Moreover, he had the Deity as his benevolent cooperator[1538] since he was just and pious and was seeking each day to do what would be pleasing and acceptable to God.[1539] Those around [him] honored him with kingly gifts and thus caused him to become extremely wealthy and enjoy the greatest glory.[1540]

*Jehoshaphat
teaches people
the law*

(15.2) 395 In the third year of his reign, calling together the leaders of the country and the priests,[1541] he directed them to go round the entire country and teach the people [living] in it, city by city, the Mosaic laws, both to observe these and to be solicitous for the worship of God.[1542] The entire crowd was so pleased by this, that there was nothing for which they were more ambitious or which they more loved than to keep the laws.[1543]

*Tribute and
military
measures*

396 The surrounding [peoples] likewise continued to cherish Josaphat and to be at peace with him.[1544] The Palestinoi paid their fixed tribute to him,[1545] while each year the Arabs delivered 360 lambs and as many kids.[1546] He fortified other great

---

[1535] Of the above 2 transitional formulae—both of which are Josephan additions—one rounds off the historian's extended (initial) presentation of Ahab (8.316-392// 1 Kgs 16:21-21:29), while the other re-directs attention to the Judean Jehoshaphat, last mentioned in 8.315. On Josephus' account of Jehoshaphat's early reign in 8.393-397 (// 2 Chronicles 17), see Begg 1993: 236-42; on his overall treatment of this king, see Feldman 1998a: 307-21.

[1536] 2 Chr 17:2a speaks of Jehoshaphat's "placing forces in all the fortified cities of Judah." Josephus omits the notices of 17:1 on Jehoshaphat's accession (already mentioned by him in 8.315) and his "strengthening himself against Israel" (in this instance, his omission likely has in view the friendly relations between Jehoshaphat and the northern kings portrayed in what follows).

[1537] On the textual problems of the Greek underlying this translation, see Marcus *ad loc.* In 2 Chr 17:2b the reference is to Ephraimite cities occupied by Jehoshaphat's father Asa, a happening mentioned in passing in 2 Chr 15:8. Josephus makes the allusion rather to the seizure of Northern cities by Abijah/Abias recorded in 2 Chr 13:19 (// 8.284). He adds the specification that Abijah took the cities during Jeroboam's reign.

[1538] Greek: εὐμενὴς καὶ συνεργός. This collocation occurs only here in Josephus. He uses the term "cooperator" (Greek: συνεργός) of God's relationship to David in *Ant.* 7.91.

[1539] This is Josephus' generalized rendition of the evaluative statements concerning Jehoshaphat of 2 Chr 17:3-4, 6. From the biblical sequence Josephus elimi-

nates, e.g., the reference to Jehoshaphat's "walking in the earlier way of his father" (17:3a) given that in his presentation Asa, Jehoshaphat's father, remains an impeccable king throughout his reign. He likewise leaves aside the mention of particular deities (Baal [17:3b]; the Asherim [17:6]) and illegitimate cultic institutions (the high places [17:6]) that the biblical Jehoshaphat either avoids or eliminates.

[1540] Compare 2 Chr 17:5b: "all Judah brought tribute to Jehoshaphat; and he had great riches and honor."

[1541] According to MT 2 Chr 17:7-8, Jehoshaphat's delegation consisted of 5 named "princes," 9 named Levites, and 2 named priests. Josephus passes over the 2nd of these groups entirely, while also omitting the names of the 1st and 3rd groups.

[1542] In 2 Chr 17:7 the delegation is directed simply "to teach." Josephus supplies a content for the teaching they are to impart, drawing on the subsequent biblical reference (17:9) to the delegation's "having the book of the law of the Lord with them."

[1543] Josephus appends this notice on the successful outcome of the teaching mission spoken of in 2 Chr 17:7-9. With the addition, he highlights the fact that, also in this regard, Jehoshaphat proved an effective king.

[1544] Josephus leaves aside the biblical reference (2 Chr 17:10) to "the fear of the Lord" as that which kept the foreign nations from making war on Judah in Jehoshaphat's time.

[1545] According to 2 Chr 17:11a, the Philistines brought Jehoshaphat "presents" and "silver for tribute."

[1546] Contrary to his usual practice, Josephus gives much lower figures for the Arabs' tribute than does

cities and towers, and had a military force available against his enemies.[1547] **397** From the tribe of Iouda there was an army of 300,000 troops, over which Ednai[1548] had the leadership. Joannes[1549] [was in charge] of 200,000; he was also leader of the 200,000 archers on foot of the tribe of Benjamin.[1550] Another general, named Chabath,[1551] provided the king with a crowd of 180,000 troops.[1552] These were in addition to those whom he [Josaphat] dispatched to the most [solidly] fortified cities.[1553]

(15.3) 398 Josaphat procured [in marriage] for his son Joram the daughter of Achab, the king of the ten tribes, whose name was Othlia.[1554] When, after some time,[1555] he came to Samareia, Achab received him and the army that followed him in a friendly fashion; he entertained them splendidly with an abundance of grain, wine and meat.[1556] He appealed to him [Josaphat] to become his ally against the king of the Syrians, so that he might recover the city of Aramatha in Galadene.[1557] **399** For the Syrian's father had taken it away from his own father, to whom it had belonged at first.[1558]

Josaphat promised his help, for he had a force that was not inferior to his.[1559]

Jehoshaphat visits Ahab in Samaria

Military alliance of two kings

---

2 Chr 17:11b (7,700 rams and 7,700 he-goats [MT LXX L; LXX B mentions only rams]). Perhaps then, Josephus had before him a variant text of 17:11b.

[1547] Josephus summarizes the notices of 2 Chr 17:12-13 on Jehoshaphat's preparation of both sites and men for military purposes.

[1548] MT (2 Chr 17:14) עדנה (Eng.: "Adnah"); LXX B Ἐδνάας; LXX L Αἰδής; Josephus Ἐδναῖος.

[1549] MT (2 Chr 17:15) יהוחנן (Eng.: "Jehohanan"); LXX BL Ἰωανάν; Josephus Ἰωάννης.

[1550] 2 Chr 17:15-16 cites 2 additional (i.e. beyond the "Adnah" mentioned in 17:14) Judean commanders, i.e. "Jehohanan" with 280,000 troops and "Amasiah" with 200,000. Thereafter, 17:17 refers to a 1st Benjamite commander, i.e. "Eliada" with his 200,000 men. Josephus conflates these data, making the one commander "Joannes" head of both a Judean and a Benjamite contingent, each consisting of 200,000 men. In so doing, he leaves unaccounted for the 280,000 men assigned to "Jehohanan" in 17:15.

[1551] MT (2 Chr 17:17) יהוזבד (Eng.: "Jehozabad"); LXX BL Ἰωζαβάδ; Josephus Χάβαθος.

[1552] 2 Chr 17:18 states that "Jehozabad" with his 180,000 (Benjamite; see 17:17) troops was next to "Eliada."

[1553] See 2 Chr 17:19, which localizes the cities in question "in Judah."

[1554] 2 Chr 18:1b speaks simply of the "marriage alliance" between Jehoshaphat and Ahab. Josephus derives the names of the couple involved, i.e. "Joram," son of Jehoshaphat, and "Athaliah," (grand) daughter of Ahab, from subsequent biblical contexts; see 2 Kgs 8:16 // 2 Chr 21:6 and 2 Kgs 8:25 // 2 Chr 22:2, respectively. He omits the notice of 2 Chr 18:1a on the "great riches and honor" acquired by Jehoshaphat, having already referred to these in 8.394 (cf. 2 Chr 17:5). On Josephus' version of the story of the death of Ahab (1 Kgs 22:1-40// 2 Chr 18:1-34) in 8.398-420, see Begg 1993: 243-69 and Sievers 1999.

[1555] Josephus' vague chronological indication here corresponds to that with which 2 Chr 18:2 begins, i.e. "after some years." 1 Kgs 22:2, by contrast, dates Jehoshaphat's arrival in Samaria "in the 3rd year," i.e. of the 3-year truce between Syria and Israel cited in 22:1 (to which Josephus will make subsequent reference; see 8.400).

[1556] Josephus elaborates on the notice, unique to 2 Chr 18:2a, concerning the welcome given Jehoshaphat and his entourage by Ahab. In particular, he has the visitors offered, not only meat, but also "grain and wine."

[1557] In 1 Kgs 22:4// 2 Chr 18:2b Ahab's request is simply that Jehoshaphat "accompany him" to "Ramoth-gilead." Josephus' formulation of the request—which stands under the influence of the plus of 1 Kgs 22:3, where Ahab declares to his servants that whereas, the city "belongs to us," they have been making no effort to take it back from the Syrian king—specifies the objective of the projected joint campaign.

[1558] This added comment accounts for the state of affairs to which Ahab alludes in his words to his servants in 1 Kgs 22:3, i.e. Ramoth-gilead "belongs to us," but is currently in the possession of the Syrians; see previous note.

[1559] Jehoshaphat's positive promise of support in Josephus' version picks up on the king's closing words to Ahab in 2 Chr 18:3bβ, i.e. "(we will be) with you in war." His appended notice on the non-inferiority of Jehoshaphat's army to that of Ahab seems to represent an interpretation of the former's declaration of solidar-

Prophetic consultation

When he had summoned his force from Hierosolyma to Samareia, the two kings advanced from the city, and each sitting on his throne, were distributing their soldiers' pay to their own soldiers.[1560] **400** Josaphat, however, directed that, if any prophets were present, he [Achab] should call them to answer concerning the expedition against the Syrian, whether they would advise him to undertake the campaign at that time.[1561] For by then peace and friendship[1562] between Achab and the Syrian had continued for three years,[1563] from the time the former had released the latter after taking him prisoner until that day.[1564]

(15.4) 401 Calling his prophets—who were about 400 in number—Achab directed them to question God as to whether he would give him, in his campaign against Ader,[1565] victory and the destruction of that city for the sake of which he was about to launch the war.[1566]

Jehoshaphat asks for second opinion

402 The prophets, for their part, advised him to set out on the campaign, for he would conquer the Syrian and make him subject, as [he had been] earlier.[1567] Perceiving from their words that they were false prophets,[1568] Josaphat asked Achab if there was yet another prophet of God "so that they might learn more precisely concerning the future."[1569]

Micaiah summoned

403 Achab said that there was. He hated him, however, because he prophesied calamities and had predicted that he would be killed, after being defeated by the Syrian king.[1570] Because of this, he now had him under guard.[1571] He was called

---

ity as cited in 1 Kgs 22:4b// 2 Chr 18:3bα: "I am as you are, my people as your people, my horses as your horses" (Chronicles lacks the reference to horses).

[1560] Josephus anticipates his reference to the 2 kings sitting on their thrones from 1 Kgs 22:10// 2 Chr 18:9. He likewise amplifies this item with reference to Jehoshaphat's bringing up (the rest of) his army and to the activity being performed by the royal pair as it awaits the arrival of those additional forces, i.e. paying their troops.

[1561] Josephus elaborates Jehoshaphat's directive that Ahab "seek the word of the Lord" of 1 Kgs 22:5// 2 Chr 18:4. In so doing, he avoids the phrase "word of the Lord," while also spelling out what it is Jehoshaphat hopes to learn from the consultation for which he is calling.

[1562] Greek: εἰρήνη καὶ φιλία. Josephus uses this collocation also in *Ant.* 12.394 (reverse order) and 18.375.

[1563] Josephus here makes a delayed use of the notice on the 3-year truce between Syria and Israel of 1 Kgs 22:1, turning this into an explanation ("for") as to why Jehoshaphat feels the need for a prophetic consultation about the advisability of a war against Syria.

[1564] To his preceding reference (drawn from 1 Kgs 22:1) to the 3-year Syrian-Israelite truce, Josephus appends this allusion to the starting point of that period, i.e. Ahab's release of the defeated Ben-hadad, as related by him in 8.388 (// 1 Kgs 20:34).

[1565] This form of the name (Greek: Ἄδερ) of Ahab's Syrian opponent as read by Niese here in 8.401 differs

from that found previously in Josephus' text, i.e. "(son of) "Adad(os)" (which Marcus and Schalit *s.v.* read in 8.401 as well); the form "Ader" recurs frequently in *Antiquities* 9, however. Ahab's question to the prophets (see next note) as cited in 1 Kgs 22:6a// 2 Chr 18:5a makes no reference either to an inquiry of the Deity by them or to the Syrian king.

[1566] Josephus expatiates considerably on the alternate question put by Ahab to the 400 prophets in 1 Kgs 22:6a// 2 Chr 18:5a, i.e. "Shall I/we go to battle against Ramoth-gilead, or shall I forbear?" In particular, the added reference to God in the question(s) he attributes to Ahab is noteworthy, given his tendency to eliminate biblical references to the Deity. The city to which Ahab alludes here is "Aramatha"; see 8.398.

[1567] Compare 1 Kgs 22:6b// 2 Chr 18:5b, where the prophets respond: "Go up; for God/the Lord will give it into the hand of the king." Josephus adds the allusion to Israel's earlier domination of the Syrians.

[1568] Josephus adds this motivation for Jehoshaphat's subsequent request for a "second opinion." On Josephus' use of the term "false prophet" (Greek: ψευδοπροφήτης), see the note to "what pleased him" at 8.236.

[1569] See 1 Kgs 22:7// 2 Chr 18:6. Josephus has Jehoshaphat spell out what he hopes to learn from the additional prophet.

[1570] Josephus elaborates on Ahab's general allusion (1 Kgs 22:8a// 2 Chr 18:7a) to the "evil" Micaiah has (purportedly) been saying about him [Ahab] with a more

Michaias,[1572] the son of Omblai.[1573] When, nonetheless, Josaphat directed that he be brought,[1574] he sent a eunuch and fetched Michaias.[1575]

404 On the way the eunuch disclosed to him that all the other prophets had predicted victory to the king.[1576] He, however, stated that it was not right for him to speak lies in God's name;[1577] he had rather to say what [God] would tell him about the king.[1578] When he came to Achab,[1579] who adjured him to tell him the truth,[1580] he said that God had shown him the Israelites in flight, pursued by the Syrians and dispersed by them on the mountains, like sheep lacking a shepherd.[1581] **405** He further said that whereas God was indicating that these [the Israelites] would return in peace to their homes, he [Achab] alone would fall in battle.[1582] When Michaias stated these things, Achab said to Josaphat: "Did I not disclose to you a short while back that this person is ill-disposed to me and prophesied the worst against me?"[1583]

Ahab–Micaiah exchange

---

specific allusion to the former's earlier announcement about the fate awaiting the king as cited in 8.392 (cf. 1 Kgs 20:42).

[1571] This addition to Ahab's reply recalls Josephus' version of the earlier confrontation between Micaiah and Ahab; see 8.392, where Ahab commands that the prophet be kept "locked under guard." In this way Josephus provides an explanation as to why Micaiah was not on hand for the initial prophetic "consultation."

[1572] MT (1 Kgs 22:8a// 2 Chr 18:7a) מיכיהו (Eng.: "Micaiah"); LXX B 1 Kgs 22:8a// LXX B 2 Chr 18:7a Μειχαίας; LXX L 1 Kgs 22:8a// LXX L 2 Chr 18:7a and Josephus Μιχαίας. Josephus has already introduced this figure by name in 8.389.

[1573] MT (1 Kgs 22:8a) ימלה (Eng.: "Imlah"); (2 Chr 18:7a) א‏ ימל (Eng.: "Imlah"); LXX B 1 Kgs 22:8a Ἰεμιάς; LXX L 1 Kgs 22:8a Ναμαλεί; LXX B 2 Chr 18:7a Ἰεμαάς; LXX L 2 Chr 18:7a Ναμαλί; Josephus Ὀμβλαῖος (so Niese; Marcus, Naber, and Schalit s.v. follow the reading Ἰεμβλαῖος of P²).

[1574] In 1 Kgs 22:8b// 2 Chr 18:7b, Jehoshaphat reacts to Ahab's invective against Micaiah with the soothing interjection "let not the king say so." Josephus depicts a more imperious Judean king whose directive here recalls his earlier enjoining Ahab to summon whatever prophets might be on hand in 8.400.

[1575] Josephus' designation for Ahab's envoy is the same term (Greek: εὐνοῦχος) used in LXX 1 Kgs 22:9 // 2 Chr 18:8. MT employs a more general term, i.e. סרים, which may denote a "eunuch," but also has the more general sense of "official."

[1576] From the messenger's words to Micaiah on the way in 1 Kgs 22:13// 2 Chr 18:12, Josephus omits the former's crass appended suggestion to the prophet: "let your word be like the word of one of them, and speak favorably." Having anticipated (see 8.399) the notice (1 Kgs 22:10// 2 Chr 18:9) on the 2 kings sitting enthroned as they await Micaiah's arrival, Josephus—for the moment, but see 8.409—leaves aside the entire se-

quence (22:10-12//18:9-11) concerning Zedekiah's prophetic performance before the royal pair during the interlude.

[1577] Greek: καταψεύσασθαι τοῦ θεοῦ. This same construction recurs in *War* 6.288 (subject: the false prophets during the siege of Jerusalem) and *Ant.* 10.178 (the survivors of Jerusalem suspect Jeremiah of doing this).

[1578] Compare 1 Kgs 22:14// 2 Chr 18:13, where Micaiah responds to the messenger's proposal: "... what the Lord says to me, that will I speak." Josephus omits the prophet's opening oath formula ("as the Lord lives").

[1579] Josephus omits the initial exchange between Ahab and Micaiah that is appended to the notice of the latter's arrival in 1 Kgs 22:15// 2 Chr 18:14, where, contrary to his previous affirmation (22:14// 18:13) about saying only what the Lord will tell him, Micaiah appears to lie in his (ironic) echoing of the 400 prophets' favorable words to the king.

[1580] In 1 Kgs 22:16// 2 Chr 18:15 Ahab's "adjuring" of Micaiah follows upon the former's realization that the latter is mocking him with his initial response to his question, in which Micaiah echoes the words of the 400 prophets (see previous note). In Josephus, Ahab's adjuring Micaiah marks the beginning of the exchange between the 2 figures.

[1581] See 1 Kgs 22:17a// 2 Chr 18:16a. Josephus adds the explicit mention of God as the source of Micaiah's "vision."

[1582] Josephus reverses the sequence of the divine word as cited by Micaiah in 1 Kgs 22:17b// 2 Chr 18:16b, where the Deity first states: "these [the Israelites] have no master," and then proceeds to enjoin "let each return to his home in peace."

[1583] See 1 Kgs 22:18// 2 Chr 18:17. Josephus amplifies the biblical Ahab's claim with the assertion that Micaiah is "ill-disposed" towards him, this recalling the king's earlier statement (8.403// 1 Kgs 22:8// 2 Chr 18:7) that he himself "hates" Micaiah.

Intervention of Zedekiah (Sedekias)

406 At that, Michaias said that it was fitting for him to pay attention to all the things spoken in advance by God.[1584] Moreover, it was the false prophets who were inciting[1585] him to make war in hope of victory, whereas he was destined to fall while fighting.[1586] Achab was reflecting [on this],[1587] but a certain Sedekias,[1588] one of the false prophets, approached and urged [the king] not to listen to Michaias,[1589] **407** for he was not speaking the truth.[1590] As proof of this, he made use of what Elias—who perceived the future better than he [Michaias] did—had prophesied.[1591] "For [Elias]," he said, "when prophesying in the city of Jezarela in the field of Naboth, had predicted that dogs would lick his [Achab's] blood, just as they had that of Naboth[1592] who, at his [Achab's] instigation, had been stoned by the crowd.[1593] **408** It was clear, therefore, that Michaias was lying,[1594] given his contradicting a better prophet in stating that he [Achab] would die within three days.[1595] But that you may know whether he is truthful and has the force of the divine spirit[1596] let him, imme-

---

[1584] This affirmation replaces the call to attention, "hear [sg., 1 Kgs 22:19/ pl., 2 Chr 18:18] the word of the Lord," with which the biblical Micaiah opens his 2nd discourse, 1 Kgs 22:19-23// 2 Chr 18:18-22.

[1585] Greek: παρορμάω. Josephus uses this same verb of the false prophet of Bethel who misleads Jeroboam in 8.245.

[1586] This is Josephus' rendering of the conclusion (1 Kgs 22:23// 2 Chr 18:22) of Micaiah's 2nd discourse, which affirms that the Lord has placed "a lying spirit" in the mouth of Ahab's prophets. Josephus thus avoids attributing a divine origin to the message of the "false prophets." To this same end, he omits the entire heavenly vision sequence as related by Micaiah in 22:19b-22// 18:18b-21, which serves to set up Micaiah's theologically problematic affirmation in 22:23// 18:22.

[1587] Josephus supplies this reference to Ahab's initial reaction to Micaiah's words.

[1588] MT (1 Kgs 22:24// 2 Chr 18:23) צדקיהו (Eng.: "Zedekiah"); LXX B 1 Kgs 22:24 Σεδεκιού; LXX L 1 Kgs 22:24// LXX BL 2 Chr 18:23 and Josephus Σεδεκίας. Josephus replaces the biblical mention of his father (MT: Chenanah) with the qualification of him as one of the "false prophets," this recalling Micaiah's allusion to these personages in 8.406. This is Josephus' first reference to Zedekiah, given his delayed utilization of the earlier biblical scene featuring Zedekiah's sign with the iron horns (1 Kgs 22:10-12// 2 Chr 18:9-11); see the note to "and their soldiers" in 8.399.

[1589] Josephus at this point has Zedekiah address the king directly and at length, whereas in 1 Kgs 22:24b// 2 Chr 18:23b he briefly queries Micaiah, asking how it is that the Lord's spirit has left himself in order to speak with his rival.

[1590] This is the thesis of the Josephan Zedekiah's speech to Ahab, which he will then proceed to prove by calling attention to the discrepancy between Micaiah's present prediction and an earlier one made by another prophet, i.e. Elijah.

[1591] Zedekiah's initial comparison of Micaiah and Elijah regarding their respective degree of insight regarding the future already serves to brand the former as an inferior prophet, who, as such, should not be listened to by the king—as Zedekiah has just urged.

[1592] Zedekiah here (loosely) recalls Elijah's words to Ahab as cited by Josephus in 8.361 (where the prophet states that Ahab's blood "will be shed" at the very spot where Naboth's body had been consumed by dogs). In fact, Zedekiah's "quotation" of Elijah here in 8.407 is closer to the wording of 1 Kgs 21:19 itself then is Josephus' own rendering of that verse in 8.361.

[1593] Josephus here has Zedekiah make summary reference to the circumstances of Naboth's death, wherein, however, the leading role was taken, not by Ahab himself, but rather by Jezebel; see 8.357-359.

[1594] With this assertion Zedekiah reiterates his earlier claim (8.407) that Micaiah "was not speaking the truth." Both assertions appear highly ironic, given that the speaker is himself "one of the false prophets" (8.406), as well as Micaiah's own previous affirmation that it was "not right for him to speak lies in God's name" (8.404).

[1595] It is difficult to perceive where the "contradiction" between Micaiah and Elijah is supposed to lie here—the latter spoke of what will happen to Ahab's corpse, while the former had, Zedekiah avers, announced the period within which the king is to die. Moreover, Zedekiah's case against Micaiah's credibility is made all the weaker by the fact that neither in Josephus nor in the Bible does Micaiah himself actually specify a time-frame for Ahab's end.

[1596] With this phrase Josephus seems to be making delayed use of Zedekiah's mention of the "spirit of the Lord" in his question to Micaiah about that spirit leaving himself to speak to his opponent in 1 Kgs 22:24b // 2 Chr 18:23b. For the phrase "the divine spirit" (Greek: τὸ θεῖον πνεῦμα) in Josephus, see note to "the divine spirit" at *Ant.* 6.166.

diately upon his being struck by me, paralyze my hand, just as Jada[1597] withered the right hand of Hieroboam, who wanted to arrest him—for I suppose that you have heard all about this event."[1598]

409 When therefore he struck Michaias[1599] and did not happen to suffer anything,[1600] Achab, being encouraged, was eager to lead his army against the Syrian.[1601] For it was fate, I suppose, that made the false prophets more convincing than the truthful one, in order that it might have a pretext for his [Achab's] end.[1602] Making iron horns, Sedekias said to Achab that God was signifying by means of these that he would subjugate all Syria.[1603]

410 Michaias, on the other hand, said that after not many days Sedekias would be seeking out one hidden inner chamber after another, searching to elude judgment for his lying speech.[1604] The king directed that he [Michaias] be brought under guard to Achamon,[1605] the ruler of the city,[1606] who was to supply him with nothing more than bread and water.[1607]

Micaiah's response and arrest

[1597] Greek: Ἰάδαος. Throughout 8.230-245 Josephus' name for Jeroboam's prophetic antagonist is "Jadon." Schalit *s.v.* reads that same form here in 8.408 as well.

[1598] Josephus adds this long preface to Zedekiah's actual striking of Micaiah (1 Kgs 22:24a// 2 Chr 18:23a); by means of the addition the former spells out what that act is supposed to prove, i.e. whether or not Micaiah is a true prophet, who, as such, like Jadon, cannot be abused with impunity. On the withering of Jeroboam's hand to which Zedekiah alludes here, see 8.233// 1 Kgs 13:4.

[1599] Josephus finally now comes to cite this biblical datum from 1 Kgs 22:24a// 2 Chr 18:23a, following the extended preceding discourse that he has Zedekiah address to the king in 8.407-408 (compare the sequence of 1 Kgs 22:24// 2 Chr 18:23, where Zedekiah speaks to Micaiah himself in conjunction with his striking him).

[1600] Josephus makes explicit this point—and thus the success of the "test" proposed by Zedekiah in 8.408—which remains implicit in the biblical accounts.

[1601] This reference to the impact of Zedekiah's initiative on Ahab is Josephus' addition. Contrast 8.407, where Ahab is said to be "reflecting" on Micaiah's earlier words.

[1602] This appended editorial reflection is a further indication of Josephus' concern to disassociate God from Ahab's death, which in the Bible, results from the king's listening to the false prophets, who have themselves been led astray by a "lying spirit" commissioned for that purpose by the Deity (see 1 Kgs 22:22-23// 2 Chr 18:22, omitted by Josephus). On Josephus' use of the concept of "fate" (Greek: τὸ χρεών), see Schlatter 1932: 43; Stählin 1974: 331-43; and Villabla i Varneda 1986: 58-62. The term appears twice subsequently in Josephus' account of Ahab's demise; see 8.412, 419.

[1603] Josephus makes his delayed use of this biblical element—which in 1 Kgs 22:11// 2 Chr 18:10 occurs prior to Micaiah's arrival—the climax to Zedekiah's efforts at persuading Ahab about Micaiah's lack of credibility. He leaves aside the notice on the remaining 400 prophets seconding Zedekiah's claim about Ahab's forthcoming triumph (22:12// 18:11).

[1604] Josephus elaborates on Micaiah's response to Zedekiah in 1 Kgs 22:25// 2 Chr 18:24, highlighting the imminence of what is announced, as well as supplying a reason for Zedekiah's coming attempt at self-concealment. With his mention of Zedekiah's "lying speech," Micaiah turns his opponent's previous claims (see 8.407, 408) about his own false speaking against him.

[1605] MT (1 Kgs 22:26// 2 Chr 18:25) אמן (Eng.: "Amon"); LXX B 1 Kgs 22:26 Σεμήρ; LXX L 1 Kgs 22:26 Ἐμμήρ; LXX B 2 Chr 18:25 Ἐμήρ; LXX L 2 Chr 18:25 Σεμμήρ; Josephus Ἀχάμων (Schalit *s. v.* suggests that this form may a corruption/conflation of the title ἄρχων [used for the figure in LXX BL 1 Kgs 22:26] and the proper name Ἀμων [cf. MT]).

[1606] This is the same title (Greek: ὁ τῆς πόλεως ἄρχων) used in LXX BL 1 Kgs 22:26 and 2 Chr 18:25.

[1607] Josephus abridges Ahab's directives as cited in 1 Kgs 22:26-27// 2 Chr 18:25-26. In particular, he passes over the name of the 2nd official to whom Micaiah is to be entrusted (Joash, son of the king, MT 22:26// 18:25), as well as the command that Micaiah be kept in prison until Ahab returns "in peace" (22:27 // 18:26). He likewise leaves aside Micaiah's retort to the king (22:28// 18:27), in which he first avers that should Ahab actually return in peace this will show that the Lord has not spoken through him, and then appeals to "all peoples" to "hear" (this concluding appeal is absent in LXX BL 22:28).

Battle started   **411** Achab and Josaphat, the king of Hierosolyma, having led up their armies, marched to Ramathe, a Galadite city.[1608] When the king of the Syrians heard of their campaign, he set his own army over against them, camping not far from Aramathe.[1609]

412 Now Achab and Josaphat had agreed[1610] that Achab would lay aside his royal robe, while the king of Hierosolyma, wearing the former's[1611] garment, would stand in the battle line; thus they would nullify what Michaias had predicted.[1612] Fate found him out, however, even without his robe.[1613] **413** For Adad,[1614] the king of the Syrians, instructed his army via its leaders to do away with no one else, but only the king of the Israelites.[1615] When battle was joined, the Syrians, seeing Josaphat standing in front of the line and supposing him to be Achab, made a rush at him, surrounding him.[1616]

Ahab wounded   **414** Once they drew near, however, they knew that it was not he [Achab], and all drew back.[1617] Fighting from early morning until evening, and being victorious, they killed no one, in accordance with the command of their king; they were seeking to do away with Achab alone, but were unable to find him.[1618] However, one of Adad's royal lads, named Aman,[1619] while shooting arrows at the enemy, wounded the king through his breastplate in the lung.[1620]

[1608] See 1 Kgs 22:29// 2 Chr 18:28. In 8.398 the contested city is called "Aramatha in Galadene." Cf. the form "Aramathe," which appears in the continuation of 8.411.

[1609] Josephus appends this notice on the Syrian's counter-move to the biblical mention of the advance of the allied kings. The text of 8.411 printed by Niese reads 2 different forms for the name of the contested city ("Ramathe," "Aramathe"), while Marcus gives the same form ("Aramathe") in both instances.

[1610] In 1 Kgs 22:30// 2 Chr 18:29 Ahab simply tells Jehoshaphat what he is to do. Josephus' reference to an "agreement" between the 2 kings is part of his wider enhancement of the status and active role of Jehoshaphat vis-à-vis Ahab, reflected also in his having the former twice earlier issue commands to the latter; see 8.400, 403.

[1611] Josephus follows the reading of LXX BL as against MT 1 Kgs 22:30a// 2 Chr 18:29a; in the former witnesses Jehoshaphat is to don Ahab's robes, while in the latter he will wear his own royal robes into battle.

[1612] Josephus supplies this indication concerning the purpose of the kings' change of clothes; it takes the place of the notice of 1 Kgs 22:30b// 2 Chr 18:29b that Ahab did in fact "disguise himself," whereupon he (MT 18:29b: they) proceeded into battle.

[1613] This reference to the operation of "fate" in Ahab's imminent demise picks up on Josephus' earlier statement (8.409), attributing Ahab's heeding of the false prophets to the influence of "fate" upon him.

[1614] The enemy king of Syria is nameless in 1 Kgs 22:31// 2 Chr 18:30. Josephus draws the name from his account of the earlier conflict between Ahab and the

Syrian king in 8.363-392 (// 1 Kings 20). Compare 8.401, where the form of the king name's read by Niese is "Ader."

[1615] See 1 Kgs 22:31// 2 Chr 18:30, where the Syrian's command to his chariot officers is that they "fight" solely with the king of Israel. Like Chronicles, Josephus lacks an equivalent to Kings' specification that the officers to whom the Syrian ruler addressed himself numbered 32.

[1616] Josephus amplifies 1 Kgs 22:32a// 2 Chr 18:31a with further details: the start of battle, Jehoshaphat's position, and the "rush" made against him. Conversely, he omits Jehoshaphat's resultant "cry" of 1 Kgs 22:32b// 2 Chr 18:31b (which adds that the Lord helped him, drawing away his assailants). Perhaps, Josephus found such a "cry" unworthy of a king whose stature he is concerned to enhance; see note to "agreed" at 8.412.

[1617] See 1 Kgs 22:33// 2 Chr 18:32.

[1618] Josephus anticipates this notice on the duration and intensity of the battle from 1 Kgs 22:35// 2 Chr 18:34. The notice likewise alludes back to the Syrian king's command as cited in 8.413.

[1619] In 1 Kgs 22:34a// 2 Chr 18:33a Ahab's wounder is a nameless "man." Josephus' name for him likely represents that of the Syrian general featured in 2 Kings 5, i.e. "Naaman" (who, in fact, is identified with Ahab's killer in Tg. 2 Chr 18:33; *Midr. Pss.* 78, 350 (*ad* Ps 78: 11); and *Midr. Sam.* 11, 80). See further Begg 1993: 261-2, n. 1744.

[1620] Josephus' specification concerning the "place" of Ahab's wound reflects the LXX reading in 1 Kgs 22:34a// 2 Chr 18:33a, i.e. "between the breastplate

415 Achab decided not make known what had happened to his army so that they would not turn to flight.[1621] Instead, he directed the charioteer to turn his chariot aside and to exit the battle; for he was badly, indeed mortally, wounded.[1622] Although he was in pain, he stood in the chariot until sunset; after losing blood,[1623] he died.[1624] **(15.6) 416** Since it was already night, the army of the Syrians withdrew to its camp; when the herald[1625] disclosed that Achab was dead, they [the Israelites] returned to their homes.[1626] Bringing the corpse of Achab to Samareia, they buried it there.[1627]

Ahab's death and burial

417 Washing out the chariot in the spring of Jezarela (which was stained by the king's blood),[1628] they acknowledged that Elias' prophecy was true, for dogs[1629] did lick up his blood, while in the future prostitutes[1630] continued to wash themselves in the spring in this [blood].[1631] He died, on the other hand, at Aramathe, as Michaias had predicted.[1632] **418** Since therefore it happened to Achab as the two prophets had said,[1633] we should think that the Deity is great and everywhere adore and honor him, nor should we imagine that what [is said] in accordance with our pleasure and will[1634] is more persuasive than the truth. Rather, we ought to suppose that nothing is more advantageous than prophecies and the foreknowledge that comes from them,

Fulfillment of two prophecies

Concluding reflections

---

and the lung"; compare MT: "between the scale armor and the breastplate."

[1621] Josephus supplies this notice on Ahab's self-sacrificing concern for the morale of his troops.

[1622] See 1 Kg 22:34b// 2 Chr 18:33b. Josephus both clarifies the meaning of the biblical Ahab's command to his driver, i.e. "turn your hand(s)," and underscores the severity of the king's wound.

[1623] Greek: λιφαιμέω. The verb is *hapax* in Josephus.

[1624] See 1 Kgs 22:35aβb// 2 Chr 18:34aβb. Josephus adds the reference to Ahab's "pain," thereby underscoring the king's heroism. His reference to Ahab's loss of blood reflects the plus of 1 Kgs 22:35bβ.

[1625] Greek: στρατοκήρυξ. This is the same term used in LXX BL 1 Kgs 22:36a (MT does not mention a "herald," but rather of a "cry" going through the camp). It is *hapax* in both Josephus and the LXX.

[1626] See 1 Kgs 22:36 (the Chronicler ends his account with the death of Ahab, 2 Chr 18:34// 1 Kgs 22:35aβ). Josephus supplies the reference to the Syrian withdrawal and to the Israelites' being informed of Ahab's demise. He likewise turns the biblical cry "every man to his city, and every man to his country" (22:36b) into the notice that the Israelites did return home.

[1627] See 1 Kgs 22:37. Josephus leaves aside the verse's opening mention of the death of Ahab, which duplicates that of 22:35aβ.

[1628] See 1 Kgs 22:38aα. Josephus appends the reference to the staining of the spring with Ahab's blood.

[1629] LXX BL 1 Kgs 22:38aβ adds "swine" in line with the plus of LXX 1 Kgs 20:19, where Elijah refers

to the licking of Naboth's blood not only by dogs (as in MT 1 Kgs 21:19) but also by "swine."

[1630] This term translates the participle of the verb ἑταίριζω, used by Josephus only once elsewhere, i.e. in relation to Delilah in *Ant.* 5.306.

[1631] Compare 1 Kgs 22:38bβ, where the use made of Ahab's blood by the dogs and prostitutes respectively is said to be "according to the word of the Lord which he spoke." Josephus replaces the biblical reference to the fulfillment of the divine "word" by a statement about recognition of the truth of a "prophecy," which is itself explicitly attributed to Elijah (see 8.407).

[1632] Josephus adds this notice on the fulfillment also of Micaiah's prediction about Ahab's end (see 8.405, where, however, Micaiah does not explicitly mention Ahab's dying at "Aramathe"), thereby highlighting the falsity of Zedekiah's claim (8.407-408) that Micaiah and Elijah had delivered "contradictory" announcements concerning the king's demise. He has no equivalent to the "source notice" for Ahab given in 1 Kgs 22:39 nor to the allusion to Ahab's "sleeping with his fathers" (22:40a), which could suggest that, contrary to the account given by both the Bible and Josephus, the king died a peaceful death.

[1633] With this transitional notice to his following appended reflections on the moral to be drawn from the circumstances of Ahab's end, Josephus underscores the status of both Elijah and Micaiah as true prophets, whose—seemingly divergent—predictions both found fulfillment.

[1634] Greek: ἡδονὴ καὶ βούλησις. These 2 terms are collocated also in *Ant.* 5.179.

[for] in that way God confers [knowledge] of what to guard against.[1635] **419** It is likewise fitting, by thinking on what happened to the king, to infer the strength of fate, which cannot be escaped, even when it is foreknown. On the contrary, it approaches human souls, flattering them with kindly hopes; by means of these, it leads them along to the point where it may conquer them.[1636] **420** It appears then that Achab's mind as well was led astray by this [fate], so that, disbelieving those who predicted his defeat, while believing those who prophesied in his favor, he died.[1637]

His son Ochozias[1638] therefore succeeded him.

[1635] This is the 1st of the lessons Josephus draws from the story of Ahab's death, i.e. (true) prophetic prediction is a helpful divine gift that, as such, needs to be respected and attended to—as Ahab failed to do. Such predictions may, moreover, be recognized by their typically unpleasing and unflattering character.

[1636] The 2nd lesson to be drawn from Ahab's death concerns the operation and efficacy of "fate" (see 8.409, 413), which, by appealing to the desires and hopes of its victims, diverts their attention from the truth of the prophetic warnings they have been given, and so leads them to destruction. In making the above points concerning "fate," Josephus offers no explanation as to how this power relates to God's own power and purposes as spoken of in what precedes—he simply juxtaposes the workings of the 2 powers in the human sphere.

[1637] Josephus applies his preceding general reflections to the particular case of Ahab in language reminiscent of his earlier editorial remark in 8.409: "it was fate, I suppose, that made the false prophets more convincing than the truthful one...."

[1638] MT (1 Kgs 22:40b) אחזיהו (Eng.: "Ahaziah"); LXX BL Ὀχοζείας; Josephus Ὀχοζίας.

BOOK NINE

(1.1) 1 The prophet Jeous[1] met King Josaphat as he was coming to Hierosolyma from his alliance with Achab, the king of the Israelites, which he had entered into against the enemy king Ader[2] of the Syrians, as we mentioned previously.[3] He reproached him for his alliance with Achab, who was an impious and vile[4] person;[5] for in this way he had caused God to become displeased.[6] He said, however, that, although he [Josaphat] had offended, he [God] would deliver him from his enemies because of his good nature.[7]

Jehu (Jeous) confronts Jehoshaphat

2 At this, the king turned to thanksgiving and sacrifices to God,[8] after which he hastened to circulate throughout the entire country over which he ruled[9] in order to teach the people the ordinances given by God through Moyses and piety towards him.[10] **3** He also appointed judges in each city of those over which he ruled as king.[11] He appealed to them to judge the mob, caring for nothing so much as what was just,[12] looking neither to the gifts nor to the rank of those who seemed prominent, on account of their wealth or family.[13] They were to render equitable

Jehoshaphat's teaching and judicial initiatives in Judah

---

[1] MT (2 Chr 19:2) יהוא (Eng.: "Jehu"); LXX B Ἰού; LXX L Ἰηού; Josephus Ἰηοῦς. Josephus omits the name of this figure's father (MT: Hanani), and gives him the title "prophet" of LXX BL as opposed to MT's "seer." Josephus has already mentioned "Jeous" in *Ant.* 8.299 (// 1 Kgs 16:2, 7) as the one who confronted the Israelite king Baasha. On Josephus' version (9.1-17) of the segment 2 Chronicles 19-20, (mostly) unparalleled in 2 Kings, focussing on "Jehoshaphat at mid-career," see Begg 2000: 5-28.

[2] This form of the Syrian king's name was used by Josephus in *Ant.* 8.401; elsewhere in *Antiquities* 8 one finds the alternative form "Adad(os)," which Marcus reads also here in 9.1.

[3] Josephus expands the reference to Jehoshaphat's return to Jerusalem in 2 Chr 19:1 with a summary allusion to what preceded this return, i.e. Jehoshaphat's involvement with Ahab's disastrous anti-Syrian campaign (see 1 Kgs 22:1-40// 2 Chr 18:1-34// *Ant.* 8.398-420).

[4] Greek: ἀσεβὴς καὶ πονηρός. Josephus' other uses of this collocation are *Ant.* 8.243, 299; 12.252, 385; 13.34.

[5] In 2 Chr 19:2bα Jehu refers more generally to "the wicked" and "those who hate the Lord." Josephus' prophet keeps attention focussed on the depravity of Ahab, Jehoshaphat's royal partner. He likewise turns the source's direct rhetorical question into an indirect address statement by Jehu.

[6] Josephus softens Jehu's announcement to Jehoshaphat in 2 Chr 19:2bβ: "because of this, wrath has gone out against you from the Lord."

[7] The Josephan prophet generalizes the 2 particulars militating in Jehoshaphat's favor cited by Jehu in 2 Chr 19:3, i.e. his elimination of "the Asherahs" (see 2 Chr 17:6b, also omitted by Josephus) and "setting his heart to seek God."

[8] Josephus adds this reference to Jehoshaphat's immediate, positive response to Jehu's word to him. The Chronicler records no such response by Jehoshaphat, but simply follows Jehu's discourse (2 Chr 19:2-3) with the notice (19:4a) that "Jehoshaphat dwelt in Jerusalem," which Josephus leaves aside.

[9] Josephus leaves aside the boundary indications for Jehoshaphat's "tour" given in 2 Chr 19:4bα, i.e. "from Beersheba to the hill country of Ephraim."

[10] Josephus renders more specific the indication concerning the outcome of Jehoshaphat's "tour" given in 2 Chr 19:4bβ: "he brought them [the people] back to the Lord...." The wording used by Josephus here recalls his description of Jehoshaphat's earlier "teaching mission" in *Ant.* 8.395 (// 2 Chr 17:7-9).

[11] 2 Chr 19:5 specifies that the judges were installed in "all the fortified cities of Judah."

[12] This opening appeal that the newly appointed judges concern themselves with "what is just" has no explicit equivalent in Jehoshaphat's address to them in 2 Chr 19:6-7.

[13] Josephus turns into an exhortation to the new judges Jehoshaphat's closing affirmation about the divine judge in 2 Chr 19:7b: "there is no perversion of justice with the Lord..., or partiality, or taking bribes." Josephus' wording of the initial portion of Jehoshaphat's charge to the judges seems modelled on his version (*Ant.* 4.216) of Moses' directives concerning

Judicial appointments in Jerusalem

decisions for all, recognizing that God sees all that is done even in secret.[14]

4 When he had taught these things in each city of the two tribes, he returned to Hierosolyma;[15] there, he also installed judges from the priests and Levites and those holding the first places in the crowd,[16] whom he urged to take care to act justly in all their judgments.[17] **5** But if some of their compatriots should have disputes about graver matters, they should send to them [the Hierosolyma judges] from the other cities.[18] And they [the judges] should give these [people] just judgment concerning their cases with greater solicitude.[19] For above all in this city, in which God's sanctuary happened to be and where the king had his residence, it was fitting that [judgments] should be solicitous and most just.[20] **6** As their rulers he designated Amasias[21] the priest and Zabadias,[22] both of the tribe of Iouda.[23] This was the way in which the king arranged matters.[24]

Enemy coalition invades Judah

(1.2) 7 At this same time, the Moabites and the Ammanites, who took along a large group of Arabs as well, were campaigning against him.[25] They encamped at Engade,[26] a city situated on Lake Asphaltitis,[27] 300 *stadia* distant from Hierosolyma.

Israel's judges in Deut 16:19-20a; see Begg 2000: 9, n. 23.

[14] Compare Jehoshaphat's opening words to the judges in 2 Chr 19:6: "consider what you do… he [the Lord] is with you in giving judgment." From Jehoshaphat's charge in 19:6-7 Josephus omits the appeal of 19:7aα: "let the fear of the Lord be upon you." On the historian's general avoidance of the key biblical expression "fear of God/the Lord," see Schlatter 1932: 155. On the divine omniscience and solicitude for human affairs highlighted by Josephus here, see further *Ant.* 1.14, 20; 10.277-280.

[15] Josephus adds this transitional phrase, linking the 2 phases of Jehoshaphat's judicial initiatives: outside Jerusalem (2 Chr 19:4b-7) and in Jerusalem itself (19:8-11).

[16] See 2 Chr 19:8a. Josephus' sequence ("priests and Levites") agrees with that of LXX B, whereas MT and LXX L have the reverse. He leaves aside both the double task assigned the Jerusalem judges ("to give judgment for the Lord and to decide disputed cases") and the mention of their "seat" being in Jerusalem of 19:8b.

[17] This initial exhortation to the Jerusalem judges— which recalls the charge Jehoshaphat gives the extra-Jerusalem judges in 9.3—is Josephus' version of the king's opening appeal to the former group in 2 Chr 19:9: "thus shall you do in fear of the Lord, in faithfulness, and with your whole heart."

[18] Josephus' phrase "graver matters" summarizes the catalogue of cases that might come before the Jerusalem judges enumerated by Jehoshaphat in 2 Chr 19:10a ("concerning bloodshed, law or commandment, statutes or ordinances").

[19] Compare 2 Chr 19:10aβ: "then you [the Jerusalem judges] shall instruct them [i.e. those submitting

cases from other cities]."

[20] This motivation for Jehoshaphat's call for just judgments by the Jerusalem judges takes the place of his appeal to those judges to decide cases in such a way that they would not bring guilt and wrath upon themselves (and their fellows) in 2 Chr 19:10b.

[21] MT (2 Chr 19:11) אמריהו (Eng.: "Amariah"); LXX BL Ἀμαρίας; Josephus Ἀμασίας. Josephus leaves aside the biblical specification that he is to have jurisdiction "over all the matters of the Lord."

[22] MT (2 Chr 19:11) זבדיהו (Eng.: "Zebadiah"); LXX B Ζαβδείας; LXX L and Josephus Ζαβαδίας. Josephus omits the name of his father (MT: Ishmael), his title ("governor of the house of Judah"), and area of competence, i.e. "all the king's matters."

[23] As Marcus (*ad loc.*) points out, Josephus' formulation here appears careless, in that one would certainly suppose that the priest Amariah was rather of the tribe of Levi.

[24] This closing formula for Josephus' account of Jehoshaphat's didactic/judicial measures in 9.2-6 takes the place of the king's concluding exhortation to the Jerusalem judges—with its reference to the Levites as their assistants—of 2 Chr 19:11b.

[25] Josephus' designation for the 3rd group coming against Jehoshaphat ("Arabs") diverges from that cited in the various witnesses to 2 Chr 20:1, i.e. MT (the Ammonites, this duplicating its 2nd group, i.e. "Ammon"), LXX B (the Meunites), and LXX L (the sons of the Ammanites, the sons of Seeir).

[26] MT (2 Chr 20:2) עין גדי (Eng.: "En-gedi"); LXX B Ἐνγάδει; LXX L Ἐγγάδδι; Josephus Ἐγγάδη (so Niese). Josephus omits the initial biblical designation for the city, i.e. "Hazazon-tamar" (MT).

[27] In 2 Chr 20:2 the invaders are said to come "from beyond the sea." Josephus' more precise designation,

(In it, the best palm trees and balsam bushes grow).[28]

8 When Josaphat heard that the enemy had crossed the lake and had already invaded the country that was ruled by him as king,[29] in his fear he summoned the population of Hierosolyma to an assembly in the sacred precinct.[30] Standing with his face towards the sanctuary,[31] he prayed and called upon God to grant him force and strength so that he might punish those campaigning [against him].[32] **9** For this was the plea of those who constructed the sacred precinct,[33] namely that he [God] would fight for that city and take vengeance on those who dared to come against [the sacred precinct], who were now on hand to take away from them the land that had been given by him as their place of residence.[34] As he [Josaphat] prayed these things he wept, and the entire crowd, along with their wives and children, kept imploring [God].[35]

Jehoshaphat leads appeal to God

10 A certain prophet named Jaziel[36] came into the middle of the assembly and cried out, saying to the crowd and the king that God was listening to their prayers and promised that he would make war on their foes.[37] He ordered [Josaphat] to lead his army out to meet the enemy on the following day,[38] **11** for he would find them at the elevation called *Exoche*[39] between Hierosolyma and Engade.[40] They were not

Prophetic assurance

---

i.e. "Lake Asphaltitis," is his frequent equivalent for the contemporary "Dead Sea." See Begg 2000: 12, n. 137.

[28] Josephus appends both of the above particulars—based presumably on his personal knowledge of the site—to the mention of "En-gedi" in 2 Chr 20:2.

[29] In 2 Chr 20:2 "some men come and tell Jehoshaphat" of the enemy advance.

[30] Josephus modifies the particulars of the fearful Jehoshaphat's initiatives according to 2 Chr 20:3, according to which "he set himself to seek the Lord and proclaimed a fast throughout all Judah." His limiting of the king's summons to the Jerusalemites might reflect the consideration that there would not have been enough time to gather people from outside the city (in the same line he also leaves aside the notice of 20:4 on people assembling from "all the cities of Judah").

[31] According to 2 Chr 20:5a, Jehoshaphat stood "in the house of the Lord, before the new court."

[32] With this opening of Jehoshaphat's prayer, Josephus anticipates and modifies the king's closing appeal (see 2 Chr 20:12a) that God himself "execute judgment" upon the invaders. The reference to the "force and strength" Jehoshaphat asks God to confer upon him is inspired by the king's confession in 20:6b: "in thy [God's] hand are power and strength...." Josephus leaves aside the king's 2 preceding rhetorical questions of 20:6a that underscore the transcendent divine power.

[33] Cf. 2 Chr 20:8b, where Jehoshaphat refers to the Israelites' building a sanctuary "for thy [the Lord's] name in the land."

[34] This portion of the Josephan Jehoshaphat's prayer combines elements drawn from the king's appeal in 2 Chr 20:7-11: the temple's function as a place of

intercession (v. 9) in the face of enemy attack such as Judah is now experiencing (vv. 10-11), notwithstanding God's previous gift of the land to the ancestors (v. 7). Josephus leaves aside the king's closing acknowledgement of powerlessness and expression of trust in God (20:12b).

[35] See 2 Chr 20:13. Josephus adds the reference to the king's "weeping," and has the assembly join in his appeal, rather than simply "standing before the Lord."

[36] MT (2 Chr 20:14) יחזיאל (Eng.: "Jahaziel"); LXX B Ὀζειήλ; LXX L Ἰεζιήλ; Josephus Ἰαζίηλος. Josephus' title, i.e. "a certain prophet" substitutes for the source's "a Levite of the sons of Asaph." He leaves aside both the Bible's genealogy of this figure and its reference to the "Spirit of the Lord coming upon" him.

[37] Josephus reproduces, in his own words, the core content of Jahaziel's opening address to king and people from 2 Chr 20:15, i.e. "the battle is not yours, but the Lord's." He leaves aside the prophet's preceding summons: "fear not, and do not be dismayed at this great multitude."

[38] Jahaziel's command in 2 Chr 20:16a is addressed to the entire people, rather than to the king alone.

[39] Greek Ἐξοχή. This common noun, meaning "prominence," appears in the plus of LXX L 2 Chr 20:16, where it is coupled with the place name Ἀσεῖς (compare MT הציץ [Eng.: "Ziz"]; LXX B Ἀσάε). Josephus took L's ἐξοχή as the actual name of the site.

[40] Josephus' localization of the site by reference to the 2 cities mentioned by him in 9.7 takes the place of the indications given by Jahaziel in 2 Chr 20:16b: "you will find them at the end of the valley, east of the wilderness of Jeruel."

to engage them, but simply to stand and see how the Deity would fight against them.[41] When the prophet said these things, the king and the crowd, falling on their faces, gave thanks to God and paid homage to him,[42] while the Levites continued playing hymns on their instruments.[43]

Invaders destroyed without a fight

(1.3) 12 Once it was daylight, the king advanced into the desert below the city of Thekoe[44] and said to the crowd that they ought to believe the things spoken by the prophet[45] and not draw themselves up for battle.[46] Rather, while the priests with their trumpets and the Levites[47] stood in front, they were to give thanks, as if their country had already been delivered from the enemy.[48]

13 The king's plan pleased [the people], and they did as he advised.[49] God cast fear and consternation[50] upon the Ammanites.[51] They, thinking one another to be

Enemy corpses stripped

enemies, killed [each other], so that of so great an army no one survived.[52] 14 Josaphat, looking out into the valley, in which the enemy happened to be encamped and seeing it full of corpses,[53] was pleased at God's unexpected help, because he had given the victory, not to their exertions, but by himself.[54] He [Josaphat] allowed his army to plunder the camp of the enemy and to strip the corpses.[55] 15 After three days of stripping, they were tired, so great was the number of those who had been

---

[41] See 2 Chr 20:17a. Josephus leaves aside Jahaziel's concluding exhortation in 20:17b, which reiterates his initial appeal "fear not, and be not dismayed" of 20:15b.

[42] See 2 Chr 20:18.

[43] 2 Chr 20:19 mentions only vocal praise by the Levites; Josephus has no equivalent to the Bible's mention of the 2 Levitical families ("the Kohathites and the Korahites") involved.

[44] MT (2 Chr 20:20a) תקוע (Eng.: "Tekoa"); LXX BL and Josephus Θεκῶε.

[45] In 2 Chr 20:20b Jehoshaphat urges the people to "believe God and his prophets." Josephus' singular term ("prophet") refers to Jahaziel and the words he has just spoken in 9.10-11.

[46] This negative injunction, reminiscent of that given by Jahaziel in 9.11, takes the place of the promise ("and you will succeed"), which Jehoshaphat attaches to his appeal for belief in the prophets in 2 Chr 20:20bβ.

[47] Greek: καὶ Ληουιτῶν. This is the reading of RO, which Niese follows. Marcus reads καὶ Ληουίτας μετὰ τῶν ὑμνούντων ("and the Levites with the singers") of MSPEZon; cf. Lat.

[48] Compare 2 Chr 20:21, where, on the basis of a consultation with the people, Jehoshaphat appoints those who are to precede the army, singing praise to the Lord. Josephus specifies the identity of those appointed, while entrusting the thanksgiving to the entire people. He likewise has Jehoshaphat arrange matters without consulting the people (see, however, next note), and omits the actual words of thanks he prescribes to be said, i.e. "Give thanks to the Lord, for his steadfast love endures for ever."

[49] This notice on the people's response to Jehoshaphat's dispositions takes the place of the reference to a "they" who begin to sing and praise in 2 Chr 20:22a. The allusion to the king's "plan" and its endorsement by the people seems to reflect the mention of Jehoshaphat's "taking counsel with the people" of 20:21, earlier passed over by Josephus; see previous note.

[50] Greek: φόβος καὶ ταραχή. This wordpair occurs also in *Ant.* 9.57; 11.175; cf. 11.141.

[51] 2 Chr 20:22b mentions the Lord's "setting an ambush against the men of Ammon, Moab, and Mount Seir...."

[52] Josephus simplifies and generalizes the presentation of 2 Chr 20:23, where the Ammonites and Moabites first fall on the "inhabitants of Mount Seir," and then turn on each other. At the same time, he also supplies a motivation for the invading forces' acting as they do, namely their mistaken perception that they are dealing with "enemies."

[53] Compare 2 Chr 20:24, where it is Judah as whole who, from the vantage point of "the watchtower of the valley," surveys the enemy corpses. Josephus anticipates his reference to the "valley" in which the slain are lying from 2 Chr 20:26. Throughout his reappropriation of 2 Chronicles 20, he highlights the role of Jehoshaphat in comparison with that of the people.

[54] Josephus appends this reference to Jehoshaphat's response to what he sees, once again insisting on Judah's deliverance as solely the work of God (see 9.10, 11, 12).

[55] See 2 Chr 20:25a. Josephus supplies the reference to the "permission" given by Jehoshaphat. His mention of the enemy "corpses" seems to reflect the MT

done away with.[56] On the third day, once all the people had been assembled at a certain hollow and ravine-like place, they blessed the force and alliance[57] of God; from this the place has the name "Hallow of Blessing."[58]

16 Bringing up his army from there to Hierosolyma, the king turned to feasting and sacrifices for many days.[59] Once, however, the foreign nations heard of the destruction of the enemy, they all were frightened of him,[60] as though God would clearly continue to be his ally in the future.[61] And Josaphat from then on possessed a splendid reputation, on account of his justice and piety towards God.[62]

Effect on other nations

17 He was also a friend of the son of Achab, who reigned as king over the Israelites.[63] He participated with him in preparing ships that were to sail to Pontus and the trading regions of Thrace.[64] The enterprise failed, however, for the boats were lost on account of their size.[65] Because of this he was no longer enthused about ships.[66] This then was the situation with Josaphat, king of Hierosolyma.[67]

Failed maritime venture

---

reading as against LXX BL's "spoils." He leaves aside the remainder of the biblical catalogue of the enemy items acquired by the Judeans.

[56] See 2 Chr 20:25b. Josephus adds the reference to the people's being "tired" as a result of their extended exertions.

[57] Greek: δύναμις καὶ συμμαχία. Josephus' one other use of this precise collocation is in *Ant.* 7.122, where it refers to the Ammonite coalition that David confronts; cf. *Ant.* 10.17; and Plutarch, *Comp. Lys. Sull.* 5.2; *Mor.* 606E. See also Jehoshaphat's prayer that God give him "force [Greek: δύναμις] and strength" in 9.8.

[58] See 2 Chr 20:26. Josephus omits the biblical specification that the gathering took place "on the 4th day," while supplying a content for the assembly's "blessing" of God on this occasion.

[59] Cf. 2 Chr 20:27-28. For the biblical reference to the army's "joy" and their advance to the temple to the accompaniment of musical instruments, Josephus substitutes mention of the king's "feasting and sacrifices." This formulation recalls 9.2, where Jehoshaphat "turns to thanksgiving and sacrifices" following Jehu's rebuke in 9.1.

[60] Compare 2 Chr 20:29a: "the fear of God came on all the kingdoms of the countries."

[61] This reference to God's "continuing to be [Jehoshaphat's] ally" recalls the assembly's blessing "the force and alliance" of God in 9.15. In 2 Chr 20:29b the nations' "fear of God" (20:29a) is prompted by their hearing that "the Lord had fought against the enemies of Israel."

[62] Compare 2 Chr 20:30, which alludes to the God-given "quiet" and "rest" enjoyed by Jehoshaphat's kingdom following the divine overthrow of the enemy coalition. Josephus' formulation recalls his notice on Jehoshaphat's earlier reign in *Ant.* 8.394, where the king's possession of "greatest glory" is attributed to his being "just and pious." Since he will, on the basis of 2 Kings 3, have more to say concerning Jehoshaphat,

Josephus omits at this point the concluding notices for the king of 2 Chr 20:31-34 (// 1 Kgs 22:41-44, 46).

[63] Josephus draws this item from 1 Kgs 22:45 (MT LXX B; LXX L's equivalent to the complex of notices concerning Jehoshaphat, MT LXX L 1 Kgs 22:41-50, stands after its 1 Kgs 16:28)// 2 Chr 20:35a, which mention Jehoshaphat's Israelite partner by his name, i.e. "Ahaziah"; Josephus introduced this figure in *Ant.* 8.420. Like Kings, Josephus lacks the qualification of the Northern king as one "who did wickedly" found in 2 Chr 20:35b.

[64] "Pontus" is in northwestern Turkey, "Thrace" in northeastern Greece. 1 Kgs 22:48a speaks of "ships of Tarshish," constructed to "go to Ophir for gold," while in 2 Chr 20:36a the ships are built "to go to Tarshish" (LXX: Θαρσείς). Marcus (*ad loc.*) suggests that with his reading "Thrace" for the biblical "Tarshish" here, Josephus "connects (or confuses)" the latter form with the name of the son of Japheth called "Tiras" in Gen 10:2. In his parallel (*Ant.* 1.125) to the Genesis text, Josephus designates Japheth's son as "Theires," and notes that the Greeks have converted the name of his subjects, i.e. the Theirians," into "Thracians." (In *Ant.* 1.127, Josephus states that the "Tarshish" of Gen 10:4 is the ancient name of "Cilicia"; see also 9.208).

[65] 1 Kgs 22:48b states that the ships were "wrecked at Ezion-geber," but supplies no reason for their loss. The explanation adduced by Josephus (the size of the ships) differs from that given in 2 Chr 20:37, where mention of the ships' destruction is preceded by a speech attributed to the prophet "Eliezer," announcing that God will destroy what Jehoshaphat has made. Like Kings, and in contrast to Chronicles, Josephus thus does not express any explicit criticism of Jehoshaphat's involvement in the Israelite ship-building enterprise.

[66] This reference to the effect of the ships' loss upon Jehoshaphat takes the place of the notice, peculiar to 1 Kgs 22:49, that Jehoshaphat refused Ahaziah's request that his servants be allowed to accompany Jehosha-

(2.1) 18 Ochozias, the son of Achab, ruled as king over the Israelites, making Samareia his residence.[68] He was vile and in all respects similar to both his parents and to Hieroboam, who first acted lawlessly and began to mislead the people.[69]

19 He had already held the kingship for two years when the king of the Moabites rebelled against him,[70] and ceased to supply the tribute that he had previously paid to his father Achab.[71] Now it happened that Ochozias fell, when descending from the roof of his house.[72] Being ill, he sent to the god *Fly*[73] of Akkaron[74]—for this was the god's name[75]—to inquire about his safety.

20 The God of the Hebrews[76] appeared, however, to the prophet Elias[77] and ordered him to meet the messengers that had been sent and to inquire of them whether the people of the Israelites did not have their own God so that their king should be sending to an alien one to ask about his safety.[78] He was further to direct them to return and tell the king that he would not come through his illness.[79]

21 When Elias did what God ordered and the messengers heard [these things] from him, they immediately returned to the king.[80] He, surprised at the quickness of their return, asked the cause.[81] They stated that a certain person had met them,

---

phat's men in the ships. Josephus' replacement disposes of the problem that the notice of 22:49 seems out of place, given that the ships have already been wrecked in 22:48b.

[67] Josephus adds this closing notice to his account of Jehoshaphat at mid-career, 9.1-17 (// 2 Chronicles 19-20).

[68] See 1 Kgs 22:51a. Josephus has already mentioned the accession of "Ahaziah" on the basis of 1 Kgs 22:40b in *Ant.* 8.420; cf. the allusion to this in 9.17. He omits the synchronization of Ahaziah's accession with the 17th (MT LXX B; LXX L: 24th) year of Jehoshaphat found in 22:51b, while holding over its reference to Ahaziah's 2-year reign until a later point; see 9.19. On Josephus' account of Ahaziah, his bad end, and its sequels (// 1 Kgs 22:51-2 Kgs 3:3) in 9.18-28, see Begg 2000: 29-46.

[69] See 1 Kgs 22:52. Josephus omits the appended reference to Ahaziah's "worshipping Baal" and "provoking the Lord" of 22:53.

[70] In both the parallel notices of 2 Kgs 1:1 and 3:5, the Moabite revolt is dated generally to "after the death of Ahab." For his more specific dating, Josephus draws on the mention of Ahaziah's reigning for 2 years in 1 Kgs 22:51b. At this juncture (see, however, 9.29) he omits the name of the rebel Moabite king cited in 3:5 as "Mesha."

[71] Josephus adds this specification concerning the form (non-payment of taxes) taken by the Moabite king's "revolt" (see 2 Kgs 1:1// 3:5) on the basis of 2 Kgs 3:4, which speaks of his earlier delivery of 100,000 lambs and the wool of 100,000 rams to the Israelite king. He will mention "Mesha" and his sheep tribute subsequently; see 9.29.

[72] See 2 Kgs 1:2a. Josephus omits the biblical specification that the incident occurred "in Samaria."

[73] Greek: θεὸς Μυῖα. In line with LXX BL 2 Kgs 1:2b, Josephus "translates" the 2nd part of the deity's name (MT: [Baal]-zebal," i.e. "[Baal] the prince") as "the fly [= Hebrew: *zebub*] god," while likewise replacing its initial element "Baal" with the more general term "god."

[74] Josephus' form of the city's name corresponds to that of LXX BL 2 Kgs 1:2b. MT has "Ekron."

[75] This appended phrase serves to underscore the odd, pejorative (LXX) name of the god to whom Ahaziah has recourse.

[76] Greek: ὁ τῶν Ἑβραίων θεός. This designation for Israel's Deity appears only here in Josephus.

[77] Compare 2 Kgs 1:3a, where it is "the angel of the Lord" who speaks to Elijah. On Josephus' angelology overall, with its tendency, as here, to eliminate biblical references to angels, see Mach 1992: 300-322. Josephus omits the Bible's designation of Elijah as "the Tishbite." The reference to God's "appearing to" Elijah here recalls Obadiah's allusion to "God's again appearing" to the prophet in *Ant.* 8.333.

[78] In 2 Kgs 1:3b the accusatory question that is to be put to Ahaziah's messengers is formulated in direct address and the designation of the offending deity is repeated in full from 1:2.

[79] See 2 Kgs 1:4a. Josephus substitutes a directive—anticipated by him from the envoys' own report of what Elijah has told them in 1:6—about the messengers' returning to their sender for the biblical messenger formula ("thus says the Lord"), just as he compresses the announcement that is to be brought to Ahaziah: "you shall not come down from the bed to which you have gone, but you shall surely die."

[80] See 2 Kgs 1:4b-5a.

[81] See 2 Kgs 1:5b. Josephus supplies the reference to Ahaziah's "surprise."

prevented them from proceeding further, and made them return "to say to you, by the command of the God of the Israelites,[82] that your illness will get worse."[83]

22 When the king directed them to indicate to him who had said these things,[84] they said that he was a hairy man, wearing a leather belt.[85] Perceiving from these things that Elias was the man indicated by the messengers,[86] he sent a military officer and fifty troops to him and directed that he be brought.[87]

Two attempts to arrest Elijah fail

23 Finding Elias seated on the top of the hill, the officer who had been sent directed him to descend and come to the king, for he had directed this.[88] If, however, he were unwilling, he would do him violence against his will.[89] But [Elias] said to him that, as a test of whether he was a truthful prophet,[90] he would pray that fire fall from heaven and destroy the soldiers and himself. He prayed,[91] and a fire-storm[92] came down and destroyed the officer and those with him.[93]

24 When their loss was disclosed to the king, he became enraged[94] and sent another military officer to Elias with as many troops as he had dispatched along with the first one.[95] Likewise this one threatened to take the prophet by violence and bring him, if he did not wish to come down.[96] When Elias prayed against him, fire made an end of him, just as it had the officer before him.[97]

25 Once he found out also about this one, the king sent off a third [officer].[98] He, however, was sensible and very gentle[99] in character.[100] Coming to the place where

Third officer secures Elijah's cooperation

---

[82] Greek: ὁ Ἰσραηλιτῶν θεός. This designation recurs in 9.60. Compare "the God of the Hebrews" in 9.20.

[83] See 2 Kgs 1:6. Josephus' compressed version of the messengers' report to the king avoids its extended verbal repetition of Elijah's communication to them of 1:3b-4a.

[84] In 2 Kgs 1:7 Ahaziah asks about the "kind of man" the messengers had encountered.

[85] See 2 Kgs 1:8a. MT speaks literally of "a man of hair" (RSV: "he [Elijah] wore a garment of haircloth"). Josephus uses the same Greek word for "hairy" (δασύς) as does LXX BL.

[86] In 2 Kgs 1:8b Ahaziah declares: "It is Elijah the Tishbite." Josephus makes the king's (interior) perception the ground for his following initiative.

[87] See 2 Kgs 1:9a. Josephus adds the royal directive about the fetching of Elijah on the basis of 1:9b, where the officer informs Elijah that the king has said that he (Elijah) is to "come down."

[88] Compare 2 Kgs 1:9b, where the officer speaks to Elijah in direct address, and calls him "man of God."

[89] This threat by the officer has no parallel in his words as reported in 2 Kgs 1:9. Josephus' addition of the threat helps provide a greater justification for Elijah's drastic and destructive response.

[90] In 2 Kgs 1:10a, Elijah, picking up on the officer's addressing him as "man of God" in 1:9b, begins his reply with the words "if I am a man of God..." (in both instances the Tg. reads "prophet of the Lord"). The phrase "truthful prophet" (Greek: προφήτης ἀληθής), recurs in *Ant.* 6.47 (Samuel); 8.296 (the future prophetic

figure who will be denied the apostate people); and 9.34 (Elisha's ironic characterization of the prophets of King Joram's parents).

[91] 2 Kgs 1:10a has Elijah express a wish and/or command regarding the descent of the heavenly fire, which then (1:10b) immediately comes about. Josephus' double reference to his "praying" for the heavenly fire points up God's control of what happens.

[92] Greek: πρηστήρ. This word is *hapax* in Josephus.

[93] See 2 Kgs 1:10b.

[94] Josephus supplies this transitional notice on the report made to the king and its emotional effect upon him.

[95] See 2 Kgs 1:11a.

[96] Just as he did with the 1st one (see note to "against his will" at 9.23) Josephus accentuates the threatening character of the 2nd officer's words; compare 2 Kgs 1:11b, where the latter enjoins Elijah: "O man of God, this is the king's order, 'Come down quickly'!"

[97] Josephus compresses the 2-part sequence of Elijah's utterance and its outcome in 2 Kgs 1:12 with its largely verbal repetition of the wording of 1:10b. In contrast to the Bible's phrase "fire of God" (2 Kgs 1:12), he speaks simply of "fire."

[98] 2 Kgs 1:13 mentions also the 50 men dispatched with this 3rd officer (who in the *Liv. Pro.* 9.3 is identified with the later prophet Obadiah).

[99] Greek: φρόνιμος... καὶ... ἐπικικής. This wordpair occurs only here in Josephus.

[100] Josephus supplies this characterization of the 3rd officer, which already sets him in contrast to his 2

Elias happened to be, he addressed him in friendly fashion.[101] He said that he [Elias] knew that it was not willingly, but in service to the royal order, that he had come to him, just as those sent before himself had come, not voluntarily but for the same cause.[102] He therefore requested him to be merciful to him and the troops present with him and descend and follow him to the king.[103]

Elijah announces death for Ahaziah

26 Responding favorably to the tactfulness of his words[104] and his diplomatic[105] manner,[106] Elias came down and followed him. When he came to the king, he prophesied to him and disclosed that God was saying [this]:[107] "since you have despised him, as though he were not God and unable to predict the truth about your illness, and have sent to [the god] of the Akkaronites to inquire of him what will be the outcome of your illness,[108] know that you will die."[109]

Joram succeeds Ahaziah

(2.2) 27 After a very short time had elapsed, he did die, as Elias had predicted;[110] his brother Joram[111] assumed the kingship, for he [Ochozias] ended his life childless.[112] This Joram[113] was very similar to his father Achab in his vileness;[114] he

---

overbearing, bullying colleagues.

[101] In 2 Kgs 1:13a the 3rd officer, like his 2 colleagues (see vv. 9b, 11b), "goes up" to Elijah. Josephus underscores his distinctiveness by having him begin, not with the peremptory orders and threats of his predecessors, but rather with a friendly greeting.

[102] Josephus prefaces the 3rd officer's words as reported in 2 Kgs 1:13b-14 with this exculpatory declaration by him.

[103] This double request replaces the 3rd officer's twice-made appeal (2 Kgs 1:13b, 14b) that his own life (and that of his men) be "precious" in Elijah's eyes. Josephus omits the officer's intervening reminiscence of the fate of his 2 colleagues in 1:14a—a matter best left unmentioned.

[104] Greek: δεξιότης τῶν λογῶν. The translation of Marcus (*ad loc.*: "[approving] of his words") fails to render the word δεξιότης of this phrase.

[105] Greek: ἀστεῖος. Josephus uses this adjective twice elsewhere: *Ant.* 7.147; 12.277.

[106] According to 2 Kgs 1:15a, Elijah's "descent" was prompted by a word of "the angel of the Lord," who tells him not to be "afraid" of the 3rd captain. Whereas in 9.20 Josephus replaces the Bible's earlier mention of an angelic intervention (1:3) with a reference to an appearance and directive of God himself, here in 9.26 he has Elijah act on his own volition. Given the demeanor of the 3rd captain, a supernatural intervention urging Elijah not to be "afraid" of the suppliant officer hardly seems necessary.

[107] See 2 Kgs 1:15b-16aα. Josephus supplies the reference to Elijah's "prophesying," which picks up on his earlier allusion to himself as a "truthful prophet" in 9.23.

[108] This is Josephus' alternative formulation of Elijah's accusatory question to Ahaziah in 2 Kgs

1:16aβbα, whose wording is largely identical to that already used in 1:3b and 6b.

[109] As in 9.20 (compare 2 Kgs 1:4a), Josephus leaves aside the announcement about Ahaziah's "not coming down from his bed" of 1:16bβ.

[110] See 2 Kgs 1:17a, where Ahaziah dies "according to the word of Elijah."

[111] MT (2 Kgs 1:17b) יהורם (Eng.: "Jehoram"); LXX BL Ἰωράμ; Josephus Ἰώραμος; in my notes I shall refer to this king by the shorter biblical (and Josephan) form of his name, i.e. "Joram," used, e.g., in 2 Kgs 9:14. On Josephus' treatment of Joram, see Feldman 1998a: 322-33.

[112] See 2 Kgs 1:17b. Josephus has no equivalent either to the divergent biblical synchronizations of Joram's accession, i.e. the 2nd (MT LXX L 2 Kgs 1:17b) year of J[eh]oram of Judah vs. the 18th year of Jehoshaphat (LXX B 2 Kgs 1:17b and 2 Kgs 3:1) or to the source notice for Ahaziah of 1:18. Josephus' specification that Joram was Ahaziah's "brother" corresponds to the plus of LXX L in 1:17b.

[113] In continuing with the presentation of Joram at this point, Josephus aligns himself with LXX BL's appendix to 2 Kgs 1:18 (1:18a-d) whereas in MT the material in question stands after the account of the "ascension" of Elijah and the succession of Elisha (2 Kings 2) in 2 Kgs 3:1-3 (to which LXX BL have an equivalent, repeating the content of their 1:18a-d, at this point as well).

[114] Josephus here accentuates Joram's depravity in comparison with MT 2 Kgs 3:2 (LXX BL present this notice twice, i.e. in their 1:18c [see previous note] and in 3:2), which affirms that the evil done by Joram was "*not* like that of his father [MT; LXX BL: brothers] and mother," in that he removed the pillar [MT; LXX BL: pillars] of Baal his father had made.

ruled as king for twelve years,[115] displaying all lawlessness and impiety[116] towards God, for, while he refrained from worshipping him, he adored foreign [deities].[117] For the rest, he was an energetic [man].[118]

28 At that time Elias disappeared from among humans,[119] and no one knows of his death until today.[120] He left behind his disciple[121] Elissai, as we have related previously.[122] Now concerning Elias and Enoch,[123] who lived before the flood, one reads in the sacred books[124] that they became invisible,[125] and no one knows of their death.[126]

Elijah's disappearance and Elisha's (Elissai's) succession

(3.1) 29 Once he obtained the kingship, Joram decided to campaign against the king of the Moabites, whose name was Meisas,[127] for, as we said earlier,[128] he had rebelled against his brother [Ochozias], after having paid a tribute of 200,000 sheep, along with their wool, to his father Achab.[129]

Joram's campaign against rebel Moab

---

[115] This figure for Joram's length of reign corresponds to that given in 2 Kgs 3:1b (MT; LXX BL supply the indication twice, i.e. in 2 Kgs 1:18ª and 3:1).

[116] Greek: παρανομία καὶ ἀσέβεια. This collocation is used once elsewhere by Josephus, i.e. in *Ant.* 10.104 (of King Zedekiah).

[117] This accusation replaces the stereotyped allusion to Joram's persisting in the sin of Jeroboam of 2 Kgs 3:3 (and LXX BL 2 Kgs 1:18ᶜ). Josephus has no equivalent to the LXX BL notice of 2 Kgs 1:18ᵈ: "and the anger of the Lord burnt against him [Joram; LXX B lacks this reference to Joram] and the house of Achab."

[118] This characterization of Joram is Josephus' addition. The term "energetic" (Greek: δραστήριος) serves to associate Joram with his mother Jezebel, of whom Josephus uses the same term in *Ant.* 8.318 (compare 2 Kgs 3:2 [and LXX BL 2 Kgs 1:18ᵇ], where Joram is said not to have done evil "like his mother").

[119] With this formulation Josephus sums up the lengthy story of Elijah's removal from the earth as told in 2 Kgs 2:1-12; cf. 2:12b: "and he [Elisha] saw him [Elijah] no more." The term "disappear" (Greek: ἀφανίζω) here is the same one used by Josephus of Moses' earthly end in *Ant.* 4.323, 326, and is also frequent in extra-biblical accounts of heavenly ascents; see Lohfink 1971: 41, n. 57 and cf. Begg 2000: 43, n. 66.

[120] Feldman (1998a: 301) points out that a similar statement occurs in Sophocles, *Oed. col.* 1655-1656, where it is affirmed that no one but Theseus can relate how Oedipus came to disappear. The notice here in 9.28 is also reminiscent of Deut 34:6b, which declares that "no man knows the place of his [Moses'] burial until this day."

[121] Greek: μαθητής; this is the same term that Josephus uses (*Ant.* 8.354) to designate Elisha in his relation to Elijah at the moment of the former's call.

[122] With this formula Josephus refers back to *Ant.* 8.354, where he alludes to the Elisha's following the Elijah "the entire time he lived as his disciple and minister." The reference to Elijah's "leaving Elisha behind"

is Josephus' summation of the account of the latter's succession to the former in 2 Kgs 2:12b-18(19-25).

[123] On Enoch and his departure from the earth, see *Ant.* 1.85 (// Gen 5:24), which speaks of his "returning to the divinity."

[124] This same phrase is used by Josephus in *Ant.* 4.326, where he refers to Moses' recording the fact of his death "in the sacred books."

[125] This phrase (Greek: ἀφανὴς γίνεσθαι), like the verb "disappear" earlier in 9.28, is part of the standard vocabulary of Greco-Roman accounts of heavenly ascents; see Lohfink 1971: 41, n. 59.

[126] This expression recalls that used of Elijah earlier in 9.28 i.e. "no one knows of his death until today."

Josephus' markedly abbreviated version of the story of Elijah's heavenly ascent as related in 2 Kings 2 likely reflects a concern that this great figure of Jewish history not be exposed to the ridicule that various Greco-Roman authors (e.g., Seneca, Lucian, Plutarch) heaped on the supposed heavenly ascents associated with various pagan figures (e.g., Romulus); see Begg 1990: 691-93; 2000: 44; and compare Tabor 1989.

Josephus here passes over Elisha's 1st miracle subsequent to Elijah's ascent, i.e. his healing of the Jericho water supply (2 Kgs 2:19-22); he does, however, recount that miracle at length elsewhere, i.e. *War* 4.460-464; see Feldman 2001: 319-20. As for the subsequent miracle ascribed to Elisha in 2 Kgs 2:23-25, namely his using 2 she-bears to maul 42 boys who had treated him with disrespect, Josephus' complete silence concerning this episode is readily understandable, given that the image of the prophet it conveys would undoubtedly prove offputting to gentile readers.

[127] MT (2 Kgs 3:4) מישע (Eng.: "Mesha"); LXX BL Μωσά; Josephus Μεισᾶς. On Josephus' rendition of the story of Joram's Moabite campaign (// 2 Kings 3) in 9.29-43, see Begg 2000: 47-65.

[128] See 9.19.

[129] Josephus' figure for Mesha's tribute of 200,000 sheep seems to conflate the indications on the Moa-

Campaign of three kings launched

30 When therefore he had mustered his own force,[130] he sent to Josaphat,[131] appealing to him, since he had been a friend of his father from the beginning,[132] to be his ally in the war he was about to undertake against the Moabites, who had rebelled against his kingship.[133] [Josaphat], for his part, not only promised to help,[134] but also to compel the king of the Idumeans, who was subordinate to him, to join the campaign.[135] **31** When these [promises] concerning the alliance with Josaphat were brought to him, Joram, bringing up his own army, came to Hierosolyma. After he had been splendidly entertained by the king of Hierosolyma,[136] they decided to make their march against the enemy through the desert of Idumea,[137] for they [the Idumeans] would not be expecting them to make their advance by this [route].[138] The three kings, namely the king [of Hierosolyma], of the Israelites, and of Idumea, marched from Hierosolyma.[139]

Water runs out

32 After following a circular route for seven days, they were severely afflicted by a lack of water for both the animals and the army, their guides having lost their way.[140] As a result, they were all in agony, especially Joram.[141] In his grief, he cried out to God, [asking] what evil he was accusing him of that he was leading three kings to hand them over to the king of the Moabites without a fight.[142]

---

bite's payment given in 2 Kgs 3:4, i.e. 100,000 lambs and the wool of 100,000 rams.

[130] See 2 Kgs 3:6.

[131] In designating, here and subsequently, Joram's Judean ally as "Jehoshaphat," Josephus agrees with MT and LXX B 2 Kings 3, whereas LXX L identifies the Judean king in question as Ὀχοζείας, i.e. the grandson of Jehoshaphat called "Ahaziah" in MT (see 2 Kgs 8:24). On the point, see Schenker 2004: 94-97 (who holds that the LXX L reading is the original one).

[132] Josephus supplies this explanation as to why Joram turned precisely to Jehoshaphat as a potential ally as he does in 2 Kgs 3:7a; on the latter's alliance with Ahab, see *Ant.* 8.398. The cross-reference points up the connection between the stories of Jehoshaphat's 2 joint campaigns with a northern king, i.e. Ahab (8.398-420) and Joram (9.29-43), which Josephus will highlight throughout his presentation of the latter incident.

[133] Compare Joram's direct address question to Jehoshaphat in 2 Kgs 3:7a: "Will you go with me to battle against Moab?"

[134] With this notice Josephus condenses Jehoshaphat's declaration in 2 Kgs 3:7b: "I will go; I am as you are, my people as your people, my horses as your horses."

[135] Josephus appends this further commitment by Jehoshaphat in order to explain how it was that the king of Edom (Idumea) also appears as a party to the campaign against Moab in what follows (see 2 Kgs 3:9). Josephus found inspiration for the addition in the notice of MT 1 Kgs 22:47, which states that in Jehoshaphat's day "there was no king in Edom, a deputy [MT: נצב; in the LXX BL equivalent of 22:47, i.e. 1

Kgs 16:28ᶠ, the Hebrew word is transliterated] was king," interpreting this to mean that Edom's ruler at this time was not an independent sovereign, but a vassal of his Judean overlord.

[136] Josephus adds this account of Joram's visit to Jerusalem and his reception there. In so doing, he depicts Jehoshaphat as reciprocating the hospitality he and his entourage had received from Ahab in Samaria, as recounted in *Ant.* 8.398 (// 2 Chr 18:2).

[137] Josephus makes the march route a matter of a joint decision by the 2 kings, whereas in 2 Kgs 3:8 Joram simply prescribes this in response to a question by Jehoshaphat. This accentuation of the stature of the Judean king characterizes Josephus' version of the story of 2 Kings 3, just as it does his retelling of Jehoshaphat's earlier involvement in Ahab's campaign against Syria (*Ant.* 8.398-420), as compared with its biblical sources (1 Kings 22// 2 Chronicles 18).

[138] Josephus appends this explanation of the coalition's choice of the desert route, despite its potential hazards that will emerge subsequently.

[139] See 2 Kgs 3:9a. Josephus appends the mention of Jerusalem as the kings' starting point in view of his notice on Joram's coming there earlier in 9.31.

[140] See 2 Kgs 3:9b. Josephus appends the explanation about the expedition's situation being due to the incompetence of the guides.

[141] With this addition Josephus highlights the effects of the lack of water on the expedition, above all on Joram, whose idea the campaign was and who, therefore, would feel especially chagrined by the turn it has now taken.

[142] Josephus amplifies Joram's assertion about the Lord's "handing over" the 3 kings to Moab (2 Kgs

33 The just[143] Josaphat encouraged him and, sending to the camp, directed that *Elisha* they ascertain whether any prophet of God had come along with them,[144] "in order *consulted* that, through him, we might learn from God what we are to do."[145] When a certain one of Joram's domestics stated that he had seen Elissai, the disciple of Elias, the son of Saphat, there,[146] the three kings, at Josaphat's urging, set out to him.[147]

34 When they came to the prophet's tent—it happened that he had pitched it outside the camp[148]—they asked him what was in store for the army, Joram in particular [doing this].[149] When [Elissai] said not to bother him,[150] but to go to the prophets of his father and mother—for they were truthful prophets[151]—, he begged him to prophesy and save them.[152]

35 He, however, swore by God[153] that he would not answer him,[154] were it not for Josaphat, who was holy and just.[155] When a certain man was brought who knew how to play the harp (for he himself had asked for him),[156] he became divinely possessed by the harp,[157] and ordered the kings to dig out many pits in the stream.[158]

3:10) with a question about what offense on his (Joram's) part has prompted God to do this. That question further underlines Joram's sense of responsibility for the expedition's predicament; see previous note. At the same time, it appears rather disingenuous, given Josephus' previous highlighting of the king's depravity; see 9.28.

[143] This characterization of Jehoshaphat (Greek: δίκαιος) recalls Josephus' earlier mentions of his "justice" (Greek: δικαιοσύνη); see *Ant.* 8.394; 9.16.

[144] Josephus accentuates Jehoshaphat's role in the proceedings with his added reference to his "encouraging" Joram and by having him "direct" that search be made for a prophet; in 2 Kgs 3:11a the Judean king simply raises the question about the availability of a prophet.

[145] Josephus spells out what Jehoshaphat has in mind when (see 2 Kgs 3:11a) he speaks of the expedition's "inquiring of the Lord" through the prophet. The formulation recalls Jehoshaphat's earlier asking Ahab to procure another prophet in order that "they might learn more precisely about the future" in *Ant.* 8.402.

[146] See 2 Kgs 3:11b. Josephus replaces the source's figurative qualification of Elisha as the one "who poured water on the hands of Elijah" with the title "disciple" previously used by him of the former figure in *Ant.* 8.353; 9.28. In the same line, Tg. substitutes its own prosaic equivalent, making Elisha the one who "served Elijah."

[147] See 2 Kgs 3:12b. The reference to Jehoshaphat's "urging" the other kings to seek out Elisha further underscores the king's leading role—alongside Joram—in the incident. It takes the place of the declaration about the "word of the Lord" being with Elisha attributed to Jehoshaphat in 3:12a.

[148] Josephus adds this notice on the site of the meeting.

[149] Josephus gives Joram the opening word in the encounter—just as he is the first to speak when the water runs out in 9.32. By contrast, in 2 Kgs 3:13a it is Elisha who initiates the discussion with his address to Joram.

[150] This directive is Josephus' elucidatory rendering of Elisha's opening question to Joram in 2 Kgs 3:13aα, which reads literally: "what to me and to you?"

[151] See 2 Kgs 3:13aβ. Josephus appends Elisha's ironic characterization of the parental prophets; on these figures, see *Ant.* 8.318, 336, 402. On the phrase "truthful prophet(s)," see note to "truthful prophet" at 9.23.

[152] Compare 2 Kgs 3:13b, where Joram responds by reiterating his claim about the Lord's handing over the 3 kings to Moab from 3:10.

[153] As usual, Josephus leaves aside the oath formula ("as the Lord of hosts lives, whom I serve") used by Elisha in 2 Kgs 3:14aα.

[154] Josephus clarifies the meaning of Elisha's response to Joram as cited in 2 Kgs 3:14bβ: "... I would neither look at you, nor see you."

[155] Josephus expands the biblical Elisha's declaration of esteem for Jehoshaphat (2 Kgs 3:14aβ) with mention of these 2 qualities of the king, the 2nd of which recalls the designation of him as "just" in 9.33. The collocation "holy and just" (Greek: ὅσιος καὶ δίκαιος) occurs also in *Ant.* 6.87; 8.245, 295 (reverse order); 15.138.

[156] See 2 Kgs 3:15a. Josephus adds the mention of the minstrel's being, not only called for by, but actually brought to, Elisha.

[157] 2 Kgs 3:15b speaks of the "power of the Lord coming upon" Elisha as the minstrel plays. On the phrase "divinely possessed" (ἔνθεος γενόμενος) in Josephus, see the note to "he became divinely possessed" at *Ant.* 6.56.

36 "For though there will be no cloud nor wind nor rain falling, you will see the river full of water,[159] so that both the army and the beasts of burden might be preserved by drinking.[160] Not only this will be for you from God,[161] but you will also conquer the enemy and capture the best and most solidly fortified cities of the Moabites. You are likewise to cut down their cultivated trees, ravage their country, and stop up their springs and rivers."[162]

Expedition gets water

(3.2) 37 After the prophet had said these things, on the following day, before the sun rose,[163] the stream ran with much [water], for God had caused rain to fall very heavily a three-days journey away in Idumea, with the result that the army and the beasts of burden found abundant drink.[164]

Moabites deceived and routed

38 When the Moabites heard that the three kings were coming against them and were making their approach through the desert,[165] their king immediately gathered his army together and directed them to pitch camp on the borders,[166] so that the enemy would not be concealed from them once they had invaded their country.[167]

39 When at sunrise they observed the water in the stream—for this was not far from the Moabite country—with a color similar to blood (for then especially the water becomes a glistening red),[168] they were deceived into thinking that their enemies had killed each other on account of their thirst, and that the river was running with their blood.[169] **40** Supposing this to be the case then, they requested the king to send them out to plunder the enemy. All rushed out, as though for ready gain, and came to the camp of the enemies [they thought] had perished.[170] But this hope of theirs was disappointed,[171] for the enemy surrounded them; some were slaughtered, while the rest dispersed in flight to their own country.[172]

---

[158] This directive takes the place of Elisha's opening announcement in 2 Kgs 3:16, i.e. "I [the Lord] will make this dry stream-bed full of pools." In Josephus' presentation, the coming of the water requires human exertion as well.

[159] See 2 Kgs 3:17a. Josephus adds the reference to the cloud.

[160] See 2 Kgs 3:17b.

[161] Compare 2 Kgs 3:18a, where Elisha calls the promised water "a light thing in the sight of the Lord."

[162] Josephus has an equivalent for each of Elisha's 5 announcements of what the Lord will enable the expedition to accomplish as cited in 2 Kgs 3:18b-19. At the same time, he reverses the sequence of the Bible's last 2 items, i.e. the stopping of the water sources and the wasting of the land. He likewise omits the specification that the latter operation is to be effected by use of "stones."

[163] This chronological indication replaces the cultic allusion of 2 Kgs 3:20a, i.e. "about the time of the offering of the sacrifice."

[164] See 2 Kgs 3:20b. Josephus supplies the explicit reference to God's role, as well as to the distance over which the water traveled to reach the expedition. His concluding mention of the army and beasts of burden finding abundant drink draws on the wording of Elisha's promise as cited in 9.36, thus underscoring its fulfillment.

[165] See 2 Kgs 3:21a. Josephus appends the reference to the expedition's march route, this picking up on his notice that the kings had decided to advance through "the desert of Idumea" in 9.31.

[166] This rendering reflects the conjecture, i.e. ὅρων of Niese (adopted also by Marcus) for the reading of the codices, i.e. ὁρῶν ("mountains").

[167] Cf. 2 Kgs 3:21b. Josephus adds explicit mention of the Moabite king's leadership role in the preparations and appends the rationale for his stationing his army at the frontier.

[168] See 2 Kgs 3:22. Josephus supplies the parenthetical specification concerning the site of the water and the notice on sunrise as the time when the water took on an especially reddish hue.

[169] See 2 Kgs 3:23a. Josephus supplies the (supposed) motivation for the kings' mutual slaughter, while making clear from the start that the Moabites were deluded in their surmise.

[170] Josephus elaborates on the Moabites' cry as reported in 2 Kgs 3:23b: "Now then, Moab, to the spoil." In particular, he highlights the king's role in the proceedings and the extent of the Moabites' delusion.

[171] This added transitional phrase highlights the contrast between what the Moabites suppose and the reality that awaits them.

[172] See 2 Kgs 3:24a. Josephus adds mention of the killing of some of the Moabites.

41 Invading the Moabite [country], the kings overthrew the cities that were in it and ravaged their fields, causing these to disappear by filling them with stones from the streams.[173] They cut down the best of the trees, covered over the waters of the springs,[174] and leveled the walls to the ground.[175]

42 Now the king of the Moabites, being hard-pressed by the siege, and seeing the city in danger of being captured by storm, made a charge with 700 men;[176] he went out in order to ride through the camp of the enemy at a spot where he supposed their guards were negligent.[177] But though he made the attempt, he was unable to flee, for it happened that the place was carefully guarded.[178] **43** Returning to the city, he performed an act of desperation and terrible necessity.[179] Leading up the eldest of his sons, who was to reign as king after him, onto the wall, so that he was visible to all his enemies, he offered him as a whole sacrifice to god.[180] When the kings observed him, they had pity on his necessity. Moved by a certain humanity and mercy,[181] they raised the siege and each one returned to his own home.[182] **44** Josaphat came to Hierosolyma and lived in peace.[183] Surviving for a short time after that campaign, he died, having lived sixty years,[184] of which he reigned as king for twenty-five. He received a magnificent burial in Hierosolyma,[185] for he was an imitator of the deeds of David.[186] **(4.1) 45** He left behind several sons, but as his

---

[173] See 2 Kgs 3:25aα. Josephus supplies the indication concerning the source of the stones that are used to cover the Moabite fields.

[174] Josephus reverses the order of the invaders' operations as cited in 2 Kgs 3:25aβ. In so doing, he has the invaders follow the sequence of Elisha's directives in 9.36.

[175] This notice seems to reflect the LXX BL reading at the opening of 2 Kgs 3:25b, i.e. "until they [the invaders] left the stones of the wall cast down...." (compare MT's [apparent] proper name: "only at Kir-haresh did the stone walls remain"). Josephus has no equivalent to the continuation of 3:25b, i.e. "...until the slingers surrounded and conquered it [Kir-haresh]."

[176] 2 Kgs 3:26a specifies that the 700 were "swordsmen."

[177] According to 2 Kgs 3:26a, the Moabite assault was made "opposite the king of Edom." Josephus supplies a rationale for the Moabite king's choosing the particular spot he does for the attempt.

[178] Josephus elaborates on the summary remark of 2 Kgs 3:26b concerning the failure of the attempt: "but they [the Moabites] could not [break through]."

[179] Josephus dramatizes the Moabite king's subsequent sacrifice of his son (2 Kgs 3:27a) with these portentous opening words. The phrase "terrible necessity" (Greek: δεινῆ ἀνάγκη) occurs only here in Josephus.

[180] Greek: ὁλοκαύτωσις τῷ θεῷ. See 2 Kgs 3:27a. Josephus spells out the purpose, i.e. visibility to the invaders, of the king's sacrificing his son "on the wall." The Bible does not state to whom (his own god? the Lord?) the king offered his son. Josephus' specification that the sacrifice was offered "to god" (Greek: τῷ θεῷ)

leaves the matter ambiguous as well.

[181] Josephus' reference to the kings' emotional response to their witnessing the sacrifice as that which prompts their subsequent withdrawal takes the place of the statement of 2 Kgs 3:27bα that "there came great wrath upon Israel" (which itself leaves ambiguous whether the "wrath" in question was that of the Moabite god or of the Lord). Josephus' alternative presentation furthers his purpose of highlighting Jewish humanity—even towards a pagan rebel and enemy; see Feldman 1998a: 326. The collocation ἀνθρώπινον καὶ ἐλεεινόν ("humanity and mercy") occurs only here in Josephus.

[182] See 2 Kgs 3:27bβ.

[183] Josephus supplies this transitional notice—itself inspired by the reference to the invaders' withdrawal in 2 Kgs 3:27bβ—to his following account of Jehoshaphat's demise, which he, in contrast to the Bible, explicitly dates to shortly after the end of the Moabite campaign.

[184] Josephus obtains this figure for Jehoshaphat's total life-span by combining the data of 1 Kgs 22:41a // 2 Chr 20:31a: acceding at age 35, Jehoshaphat ruled for 25 years.

[185] See 1 Kgs 22:50a// 2 Chr 21:1a. Josephus supplies the characterization of Jehoshaphat's burial as "magnificent."

[186] In 1 Kgs 22:43a// 2 Chr 20:32a Jehoshaphat's good conduct is associated with that of his own father Asa. Josephus' paralleling of Jehoshaphat rather with David here recalls his introduction of the former king in *Ant.* 8.315, where the same linkage is made.

successor he appointed the oldest, Joram[187] (for he had the same name as his wife's brother, who was reigning as king over the Israelites, the son of Achab).[188]

Elisha's great deeds

46 Coming to Samareia from the Moabite country, the king of the Israelites[189] had with him the prophet Elissai, whose actions I wish to relate, for they are splendid and worthy of history, just as we have come to know them in the sacred books.[190]

Elisha assists widow

(4.2) 47 Thus it is told that the wife of Achab's steward Obedias[191] approached him and said that he was not unaware of how her husband had preserved the prophets from being done away with by Jezabele, the wife of Achab, for, she said, 100 of them who were in hiding were fed by him,[192] who had borrowed money [to do this].[193] And now, after the death of her husband, she and her children were being driven into slavery by the creditors.[194] She appealed to him, in view of her husband's beneficial deed, to take pity and award her some help.[195]

48 Upon his inquiring what she had in her house, she said that she had nothing but a very little oil in a jar.[196] But the prophet directed her to go off and borrow many empty vessels from her neighbors and then, having closed the doors of her room, to pour all the oil from her one vessel into the others, for God would fill them.[197] **49** The woman did what she was directed,[198] ordering her children[199] to

---

[187] Josephus abbreviates the content of 2 Chr 21:2-3, omitting the names of Jehoshaphat's 6 other sons and the mention of the gifts he gave them.

[188] With this parenthetical remark Josephus highlights the noteworthy coincidence that the contemporary kings of Judah and Israel both bore the same name. The notice recalls Josephus' account of the Israelite Joram's accession in 9.27 and the mention of Jehoshaphat's marrying his son Joram to Athaliah, daughter of Ahab (and thus sister of Joram of Israel) in *Ant.* 8.398.

[189] This transitional reference to Joram's return to his capital parallels Josephus' notice on Jehoshaphat's coming back to Jerusalem in 9.44. Both notices are Josephus' elaboration of the general remark about the invaders' returning home in 2 Kgs 3:27bβ.

[190] With this (biblically unparalleled) notice on Elisha's returning with Joram to Samaria, Josephus makes the transition to his long subsequent account (9.47-94// 2 Kgs 4:1-8:15) concerning Elisha's activities; on this, see Begg 2000: 67-112 and Feldman 1998a: 334-51. The phrase "sacred books" recalls the mention of these writings as recording the "disappearances" of Elijah and Enoch in 9.28.

[191] 2 Kgs 4:1 (MT and LXX BL) does not name the woman's late husband, whom it simply designates as "one of the sons of the prophets." Josephus' identification of him with Ahab's official "Obadiah" is paralleled in the Tg. on 2 Kgs 4:1 and elsewhere in Jewish and Christian tradition; see Begg 2000: 68, n. 7. The identification seems to have been inspired by the verbal link between the woman's characterization of her husband as Elisha's "servant" who "feared the Lord" (4:1bα) and Obadiah's presentation of himself to Elijah

in 1 Kgs 18:12: "I your servant have revered [feared] the Lord from my youth."

[192] The widow's allusion of her husband's support for the endangered prophets here takes the place of her brief reference to his having "feared the Lord" in 2 Kgs 4:1bα. The wording of the allusion is drawn from Josephus' account of Obadiah's support for the prophets in *Ant.* 8.330 (// 1 Kgs 18:4, 13).

[193] This detail lacks a basis in either Josephus' earlier account of Obadiah's initiative (*Ant.* 8.330) or its biblical source, i.e. 1 Kgs 18:4, 13. It is, however, paralleled in the Tg. on 2 Kgs 4:1 and other Jewish writings; see Begg 2000: 69, n. 10. Such borrowing on the husband's part explains how he incurred the debt, which the creditor(s) is now demanding be satisfied.

[194] See 2 Kgs 4:1bβ, where the woman speaks of a single "creditor," who is above to enslave her 2 children. Josephus highlights the threatening situation by having the woman herself face enslavement, along with her children at the hands of several creditors.

[195] Josephus supplies this closing appeal by the woman, who in 2 Kgs 4:1 simply presents the facts of her situation to Elisha.

[196] See 2 Kgs 4:2. Josephus omits Elisha's opening question ("what shall I do for you?") given that, in his own presentation, the woman ends her words to the prophet with an explicit plea for his assistance; see previous note.

[197] See 2 Kgs 4:3-4. Josephus expands Elisha's instructions to the woman with the concluding promise of God's "filling" the vessels.

[198] With this formula Josephus summarizes the various actions performed by the woman in 2 Kgs 4:5 in accordance with Elisha's directives to her in 4:3-4.

bring each of the vessels. Then when they were all filled and none was empty,[200] she came to the prophet and reported these things.[201]

50 He advised her to go off, sell the oil, and pay the creditors what they were owed; there would also be something left over from the sale-price of the oil that she might use for feeding her children.[202] Thus Elissai relieved the woman's needs and freed her from the arrogance of her creditors.[203]

(4.2) 51 ...[204] Elissai sent off quickly to Joram, urging him to be on his guard at that place, for some Syrians were in ambush there to do away with him.[205] Persuaded by the prophet, the king no longer went out hunting.[206]

Elisha warns Joram

52 Now Ader,[207] having failed in his plot,[208] became wrathful,[209] as if it were his own people who had informed Joram of the trap.[210] Summoning them, he called them betrayers of his secrets and threatened them with death, since his scheme, which he had entrusted to them alone, had been revealed to the enemy.[211] **53** One of those present said, however, that he was mistaken; nor should he suppose that they had informed the enemy of his dispatch of those who were to do away with

Ben-hadad (Ader) learns of Elisha's clairvoyance

---

[199] Josephus' plural accords with the reading of LXX BL 2 Kgs 4:6a, whereas MT has the singular, "son" in this instance (though elsewhere in the pericope it too uses the plural).

[200] Josephus expatiates on the son's (MT; LXX: sons'; see previous note) statement to the woman in 2 Kgs 4:6aβ: "there is not another [vessel]." He leaves aside the notice of 4:6b about the cessation of the oil at this point.

[201] 2 Kgs 4:7a (MT and LXX BL) uses the title "man of God" for Elisha. Josephus' substitution of "prophet" is paralleled in Tg.

[202] Cf. 2 Kgs 4:7b, where Elisha tells the woman that she and her son(s) can live off the oil that remains once her debts have been paid.

[203] Josephus supplies this closing notice to the biblical story of Elisha's "oil miracle" (2 Kgs 4:1-7), underscoring the efficacy of the prophet's intervention.

[204] The dots in the translation above point to the fact that the extant text of Josephus moves abruptly from Elisha's closing word to the woman (9.50// 2 Kgs 4:7b) to the prophet's warning King Joram about the Syrians (9.51// 2 Kgs 6:9), with no parallel to the intervening biblical segment, i.e. 2 Kgs 4:8-6:8, which relates a series of additional miracles by Elisha. It seems clear that a lacuna has to be posited, either in the text of Josephus or in that of the biblical witnesses used by him at this point. For one thing, *Ant.* 9.51, with its reference to "that place," presupposes a preceding notice identifying the site and mentioning the Syrian advance towards it. In addition, Josephus' statement in 9.46, announcing his intention of recounting Elisha's memorable miracles, suggests that he would indeed have made use of the miracle stories of 2 Kgs 4:8-6:8, if he

had these before him. It remains, unclear, however, just how much of the segment in question was absent from Josephus' biblical text(s) or, alternatively, how extensive his own original, but now missing, parallel to this segment may have been. See further Begg 2000: 71-72 and n. 24.

[205] Josephus spells out the hostile intention behind the Syrians' "going down" to the spot about which Elisha warns Joram in 2 Kgs 6:9.

[206] This notice on Joram's compliance with Elisha's directive replaces the reference in 2 Kgs 6:10a to Joram's "sending to the place" about which the prophet had cautioned him (see 6:9). Josephus leaves aside the notice of 6:10b, which states that Elisha's warnings ensured Joram's safety on several occasions.

[207] In the biblical account the Syrian king is not identified by his name ("Ben-hadad") until 2 Kgs 6:24. The form of the king's name here is that read by RMSPEZon and printed by Niese. Marcus adopts the conjecture of J. Hudson, i.e. Ἄδαδος. Both forms of the name appear elsewhere in Josephus' text; for the form "Ader," see *Ant.* 8.401 and 9.1.

[208] Josephus adds this transitional phrase that recalls Elisha's warning about the Syrian "ambush" against Joram in 9.51.

[209] 2 Kgs 6:11a speaks of the king's mind being "greatly troubled."

[210] Josephus elucidates the vague reference to "this thing" that is said to disturb the king's mind in 2 Kgs 6:11a.

[211] Josephus dramatizes the king's reproach to his officials, which in 2 Kgs 6:11b is formulated more indirectly, via his question: "will you not show me who of us is for the king of Israel?"

Elisha's servant shown God's support of prophet

him [Joram].[212] He should know rather that it was the prophet Elissai who was reporting everything to him [Joram] and revealing what he [Ader] intended.[213] He [Ader] then ordered that they send to learn in what city Elissai was residing.[214]

54 Those who had been sent came and announced that he was in Dothaein.[215] Ader therefore dispatched a large force of horses and chariots to the city that they might take Elissai. They encircled the entire city by night and kept it under guard.[216] Just at dawn, the prophet's minister[217] learned of this and that the enemy was seeking to take Elissai; he disclosed this to him, running to him with shouting and consternation.[218]

55 He encouraged his attendant[219] not to be afraid,[220] however, and appealed to God—relying on whom as his ally he was fearless[221]—to show his minister his own power and presence, so far as this was possible, in order that, thus encouraged, he might have good hope.[222] God, for his part, heard the prayers of the prophet and granted the attendant to observe a crowd of chariots and horses encircling Elissai.[223] As a result, he put aside his fear, reanimated by the sight of the evident alliance [between God and Elissai].[224]

Blinded Syrians led to Samaria

56 After these things Elissai appealed to God to blind[225] the enemies' sight by casting darkness[226] upon them, in virtue of which they would be unaware of him.[227]

---

[212] Josephus elaborates on the courtier's initial response in 2 Kgs 6:12: "None, my lord, O king." The wording of his version recalls the reference to the Syrians' being in ambush "to do away with" Joram in 9.51.

[213] In 2 Kgs 6:12b the courtier affirms that Elisha is reporting to Joram "the words that you [the Syrian king] speak in your bedchamber."

[214] Josephus' version of the king's command (2 Kgs 6:13a) omits its attached statement of intention, i.e. "that I may send and seize him [Elisha]." He will, however, make use of this item in connection with the Syrian's 2nd sending; see 9.54.

[215] MT (2 Kgs 6:13b) דֹתָן (Eng.: "Dothan"); LXX BL Δωθάειμ; Josephus Δωθαείν.

[216] See 2 Kgs 6:14. Josephus' reference to the purpose of the king's "sending" is derived from his earlier directive as cited in 6:13a; see note to "was residing" at 9.53.

[217] Greek: διάκονος. This is the same designation used of Elisha himself in his relationship to Elijah in *Ant.* 8.354. 2 Kgs 6:15 calls the figure "the servant (LXX BL λειτουργός) of the man of God" (MT LXX L; LXX B: of Elisha).

[218] Josephus dramatizes the distress of the servant, who in 2 Kgs 6:15b says: "Alas, my master! What shall we do?"

[219] Greek: θεράπων. In 9.54-55 Josephus alternates between this term and the word "minister" (Greek: διάκονος) to designate Elisha's companion.

[220] In 2 Kgs 6:16 Elisha motivates his exhorting his servant not to be afraid with the statement "for those who are with us are more than those who are with them [the Syrians]."

[221] Josephus supplies this characterization of Elisha, which places him in sharp contrast with his fear-filled servant.

[222] In 2 Kgs 6:17a Elisha prays: "O Lord, open his [the servant's] eyes that he may see." Josephus has the prophet spell out what he wants God to show the servant and the intended purpose of this. The expression "show his [God's] power and presence (Greek: δύναμις καὶ παρουσία)" has a parallel in Solomon's prayer that God "show his power and providence (Greek: δύναμις καὶ πρόνοια)" on the occasion of the dedication of the temple in *Ant.* 8.109. On Josephus' use of the word παρουσία ("presence") in connection with God's self-manifestation, see Schlatter 1932: 30-31.

[223] Compare 2 Kgs 6:17b, where the servant is shown the "mountain full of horses" and "chariots of fire round about Elisha."

[224] Josephus appends this notice on the effect of what he sees upon the servant, thus highlighting the fulfillment of Elisha's request for the vision from God. Its term "alliance" (Greek: συμμαχία) recalls the reference to God's being Elisha's "ally" (Greek: σύμμαχος) earlier in 9.55.

[225] Greek: ἀμαυρόω. God is the subject of this verb also in *Ant.* 1.202, where he "blinds" the Sodomites. Josephus' only other use of the verb is in *Ant.* 8.268 (Ahijah's eyes are "blinded" by age).

[226] Greek: ἀχλύς. Josephus' 2 uses of this noun are here in 9.56 and in the immediately following 9.57.

[227] See 2 Kgs 6:18a. Josephus amplifies Elisha's prayer with an indication concerning how the requested blinding of the Syrians is to be accomplished (i.e. by God's casting of "darkness" upon them) and a reference

When this occurred as well,[228] he advanced into the middle of the enemy and asked whom they had come to seek. Upon their saying that it was the prophet Elissai,[229] he promised to hand him over, if they would follow him to the city where he was.[230]

57 They readily followed, with the prophet as their guide and their sight and minds darkened[231] by God.[232] Having brought them to Samareia, Elissai ordered King Joram to close the gates and surround the Syrians with his own force,[233] while he himself prayed to God to clear the eyes of the enemy and eliminate their darkness.[234] They, when their blindness[235] was removed, found themselves in the middle of their enemies.[236]

58 The Syrians, as was natural, were in terrible terror and helplessness[237] in the face of such a divine and unexpected event.[238] But when King Joram inquired of the prophet whether he should direct that they be shot down,[239] Elissai prevented him from doing this.[240] For, he said, whereas by the law of war it was just to kill those who had been captured,[241] these men had perpetrated no harm on his country and had come to them unknowingly, [under the influence] of divine power.[242]

Syrians spared by Joram

59 He advised him to share hospitality and his table with them and to dismiss them unharmed.[243] Obeying the prophet,[244] therefore, Joram, quite splendidly and

---

to the purpose of their blinding.

[228] Cf. 2 Kgs 6:18b, which states that God struck the Syrians with blindness in accordance with Elisha's prayer.

[229] Josephus prefaces Elisha's words to the Syrians as reported in 6:19a with this sequence concerning the initial exchange between him and them.

[230] From Elisha's words to the Syrians in 2 Kgs 6:19aα Josephus omits his opening statement: "this is not the way, and this is not the city." He likewise reverses the sequence of prophetic command ("follow me") and promise ("I will bring you to the man whom you seek") to the Syrians of 6:19aβ.

[231] Greek: ἐπισκοτέω. Josephus uses this verb with God as subject also in *War* 5.343 (God "darkens" counsels). Its other occurrences in his corpus are in *War* 5.246; *Ant.* 5.205; 8.106; *Apion* 1.214.

[232] Josephus elaborates on the summary notice of 2 Kgs 6:19b: "and he [Elisha] led them [the Syrians] to Samaria," highlighting the fulfillment of Elisha's prayer in 9.56.

[233] Josephus adds mention of these precautionary measures that Elisha enjoins on the king.

[234] See 2 Kgs 6:20a. Josephus' appended phrase "remove their darkness" recalls Elisha's earlier prayer that God "cast darkness upon" the Syrians in 9.56.

[235] Greek: ἀμαύρωσις. This noun cognate of the verb ἀμαυρόω ("to blind") of 9.56 is *hapax* in Josephus.

[236] Compare 2 Kgs 6:20bβ: "...and lo, they [the Syrians] were in the midst of Samaria." Josephus' version, with its reference to the Syrians' being among their "enemies," highlights the threat facing them.

[237] Greek: ἔκπληξις καὶ ἀμηχανία. This collocation occurs only here in Josephus. The phrase "terrible terror" (Greek: δεινῆ ἔκπληξις) occurs also in *War* 2.538; 6.180.

[238] Josephus supplies the reference to the Syrians' emotional state. He uses the collocation "divine and unexpected" (Greek: θεῖος καὶ παράδοξος) of the manna in *Ant.* 3.30 and of God's providence in 10.214.

[239] In 2 Kgs 6:21a Joram twice asks Elisha—whom he addresses as "my father"—"shall I slay them [the Syrians]?" Josephus has the king specify the manner in which he envisages the captives being put to death.

[240] Compare Elisha's opening response to Joram in 2 Kgs 6:22aα: "you shall not slay them."

[241] This statement appears to be a reversal of the thrust of Elisha's rhetorical question in 2 Kgs 6:22aβ: "would you [Joram] slay those whom you have taken with your sword and your bow?" (RSV). Whereas the biblical prophet thus intimates that even those captured in war are not to be put to death, Josephus' Elisha affirms that such captives may legitimately be executed (conceivably, however, Josephus read Elisha's question as a statement, i.e. "you [do] slay those...").

[242] Josephus here amplifies Elisha's word to Joram of 2 Kgs 6:22a with a contrast between those who might be legitimately put to death (enemies captured in war) and those, who like Joram's captives, may not be executed; see previous note. The phrase "divine power (Greek: θεία δύναμις) occurs also in *Ant.* 19.69; cf. 18.288; it recalls the expression "divine [θεῖος] and unexpected event" used earlier in 9.58, as well as Elisha's appeal that God show his "power [Greek: δύναμις] and presence" in 9.55.

[243] Compare 2 Kgs 6:22b, where Elisha urges Joram to set "bread and water" before the Syrians that they might "eat and drink and go to their master."

Benhadad (Ader) besieges Samareia lavishly[245] feasted the Syrians, and then dismissed them to Ader their king.[246]

(4.4) 60 When they came and disclosed to him what had happened, Ader marveled at its unexpectedness and at the manifestation and power of the God of the Israelites,[247] as also at the prophet, with whom the Deity was so obviously present.[248] Being afraid of Elissai, he decided then no longer to secretly attack the king of the Israelites. Rather, he resolved to make war openly, thinking that he was superior to the enemy in the size of his army and his force.[249] **61** He campaigned with a large force against Joram, who, not regarding himself as a match for the Syrians, shut himself up in Samareia, putting his confidence in the solidity of the walls.[250] Ader, reasoning that he would capture the city, if not by means of engines, then at any rate by subduing the Samareians through famine and the lack of provisions, launched a siege of the city.[251]

Scarcity in city **62** The supply of necessities failed Joram to such an extent that, due to the overwhelming scarcity, a donkey's head was being sold in Samareia for eighty pieces of silver,[252] while the Hebrews were buying a *sextarius*[253] of dove's dung in place of salt for five [silver pieces].[254]

Joram's inspection **63** Joram was in fear that, because of the famine, someone might betray the city to the enemy;[255] each day he used to inspect the walls and the guards,[256] spying out whether there was any one from [the enemy] inside, precluding by his visibility and attentiveness any one's even wishing such a thing or from acting [on this], if he had already formed such a plan.[257]

---

[244] Josephus adds this transitional phrase that underscores the king's readiness to do what Elisha tells him.

[245] This collocation (Greek: λαμπρῶς καὶ φιλοτίμος) recurs in 9.272; 15.194 (reverse order).

[246] See 2 Kgs 6:23a.

[247] This designation for the Deity was used previously in 9.21.

[248] Josephus elaborates on the mention of the Syrians' return to their king in 2 Kgs 6:23bα, highlighting the effect of their report upon him. The expression "manifestation and power" (Greek: ἐπιφάνεια καὶ δύναμις) recurs in *Ant.* 17.96; cf. the phrase "divine power" (Greek: θεία δύναμις) in 9.58. The mention of God's being "present" (Greek: πάρειμι) with Elisha recalls the prophet's prayer in 9.55 that God show his "power and presence (Greek: παρουσία)" to his servant.

[249] Josephus introduces this contrast between the 2 forms of warfare successively adopted by the Syrian king so as to obviate the seeming discrepancy between 2 Kgs 6:23bβ (the Syrians cease their raids on Israel) and 6:24 (Ben-hadad moves his army against Samaria).

[250] In 2 Kgs 6:24 all attention is focussed on Ben-hadad's initiatives, with nothing being said of Joram's counter-moves. Josephus, by contrast, highlights the tactics adopted by the latter in countering the Syrian advance and his motivation for adopting these. The addition here is reminiscent of Josephus' (likewise added) remarks on Ahab's response to an earlier Syrian

attack, i.e. shutting himself up behind the walls of Samaria, in *Ant.* 8.364.

[251] Josephus elaborates on the summary reference to Ben-hadad's "besieging" Samaria in 2 Kgs 6:24b with mention of the various possibilities (engines, famine) available to him for subjugating the city.

[252] Josephus' figure agrees with that of MT 2 Kgs 6:25bα against LXX BL, which read 50. Both biblical witnesses speak more specifically of silver "shekels."

[253] This is Josephus' replacement for the unit of measure cited in 2 Kgs 6:25bβ, i.e. "the 4th part of a kab." According to *Ant.* 8.57 there were 72 *sextarii* to a *bath*.

[254] Josephus adds the indication concerning the intended use of the "dove's dung" cited in 2 Kgs 6:25bβ.

[255] Josephus supplies this reference to Joram's emotional state, which prompts the action attributed to him in 2 Kgs 6:26a, i.e. passing along on the wall.

[256] 2 Kgs 6:26a seems to refer to Joram's one-time passing along the walls, where he is accosted by a woman in distress. Josephus makes this a daily routine of the king, thereby underscoring his solicitude for the city's safety. He adds the reference to Joram's oversight of the "guards."

[257] Josephus appends this elaborate allusion to the considerations behind Joram's inspection (cf. 2 Kgs 6:26a).

64 A certain woman cried out: "Be merciful, O master!"[258] Thinking she was going to request something in the way of food, he in his wrath[259] cursed her by God,[260] saying that he had nothing either from the threshing floor or from the wine press that he might provide for her who asked.[261]

Joram informed of case of cannibalism

65 She, however, said she needed none of these things, nor was she troubling him about food;[262] rather, she was requesting him to give judgment against another woman.[263] He then commanded her to speak and instruct [him] about what she was seeking.[264] She said that she was living together with the other woman, who was her neighbor and friend.[265] Given the hopelessness of the famine and the scarcity,[266] they were going to murder their children (each had a little male child)[267] and feed each other for one day.[268] **66** "And I," she said, "did indeed slaughter my [child] first[269] and on the next day we both ate mine.[270] Now however, she does not wish to do the same, but in violation of our agreement, has caused her son to disappear."[271]

67 When he heard this, Joram grieved greatly; he tore his clothes and let out a terrible cry.[272] Then, being full of wrath against the prophet Elissai,[273] he swore that he would do away with him[274] because he was not asking God to give them a way of escaping the calamities that surrounded them.[275] He immediately dispatched [a man] to cut off his head.[276]

Joram orders Elisha's execution

---

[258] In 2 Kgs 6:26b the woman exclaims: "help, my lord, O king!"

[259] Josephus supplies the indication concerning the king's emotional response to the woman's appeal.

[260] This is Josephus' version of the king's opening words to the woman in 2 Kgs 6:27, i.e. "(if the Lord will not help you...," which he takes as a "curse."

[261] In 2 Kgs 6:27 the king expresses his inability to help the woman in the form of a rhetorical question mentioning the 2 sources of commodities (the threshing floor and wine press) from which he has nothing to give her. Josephus "holds over" the king's appended question "what is your trouble?" of 6:28a until after the woman has stated the nature of her request, both positively and negatively; see 9.65.

[262] Josephus adds this initial assurance by the woman.

[263] Josephus supplies this initial, summary statement by the plaintiff about what she is asking of the king.

[264] This is Josephus' (delayed) version of the king's question to the woman ("what is your trouble?") of 2 Kgs 6:28a.

[265] In 2 Kgs 6:28b the plaintiff refers to the one she is accusing simply as "this woman." The added details about the latter supplied by Josephus' speaker underscore the closeness of the relationship between them and so likewise the reprehensibility of the other woman's deed.

[266] Josephus supplies this motivation for the appalling plan devised by the 2 women as cited by the plaintiff in 2 Kgs 6:28b.

[267] The plaintiff's statements in 2 Kgs 6:28-29 provide no indication concerning the age of the women's sons.

[268] In 2 Kgs 6:28b the plaintiff presents the plan as something thought up by the other woman on her own. Given the closeness of their relationship as previously described by her, Josephus depicts it rather as a matter of a joint agreement by them.

[269] According to 2 Kgs 6:29aα, the 2 women jointly "boiled" the plaintiff's son.

[270] See 2 Kgs 6:29aβ.

[271] In 2 Kgs 6:29b the plaintiff mentions her calling on the other woman to produce her son so that they might eat him and the latter's hiding of the child. Josephus' reference to the existing "agreement" between the pair reflects the plaintiff's allusion to their joint decision in 9.65 and underscores the wrongfulness of the other woman's deed.

[272] 2 Kgs 6:30a mentions only Joram's tearing of his clothes; Josephus accentuates his distress in the face of the shocking case just told him. On the other hand, he leaves aside the mention (6:30b) of the people's seeing the "sackcloth" the king is wearing beneath his clothes, given that nothing further is made of this item in what follows.

[273] Josephus adds this reference to the king's emotional state, which recalls the mention of his "wrath" in the face of the woman's appeal in 9.64.

[274] Josephus leaves aside Joram's oath formula ("may God do so to me, and more also, if..."), and generalizes his threat to see to it that Elisha's head will not remain on his shoulders by the following day of 2 Kgs 6:31.

[275] Josephus supplies this explanation as to what lies behind Joram's vehement outburst in 2 Kgs 6:31. The phrase "ask God" (Greek: δεῖται τοῦ θεοῦ) is used of 2 other prophetic figures by Josephus, i.e. Deborah (*Ant.* 5.201) and Isaiah (10.12).

Elisha warns his disciples

68 The one [sent] to do away with the prophet made haste.[277] The king's wrath was not, however, concealed from Elissai, who was sitting in his home with his disciples.[278] He reported to them that Joram, the son of the murderer, had sent a man to remove his head.[279] **69** "But you," he said, "when the one who has been ordered to do this arrives, be on your guard against him as he is about to enter; press against the door and keep him in check.[280] For the king has had second thoughts and will follow him, coming to me."[281] And they did what had been directed when the one sent by the king to do away with Elissai came.[282]

Joram confronts Elisha

70 Joram, however, regretted his wrath against the prophet, and fearing that the one ordered to kill him might [already] be doing this, hurried to prevent the murder from happening and to preserve the prophet.[283] When he arrived at his house, he censured him because he was not imploring God for release from their present calamities, but rather was ignoring those who were being afflicted by these.[284]

Elisha's assurances believed

71 Elissai, however, promised[285] that on the following day, at that [same] hour when the king had arrived at his house, there would be a great supply of food and two *sata* of barley would be sold in the market for a shekel and a *saton* of the finest wheat flour would be bought for a shekel.[286] **72** These [words] restored their joy to Joram and those who were present. For they did not hesitate to believe the prophet, given the truth of their past experiences; what was expected likewise made the lack and misery on that day easy for them to bear.[287]

Officer–prophet exchange

73 However, the leader of the third division, a friend of the king, whom he was then holding up as he leaned upon him,[288] said: "you are saying unbelievable things,

---

[276] Josephus supplies this appendix to the king's outburst in 2 Kgs 6:31, anticipating the mention of Joram's having "dispatched a man from his presence" and Elisha's allusion to the king's "sending to take off my head" in 6:32.

[277] Josephus adds this reference to the executioner's alacrity in carrying out his mandate.

[278] 2 Kgs 6:32aα has Elisha sitting with "the elders." Josephus adds the reference to the prophet's clairvoyance—with its allusion to the king's "wrath" as mentioned in 9.67—in light of his subsequent announcement to his companions in 6:32b.

[279] In 2 Kgs 6:32bα Elisha uses the Semitic idiom "son of this murderer" to designate Joram himself as a murderer. Josephus takes the expression as referring not to Joram personally, but rather to his father Ahab, the murderer of Naboth; see Marcus *ad loc.*

[280] See 2 Kgs 6:32bβ.

[281] With this announcement, Josephus clarifies Elisha's concluding rhetorical question in 2 Kgs 6:32bγ, i.e. "is not the sound of his master's [i.e. the king's] feet behind him [the executioner dispatched by Joram]?" He thereby highlights the clairvoyance of the prophet, who even at a distance knows of the king's change of plans.

[282] Josephus adds this notice on the prophet's disciples' carrying out the orders given them regarding the king's agent as cited in 2 Kgs 6:32b.

[283] Josephus supplies this sequence on Joram's

change of mind and resultant initiative, which serves to confirm the accuracy of Elisha's clairvoyant announcement in 9.69.

[284] This notice on Joram's words to Elisha, which recalls the reference to the king's "wrath" at the prophet's failure to intercede with God in 9.67, takes the place of the king's words to Elisha in 2 Kgs 6:33b: "This trouble is from the Lord! Why should I wait for the Lord any longer?"

[285] From Elisha's announcement in 2 Kgs 7:1 Josephus characteristically omits its opening summons ("hear the word of the Lord") and messenger formula, "thus says the Lord."

[286] Josephus' unit of measure replaces those of MT (הָאְס, RSV: "measure") and LXX BL (μέτρον, "measure") 2 Kgs 7:1b. He reverses the biblical sequence, in which the "fine meal" is cited before the "barley" (so MT LXX L; LXX B mentions only the former). As Marcus (*ad loc.*) notes, in 9.85 Josephus equates the *saton* with 1.5 Italian *modii*.

[287] Josephus adds this sequence concerning the believing response to Elisha's announcement on the part of Joram and those with him. The effect is to throw into relief the skepticism of the officer in what follows, who is alone in adopting such a stance.

[288] To the data concerning Elisha's challenger given in 2 Kgs 7:2a, Josephus adds the mention of his being Joram's "friend."

O prophet.[289] Just as God is unable to rain down torrents of barley or the best wheat flour from the sky, so also it is impossible that the things said by you just now will come about."[290] But the prophet said to him: "You shall indeed see this fulfilled, but shall have no share in the benefits."[291]

(4.5) 74 The things predicted by Elissai therefore came about in this way.[292] There was a law in Samareia that those with leprosy and whose bodies were not clean of this were to stay outside the city.[293] Now then, there were four men who for this reason were staying in front of the gates; because of the excess of the famine no one was any longer bringing food out to them, **75** who were themselves prevented by law from entering the city.[294] They reasoned that, even if they were allowed [to do this], they would be miserably destroyed by the famine, while they would suffer the same [fate] if they remained there, given their lack of food.[295] They resolved to surrender themselves to the enemy, so that if they were spared by them they would live, while if they were done away with, they would die a good death.[296]

76 Having settled on this scheme, they came by night to the camp of the enemy.[297] God had, however, already begun to frighten the Syrians and throw them into consternation.[298] He caused the noise of chariots and horses like those of an advancing army to sound in their ears, and was bringing this suspicion ever nearer to them.[299]

77 They were naturally so disturbed by this, that leaving their tents, they ran together to Ader,[300] saying that Joram, the king of the Israelites, had hired as allies the king of the Egyptians and those [kings] of the islands,[301] and was bringing these against them, for they were close enough that their noise could be heard.[302] **78** While

Lepers decide to surrender to Syrians

Flight of Syrians

---

[289] Josephus supplies this initial assertion by the officer, which establishes an immediate verbal contrast between him and Elisha's other hearers, who, according to 9.72, "did not hesitate to believe the prophet."

[290] Josephus transposes into an emphatic denial the officer's rhetorical question in 2 Kgs 7:2aβ: "if the Lord himself should make windows in heaven, could this thing be?" The Josephan officer's claim likewise picks up on the wording of Elisha's announcement of the coming surpluses of barley and fine wheat flour in 9.71.

[291] See 2 Kgs 7:2b.

[292] Josephus supplies this transition to the following story of the lepers (2 Kgs 7:3-10), which will eventuate in the realization of Elisha's prediction to the officer.

[293] Josephus supplies this reference to a (purported) Samaritan law in order to explain why, during an enemy siege, the 4 lepers should be outside the city's walls, as reported of them in 2 Kgs 7:3a. He may have found inspiration for the idea of such a "Samaritan law" in the injunction of Lev 13:46 that a leper is to "dwell alone in a habitation outside the camp"; cf. Josephus' own statement (*Ant.* 3.261, 264) that Moses excluded lepers "from the city," and *m. Kelim* 1.7, which prescribes that lepers are to be sent outside the walls of a city.

[294] These remarks, highlighting the lepers' predicament—and thus preparing for the desperate initiative they will now take— expatiate on the summary reference to their being "at the entrance of the gate" in 2 Kgs 7:3 in light of Josephus' preceding statement about "the law" governing their situation.

[295] See 2 Kgs 7:3b-4a.

[296] According to 2 Kgs 7:4b the lepers resolve to go to the Syrian camp, to live if they are spared and to "but die" if they are not. The verb εὐθανατέω ("to die a good death") is *hapax* in Josephus.

[297] See 2 Kgs 7:5a.

[298] Anticipating the notice on God's dealings with the Syrians from 2 Kgs 7:6, Josephus prefaces this with mention of the effect of the divine initiative upon them.

[299] See 2 Kgs 7:6a. Josephus appends the notice on the increasing proximity of the noise.

[300] Josephus dramatizes the scene with his added reference to the frightened Syrians abandoning their quarters and hurrying to find their king. By contrast, the account of the Syrians' flight in 2 Kgs 7:6-7 nowhere mentions the king.

[301] Compare 2 Kgs 7:6b: "the kings of the Hittites and the kings of Egypt."

[302] Josephus appends this explanation for the Syr-

they were speaking, Ader—for already his ears were resounding like those of the crowd—paid attention.[303] With much disorder and confusion,[304] leaving their horses and other beasts of burden as well as uncountable wealth in the camp, they proceeded to flee.[305]

Lepers in Syrian camp

79 Now the lepers, who were proceeding from Samareia to the camp of the Syrians, as we mentioned a short while ago,[306] when they reached the camp, perceived the great quiet and silence[307] there.[308] They went inside and, rushing into a tent, found no one. Having eaten and drunk, they carried off a garment and much silver, which they brought outside the camp and hid.[309]

Empty camp reported

80 Then they went into a another tent and, in like manner, also brought out the things in it;[310] they did this four times, meeting no one at all.[311] Concluding then that the enemy had withdrawn,[312] they regretted not having disclosed these things to Joram and the citizens.[313]

81 Coming to the wall of Samareia and crying up to the guards, they reported to them the situation regarding the enemy.[314] The [guards] announced this to those guarding the king.[315] Once he learned [the matter] from them, Joram summoned his friends and the leaders.[316] **82** When they had come, he told them that he suspected that the withdrawal of the king of the Syrians, "who has despaired of destroying us by famine, was a trap and a scheme, so that when, upon his pretending to flee, we go out to plunder the camp, he might suddenly fall upon and kill them and capture the city without a fight.[317] I urge you therefore to keep it [the Syrian camp] under guard and not to advance at all, putting excessive confidence in the enemy's withdrawal."[318]

Israelite leaders deliberate about report

83 Someone stated that he [Joram] did excellently and was most sagacious to be

---

ians' "knowing" the identity of the foreign mercenaries to their word in 2 Kgs 7:6b (which they there address to one another, rather than to the king as in his version).

[303] Continuing to highlight the king's involvement in the proceedings, Josephus adds this notice on his reaction to the report made him and the approaching noise that he hears for himself.

[304] Greek: ἀταξία καὶ θόρυβος. This wordpair occurs only here in Josephus.

[305] See 2 Kgs 7:7. Josephus adds the references to the fugitives' emotional state and to their abandoned "wealth," the latter with an eye to the subsequent course of the story, where (7:8) the lepers carry off "silver and gold."

[306] After the interlude concerning the Syrians' flight (9.76b-78), Josephus returns to the Samaritan lepers with this added allusion to his previous mention of them in 9.76a.

[307] Greek: ἡσυχία καὶ ἀφωνία. This collocation is *hapax* in Josephus.

[308] Cf. 2 Kgs 7:5bβ, which states that "there was no one there" at the moment of the lepers' arrival in the Syrian camp.

[309] See 2 Kgs 7:8a, which mentions the lepers' carrying off gold and clothing as well.

[310] See 2 Kgs 7:8b.

[311] Josephus appends this notice on the lepers' plundering 2 additional tents unimpeded. He thereby makes clear that the camp was completely empty.

[312] Josephus adds this transitional notice on the lepers' inference.

[313] Josephus' lepers appear less mercenary in their thinking than do their biblical counterparts (see 2 Kgs 7:9), whose decision to report their discovery is motivated by fear of punishment should they delay in doing this.

[314] Josephus generalizes the lepers' detailed report to the city "gatekeepers" about their experiences in the Syrian camp as cited in 2 Kgs 7:10.

[315] Cf. 2 Kgs 7:11, where the gatekeepers "call out," and the matter "is told within the king's household."

[316] In 2 Kgs 7:12aα the king "rises in the night" and addresses "his servants."

[317] Joram's discourse in 2 Kgs 7:12aβb speaks of what the Syrians in general have devised. Josephus' highlighting of the role of the Syrian king in particular accords with his previous focus on him in his account of the Syrian flight in 9.77-78.

[318] Josephus appends this practical conclusion to the king's remarks about the Syrians' (purported) stratagem as cited in 2 Kgs 7:12aβb.

suspicious.[319] He advised him, however, to send two horsemen to search out the whole [route] as far as the Jordan,[320] so that, if they should be taken by the enemy in ambush and destroyed, he [Joram] would guard his army against suffering a similar [fate] due to a credulous advance.[321] "You will," he said, "only add the horsemen to those killed by the famine, should they be captured by the enemy and eliminated."[322]

84 Approving this plan, he [Joram] then sent the scouts out.[323] They traversed a route empty of the enemy, but found it full of grain and weapons, which they had cast aside and left behind so as not to be encumbered in their flight.[324] When he heard this, the king released the crowd to plunder the things that were in the camp.[325]

Syrian flight confirmed

Syrian camp plundered

85 What they gained in doing this was neither valueless nor small, but rather much gold, much silver, herds of all sorts of beasts, as well as vast quantities of wheat and barley, such as they had not even dreamed of hoping for.[326] They were relieved of their earlier calamities, and had such abundance that two *sata* of barley were sold for a shekel and a *saton* of fine wheat flour for a shekel as well, according to the prophecy of Elissai.[327] (The *saton* is equivalent to one and a half Italian *modii*.)[328]

86 The only one who did not enjoy all these good things was the leader of the third division.[329] For he, having been stationed at the gate by the king, in order that he might restrain the rush of the crowd so that they would not endanger one another by their pushing, was eliminated, being trampled down by them.[330] He suffered this

Unbelieving officer killed

---

[319] Josephus prefaces the retainer's reply (2 Kgs 7:13) with this initial flattering word, designed to win the king's favorable attention for the proposal he is about to make.

[320] The servant's proposal in 2 Kgs 7:13 is that *5 horses* be used for reconnoitering purposes. Josephus derives his reference to "2 horsemen" from 7:14, where "2 mounted men" are dispatched by the king. He adds the specification concerning the end-point of the proposed pursuit on the basis of 7:15a, which has the scouts (cf. 7:14) going "as far as the Jordan."

[321] Josephus amplifies the retainer's proposal (2 Kgs 7:13) with this statement concerning the purpose of his suggestion, i.e. to sacrifice—if need be—the band of scouts, in order to keep the entire army from being ambushed and destroyed.

[322] Compare 2 Kgs 7:13, where the speaker affirms that Joram has nothing to lose in dispatching the scouts, seeing that if he does not do this all those still alive in the city will certainly die—as had so many already. The point of Josephus' speaker is somewhat different: the death of the scouts would only be another (small) addition to all those that have already occurred.

[323] See 2 Kgs 7:14. Josephus supplies the reference to Joram's "approval," while leaving aside the wording of his order to the scouts: "go and see."

[324] See 2 Kgs 7:15a; Josephus leaves aside the reference to the scouts' pursuit extending to the Jordan, which he made part of the retainer's proposal in 9.83;

see note to "as far as the Jordan" at 9.83. Conversely, he adds the reference to the absence of the Syrians from the pursuit route and substitutes "grain" for the "garments," which the biblical pursuers encounter.

[325] Cf. 2 Kgs 7:15b-16a. In 7:16a the people "go out" on their own; Josephus makes them do so with the king's permission— compare his similar insistence on the role of the Syrian king in what precedes.

[326] Josephus supplies this notice on the range of valuable items acquired by the people in the Syrian camp. His specific mention of wheat and barley prepares for his following statement, based on 2 Kgs 7:16b, concerning the new, changed price of these items. His reference to the gold and silver discovered in the Syrian camp is inspired by 2 Kgs 7:8a, where the lepers plunder these metals from the enemy tents.

[327] See 2 Kgs 7:16b. Josephus substitutes the reference to the "prophecy of Elissai" for the biblical phrase "according to the word of the Lord."

[328] With a view to making the details of the biblical presentation more readily understandable to a Roman audience, Josephus appends this notice on the "Italian" equivalent of the *saton*; see 9.71 and the note to "for a shekel" there.

[329] Josephus supplies this heading to the story of the officer's fate as described in 2 Kgs 7:17-20.

[330] See 2 Kgs 7:17abα. Josephus supplies a motivation for the king's stationing the officer at the gate, i.e. to keep those exiting from trampling each other—

[fate] and died in this manner, the death Elissai had prophesied to him,[331] when he, alone of all of them, did not believe the things said by him [Elissai] concerning the coming abundance of provisions.[332]

Ben-hadad (Ader) sick

(4.6) 87 Now Ader, the king of the Syrians, having escaped to Damascus and learned that the Deity had inflicted fright and consternation[333] upon him and his entire army, and that it was not a matter of the enemy's advance, became dejected at having God very hostile[334] to him[335] and fell sick.

Elisha–Hazael (Azael) encounter

88 The prophet Elissai traveled to Damascus at that time.[336] Knowing this, Ader sent Azael,[337] the most trusted of his domestics, to meet him and bring him gifts.[338] He directed him to inquire about his sickness and whether his coming through this was at risk.[339]

89 Azael, joined up with Elissai, along with forty camels, which were bearing the best and most costly gifts from what was in Damascus and the palace. After greeting him in a friendly way,[340] he said that he had been sent to him by King Ader to bring him gifts and to inquire about his sickness and whether he would recover from it.[341]

90 Now the prophet, although he directed Azael not to announce anything bad to the king,[342] said that he would die.[343] When he heard this, the king's domestic was

---

ironically, the very thing they end up doing to him.

[331] Compare the fulfillment notice of 2 Kgs 7:17bβ: "... as the man of God had said when the king came down to him."

[332] This allusion to the officer's earlier stance towards Elisha's announcement recalls 9.73. It takes the place of the extended recapitulation of the prophet-officer exchange of 2 Kgs 7:1-2 in 7:18-19 (plus the renewed notice on the officer's death in 7:20// 7:17bα).

[333] Greek: δέος καὶ ταραχή. This collocation recurs in *War* 5.91; *Ant.* 6.24 (both times in reverse order). The phrase is reminiscent of the wording of 9.76: "God had already begun to frighten the Syrians and throw them into consternation."

[334] Greek: τῷ δυσμενῆ τὸν θεὸν ἔχειν. This is Josephus' only use of this phrase with God as subject.

[335] Josephus prefaces the notice on the sickness of the Syrian king (// 2 Kgs 8:7a) with this elaborate reintroduction of the figure and his flight (see 9.78) after a segment focussed on the scene at the abandoned Syrian camp in 9.79-86. In so doing he passes over the incident (2 Kgs 8:1-6) featuring the Shunammite woman and her recovery of her property (he has no equivalent either to the previous account of this woman and her dealings with Elisha in 2 Kgs 4:8-41; see the opening note at 9.51).

[336] See 2 Kgs 8:7aα. Neither the Bible nor Josephus provides a motivation for Elisha's going to Damascus. Rabbinic tradition (see, e.g., *b. Sotah* 47a; *b. Sanh.* 107b; *y. Sanh.* 10.29b) represents him as traveling there to try to reclaim his servant Gehazi (see 2 Kgs 8:4, etc.) from the idolatry into which he had fallen. The Christian author Theodoret (*Quaestio* 23; PG 80, c. 763) avers that Elisha made the trip with a view to carrying

out the divine mandate given Elijah in 1 Kgs 19:15, i.e. to anoint Hazael as king of Syria.

[337] MT (2 Kgs 8:8) חזהאל (Eng.: "Hazael"); LXX B ʿΑζαήλ; LXX L ʾΑζαήλ; Josephus ʾΑζάηλος.

[338] See 2 Kgs 8:7b-8a. Josephus supplies the reference to Hazael's "trusted" status; thereby, he accentuates the perfidy of his subsequent assassination of his master. He uses the same plural form δῶρα ("gifts") as does LXX L 2 Kgs 8:8a to designate what Hazael is to take with him, whereas MT employs the singular term מנחה (RSV: "present"), transliterated by LXX B as μαννα, for this.

[339] See 2 Kgs 8:8b.

[340] See 2 Kgs 8:9a. Josephus accentuates both the lavishness and the cordiality of the reception given Elisha by Hazael, adding the characterization of his gifts as "the best and most costly" and the mention of his "friendly" greeting.

[341] See 2 Kgs 8:9b. Josephus' Hazael prefaces his transmission of the king's "inquiry" with mention of the gifts he has been sent to bring Elisha, while omitting his biblical counterpart's designation of his master as "your [Elisha's] son."

[342] In the line of the *ketiv* in MT 2 Kgs 8:10a, where Elisha instructs Hazael to tell the king "you will certainly *not* [Hebrew לא] recover," Josephus' formulation attenuates the lie, which the prophet enjoins Hazael to bring his master in the *qere* (as well as LXX BL), i.e. "go, say *to him* [Hebrew לו] 'you shall certainly recover'." His Elisha simply directs Hazael to refrain from giving the king a negative report.

[343] In 2 Kgs 8:10b Elisha attributes his knowledge of the king's upcoming death to the Lord's "showing" him this.

grieved,[344] while Elissai wept and shed many tears,[345] foreseeing the calamities the [Israelite] people were going to suffer after the death of Ader.[346]

91 When Azael questioned him about the cause of his dismay,[347] he stated: "I weep in pity for the crowd of the Israelites, at the terrible things they will suffer from you; for you will kill the best of them, and burn their most solidly fortified cities; you will eliminate their children, dashing them against stones, and will rip open pregnant women."[348]

92 Azael then said: "What is this so great strength that has come to me that I should do these things?"[349] [Elissai] stated that God had disclosed this to him, that he [Azael] was about to reign as king over Syria.[350] Azael therefore went to Ader and announced good things about his illness.[351] The next day, however, he placed a moist netting upon him and destroyed him by suffocation.[352]

Hazael assassinates Ben-hadad

93 He took over the rule,[353] being an energetic[354] man and enjoying great loyalty from the Syrians and the population of Damascus by whom, even until today, Ader himself and Azael, who ruled after him, are honored as gods, on account of their benefactions and their building of sanctuaries, with which they adorned the city of the Damascenes. **94** They stage a procession every day in honor of these kings and glory in their antiquity, not knowing that they are rather recent, being only 1,100 years old.[355] When, however, Joram, the king of the Israelites, heard of the death of

Notice on later Syrian history

Peace between

---

[344] With his mention of Hazael's "grieving" at this point, Josephus modifies and clarifies the formulation of 2 Kgs 8:11a (MT LXX B): "and he fixed his gaze and stared at him, until he was ashamed" (RSV), where the subject of the various actions cited remains uncertain—who does the "staring" and who ends up being "ashamed"? (in LXX L the reference is to Hazael's presenting himself before Elisha and laying his gifts before him until he [Hazael] is ashamed, i.e. by Elisha's lack of response to the gifts.)

[345] See 2 Kgs 8:11b: "and the man of God wept."

[346] Josephus supplies this motivation for Elisha's "weeping" (2 Kgs 8:11b) on the basis of the prophet's subsequent reply to Hazael in 8:12b.

[347] Compare Hazael's question to Elisha in 2 Kgs 8:12a: "why does my lord weep?"

[348] See 2 Kgs 8:12b. In the biblical Elisha's catalogue of the 4 particular atrocities Hazael will commit, the 2nd item concerns his "slaying the young men with the sword." Josephus places his version of this item ("you will kill the best of them") in 1st position. He likewise has Elisha refer, perhaps under the influence of Ps 137:9 ("happy shall he be who takes your [Babylon's] little ones and dashes them against the rock!"), to the Israelite children being dashed "against stones" rather than "in pieces."

[349] In 2 Kgs 8:13a Hazael, referring to himself as Elisha's "servant" and "but a dog," asks how he is to accomplish "this great thing." Josephus' Hazael dispenses with such self-deprecation.

[350] See 2 Kgs 8:13b. Here, in contrast to the earlier

case of 8:10b (see note to "he would die" at 9.90), Josephus does reproduce Elisha's invocation of God's revelation to him.

[351] Josephus passes over Ben-hadad's question to Hazael in 2 Kgs 8:14aβ ("what did Elisha say to you?") which evokes the latter's (fraudulent) favorable announcement in 8:14b.

[352] See 2 Kgs 8:15a. According to the RSV's rendering, the object used by Hazael in killing the king was "a coverlet" (MT: מכבר).

[353] See 2 Kgs 8:15b.

[354] The epithet "energetic" (Greek: δραστήριος), which Josephus applies to Hazael, is the same used by him of Jezebel (*Ant.* 8.318) and Joram of Israel (9.27). Marcus (*ad loc.*) suggests that the remarks on Syrian conditions that Josephus appends to his notice on Hazael's accession (// 2 Kgs 8:15b) in 9.93-94a may derive from Nicolaus of Damascus, whom he quotes by name when speaking of the succession of Syrian kings in *Ant.* 7.100.

[355] Marcus (*ad loc.*) points out that the historically correct figure for the interval between the reigns of these kings (*ca.* 850 BCE) and Josephus' own time (*ca.* 100 CE) would be "less than 1000 years." In any case, Josephus' remark here allows him to downplay the antiquity of these Syrian divinized rulers at a time when a people's antiquity was so greatly prized (and controverted); see *Apion* 1.3, where he states that he is writing this work "to instruct all those who desire to know the antiquity of our race." See further Droge 1996.

Israel and Syria

Ader, he was relieved of the fears and the fright he had because of him, and gladly accepted peace.[356]

Deprevity of Joram of Judah

(5.1) 95 Now Joram, the king of Hierosolyma—for, as we mentioned previously, he had the same name as the other[357]—, once he took over the rule, immediately proceeded to the slaughter of his brothers and those of his fathers' friends who were leaders as well.[358] In so doing, he made a beginning and a display of his vileness. He in no way differed from the kings of the people who first acted lawlessly against the ancestral customs of the Hebrews and the worship of God.[359] **96** Now it was Othlia,[360] the daughter of Achab, who was married to him, who taught him to be vile and pay homage to foreign gods.[361] God, nevertheless, on account of his promise to David, did not wish to annihilate his family,[362] even though Joram did not cease from daily doing something new in the way of impiety and the violation of the native observances.[363]

Revolts against Joram

97 When the Idumeans revolted against him at that time and, after killing their former king, who had been subject to his father, had installed the one they wished,[364] Joram, together with his accompanying horsemen and chariots, invaded Idumea at night.[365] He destroyed those on the border of his own kingdom, but did not advance further.[366] **98** He profited not at all by doing this, however, for they all revolted against him,[367] as did also those inhabiting the country called Labina.[368] He was so

Joram promotes idolatry

---

[356] This added reference to the Israelite Joram's reaction to the death of "Ader" (Bible: Ben-hadad) recalls the account of the conflict between the 2 kings related in 9.60-87. The Bible does not mention such a "peace" between Joram and Ben-hadad's successor, Hazael.

[357] This parenthetical note refers back to 9.45, where Josephus introduces Joram of Judah and notes the fact of his having the same name as his Israelite counterpart. On Josephus' depiction of Joram in 9.95-104, for which he bases himself on the more elaborate account of 2 Chr 21:4-22:4, as opposed to the summary presentation of 2 Kgs 8:16-24, see Begg 2000: 113-27.

[358] 2 Chr 21:4 speaks of "some of the princes of Israel" as those killed by Joram along with his brothers.

[359] This is Josephus' elaborated rendering of the formula of 2 Kgs 8:18aα// 2 Chr 21:6aα: "he [Joram] walked in the ways of the kings of Israel, as the house of Ahab had done...."

[360] Greek: Ὀθλία. This is the form of the name—corresponding to that used elsewhere by Josephus—conjectured by Niese and seconded by Marcus for the reading Γοθολία of the codices here in 9.96.

[361] In attributing Joram's following the ways of the Israelite kings to the influence of his wife, 2 Kgs 8:18a // 2 Chr 21:6a do not mention her name. Josephus has already cited the queen's name when relating her marriage to Joram in *Ant.* 8.398. Here he underscores her active role in leading Joram astray with his reference to her "teaching" him his aberrations.

[362] Josephus passes over the actual content of the divine "promise" to David cited in 2 Kgs 8:19// 2 Chr 21:7, i.e. "to give him and his sons a lamp for ever,"

likely given the fact that by his day the Davidic dynasty had not ruled for several centuries. In speaking of God's unwillingness to destroy the Davidic line, Josephus agrees with 2 Chr 21:7 against 2 Kgs 8:19 (where it is "Judah," which God will not exterminate).

[363] Josephus' accusation embellishes the reference to Joram's doing "what was evil in the sight of the Lord" of 2 Kgs 8:18b// 2 Chr 21:6b (where it precedes the notice on the Lord's nevertheless abiding by his covenant with David in 8:19// 21:7).

[364] See 2 Kgs 8:20// 2 Chr 21:8, where "Edom" revolts against Judah's rule. Josephus supplies the reference to the prior killing of the Idumean vassal king in light of the (also added) reference to this figure as being under Judean authority that he attributes to King Jehoshaphat in 9.30; see note to "to join the campaign" there.

[365] See 2 Kgs 8:21a// 2 Chr 21:9a. Josephus adds the reference to Joram's "horsemen" to the biblical mention of his "chariots." Like Chronicles, he has no equivalent to the place name ("Zair"), to which Joram is said to "pass over" in Kings.

[366] Compare 2 Kgs 8:21b, where once Joram "smites" the surrounding Edomites, his own army "flees home" (In 2 Chr 21:9b only the "smiting" of the Edomites is mentioned). Josephus' rewording of Kings' double notice seems designed to attenuate the discrepancy between its parts—why would the Judeans flee home after having smitten the enemy?

[367] Cf. 2 Kgs 8:22a// 2 Chr 21:10a, which refer to Edom's revolting "from the rule of Judah to this day." Given that by his own time Edom's revolt against Judah

insane,[369] however, that he compelled his people to ascend the heights of the mountains and pay homage to alien gods.[370]

(5.2) 99 While he was doing these things and had completely expelled the ancestral ordinances from his mind,[371] a written communication was brought from the prophet Elias.[372] In it God disclosed that he [Joram] would receive a severe judgment from him[373] because, rather than being an imitator of his own ancestors,[374] he had followed the impieties of the kings of the Israelites[375] and compelled both the tribe of Iouda and the citizens of Hierosolyma, to abandon the holy [worship][376] of their native God in order to adore idols,[377] just as Achab had forced the Israelites [to do].[378] 100 In addition, he had murdered his brothers and killed good and just men.[379] In his letter the prophet also indicated the punishment that he [Joram] was about to undergo for these things,[380] namely the annihilation of his people and the butchery of his wives and children.[381] 101 Moreover, he would die of an illness of the abdomen, after having been greatly tormented and his insides having fallen out, due to their excessive internal decay.[382] He would thus see his own misfortune,

Elijah's message of doom for Joram

---

had long ceased, Josephus speaks rather of a general revolt of the entire Edomite population in response to Joram's killing those on the frontier (see 9.97).

[368] MT (2 Kgs 8:22a// 2 Chr 21:10bα) לבנה (Eng.: "Libnah"); LXX B 2 Kgs 8:22a Σεννά; LXX L 2 Kgs 8:22a and LXX BL 2 Chr 21:10bα Λοβνά; Josephus Λαβίνα. Like Kings, Josephus has no equivalent, at this juncture, to the motivation for the revolts of Edom and Libnah cited in 2 Chr 21:10bβ: "because he [Joram] had forsaken the Lord, the God of his fathers."

[369] Josephus' 2 remaining uses of this adjective (Greek: ἐμμανής) are in *War* 4.233; 7.75, both times in the plural.

[370] See 2 Chr 21:11 (no parallel in 2 Kgs 8:16-24), which charges Joram with "making high places in the hill country of Judah" and "making Judah go astray." The mention of the "heights of the mountains," which Joram forces his people to ascend here recalls Josephus' allusion (*Ant.* 8.265) to Jeroboam's "erecting altars on the high mountains." Similarly, the reference to the "alien gods" whom Joram compels his people to serve is reminiscent of the notice on his wife's teaching Joram himself to worship "foreign gods" in 9.96.

[371] Josephus adds this transitional phrase, with its reminiscence of the expression "ancestral customs" of 9.95.

[372] See 2 Chr 21:12a; 2 Kgs 8:16-24 has no equivalent to the sequence concerning Elijah's communication and its sequels of 2 Chr 21:12-18, which Josephus utilizes in 9.99-104. The codices SP follow the words "Elijah the prophet" in 9.99 with the phrase "who was still on earth," this indicating that the incident of Elijah's letter took place prior to his removal to heaven recounted in 2 Kgs 2:11 (cf. 9.28).

[373] Josephus prefaces Elijah's opening accusation (2 Chr 21:12b-13) with this initial, general indication about what awaits the reprobate king.

[374] 2 Chr 21:12b accuses Joram more specifically of not walking in the ways of Jehoshaphat and Asa, his father and grandfather, respectively.

[375] In 2 Chr 21:13aα Elijah charges Joram with having "walked in the ways of the kings of Israel."

[376] Greek: θρησκείαν. The word is absent in RO and omitted by Niese, but read by Marcus in accordance with the other codices.

[377] Josephus provides a content for the charge, made by Elijah in 2 Chr 21:13aβ, that Joram "had led Judah and the inhabitants of Jerusalem into unfaithfulness" that recalls his previous references to the worship of other gods that Joram both practiced and promoted; see 9.96, 98. The phrase "adore idols" (Greek: σέβειν τὰ εἴδολα) recurs in 9.205 in connection with the Israelite king Jeroboam II.

[378] In 2 Chr 21:13aβ Elijah alludes to "the house of Ahab's" having led Israel "into unfaithfulness."

[379] Elijah's concluding charge in 2 Chr 21:13bβ mentions only Joram's killing of his brothers, whom it qualifies as "better than yourself." Josephus' version adds a reference to Joram's other victims (called those of his father's "friends who were leaders as well" in 9.95), transferring the biblical epithet for the brothers to these figures.

[380] This added transition to the announcement of punishment component of Elijah's letter (// 2 Chr 21:14-15) picks up on the opening words of 9.99: "... God disclosed that he [Joram] would receive a severe judgment from him."

[381] 2 Chr 21:14 mentions a "great plague" that the Lord will "bring upon" Joram's people, household, and possessions. Josephus avoids explicitly attributing the coming disasters to God. He likewise reverses the biblical order, where Joram's children are cited prior to his wives.

[382] The Josephan Elijah's announcement to Joram

Judah invaded

(5.3) 102 Not long afterwards, a army of those Arabs living in the vicinity of Ethiopia and of foreign nations[385] invaded Joram's kingdom and plundered both the country and the house of the king.[386] They likewise slaughtered his sons and wives.[387] Of his children there was left [only] one, named Ochozias,[388] who escaped the enemy.

Joram's death and burial

103 After this misfortune he [Joram] suffered for a very long time from the illness foretold by the prophet, for the Deity struck at his stomach in his wrath.[389] He died pitiably, looking on as his insides fell out.[390] The people showed contempt even for his dead body.[391] **104** For they reasoned, I suppose, that he died in this way in accordance with God's fury.[392] [They did not find him] worthy of obtaining an interment befitting kings, nor did they inter him in the tombs of his ancestors or show him other honor. They buried him rather as a commoner.[393] He had lived forty

---

here recalls Josephus' description of Herod's final illness in *Ant.* 17.69: "there was also an ulceration of the bowels and intestinal pains that were particularly terrible."

[383] Josephus' Elijah expatiates on the announcement of Joram's malady in 2 Chr 21:15, adding, e.g., mention of the king's helplessness in the face of this and the fact that he will ultimately die of it.

[384] Josephus rounds off his citation of Elijah's letter in 9.99-101 (// 2 Chr 21:12-15) with this closing formula.

[385] Like MT 2 Chr 21:16 ("the Philistines and the Arabs who are near Ethiopia") Josephus speaks of 2 groups of invaders, whereas LXX BL mentions 3 such groups, i.e. "the Philistines, the Arabs, and those near the Ethiopians." He uses the same term, i.e. ἀλλόφυλοι, which in LXX BL 2 Chr 21:16 designates the "Philistines." In my translation, however, I, in contrast to Marcus' "Philistines," render this word by "foreign nations," given that Josephus' consistent designation for the Philistines is "Palestinoi." 2 Chr 21:16 mentions the Lord's "stirring up the anger" of the invaders. As in his version of 2 Chr 21:14 in 9.100, Josephus avoids a biblical formulation attributing Joram's misfortunes directly to God.

[386] 2 Chr 21:17a explicitly mentions only the plundering of the palace. Josephus magnifies the calamity by having the invaders despoil the entire country.

[387] According to 2 Chr 21:17bα, Joram's "sons and wives" were part of the plunder taken by the invaders. By stating that the king's family members were actually put to death, Josephus brings their fate into line with Elijah's announcement of their "butchery" in 9.100. Like MT, he does not mention the loss also of Joram's "daughters," as do LXX BL.

[388] MT (2 Chr 21:17) יהואחז (Eng.: "Jehoahaz"); LXX B Ὀχοζείας; LXX L and Josephus Ὀχοζίας. Else-

where, in both Kings and Chronicles, this son and successor of Joram is called "Ahaziah" (Hebrew: אחזיהו). Josephus leaves aside the Chronicler's specification that Jehoahaz/Ahaziah was Joram's "youngest son."

[389] See 2 Chr 21:18. Here, in contrast to his procedure with 2 Chr 21:14 in 9.100 and 2 Chr 21:16 in 9.102, Josephus follows the Bible in attributing Joram's misfortunes directly to God. He adds the allusion to the fulfillment of Elijah's announcement (see 9.101// 2 Chr 21:15). His reference to the prolonged duration of Joram's illness reflects the indication of 2 Chr 21:19 that it was "at the end of 2 years" that the king's bowels finally fell out.

[390] This detail about Joram's witnessing the falling out of his insides lacks an explicit equivalent in the Chronicler's account of the king's demise in 2 Chr 21:19a. It does, however, correspond to the wording of the Josephan Elijah's announcement in 9.101.

[391] With this remark Josephus synthesizes the 2 separate notices on the popular reaction to the death of Joram in 2 Chr 21:19b (the people make no fire in his honor as was done for his ancestors) and 21:20bα (Joram "departed to no one's regret").

[392] Greek: κατὰ μῆνιν θεοῦ; Josephus' other uses of this phrase are in *Ant.* 1.164; 2.344; 4.8; 9.236; 15.234. Josephus appends this explanation—recalling his previous notice on the "Deity striking at Joram's stomach in his wrath" (9.103)—for the people's contemptuous treatment of the king's body.

[393] Josephus elaborates on 2 Chr 21:20bβ, which states that, whereas Joram was buried "in the city of David" (so also 2 Kgs 8:24bα), he was not interred in "the tomb of the kings." He thereby accentuates the contrast between the dishonorable burial given Joram and the "magnificent" obsequies accorded his father Jehoshaphat (see 9.44).

years[394] and reigned as king for eight. The population of Hierosolyma handed over the rule to his son Ochozias.[395]

(6.1) 105 Now Joram, the king of the Israelites,[396] hoping after the death of Ader to win back the Galadite city of Aramotha[397] from the Syrians, campaigned against it with a large expedition.[398] In the course of the siege he was shot by one of the Syrians, though not fatally.[399] He returned to the city of Jezarela[400] to be treated there for his wound, while leaving his entire army, with Jeous,[401] the son of Amases,[402] as its leader, at Aramotha, for he had already taken it by storm.[403]

Joram of Israel wounded while on campaign

106 It was his intention, once he was cured, to make war on the Syrians.[404] However, Elissai the prophet, giving one of his disciples[405] the holy oil[406] sent him

Jehu (Jeous) anointed at

---

[394] Josephus computes Joram's total lifespan by combining the figures for his age at accession (32 years) and length of reign (8), as cited in 2 Kgs 8:17// 2 Chr 21:20aα.

[395] In attributing Ahaziah's accession to the efforts of the people of Jerusalem, Josephus follows 2 Chr 22:1a, as opposed to 2 Kgs 8:24b, which does not ascribe such a role to them.

[396] *Ant.* 9.105-139 features events in the Northern Kingdom, namely the elimination of Joram and all those associated with him by the usurper Jehu. On this segment (// 2 Kgs 8:25-10:36; cf. 2 Chr 22:2-9), see Begg 2000: 129-66; Mulzer and Krieger 1996; and Feldman 1998a: 352-62.

[397] Greek Ἀραμώθα; this is the reading of RO, which Niese follows. Marcus reads Ἀραμάθη with MSP, the reading found in Josephus' earlier mention of the site (biblical "Ramoth-gilead") in *Ant.* 8.398.

[398] See 2 Kgs 8:28a, which mentions the joint attack on "Ramoth-gilead" by Joram of Israel and Ahaziah of Judah. Josephus amplifies this notice with a reference to the occasion for the attack, namely, the death of the Syrian King "Ader" (see 9.92) and the motivation behind it, namely, Joram's desire to recover the town (which had been lost to the Syrians in the time of Ahab's father (see *Ant.* 8.398-399). Conversely, he holds over mention of Ahaziah's involvement in the campaign until after he has related the wounding and withdrawal of Joram to Jezreel; see 9.112.

[399] Josephus adds details to the summary reference to Joram's being "wounded" by the Syrians in 2 Kgs 8:28b. His mention of the king's being (non-fatally) "shot" by a Syrian both associates and contrasts Joram with his father Ahab, who likewise was "shot" by a Syrian archer (*Ant.* 8.414), though in his case "fatally" (8.415).

[400] MT (2 Kgs 8:29) יזרעאל (Eng.: "Jezreel"); LXX B Ἰσραήλ; LXX L Ἰεζραήλ; Josephus Ἰεζαρήλη (this is the form read by Marcus; Niese reads Ἰεζέρηλη with RO).

[401] MT (2 Kgs 9:2) יהוא (Eng.: "Jehu"); LXX B

Εἰού; LXX L Ἰού; Josephus Ἰηοῦς. Josephus mentioned this figure earlier in *Ant.* 8.352 (// 1 Kgs 19:16-17), where Elijah is told to appoint him king and informed of his task of executing the impious, matters that are now about to be realized.

[402] According to MT and LXX B 2 Kgs 9:2, Jehu was "the son of Jehoshaphat, the son of Nimshi." LXX L calls him "the son of Nimshi, the son of Jehoshaphat." Marcus and Schalit (*s.v.*) read the name of Jehu's father here in 9.105 as Νεμεσαῖος, whereas the form attested by the codices and adopted by Niese is Ἀμασῆς.

[403] Josephus supplies this notice on Jehu's being left in captured Ramoth-gilead with a view to the continuation of the biblical account, where Jehu's presence at the city in a leadership capacity is presupposed. The notice replaces the mention, repeated in 1 Kgs 9:16b, of the visit to the wounded Joram by Ahaziah of Judah of 8:28b, which Josephus will utilize only in 9.112.

[404] Josephus adds this notice on Joram's plans; the notice is full of irony in that Joram, rather than being "cured," is about to be assassinated by Jehu.

[405] MT and LXX 2 Kgs 9:1 designate Elisha's agent as "one of the sons of the prophets," while Tg. speaks of "one of the students of the prophets" (Aramaic: מתלמידי נבייא). Josephus mentioned Elisha's "disciples" in 9.68.

[406] Greek: τὸ ἅγιον ἔλαιον. In 2 Kgs 9:3 the reference is rather to the "flask of oil" that is to be used. Josephus' qualification of the anointing oil as "holy" serves to assimilate Jehu's anointing to those of Saul (see *Ant.* 6.83), David (*Ant.* 6.157) and Solomon (see *Ant.* 7.355), all of whom are anointed with "holy oil." By contrast, the Talmud (see, e.g., *b. Meg.* 14a) distinguishes between the biblical kings Saul and Jehu who are anointed from a "flask" (see 1 Sam 10:1 and 2 Kgs 9:3, 6, respectively) and whose lines ruled for only a limited time on the one hand and David and Solomon, both of whom are anointed from a "horn" (see 1 Sam 16:13 and 1 Kgs 1:39, respectively) and whose dynasty was chosen to rule forever on the other.

Elisha's direction

to Aramotha to anoint Jeous and to state that the Deity had selected him as king.[407] In addition to these things that he was to say, he directed him, as he was sending him off, to make the journey like a fugitive, so that he might get away from there concealed from everyone.[408]

107 Once he was in the city, he found Jeous sitting among the leaders of the army, as Elissai had foretold to him.[409] Approaching him, he said that he wished to converse with him about certain matters.[410]

108 Upon his standing up and following him into the inner room, the young man took the oil, poured it on his head and said that God was designating him king[411] for the annihilation of the family of Achab and so that the blood of the prophets whom Jezabele had lawlessly killed might be avenged.[412] **109** [God was doing this] in order that their house might be utterly exterminated on account of its impiety like those of Hieroboam the son of Nabatai and Basa,[413] and that no seed be left to the family of Achab.[414] When he had said these things, he rushed out of the inner room, solicitous not to be seen by anyone in the army.[415]

Jehu acclaimed king by officers

(6.2) 110 Jeous, for his part, proceeded to the place where he had been sitting with the leaders. When they inquired and appealed to him to tell them why the young man had come to him and at the same time called him a madman,[416] he said, "you have indeed perceived rightly, for the words he spoke were those of a madman."[417] **111** But when, in their solicitude, they begged to hear,[418] he stated that

---

[407] Josephus lacks an equivalent to several of the circumstantial details mentioned in Elisha's directive to his agent as cited in 2 Kgs 9:1b-3a: he is to "gird his loins," seek out Jehu, and summon him away by himself into an "inner chamber." Exceptionally, he does reproduce the biblical term "anoint" of 9:3a; in the continuation of his Jehu account he will, however, use more general equivalents for the word.

[408] In 2 Kgs 9:3b Elisha instructs his agent: "open the door and flee; do not tarry." Josephus supplies a motivation for the latter's prescribed manner of travel, namely to avoid being observed.

[409] See 2 Kgs 9:4-5a. Josephus appends mention of the fulfillment of the prophet's prediction, thus highlighting Elisha's clairvoyance.

[410] 2 Kgs 9:5b has Elisha's envoy address Jehu with the words: "I have an errand for you, O commander." Josephus eliminates the attached exchange between the pair concerning the identity of the intended recipient of the envoy's message. That exchange might appear superfluous, given that in Josephus' presentation the envoy goes up to Jehu and addresses himself specifically to him.

[411] See 2 Kgs 9:6. Here (compare 9.106), Josephus replaces the biblical term "anoint" with a more general word, i.e. "designate."

[412] See 2 Kgs 9:7, which mentions "the blood of all the servants of the Lord" in addition to that of "my [God's] servants the prophets." Josephus adds the qualification about Jezebel's slaying the prophets (see *Ant.*

8.344) "lawlessly" (Greek: παρανόμως).

[413] See 2 Kgs 9:9. Earlier (see *Ant.* 8.288), Josephus designated the founder of the 2nd Israelite dynasty as "Basanes" (biblical Baasha).

[414] See 2 Kgs 9:8. Josephus adds the reference to the "impiety" of Ahab's line and rewords the vulgar biblical expression "those pissing against the wall" used of Ahab's male descendants. He has no equivalent to the renewed reference to the fate awaiting Jezebel (see 9:7; cf. 9.108), with which Elisha's agent concludes his discourse in 9:10a.

[415] Josephus elaborates the summary notice about the envoy's opening the door and fleeing of 2 Kgs 9:10b with a reminiscence of the motivation behind this, i.e. concealment, previously introduced by him in his version of Elisha's instructions to the messenger in 9.106 (compare 2 Kgs 9:3b).

[416] See 2 Kgs 9:11a. Josephus leaves aside the officers' opening query to Jehu, i.e. "is all well?"

[417] Josephus aligns the wording of Jehu's response with that of the officers' question to him. Both times, the Greek word qualifying Elisha's agent as a "madman" is a form of the verb μαίνομαι. Compare Jehu's statement to his colleagues in 2 Kgs 9:11b: "you know the fellow and his talk."

[418] Josephus attenuates the sharpness of the officers' response (2 Kgs 9:12a) to Jehu's evasive reply (9:11b; see previous note) to them: "that is not true; tell us now." On the apologetic concern behind Josephus' modification of the biblical presentation here with its

he [Elissai's disciple] had affirmed that God had selected him as king of the crowd.[419] When he said this, each man stripped himself and spread his garment out under him.[420] By blowing their horns, they signified that Jeous was king.[421]

112 Having gathered the army,[422] he was about to march out against Joram to the city of Jezarela, in which, as we said before, he was being healed of the wound that he had received at the siege of Aramotha.[423] Now it happened that Ochozias, the king of Hierosolyma, had also come to Joram, for he was the son of his sister, as we also said before. Given their relationship, he had come to ascertain how things were going with his wound.[424]

Jehu advances against Joram and visitor Ahaziah (Ochozias) of Judah

113 Wishing to fall suddenly upon those around Joram,[425] Jeous requested that none of his soldiers run off to report these things to Joram, for that would be a splendid demonstration of their loyalty to him and of their having appointed him king on account of their being thus disposed towards him.[426]

Jehu's advance concealed from Joram

114 Pleased by what was said, they guarded the roads so that no one might escape to Jezarela to report him [Jeous] to those who were there.[427] Jeous, taking the elite of his horsemen, and sitting in his chariot, went to Jezarela.[428] Once he was near, the lookout whom King Joram had stationed to look out for those coming towards the city, seeing Jeous drawing near with a crowd, announced to Joram that a band of horsemen was drawing near.[429]

Jehu's approach announced

115 He immediately directed that one of the horsemen be sent out to meet [them] and to find out who was approaching.[430] So the horseman came to Jeous and asked

Joram's messenger join Jehu

---

seeming substantiation of contemporary charges about the Jews' untrustworthiness, see Feldman 1998a: 355, 362.

[419] See 2 Kgs 9:12b. As in 9.108, Josephus replaces the Bible's verb "anoint" with a more general term.

[420] Compare 2 Kgs 9:13a, where Jehu's hearers place their garments "on the bare steps" (RSV).

[421] See 2 Kgs 9:13b.

[422] Josephus supplies this transitional phrase in order to prepare for the continuation of the account in which Jehu appears surrounded by his troops.

[423] See 2 Kgs 9:14a, which speaks of Jehu's "conspiring against" Joram. Josephus appends the allusion to his earlier account of Joram's coming to Jezreel (9.105) under the influence of the parenthetical notice of 9:14b-15a, with its recapitulation of the events told in 8:28-29.

[424] Josephus here combines the data of 2 Kgs 8:27, 29b (earlier passed over by him) and 9:16 concerning the relationship between Ahaziah and Joram and the former's visit to the latter following his wounding, likewise rendering more specific the indication of 8:29b ("for he [Joram] was sick") concerning the purpose of the Judean's visit. Contrary to his wording here in 9.112, Josephus in fact has not previously explicitly identified Ahaziah's mother as the sister of Joram of Israel; see, however, 9.96, where "Othlia," daughter of Ahab (and so sister of his son Joram) is cited as the wife

of Joram of Judah, the father of "Ochozias" (see 9.102, 104).

[425] Josephus supplies this motivation for the request Jehu is about to make of his men (// 2 Kgs 9:15b).

[426] Josephus here spells out the import of the formula with which Jehu introduces his appeal (2 Kgs 9:15b) to his men that none of them bring news of what has happened to Jezreel, i.e. "if this is in your mind...."

[427] Josephus supplies this notice on the efficacy of Jehu's appeal to his men (2 Kgs 9:15b).

[428] See 2 Kgs 9:16a (and the initial announcement of Jehu's intended advance in 9.112). Josephus adds the reference to the elite cavalry force's accompanying Jehu in order to prepare the Jezreel lookout's subsequent report of seeing, not just a lone individual (Jehu), but "a company" (see 9:17a).

[429] Josephus embellishes the notice on the watchman's report of 2 Kgs 9:17a with, e.g., mention of the king's having stationed him and the reason for this. In the same line he has the watchman make his report specifically to Joram. The reference to "a band of horsemen" in the watchman's report (compare 9:17b: a company) echoes Josephus' added reference to Jehu's taking along the "elite of his horsemen" earlier in 9.114.

[430] In 2 Kgs 9:17b the question that Joram directs to be asked of those approaching runs: "Is it peace?"

about how things were in the camp, for the king had inquired about this.[431] He [Jeous] however, directed him not to concern himself at all about these matters, but rather to follow him.[432]

116 Seeing this, the lookout reported to Joram that the horseman had joined up with the crowd of those approaching and was coming along with them.[433] When the king sent a second man, Jeous ordered him to do the same thing.[434]

Joram and Ahaziah set out to meet Jehu

117 When the lookout disclosed this too to Joram, he finally mounted his chariot and went out to meet him [Jeous] together with Ochozias, the king of Hierosolyma (for he was present, as we stated earlier, to see how things were going with his wound, given their relationship).[435] Jeous, for his part, was driving somewhat slowly[436] and with moderation.[437]

Jehu kills Joram in fulfillment of Elijah's prediction

118 Coming upon him in the field of Naboth,[438] Joram inquired if everything was alright in the camp.[439] Jeous, however, bitterly defamed him, even calling his mother a sorceress.[440] Fearing his [Jeous'] intentions and surmising that he was thinking nothing good, the king turned the chariot[441] as it was and fled, telling Ochozias that he had been taken in by a trap and deceit.[442] Jeous, however, shot and hit him, the arrow penetrating through his heart.[443] **119** Immediately falling to his knees, Joram expired.[444] Jeous, for his part, ordered Badak,[445] the leader of the third division, to

---

[431] Josephus elucidates the question the messenger poses to Jehu in 2 Kgs 9:18a in accordance with the king's instructions in 9:17b, i.e. "Thus says the king, 'Is it peace'?" See previous note.

[432] Compare 2 Kgs 9:18b, where Jehu first picks up on the messenger's question to him ("is it peace?," 9:18aβ) with his counter-question, "what have you to do with peace?," and then orders him "turn round and ride behind me."

[433] As in 9.114 (compare 2 Kgs 9:17a), Josephus has the watchman make his 2nd report (see 9:18c) specifically to the king.

[434] Josephus abbreviates the exchange between the 2nd rider and Jehu in 2 Kgs 9:19, with its verbatim repetition of the earlier such exchange (9:18ab).

[435] Josephus combines into a continuous sequence the events recounted in 2 Kgs 9:20a (report of the 2nd horseman's joining the advancing party) and 9:21a (the 2 kings' going forth to meet Jehu), while holding over the intervening notice on Jehu's own approach (9:20b; see note to "slowly" at 9.117). He adds the reminder concerning Ahaziah's presence in Jezreel at this moment, reutilizing the wording of 9.112.

[436] Greek: σχολαίτερον. Josephus only other use of the adjective σχολαῖος is in *War* 7.98.

[437] Josephus' characterization of Jehu's driving corresponds to that of Tg. 2 Kgs 9:20b (Aramaic: בניח, "with gentleness"), whereas both MT and LXX speak rather of the "wildness" of his driving. In all the biblical witnesses, the description of Jehu's driving style is part of the watchman's final report (see 9:20b), whereas Josephus presents it as a narrative editorial remark.

[438] Josephus omits the designation of Naboth as

"the Jezreelite" from 2 Kgs 9:21bβ, where the 2 kings encounter Jehu at Naboth's property.

[439] Joram's question in 9:22a runs: "Is it peace, Jehu?" Josephus has the king reiterate the question the first messenger posed to Jehu in 9.115.

[440] Josephus turns into a curse/invective Jehu's rhetorical question to Joram in 2 Kgs 9:22b: "What peace can be, so long as the harlotries and the sorceries of your mother are so many?" The text read by RO and followed by Niese uses only 1 epithet for Jezebel ("sorceress," Greek: φαρμακός, a Josephan *hapax*), whereas MSPLat (followed by Marcus) qualify her with 2 terms ("sorceress and harlot [Greek: πόρνη, also a Josephan *hapax*]"), as in the Bible (where the corresponding terms appear in reverse order).

[441] In his explicit mention of Joram's "turning his chariot," Josephus goes together with OL 2 Kgs 9:23aα against MT and LXX BL, where the king "turns his hands."

[442] Josephus elaborates the notice of 2 Kgs 9:23 concerning Joram's flight and his warning Ahaziah of "treachery," adding the reference to the former's mental state that prompts his initiatives.

[443] 2 Kgs 9:24abα features several additional details: Jehu's shooting "with full strength" and striking Joram "between the shoulders."

[444] Josephus agrees with LXX BL 2 Kgs 9:24bβ in portraying Joram as sinking "to his knees"; MT has him "sink in his chariot" (the forms "his knees" and "his chariot" only differ by one consonant in Hebrew). Josephus adds the explicit mention of the king's death.

[445] MT (2 Kgs 9:25) בדקר (Eng.: "Bidkar"); LXX B Βαδεκά; LXX L Βαδέκ; Josephus Βάδακος (Schalit *s.v.*

toss the corpse of Joram onto the field of Naboth, reminding him of the prophecy of Elias that he prophesied to his [Joram's] father Achab when the latter killed Naboth, namely, that he himself and his family would perish in that very spot.[446] **120** For, he had heard the prophet saying these things while sitting in the back of Achab's chariot.[447] And so it happened in accordance with his [Elias'] prediction.[448] When Joram fell, Ochazias, frightened for his own safety, steered his chariot off onto another road, thinking to hide himself from Jeous.[449] **121** He, however, pursued and overtook him at a certain ascent, where he shot and wounded him.[450] [Ochozias, for his part,] abandoned his chariot, mounted a horse, and fled from Jeous to Magiaddo,[451] where, shortly afterwards, he died while being healed of his wound.[452] He was brought to Hierosolyma and buried there,[453] after reigning one year as king.[454] He was vile and worse than his father.[455]

Ahaziah assassinated by Jehu

(6.4) 122 As Jeous was entering Jezarela, Jezabele, beautified and standing on the tower,[456] said: "a fine slave who has killed his master!"[457] Looking up at her, he

Jezebel killed in accordance

---

reads Βάδακρος in line with the MT form).

[446] See 2 Kgs 9:25a, 26a. Josephus leaves aside the reference to "the blood of Naboth's sons" from Jehu's citation of the prophetic word (v. 26a), seeing that the story of Naboth's murder in 1 Kings 21 (MT and LXX B 1 Kings 20; the plus in LXXL 1 Kgs 20:27 does refer to Jezebel's having smitten Naboth *and his son*) makes no mention of them, while holding over for a later point (see 9.120) the allusion to the prophecy's being delivered as Jehu and Bidkar ride behind Ahab of 9:25b. Conversely, he introduces mention of Elijah as the bearer of the word and adds the notice on Ahab's family being requited at the spot along with him, in line with his version of Elijah's original word to the king in *Ant.* 8.361. Finally, he passes over the repetition of Jehu's directive to Bidkar about the disposition of Joram's corpse of 9:26b= 9:25a.

[447] According to Jehu's statement in 2 Kgs 9:25b, both he and Bidkar were riding behind Ahab when the Lord uttered his word against the king.

[448] Compare 2 Kgs 9:26b, where Jehu reiterates his command to Bidkar from 9:25a and adds that he [Bidkar] is to dispose of the king's corpse "in accordance with the word of the Lord." The Greek term translated "prediction" here, i.e. πρόρρησις, occurs 18 times in Josephus, but never in the LXX. The above formula "according to the prediction," recurs in *Ant.* 1.258; 2.229.

[449] Josephus embellishes the notice on Ahaziah's flight of 2 Kgs 9:27a with mention of the fugitive king's feelings and thoughts. His reference to "another road" replaces the more specific route cited in the Bible, i.e. "in the direction of Beth-haggan."

[450] 2 Kgs 9:27bβ specifies the site of Ahaziah's wounding as "the ascent of Gur, which is by Ibleam." According to 9:27aβ, Jehu commands unspecified others to shoot Ahaziah. Josephus has him shoot the king himself, just as he did Joram earlier.

[451] MT (2 Kgs 9:27) מגדו (Eng.: "Megiddo"); LXX B Μαγεδαών; LXX L Μαγεδδώ; Josephus Μαγιάδδω (I adopt this as the more difficult reading with Niese, in preference to Lat's more biblical form *Mageddon*).

[452] See 2 Kgs 9:27c. Josephus adds the reference to Ahaziah's (unsuccessful) "treatment," thus establishing a parallel between him and Joram, who likewise undergoes treatment after being "shot"; see 9.105. Josephus' account of Ahaziah's demise follows that given in 2 Kgs 9:27-28a, as opposed to the rather different version found in 2 Chr 22:9a, where Ahaziah is apprehended while hiding in Samaria, brought to Jehu, and "put to death" at an unspecified site.

[453] See 2 Kgs 9:28, which specifies that Ahaziah's servants conveyed his corpse to Jerusalem "in a chariot" and that he was "buried in his tomb with his fathers in the city of David." Contrast 2 Chr 22:9b, where Ahaziah seems to be buried somewhere in the North, with Jehu's men performing the task.

[454] Josephus derives this datum from 2 Kgs 8:26// 2 Chr 22:2. He has no equivalent to the divergent biblical notices on Ahaziah's age at accession, i.e. 22 in MT LXX BL 2 Kgs 8:26 and LXX L 2 Chr 22:2; 20 in LXX B 2 Chr 22:2; and 42 in MT 2 Chr 22:2.

[455] This closing, negative evaluation of Ahaziah is inspired by the more detailed judgments of 2 Kgs 8:27 // 2 Chr 22:3-4, which associate the reprobate Judean king with the "ways of the house of Ahab." Josephus has no equivalent to the extraneous chronological notice of 2 Kgs 9:29, which synchronizes Ahaziah's accession with the 11th regnal year of Joram of Israel.

[456] 2 Kgs 9:30 represents Jezebel, eyes painted and head adorned, "looking out the window" as Jehu comes to Jezreel. Josephus makes the queen's location more specific.

[457] In 2 Kgs 9:31 Jezebel uses the name "Zimri," the assassin of King Elah of Israel (see 1 Kgs 16:10), in her sarcastic address to the regicide Jehu. Likely finding

with Elijah's prediction

inquired who she was and directed her to come down to him.[458] Finally, he ordered the eunuchs to throw her from the tower.[459] **123** When she was heaved down, the wall was splattered with her blood, and she died, after being trampled by the horses.[460] While these things were happening, Jeous entered the palace with his friends; he refreshed himself from the journey with food and other things.[461] He then ordered the domestics to gather Jezabele up to bury her on account of her family, for she was [descended] from kings.[462] **124** But those who had been ordered [to see to] her interment found nothing of her body except the extremities,[463] for all the rest had been consumed by dogs.[464] When Jeous heard these things, he marveled at the prophecy of Elias, for he had predicted that she would perish in Jezarela in this way.[465]

Sons of Ahab executed at Jehu's demand

(6.5) 125 Now there were seventy sons of Achab who were being brought up in Samareia.[466] Jeous sent two written communications,[467] one to their tutors,[468] the other to the rulers of the Samareians.[469] [In these] he said that they should appoint the bravest of Achab's sons king,[470] for he [that son][471] had a crowd of chariots, horsemen, and weapons, as well as an army and fortified cities.[472] Doing this, they

---

the allusion too subtle for his intended audience, Josephus has her mockingly address Jehu as Joram's "fine slave."

[458] Josephus adds this initial address by Jehu to Jezebel herself, responding to her own previous words to him. Contrast 2 Kgs 9:32aβ, where he immediately asks "Who is on my side?"

[459] Josephus compresses the sequence of 2 Kgs 9:32aβ-33aα, where Jehu first asks, "Who is on my side?"; in response, 2 or 3 eunuchs look out at him, and Jehu directs them to throw Jezebel down. The reference to the "tower" recalls its mention earlier in 9.122.

[460] See 2 Kgs 9:33aβb, where Jezebel's blood also splatters on the horses. Josephus adds explicit mention of Jezebel's death, just as he did with Joram in 9.119 (compare 2 Kgs 9:24).

[461] Josephus elaborates the notice of 2 Kgs 9:34a about Jehu's eating and drinking even as Jezebel is meeting her violent end with various details: Jehu enters "the palace"; he is accompanied by his entourage; and refreshes himself after his travels.

[462] See 2 Kgs 9:34b. Josephus specifies to whom Jehu gives his command, while leaving aside the king's pejorative designation of Jezebel as "this cursed woman."

[463] 2 Kgs 9:35 makes explicit mention of Jezebel's skull, feet, and the palms of her hands.

[464] Josephus amplifies the notice of 2 Kgs 9:35 concerning the finding of Jezebel's extremities with this indication about the fate of the rest of the queen's body under the inspiration of 9:36, where Jehu quotes Elijah's announcement (see 1 Kgs 21:23) that "dogs shall eat the flesh of Jezebel."

[465] With this formulation Josephus makes summary allusion to the core content of the extended quotation

of Elijah's word about Jezebel's being consumed by dogs (see 1 Kgs 21:23; compare *Ant.* 8.361, where the Josephan Elijah speaks of Jezebel's blood being shed in the place where dogs had eaten Naboth's body) made by Jehu in 2 Kgs 9:36-37. In so doing, he turns the biblical Jehu's statement into a notice on his wonderment at seeing the prophet's word so dramatically realized. From Jehu's citation of Elijah's word Josephus omits the vulgar announcement (not previously attributed to the prophet either by the Bible or himself) of 9:37: "and the corpse of Jezebel shall be dung upon the face of the field in the territory of Jezreel, so that no one can say, 'This is Jezebel'."

[466] See 2 Kgs 10:1a. Josephus derives his indication about the sons' being "brought up" in Samaria from 10:6b.

[467] Josephus' plural form corresponds to MT 2 Kgs 10:1b's "letters," whereas LXX BL have the singular "letter."

[468] Greek: παιδαγωγοί. On the term, see Spicq 1978 (II): 639-41.

[469] 2 Kgs 10:2b mentions 3 categories of recipients of Jehu's letters: the rulers of the city (LXX BL; MT: of Jezreel), the elders, and the guardians of Ahab's sons. Josephus reduces the 3 groups to 2, each of whom receives a letter from Jehu.

[470] Josephus anticipates this core content of Jehu's message from 2 Kgs 10:3a.

[471] Greek: αὐτῷ. This is the reading of RO adopted by Niese. Marcus reads αὐτοῖς ("they," i.e. the Samaritan officials to whom Jehu is writing) with MSPLat.

[472] Josephus expands the 4-part catalogue of resources available in Samaria that he takes over from 2 Kgs 10:2 with mention of "an army."

would render judgment on behalf of their master.[473] **126** He wrote these things, wishing to test the mind of the Samareians.[474] When they read the letters, the rulers and the tutors were terrified. They reasoned that they could do nothing in this regard,[475] for Jeous had already defeated two very great kings.[476] They wrote back, affirming that he was their master and that they would do whatever he directed.[477]

127 To this he wrote back, directing them to obey him[478] and, once they had cut off the heads of Achab's sons, to send [these] to him.[479] Summoning the sons' tutors, the rulers ordered them to kill them[480] by cutting off their heads and to send [these] to Jeous. They did this, showing no compassion at all; collecting the heads in a wicker basket, they sent them off to Jezarela.[481]

128 Once these were brought, it was announced to Jeous, who was dining with his friends, that the heads of Achab's sons had been brought.[482] He directed that heaps of these be erected in front of the gate on either side.[483] **129** Once this was done, he went out to see [them] at dawn. When he had observed them, he began to say to the people who were present[484] that he had indeed campaigned against his master [Joram] and killed him, but had not done away with these [Achab's sons].[485] He requested them to recognize that everything concerning the family of Achab had happened in accordance with the prophecy of God and that his house, just as Elias had predicted, had perished.[486]

130 After he had likewise destroyed those of Achab's relatives who were found

Jehu addresses people about heads of Ahab's sons

Jehu kills

---

[473] This concluding statement of Jehu's message is Josephus' version of the (mock) exhortation of 2 Kgs 10:3b, in which Jehu urges the recipients to "fight for your master's house."

[474] Josephus adds this comment explaining the purpose behind Jehu's letters and their ironically-intended content: by means of his insolently provocative words Jehu aims to find out whether the leadership of Samaria is at all disposed to resist him.

[475] Greek: πρὸς τοῦτο. This is the reading of RO, which Niese follows. Marcus reads πρὸς τοῦτον ("in his [Jehu's] regard") with MSPLat.

[476] See 2 Kgs 10:4. Josephus' term "reasoned" replaces the more generic "said," introducing the biblical recipients' words to one another concerning Jehu's invincibility.

[477] See 2 Kgs 10:5, which attributes the collective answer sent to Jehu to "he who was over the palace and the city," along with the elders and the guardians. Josephus omits the respondents' closing protestation: "we will not make any one king; do whatever is good in your [Jehu's] eyes."

[478] 2 Kgs 10:6α formulates Jehu's response to the Samarians conditionally: "(if you are on my side) and if you are ready to obey me...."

[479] In 2 Kgs 10:6αβ Jehu's directive is that the recipients themselves are to come to him at Jezreel with the heads of Ahab's sons on the following day. Josephus' rewording of this demand might reflect the consideration that the recipients would have found the command that they appear before Jehu in person too

intimidating to act on.

[480] The sequence of 2 Kgs 10:6b-7 suggests that those responsible for the killing of Ahab's sons were the "great men of the city who were bringing them up" (v. 6b). Josephus differentiates: the governors give the command for the sons' execution, leaving it to their tutors to carry this out.

[481] See 2 Kgs 10:7. Josephus adds the editorial comment about the utter lack of compassion with which the executions were carried out.

[482] See 2 Kgs 10:8a. Josephus appends the remark about Jehu's "dining," which recalls the mention of his "refreshing himself with food and other things" as Jezebel meets her end in 9.123 (// 2 Kgs 9:34). The repetition of the motif highlights Jehu's cold-bloodedness.

[483] In 2 Kgs 10:8b Jehu specifies that the heaps are to be left "until the morning."

[484] See 2 Kgs 10:9a. Josephus omits Jehu's opening words to the Jezreelites: "you are innocent," which might seem unmotivated— what question can there be of their guilt or innocence in the matter at hand?

[485] Jehu's reference to the heaps of heads before him is formulated as a question in 2 Kgs 10:9b: "but who struck down all these?" The Josephan Jehu more emphatically affirms his non-responsibility for their deaths.

[486] See 2 Kgs 10:10. Josephus re-formulates the biblical Jehu's reference to the "word of the Lord" not "falling to the ground." On the expression "the prophecy of God," see the note on this phrase at *Ant.* 6.136.

Judeans on wax to Samaria

among the Jezarelites,[487] he went to Samareia. On the way he encountered members of the household of Ochozias, the king of Hierosolyma,[488] and asked them why they had come at that time.[489] **131** They said that they had come to greet Joram and their own King Ochozias[490] (for they did not know that both of them had been murdered by him).[491] Jeous, for his part, ordered them to be arrested and done away with; they were forty-two in number.[492]

Jehu meets Jehonadab (Jonadab)

(6.6) 132 After them [Ochozias' relatives], he was met by a good and just man, named Jonadab,[493] who had been his friend for a long time.[494] After greeting him, he [Jonadab] began to extol all that he [Jeous] had done, in accordance with the will of God, in exterminating the house of Achab.[495] **133** Jeous appealed to him to ascend his chariot,[496] in order to accompany him to Samareia, saying he would show [him] how he would spare no vile person, but would punish the false prophets and false priests, and those who misled the crowd[497] so that they abandoned the worship of the greatest God and paid homage to foreign ones. It was indeed the finest and most pleasant of spectacles for a kind and just[498] man [to see][499] the vile requited.[500]

Jehu's violent

134 Persuaded by these [words], Jonadab ascended the chariot and went to

---

[487] 2 Kgs 10:11 identifies Jehu's Jezreelite victims as all Ahab's "great men, familiar friends, and priests."

[488] See 2 Kgs 10:12-13aα, which designates those whom Jehu meets on the way as Ahaziah's "kinsmen." Josephus omits the localization of the encounter cited in v. 12, i.e. "Beth-eked of the Shepherds."

[489] See 2 Kgs 10:13aβ, where Jehu's question to the Judeans is "who are you?"

[490] From the Judeans' response to Jehu in 2 Kgs 10:13b Josephus omits their opening self-identification as "kinsmen of Ahaziah." He likewise modifies the biblical statement concerning the purpose of their journey, i.e. "to visit the royal princes and the sons of the queen mother."

[491] Josephus appends this explanatory comment, which accounts both for the Judeans' coming to visit 2 kings who are already dead and the unguarded way in which they speak to the kings' killer.

[492] See 2 Kgs 10:14. Josephus omits the site of the massacre ("the pit of Beth-eked") and the concluding biblical statement that Jehu "spared none of them." In his account of the Judeans' fatal encounter with Jehu, Josephus follows the version of 2 Kgs 10:12-14 in preference to 2 Chr 22:8 (where Jehu meets the "princes of Judah and the sons of Ahaziah's brothers, who attended Ahaziah" and kills them personally).

[493] MT (2 Kgs 10:15) יהונדב (Eng.: "Jehonadab"); LXX BL Ἰωναδάβ; Josephus Ἰωνάδαβος.

[494] Josephus' notices on the qualities of Jehonadab and his long-standing relationship with Jehu replace the mention of his father's name ("Rechab") in 2 Kgs 10:15aα. Josephus' added reference to the existing relationship between the pair seems inspired by Jehu's opening question (which he does not reproduce) to Jehonadab in 2 Kgs 10:15aβ, where LXX BL (followed by RSV) reads "Is your heart true to my heart as mine is to your heart?" for MT's "Is it right with your heart, as my heart is with your heart?"

[495] Jehonadab's praise of Jehu's bloody initiatives takes the place of the opening exchange between the 2 men as cited in 2 Kgs 10:15aβ, where Jehu asks whether Jehonadab is as devoted to him as he is to Jehonadab and receives an affirmative answer. On Josephus' earlier utilization of the content of this exchange in his reference to the long-standing friendship between the pair, see previous note.

[496] Josephus compresses the content of 2 Kgs 10:15bβγ, where Jehu asks Jehonadab to give him his hand and, upon his doing so, draws him up into his chariot.

[497] The 3 categories of persons cited by Jehu here all have their equivalents in Josephus' story of the "Bethel confrontation" under Jeroboam I; for "false prophets," see *Ant.* 8.242; for "false priests," see 8.232; and for "those who misled the crowd," see the phrase "to mislead the people" used of Jeroboam in 8.229.

[498] This 2-fold characterization of Jehonadab by Jehu picks up on Josephus' introduction of him as "a good and just man" in 9.132. On the collocation "kind and just" (Greek: χρηστὸς καὶ δίκαιος), see the note to "just and kind" at *Ant.* 6.294.

[499] Greek: ἰδεῖν. This word is absent in ROM and omitted by Niese. Marcus reads it with SP (and possibly Lat).

[500] Josephus expatiates considerably on Jehu's reference to his "zeal for the Lord," which he invites Jehonadab to witness in Samaria in 2 Kgs 10:16a. At the same time, he avoids the Bible's problematic "zeal-terminology," which could convey the idea that Jehu was a proto-Zealot; see Feldman 1998a: 358-9.

Samareia.[501] Searching out all Achab's relatives, Jeous killed them.[502] Wishing none measures in
Samaria of the false prophets or priests of Achab's gods to escape punishment, he arrested all of them by deception and trickery.[503] **135** For, assembling the people, he said that he wished to pay homage to twice as many gods as those that Achab had introduced,[504] and requested that their [Achab's gods'] priests, prophets, and slaves be present.[505] For he was about to offer costly and great sacrifices to Achab's gods.[506] He would, on the other hand, penalize with death any of the priests who failed to appear.[507] (Now Achab's god was called Baal).[508] **136** Fixing the day on which he would make the sacrifices, he sent throughout the entire country of the Israelites those who were to bring the priests of Baal to him.[509] Jeous then directed the priest[510] to give vestments to everyone. When they had received these,[511] he proceeded into the house with his friend Jonadab and ordered that search be made in order that there be no foreigner or stranger among them, for he did not wish any alien to be on hand for their sacred [rituals].[512]

137 Once they said that no stranger was present, and they had initiated the sacrifices,[513] he stationed eighty[514] men around [the Baal temple] whom he knew to

---

[501] Cf. 2 Kgs 10:16b-17aα. Josephus adds the reference to Jehonadab's being "persuaded" by Jehu's preceding discourse.

[502] See 2 Kgs 10:17aβb. Josephus passes over the Bible's concluding reference to Jehu's initiative being in accordance with "the word of the Lord which he spoke to Elijah."

[503] Josephus provides this heading to the following story of Jehu's elimination of the Baal cult (2 Kgs 10:18-28), anticipating the notice of 2 Kgs 10:19bβ ("but Jehu did it with cunning in order to destroy the worshipers of Baal"); the heading makes the king's anti-Baal intentions clear from the start. The Bible, by contrast, seems at the outset to represent Jehu as actually going over to Baal. The collocation "deception and trickery" (Greek: ἀπάτη καὶ δόλος) occurs also in *Ant.* 7.32; 12.4 (reverse order); 18.326 (reverse order); *Apion* 2.200.

[504] Jehu's opening word to the assembly in 2 Kgs 10:18 runs: "Ahab served Baal a little, but Jehu will serve him much." For the biblical contrast between a lesser and a greater service of a single god (Baal), Josephus substitutes that between Ahab's deities and the still greater number of gods Jehu (purportedly) intends to worship.

[505] 2 Kgs 10:19aα has Jehu mention the same 3 categories of persons, though citing them in the order prophets, servants/slaves, and priests. Whereas the Bible designates the groups in question as associated with the single deity Baal, Josephus links them more generally with Ahab's various "gods" to whom he has Jehu refer in what precedes.

[506] See 2 Kgs 10:19aβ, where Jehu announces his intention of offering "a great sacrifice to Baal." Josephus continues his generalizing of the Bible's mention of Baal.

[507] See 2 Kgs 10:19bα, where Jehu declares "whoever is missing shall not live."

[508] With this parenthetical comment Josephus makes use of the biblical association of Ahab with the god Baal in particular. The notice recalls *Ant.* 8.318, where Josephus mentions the building of a temple to "the Tyrian god Belias" (1 Kgs 16:32: Baal) by Ahab's wife Jezebel. It takes the place of the editorial remark of 2 Kgs 10:19bβ ("but Jehu did it with cunning in order to destroy the worshipers of Baal"), already anticipated by Josephus in 9.134.

[509] Cf. 2 Kgs 10:20-21. Josephus goes beyond v. 21aα in specifying that Jehu sent to summon the "priests of Baal," just as he rewords Jehu's order in v. 20, i.e. "sanctify a solemn assembly for Baal." He leaves aside the statement of v. 21aβb that all the Baal worshipers without exception did in fact assemble and then proceeded to completely fill "the house of Baal."

[510] Greek: τῷ ἱερεῖ. This is the reading of ROLat that Niese and Marcus follow. MSPE (and possibly Zon) read τοῖς ἱεροῦσι ("the priests)."

[511] See 2 Kgs 10:22, where Jehu's directive about the vestments is made to "him who was in charge of the vestments."

[512] See 2 Kgs 10:23. Josephus supplies the rationale for Jehu's "search order" (which in the Bible concerns the presence of "servant(s) of the Lord" among the Baal worshippers).

[513] Josephus agrees with MT and LXX L 2 Kgs 10:24a in making the Baal worshipers the ones to commence the sacrifices, whereas in LXX B it is Jehu himself who does this. He adds the reference to Jehu's being informed of the outcome of the search he had ordered (see 9.136).

be the most faithful of his troops,[515] directing them to kill the false prophets and now to punish them on behalf of the ancestral laws that had already been neglected for a long time.[516] He threatened that *their* lives would be taken in place of any who escaped.[517]

138 They, for their part, slaughtered all the men and set fire to the house of Baal;[518] thus they cleansed Samareia of foreign customs.[519] This Baal was the god of the Tyrians.[520] Achab, wishing to gratify his father-in-law Ithobal, who was king of the Tyrians and Sidonians, had constructed a sanctuary for him in Samareia; he had also appointed prophets and honored him with all devotion.[521]

Jehu tolerates calf-cult

139 After eliminating this god, Jeous allowed the Israelites to pay homage to the golden heifers.[522] God, through the prophet,[523] predicted to him, who had brought about and taken care of the requital of the impious,[524] that his descendants for four generations would rule as kings over the Israelites.[525] And thus things stood with Jeous.[526]

---

[514] This figure agrees with that read by MT and LXX B 2 Kgs 10:24bα. LXX L and some OL witnesses give a much higher figure, i.e. 3,000.

[515] Josephus appends this characterization of those selected by Jehu. He thereby accounts for the king's choice of precisely these men for their intended mission.

[516] Josephus prefaces Jehu's threatening word to the 80 (// 2 Kgs 10:24bβ) with this extended statement by the king about what he is asking them to do. This statement both anticipates and elaborates the order given by Jehu to "the runners and the third men" (RSV: the guard and the officers) in MT and LXX B 10:25aβ (LXX L reads "the runners and the 3,000"), i.e. "go in and slay them [the worshipers of Baal]; let not a man escape." (The biblical presentation in 10:24-25 leaves it unclear whether the 80 of v. 24 are the same as the "the runners and the third men" of v. 25; Josephus simplifies matters by mentioning only the former group). The term "false prophets" used in Jehu's word to the 80 here recalls the king's remark to Jehonadab about his intended victims in 9.134.

[517] This threat corresponds to Jehu's warning to the 80 in 2 Kgs 10:24bβ: "the man who allows any of those whom I give into your hands to escape shall forfeit his life."

[518] From the lengthy catalogue of anti-Baal measures perpetrated by Jehu's men in 2 Kgs 10:25b-27, Josephus selects just these 2 for explicit mention.

[519] This summary formula takes the place of the various additional anti-Baal measures performed by Jehu's men according to 2 Kgs 10:25-27: casting out of the bodies of the Baal-worshipers, removal and demolition of the "pillar(s) of Baal," demolition of the house of Baal, and its transformation into a latrine "to this day." On Josephus' non-usage of the last of these items as reflective of his concern not to offend gentile religious sensibilities, see Feldman 1998a: 355-6.

[520] This parenthetical notice recalls the reference to

"the Tyrian god whom they call Belias" in *Ant.* 8.318 and Josephus' statement "now Achab's god was called Baal" in 9.135.

[521] This appendix to Josephus' account of Jehu's elimination of the Baal-cult in Samaria recalls *Ant.* 8.318, where, however, the building of the temple for Baal/Belias as well as the appointment of his (false) prophets is attributed, not, as here, to Ahab himself, but rather to his wife Jezebel.

[522] See 2 Kgs 10:28-29. Josephus omits the stereotyped terminology used of the "golden calves" in v. 29, where they are called "the sins of Jeroboam which he made Israel to sin." He likewise rewords the biblical reference to Jehu's "not turning aside" from Jeroboam's idols, with its suggestion that the king personally participated in their cult, into a reference to Jehu's (merely) "allowing" such participation by his people.

[523] In 2 Kgs 10:30 God speaks to Jehu directly. Josephus' reference to a prophetic intermediary has a counterpart in *S. 'Olam Rab.* 19.1, where the prophet in question is identified as Jonah.

[524] Compare 2 Kgs 10:30a, where the reference to Jehu's God-pleasing deed of eliminating the house of Ahab functions as part of the divine word itself and as the grounds for ("because...") God's following promise to the king.

[525] In 2 Kgs 10:30b God promises Jehu that his sons to the 4th generation "shall sit on the throne of Israel." Josephus at this point leaves aside the censure of Jehu (10:31) for his failure to walk carefully in the law of the Lord and his persistence in the "sins of Jeroboam" (see 10:29); he will, however, draw on the content of 10:31 subsequently, see 9.160.

[526] With this formula Josephus breaks off his account of Jehu in order to shift attention to the career of Athaliah in Judah to which he devotes 9.140-156 (// 2 Kgs 11:1-20// 2 Chr 22:10-23:21). By contrast, 2 Kgs 10:32-36 first completes the presentation of Jehu, prior

(7.1) **140** When Othlia, the daughter of Achab,[527] heard of the deaths of her brother Joram and of Ochozias her son and the annihilation of the royal family,[528] she became solicitous to leave no one of the house of David and to exterminate the whole family in order that there be no king from it.[529] **141** And this, she imagined, she accomplished;[530] one son of Ochozias was, however, preserved. He escaped death in this manner:[531] Ochozias had a sister by the same father, whose name was Osabethe;[532] the high priest Iodas[533] married her. **142** She entered the palace and found, among those who had been slaughtered, the one-year old Joas[534]—for that was his name—hidden along with his nurse. She carried him together with her [the nurse] and shut him up in a bedroom.[535] She and her husband Iodas secretly raised him for six years in the sacred precinct, during which time Othlia reigned as queen over Hierosolyma and the two tribes.[536]

(7.2) **143** In the seventh year Iodas conferred with certain men, five in number, who were commanders of hundreds.[537] He persuaded them to be part of an undertaking against Othlia and to secure the kingship for the boy. When he had received oaths, by which he was confirmed in his fearlessness for the future as far as his accomplices were concerned, he was encouraged in his hopes regarding Othlia.[538]

144 The men whom the priest Iodas had taken as participants in the deed went around the entire country. When they had assembled the priests and Levites from

Athaliah (Othia) massacres Davidids Joash (Joas) rescued

High priest Jehoiada (Iodas) prepares coup

---

to beginning the Athaliah story in 11:1.

[527] 2 Kgs 11:1a// 2 Chr 22:10a designate Athaliah rather as "the mother of Ahaziah." Josephus' qualification of her as Ahab's "daughter" recalls *Ant.* 8.398; 9.96, where the same identification occurs. On Josephus' version of the story of Athaliah (9.140-156// 2 Kgs 11:1-20// 2 Chr 22:10-23:21), see Begg 2000: 167-87.

[528] 2 Kgs 11:1a// 2 Chr 22:10a mention Athaliah's hearing of the death of Ahaziah alone. Josephus supplies a further motivation for her subsequent bloody initiatives, i.e. the killing also of her brother Joram and of the Judean royal family.

[529] 2 Kgs 11:1b// 2 Chr 22:10b mention Athaliah's extermination of the Judean royal family as a fact, rather than as something intended by her; see, however, next note.

[530] With this phrase Josephus alludes to the virtual extermination of the Judean royal line perpetrated by Athaliah according to 2 Kgs 11:1b// 2 Chr 22:10b; see previous note.

[531] Josephus adds these transitional notices to the story of the survival of a single Judean royal male, which he is about to relate on the basis of 2 Kgs 11:2-3// 2 Chr 22:11-12.

[532] MT (2 Kgs 11:2) יהושבע (Eng.: "Jehosheba"); (2 Chr 22:11) יהושבעת (Eng.: "Jehoshabeath"); LXX B (2 Kgs 11:2// 2 Chr 22:11) Ἰωσαβεέ; LXX L (2 Kgs 11:2 // 2 Chr 22:11) Ἰωσάβεαι; Josephus Ὠσαβέθη. Josephus' indication about the woman's familial relationship corresponds to the references to her as "daughter

of King Joram" and "sister of Ahaziah" in 2 Kgs 11:2/ / 2 Chr 22:11b.

[533] MT (2 Chr 22:11) יהוידע (Eng.: "Jehoiada"); LXX BL Ἰωδάε; Josephus Ἰώδας. In 2 Kings 11, Jehoiada's name appears only in 11:4, and his relationship to Jehosheba (see 11:2) is not spelled out explicitly.

[534] MT (2 Kgs 11:2// 2 Chr 22:11) יואש (Eng.: "Joash"); LXX Ἰωάς; Josephus Ἰώασος.

[535] See 2 Kgs 11:2a// 2 Chr 22:11b. Josephus adds the preliminary detail about Jehosheba's "entering the palace," where she comes upon Joash as well as the mention of the infant's age.

[536] See 2 Kgs 11:2bβ-3// 2 Chr 22:12. Josephus' attributing the custody of the child to the couple jointly corresponds to the wording of Chronicles, whereas Kings speaks of Joash's "remaining with her [Jehosheba]" for the 6-year period. Josephus specifies the domain ruled by Athaliah, which both biblical passages simply designate as "the land."

[537] Josephus here follows the presentation of 2 Chr 23:1 (although omitting the names of the 5 commanders cited there) rather than 2 Kgs 11:4a, where Jehoiada summons to the temple "the captains of the Carites and of the guards."

[538] With this appended notice Josephus spells out the content of the agreement that Jehoiada "enters into with" the 5 commanders according to 2 Chr 23:1. Once again, he avoids the term διαθήκη (= Hebrew ברית) used here by LXX L.

this [the country], along with the heads of the tribes, they came to Hierosolyma, bringing [them] to the high priest.[539]

145 He asked for their sworn pledge[540] that they would keep secret what they would learn from him, who needed both their silence and their cooperation.[541] Once they had sworn and there was security for him to speak,[542] he brought forward the one from the family of David whom he had reared,[543] and said: "This is our[544] king from that house that, as you know, God prophesied to us would reign as king for all time.[545] **146** I urge a third part of you to guard him in the sacred precinct, while [another] third takes its position at all the gates of the sacred enclosure. In addition, let the [final third] guard the gate that opens out on and leads into the palace.[546] Let the rest of the crowd be on hand, unarmed, in the sacred precinct.[547] Permit no trooper to enter, but only a priest."[548]

147 He further enjoined that, in addition to these, a detachment of priests and Levites be around the king himself to protect him as a bodyguard with their swords drawn and to do away with on the spot anyone venturing to enter the sacred precinct armed. Fearing nothing, they were to remain on guard over the king.[549]

148 Once those with whom the high priest consulted had been persuaded by these [words], they disclosed their intention by their action.[550] Opening the armory in the sacred precinct that David had constructed,[551] Iodas distributed to the commanders of hundreds, as also to the priests and Levites,[552] all the spears and quivers[553] that he

---

[539] See 2 Chr 23:2. Josephus adds the priests as a 3rd group of those summoned alongside the Bible's Levites and "heads of the fathers' houses of Israel."

[540] Josephus' phrase "sworn pledge" seems to reflect the reference in 2 Kgs 11:4bα to Jehoiada's "making a covenant" with the assembled military men (see 11:4a) and "putting them under oath." Compare 2 Chr 23:3a: "all the assembly made a covenant with the king."

[541] Josephus supplies a content for the "covenant" and the "oath" initiated by Jehoiada in 2 Kgs 11:4bα, likewise adducing the considerations that inspired these initiatives.

[542] Josephus supplies this transitional phrase.

[543] See 2 Kgs 11:4bβ.

[544] Greek: ἡμῖν. This is the reading of RO, which Niese follows. Marcus reads ὑμῖν ("your") with MSPLatZon.

[545] Compare Jehoiada's declaration to the assembly in 2 Chr 23:3b (no equivalent in 2 Kings 11): "this is the king's son. Let him reign as God spoke concerning the sons of David."

[546] Josephus agrees with 2 Chr 23:4-5a and 2 Kgs 11:5-6 in distinguishing 3 guard detachments assigned by Jehoiada to their various positions. Otherwise, he leaves aside many particulars cited by one or other of his sources (or by both of them), e.g., the identification of the guards as "priests and Levites" (23:4a), the 2 divisions making up the 3rd detachment (11:6), and the references to the sabbath as the time when the guards

come on/off duty.

[547] Josephus draws this further directive from 2 Chr 23:5b, adding the specification that the people are to remain "unarmed."

[548] This directive represents Josephus' version of 2 Chr 23:6a: "let no one enter the house of the Lord except the priests and the ministering Levites, for they are holy." Josephus drops the Levites as those entitled to enter along with the priests, while adding the prohibition of entry by soldiers.

[549] See 2 Chr 23:7, where it is the Levites alone who are assigned to guard the king (in 2 Kgs 11:7-8 Jehoiada directs the 3rd guard-detachment with its 2 divisions to watch over him).

[550] Josephus' indeterminate reference to "those persuaded" by Jehoiada covers both the groups who are said to act on the priest's instructions in 2 Kgs 11:9a (the captains) and 2 Chr 23:8a (the Levites and all Judah), respectively. He leaves aside the allusions to those coming on and off duty on the sabbath common to 2 Kgs 11:9b and 2 Chr 23:8b.

[551] Josephus adds this reference to the "repository" of the weapons Jehoiada is about to distribute. He had not previously mentioned David's building such a structure.

[552] According to 2 Kgs 11:10 // 2 Chr 23:9, it is only the "captains" who received weapons from Jehoiada. Josephus adds the 2 clerical groups who have figured so prominently in what precedes as recipients.

[553] Josephus' mention of these 2 items corresponds

found in it, as well as whatever other sort of weapon he came upon.[554] He stationed those who had been armed in a circle around the sacred precinct with their hands joined, thus blocking access to those who did not belong [there].[555]

149 Jointly leading the boy into the center, they placed the royal crown on him,[556] while Iodas appointed him king, anointing him with the oil.[557] The crowd rejoiced and applauded, crying out "may the king be saved."[558]

Joah acclaimed king

(7.3) 150 Hearing the noise and the unexpected acclamations, Othlia was greatly disconcerted in mind.[559] She rushed out of the palace with her own body of soldiers.[560] Once she came to the sacred precinct, the priests let her enter, but those standing around in a circle kept the troops following her from entering, as had been ordered by the high priest.[561]

Athaliah executed after coming to temple

151 When Othlia saw the boy standing on the platform[562] and wearing the royal crown,[563] she tore her garments and, crying out terribly, directed that he who had conspired against her and was intent on depriving her of her rule be put to death.[564]

---

to the reading of LXX L 2 Kgs 11:10 (where they appear in reverse order). In MT LXX B 2 Kgs 11:10 the reference is to "spears and shields." MT 2 Chr 23:9 speaks of "spears and large and small shields," LXX B 2 Chr 23:9 of "swords and large shields and weapons," and LXX L 2 Chr 23:9 of "spears and small shields and weapons."

[554] This 3rd item reflects the reading "weapons" of LXX BL 2 Chr 23:9; see previous note.

[555] Josephus adapts the notice of 2 Chr 23:10, which has Jehoiada placing "all the people" with their weapons to guard the king in a line extending from the south to the north side of the temple. (In 2 Kgs 11:11 "the guards" take their stand, weapons in hand, in the same formation.) Josephus' (added) motivation of the priest's measure recalls Jehoiada's directive as cited in 9.146: "permit no trooper to enter, but only a priest."

[556] In making an unspecified collectivity ("they") the subject of Joash's crowning Josephus agrees with MT 2 Chr 23:11, whereas the other witnesses to 23:11, as well as those to 2 Kgs 11:12, have Jehoiada act as sole "crowner." Josephus leaves aside the biblical reference to "the testimony" (RSV) given Joash on this occasion, perhaps because—like modern scholars—he was uncertain what this object was.

[557] Josephus agrees with LXX BL 2 Kgs 11:12 in making Jehoiada alone appoint Joash king. By contrast, the subject is an unspecified "they" in MT 11:12, and "Jehoiada and his sons" in the various witnesses to 2 Chr 23:11. Josephus adds the mention of Joash's being "anointed with oil"—rather surprisingly given his general tendency to reword biblical anointing/messiah language.

[558] See 2 Kgs 11:12bβ for mention of the people's applauding and acclaiming the king (2 Chr 23:11bβ cites only the latter point). Josephus adds the reference to the crowd's "rejoicing."

[559] See 2 Kgs 11:13a// 2 Chr 23:12a. Josephus' ref-

erence to the queen's hearing the "acclamations" reflects the reading peculiar to 2 Chr 23:12a, which states that Athaliah heard the noise of the people "(running and) praising the king." Josephus appends the remark on Athaliah's emotional state upon hearing the commotion.

[560] Josephus supplies these preliminary details about Athaliah's response to what she has just heard. Mention of the "soldiers" she takes with her serves to prepare subsequent elements of his presentation of the queen's demise.

[561] Josephus elaborates the notices of 2 Kgs 11:13b// 2 Chr 23:12b, which simply mention Athaliah coming (alone) to the temple. His expansion narrates the carrying out of Jehoiada's orders about who is (not) to be allowed access as cited in 9.146, 148.

[562] The translation follows the Greek reading (ἐπὶ τῆς σκηνῆς) adopted by Niese, Marcus, etc.; compare LXX BL 2 Chr 23:13 ἐπὶ τῆς στάσεως αὐτοῦ, "at his station." The codices RO read rather ἐπὶ τῆς στήλης ("at the pillar") in accordance with MT LXX BL 2 Kgs 11:14 and MT 2 Chr 23:13.

[563] Neither 2 Kings 11 nor 2 Chronicles 23 mentions Athaliah's "seeing" Joash in his crown (cf. 9.149). The reference takes the place of the enumeration of the things Athaliah does see and hear in the temple according to 2 Kgs 11:14a// 2 Chr 23:13a, i.e. the captains and trumpeters surrounding the king, the people of the land rejoicing and blowing trumpets (23:13a adds the singers with their musical instruments). Josephus keeps Athaliah's attention focussed on Joash himself.

[564] In 2 Kgs 11:14b// 2 Chr 23:13b Athaliah's rending her clothes is accompanied by the double exclamation "Treason! Treason!" The directive Josephus ascribes to the queen presupposes his earlier mention (9.150) of the soldiers she took with her (but who are now unable to obey her current command, since they were kept from following her into the temple itself).

Calling the commanders of the hundreds, Iodas directed them to lead Othlia to the Kedron [Kidron] valley and do away with her there,[565] for he did not wish to defile the sacred precinct by punishing the reprobate on the spot.[566] **152** He also ordered that if anyone approached to help her, he was to be done away with.[567] Taking hold therefore of Othlia, those ordered to do away with her brought her to the gate of the king's mules and there executed her.[568]

Sequels to Athaliah's death

(7.4) 153 Once Othlia's case had thus been adroitly disposed of in this way,[569] Iodas called together the populace and the troops to the sacred precinct[570] and made them swear to be loyal to the king and take care for his safety and ongoing rule.[571] Then he compelled the king himself to pledge that he would honor God and not transgress the laws of Moyses.[572]

154 After this they rushed into the house of Baal that Othlia and her husband Joram had constructed as an outrage against the ancestral God and in honor of Achab's god.[573] They tore it down[574] and killed Mathan[575] who held its priesthood.

155 Iodas now entrusted the oversight and custody of the sacred precinct to the priests and Levites in accordance with the arrangements of King David, directing them twice a day to offer the customary sacrifices of the whole sacrifices and, following the law, to burn incense.[576] He also appointed some of the Levites and gatekeepers to guard the sacred enclosure so that no one who had been defiled should secretly be present.[577]

---

[565] In 2 Kgs 11:15a// 2 Chr 23:14a Jehoiada's initial command to the captains runs simply: "Bring her [Athaliah] out between the ranks." Josephus' added mention of the "Kedron [Bible: Kidron] valley" as the prescribed site of Athaliah's execution may be inspired by the biblical references (see, e.g., 1 Kgs 15:13; 2 Kgs 23:4, 6, 12) to this valley as *the* place for the disposal of idolatrous phenomena of all kinds.

[566] Josephus spells out the grounds for Jehoiada's prohibition "do not slay her [Athaliah] in the house of the Lord" as cited in 2 Kgs 11:15b// 2 Chr 23:14b.

[567] Josephus, having first disposed of the topic of the queen's fate, now makes delayed use of this further command, which the biblical Jehoiada attaches to his directive about bringing Athaliah out between the ranks in 2 Kgs 11:15a// 2 Chr 23:14a ("slay with the sword any who follows her").

[568] See 2 Kgs 11:16// 2 Chr 23:15, which speak of the "horse gate" and associate this with the entrance of the palace.

[569] Josephus supplies this transitional phrase, rounding off his account of Athaliah's demise and leading into the sequels that he is about to narrate.

[570] This "summons" is Josephus' addition.

[571] This 1st initiative by Jehoiada seems inspired by the reference in MT LXX B 2 Kgs 11:17b to the priest's mediating a 2nd, additional covenant—one not mentioned in either LXX L 2 Kgs 11:17b or 2 Chr 23:16—"between the king and the people." Josephus spells out the content of this agreement in so far as it obligates the people.

[572] Neither 2 Kgs 11:17 nor 2 Chr 23:16 mentions such a commitment imposed by Jehoiada on Joash alone. Conversely, both these texts cite a "covenant" established by Jehoiada, whereby king *and people* acknowledge their status as "God's people." Josephus makes the biblical, God-oriented agreement one assumed exclusively by Joash, at the same time giving it a more definite content.

[573] See 2 Kgs 11:18aα// 2 Chr 23:17aα. Josephus appends an explanation of the origin of this temple, not previously mentioned in either the Bible or his own presentation. Cf. 2 Chr 24:7, where the sons of Athaliah are charged with having used the "dedicated things" of the temple "for the Baals." On Baal as Ahab's god, see 9.135.

[574] 2 Kgs 11:18aβ// 2 Chr 23:17aβ mention also the smashing of the "altars and images" for Baal. Josephus' omission of these particulars is reminiscent of his abbreviation of the detailed description of the desecration of the Baal temple in Samaria (2 Kgs 10:25b-27) in 9.138.

[575] MT (2 Kgs 11:18b// 2 Chr 23:17b) מתן (Eng.: "Mattan"); LXX B 2 Kgs 11:18b Μαγθάν; LXX L 2 Kgs 11:18b// LXX BL 2 Chr 23:17b Ματθάν; Josephus Μάθαν. The biblical texts add that Mattan was killed "before the altars."

[576] See 2 Chr 23:18b (no parallel in 2 Kings 11), from which Josephus omits the indication that the sacrificial activity of the priests and Levites was to be accompanied "by rejoicing and singing."

[577] Cf. the references to Jehoiada's stationing of

(7.5) 156 When he had arranged each of these [matters], he took along the commanders of hundreds, the leaders, and the entire people from the sacred precinct, and brought Joas to the palace.[578] When he was seated on the royal throne, the crowd, after expressing its good wishes, turned to feasting, banqueting for many days.[579] The city, however, was quiet following the death of Othlia.[580]

157 Joas was seven years old when he assumed the kingship.[581] His mother's was named Sabia;[582] her native city was Bersabee.[583] He made much of keeping the ordinances and was lavish in his worship of God during the whole time Iodas lived.[584] **158** Once he came of age, he married the two wives whom the high priest gave him, by whom he had both male and female children.[585] The matters relating to King Joas, how he escaped Othlia's plot and assumed the kingship, we have related then with these [words].[586]

Joash's reign begins

(8.1) 159 Now Azael, the king of the Syrians,[587] was making war on the Israelites and their king Jeous;[588] he destroyed the country beyond the Jordan to the east belonging to the Roubenites, the Gadites, and the Manassites, as well as all Galaditidis and Batanaia.[589] He burned and plundered everything, and did violence to all who [came] into his hands.[590] **160** For Jeous was not quick to take vengeance on him for devastating his country. He [Jeous] died,[591] having become a despiser of

End of Jehu's reign

---

temple police 2 Kgs 11:18bβ and 2 Chr 23:18aα, 19. Josephus lacks an equivalent to the notice of 23:18aβ that these forces were to be under the direction of the priests and Levites.

[578] See 2 Kgs 11:19a // 2 Chr 23:20a. Josephus omits mention of the gate through which the procession proceeds according to the biblical texts, i.e. "the gate of the guards" (2 Kgs 11:19a)/ "the upper gate" (2 Chr 23:20a).

[579] See 2 Kgs 11:19b-20a// 2 Chr 23:20b-21a. Josephus expatiates on the biblical references to the people's "rejoicing" following the enthronement of Joash.

[580] See 2 Kgs 11:20b// 2 Chr 23:21b.

[581] See 2 Kgs 12:1 (MT; Eng. 11:21) // 2 Chr 24:1aα. Josephus lacks an equivalent to the synchronism of Joash's accession with the 7th year of Jehu of Israel given in 2 Kgs 12:2aα (MT; Eng. 12:1aα). On Josephus' portrayal of Joash in 9.157-171 (// 2 Kgs 12:1-22 [MT; RSV 11:21-12:20]// 2 Chr 24:1-27), see Begg 2000: 189-206.

[582] MT (2 Kgs 12:2// 2 Chr 24:1) צביה (Eng.: "Zibiah"); LXX BL 2 Kgs 12:2// LXX B 2 Chr 24:1 Ἀβιά; LXX L 2 Chr 24:1 and Josephus Σαβία.

[583] MT (2 Kgs 12:2// 2 Chr 24:1) באר שבע (Eng.: "Beersheba"); LXX BL 2 Kgs 12:2// LXX B 2 Chr 24:1 and Josephus Βηρσάβεε; LXX L 2 Chr 24:1 Βηρσάβει.

[584] Josephus' formulation follows 2 Chr 24:2 in its restricting Joash's good behavior to the lifetime of Jehoiada. Compare 2 Kgs 12:3, where the king's life-long ("all his days") righteousness is attributed to the instruction of Jehoiada. Josephus has no counterpart to

the notice of 2 Kgs 12:4 about the continuation of the cult on the high places under Joash, which qualifies the affirmation about the king's righteousness in 12:3.

[585] See 2 Chr 24:3 (no equivalent in 2 Kings 12). The MT wording in 24:3 leaves it uncertain which of the 2 men married the 2 wives—Joash (so RSV) or Jehoiada. LXX BL resolves the matter one way, making Jehoiada the one who marries them, Josephus the other.

[586] With this formula Josephus provisionally concludes his presentation of Joash, which he will then resume in 9.161, after an interlude (9.159-160) dealing with the end of Jehu's reign that itself picks up on his last mention of this king in 9.139.

[587] On this king (biblical "Hazael") and his usurpation, see the segment 9.87-94, which concludes (9.94) with mention of the peace between him and Joram of Israel, a peace that gives way to conflict now in the time of Joram's successor Jehu.

[588] Josephus omits the divine involvement in Hazael's attacks highlighted in 2 Kgs 10:32a: "in those days the Lord began to cut off parts of Israel."

[589] Of the Israelite place names cited in 2 Kgs 10:33, Josephus has no equivalent to the phrase "from Aroer, which is by the valley of the Arnon," as well as the 1st of its 2 mentions of "Gilead."

[590] 2 Kgs 10:32b merely states that Hazael "defeated them [the Israelites] throughout the territory of Israel." Josephus' elaboration concerning the Syrian's depredations recalls the predictions of his future activities made by Elisha in 9.91 (// 2 Kgs 8:12b).

[591] See 2 Kgs 10:35aα: "so Jehu slept with his fathers."

[his duties towards] the Deity and contemptuous of holiness and the laws,[592] after ruling as king over the Israelites for twenty-seven years.[593] He was buried in Samareia,[594] leaving as the successor to his rule his son Joaz.[595]

Joash's plan for restoration of temple fails

(8.2) 161 A certain urge to restore the sanctuary of God took hold of Joas, the king of Hierosolyma;[596] calling the high priest Iodas, he directed him to send the Levites and priests[597] throughout the entire country to ask for a half-shekel of silver per head[598] for the repair and restoration of the sanctuary that had fallen into decay under Joram and Othlia and her children.[599]

162 The high priest did not do this, however, perceiving that no one would be [sufficiently] generous to hand over the silver.[600] In the twenty-third year of his kingship,[601], however, the king summoned both him and the Levites[602] and asked why they had disregarded what he had ordered.[603] He also directed them in the future

---

[592] These negative remarks concerning Jehu at the end of his reign take the place of the source notice for him of 2 Kgs 10:34. They represent Josephus' delayed utilization of the evaluation of the king given in 2 Kgs 10:31: "Jehu was not careful to walk in the law of the Lord the God of Israel...."

[593] The figure given in both MT and LXX BL 2 Kgs 10:36 for Jehu's length of reign is *28* years. Josephus' divergent figure is, however, paralleled in several OL manuscripts; see Mulzer and Krieger 1996: 67, n. 131.

[594] See 2 Kgs 10:35aβ.

[595] MT (2 Kgs 10:35b) יהואחז (Eng.: "Jehoahaz"); LXX BL Ἰωαχάζ; Josephus Ἰώαζος. Josephus will resume his account of this king in 9.172 (// 2 Kgs 13:1), after concluding his presentation of Joash of Judah in 9.161-171. He has no equivalent to the long plus, with its combination of elements drawn from 2 Kgs 8:25-9:28, that follows 2 Kgs 10:36 in LXX L.

[596] Josephus dramatizes the king's decision to restore the temple as cited in 2 Chr 24:4.

[597] In 2 Chr 24:5a Joash personally dispatches the priests and Levites on their mission; Josephus has him work through the head priest Jehoiada, this perhaps reflecting his personal conception of the primacy of the priesthood in Jewish life. In 2 Kgs 12:5-6 (MT; Eng. 12:4-5) no such "mission" is mentioned; rather, Joash issues directives to the priests about collecting various monies from the people and using these for the repair of the temple.

[598] In 2 Chr 24:5a itself the priests and Levites are simply instructed to collect "money" for the temple's repair. Josephus' specification of the amount is inspired by the Chronicler's subsequent references (see 24:6, 9) to "the tax levied by Moses" for the tent of testimony in the desert. These references, in turn, allude to Exod 30:11-16 (cf. *Ant.* 3.194-196), where Moses asks for "half a shekel" from each Israelite on behalf of the sanctuary that is to be constructed.

[599] To the king's directive about the collected money being used for the repair of the temple in 2 Chr

24:5a, Josephus adds an explanation as to why such repair is needed, i.e. the neglect of the edifice by Joash's immediate predecessors. The wording of this addition is partially inspired by Joash's subsequent statement in 2 Chr 24:7, where he recalls that the sons of Athaliah "broke into" the temple and used its votive offerings "for the Baals." See also 9.154, where Athaliah and Joram are charged by Josephus with having built a temple for Baal in Jerusalem.

[600] Josephus continues to highlight Jehoiada's personal role in the affair. By contrast, Joash's directive about repairing the temple is disregarded by "the priests" collectively in 2 Kgs 12:7 (MT; Eng. 12:6) and by "the Levites" in 2 Chr 24:5b. Josephus likewise supplies a rationale—lacking in both biblical texts—for the non-fulfillment of the king's command.

[601] Josephus derives this dating indication for Joash's new initiative—unparalleled in 2 Chronicles 24—from 2 Kgs 12:7 (MT; Eng. 12:6) which states that by the king's 23rd year the priests had failed to do anything regarding the repair of the temple.

[602] In 2 Kgs 12:8a (MT; Eng. 12:7a) those confronted by Joash are Jehoiada and the other priests, while in 2 Chr 24:6a it is Jehoiada alone. Josephus' added mention of the Levites is noteworthy, given his tendency to leave aside biblical mentions of them elsewhere (compare his mention of the Levites before the priests in 9.161, as against 2 Chr 24:5a's "priests and Levites"). He may, however, have found inspiration for his introduction of them here in the accusatory question Joash addresses to Jehoiada in 2 Chr 24:6b, in which the Levites do figure; see next note.

[603] Josephus generalizes the wording of the alternative accusatory questions attributed to the king in 2 Kgs 12:8aβ (MT; Eng. 12:7aβ) ("Why are you [Jehoiada and the other priests] not repairing the house?") and 2 Chr 24:6b ("Why have you [Jehoiada] not required the Levites to bring in from Judah and Jerusalem the tax levied by Moses...?"), respectively.

to take care of the repair of the sanctuary.⁶⁰⁴ The high priest devised a scheme for collecting the funds that the crowd gladly adopted.⁶⁰⁵ **163** He constructed a wooden collection chest that he enclosed on all sides, while opening a single hole in it.⁶⁰⁶ Then placing it in the sacred precinct next to the altar,⁶⁰⁷ he directed each person to throw into it, through the hole, whatever he wished for the repair of the sanctuary.⁶⁰⁸ The entire people was favorable to this and, by their emulation and joint contributions, they assembled much silver and gold.⁶⁰⁹

Jehoiada's alternative plan wins popular approval

164 When the scribe and [priest]⁶¹⁰ of the storehouses had emptied the collection box⁶¹¹ and counted what had been collected in the presence of the king,⁶¹² they put it back in the same place.⁶¹³ Once it seemed that a sufficient amount of money had been thrown in, the high priest Iodas and King Joas sent to hire stone-masons and carpenters as well as large timbers and the best materials.⁶¹⁴

Use of proceeds from collection

165 When the sanctuary had been repaired,⁶¹⁵ they employed the remaining gold

---

⁶⁰⁴ In 2 Kgs 12:8b (MT; Eng. 12:7b) Joash enjoins the priests to no longer take money from their acquaintances, but rather to "hand it [the money] over for the repair of the house." Given his modification of the king's order, Josephus leaves aside the notice of 12:9 (MT; Eng. 12:8) on the priests' response to Joash's words to them, i.e. their agreeing to no longer take money from the people or repair the house.

⁶⁰⁵ Josephus' addition of this notice provides a lead-in to the subsequent course of the story, once again highlighting Jehoiada's role. The reference to the people's enthusiastic endorsement of the priest's plan may be inspired by the mention of all the princes and people "rejoicing" as they place their contributions in the collection chest in 2 Chr 24:10.

⁶⁰⁶ See 2 Kgs 12:10a (MT; Eng. 12:9a); compare 2 Chr 24:8a, where "they" make the chest at the king's command. Josephus adds the detail about the chest's being "enclosed on all sides."

⁶⁰⁷ See 2 Kgs 12:10aβ (MT; Eng. 12:9aβ), which adds that the chest was located to the right of the altar "as one entered the house of the Lord"; compare 2 Chr 24:8b, which situates the chest "outside the gate of the house of the Lord."

⁶⁰⁸ Compare 2 Chr 24:9, where a "proclamation is made"—by whom or at whose instance it is not said—throughout the land, calling for the Mosaic sanctuary tax to be brought. Josephus earlier had Joash enjoin—unsuccessfully—the collection of that tax (see 9.161). He now portrays Jehoiada leaving the amount up to the individual giver, this time with positive results.

⁶⁰⁹ With this notice on the response to Jehoiada's initiative Josephus combines 2 Chr 24:10 (the princes and people "rejoice" as they place their contributions in the chest) and 24:11bβ (the designated officials "collect money in abundance"). In 2 Kgs 12:10b (MT; Eng. 12:9b), by contrast, it is the priests who place the contributions of those who have come to the temple in the chest. Josephus has made prior reference to the general

enthusiasm for Jehoiada's collection plan in 9.162.

⁶¹⁰ Greek: καὶ ἱερεύς. This phrase, bracketed by Niese, is absent in the codices RO. Marcus omits Niese's brackets.

⁶¹¹ In 2 Chr 24:11b it is the "king's secretary [literally: scribe] and the officer of the high priest" who "empty" the chest (which had previously been brought to them by Levites—a detail omitted by Josephus). 2 Kgs 12:11 (MT; Eng. 12:10) does not mention an "emptying" of the chest; rather, it describes the king's secretary and the high priest "counting" and "tying up in bags" the collected monies. Josephus will mention the counting of the monies in the continuation of his account; see next note.

⁶¹² Josephus' mention of the "counting" of the money by the 2 officials corresponds to 2 Kgs 12:11 (MT; Eng. 12:10), which, however, does not state that this was done in the king's presence.

⁶¹³ See 2 Chr 24:11aβ. Josephus omits the appended notice of 24:11bα that the officials performed their task "day after day," thereby collecting "money in abundance" (Josephus has anticipated the latter notice in 9.163 and will make renewed use of in the continuation of 9.164).

⁶¹⁴ Josephus conflates the rather different notices on the (initial) use made of the collected monies found in 2 Kgs 12:12-13 (MT; Eng. 12:11-12) and 2 Chr 24:12. Like the latter text, he has king and priest take an initiative with the assembled funds (in 2 Kgs 12:12 [MT; Eng. 12:11] the king's secretary and Jehoiada do this), while in line with the former passage (see 12:13 [MT; Eng. 12:12]) he mentions the purchase of needed supplies as well. In contrast to both biblical accounts, he cites only 2 categories of hired workers. Josephus' opening transitional phrase concerning the availability of sufficient amounts of money picks up on the reference to the officials' collecting "money in abundance" in 2 Chr 24:11bβ; see previous note.

⁶¹⁵ This transitional phrase summarizes the more

*Death of
Jehoiada*

*Joash and
leaders ignore
prophets'
warnings*

and silver (which was not negligible) for bowls, wine jugs, drinking vessels, and other vessels;[616] they likewise continued to furnish the altar abundantly with costly daily sacrifices.[617]

As long as Iodas lived, these things were carried out with fitting solicitude.[618] **(8.3) 166** But when he died,[619] after having lived 130 years, a man just and kind in all things,[620] and was buried in the royal tombs in Hierosolyma because he had restored the kingship to the family of David,[621] King Joas gave up his concern for God.[622] **167** The chiefs of the crowd degenerated together with[623] him so that they offended against what was just and regarded as best among them.[624] God, however, was displeased by this change on the part of the king and the others[625]; he sent the prophets to raise their voices against[626] what they were doing and to make them cease from vileness.[627]

168 They, however, had so strong a lust and terrible desire[628] for this that, neither by what those who were before them had suffered, along with entire household, in punishment for their outrages against the ordinances nor by what the prophets kept predicting, were they persuaded to change their minds and turn away from those things to which they had turned when acting lawlessly.[629] Rather, the king,

---

expansive notice on the temple work and its completion of 2 Chr 24:13-14aα.

[616] This notice agrees with 2 Chr 24:14a concerning an additional use made of the leftover monies. By contrast, 2 Kgs 12:14 (MT; Eng. 12:13) declares that the remaining funds were *not* used to procure such vessels for the temple. Josephus omits the preliminary detail of 2 Chr 24:14a, according to which those involved in the temple's repair brought the remaining monies "before the king and Jehoiada." Conversely, he adds the parenthetical reference to the magnitude of the still available funds that made possible the realization of several other projects connected with the temple.

[617] See 2 Chr 24:14b; compare 2 Kgs 12:17 (MT; Eng. 12:16), which states that the monies deriving from the guilt and sin offerings were not brought into the temple, given that these belonged to the priests. Josephus' wording accentuates the opulence of the sacrificial cult made possible by the magnitude of what had been collected.

[618] Josephus adapts the final words of 2 Chr 24:14b (the sacrifices are offered "all the days of Jehoiada"), making these a transition that sums up the first, good period of Joash's rule and intimates the change for the worse that is about to set in.

[619] Josephus here begins his version (9.166-169) of a segment, 2 Chr 24:15-22, which has no parallel in 2 Kings 12.

[620] See 2 Chr 24:15. To the Chronicler's notice on Jehoiada's lifespan, Josephus adds a double characterization of the priest, employing the same collocation (Greek: δίκαιος καὶ χρηστός) used, in reverse order, of Jehonadab in 9.133.

[621] See 2 Chr 24:16. Josephus' motivation for the

special burial honor accorded Jehoiada, with its reference to the priest's overthrow of the usurper Athaliah (see 9.140-156), is more specific than that given by the Chronicler, i.e. "...because he [Jehoiada] had done good in Israel, and towards God and his house."

[622] Greek: ἐπιμέμεια πρὸς τὸν θεόν; the phrase occurs only here in Josephus. He prefaces the story of 2 Chr 24:15-22 with this notice on Joash's defection, thereby highlighting the king's personal responsibility for what now happens.

[623] Greek: συνδιαφθείρω. This is the same verb used in *Ant.* 8.252 in Josephus' reflection on subjects' degenerating along with their depraved rulers.

[624] Josephus generalizes and compresses the account of Joash's defection given in 2 Chr 24:17-18a, where the king listens to those "princes of Judah" who pay him homage (v. 17) with the result that "they" (king and princes) forsake the temple and serve "the Asherim and the idols" (v. 18a).

[625] Compare 2 Chr 24:18b: "wrath came upon Judah and Jerusalem for this their [the king and princes'] guilt."

[626] Greek: διαμαρτύρομαι. The word is *hapax* in Josephus.

[627] See 2 Chr 24:19abα, where the prophets' mission is to "bring them back to the Lord."

[628] Greek: δεινῆ ἐπιθυμία. Josephus uses this expression of Herod's urge to scratch himself in *Ant.* 17.169; related expressions occur in *Ant.* 6.279 and 7.168. The wordpair "lust and desire" (Greek: ἔρως καὶ ἐπιθυμία) is *hapax* in Josephus.

[629] Josephus dramatizes the summary notice of 2 Chr 24:19bβ: "but they would not give heed," attributing the hearers' recalcitrance to the prophets' appeal to

unmindful of his father's benefactions, even directed that Zacharias,[630] the son of the high priest Iodas, be killed in the sacred precinct by throwing [stones].[631] **169** [He did this] because God had appointed [Zacharias] to prophesy.[632] Standing in the middle of the crowd,[633] he advised both them and the king to do what was just, and predicted that they would undergo great punishment if they were not persuaded.[634] But as Zacharias was dying, being put to death in a cruel and violent[635] way, he made God the witness and avenger[636] of what he suffered in return for his kind advice and the things his father had obtained for Joas.[637]

Martryed Zechariah's (Zacharias') prayer for vengeance

(8.4) 170 It was not long, however, before the king paid the penalty for his acting lawlessly.[638] For Azael, the king of the Syrians, invaded his country.[639] After subjugating and looting Gitta, he was about to campaign against him in Hierosolyma.[640] In his fear,[641] Joas emptied all the treasuries of God and of the palace and tore down the votive offerings. He sent them to the Syrian, purchasing with them his not being besieged and his [Azael's] not endangering everything.[642]

Joash buys off invader Hazael

171 The Syrian, persuaded by the magnitude of these sums, did not lead his army against Hierosolyma.[643] When, however, Joas fell [victim] to a serious disease,[644] he

Assassination and burial of Joash

---

their intense urge for depravity.

[630] MT (2 Chr 24:20) זכריה (Eng.: "Zechariah"); LXX B Ἀζαρίας; LXX L and Josephus Ζαχαρίας.

[631] Reversing the biblical order, Josephus speaks of Zechariah's murder (// 2 Chr 24:21) at the instigation of Joash, unmindful of what he owed the former's father (// 24:22a), prior to citing Zechariah's own prophetic intervention (// 24:20).

[632] This is Josephus' characteristic rewording of the reference to the spirit of God's "taking possession of" Zechariah in 2 Chr 24:20aα.

[633] 2 Chr 24:20aβ has Zechariah standing "over the people."

[634] Josephus gives a free rendering of Zechariah's warning in 2 Chr 24:20b, where he 1st asks the people why they are "transgressing the commandments of the Lord" with their resultant inability to "prosper," and then announces that their "forsaking the Lord" has prompted the Lord to "forsake" them. In so doing, he also makes Joash a distinct addressee of Zechariah's words.

[635] Greek: πικρῶς καὶ βιαίως. This collocation is *hapax* in Josephus.

[636] Greek: μάρτυς καὶ δικαστής. Josephus uses this same collocation, though with a reversal of its elements, of God in *Ant.* 4.46.

[637] See 2 Chr 24:22b. Josephus expatiates on both the brutality of Zechariah's death and the grounds for his prayer that God deal appropriately with Joash.

[638] Josephus supplies this heading to the following story of Joash's calamity, highlighting the connection between this and his previous treatment of Zechariah. His inspiration for it is likely the "theological commentary" appended to the story of the Syrian invasion (2 Chr 24:23) in 24:24a, ascribing Israel's defeat to the Lord's punishment for its forsaking him.

[639] Like 2 Kgs 12:18 (MT; Eng. 12:17), Josephus has no parallel to the indication of 2 Chr 24:23a that the Syrian attack came "at the end of the year."

[640] In his mention of Hazael's initial capture of "Gath," prior to his move against Jerusalem, Josephus agrees with 2 Kgs 12:18 (MT; Eng. 12:17) against 2 Chr 24:23b, where the former event is not cited.

[641] Josephus supplies this reference to Joash's emotional state in the face of the Syrian invasion.

[642] See 2 Kgs 12:19a (MT; Eng. 12:18a). From the biblical passage Josephus omits the names of the 3 prior Judean kings whose "votive gifts" Joash hands over to the Syrian, while adding reference to the intended purpose of Joash's initiative, i.e. delivery from still greater calamities. In contrast to both Kings and Josephus, 2 Chr 24:23b avers that the Syrians, upon coming to Judah and Jerusalem, destroyed the princes of the people and themselves dispatched spoil to Hazael. Josephus has no equivalent to the "theological commentary" on the Syrian invasion of 2 Chr 24:24a, which, however, he has drawn from in formulating his introduction to the episode of Joash's punishment at the start of 9.170; see the note to "penalty for his acting lawlessly" there.

[643] See 2 Kgs 12:19b (MT; Eng. 12:18b), whose notice on Hazael's withdrawal Josephus expands with mention of the king's motivation for this.

[644] 2 Kings 12 makes no mention of such a disease that provides the occasion for Joash's assassination. In 2 Chr 24:25aα Joash is left "severely wounded" by the departing Syrians—a presentation that Josephus modifies, turning Joash's affliction into a "disease" that befalls the king given the fact that in his (Kings-based) previous account, the Syrians do not actually get their hands on Jerusalem or Joash.

was assaulted by his friends, who, avenging the death of Zacharias, the son of Iodas, plotted against the king, and was destroyed by them.[645] **172** He was buried in Hierosolyma, but not in the tombs of his ancestors,[646] since he was impious.[647] He had lived forty-seven years;[648] his son Amasias[649] succeeded to the kingship.

Jehoahaz (Joaz) of Israel

(8.5) 173 In the twenty-first year of King Joas, Joaz, the son of Jeous, assumed the leadership of the Israelites in Samareia.[650] He exercised it for seventeen years;[651] though not an imitator of his father, he was as impious as those who previously were contemptuous of God.[652]

Syrian threat, Jehoahaz' appeal, and God's positive response

174 The king of the Syrians campaigned against him, destroyed his cities, which were both great and many, and ruined his army: he humbled him and contracted such a great force to 10,000 troops and 50 horsemen.[653] **175** The people of the Israelites suffered these things in accordance with the prophecy of Elissai when he predicted that Azael, after killing his master, would rule as king over the Syrians and Damascenes.[654] Faced with such difficult calamities,[655] Joaz had recourse to prayer and supplication to God to deliver him from the hands of Azael, appealing to him not to overlook what was being done by him.[656] **176** God, for his part, accepted

---

[645] See 2 Kgs 12:22a (MT; Eng. 12:21a)// 2 Chr 24:25aβ, where it is Joash's "servants" who assault him, killing him "on his bed" according to Chronicles. Like the Chronicler, Josephus does not mention the places associated with Joash's killing cited in 2 Kgs 12:22. He likewise passes over the names of his 2 assassins listed in both 2 Kgs 12:22a (MT; Eng. 12:21a: Jozacar and Jehozabad) and 2 Chr 24:26 (Zabad and Jehozabad).

[646] Josephus' notice on Joash's being denied burial in the tombs of his predecessors agrees with 2 Chr 24:25bβ against 2 Kgs 12:22bα (MT; Eng. 12:21bα), which states that he was buried "with his fathers in the city of David."

[647] Josephus adds this explanation as to why Joash, as stated in 2 Chr 24:25bβ, was denied burial with the earlier Judean kings.

[648] Josephus obtains this figure for Joash's life-span by combining the years of his age at accession (7) and length of reign (40) as cited in 2 Kgs 12:1-2a (MT; Eng. 11:21-12:1a)// 2 Chr 24:1a.

[649] MT (2 Kgs 12:22bβ) אמציה (Eng [12:21bβ]: "Amaziah")/ (2 Chr 24:27b) אמציהו (Eng.: "Amaziah"); LXX BL 2 Kgs 12:22 Ἀμεσσείας; LXX BL 2 Chr 24:27b; Josephus Ἀμασίας. Josephus has no equivalent to the (disparate) source notices for Joash of 2 Kgs 12:20 (MT; Eng. 12:19) and 2 Chr 24:27a.

[650] MT and LXX BL 2 Kgs 13:1a date Jehoahaz' accession to the *23th* year of Joash of Judah. On Josephus' account of the Israelite King Jehoahaz and his successor Joash in 9.173-185 (// 2 Kings 13), see Begg 2000: 207-24. Josephus mentioned Jehoahaz' succession to his father Jehu in 9.160.

[651] This figure corresponds to that given in MT and LXX BL 2 Kgs 13:1b for Jehoahaz' length of reign.

[652] 2 Kgs 13:2 simply "credits" Jehoahaz with per-

sisting in the sins of Jeroboam I, a charge generalized in the 2nd part of Josephus' evaluation. His initial reference to Jehoahaz' not "imitating" his father Jehu (whom he calls a "despiser of [his duties towards] the Deity and contemptuous of holiness and the laws" in 9.160) may have in view the fact of the former's appealing to God—as Jehu did not—in face of the Syrian threat as cited in 2 Kgs 13:4. Josephus' designation of Jehoahaz as nevertheless "impious" parallels him with Joash of Judah, against whom the same charge is made in 9.172.

[653] From the notice on Hazael's reduction of Israel's armed forces in 2 Kgs 13:7, which he anticipates here (in 1 Kings 13 the notice appears only after mention of Jehoahaz' appeal and the Lord's resultant delivery of Israel in 13:4-6) Josephus omits the detail about Israel's being left with only 10 chariots, as well as the figurative reference to the Syrian's making Jehoahaz' troops "like the dust at threshing." Conversely, he introduces mention of Hazael's "destroying" the Israelite cities, likely under the influence of Elisha's announcement concerning the Syrian's future hostile initiatives as cited in 9.91, to which he will make explicit allusion in 9.175.

[654] Josephus' (added) allusion to Elisha's prediction to Hazael as cited in 9.91 (// 2 Kgs 8:12b) underscores the fulfillment of that prediction. Compare 2 Kgs 13:3, which highlights the divine role in Syria's subjugation of Israel, though without explicit mention of Elisha's prediction of this.

[655] Josephus supplies this transitional phrase, which underscores the desperateness of the situation that prompts Jehoahaz' turning to God.

[656] See 2 Kgs 13:4a; Josephus supplies a content for Jehoahaz' appeal as mentioned there.

the king's change of mind as a virtue and, because he preferred to admonish the powerful rather than to annihilate them completely,[657] gave him respite from war and its dangers.[658] Obtaining peace, the country reverted to its earlier state and prospered.[659]

177 After the death of Joaz,[660] his son Joas[661] received the rule. Joas had already been ruling as king for thirty-seven years over the tribe of Iouda when this Joas assumed the rule of the Israelites in Samareia (for he had the same name as the king of Hierosolyma) and exercised it for sixteen years.[662] **178** He was a good man, not at all like his father in nature.[663]

Joash (Joas) of Israel introduced

At that time, Elissai the prophet, being already an old man, fell ill and the king of the Israelites came to visit him.[664] **179** Finding him *in extremis*, he began to weep [seeing him][665] and lament, calling him his father and weapon,[666] for thanks to him, he no longer employed weapons against the adversary, but defeated his enemies without a fight by means of his prophecies.[667] But now, in departing this life, he was leaving him without a weapon against the Syrians and their wars.[668] **180** It was not, he said, secure for him to go on living. Rather, it was better for him to follow him [Elissai] in death and die with him.[669]

Dying Elisha's promises for Joash

---

[657] See 2 Kgs 13:4b, which attributes God's favorable response to his seeing "the oppression of Israel."

[658] Compare 2 Kgs 13:5a, which mentions the Lord's giving Israel "a savior," this resulting in their "escaping from the hand of the Syrians." Josephus passes over this savior figure, whom the Bible leaves unnamed and whose identity remains a mystery.

[659] Josephus expatiates on the notice of 2 Kgs 13:5b, which states that the Israelites "dwelt in their homes as formerly." He leaves aside both the reference to the mysterious "savior" God is said to give the Israelites in 13:5a (see previous note) and the affirmation of 13:6 that, notwithstanding their experience of God's benefits, the people persisted in Jeroboam's sin and that the Asherah still remained in Samaria.

[660] Compare 2 Kgs 13:9aα: "Jehoahaz slept with his fathers."

[661] MT (2 Kgs 13:9b) יוֹאָשׁ (Eng.: "Joash"; in the continuation of 2 Kings 13 this form of the king's name will alternate with a longer one, i.e. יְהוֹאָשׁ, Eng. "Jehoash"); LXX BL Ἰωάς; Josephus Ἰώασος. Josephus leaves aside both the source notice for Jehoahaz (2 Kgs 13:8) and the mention of his burial (13:9aβ).

[662] Josephus' figures for the synchronization of the Israelite Joash's accession with the regnal year of his Judean counterpart and the former's length of reign correspond to those cited in 2 Kgs 13:10 (MT and LXX BL). He supplies the parenthetical allusion to both contemporary kings having the same name (compare his similar notices on the 2 Jorams in 9.46, 94).

[663] Josephus' evaluation of Joash of Israel diverges dramatically from that given in 2 Kgs 13:11, which simply makes him one more adherent to the sins of

Jeroboam I. The change has a partial equivalent in Josephus' judgment on Jehoahaz in 9.173, as compared with that of 2 Kgs 13:2. The evaluation seems to be based on the fact of Joash's friendly, non-accusatory, reception by God's prophet Elisha in what follows—something that in the Bible itself comes as a surprise, given its negative judgment on the king in 2 Kgs 13:11.

In MT and LXX B the evaluation of Joash (2 Kgs 13:11) is followed immediately by their concluding notices for this king (13:12-13). Like LXX L (where the content of 13:12-13 appears after 13:25), Josephus tells of Joash's death, burial, and succession by his son Jeroboam only after he has drawn on the further biblical data concerning Joash found in 2 Kgs 13:14-25; see 9.185.

[664] See 1 Kgs 13:14a. Josephus adds the reference to Elisha's advanced age.

[665] Greek: βλέποντος αὐτοῦ. This phrase, bracketed by Niese, is absent in M (RO lacks the word αὐτοῦ). Marcus prints it without brackets.

[666] See 2 Kgs 13:14b, where Joash twice calls Elisha his "father," and then designates him as "the chariots of Israel and its horsemen." Josephus synthesizes the latter phrase with the term "weapon" which he has Joash apply to Elisha.

[667] With these added words Josephus has Joash spell out the reason for his giving Elisha's the military title ("weapon"; compare 2 Kgs 13:14b: "the chariots of Israel and its horsemen") he does.

[668] Josephus appends this affirmation about what the imminent loss of the "weapon" that Elisha has been for Joash will entail for the king.

[669] Josephus rounds off his expansion of Joash's

Elissai comforted the king who was bewailing these things and directed him to have a bow brought to him and to string this.[670] When the king then had made the bow ready to shoot, he [Elissai] grasped his hands and directed him to shoot.[671] He let fly three arrows, and then stopped.[672]

181 "If," he [Elissai] said, "you had released more [arrows], you would have uprooted the kingdom of the Syrians. Since, however, you were satisfied with only three, that same number of times you will join battle with the Syrians and defeat them, so that you might recover the country they cut off from your father."[673] When the king heard this, he was relieved.[674]

182 A short while afterwards, the prophet died, a man outstanding in justice and clearly an object of God's solicitude.[675] For he accomplished marvelous and surprising[676] deeds through his prophecy and was worthy of a splendid memory among the Hebrews.[677] He received a magnificent funeral, as was appropriate for a friend of God.[678]

*Power of
Elisha's corpse*

183 It also happened at that time that some robbers tossed a man whom they had done away into Elissai's grave;[679] when the corpse came into contact with his

---

summary address to Elisha in 2 Kgs 13:14b with this declaration by the king of his inability (or unwillingness) to carry on without the benefit of Elisha's presence.

[670] See 2 Kgs 13:15-16a. Josephus supplies the allusion to Elisha's "comforting" the king, thereby accentuating the cordiality of their relationship. He likewise compresses into a single continuous command the 2 separate orders concerning the bow given by Elisha in 13:15a, 16a with the notice on Joash's compliance with the 1st order supervening in v. 15b.

[671] See 2 Kgs 13:16b-17a. Continuing to compress the biblical account, Josephus leaves aside the prophet's command that Joash open the window towards the east and the latter's doing this (13:17aα).

[672] 2 Kgs 13:17aβ does not specify how many arrows Jehoash actually "shot." Josephus derives the figure from 2 Kgs 13:18, which has the king performing another action with the arrows, i.e. striking the ground with them, a total of 3 times.

[673] Josephus draws this commentary by Elisha concerning Joash's action with the arrows, not from his affirmation regarding the 1st of these actions, i.e. his shooting them, as cited in 2 Kgs 13:17b (where Elisha affirms that, as signified by the flight of the arrows, Joash will annihilate the Syrians "at Aphek"), but rather from the prophet's remarks (2 Kgs 13:19) on Joash's 2nd action with the arrows—which Josephus does not record himself—, namely, his striking the ground with them a total of 3 times. He likewise passes over the opening reference in 13:19 to Elisha's "anger" at Joash and the former's declaration there that, had he struck the ground 5 or 6 times, Joash would have made a full end of Syria. Conversely, he introduces the allusion to

the intended outcome of Joash's engaging the Syrians, i.e. to recover the territories Jehoahaz had lost to them (Josephus apparently draws this allusion from 2 Kgs 13:25a, which refers to Jehoash's recovering the cities which Hazael "had taken from Jehoahaz his father in war").

[674] Josephus supplies this reference to Joash's reaction to the prophet's favorable announcement (see 2 Kgs 13:19) to him.

[675] Josephus expands the mention of Elisha's death (2 Kgs 13:20aα) with a double characterization of him, whose 2nd component, i.e. "(clearly an) object of God's solicitude" (Greek: σπουδασθείς ὑπὸ τοῦ θεοῦ), occurs only here in Josephus; cf., however, the reference to the Deity's being "clearly present" to Elisha in 9.60.

[676] Greek: θαυμαστὰ καὶ παράδοξα. This wordpair is *hapax* in Josephus.

[677] Josephus' summation of Elisha's career here recalls the language with which he introduces his account of him in 9.46, where he announces his intention of relating the prophet's deeds as found in "the sacred books," given that "they are splendid and worthy of history."

[678] Just as he did with the Bible's summary notice (2 Kgs 13:20aα) on Elisha's death (see note to "God's solicitude" at 9.182), Josephus expatiates on its jejune mention (13:20aβ) of the prophet's burial. He uses the term "friend of God" (Greek: θεοφιλής) for David in *Ant.* 6.280.

[679] 2 Kgs 13:20b-21a (MT and LXX BL) distinguishes between 2 groups of persons, i.e. the "marauding" Moabites and those (presumably Israelites) burying the dead man, who, on the Moabites' appearance, toss his corpse into Elisha's grave. Josephus' iden-

[Elissai's] body, he was revived.[680] We have now disclosed the matters relating to the prophet Elissai, the things he predicted while alive, and how, after his death, he still had divine power.[681]

(8.7) 184 Upon the death of Azael, the king of the Syrians, the kingship came to his son Addas.[682] Against him Joas, the king of the Israelites, launched a war.[683] Having vanquished him in three battles, he took away all the country and whatever cities and villages his [Addas'] father Azael had confiscated from the kingdom of the Israelites.[684] 185 Now this came about in accordance with the prophecy of Elissai.[685] Then it happened that Joas also died and was interred in Samareia, while the rule passed to his son Hieroboam.[686]

Joash's victories over Syria and death

(9.1) 186 In the second year of Joas' kingship over the Israelites, Amasias[687] began to rule as king over the tribe of Iouda in Hierosolyma; his mother's name

Amaziah (Amasias) of

---

tification of the buriers with the "robbers"—whose nationality he leaves unmentioned—has a parallel in the OL MS L 115; see Schenker 2004: 143-5. Whereas, however, L 115 (like MT and LXX BL) leaves indeterminate the circumstances behind the death of the man who corpse ends up being placed in Elisha's grave, Josephus has him killed by the robbers themselves. On the proposed identifications of the dead man (e.g., the false prophet Zedekiah [1 Kgs 22:24], the son of the Shunammite woman previously resuscitated by Elisha [2 Kgs 4:18-37], and Shallum, the husband of the prophetess Huldah [2 Kgs 22:14]) in Jewish tradition, see Begg 2000: 220, n. 62.

[680] See 2 Kgs 13:21b. Josephus omits the biblical detail about the revived man's "standing upon his feet."

[681] With this appended notice, Josephus concludes his presentation of Elisha's mighty deeds he began in 9.46. The phrase "divine power" (Greek: δύναμις θεία) was employed of Elisha in 9.58; cf. *Ant.* 8.408 (Micaiah).

[682] MT (2 Kgs 13:24) בֶּן־הֲדַד (Eng.: "Ben-hadad"); LXX BL υἱὸς Ἀδερ; Josephus Ἀδδάς (this is RO's reading that Niese follows; Marcus and Schalit [*s.v.*] adopt the conjecture of J. Hudson, i.e. Ἄδαδος). Josephus has no equivalent to the MT LXX B sequence of 2 Kgs 13:22-23, which unexpectedly reintroduces the figure of the long-dead Jehoahaz, his conflict with the Syrians, and the Lord's continued solicitude for Israel from 2 Kgs 13:3-7 (LXX L situates its parallel to 13:23 after 13:7) following the account of Elisha's death and burial in 13:20-21. He likewise lacks a parallel to the plus of LXX L that follows its rendering of 13:22 (MT LXX B): "And Hazael took the Philistine [Greek: τὸν ἀλλόφυλον] out of his [Jehoahaz'] hand, from the sea of the West to Aphek." On this plus see Schenker 2004: 113-5, who regards it as part of the original text of Kings.

[683] Josephus supplies this introductory heading to the biblical account of Joash's successes against the

Syrians (2 Kgs 13:25).

[684] See 2 Kgs 13:25, whose sequence Josephus rearranges, mentioning Joash's triple defeat of Ben-hadad (13:25bα) in 1st place. He likewise eliminates the biblical's verse's double mention of the recovery of the Israelite cities.

[685] Josephus appends this fulfillment notice, calling attention to the realization of Elisha's promise to Joash as cited in 9.181 (// 2 Kgs 13:19). Compare his (likewise added) reference in 9.175 to the fulfillment, in Jehoahaz' time, of "the prophecy of Elissai" (see 9.91) concerning the devastation of Israel by Hazael.

[686] As pointed out in the note to "in nature" at 9.178, Josephus, in relating Joash's death, burial, and succession by his son at this point, aligns himself with the sequence of LXX L, where the notices in question stand after its rendering of 13:25 (MT), whereas in MT and LXX B they occur at a much earlier point, i.e. as 13:12-13. From the biblical complex of items concerning Joash's end, Josephus omits the source notice of 13:12 (MT LXX B). In his mention of Joash's burial he goes together with MT 13:13aβ (and its equivalent in LXX L after 13:25), against LXX B 13:13, which does not cite this event.

Finally to be noted is the text-critical problem concerning the form of the name of Joash's successor in 9.185. Niese reads the name as "Joas," i.e. the same as that of the previous king, on the basis of ROMS. Given, however, that in 2 Kgs 13:13b the new king's name is "Jeroboam" (II), Marcus and Schalit (*s.v.*) read "Hieroboam," a reading attested in Codex Vaticanus as cited by J. Hudson (see Marcus' note, *ad loc.*) and throughout 9.205-215. I adopt the later reading.

[687] Josephus' synchronism for Amaziah's accession, previously cited by him in 9.171, agrees with that given in 2 Kgs 14:1 (MT and LXX BL). On his portrayal of this king in 9.186-204 (// 2 Kgs 14:1-22// 2 Chr 25:1-26:2), see Begg 2000: 225-49.

Judah executes father's assassins

was Ioade,[688] by birth a native of the city. He showed marvelous care for what was just,[689] even while still a youth.[690] Once he had embarked on public affairs and governance, he realized that he ought first to avenge his father Joas and punish the friends who had attacked him.[691] **187** Arresting these, he executed them all; however, he did no harm to their children, following the laws of Moyses, who did not sanction requiting children for their fathers' offenses.[692]

Amaziah prepares forces for campaign

188 Then, selecting an army from the tribes of Iouda and Benjamin of those who were in their prime and about twenty years of age, and having enlisted about 300,000 of these, he designated commanders of hundreds.[693] He likewise sent to the king of the Israelites to hire 100,000 soldiers for 100 talents of silver,[694] for he had decided to launch a campaign against the nations of the Amalekites, the Idumeans, and the Gabalites.[695]

At prophet's urging Amaziah dismisses Israelite mercenaries

189 When he had made preparations for the campaign and was about to march out,[696] the prophet[697] advised him to dismiss the Israelite army, for they were impious,[698] and God predicted defeat for him, should he use such allies.[699] He would, however, prove superior to the enemy, even though battling with only a few [on his side], if God wished this.[700]

---

[688] MT (2 Kgs 14:2b) יהועדין (Eng.: "Jehoaddin") / (2 Chr 25:1b) יהועדן (Eng.: "Jehoaddan"); LXX BL 2 Kgs 14:2b// LXX L 2 Chr 25:1b Ἰωαδείμ; LXX B 2 Chr 25:1b Ἰωννά; Josephus Ἰωάδη.

[689] Greek: τοῦ δικαίου προνοέω. This same phrase is used in Jehoshaphat's charge to the judges he has just named in 9.3.

[690] Josephus' highlighting of Amaziah's (moral) "precocity" is paralleled in his treatment of several other kings, i.e. Solomon (*Ant.* 8.21) and Josiah (10.50). His statement on the matter finds support in the notice of 2 Kgs 14:2aα// 2 Chr 25:1a (Amaziah acceded at age 25) taken together with that of 2 Kgs 14:5// 2 Chr 25:3 (Amaziah acted against his fathers' assassins "as soon as the royal power was in his hand"). The statement takes the place of the (qualifiedly) positive judgments pronounced on Amaziah by 2 Kgs 14:3-4// 2 Chr 25:2, the former passage mentioning the king's toleration of the high-place cult.

[691] 2 Kgs 14:5a// 2 Chr 25:3 mention merely the fact of Joash's executing his father's assassins. Josephus supplies the reference to the king's thought processes that precede this initiative. On Joash's assassination by "friends" (as opposed to the "servants" of the Bible), see 9.172.

[692] See 2 Kgs 14:5b-6// 2 Chr 25:4. In contrast to both biblical texts, Josephus does not quote the wording of Deut 24:16 (cited by him in *Ant.* 4.289), but simply alludes in a general way to the "laws of Moyses" and what he did not permit.

[693] See 2 Chr 25:5; this is the beginning of a segment (2 Chr 25:5-10), without parallel in 2 Kings 14, concerning the preparations for Amaziah's Edomite war, which Josephus will utilize in 9.188-190.

[694] In 2 Chr 25:6 Amaziah hires the mercenaries "from Israel." Josephus specifies that he procured them from the Israelite king.

[695] Josephus appends this explanation of the purpose behind Amaziah's military preparations, as related in 2 Chr 25:5-6. He anticipates the name of the 2nd targeted people from 2 Kgs 14:7// 2 Chr 25:11, where it is called, respectively, "the Edomites" and "the men of Seir." The 3 peoples cited by Josephus appear together as enemies of Israel in Ps 83:6; see also Tg. 2 Chr 25:14, where the MT reference to "the gods of the men of *Seir*" becomes "the idols of the men of *Gebal*." Cf. further Begg 2000: 228-9.

[696] Josephus supplies this transitional phrase.

[697] MT LXX BL 2 Chr 25:7 calls Amaziah's anonymous interlocutor "a man of God." Josephus' designation finds a parallel in Tg.'s "the prophet of the Lord." *S. ʿOlam Rab.* 20.21 identifies the anonymous biblical figure with Amoz, the father of Isaiah (Isa 1:1) and brother of Amaziah himself.

[698] Compare 2 Chr 25:7, where the man of God motivates his warning against Amaziah's allowing the mercenaries to accompany him with the declaration "for the Lord is not with Israel, with all these Ephraimites."

[699] Compare 2 Chr 25:8a, where Amaziah is warned that if allows the mercenaries to accompany him (see 25:7), "... God will cast you down before the enemy."

[700] The biblical man of God concludes his words to Amaziah in 2 Chr 25:8b with a reference to God's "power to help or cast down." Josephus has the prophet end with a more definite assurance for Amaziah, should he obey his admonition.

190 The king was unhappy about the hire-price he had already given the king of the Israelites,[701] but the prophet urged him to do what seemed good to God, for there would be much wealth for him from him [God].[702] He did, in fact, dismiss them, saying that he was giving them the hire-price as a gift, while he himself campaigned with his own force against the above-mentioned nations.[703]

191 Defeating them in battle, he killed 10,000 of them,[704] and took as many alive.[705] These he led to the great rock that is opposite Arabia,[706] from which he cast them down. He also led away much plunder and uncountable riches from those nations.[707]

Amaziah's victory

192 While Amasias was engaged in these things, those of the Israelites whom he had dismissed after hiring them became indignant at this and thought their dismissal an outrage, for [they claimed] they would not have suffered this if they were not held in contempt. They came against his kingdom and, advancing as far as Bethsemeron,[708] plundered the country, took many beasts of burden, and killed 3,000 people.[709]

Dismissed Israelites run amok

(9.2) 193 Amasias, for his part, became elated over his victory and achievements and because of them began to overlook God.[710] He continued rather to adore those [gods] that he had brought from the country of the Amalekites.[711]

Amaziah worships gods of enemy

---

[701] Josephus turns the king's question to the man of God about the money already paid by him of 2 Chr 25:9a into an editorial remark about Amaziah's state of mind in face of the prophet's preceding admonition.

[702] Josephus prefaces the prophet's response of 2 Chr 25:9b, assuring Amaziah of divine compensation, with a call to do what pleases God.

[703] Josephus combines the notices of 2 Chr 25:10a (Amaziah dismisses the mercenaries) and 11a (Amaziah leads out his own troops), while leaving for a later point (see 9.192) the intervening mention of the mercenaries' angry response to their dismissal (25:10b). The "nations" to which Josephus alludes here are the 3 named in 9.188.

[704] Josephus draws this datum from 2 Kgs 14:7a// 2 Chr 25:11b, while omitting the biblical identification of the battle site, i.e. "the Valley of Salt". Given that in his presentation Amaziah's campaign is directed against 3 distinct peoples (see 9.188, 190), he likewise does not take over the Bible's identifications of the casualties as "Edomites" (14:7a)/ "men of Seir" (25:11b).

[705] Josephus draws his mention of these 10,000 live captives from 2 Chr 25:12a (no parallel in 2 Kgs 14:7).

[706] Compare 2 Chr 25:12, where the captives are hurled from "the top of a rock" (MT: הסלע). In MT 2 Kgs 14:7b the word סלע seems to be the proper name of a site (RSV: "Sela"), which Amaziah captures and re-names "Joktheel." Josephus' notation concerning the location of the "rock" (Greek: πέτρα) from which the captives are hurled has a counterpart in *Ant.* 4.82, where he localizes Aaron's death at "a place in Arabia ... now called Petra" (Greek: Πέτρα). Whereas 2 Chr 25:12 at-

tributes the killing of the captives to the Judeans in general, Josephus' formulation ascribes the deed to Amaziah personally.

[707] This notice has no equivalent in either biblical account of Amaziah's Edomite campaign. By means of the addition, Josephus highlights the realization of the prophet's promise in 9.190 that, if Amaziah does what "seems good to God," he will gain "much wealth from him [God]."

[708] MT (2 Chr 25:13) בית־חורון (Eng.: "Beth-horon"); LXX BL Βαιθωρών; Josephus Βηθσεμήρων. The Bible states that the irate mercenaries overran a territory extending "from Samaria to Beth-horon."

[709] Josephus combines into a continuous sequence the separate notices of 2 Chr 25:10b (earlier passed over by him) and 13 concerning the mercenaries' reaction to their dismissal by Amaziah. He adds the reference to the beasts of burden seized by them. The segment 2 Chr 25:13-16 concerning events contemporaneous with and immediately subsequent to Amaziah's victory, which Josephus reproduces in 9.192-196a, has no parallel in 2 Kings 14.

[710] Josephus prefaces the Chronicler's following story (2 Chr 25:14-16; no parallel in 2 Kings 14) of Amaziah's worship of the conquered enemy gods with this explanatory remark that portrays the king's initiative as an instance of success-induced *hubris*. This is Josephus' only use of the expression "overlook God" (Greek: θεὸν ὑπεροράω).

[711] Compare 2 Chr 25:14, which speaks of Amaziah's bringing back "the gods of the men of Seir" and worshiping these. Josephus highlights the senselessness of the king's deed by making the gods in question

Prophet–king confrontation

194 The prophet approached him[712] and said that he was astonished that he [Amasias] should think these to be gods who had neither profited their own people by whom they were honored, nor delivered them from his hands. Instead, they had overlooked[713] [the fact] that many of them had been annihilated and that they themselves had been taken captive. For they had been brought to Hierosolyma in this way, as someone might lead an enemy he had taken prisoner.[714]

195 With these [words] he provoked the king to wrath;[715] he ordered the prophet to keep quiet, threatening to punish him if he meddled.[716] [The prophet] said that he would be quiet, but predicted that God would not leave unpunished[717] the innovations he [Amasias] had initiated.[718]

Amaziah challenges Joash of Israel

196 Amasias, however, could not restrain himself because of his successes,[719] which he had received from the very God against whom he was committing his outrages.[720] Becoming prideful,[721] he wrote[722] to Joas, the king of the Israelites, directing him, along with all his people, to obey him, just as they had earlier obeyed his ancestors David and Solomon. If he did not wish to be reasonable,[723] he should realize that the rule would be decided by war.[724]

Joash warns Amaziah

197 Joas wrote back[725] as follows: "King Joas to King Amasias.[726] On Mount

those of Israel's arch-enemy, the Amalekites (whom he mentioned as the 1st of the 3 peoples against whom Amaziah campaigns in 9.188).

[712] Josephus omits the opening reference to God's "anger" at Amaziah in 2 Chr 25:15a, which prompts him to dispatch "a prophet." In the OL text of 2 Chr 25:15 cited by Lucifer Calaritanus, *De non parcendo in Deum delinquientibus* 5.36 Amaziah's interlocutor is called "Baneas." Whereas 2 Chronicles 25 uses different designations for the one confronting the king, i.e. "man of God" (v. 7) and "prophet" (v. 15), thus leaving it unclear whether the reference is to the same figure, Josephus uses the identical title ("the prophet"; see 9.189, 194) both times, this suggesting a double intervention by a single divine envoy.

[713] Greek: ὑπεροράω. This is the same verb used in 9.193 of Amaziah's "overlooking God."

[714] Josephus expands considerably on the prophet's summary allusion to the impotence of the captured gods in 2 Chr 25:15b, highlighting the foolishness of Amaziah's adopting their worship.

[715] Josephus supplies this reference to the king's emotional state upon hearing the prophet's words.

[716] See 2 Chr 25:16a, where Amaziah's response to the prophet concludes with the threatening question "why should you be put to death?"

[717] Greek: ἀμελέω. Josephus uses this verb with God as subject also in *Ant.* 4.13; 5.31; 11.300.

[718] See 2 Chr 25:16b, where the prophet predicts the divine destruction of Amaziah for having adopted the enemy gods and not listening to his advice. Josephus' reference to Amaziah's "innovations," using a participial form of the verb νεωτερίζω, introduces a

Greek root that he frequently applies to the reprobate activities of the Jewish rebels of his own time to whom Amaziah is hereby assimilated; see Begg 2000: 237, n. 47.

[719] Josephus' wording here has a close parallel in his comment about most people's inability to retain self-mastery when successful in *Ant.* 6.63.

[720] Josephus adds this psychological note that recalls his (also added) reference to Amaziah's "becoming elated over his victory and achievements" in 9.193 and highlights the irony of the situation, in which the king abandons the source of his victory in order to devote himself to the defeated foreign gods.

[721] Greek: φρονηματίζομαι. Josephus' one remaining use of this verb is in *Ant.* 5.222, where it has the sense "to take heart, summon up courage."

[722] In 2 Kgs 14:8 Amaziah sends "messengers" to Joash, while in 2 Chr 25:17 he simply "sends" to him.

[723] Greek: εὐγνωμοέω. Josephus' only other use of this verb is in *Ant.* 17.240.

[724] Josephus elaborates on Amaziah's cryptic challenge to Joash as cited in 2 Kgs 14:8// 2 Chr 25:17: "Come, let us look one another in the face." In particular, he adds the demand that Joash and his people submit to the Davidic dynasty, of which Amaziah is the current representative.

[725] Josephus' Joash responds in writing to Amaziah's written message to himself, whereas in 2 Kgs 14:9a// 2 Chr 25:18a he simply "sends" to the latter.

[726] Josephus supplies this standard epistolary salutation formula in line with his depiction of Joash responding to Amaziah in writing; see previous note.

Liban there was a very tall and lofty cypress[727] and a thistle. The latter sent to the cypress in order to betroth its daughter to the cypress's son in marriage. While it was saying these things, a certain wild beast passed by and trampled down the thistle.[728] **198** This then will be a lesson to you[729] not to strive after great things nor, because you were lucky in battle against the Amalekites, should you be conceited[730] about that and expose your kingdom to dangers."[731]

(9.3) 199 When Amasias read this, he was still more incited to [undertake] the campaign, God, I suppose, inducing[732] him into this, in order that he might exact judgment on him for his acting lawlessly towards himself.[733] Once he had set out with his force against Joas and was about to join battle, God instilled in Amasias' army a sudden fear and dismay,[734] as he does with those towards whom he is not benevolent, and it turned to flight.[735] **200** Before it even came to combat, they were scattered in their fright, and it happened that Amasias, who had been left alone, was taken captive by the enemy.[736] Joas threatened him with death, if he did not persuade the Hierosolymites to open the gates to receive him into the city along with his army.

201 Amasias, out of necessity and fright[737] for his life, did cause the enemy [king] to be admitted.[738] And he, after breaching some of the wall for about 400 cubits,[739] entered Hierosolyma in his chariot through the breach, leading Amasias captive.[740]

Amaziah's army panicked; king captured

Joash's measures in Jerusalem

---

[727] 2 Kgs 14:9 and 2 Chr 25:18 both speak of a "cedar." Josephus adds the double characterization of the tree, thereby accentuating the discrepancy between it and the low-lying "thistle."

[728] See 2 Kgs 14:9aβ// 2 Chr 25:18aββb.

[729] This added phrase makes explicit the intended link between Joash's fable (2 Kgs 14:9// 2 Chr 25:18) and the admonition he proceeds to address to Amaziah (14:10// 25:19).

[730] Greek: γαυρόομαι. This verb is *hapax* in Josephus. It recalls the reference to Amaziah's "becoming prideful" in 9.196.

[731] See 2 Kgs 14:10// 2 Chr 25:19. In both biblical texts the reference is to Amaziah's smiting "Edom." As in 9.193, Josephus substitutes mention of the Amalekites, this suggesting that they were Amaziah's primary target among the 3 peoples attacked by him (see 9.188).

[732] Greek: παρομάω. Josephus uses this verb with God as subject twice elsewhere (*Ant.* 4.111; 11:3), both times in a positive sense. Compare *Ant.* 8.409 and 10.76, where the subject is "fate" and "destiny," respectively and where the term has the negative sense of "to lead astray."

[733] Like 2 Chr 25:20, but in contrast to 2 Kgs 14:10, Josephus makes explicit reference to the divine agency operative in Amaziah's refusal to heed Joash's warning. His allusion to Amaziah's "dealing lawlessly" takes the place of the Chronicler's mention of "their [the Judeans'] seeking the gods of Edom" as that which prompts God to cause the king to disregard the warning given him.

[734] Greek: φόβος καὶ κατάπληξις. This collocation

occurs only here in Josephus.

[735] Josephus goes beyond 2 Kgs 14:11b-12// 2 Chr 25:21-22 in making explicit and emphatic mention of the divine involvement in Judah's defeat, this recalling his immediately preceding reference (9.199) to God's "inducing" Amaziah to disregard Joash's warning. Conversely, he leaves aside the biblical localization of the battle-site, i.e. "Beth-shemesh which belongs to Judah."

[736] See 2 Kgs 14:13aα// 2 Chr 25:23aα. Josephus amplifies the biblical notices on Amaziah's capture with mention of the scattering of the Judean army and the king's abandonment.

[737] Greek: ἀνάγκη καὶ δέος. This wordpair occurs also in *War* 5.427.

[738] Neither 2 Kings 14 nor 2 Chronicles 25 mentions these developments surrounding Joash's arrival at Jerusalem (14:13aβ// 25:23aβ). The addition helps explain how the Israelite king got immediate and uncontested control of the city, as the biblical accounts presuppose. It likewise highlights the contrast between Amaziah's earlier "elation" (9.190) and his present craven fear for his life.

[739] See 2 Kgs 14:13b// 2 Chr 25:23b. Josephus omits the biblical indication concerning the precise stretch of wall leveled by Joash, i.e. "from the Ephraim Gate to the Corner Gate."

[740] Josephus adds this item—with its reminiscence of contemporary Roman triumphal processions—to the biblical accounts of Joash's measures at Jerusalem (2 Kgs 14:13-14// 2 Chr 25:23-24). The addition highlights, yet again, the humiliation of the once "proudful" (9.198) Amaziah, who earlier brought the captured

202 Having become lord of Hierosolyma in this way,[741] [Joas] removed the treasures belonging to God and carried off whatever gold and silver Amasias had in his palace. Then, dismissing him from his captivity, he set out for Samareia.[742]

Amaziah's assassination and burial

203 These matters concerning the Hierosolymites occurred in the fourteenth year of Amasias' reign.[743] Afterwards, when plotted against by his friends,[744] he fled to the city of Lachisa.[745] He was done away with by the plotters, who sent [men] there to kill him.[746] Bringing his body to Hierosolyma, they interred it royally.[747] **204** Amasias ended his life thus because of the innovations involved in his neglect of God,[748] after living fifty-four years[749] and reigning as king for twenty-nine.[750] His son named Ozias[751] succeeded him.[752]

Jeroboam II (Hieroboam) introduced

(10.1) 205 In the fifteenth year of the reign of Amasias,[753] Hieroboam,[754] the son of Joas, began his reign of forty[755] years as king of the Israelites in Samareia. This

---

enemy gods to Jerusalem (see 9.194), but is now himself "led captive" into the city.

[741] Josephus supplies this transitional phrase.

[742] See 2 Kgs 14:14// 2 Chr 25:24. Josephus' explicit reference to Joash's release of Amaziah takes the place of the biblical statement that Joash carried off "hostages" (MT LXX L 2 Chr 25:24 mention an "Obed-edom" by name) as well as the temple and palace treasures. He has no parallel to the complex of closing notices for Joash, paralleling those already given in 2 Kgs 13:12-13, which in MT and LXX B 2 Kgs 14:15-16 immediately follow mention of the king's return to Samaria in 14:14; see following note.

[743] Josephus obtains this date for Jerusalem's capture by Joash on the basis of the figures given in 2 Kgs 14:2a// 2 Chr 25:1a (Amaziah ruled a total of *29* years) and 2 Kgs 14:17// 2 Chr 25:25 (Amaziah survives Joash's death—which Josephus, in accord with the sequence of MT LXX 2 Kgs 14:14-16 [see previous note], presupposes to have taken place immediately after his return from Jerusalem—by *15* years). Subtracting 15 from 29, Josephus arrives at Amaziah's 14th regnal year as the date of Joash's triumph.

[744] In 2 Kgs 14:19aα// 2 Chr 25:27aα an unspecified "they" conspires against Amaziah, Chronicles adding that the conspiracy arose "from the time when he [Amaziah] turned away from the Lord." Josephus heightens the pathos of the episode by making the conspirators the king's own "friends." In so doing, he likewise establishes a more specific link between Amaziah and his father Joash, who also, in Josephus' presentation, is assassinated by his "friends" (see 9.172).

[745] MT (2 Kgs 14:19aβ// 2 Chr 25:27aβ) לכיש (Eng.: "Lachish"); LXX BL Λαχείς; Josephus Λάχισα (this is the reading of ROE, followed by Niese; Marcus reads Λάχεισα with MS).

[746] See 2 Kgs 14:19b// 2 Chr 25:27b.

[747] 2 Kgs 14:20// 2 Chr 25:28 specify that the corpse was conveyed "upon horses" and that Amaziah was buried "with his fathers in the city of David."

[748] Josephus appends this theological commentary on Amaziah's sorry end. Its phrase "neglect of God" (Greek: πρὸς τὸν θεὸν ὀλιγωρία, used also in *Ant.* 5.179 [the Israelites' "neglect of the Deity"] and 9.257 [subject: King Ahaz]) recalls the reference to the king's "beginning to overlook God" in 9.193, while its term "innovations" represents the same Greek participle employed by the prophet in his denunciation of Amaziah in 9.194.

[749] Josephus obtains this figure for Amaziah's lifespan by combining the notices of 2 Kgs 14:2a// 2 Chr 25:1a on the king's age at accession (25) and length of reign (29).

[750] This figure for Amaziah's length of reign corresponds to that cited in 2 Kgs 14:2a// 2 Chr 25:1a.

[751] MT (2 Kgs 14:21) עזריה (Eng.: "Azariah")/ (2 Chr 26:1) עזיהו (Eng.: "Uzziah"); LXX BL 2 Kgs 14:21 Ἀζαρίας; LXX B 2 Chr 26:1 Ὀχοζείας; LXX L 2 Chr 26:1 and Josephus Ὀζίας.

[752] See 2 Kgs 14:21// 2 Chr 26:1. Josephus leaves aside the biblical indication that Azariah/Uzziah was made king by "all the people of Judah." He likewise passes over the source notice for Amaziah of 2 Kgs 14:18// 2 Chr 25:26.

[753] This synchronism for Jeroboam's accession agrees with that given in 2 Kgs 14:23 (MT LXX BL). Following the sequence of 2 Kings 14, Josephus "interrupts" his account of Azariah/ Uzziah of Judah in order to give his presentation of Jeroboam II (into which he incorporates a greatly compressed version of the story of Jonah) in 9.205-216; on this complex, see Begg 2000: 251-72; on the Josephan Jonah, see Feldman 1998a: 393-415.

[754] MT (2 Kgs 14:23) ירבעם (Eng.: "Jeroboam"); LXX BL Ἱεροβοάμ; Josephus Ἱερόβοαμος. On the text-critical problem of this king's name in 9.185, where Josephus first mentions him, see note to "Hieroboam" there.

[755] MT and LXX BL* 2 Kgs 14:23b assign Jeroboam II a *41*-year reign. The LXX L MSS 127 and 93

king was an insulter of God[756] and terribly lawless; he adored idols[757] and committed many perverse and strange acts.[758] To the people of the Israelites, however, he was the cause of countless good things.[759]

206 A certain Jonas[760] prophesied to him[761] that he ought to make war on the Syrians in order to defeat their force and enlarge his own kingdom, in the northern part as far as the city of Amath, and on the south to Lake Asphaltitis.[762] **207** For these were of old the borders of Chananaia, as the general Iesous had fixed them in ancient times.[763] Campaigning therefore against the Syrians, Hierobam[764] subjugated their entire country, as Jonas had prophesied.[765]

(10.2) 208 Having promised to transmit an accurate [account] of events, I have thought it necessary, however, to relate as well whatever I found recorded in the Hebrew books concerning this prophet.[766] For he was directed by God[767] to go to the kingdom of Ninuos,[768] and once there to proclaim in the city that it would lose its rule.[769] Being frightened,[770] however, he did not go off [there], but ran away from God[771] to the city of Iope.[772] Finding a boat and embarking,[773] he sailed for Tarsos[774]

Jeroboam recovers Israelite territory in accordance with prophecy of Jonah (Jonas)

Jonah evades God's commission

---

give him a markedly shorter reign, of, respectively, 16 and 15 years.

[756] Greek: εἰς τὸν θεὸν ὑβριστής. This expression is *hapax* in Josephus.

[757] Greek: εἴδωλα σέβομαι. Josephus uses this same phrase of the reprobate King Joram of Judah in 9.99.

[758] This is Josephus' free variation on the stereotyped language of 2 Kgs 14:24, which charges Jeroboam II with persisting in the sins of the first Jeroboam.

[759] Josephus supplies this transitional notice that has in view the Jeroboam's military achievements he will relate in 9.206-207.

[760] MT (2 Kgs 14:25) יונה (Eng.: "Jonah"); LXX BL Ἰωνᾶ; Josephus Ἰωνᾶς. Josephus omits the biblical name of the prophet's father ("Amittai") and his place of origin ("Gath-heper"), as well as his title ("his [God's] servant").

[761] In having Jonah address Jeroboam directly, Josephus goes beyond the wording of 2 Kgs 14:25 itself, which merely states that the king's conquests were "in accordance with the word which he [God] spoke by his servant Jonah...."

[762] The area recovered by Jeroboam according to 2 Kgs 14:25 extended "from the entrance of Hamath as far as the Sea of the Arabah [i.e. the Dead Sea]." Josephus here turns into a prophetic exhortation concerning what Jeroboam ought to do the biblical notice about what he actually did achieve (which he will subsequently also reproduce in shortened form; see 9.208). On "Lake Asphaltitis" (= the Dead Sea"), see note to "Lake Asphaltitis" at 9.7.

[763] Josephus supplies this reminiscence of Joshua's earlier fixing of Israel's borders (see *Ant.* 5.80-89), perhaps under the inspiration of the reference in 2 Kgs 14:25a to Jeroboam's "*restoring* the border of Israel."

[764] There is the alternative Josephan form of the

king's name, found in 9.228 as well. Elsewhere, Josephus gives the name as "Hieroboam."

[765] With this statement Josephus reproduces—in shortened form—the content of the notice of 2 Kgs 14:25 on Jeroboam's achievements, while also underscoring the realization of Jonah's prophetic announcement as formulated by him in 9.206.

[766] By means of this notice Josephus makes the transition to the condensed version of the Book of Jonah (9.208-214) that he incorporates into his account of Jeroboam II (9.205-207, 215// 2 Kgs 14:23-29), inspired by the fact that the Kings passage itself mentions "Jonah" in 14:25. Whereas neither Kings nor the Book of Jonah ever applies the title "prophet" to Jonah, Josephus does so a total of 4 times in 9.208-214; cf. also his double mention of Jonah's "prophesying" in 9.206, 207.

[767] This formulation replaces the stereotypical expression of Jonah 1:1: "the word of the Lord came to...."

[768] MT (Jonah 1:1) נינוה (Eng.: "Nineveh"); LXX Νινευή; Josephus Νινύος (this is the reading of RO, which Niese follows; Marcus reads Νίνος with MSP). Josephus mentions the founding of "Ninos" by "Assouras" (Asshur) in *Ant.* 1.143 // Gen 10:11.

[769] In Jonah 1:2a Jonah is instructed simply to "cry against" Nineveh; Josephus supplies a content for this "cry." Conversely, he leaves aside the motivation for God's sending Jonah to the city cited in 1:2b, i.e. "for their wickedness has come up before me."

[770] Josephus supplies this reference to the emotional state that prompts Jonah's attempt to evade his commission.

[771] Josephus avoids the anthropomorphic reference to Jonah's fleeing the Lord's "face" of Jonah 1:3aα. The phrase "run away from God" (Greek: ἀποδιδράσκει τὸν

Storm at sea
leads to
Jonah's being
thrown
overboard

in Cilicia.[775] **209** Now a very severe storm arose and the vessel was in danger of sinking.[776] The sailors, the pilots, and even the ship owner[777] made vows of thank-offerings, should they escape the sea.[778] Jonas, on the other hand, wrapped himself up and kept to himself, not imitating what he saw the others doing.[779] **210** When the waves increased still more and the sea was made even more violent by the winds,[780] they [the sailors] surmised—as was natural—that one of those sailing with them was the cause of the storm and resolved to learn who this might be by means of the lot.[781] **211** When therefore the prophet was taken by their lot-casting,[782] they inquired where he was from and what his occupation was.[783] He said that he was a Hebrew by race[784] and a prophet of the greatest God.[785] He therefore advised them, if they wished to elude the present danger, to eject him into the open sea, for he was the cause of the storm.[786]

212 At first, they did not dare [to do this], judging it an impiety for them to cast out to certain loss a man who was a stranger and who had entrusted his life to them.[787] Finally, however, with calamity pressing heavily upon them and with the

---

θεόν) occurs also in *War* 3.373, where Josephus uses it in his address to his compatriots, urging them not to commit suicide.

[772] MT (Jonah 1:3) יפו (Eng.: "Joppa"); LXX Ἰώππη; Josephus Ἰόπη.

[773] Josephus omits the reference to Jonah's "paying his fare" and the 2nd mention of his going "away from the face of the Lord" of Jonah 1:3b.

[774] MT (Jonah 1:3) תרשיש (Eng.: "Tarshish"); LXX Θαρσις; Josephus Τάρσος.

[775] Jonah 1:3 does not further identify "Tarshish"; Josephus makes the same linkage between "Tarsos" and "Cilicia" in *War* 7.238.

[776] See Jonah 1:4. Josephus omits the biblical reference to the Lord's role in sending the storm.

[777] Jonah 1:5 mentions only the sailors in general. The term ναύκληρος ("ship owner") is *hapax* in Josephus.

[778] Jonah 1:5aα speaks more generally of "each man crying to his god." Josephus' wording may be inspired by Jonah 1:16, where, following the cessation of the storm, the sailors "offer a sacrifice to the Lord and make vows." Josephus leaves aside the reference (Jonah 1:5aβ) to the sailors' casting the ship's cargo into the sea.

[779] Josephus modifies the description of Jonah 1:5b, where the fugitive prophet descends into the inner part of the ship and there goes to sleep; in his presentation Jonah seems to remain on deck, but refrains from joining his shipmates' vow-making. Josephus omits the confrontation, recounted in Jonah 1:6, between Jonah and the ship's captain in the hull of the ship, in which Jonah is called on to "cry to his god" as the others are doing.

[780] Anticipating the notice of Jonah 1:11b ("for the sea grew more and more tempestuous"), Josephus mentions this development at this point, so as to account for the sailors' recourse to a new expedient, i.e. the casting of the lot to identify the guilty party as recounted in Jonah 1:7a.

[781] See Jonah 1:7a. Josephus supplies the reference to the sailors' "surmise," which leads to their decision to use the lot.

[782] See Jonah 1:7b.

[783] Of the 4 questions that the sailors address to Jonah in Jonah 1:8, Josephus passes over the 1st and 4th, i.e. those concerning the source of their affliction and his country, respectively.

[784] In having Jonah call himself a "Hebrew," Josephus agrees with MT Jonah 1:9a, whereas in LXX he identifies himself as a "servant/slave [Greek: δοῦλος] of the Lord."

[785] This is the same designation (Greek: προφήτης τοῦ μεγίστου θεοῦ) Josephus uses of Elijah in *Ant.* 8.319. It takes the place of Jonah's claim to be one who "fears the Lord" in Jonah 1:9b. Josephus omits the appended account of the crew's further questions to Jonah in 1:10-11a, as well as the reference to the worsening of the storm in 1:11b (anticipated by him in 9.210).

[786] See Jonah 1:12. In Josephus Jonah offers this advice on his own, whereas in Jonah 1:11-12 he does so in response to a question by the crew. Jonah's admission here about his being the "cause of the storm" confirms the crew's "surmise" on the matter as cited in 9.210.

[787] This notice takes the place of the mention of the crew's "rowing hard towards land" as their first, implicitly negative response to Jonah's proposal (Jonah 1:12) in Jonah 1:13a. In reworking the biblical presentation here, Josephus likewise supplies a (positive) rationale

vessel on the verge of going under, being urged on as well by the prophet and being fearful for their own safety, they cast him into the sea.[788]

213 The storm subsided.[789] The story, however, has it[790] that [Jonas], having been swallowed up by a whale for three days and as many nights,[791] was spit out[792] on [the shore of] the Euxine Sea, alive and uninjured in body.[793] **214** From there, once he had prayed God to grant him pardon for his offenses,[794] he went off to the city of Ninos.[795] Standing where he could be heard,[796] he proclaimed that, after a little [while], they would in a very short time[797] forfeit their rule of Asia;[798] having disclosed these things, he departed.[799] I have related the account about him as I found it recorded.[800]

Rescued by fish, Jonah carries out mandate

---

for the crew's initial unreadiness to do as Jonah had suggested.

[788] Josephus combines the notices of Jonah 1:13b (the storm prevents the sailors from making any headway) and 1:15a (their throwing Jonah into the sea), passing over their intervening appeal "to the Lord" in 1:14, in which they appear to become Jewish converts; see next note.

[789] See Jonah 1:15b. Josephus omits the content of 1:16, where the crew responds to their delivery with "fear of the Lord," sacrifices, and vows, just as he left aside their earlier appeal to the Lord's mercy prior to their casting Jonah overboard (1:14). In both instances, sensitivity to Roman concerns over the issue of Jewish "proselytizing" appears to be operative; see Feldman 1998a: 409-10.

[790] Greek: λόγος. With this formula Jonah invites his readers to make up their own minds about the following "fish story." Feldman (1998a: 403) points out that Herodotus (1.24) uses a similar formula ("they say [λέγουσι]") in introducing the mythological tale of Arion who, having been thrown overboard, is rescued by a dolphin.

[791] See Jonah 2:1 (Eng. 1:17). As in the case of the storm (see 9.209), Josephus omits the biblical reference to God's role in the fish's swallowing Jonah. He reserves to a later point his version of the thanksgiving psalm that Jonah pronounced during his time in the fish according to Jonah 2:2-10 (Eng. 2:1-9); see 9.214.

[792] Greek: ἐκβράζω. Josephus's one other use of this verb is in *War* 3.427.

[793] In Jonah 2:11 (Eng. 2:10) the fish, at the Lord's command, vomits Jonah out "on dry land." Marcus (*ad loc.*) suggests that Josephus' added specification that the site was "on [the shore of] the "Euxine [Black] Sea" reflects his assumption that this body of water "would be the nearest sea to Nineveh," Jonah's God-designated destination according to 9.209.

[794] This allusion to Jonah's prayer both drastically condenses and gives a different content to Jonah's "thanksgiving psalm" as cited in Jonah 2:2-10 (Eng. 2:1-9), turning the biblical prophet's extended reminis-

cence of his affliction, his appeal to God and the latter's hearing of this, as well as his concluding promise of praise and statement of confidence there into a summary notice on Jonah's asking pardon for his (unspecified) "offenses." In addition, Josephus has Jonah utter his prayer after, rather than during, his confinement in the fish.

[795] See Jonah 3:3aα. Josephus omits the biblical references to the new divine word to Jonah (Jonah 3:1-2, 3aβ) that prompts him to finally head for Nineveh. In his presentation, Jonah, having recognized the wrongfulness of his earlier shirking of his commission, now does this on his own.

[796] This transitional phrase replaces the biblical notices on the vast size of Nineveh (Jonah 3:3b) and Jonah's proceeding a day's journey into it (3:4a).

[797] Greek: πάνυ χρόνον; this is the reading of ROSPELat, which Niese and Marcus follow. M and the *Ed. pr.* have πάλιν ("again").

[798] Jonah's message in Jonah 3:4b is more precise and ominous: within 40 (MT; LXX 3) days Nineveh will be "overthrown." Josephus' rendering of the prophet's proclamation picks up on the words that God confides to Jonah in 9.209, now with the added specification that Nineveh will be deprived of its rule over Asia within "a very short time."

[799] Josephus appends this notice concerning what Jonah did once he had delivered his message in Nineveh as recounted in Jonah 3:4b.

[800] This closing formula for Josephus' Jonah story (9.208-214) reads oddly in that, in fact, he leaves completely unused the whole concluding and climatic portion of the book (Jonah 3:5-4:11), featuring Nineveh's repentance, God's relenting, and the disputation between Jonah and the Deity regarding the latter's sparing of the city. Two main factors would seem to be at work in this large-scale omission on Josephus' part, namely Roman concerns about conversions to Judaism (for which the repentance of Nineveh—like the sailors' previous turning to the Lord, also eliminated by Josephus—might seem a precedent) and the realization that gentile readers would likely find Jonah's resent-

Zechariah (Zacharias) succeeds Jereboam

215 King Hieroboam, after living a life of total well-being[801] and ruling for forty years,[802] died and was buried in Samareia.[803] His son Zacharias[804] succeeded to the kingship.

Uzziah (Ozias) of Judah introduced

216 In the same way also Ozias,[805] the son of Amasias, when Hieroboam had already been reigning as king for fourteen years,[806] began to rule as king over the two tribes in Hierosolyma; his mother's name was Achia,[807] by birth a native of the city. He was good and just[808] by nature, magnanimous, and most industrious[809] regarding affairs.[810]

Uzziah's military ventures

217 Campaigning against the Palestinoi[811] and vanquishing them in battle, he took their cities, Gitta[812] and Iamneia,[813] by storm and tore down their walls.[814] After this campaign he invaded the Arabs bordering on Egypt[815] and, having founded a city on the Red Sea, stationed a garrison in it.[816]

---

ment at God's sparing of a pagan city as conveyed in the concluding dialogue between him and the Deity offputting. See further Begg 2000: 271-2 and Höffken 2001: 399-400 (who argues that Josephus' non-mention of the Ninevites' repentance and God's acceptance of this is to be explained rather in terms of the historian's subsequent presentation in which Nineveh, in accordance with Nahum's prediction, is destroyed [see 9.239-242]; this happening, according to Höffken, would make better sense if, as in Josephus' account, there has been no previous repentance by the city and pardoning of it by God).

[801] This added notice on the positive course of Jeroboam's life recalls Josephus' statement in 9.205 that, his personal depravity notwithstanding, the king was a source of "countless good things" to his people.

[802] Josephus repeats this datum from 9.205, once again diverging from 2 Kgs 14:23b, which assigns Jeroboam *41* regnal years.

[803] Compare 2 Kgs 14:29a, which mentions Jeroboam's death, but not his burial. Josephus omits the source notice for the king (2 Kgs 14:28).

[804] MT (2 Kgs 14:29b) זכריה (Eng.: "Zechariah"); LXX B Ἀζαρίας υἱὸς Ἀμεσσείου; LXX L and Josephus Ζαχαρίας.

[805] Josephus introduced "Ozias," called alternatively "Uzziah" in 2 Chronicles and "Azariah" in 2 Kings, in 9.204. On Josephus' presentation (9.216-227) of this king—which follows the more expansive account of 2 Chr 26:3-23 in preference to the summary treatment given him in 2 Kgs 15:1-7—, see Begg 2000: 273-84.

[806] Josephus' synchronism for Uzziah/Azariah's accession differs markedly from that of 2 Kgs 15:1 (MT LXX BL*), which dates that event to Jeroboam's *27th* year (the LXX L MS 127 reads 25th).

[807] MT (2 Kgs 15:2b) יכליהו (Eng.: "Jecoliah")/ (2 Chr 26:3b) יכיליה (Eng.: "Jecoliah"); LXX B 2 Kgs 15:2b Χαλειά; LXX L 2 Kgs 15:2b// LXX L 2 Chr 26:3b Ἰεχελειά; LXX B 2 Chr 26:3b Χααιά; Josephus Ἀχία.

Josephus agrees with all the biblical textual witnesses in calling her a Jerusalemite.

[808] Greek: ἀγαθὸς καὶ δίκαιος. This collocation is used of Jehonadab in 9.132.

[809] Greek: φιλοπονώτατος. This is Josephus' only use of the superlative form of the adjective φιλόπονος ("industrious").

[810] This evaluation replaces the stereotyped reference to Uzziah/Ahaziah's "doing what was right in the eyes of the Lord" as his father had done of 2 Kgs 15:3 // 2 Chr 26:4. Josephus has no equivalent to the respective "qualifications" of their positive judgments of the king found in the biblical texts, i.e. his toleration of the cult on the high places (2 Kgs 15:4) and his seeking God and being prospered by God (only) during the lifetime of "Zechariah" (2 Chr 26:5).

[811] See 2 Chr 26:6aα. Josephus here begins his reproduction (9.217-226) of a long segment of 2 Chronicles 26 (vv. 6-20a) that lacks a parallel in 2 Kings 15.

[812] MT (2 Chr 26:6) גת (Eng.: "Gath"); LXX BL Γέθ; Josephus Γίττα.

[813] MT (2 Chr 26:6) יבנה (Eng.: "Jabneh"); LXX B Ἀβεννήρ; LXX L Ἰαβνή; Josephus Ἰάμνεια (this is the reading proposed by J. Hudson on the basis of Codex Vaticanus, and adopted by Niese and Marcus; the remaining codices read Ἰαμνία). 2 Chr 26:6 adds a 3rd city, i.e. "Ashdod" (MT)/ "Azotos" (LXX BL).

[814] See 2 Chr 26:6aβ. Josephus adds the mention of Uzziah's initial "storming" of the cities. Conversely, he leaves aside the statements of 26:6b-7a about Uzziah's building cities in the territory of Ashdod/Azotus (see previous note) and elsewhere in Philistine territory and God's helping him against the Philistines.

[815] 2 Chr 26:7b mentions God's assistance in Uzziah's campaign against "the Arabs," whom it localizes "in Gurbal" and with whom it associates the "Meunites."

[816] Josephus here makes his delayed use of the "stray" notice on Azariah's/Uzziah's "building" of

218 Then, after subjugating the Ammanites and fixing the tribute they were to pay and gaining control of everything up to the borders of the Egyptians,[817] he began to be concerned for the future of Hierosolyma.[818] For whatever [part] of the walls had fallen down, due either to [the passage of] time or the neglect of the kings before him, this he rebuilt and constructed.[819] He did the same with whatever had been torn down by the king of the Israelites [Joas] when, after taking his father Amasias captive, he entered the city.[820] **219** He also erected many towers, each fifty cubits [in height].[821] He likewise installed garrisons in the desert regions and dug many conduits for water.[822] He had vast numbers of beasts of burden and other animals, for the country was suitable for grazing.[823] **220** Being very interested in agriculture,[824] he concerned himself with the soil, cultivating it with plants and seeds of every kind.[825]

He had a select army around himself of 370,000 men,[826] over which were leaders, military officers, and commanders of thousands who were of noble birth and of quite irresistible[827] prowess, 2,000 in number.[828] **221** He arranged his entire army into phalanxes[829] and armed them, giving to each a sword, a shield, and a breastplate of bronze, as well as bows and slings.[830] In addition to these things, he constructed many machines for sieges, including rock-throwers, spear-throwers, and grappling irons [and hooks],[831] and things similar to these.[832]

Uzziah's building, agricultural, and army initiatives

"Elath" (2 Kgs 14:22)/ "Eloth" (2 Chr 26:2), incorporating it within his sequence concerning Uzziah's military achievements. In utilizing this notice here Josephus omits the actual name of the city in question, while appending an indication concerning its location. His mention of the "garrison" Uzziah situates there replaces the biblical statements that the king "restored" the site "to Judah" following the death of his father (Amaziah).

[817] Compare 2 Chr 26:8, where the Ammonites pay tribute to Uzziah and his "fame" reaches even to the borders of Egypt, due to his "strength." Josephus' rendering highlights the effective control over the peoples/ regions achieved by Uzziah.

[818] Josephus supplies this transition to the next category of Uzziah's achievements, i.e. his building activities; see 2 Chr 26:9-10.

[819] Compare 2 Chr 26:9, which mentions 3 specific sites fortified by Uzziah in Jerusalem: the "Corner Gate," the "Valley Gate," and the "Angle."

[820] Josephus appends this reference to the damage done by Joash of Israel in Jerusalem in the time of Amaziah as described in 9.201.

[821] 2 Chr 26:9 does not specify the size of the towers built by Uzziah in Jerusalem.

[822] Cf. 2 Chr 26:10a, which mentions Uzziah's building "towers" in the desert.

[823] See 2 Chr 26:10bα. Josephus' reference to the "grazing" potential of the region takes the place of the biblical specification concerning the sites where

Uzziah maintained his herds, i.e. "both in the Shephelah and in the plain."

[824] Greek: γεωργικός. The term is *hapax* in Josephus.

[825] Cf. 2 Chr 26:10b, where Uzziah's "love for the soil" motivates his stationing of "farmers and vine-dressers in the hills and in the fertile lands." Uzziah's excessive enthusiasm for agriculture to the detriment of his study of the Law is censured, e.g., in *Gen. Rab.* 22.3.

[826] The figure given in 2 Chr 26:13 is 307,500.

[827] Greek: ἀνυπόστατοι. This adjective is used only here in the *Antiquities*; it appears 6 times in the *War*.

[828] 2 Chr 26:12 numbers the "heads of the fathers' houses" in Uzziah's day as 2,600.

[829] Josephus here alludes to the ordering of Uzziah's army as described in 2 Chr 26:11, while omitting the names of the 3 figures responsible for this.

[830] The catalogue of weapons prepared by Uzziah for his men in 2 Chr 26:14 mentions "spears" rather than "swords," refers also to "helmets," and ends with "stones for slinging."

[831] This phrase (Greek: καὶ ἀρτῆρας) is found only in SP; bracketed by Niese, it is omitted by Marcus.

[832] Josephus expatiates on the reference to Uzziah's "engines... to shoot arrows and great stones" of 2 Chr 26:15a, doubtless drawing on his personal knowledge of contemporary siege equipment. He leaves aside the notice of 26:15b concerning the spread of Uzziah's fame, due to his being "marvelously helped until he was strong."

Uzziah's hubris

(10.4) 222 When he had attained such a state of organization and perfection, his mind was corrupted by arrogance[833] and, puffed up[834] with mortal prosperity,[835] he neglected the strength that is deathless[836] and endures for all time, namely piety towards God and the keeping of the ordinances.[837] **223** Because of his success, he slipped and fell into the offenses of his father into which the splendor of good things and the greatness of his affairs had led the latter, [who was] unable to manage them

Uzziah's incense offering

rightly.[838] During the celebration of a festival day and a feast of the entire people, he donned priestly attire and entered the sacred enclosure to offer incense to God on the golden altar.[839] **224** The high priest Azarias,[840] along with eighty priests who

Priests warn Uzziah

were with him,[841] prevented him, for, they said, it was not allowed [for him] to offer incense—it was only permitted to those of the family of Aaron to do this. They cried out for him to go out and not act lawlessly against God.[842] In his wrath, he threatened them with death if they did not keep quiet.[843]

Earthquake and Uzziah's leprosy

225 Meanwhile, a great earthquake shook the earth[844] and the sanctuary was split open.[845] A dazzling ray of sunlight shone through and fell on the face of the king, with the result that leprosy[846] immediately appeared upon him.[847] In front of the city

---

[833] Greek: διεφθάρη τὴν διάνοιαν. Josephus uses this construction twice elsewhere: *Ant.* 9.261 (of the people in Ahaz' time) and 11.332 (of Alexander the Great).

[834] Greek: χαυνόω; the verb is *hapax* in Josephus.

[835] Greek: θνητὴ περιουσία; this phrase is *hapax* in Josephus.

[836] Greek: ἀθάνατος ἰσχύς. This phrase occurs also in *Ant.* 18.14.

[837] Josephus expatiates on 2 Chr 26:16abα: "but when he [Uzziah] was strong he grew proud to his destruction. For he was false to the Lord his God...." His rendering of this notice highlights the familiar nexus between "satiety" and *hubris*, that will prove operative also in Uzziah's case.

[838] Further accentuating Uzziah's fatal turn, Josephus appends a reference to the similar course taken by his father Amaziah before him; see 9.193, 196.

[839] Josephus elaborates on the summary description of Uzziah's cultic crime given in 2 Chr 26:16bβ, adding mention of the occasion and the vestments worn by the king. For the Chronicler's reference to the "altar of incense," he substitutes "the golden altar" (on this, see *Ant.* 3.243; 8.90).

[840] MT (2 Chr 26:17) עזריהו (Eng.: "Azariah"); LXX BL and Josephus Ἀζαρίας.

[841] Josephus omits the characterization of the priests as "men of valor" from 2 Chr 26:17.

[842] See 2 Chr 26:18. Josephus modifies the biblical conclusion of the priests' words to Uzziah, namely "go out of the sanctuary; for you have done wrong, and it will bring you no honor from the Lord God." In Chronicles, Uzziah is charged with having already done wrong; in Josephus he is warned not to do so. The

phrase "act lawlessly against God" (Greek: παρανομεῖν εἰς τὸν θεόν) used of Uzziah here represents a further verbal link between Josephus' account of this king and his father Amaziah, to whom the same construction is applied in 9.199.

[843] Josephus expands the mention of Uzziah's "anger" in 2 Chr 26:19aα with an allusion to his threatening the priests who are confronting him. The added threat is reminiscent of the one King Amaziah directs against the prophet who is admonishing him in 9.194. Conversely, Josephus passes over the mention of the angry king's having "a censer in his hand to burn incense" of 26:19aβ.

[844] 2 Chronicles 26 itself makes no mention of an earthquake in connection with Uzziah's offense. Josephus draws the item from another biblical context, i.e. Zech 14:5, which alludes to "the earthquake in the days of Uzziah king of Judah."

[845] Josephus supplies this indication on the effect of the earthquake as a preparation for what happens next, i.e. the ray of sunlight penetrating through the split-open temple and striking Uzziah's face.

[846] In the Bible (and Josephus) "leprosy" is a general term for a variety of skin-diseases, whereas in today's usage the term is used more restrictively to designate "Hansen's disease." See Wright and Jones (1992: 4:277-82).

[847] Josephus dramatizes the reference to leprosy "breaking out on Uzziah's forehead" in 2 Chr 26:19 (cf. 2 Kgs 15:5: "and the Lord smote the king, so that he was a leper..."). His reference to the "ray of sunlight" as the "carrier" of the leprosy is, as Marcus (*ad loc.*) notes, likely based on the Chronicler's use of the Hebrew ver-

at [the place] called *Eroge*,[848] half of the western hill was broken off; after rolling four *stadia*, it came to rest on the eastern hill, so that the passageways and the royal parks were blocked.[849]

Uzziah's end

226 When the priests saw the king's face stricken with leprosy, they told him of his misfortune and directed him to exit the city as an accursed person.[850] He, for his part, out of shame at the terrible thing that had happened and because there was no question of frank speech by him any longer, did as he was directed.[851] For, on account of a state of mind that went beyond the human and the impieties against God that [stemmed] from this, he underwent a pitiable and lamentable[852] judgment.[853]

227 He continued for a certain time outside the city, living the life of a private citizen,[854] while his son Jotham[855] assumed the rule.[856] Then, out of grief and dejection[857] at what had occurred, he died.[858] He lived sixty-eight years,[859] of which he reigned as king for fifty-two.[860] He was interred alone in his own tomb.[861]

---

bal stem זרה (RSV "break forth") in connection with the king's leprosy in that in, e.g., Exod 22:2, this root refers to the "shining" of the sun. For other proposals regarding the background of/parallels to this element of Josephus' account, see Begg 2000: 282, n. 38.

[848] Scholars have proposed 2 different biblical "inspirations" for this site-name, i.e. the locality "Enrogel" mentioned in 1 Kgs 1:9 and the phrase גיא־הרי (RSV: "the valley of my [God's] mountains") cited in Zech 14:5, a passage utilized by Josephus earlier in 9.225; see note to "a great earthquake shook the earth" there and cf. Begg 2000: 282, n. 40.

[849] Josephus here adapts the (eschatological) announcement of Zech 14:4-5a: "...the Mount of Olives shall be split in two from east to west by a very wide valley; so that one half of the Mount shall withdraw northward, and the other half southward. And the valley of my [God's] mountains shall be stopped up...." In making a connection between this announcement and Uzziah's calamity, he bases himself on the allusion in Zech 14:5b—incorporated by him at the opening of 9.225—to "the earthquake in the days of Uzziah."

[850] Greek: ἐναγής. Josephus expatiates on the reference to the priests' "thrusting Uzziah out" of 2 Chr 26:20bα, citing the words used by them in doing this. The Josephan priests' words are reminiscent of those with which Shimei assaults the fleeing David in *Ant.* 7.208 ("he directed him to exit the land as an accursed [Greek: ἐναγής]... person").

[851] Compare 2 Chr 26:20bβ: "... he himself [Uzziah] hastened to go out...." The king's earlier "frank speech" (Greek: παρρησία), to which Josephus alludes here, is his threat against the priests as cited in 9.224.

[852] Greek: ταλαίπωρός καὶ οἰκτρός. This collocation occurs only here in Josephus.

[853] Josephus expatiates on the summary reference to "God's having smitten him [Uzziah]" in 2 Chr 26:20bγ.

[854] This is Josephus' rendering of the reference to

"the separate house," in which Azariah/Uzziah lived for the rest of his life according to 2 Kgs 15:5a// 2 Chr 26:21a (which adds "for he was excluded from the house of the Lord"). On the prescription that lepers are to remain outside the city, see note to "stay outside the city" at 9.74.

[855] MT (2 Kgs 15:5b// 2 Chr 26:21b) יותם (Eng.: "Jotham"); LXX B 2 Kgs 15:5b Ἰωναθάν; LXX L 2 Kgs 15:5b// LXX BL 2 Chr 26:21b Ἰωαθάμ; Josephus Ἰώθαμος.

[856] 2 Kgs 15:5b// 2 Chr 26:21b speak of Jotham's being "over the household, judging the people of the land."

[857] Greek: λυπή καὶ ἀθυμία. Josephus' only other use of this collocation is in *Ant.* 5.36, where it refers to the Israelites' reaction to their defeat before Ai.

[858] Josephus adds the reference to Azariah/Uzziah's emotional state to the mention of his death ("he slept with his fathers") in 2 Kgs 15:7aα// 2 Chr 26:23aα. He omits the preceding source notice for Azariah/Uzziah of 2 Kgs 15:6// 2 Chr 26:22.

[859] Josephus obtains this figure for Azariah/Uzziah's life-span by combining the figures for his age at accession (16) and length of reign (52) given in 2 Kgs 15:2a // 2 Chr 26:3a.

[860] This figure for Azariah/Uzziah's length of reign corresponds to that cited in 2 Kgs 15:2a// 2 Chr 26:3a.

[861] Josephus' indication concerning the burial place of Azariah/Uzziah differs from those of both 2 Kgs 15:7bα ("... with his fathers in the city of David") and 2 Chr 26:23bα ("with his fathers in the burial field which belonged to the kings, for they said, 'he is a leper'"). His formulation stresses that the king's "isolation," begun when he contracted leprosy, persisted even after his death. Josephus leaves aside the notice on Jotham's accession of 15:7bβ// 26:23bβ, having already mentioned this event on the basis of 2 Kgs 15:5b // 2 Chr 26:21b earlier in 9.227.

Zechariah assassinated

(11.1) 228 When Zacharias,[862] the son of Hierobam, had ruled as king over the Israelites for six months,[863] he died, treacherously murdered by a certain friend[864] of his named Sellem,[865] the son of Jabes.[866]

Menahem's (Manaem's) violent reign

The latter, having assumed the kingship after him, exercised it for no more than thirty days.[867] **229** For, when the general Manaem,[868] who at that time was in the city of Tharse,[869] heard what had happened to Zacharias, he took his entire army and came to Samareia. Joining battle, he did away with Sellem and, having installed himself as king,[870] went from there to the city of Thapsa.[871] **230** Those inside, however, barred the gates with a cross-bar and did not admit the king.[872] Taking vengeance on them, he ravaged their country round about,[873] and, besieging their city, took it by storm. **231** Resentful at what the Thapsians had done, he slaughtered them all; he neither spared infants nor refrained from excesses of cruelty and savagery.[874] For what was unpardonable to inflict on those belonging to other nations, should these be subjected, this he perpetrated on his compatriots.[875]

232 Having then become king in this way, Manaem held on for ten years, a brutal

---

[862] Josephus introduced this king, successor of Jeroboam II, in 9.215. On Josephus' presentation of the northern kings Zechariah-Pekah in 9.228-235 (// 2 Kgs 15:8-31), see Begg 2000: 285-93.

[863] See 2 Kgs 15:8b. Josephus omits the synchronization of Zechariah's accession with Azariah's 38th (the LXX L MS 127 reads 28th) year given in 15:8a. Perhaps in view of the extreme brevity of Zechariah's reign, he also omits the negative evaluation of him found in 15:9 (see the similar case of the week-long reign of Zimri whose biblical condemnation [1 Kgs 16:19] Josephus passes over when mentioning this king in *Ant.* 8.307).

[864] Josephus adds the pathetic detail about Zechariah's assassin being a friend of his; he made a similar addition concerning the killers of the Judean Kings Joash (9.171) and Amaziah (9.203).

[865] MT (2 Kgs 15:10) שלם (Eng.: "Shallum"); LXX B Σελλούμ; LXX L Σελλήμ; Josephus Σέλλημος.

[866] MT (2 Kgs 15:10) יבש (Eng.: "Jabesh"); LXX BL Ἰαβείς; Josephus Ἰάβησος. Josephus omits the varying source indications concerning the site of Zechariah's assassination: "before the people" (MT)/ "in Keblaam" (LXX B)/ "in Ieblaam" (LXX L).

[867] Josephus combines the notices of 2 Kgs 15:10b (Shallum's assuming the kingship) and 13b (his 1-month reign). He leaves aside the intervening segment 15:11-13a: the source notice for Zechariah (v. 11), the fulfillment notice for the prediction (2 Kgs 10:30// 9.139) that Jehu's descendants would rule to the 4th generation (v. 12), and the synchronization of Shallum's accession with the 39th year of Azariah of Judah. The non-utilization of the fulfillment notice of 15:12 is surprising, given Josephus' tendency to add such notices where the Bible itself lacks them (see, e.g., notices where the Bible itself lacks them (see, e.g.,

9.184). The omission may be a function of his wide-going abbreviation of the entire biblical account (2 Kgs 15:8-31) concerning the Israelite kings Zechariah-Pekah.

[868] MT (2 Kgs 15:14) מנחם (Eng.: "Menahem"); LXX BL Μαναήμ; Josephus Μαναῆμος. Josephus omits the name of this figure's father (MT: Gadi), even as he supplies him with the title "general."

[869] MT (2 Kgs 15:14) תרצה (Eng.: "Tirzah"); LXX B Θαρσειλά; LXX L Θερσά; Josephus Θάρσε.

[870] Josephus embellishes the notice of 2 Kgs 15:14 concerning Menahem's assassination of and succession to Shallum with further details: his hearing of Zechariah's murder, bringing his army with him to Samaria, and engaging Shallum. Conversely, he omits the attached source notice for Shallum, 2 Kgs 15:15.

[871] MT (2 Kgs 15:16) תפסח (Eng.: "Tiphsah"); LXX BL Θερσά; Josephus Θαψά.

[872] Josephus turns the notice of 2 Kgs 15:16aβ about the townsfolk of Tiphsah "not opening" to Menahem into a statement about their barring the gates to him.

[873] 2 Kgs 15:16 specifies "its [i.e. Tiphsah's] territory from Tirzah on."

[874] Greek: ὠμότης καὶ ἀγριότης. This collocation is *hapax* in Josephus. The term ἀγριότης appears twice elsewhere in his corpus: *War* 7.7 (of the Jewish rebels) and *Ant.* 16.363 (of Herod). In applying the term to Menahem Josephus thus places him in very bad company.

[875] Josephus both generalizes and offers a strongly negative judgment upon the single specific atrocity attributed, without explicit commentary, to Menahem in 2 Kgs 15:16bβ: "he ripped up all the women who were with child."

man, the cruelest[876] of all.[877] When Phoul,[878] the king of the Assyrians, campaigned against him, he did not meet the Assyrians in a contest of battle.[879] Rather, persuaded by the thousand silver talents he received, Phoul withdrew and terminated the war.[880] **233** This head-tax the crowd paid to Manaem, being taxed fifty drachmas a head.[881]

Menahem buys off Assyrians

After this, he died and was interred in Samareia;[882] he left behind as the successor to his kingship his son Phakeas,[883] who, emulating his father's cruelty,[884] ruled for only two years.[885] **234** He was then treacherously murdered;[886] while at a banquet with friends, he died, having been plotted against by a certain Phakeas,[887] who was the captain of a thousand[888] and son of Romelias.[889] This Phakeas exercised his rule for twenty years,[890] being both impious and lawless.[891]

Menahem's son Pekahiah (Phakeas) overthrown by Pekah (Phakeas)

235 Now the king of the Assyrians, Thaglathphallasar[892] by name, campaigned

Assyrian

---

[876] Greek: ὠμότατος. This superlative adjectival form echoes the noun ὠμότης used of Menahem in 9.231.

[877] See 2 Kgs 15:17b. Omitting the notice of 15:17a, in which Menahem's accession is synchronized with the 39th (LXX L MS 127: 28th) year of Azariah, Josephus proceeds to give his own version of the stereotyped judgment formula for Menahem of 15:18, this continuing his earlier stress (see 9.231) on the king's egregious "cruelty." The terminology used by Josephus in 9.231-232 to highlight Menahem's brutality recurs in his account of the degenerate Parthian prince Orodes in *Ant.* 18.44.

[878] MT (2 Kgs 15:19) פּוּל (Eng.: "Pul"); LXX BL Φουά; Josephus Φοῦλος.

[879] Josephus supplies this item, thereby insinuating that Menahem was not only cruel towards those weaker them himself (see 9.231-232a), but also cowardly vis-à-vis the more powerful.

[880] Josephus combines the data of 2 Kgs 15:19bα (Menahem gives Pul 1,000 shekels) and 15:20b (Pul's withdrawal), leaving aside the reference (15:19bβ) to the purpose of Menahem's payment, i.e. that Pul might confirm his kingship. He likewise substitutes an equivalent value ("talents") for the Bible's "shekels."

[881] According to 2 Kgs 15:20a the head tax was "50 shekels of silver" and levied by Menahem (only) on the "wealthy men." As Marcus (*ad loc.*) points out, Josephus elsewhere (see, e. g., *Ant.* 3.195; 8.189) equates the biblical shekel, not with the "drachma" as here in 9.233, but rather with the "tretradrachm." Josephus omits the source notice for Menahem, 2 Kgs 15:21.

[882] To the mention of Menahem's death that he draws from 2 Kgs 15:22a, Josephus adds the reference to his burial place.

[883] MT (2 Kgs 15:22b) פְּקַחְיָה (Eng.: "Pekahiah"); LXX B Φακεσίας; LXX L Φακεεία; Josephus Φακέας.

[884] This allusion to Pekahiah's imitating his father's characteristic "cruelty" (Greek: ὠμότης; see 9.231-232a) takes the place of the stereotyped judgment notice for the former of 2 Kgs 15:24.

[885] Josephus' figure for Pekahiah's length of reign agrees with given in MT LXX B 2 Kgs 15:23b (LXX L* assigns him 10 years, the LXX L MS 127 12 years). Josephus leaves aside the notice of 15:23a, synchronizing Pekahiah's accession with the 50th (LXX L MS 127: 40th) year of Azariah (Uzziah) of Judah.

[886] Greek: δολοφονέω; this is the same verb used of Shallum's assassination of Zechariah in 9.228.

[887] MT (2 Kgs 15:25) פֶּקַח (Eng.: "Pekah"); LXX B Φάκεε, LXX L Φάκεια; Josephus Φακέας (in Josephus both this regicide and his victim bear the same name, i.e. "Phakeas"). According to 2 Kgs 15:25a, Pekahiah was murdered "in the citadel of the king's house" (MT adds 2 place names, i.e. Argob and Arieh). Josephus' version accentuates the pathos of the king's end—he is killed in the relaxed, intimate setting of a banquet while surrounded by friends.

[888] According to 2 Kgs 15:25, Pekah's plot against Pekahiah involved (a mere) "50 men of the Gileadites." Josephus makes him commander of a much larger force.

[889] MT (2 Kgs 15:25) רְמַלְיָהוּ (Eng.: "Remaliah"); LXX BL ʽΡαμελίου; Josephus ʽΡομελίας. Josephus omits the appended source notice, 15:26, for the murdered Pekahiah.

[890] Josephus reproduces this (historically problematic) chronological datum from 2 Kgs 15:27b (MT LXX BL*; the LXX L MS 127 reads 30 years). He omits the synchronization of Pekah's accession with the 52nd year of Azariah of Judah of 15:27a.

[891] Greek: ἀσεβὴς καὶ παράνομος. This is Josephus' only use of this wordpair. It represents a free rendering of the stereotyped judgment notice on Pekah as one who continued the sins of Jeroboam I in 2 Kgs 15:28.

[892] MT (2 Kgs 15:29) תִּגְלַת פִּלְאֶסֶר (Eng.: "Tiglath-pileser"); LXX B ᾽Αλγαθφελλασάρ; LXX L Θεγλαθφαλασάρ; Josephus Φαγλαθφαλλάσαρ. Apparently, neither the Biblical authors nor Josephus realized that "Pul" (see 9.232// 2 Kgs 15:19) and "Tiglath-pileser" were one and the same person, the former name being the Babylonian throne name of the Assyrian king.

campaign against Israel against the Israelites. Having subjugated all Galadene and the country beyond the Jordan, as well as that called Galilee, Kudissa, and Asora,[893] he took the inhabitants captive and resettled them in his own kingdom.[894] This may suffice concerning the king of the Assyrians.[895]

Achievements of King Jotham of Judah **236** Jotham,[896] the son of Ozias, ruled as king of the tribe of Iouda in Hierosolyma;[897] his mother, a native of the city, was named Ierase.[898] This king lacked not a single virtue; he was pious towards God and just to humans.[899] He was also concerned for the city.[900] **237** For, whatever was in need of repair and beautification he dealt with in lavish fashion. He set up porticos and vestibules in the sanctuary and re-erected those portions of the walls that had fallen down, building high and impregnable towers. He likewise devoted much attention to whatever else had been neglected throughout his kingdom.[901]

238 He also campaigned against the Ammanites. After defeating them in battle,[902] he imposed on them an annual tax of 100 talents and 10,000 cors of wheat, and as many of barley.[903] He so enlarged his kingdom that it was deserving of respect[904] by its enemies and [a source of] well-being to the natives.[905]

---

[893] 2 Kgs 15:29a mentions 8 specific cities or regions overrun by Tiglath-pileser. Of these, Josephus has an equivalent to 4 (Gilead, Galilee, Kadesh [Josephus: Kudissa] and Hazor [Josephus: Asora]), while his 5th listing, i.e. "the country beyond the Jordan," has a more general character. He leaves aside the remaining biblical place names, viz. Ijon, Abel-beth-maacah, Janoah, and the land of Naphtali.

[894] See 2 Kgs 15:29b.

[895] With this formula Josephus rounds off his sequence on the northern kings Zechariah through Pekah (9.228-235), prior to reverting to the southern King Jotham in 9.236.

[896] Greek: Ἰώθαμος; this is the form of the king's name read by MSP, which Marcus and Schalit *s.v.* follow; Niese reads rather Ἰωσᾶς. Josephus introduced this king in 9.227; on Josephus' treatment of him in 9.236-243 (// 2 Kgs 15:32-38// 2 Chr 27:1-9) with its incorporation of a citation from Nah 2:9-13 [Eng. 2:8-12], see Begg 2000: 297-313.

[897] See 2 Kgs 15:32// 2 Chr 26:23b. Like the Chronicler, Josephus lacks an equivalent to Kings' opening synchronization of Jotham's accession with the 2nd year of Pekah of Israel.

[898] MT (2 Kgs 15:33b) ירושא (Eng.: "Jerusha")/ (2 Chr 27:1b) ירושה (Eng.: "Jerusha"); LXX B 2 Kgs 15:33b Ἐρούς; LXX L 2 Kgs 15:33b// LXX L 2 Chr 27:1b Ἱερούσα; LXX B 2 Chr 27:1 Ἱερουσσά; Josephus Ἱεράση. Josephus omits the name of her father (MT: Zadok).

[899] This is Josephus' free rendering of the notice on Jotham's "doing what was right in the eyes of the Lord, according to all his father Uzziah had done" of 2 Kgs 15:34// 2 Chr 27:2a. He omits the qualifications at-

tached to the favorable biblical judgments on the king in 15:35a// 27:2b, which mention the people's persistence in dubious practices during Jotham's reign.

[900] Josephus supplies this transition to his following treatment of Jotham's building activities in 9.237.

[901] In relating Jotham's building measures, Josephus follows the more expansive account of 2 Chr 27:3-4, as opposed to the summary notice of 2 Kgs 15:35b: "he built the upper gate of the house of the Lord" (// 2 Chr 27:3a). In his reproduction of the Chronicler's account, Josephus also, however, makes a variety of changes: he adds the prefatory reference to the king's lavishness as a builder; speaks in more general terms of his temple and wall constructions (omitting the mention of "Ophel" from 27:3b); and seems to depict Jotham's towers as being erected—not "on the wooded hills" (so 27:4b)—but rather as part of the fortifications of Jerusalem itself. Finally, he has no equivalent to the notice of 27:4a on Jotham's "building cities in the hill country of Judah."

[902] See 2 Chr 27:5a, which designates "the king of the Ammonites" as Jotham's opponent. 2 Kings 15 does not mention this campaign.

[903] See 2 Chr 27:5b, which specifies that the talents were "of silver," and refers to the payments being made by the Ammonites over a period of 3 years.

[904] Greek: ἀκαταφρόνητος. This adjective is *hapax* in Josephus.

[905] This summary notice concerning Jotham's various achievements replaces the theological remark of 2 Chr 27:6 ("so Jotham became mighty, because he ordered his ways before the Lord his God"). Josephus likewise leaves aside the source notices for Jotham of 2 Kgs 15:36// 2 Chr 27:7.

*Prophecy of
Nahum
(Naoum)
against Assyria*

(11.3) 239 There was at this time[906] a certain prophet, Naoum[907] by name, who prophesying about the overthrow of the Assyrians and Ninos,[908] said that Ninuas[909] would be an agitated pool of water.[910] "For the entire populace would be so disconcerted and thrown into confusion that they would say to one another as they rushed off to flee:[911] 'stand and remain, and plunder gold and silver for yourselves.'[912] **240** But there will be no one willing.[913] For they will prefer to save their lives rather than their possessions.[914] For there will be terrible mutual strife, lamentation and paralysis of their limbs,[915] and their faces will be completely blackened by fear.[916] **241** Where will be the dwelling place of the lions and the mother of the young lions?[917] God says to you, Ninuas, that I shall cause you to disappear and lions will no longer go from you to govern the world."[918]

---

[906] Josephus' placing of Nahum's ministry in the reign of Jotham has no explicit biblical basis; neither Kings nor Chronicles mentions that prophet in connection with Jotham's rule, just as the Book of Nahum itself provides no direct indications as to when Nahum prophesied. Contemporary scholarship, for its part, generally dates Nahum's activity a century or more after the reign of Jotham (*ca.* 742-*ca.* 735 BCE), i.e. in that of Josiah (*ca.* 640-*ca.* 609), prior to the fall of Nineveh and the demise of the Assyrian empire in 612. On Josephus' utilization of the Book of Nahum in 9.239-242, see Weill 1923 and Begg 2000: 301-10.

[907] MT (Nah 1:1) נחום; LXX Ναούμ; Josephus Ναοῦμος.

[908] Josephus' indication concerning the content of Nahum's prophecy reflects the announcements of the coming overthrow of "Assyria" in Nah 3:18 and of its capital "Nineveh" in 2:9 (MT; Eng. 2:8); 3:7 (cf. also the mention of the city in the expanded LXX title of the book). His designation of the Assyrian capital as "Ninos" corresponds to his usage in *Ant.* 1.143; 9.208, 214 (here in his reproduction of the Book of Jonah). The codices employ a variety of alternate forms for the city's name in 9.239-242.

[909] MT (Nah 2:9) נינוה (Eng. [2:8]: "Nineveh"); LXX Νινευή: Josephus Νινύας. Having used the alternative name "Ninos" in what immediately precedes, Josephus shifts to this more LXX-like form of the city's name for his subsequent reproduction of Nah 2:9 (MT; Eng. 2:8).

[910] Josephus' phrase here (Greek: κολυμβήθρα ὕδατος) corresponds exactly to that of LXX Nah 2:9a (MT; Eng. 2:8a); compare MT: ["Nineveh is like a pool] from the days that she has become and they...."

[911] With this phrase Josephus expatiates on the reference to a "fleeing" by those spoken of in Nah 2:9 (MT; Eng. 2:8).

[912] Josephus here combines the imperatives of Nah 2:9bα (MT; Eng. 2:8bα) ("halt! halt!") and 2:10a (MT; Eng. 2:9a) ("plunder the silver, plunder the gold").

[913] Compare Nah 2:9bβ (MT; Eng. 2:8bβ): "but

none turns back."

[914] Nah 2:10b (MT; Eng. 2:9b) couples the calls to "plunder" of 2:10a (MT; Eng. 2:9a) with a remark about their being "no end of treasure or wealth of every pleasant thing." Josephus replaces this remark with an explanation ("for") as to why those summoned to stop and plunder precious metals for themselves (9.239) will be unwilling to do so.

[915] Compare Nah 2:11a (MT; Eng. 2:10a): "Desolate! Desolation and ruin! Hearts faint and knees tremble, anguish is on all loins."

[916] The meaning of the MT reference to the condition of the Ninevites' "faces" at the end of Nah 2:11 (MT; Eng. 2:10) is uncertain; some take its term פָארוּר in the sense of "glowing, redness," others rather as an allusion to the "paleness" of their faces (so RSV). Josephus' mention of the faces' "blackness" is in line with the understanding evidenced by the renderings of Tg., LXX, and Vulg. On the other hand, he lacks an equivalent to those versions' comparison of the blackness of the fugitives' faces with that of a "pot," citing instead the reason ("fear") for the blackened appearance of the Ninevites' complexions. See further Begg 2000: 305-6.

[917] The rhetorical question posed in Nah 2:12a (MT; Eng. 2:11a) concerns the fate of the lions' "den" and "pasture" (this 2nd term is often emended to "cave," see RSV). Josephus' rendering turns this single question into 2 distinct ones, the 1st dealing with the lions' abode, the 2nd concerning the mother lioness. He may have found inspiration for his allusion to the latter figure in Nah 2:13aβ (MT; Eng. 2:12aβ) ("[the lion] strangled prey for *his lionesses*") and/or in the allegory of the lioness and her 2 cubs in Ezek 19:1-9; see Begg 2000: 306-7.

[918] Josephus substitutes this direct-address divine announcement concerning the coming overthrow of Nineveh, portrayed as the source of marauding lions, for the statements about the lion's (= Nineveh's) past successes as a hunter featured in Nah 2:13 (MT; Eng.

242 This prophet prophesied many other things about Ninue in addition to these that I did not think it necessary to speak of, but have passed over in order not to seem tiresome[919] to my readers.[920] Everything predicted regarding Ninue did, however, come about after 115 years.[921] This may suffice concerning these matters.[922]

Ahaz' (Achaz') deviations

(12.1) 243 Now Jotham died, after living forty-one years,[923] of which he reigned as king for sixteen;[924] he was buried in the royal graves.[925] The kingship came to his son Achaz,[926] who was impious towards God[927] and transgressed the ancestral laws[928]; he imitated the Israelite kings.[929] He erected altars in Hierosolyma;[930] on these he sacrificed to idols,[931] to whom he even offered his own son[932] as a whole sacrifice[933] according to the custom of the Chananaians,[934] and performed many

---

2:12). He thereby invests Nahum's prediction of Nineveh's fate with a heightened authority and solemnity.

[919] Greek: ὀχληρός. Josephus uses this adjective 3 other times: *Ant.* 15.345; 16.22; 20.162.

[920] With this formula Josephus begins his closing notice (9.242) for the preceding "Nahum interlude" (9.239-41). By means of it Josephus acknowledges that he has not reproduced the content of Nahum's book integrally, given his concern not to tax readers' patience with such digressions from his main story line, i.e. the account of the Jewish kings and their deeds. Overall, Josephus' rather close and extended citation of the poetic language of Nah 2:9-13 (MT; Eng. 2:8-12) is quite exceptional in his handling of the prophetic books, the vast bulk of whose oracles he simply passes over, even as he gives prosaic content summaries of those oracles he does reproduce.

[921] The chronology of this statement is problematic for the modern historical-critical view that dates Nahum's predictions of Nineveh's fall a few decades at most prior to the city's destruction in 612 BCE (see note to "at this time" at 9.239). On the other hand, that chronology does (more or less) cohere with Josephus' own dating of Nahum's activity during the reign of Jotham (742-735 BCE). See further Begg 2000: 309, n. 66.

[922] Josephus uses a similar closing formula to round off his account of Tiglath-pileser in 9.235.

[923] Josephus arrives at this figure by combining the data of 2 Kgs 15:33// 2 Chr 27:1 [= 27:8] on Jotham's age at accession (25) and length of reign (16 years).

[924] See 2 Kgs 15:33b// 2 Chr 27:1b (=27:8b). Josephus has no equivalent to the biblical source notices (2 Kgs 15:36// 2 Chr 27:6) for Jotham (or to the mention—unique to 2 Kgs 15:37—of the Lord's sending the kings of Syria and Israel against Judah in Jotham's day).

[925] 2 Kgs 15:38aβ// 2 Chr 27:9aβ specify that Jotham was buried "in the city of David."

[926] MT (2 Kgs 15:38b// 2 Chr 27:9b) אחז (Eng.:

"Ahaz"); LXX BL 2 Kgs 15:38b// LXX L 2 Chr 27:9b Ἀχάζ; LXX B 2 Chr 27:9b Ἀχάς; Josephus Ἄχαζος. Josephus has no counterpart to the synchronization of Ahaz' succession with the 17th (LXX L MS 127: 18th) year of Pekah of Israel given in 2 Kgs 16:1. On Josephus' treatment of Ahaz in 9.243-257 (// 2 Kgs 16:1-20// 2 Chr 28:1-27), see Begg 2000: 315-32.

[927] This overall negative characterization of Ahaz is Josephus' counterpart to the general evaluation of him given in 2 Kgs 16:2b// 2 Chr 28:1b, where he is charged with not "doing what was right in the eyes of the Lord, like his father David." Josephus' reference to Ahaz' being "impious towards God" sets him in sharp opposition to his father Jotham, of whom 9.236 states "he was pious towards God."

[928] Greek: τοὺς πατρίους παραβὰς νόμους. This construction recurs, in positive terms, in *Ant.* 10.214, where Daniel's relatives are said to be "unwilling to transgress the ancestral laws."

[929] See 2 Kgs 16:3aα// 2 Chr 28:2a: (Ahaz) "walked in the ways of the kings of Israel." Josephus adds the reference to Ahaz' transgression of the laws.

[930] Josephus anticipates this reference to Ahaz' altar-building in Jerusalem from 2 Chr 28:24bβ.

[931] Josephus generalizes the references to Ahaz' making "molten images for the Baals and burning incense in the valley of the son of Himnon" of 2 Chr 28:2b-3a and to his "sacrificing and burning incense on the high places, and on the hills, and under every green tree" of 2 Kgs 16:4// 2 Chr 28:4.

[932] In his mention of a single "son" offered by Ahaz, Josephus agrees with MT and LXX B 2 Kgs 16:3b against LXX L 2 Kgs 16:3b// MT LXX BL 2 Chr 28:3b, which read the plural "sons."

[933] In explicitly designating Ahaz' initiative with his son as a "whole sacrifice" (or "holocaust"), Josephus differs from both biblical accounts of the king, which speak, respectively, of his "passing his son(s) through fire" (2 Kgs 16:3b) and of his "burning them [the sons] in the fire" (2 Chr 28:3b). Ahaz' deed as portrayed by Josephus is reminiscent of that of the pagan

similar things in addition.⁹³⁵

244 While he was thus behaving in this crazed way,⁹³⁶ Raases,⁹³⁷ the king of the Syrians and Damascenes, and Phakeas,⁹³⁸ the king of the Israelites, campaigned against him—for they were friends.⁹³⁹ Driving him back into Hierosolyma, they kept besieging the city for a long time, though without success, on account of the solidity of the walls.⁹⁴⁰

245 When, however, the king of the Syrians⁹⁴¹ captured the city of Elath⁹⁴² on the Red Sea,⁹⁴³ he killed the inhabitants and populated it with Syrians.⁹⁴⁴ Having likewise destroyed the Judeans in the garrisons and the surrounding [country] and driven off much spoil, he departed for Damascus with his army.⁹⁴⁵ **246** But the king of the Hierosolymites, knowing that the Syrians had retired to their homes and thinking himself militarily equal⁹⁴⁶ to the force of the king of Israel, set out against

Failed siege of Jerusalem

Syrian attacks on Judah

Israel defeats Judah

Moabite king who makes a "whole sacrifice" of his own eldest son (see 9.43); he, however, at least had his desperate military situation as an extenuating circumstance for his doing this, a fact which makes the Judean King Ahaz' (unprovoked) child sacrifice appear all the more reprehensible.

⁹³⁴ Compare the association of Ahaz' exposure of his son(s) to fire with "the abominable practices of the nations whom the Lord drove out before the people of Israel" in 2 Kgs 16:3b// 2 Chr 28:3b.

⁹³⁵ This summarizing formula encompasses the remaining specific crimes alleged against Ahaz in the indictments of 2 Kgs 16:3b-4// 2 Chr 28:2b-4; see note to "to idols" at 9.243.

⁹³⁶ Josephus adds this qualification of Ahaz' behavior as a transition to his account of its (military) consequences. In characterizing Ahaz as "acting crazily" (Greek: μαίνομαι), Josephus links him with his reprobate predecessor Joram of Judah, whom he calls "insane" (Greek ἐμμανής) in 9.98.

⁹³⁷ MT (2 Kgs 16:5) רצן (Eng.: "Rezin"); LXX BL Ῥαασσών; Josephus Ῥαασής (this is the reading of RO, which Niese follows; Marcus reads Ἀράσης with ME). 2 Chr 28:5 does not name "the king of Syria" to whom it has God hand Ahaz over.

⁹³⁸ MT (2 Kgs 16:5) פקח (Eng.: "Pekah"); LXX B Φάκεε; LXX L Φάκεαι; Josephus Φακέας. Having mentioned the name of this king's father in 9.234 (// 2 Kgs 15:25), Josephus omits its repetition in 16:5 (the MT of both biblical texts call Pekah's father "Remaliah"; compare "Romelias" in 9.234).

⁹³⁹ Josephus here follows the presentation of 2 Kgs 16:5a, according to which Rezin and Pekah launch a joint (unsuccessful) attack on Jerusalem; to this he adds an explanation of the kings' cooperation, i.e. the fact of their being "friends." By contrast, 2 Chr 28:5-7 seems to speak of separate (successful) campaigns by the 2 rulers.

⁹⁴⁰ See 2 Kgs 16:5b. Josephus appends the expla-

nation of the failure of the siege.

⁹⁴¹ 2 Kgs 16:6a repeats the name of the Syrian king (Rezin [MT]/Raasson [LXX BL]) from 16:5. The mention of "the king of Aram/Syria" in 16:6a is often emended to "king of Edom" (thus RSV). Josephus' reading corresponds to that MT LXX BL, however.

⁹⁴² MT (2 Kgs 16:6) אילת (Eng.: "Elath"); LXX BL Αἰλάθ; Josephus Ἡλαθοῦς.

⁹⁴³ Josephus appends this localization of "Elath"; cf. *Ant.* 8.163. Whereas he refers to the Syrian "capture" of the city, 2 Kgs 16:6 speaks of its being "recovered"—an allusion to 2 Kgs 14:22a// 2 Chr 26:2a, where Azariah/Uzziah rebuilds Elath/Eloth and "restores" this to Judah (compare 9.217, which alludes, without naming the site, to Uzziah's "founding a city on the Red Sea," i.e. the same body of water mentioned by Josephus here in 9.245).

⁹⁴⁴ Compare 2 Kgs 16:6b, where, once the king of Syria "expels" the Judeans from Elath, the city is occupied by Syrians, who have remained there "to this day." Josephus' identification of the new inhabitants of Elath as "Syrians" agrees with the MT *ketiv*, whereas the *qere* (as well LXX BL Tg. and Vulg.) designate them as "Edomites"; see note to "the king of the Syrians" at 9.245.

⁹⁴⁵ Having reproduced the content of 2 Kgs 16:5-6 (the Israelite/Syrian failure before Jerusalem; the Syrian capture of Elath), Josephus now switches to the Chronicler's alternative account of military developments under Ahaz given in 2 Chr 28:5-15. Here at the outset of this segment (9.245b-251), he presents his version of 28:5a, omitting its initial reference to God's giving Ahaz into the hand of the king of Syria, while adding mention of where the Syrian's massacres of the Judeans took place.

⁹⁴⁶ Greek: ἀξιόμαχος. Compare 9.61, where Joram of Israel is said "not to think himself militarily equal [Greek: ἀξιόμαχος] to the Syrians."

him. When he joined battle, he was vanquished,[947] in accordance with the fury of God[948] that he felt towards his [Achaz'] many and great impieties. **247** For 120,000 of his [men] were done away by the Israelites on that day.[949] Their general Zacharis[950] killed in battle the son of King Achaz, named Amasias.[951] They also took prisoner[952] Erkam,[953] the steward of the entire kingdom[954] and Elikas,[955] general of the tribe of Iouda.[956]   From the Benjamite tribe[957] they led away women and children;[958] plundering much spoil, they withdrew to Samareia.[959]

Prophet Oded calls for release of Judean captives

(12.2) 248 But a certain Oded,[960] who was a prophet at this time in Samareia,[961] meeting the army before the walls,[962] disclosed in a loud voice that their victory was not due to their own strength, but rather to the rage of God[963] that he felt against King Achaz[964] **249** He further blamed them because, not being satisfied with their success against him [Achaz], they had dared to take captive those of the tribe of Iouda and Benjamin who were their relatives.[965] He advised them to dismiss these [captives] unharmed to their homeland. For if they disobeyed, they would undergo judgment by God.[966]

---

[947] Josephus supplies this elaborate preface concerning Ahaz' thinking and initiatives to the summary theological notice of 2 Chr 28:5b on the Judean's "also being given [namely, by God] into the hand of the king of Israel," which he will utilize in what follows.

[948] Greek: κατὰ μῆνιν τοῦ θεοῦ; on this formula, Josephus' version of the phrase "he [Ahaz] was also given into the hand of the king of Israel..." of 2 Chr 28:5b, see 9.104, where it is used of God's stance towards the reprobate Joram of Judah.

[949] This figure for the Judean casualties corresponds to that given in 2 Chr 28:6a.

[950] MT (2 Chr 28:7) זִכְרִי (Eng.: "Zichri"); LXX B Ἐζεκρει; LXX L Ζεχρεί; Josephus Ζάχαρις (this is the reading of the codices, which Niese follows; Marcus reads Ζαχαρίας, the conjecture of J. Cocceius). 2 Chr 28:7 designates the Israelite commander as a "mighty man of Ephraim."

[951] MT (2 Chr 28:7) מַעֲשֵׂיָהוּ (Eng.: "Maaseiah"); LXX BL Μασαίαν; Josephus Ἀμασίας.

[952] This rendering reflects the plural form (Greek: ἔλαβον) read by Niese on the basis of ROS²; Marcus reads the singular ἔλαβεν (subject: Zichri) with S¹P. In 2 Chr 28:7 Zichri is credited with personally "killing" the 2 Judean officials mentioned, in addition to the king's son Maaseiah.

[953] MT (2 Chr 28:7) עַזְרִיקָם (Eng.: "Azrikam"); LXX B Ἐγδρεικάν; LXX L Ἐζρεικάμ; Josephus Ἐρκάμ.

[954] MT 2 Chr 28:7 calls Azrikam "the commander of the house [i.e. palace]."

[955] MT (2 Chr 28:7) אֶלְקָנָה (Eng.: "Elkanah"); LXX B Εἰλκανά; LXX L Ἐλκανάν; Josephus Ἐλικάς.

[956] 2 Chr 28:7 calls Elkanah "next in authority to the king."

[957] 2 Chr 28:8a speaks more generally of the Israelites' capture of their "kinsfolk" (literally: brothers).

Marcus (*ad loc.*) suggests 2 possible explanations for Josephus' mention of the "Benjamites" here: the reference might reflect a misreading of the Hebrew word בנים ("sons") from the continuation of 28:8, or, alternatively, it could be designed to prepare the notice of 9.251 (// 2 Chr 28:15) about the Israelites' captives being brought back to Jericho, a *Benjamite* city according to Josh 18:11-12.

[958] 2 Chr 28:8a distinguishes between "sons" and "daughters."

[959] See 2 Chr 28:8b.

[960] MT (2 Chr 28:9) עֹדֵד (Eng.: "Oded"); LXX BL Ὠδήδ; Josephus Ὠδηδάς.

[961] 2 Chr 28:9aα calls Oded "a prophet of the Lord" who "was there" (i.e. in Samaria; see 28:8).

[962] See 2 Chr 28:9aβ. Josephus specifies the site of the encounter.

[963] Greek: χολὸς τοῦ θεοῦ; Josephus' other uses of this phrase are in *War* 7.34; *Ant.* 6.16; *Apion* 1.236 ("rage of the gods"). Compare the equivalent expression μῆνις τοῦ θεοῦ ("fury of God") in 9.246.

[964] In 2 Chr 28:9bα Oded attributes Israel's victory more generally to God's being "angry with Judah." Josephus keeps attention focussed on Ahaz and God's stance towards him.

[965] Compare Oded's accusations against the Israelites in 2 Chr 28:9bβ-10: they have slain the hapless Judeans in a "rage that has reached up to heaven" (v. 9bβ); they intend to enslave the male and female inhabitants of Judah and Jerusalem (v. 10a), this in spite of their having sins of their own against the Lord (v. 10b). Here again (see note to "the Benjamite tribe" at 9.247), Josephus introduces a reference to "Benjamin" where the Bible lacks this.

[966] See 2 Chr 28:11, where Oded's discourse to the Israelites concludes with the words "for the fierce wrath

250 The people of the Israelites came together in assembly and deliberated about these matters.[967] A certain Barachias,[968] who was among those most respected in the commonwealth, and three others with him,[969] said that he would not allow the troops to bring them [the captives] into the city, "in order that we not all be annihilated by God.[970] For we have [already] sufficiently offended against him, as the prophets say, so as not to commit new impieties in addition to this."[971]

Oded's proposal seconded

251 When they heard this, the soldiers agreed to do what seemed advantageous to them.[972] The above-mentioned men therefore took the captives and released them. They showed concern for them, and giving them provisions for the journey to their homeland, dismissed them unhurt.[973] Not only that, but the four also went with them; having accompanied them as far as Jericho (which is not far from Hierosolyma),[974] they returned to Samareia.[975]

Captives restored

(12.2) 252 After suffering all these things from the Israelites,[976] King Achaz, sending to Thaglathphallasar,[977] the king of the Assyrians, appealed to him to grant him an alliance against the enemy, namely the Israelites and the Syrians and Damascenes, promising to give [him] a lot of money.[978] He also sent him splendid gifts.[979]

Ahaz asks for alliance with Tiglath-pileser

253 Once the messengers had come to him with their request, [Thaglathphallasar]

Tiglath-pileser

---

of the Lord is upon you." Josephus substitutes a warning about what God will do, should the hearers disregard Oded's summons to repatriate the captives.

[967] Josephus supplies this transition to his following account of the Israelites' response (// 2 Chr 28:12-15) to Oded's warning.

[968] MT (2 Chr 28:12) ברכיהו (Eng.: "Berechiah"); LXX B Ζαχαρίας; LXX L and Josephus Βαραχίας. Josephus omits the name of the father (MT: Meshillemoth) of this figure—who in the 4-man listing of 28:12 appears in 2nd place.

[969] 2 Chr 28:12 supplies the names and patronymics of these 3 (whom, along with "Berechiah" himself, it designates as "chiefs of Ephraim").

[970] See 2 Chr 28:13aα. The reference to the threat of divine "annihilation" is Josephus' addition to the leaders' prohibition of bringing the captives into Samaria there.

[971] See 2 Chr 28:12aβb, where the leaders allude to Israel's already existing guilt and the captors' intention of increasing this. Josephus adds the reference to "what the prophets say," thereby conferring a heightened authority on the leaders' own words; the plural form ("prophets") would seem to have in view not only the just-mentioned Oded (see 9.248), but such earlier northern prophets as Ahijah, Jehu, Elijah, and Elisha and their threatening announcements.

[972] Josephus supplies this notice on the army's assent to the leaders' admonition.

[973] The wording of this notice recalls Oded's advising the Israelites "to dismiss these [captives] unharmed to their homeland" in 9.249.

[974] Josephus' added localization of Jericho in relation to Jerusalem takes the place of the former's identification as "the city of palm trees" in 2 Chr 28:15. Josephus omits the further biblical notice about the Israelite leaders' turning the captives over to their relatives at the site.

[975] See 2 Chr 28:15bβ. Josephus omits or generalizes various items from the preceding catalogue (28:15a) of the leaders' benefactions to the captives, i.e. their clothing them, giving them sandals, anointing them, and carrying the feeble on asses.

[976] Josephus adds this phrase as a transition to his account of Ahaz' next move.

[977] See 2 Kgs 16:7 (2 Chr 28:16 does not mention the Assyrian king's name). Josephus made initial mention of this figure in 9.235 (// 2 Kgs 15:29).

[978] See 2 Kgs 16:7. Josephus turns Ahaz' initial biblical statement to Tiglath-pileser ("I am your servant and your son") into this request for an "alliance." He likewise has Ahaz add the promise of "a lot of money." The Chronicler's parallel to 2 Kgs 16:7 in 2 Chr 28:16 simply mentions Ahaz' asking the Assyrian king "for help." Josephus has no equivalent to the extended attached motivation for Ahaz' initiative cited in 28:17-19, i.e. attacks upon Judah by both the Edomites and the Philistines as divine punishment for Ahaz' apostasy.

[979] Josephus embellishes the reference to the "present" that Ahaz sends to Tiglath-pileser in 2 Kgs 16:8b, while delaying his use of the notice of 16:8a concerning the "source," namely, the silver and gold of temple and palace, of Ahaz' offering until a later point; see 9.254.

overruns Syria and Israel

came as an ally to Achaz.[980] Campaigning against the Syrians, he ravaged their country, took Damascus by storm, and killed King Arase.[981] He transported the Damascenes to upper Media and, moving certain of the Assyrian nations, settled them in Damascus.[982] **254** Devastating the land of the Israelites, he carried many away captives from it.[983] When he [Thaglathphallasar] had perpetrated these things on the Syrians, the king [Achaz] took the gold that was in the royal treasuries and the silver in the sanctuary of God. Moreover, if there was any outstanding votive offering, he removed this, and coming to Damascus with it, gave it to the king of the Assyrians in accordance with their agreements.[984] Having declared his gratitude to him [Thaglathphallasar] for everything, he [Achaz] returned to Hierosolyma.[985]

Ahaz presents gifts to Tiglath-pileser

Further cultic misdeeds of Ahaz

255 This king was, however, so foolish and oblivious[986] to what was to his advantage that, when warred on by the Syrians, he not only did not cease to pay homage to their gods, but continued to adore them,[987] just as if it were they who had urged him on to victory.[988] **256** Having been defeated again,[989] he began to honor the gods of the Assyrians and seemed to honor all [others], rather than the ancestral and true[990] God, who, being wrathful against him,[991] was the cause of his defeat.[992]

---

[980] The wording of this notice picks up on Ahaz' request for an "alliance" in 9.252; 2 Kgs 16:9a speaks simply of the Assyrian king's "hearkening to" Ahaz. Compare 2 Chr 28:20, where Tiglath-pileser responds to Ahaz' appeal for help (28:16), by attacking Ahaz himself.

[981] MT (2 Kgs 16:9) רצין (Eng.: "Rezin"); LXX Ῥαασσών; Josephus Ἀρασή (in 9.244 Josephus calls the [same] Syrian king Ῥαασής; Schalit *s.v.* reads this form also here in 9.253).

[982] 2 Kgs 16:9bα speaks of the Syrians being exiled to "Kir"; Josephus adds the reference to the bringing in of a new population to their former territory, thereby answering the question of what became of the newly depopulated Syrian region.

[983] With this added notice Josephus presents Tiglath-pileser acting on Ahaz' request (9.252// 2 Kgs 16:7) that he move, not only against Syria, but also against Israel.

[984] For his notice on the fulfillment of the kings' previous "agreements" (see 9.252-253), Josephus draws on the mention in 2 Kgs 16:8a (cf. 2 Chr 28:21b, which adds that Ahaz' tribute "did not help him") of Ahaz' despoiling the treasures of the temple and the palace in order to provide a "present" (16:8b) for the Assyrian king (in 2 Kgs 16:8-9 Ahaz makes his payment to Tiglath-pileser's prior to the latter's move against Syria, whereas Josephus has him do this both before [9.252] and after [9.254] the Assyrian initiative). Josephus likewise expands the notice of 2 Kgs 16:8a with mention of Ahaz' stripping of the "votive offerings"; his inspiration here may be the listing of temple furnishings that Ahaz is said to have removed in 2 Kgs 16:17-18. Finally, he depicts Ahaz bringing his (2nd) "contribution" to Tiglath-pileser at Damascus in person, likely

under the influence of 2 Kgs 16:10, where the former goes to the Syrian capital to meet the latter.

[985] 2 Kings 16 does not explicitly mention such a return by Ahaz after his visit to Tiglath-pileser at Damascus cited in v.10.

[986] Greek: ἀνόητος καὶ ἀσυλλόγιστος. This is Josephus' only use of this collocation. In its 3 remaining uses (*Ant.* 4.161; 8.174; 12.40) in his corpus, the adjective ἀσυλλόγιστος has the meaning "countless, huge."

[987] With this formulation, compare the notice (9.193) that Amaziah "continued to adore those [gods] that he had brought from the country of the Amalekites."

[988] For this element of his Ahaz story, Josephus reverts to the account of 2 Chr 28:22-23, which speaks of Ahaz' infidelity to the Lord becoming still greater in that, under duress, he turned to worshiping the gods of the victorious Syrians, doing this to his own ruin.

[989] This reference to Ahaz's being defeated "again" (i.e. after his initial defeat by the Syrians cited in 9.255; see 2 Chr 28:5 and cf. 2 Kgs 16:6) seems to reflect the mention of Tiglath-pileser's "afflicting" Ahaz (see 2 Chr 28:20) rather than providing him with the help he had requested (see 28:16).

[990] Greek: πατρῷος καὶ ἀληθῶς. This wordpair occurs only here in Josephus.

[991] This phrase recalls the mentions of God's "fury" and "rage" against Ahaz in 9.246 and 248, respectively.

[992] This notice on Ahaz's worship also of the Assyrian gods seems to have in view the detailed account (2 Kgs 16:10-18; no parallel in 2 Chronicles 28) of the king's constructing an altar in the temple complex like that which he had seen in Damascus at the time of his meeting with Tiglath-pileser there (see

257 He attained to such a degree of neglect and contempt[993] [of God] that he finally even closed the sanctuary, forbade the offering of the customary sacrifices, and stripped it [the sanctuary] of its votive offerings.[994] After outraging God in this way[995] he died, having lived thirty-six years[996] and ruled for sixteen.[997] He left his son Ezekias[998] as his successor.

Hezekiah (Ezekias) succeeds Ahaz

(13.1) 258 Phakeas[999] the king of the Israelites, also died at this same time, after being plotted against by a certain friend[1000] named Osees.[1001] The latter exercised the kingship for nine years;[1002] he was vile and a neglector of God.[1003] **259** The king of the Assyrians, Salmanassas,[1004] campaigned against him, and having defeated him—for Osees did not have God benevolent[1005] [towards him] or as his ally[1006]—

Hoshea (Osees) overthrows Pekah (Phakeas) and is subjugated by Assyrians

---

16:10-16), undertaking this and other related cultic measures "because of the king of Assyria" (16:18).

[993] Greek: ὀλιγωρία καὶ καταφρόνησις, a collocation that occurs also in *Ant.* 4.190 (where Moses warns the people about falling into such a stance with regard to virtue). Josephus supplies this transitional phrase, underscoring the wrongfulness of Ahaz' behavior; compare his similar formulations in 9.244, 255.

[994] Josephus makes selective, rearranged, and modified use of the closing summation concerning Ahaz' cultic transgressions of 2 Chr 28:24-25a (which itself seems to represent a reworking of the account of the cultic measures undertaken by Ahaz in Jerusalem under the influence of what he saw in Damascus in 2 Kgs 16:10-18), i.e. his cutting up of the temple vessels (v. 24a), closing of the temple doors (v. 24b), making altars throughout Jerusalem (v. 24c; Josephus anticipated this item already in his initial account of Ahaz' cultic violations in 9.243), and constructing "high places" in the cities of Judah (v. 25a). To the mention of Ahaz' closing the temple doors (28:24b), Josephus appends a reference to the consequence of this initiative, i.e. the termination of the "customary sacrifices."

[995] In 2 Chr 28:25b Ahaz' reprobate cultic initiatives (28:24-25a) are qualified as "provoking to anger the Lord, the God of his fathers." Josephus' reference to Ahaz' "outraging [Greek: ὑβρίζω] God" serves to associate the king with the notorious Jeroboam I, of whom he uses the same expression in *Ant.* 8.277.

[996] Josephus obtains this figure for Ahaz' life-span by combining those given for his age at accession (20 years) and length of reign (16) in 2 Kgs 16:2a// 2 Chr 28:1a.

[997] Josephus draws this figure for Ahaz' length of reign from 2 Kgs 16:2a// 2 Chr 28:1a.

[998] MT (2 Kgs 16:20b// 2 Chr 28:27b) חזקיהו (Eng.: "Hezekiah"); LXX BL and Josephus Ἐζεκίας. Josephus omits both the source and burial notices for Ahaz of 2 Kgs 16:19// 2 Chr 28:26 and 16:20a// 28:27a, respectively.

[999] Josephus introduced this figure and his coup

against "Pekahiah" in 9.234 (// 2 Kgs 15:25).

[1000] As he did with Zechariah (see 9.228), Josephus goes beyond the Bible (2 Kgs 15:30) itself in attributing Pekah's assassination to a "friend."

[1001] MT (2 Kgs 15:30a) הושע (Eng.: "Hosheha"); LXX BL Ὠσῆε; Josephus Ὠσήης. Josephus lacks an equivalent to the naming of the assassin's father (MT: Elah), the dating of his coup in the 20th year of Jotham of Israel (15:30b MT LXX B; LXX L lacks the synchronization), and the appended source notice for Pekah of 15:31.

[1002] For this notice on Hoshea's length of reign Josephus draws on the resumption of the biblical account of Israel's last king in 2 Kgs 17:1. He leaves aside that verse's synchronization of Hoshea's accession with Ahaz' 12th (LXX L MS 82: 10th; LXX L MS 127: 14th) year—a datum that conflicts with 2 Kgs 15:30b (also omitted by Josephus; see previous note), which states that Hoshea acceded in the 20th year of Jotham.

[1003] Josephus leaves aside the enigmatic qualification of the negative judgment on Hoshea ("he did what was evil in the sight of the Lord") found in 2 Kgs 17:2, i.e. "yet not as the kings of Israel who were before him (so MT LXX B; LXX L charges Hoshea with doing evil "beyond" all his predecessors). See further von Mutius 1980. His reference to Hoshea's being "neglectful [Greek: ὀλίγωρος] of God" (a phrase that occurs only here in his writings) is reminiscent of his mention of Ahaz' "neglect [Greek: ὀλιγωρία] [of God]" in 9.257.

[1004] MT (2 Kgs 17:3) שלמנאסר (Eng.: "Shalmaneser"); LXX B Σαμεννάσαρ; LXX L Σαλμανάσσαρ; Josephus Σαλμανάσσας.

[1005] Greek: εὐμενής. With this phrase, compare Josephus' reference to God's panicking the army of Amaziah of Judah, as he does "when he is not benevolent [Greek: εὐμενής]" in 9.199.

[1006] Greek: σύμμαχος. The above collocation "benevolent and an ally" (Greek: εὐμενής καὶ σύμμαχος) used in reference to God has a counterpart in *Ant.* 4.296, where it is employed of God's (positive) stance towards the Israelites.

Hezekiah introduced

made him [subservient]^{1007} and imposed tribute on him to pay.^{1008}

260 In the fourth year of the kingship of Osees,^{1009} Ezekias, the son of Achaz and Abias,^{1010} a native of the city,^{1011} began to reign as king in Hierosolyma. By nature, he was kind, just and pious.^{1012} For when he first assumed the kingship, he supposed nothing more necessary and advantageous, both for himself and his subjects, than the worshiping of God.^{1013} Calling together the people, along with the priests and the Levites, he addressed them in these words:^{1014}

Hezekiah's address about state of Judah's cult

261 "You are not unaware that, due to the offenses of my father, who transgressed reverence and honor^{1015} towards God, you have experienced many and great calamities. You yourselves were corrupted in mind by him and induced to pay homage to what he thought were gods.^{1016} **262** I urge you, who have indeed learned what a terrible thing impiety is, to give this up already now.^{1017} Let the priests and Levites likewise cleanse themselves from their prior pollutions.^{1018} Coming thus

---

^{1007} Greek: ὑπήκοον. This term is absent in RO and omitted by Niese.

^{1008} Josephus expands the mention in 2 Kgs 17:3 of Hoshea's paying tribute to Shalmaneser with a notice on the background to his doing this, i.e. the latter's defeat of the former, itself due to God's non-support for Hoshea.

^{1009} Josephus' synchronization of Hezekiah's accession agrees with that found in the LXX L MS 127 of 2 Kgs 18:1 (MT and LXX BL* date the event to Hoshea's *3rd* year). At this point, Josephus interrupts his account of the demise of the Northern Kingdom (// 2 Kings 17), in order to relate the early reign of Hezekiah, whom he introduced in 9.257. On Josephus' treatment of Hezekiah's beginnings in 9.260-276 in relation to its biblical sources, i.e. 2 Kgs 18:1-7 and 2 Chr 29:1-31:21, see Begg 2000: 339-65. See further the synthetic treatment of the Josephan Hezekiah in Feldman 1998a: 363-75.

^{1010} MT (2 Kgs 18:2b) אבי (Eng.: "Abi")/ 2 Chr 29:1b אביה (Eng.: "Abijah"); LXX B 2 Kgs 18:2b Ἀβού; LXX L Ἀβούθ; LXX B 2 Chr 29:1b Ἀββά; LXX L 2 Chr 29:1b and Josephus Ἀβίας.

^{1011} Josephus' identification of Hezekiah's mother as a Jerusalemite takes the place of the biblical (2 Kgs 18:2b// 2 Chr 29:1b) mentions of her father's name (MT: Zechariah).

^{1012} This triple qualification of Hezekiah takes the place of the stereotyped formula of 2 Kgs 18:3// 2 Chr 29:2: "he did what was right in the eyes of the Lord, according to all that David his father had done." Josephus' characterization of Hezekiah as "pious" sets him in sharp contrast to his father Ahaz, whom he calls "impious towards God" in 9.243.

^{1013} Josephus supplies this transitional notice to his account, based on 2 Chr 29:3-31:21, of Hezekiah's restoration of the temple cult. Its wording represents a generalization of the reference— not reproduced by

him—to Hezekiah's opening and repairing the temple doors already in the 1st month of the 1st year of his reign in 29:3.

^{1014} See 2 Chr 29:4-5aα. Josephus omits the biblical mention of the site of the assembly ("the square on the east," v. 4), while making also the people as a whole an addressee of Hezekiah's discourse. He likewise passes over the content of 29:3, which narrates Hezekiah's opening and repair of the temple doors in the 1st month of the 1st year of his reign (see, however, previous note). In 29:5aβ Hezekiah addresses himself specifically to the Levites. Josephus, in line with his tendency to downplay the Levites' role in his history, has him speak to all 3 assembled groups.

^{1015} Greek: ὁσία καὶ τιμή. This collocation occurs only here in Josephus. Its noun τιμή ("honor") echoes the double use of the verb τιμάω ("to honor") of Ahaz' worship of other gods in 9.256.

^{1016} Josephus has Hezekiah commence his speech to the assembly with a reminder, based on 2 Chr 29:6-9, of their sin-filled recent history and the God-inflicted consequences of this. In his version of the biblical segment he accentuates Ahaz' personal culpability vis-à-vis that of the people (whom Ahaz "corrupted in mind" and "induced" into false worship). At the same time, he leaves out much of the Chronicler's expansive detail concerning the themes of sin (the neglect of the temple cult, v. 7) and punishment (Judah and Jerusalem have become an object of derision to the nations, v. 8; the slaughter and exiling of the population, v. 9).

^{1017} This general appeal to the entire assembly to renounce "impiety" has no explicit counterpart in Hezekiah's speech of 2 Chr 29:5-11.

^{1018} Greek: καθᾶραι... μιασμάτων. This phrase occurs also in *War* 6.48; *Ant.* 5.42; 9.273. With the phrase Josephus reverts to the opening of Hezekiah's biblical speech in 2 Chr 29:5aβ, where, however, it is the Levites alone who are called to "sanctify themselves."

together, let them open the sacred precinct.[1019] Once they have cleansed it, let them restore it to its ancient and ancestral[1020] honor through the customary sacrifices.[1021] For thus we shall make God benevolent[1022] and turn away his wrath."[1023]

Priests act on Hezekiah's directives

(13.2) 263 When the king had said this,[1024] the priests opened the sacred precinct. Once they had opened it, [they prepared][1025] the vessels of God; tossing out the pollutions, they offered the customary sacrifices on the altar.[1026]

Celebration of feast of unleavened bread

Sending round to the country under him, the king called the people[1027] to Hierosolyma to celebrate the feast of Unleavened Bread,[1028] for this had not taken place for a long time, on account of the lawlessness of the above-mentioned kings.[1029]

Hezekiah invites

264 He also sent out to the Israelites,[1030] calling on them to abandon the [mode

---

[1019] This directive is without parallel in Hezekiah's instructions as cited in 2 Chr 29:5. Compare 29:3, where prior to beginning his discourse, Hezekiah himself "opens" the temple doors. Such an "opening" of the sacred precinct is necessary, given that in 9.257 Ahaz is said to have "closed the sanctuary."

[1020] Greek: ἀρχαῖος καὶ πάτριος. These terms are collocated also in *Ant.* 10.72; 12.280, 301; cf. 18.11.

[1021] Josephus expands the biblical Hezekiah's command that the temple be sanctified and the "filth" removed from it (2 Chr 29:5b) with a positive directive to the cultic officials about their reactivating the sacrificial system. Conversely, he leaves aside the king's closing words in 29:11, where he urges the Levites (see v. 5aβ) not to be negligent in view of God's choice of them to minister to him and burn incense.

[1022] Greek: εὐμενής. Compare 9.259, which states that Hoshea "did not have God benevolent (Greek: εὐμενής)" to himself.

[1023] This concluding affirmation is Josephus' version of Hezekiah's declaration (2 Chr 29:10) of his intention to make a covenant with the Lord so that "his fierce anger might turn away from us." Characteristically, Josephus omits the biblical reference to a "covenant." The noun "wrath" here recalls the cognate verb "to be wrathful" used of God's stance towards Ahaz in 9.256.

[1024] Josephus passes over the entire segment 2 Chr 29:12-15 featuring the response on the part of 15 named Levites to the directives given them in particular by Hezekiah in 29:5-11. Here again (see note to "in these words" at 9.260), Josephus evidences a tendency to downplay the Levites' part in biblical history.

[1025] Greek: ηὐτρέπισαν. This verb is absent in ROM and omitted by Niese; Marcus reads it with MSP.

[1026] Josephus brings his (greatly abbreviated) version of the priests' cultic initiatives as related 2 Chr 29:16-19(20-36) into line with the directives given them (and the Levites) by Hezekiah in 9.262, i.e. they are to open and cleanse the temple, and then offer "the

customary sacrifices." The concluding reference to the priests' sacrificing here in 9.263 represents Josephus' initial utilization of the extended biblical sequence (29:20-36) concerning the series of sacrifices that are offered already prior to the Passover observance as described in 2 Chronicles 30.

[1027] At this point Josephus begins his version of 2 Chronicles 30, the account of Hezekiah's pan-Israelite Passover. 2 Chr 30:1 (cf. 30:5) speaks initially of Hezekiah's general, simultaneous summons "to all Israel and Judah." Josephus distinguishes his convoking first his own "people" (9.263b) and then the inhabitants of the Northern Kingdom (9.264a).

[1028] In 2 Chr 30:1 the feast is designated as "Passover." Josephus draws his alternative, related designation from 2 Chr 30:13.

[1029] Josephus appends this explanatory remark as to why a special summoning of the Judeans to the legally required observance of the feast of Passover/Unleavened Bread should be necessary. The reference to "the lawlessness of the... kings" alludes above all to Ahaz, who closed the temple and prohibited its sacrifices; see 9.257.

[1030] 2 Chr 30:1 mentions Ephraim and Manasseh in particular. Josephus leaves aside the appended parenthetical details (30:2-4) about the decision taken in Jerusalem to keep the Passover in the 2nd—rather than the prescribed 1st month—given the priests' failure to sanctify themselves in sufficient numbers. The priest Josephus understandably omits this mention of such a failure on the priests' part and its consequences for the date of Hezekiah's Passover. Subsequently too, Josephus will disregard biblical indications (see 2 Chr 30:13, 15) that Hezekiah's Passover was in fact celebrated in the 2nd month, just as earlier he left aside the Pentateuch's legal basis (see Num 9:9-12) for such a "delayed Passover" in the case of those who are "unclean" at the time of its regular celebration in the 1st month.

Israelites to participate in feast

of] life that had been theirs until now[1031] and to revert to their ancient practice and adoration of God.[1032] For he would permit them as well to come to Hierosolyma to celebrate the feast of Unleavened Bread and join in the festive assembly.[1033] He said that he was urging this, not because he wished to make them subject to himself, but for the sake of their own advantage, for thus they would be blessed.[1034]

General rejection of Hezekiah's and prophets' appeals

265 Yet not only did the Israelites give no credence to the messengers who came to them and related [the words of] their king to them; they even ridiculed the messengers as foolish.[1035] Similarly, they kept scorning the prophets, who likewise urged these things and predicted what they would experience if they did not shift to piety towards God;[1036] they spat on[1037] them [the prophets] and finally seized and killed them.[1038] **266** Not satisfied with their lawless deeds up till this point, they devised still worse things than the above-mentioned [offenses], from which they only desisted when God, avenging their impiety, made them subordinate to their enemies. We shall, however, relate these matters presently.[1039]

Some Israelites come to

267 Many of the tribes of Manasseh, Zebul and Issachar, however, persuaded by what the prophets were urging,[1040] did turn back to piety.[1041] All these ran together

---

[1031] Compare the "negative" opening exhortations of Hezekiah's message to the northerners (2 Chr 30:6b-9), i.e. not be like their "faithless" relatives (v. 7), nor "stiff-necked" like their ancestors (v. 8a).

[1032] Josephus here synthesizes the "positive" exhortations that Hezekiah directs to the northerners in 2 Chr 30:6a ("return to the Lord...") and 30:8aββ ("... yield yourself to the Lord, and come to his sanctuary... and serve the Lord...").

[1033] Josephus adds this assurance by Hezekiah, with its reference to the specific occasion (see 9.263) to which the northerners are being urged to come. The verb συμπανηγυρίζω ("to join in the festive assembly") is *hapax* in Josephus.

[1034] This concluding assertion by Hezekiah concerning his good intentions vis-à-vis the northerners takes the place of the recurrent theological motivations that the biblical king appends to his appeal, stressing that if the northerners respond to the appeal, God's favor will return to them (see 30:6b, 8bβ-9).

[1035] Compare the negative response to Hezekiah's appeal reported in 2 Chr 30:10b: "... but they [the northerners] laughed them [Hezekiah's messengers] to scorn, and mocked them." In what follows Josephus expands considerably on this summary notice; see 9.265b-266.

[1036] Josephus appends this reference to the northerners' disregard of (their own) prophets, whose message reinforces that of Hezekiah's messengers. The notice seems inspired by 2 Kgs 17:13-14, where, in the context of a review of the causes of the demise of the Northern Kingdom, mention is made to the succession of prophets and seers the Lord sent to the Israelites, urging them to repent, but who met with stubborn disbelief. The reference to "the prophets" and their warnings

here in 9.265 likewise recalls 9.250, where the leading men of Samaria, when urging the release of the southern captives, remind the Israelites of what "the prophets" have been telling them about Israel's own sins (in this instance the Israelites do act in accordance with the prophets' warnings, whereas in 9.265 they do not—thereby ensuring their imminent doom).

[1037] Greek: διαπτύω. Josephus only use of this verb is in *Ant.* 1.166. In a metaphorical sense it means "to reject, despise."

[1038] This notice on the northerners' killing of the prophets is a further Josephan creation, which highlights the former's hopeless depravity and so helps account for their eventual annihilation that Josephus will shortly relate.

[1039] Josephus' elaboration of the notice on 2 Chr 30:10b on the Israelites' negative response to Hezekiah's appeal culminates in this remark, foreshadowing the catastrophic consequences of their obstinacy, which he will relate in 9.277-291.

[1040] According to 2 Chr 30:11, it was only a "few men" of the tribes of Asher, Manasseh, and Zebulun who responded positively to the appeal of Hezekiah's messengers. In Josephus' presentation the northerners' respond rather to the message of their own "prophets" as featured in the addition of 9.265b-266.

[1041] Compare 2 Chr 30:11: "they [the Israelite minority] humbled themselves." Josephus' alternative language ("they turned back to piety") picks up his reference to the prophets' urging the northerners to "shift to piety towards God" in 9.265. Josephus leaves aside the appended notice of 30:12 about the "hand of God" operating on the Judeans, causing them to act with one accord in carrying out the Passover project of Hezekiah and his princes.

to Hierosolyma to Ezekias that they might pay homage to God.[1042]

(13.3) 268 When they arrived, King Ezekias went up to the sacred precinct, together with the leaders and the entire people.[1043] He offered on his own behalf seven bulls and as many rams, as well as seven lambs and as many he-goats.[1044] Laying their hands on the heads of the victims, the king himself and the leaders told the priests to present a pleasing sacrifice;[1045] **269** the latter sacrificed and offered whole victims.[1046] The Levites stood round in a circle[1047] with their musical instruments;[1048] they sang hymns to God and played their harps, as they had been taught by David,[1049] while the remaining priests blew the trumpets they held, [accompanying] those who sang the hymns.[1050] While this was happening, the king and people, falling on their faces, were paying homage to God.[1051]

Jerusalem Festal sacrifices offered

270 Then he [Ezekias] sacrificed 70 cattle, 100 rams, and 200 lambs;[1052] for their feasting he donated to the crowd 600 cattle and 3,000 other sorts of beasts.[1053] The priests did everything in accordance with the law.[1054] The king was delighted with this; he feasted with the people, declaring his gratitude to God.[1055]

[1042] Josephus elaborates on the concluding word of 2 Chr 30:11 ("[the righteous northerners] came to Jerusalem") with mention of the purpose of their coming.

[1043] Cf. 2 Chr 30:13, which refers to "many people," a "great assembly" convening in Jerusalem. Having omitted the Chronicler's earlier notice that Hezekiah's Passover will have to celebrated, not in the 1st, but rather in the 2nd month (2 Chr 30:2-4; see note to "the people" at 9.263), Josephus likewise does not reproduce the related indication of 30:13 that the people assembled "in the 2nd month." He leaves for a later point (see 9.273) the appended biblical reference to the assembly's cleansing Jerusalem of idolatrous objects (30:14), prior to its initiating the celebration of the feast itself. In fact, at this point, Josephus appears to conflate the content of 30:13 (the people's assembling in Jerusalem) with the opening of a segment (29:20-30)—earlier passed over by him—dealing with a initial set of sacrifices, preceding the celebration of passover; see 29:20, with its mention of king and officials going to the temple.

[1044] See 2 Chr 29:21a, where "they" (i.e. the king and his officials, 29:20) bring 7 of each of the 4 categories of beasts "as a sin offering for the kingdom and for the sanctuary and for Judah."

[1045] Greek: καλλιερέω; the verb recurs in 9.271. See 2 Chr 29:21b. Josephus here anticipates (and generalizes) the reference in 29:23b, where the king and assembly lay their hands on the he-goats (nothing is said of this being done with the 3 other categories of victims cited in 29:21a).

[1046] With this phrase Josephus summarizes the extended description of the actual performance of the (pre-Passover) sacrifices by the priests in 2 Chr 29:22-24.

[1047] 2 Chr 29:25a speaks of Hezekiah's "stationing" the Levites.

[1048] 2 Chr 29:25a specifies "cymbals, harps, and lyres."

[1049] Josephus here combines elements drawn from 2 Chr 29:25-28: the singing (see vv. 27b, 28aβ), the harps (v. 21a), and David as a musical authority (v. 21b, which likewise cites the prophetic figures Gad and Nathan; cf. also the mention of Asaph alongside David in v. 30a). On David's instructing the Levites in their musical roles, see *Ant.* 7.305-306.

[1050] Cf. the phrase "the priests with their trumpets" at the end of 2 Chr 29:26, as well as the references to "trumpets" in v. 27 and to "trumpeters sounding" as the "singers sing" in v. 28.

[1051] Josephus combines 2 Chr 29:28a ("the whole assembly" worships) and 30b ("they [i.e. the Levites, acting on the directive of Hezekiah and the princes, v. 30a] bow down and worship").

[1052] In 2 Chr 29:31-32 these 3 categories of victims are provided by the assembly, at Hezekiah's direction, as "burnt offerings." Josephus highlights Hezekiah's personal contribution to the national cult.

[1053] Compare 2 Chr 29:33, where the 600 bulls and 3,000 sheep cited are designated as "consecrated offerings" and their donor is not explicitly identified. Here too (see previous note), Josephus highlights the king's personal contribution—this time as the one who provides his people with the makings of a feast.

[1054] This is the priest Josephus' substitution for the (critical) allusion, in 2 Chr 29:34, to the lack of sufficient priests and the greater cultic zeal of the Levites who fill in for the missing priests on this occasion. Josephus leaves aside biblical notice (2 Chr 29:35) on the additional sacrifices by means of which the temple cult was re-activated.

[1055] Cf. 2 Chr 29:36a, where king and people "rejoice" over what God has done for them. Josephus adds

Passover (Phaska) celebrated

271 Once the feast of Unleavened Bread had been observed, they sacrificed the so-called *Phaska*[1056] and then offered the other sacrifices for seven days.[1057] To the crowd, in addition to their own presentation of pleasing sacrifices, the king donated 2,000 bulls and 7,000 [other] animals.[1058] The leaders also did the same, for they gave them 1,000 bulls, plus 1,040 [other] animals.[1059] **272** The feast, which had not been celebrated in this way from [the time] of King Solomon was for the first time carried out splendidly and lavishly.[1060]

Indolatry purged

Once the things [pertaining to] the feast had been completed, they went out into the country and purified it.[1061] **273** They likewise cleansed the city of every idolatrous pollution.[1062]

Hezekiah's cultic provisions

The king arranged that the daily sacrifices be offered from his own [property] in accordance with the law.[1063] He fixed the tithes to be given to the priests and Levites by the crowd, as well as the first fruits,[1064] so that they [the priests and Levites] might

---

the reference to the parties' joint "feasting." He leaves aside the (extraneous) comment of 29:36b: "for the [which?] thing came about suddenly."

[1056] Whereas 2 Chr 30:1-2 has Hezekiah summoning people to a celebration of Passover, the account of the actual observance in 30:13-22 oscillates between references to "Passover/the Passover lamb" (vv. 15, 16, 18) and the "feast of Unleavened Bread" (vv. 13, 21). Here in 9.271, Josephus, reversing the standard biblical sequence of the 2 observances (see, e.g., Exod 12:1-20), differentiates between the earlier "feast of Unleavened Bread" (to which Hezekiah summons Judeans and northerners in 9.263-264) and the subsequent Passover sacrifice. See further Feldman (BJP 3: 303 n. 716) on *Ant.* 3.248-249, where questions about the relationship between the 2 festivals also arise. On the Passover in Josephus overall, see Colautti 2002.

[1057] See 2 Chr 30:22b, which mentions the people's "sacrificing peace offerings for the 7 days of the festival" (i.e. of Unleavened Bread (see 30:21—in Josephus this feast precedes "Passover" and its appended sacrifices). Josephus leaves aside the details concerning Hezekiah's Passover as reported in 2 Chr 30:15-22a, these including the references to the "priests and Levites being put to shame" (30:15bα) and to the northerners' consuming the Passover lamb notwithstanding their state of ritual impurity (30:18a), so that Hezekiah must pray (30:18b-19) for their pardon by God, who grants this (30:20). Josephus thus avoids ascribing such cultic irregularities to the participants on this momentous occasion, when the illegalities of Ahaz' reign are to be reversed.

[1058] See 2 Chr 30:24a. Josephus accentuates Hezekiah's generosity to the people by doubling the number of cattle—1,000 according to the Chronicler—that he denotes to the people. He leaves aside the preceding notice of 30:23, with its reference to a communal decision to extend the (now-concluded) 7-day observance

of the feast of Unleavened Bread for an additional 7 days—something not envisaged in the pentateuchal regulations concerning Passover/Unleavened Bread.

[1059] In 2 Chr 30:24b the figures for the princes' donation are 1,000 bulls and *10,000* sheep. Whereas Josephus magnifies Hezekiah's personal donation (see previous note), he drastically reduces the Chronicler's figure for the non-bovine animals contributed by the royal officials.

[1060] See 2 Chr 30:26. Josephus omits the listing of the festival participants given in 30:25 as well as the mention (30:27) of the priests and Levites' blessing the people such that their voices reach God's habitation in heaven.

[1061] Josephus here generalizes the catalogue of iconoclastic measures perpetrated outside Jerusalem following Hezekiah's Passover as cited in 2 Chr 31:1a. He leaves aside the attached notice (31:1b) on the subsequent return of the Israelites to their homes.

[1062] This is Josephus' "delayed" and generalized version of 2 Chr 30:14, which speaks of the people's removal of the idolatrous altars from Jerusalem to the Kidron valley, prior to (rather than after, so Josephus) Hezekiah's Passover festival. Compare 2 Kgs 18:4, which enumerates a series of iconoclastic measures initiated by Hezekiah, including his destruction of the bronze serpent, Nehustan, which Moses himself had made (Josephus omits not only this reference, but also the entire episode to which it refers, i.e. Num 21:4-9, with its seeming imputation of idol-making to Moses himself).

[1063] See 2 Chr 31:3, which enumerates the various kinds of sacrifices for which the king provides the victims. Josephus omits the preceding notice (31:2) on Hezekiah's appointing the various divisions of priests and Levites.

[1064] 2 Chr 31:4a speaks more generally of the "portion due the priests and Levites."

always persevere in their worship and be single-minded[1065] in their cult of God.[1066]

274 The crowd collected every sort of fruit for the priests and Levites.[1067] The king constructed storehouses[1068] and chambers for these and made a distribution to each of the priests and Levites, along with their children and wives.[1069] Thus they returned again to their ancient worship.[1070]

275 When he [had effected] these things in the above-mentioned way,[1071] the king, launching a war, went out against the Palestinoi. After defeating them, he subjugated all the enemy cities from Gaza as far as Gitta.[1072] But then the king of the Assyrians sent and threatened to overthrow his entire rule if he did not render the tribute his father had earlier paid.[1073] **276** Ezekias, however, thought nothing of his threats. Rather, he was encouraged by his piety towards the Deity[1074] and by the prophet Hesaias[1075] [Isaiah], by whom he was accurately informed concerning everything that what was to be. Let this suffice concerning this king for the present.[1076]

Hezekiah subjugates philistines

Hezekiah disregards Assyrian threat

(14.1) 277 Now when it was announced to Salmanasses, the king of the Assyrians,[1077] that Osees, the king of the Israelites, had sent secretly to Soas,[1078] the king of the Egyptians, appealing to him for an alliance against him,[1079] he, becoming

Assyrian campaign against rebel Hoshea

[1065] Greek: ἀχώριστος. This term occurs only 1 other time in the Josephan corpus, namely in *War* 1.388, and there only in some MSS.

[1066] Greek: θεραπεία τοῦ θεοῦ. This expression occurs also in *Ant.* 3.251; cf. *Ant.* 4.70. Compare the motivation attached to Hezekiah's order that the people provide the priests and Levites with their portions in 2 Chr 31:4b: "that they [the clerical orders] might give themselves to the law of the Lord."

[1067] See 2 Chr 31:5, which provides an extended list of the items collected. Josephus has no equivalent to the following biblical sequence (31:6-10) concerning the people's "heaping up" their contributions and the discussion regarding these heaps between Hezekiah and the cultic officials.

[1068] In 2 Chr 31:11 some collectivity ("they"- the cultic officials?, the people as a whole?) prepares the temple storehouses according to the king's directives. Josephus accentuates Hezekiah's personal involvement in the project.

[1069] Josephus condenses the extended account given in 2 Chr 31:12-19 concerning the procedures for the distribution of the people's contributions to the priests and Levites. He likewise attributes the distribution directly to Hezekiah, whereas in Chronicles the king works through priestly and Levitical overseers appointed by him.

[1070] This brief conclusion to Josephus' account of Hezekiah's cultic reform (9.260-274) takes the place of the more expansive summary of the king's (cultic) achievements in 2 Chr 31:20-21. Its phrase "ancient worship" recalls the expressions "ancient and ancestral honor" of 9.262 and "ancient custom" in 9.264.

[1071] Josephus supplies this transition to his account

of the (initial) military events of Hezekiah's reign in what follows.

[1072] For this notice Josephus draws on 2 Kgs 18:8, where the king's Philistine conquests extend "as far as Gaza and its territory, from watchtower to fortified city."

[1073] Compare 2 Chr 32:1, where, following Hezekiah's cultic reforms (2 Chronicles 29-31), the Assyrian king Sennacherib invades Judah, with the intention of subjugating its fortified cities (in 2 Kgs 18:7b the reference is rather to Hezekiah's rebelling against the king of Assyria and refusal to serve him). Josephus replaces the Chronicler's indication concerning the intention behind the Assyrian invasion with an allusion to the tribute Ahaz had paid the Assyrians; see 9.252, 254.

[1074] See 9.260, where, when introducing Hezekiah, Josephus characterizes him as "pious."

[1075] MT (2 Kgs 19:2, etc.) יְשַׁעְיָהוּ (Eng.: "Isaiah"); LXX BL Ἡσαίας; Josephus Ἡσαίας.

[1076] Josephus rounds off his initial presentation of Hezekiah with these notices (which have no precise parallel in the biblical accounts) on Hezekiah's response to the first emergence of the Assyrian threat and his relationship to the prophet Isaiah.

[1077] Josephus introduced this king and his initial dealings with Hoshea of Israel in 9.259. On Josephus' account of the end of the Northern Kingdom in 9.277-291 (// 2 Kgs 17:4-41; 18:9-12), see Begg 2000: 367-86.

[1078] MT (2 Kgs 17:4) סוֹא (Eng.: "So"): LXX B Σηγώρ; LXX L Ἀδραμέλεχ τὸν Αἰθίοπα; Josephus Σώας. The identity of this figure remains a mystery.

[1079] 2 Kgs 17:4 does not mention the intended purpose of Hoshea's "sending" to King So; it notes, rather

enraged, campaigned against Samareia in the seventh year of the reign of Osees.[1080]

Samaria captured and people deported

278 When the king did not admit him,[1081] he besieged Samareia for three years and took it by storm in the ninth year of Osees' reign as king and in the seventh of that of Ezekias, the king of the Hierosolymites.[1082] He utterly[1083] exterminated the leadership of the Israelites,[1084] and transported the entire people to Media and Persia,[1085] among them also King Osees whom he took alive.[1086] **279** Moving other nations from a certain river called the Chouthas[1087]—for there is a river in the country of the Persians bearing this name[1088]—he settled them in Samareia and the country of the Israelites.[1089]

Chronological remarks

280 The ten tribes of the Israelites were transported from Judea[1090] 947 years from the time when their ancestors went out from Egypt and occupied the country under their general Iesous[1091] From [the time] when, revolting against Roboam the grandson of David, they handed the kingship over to Hieroboam, as I have related earlier,[1092] it was 240 years, seven months, and seven days.[1093]

Causes of Israel's demise

281 And this end came upon the Israelites for their transgressing against the

---

that the former in connection with this initiative, ceased paying tribute to Assyria.

[1080] 2 Kgs 17:4 itself does not provide a date for the Assyrian move against Hoshea. The parallel text 2 Kgs 18:9 (MT; LXX BL) however, gives the same date for this initiative as does Josephus, adding that this was also the 4th year of Hezekiah.

[1081] According to the sequence of 2 Kgs 17:4b-6, Hoshea had already been captured by Shalmaneser (v. 4b) prior to the latter's laying siege to Samaria (v. 5). Perhaps finding it implausible that Shalmaneser could have gotten his hands on Hoshea before capturing his capital, Josephus presents the Assyrian siege and capture of Samaria as preceding the seizure of Hoshea himself, who he portrays as refusing admittance to the advancing Assyrians, thereby necessitating the siege of the city that will lead to his own capture (see 9.278b).

[1082] Josephus agrees with MT LXX BL 2 Kgs 17:5b-6 and 18:10 in dating the fall of Samaria to the 9th year of Hoshea, following a 3-year siege. The latter text further places the event in the *6th* year of Hezekiah (the LXX MS 127 reads 12th here). It might be noted that Josephus' dating indications in 9.277-278 concerning the course of the siege appear internally inconsistent: the siege begins in Hoshea's 7th year, lasts 3 years, and ends in Hoshea's 9th year, rather than the expected 10th.

[1083] Greek: ἄρδην. This term occurs only here in the *Antiquities*; it is used 4 times in the *Life* (102, 306, 375, 384).

[1084] The accounts of the Assyrian measures against Israel in 2 Kgs 17:4-6 and 18:9-12 do not explicitly mention such an annihilation of the Israelite leaders. Josephus may have derived his inspiration for the item from the biblical description of the Babylonians' executing the Jerusalem leadership following their capture

of the city; see 2 Kgs 25:18-21 (// *Ant.* 10.149). In introducing the item here, he reinforces the parallelism between the respective ends of the 2 capitals.

[1085] Josephus generalizes the wording of 2 Kgs 17:6 // 18:11, where the Israelites are carried initially "to Assyria" and then settled "in Halah, and on the Habor, the river of Gozan, and in the cities of the Medes." Josephus may have derived his combination "Media and Persia" from the use of the phrase "the Medes and the Persians" in such biblical texts as Dan 5:28; 6:8.

[1086] As pointed out in the note to "admit him" at 9.278, 2 Kgs 17:4b represents Hoshea as being captured *prior to*, rather than after, the Assyrian siege of Samaria.

[1087] MT (2 Kgs 17:24) כותה (Eng.: "Cuthah"); LXX B Χουνθά; LXX L Χωθά; Josephus Χουθᾶς.

[1088] Josephus supplies this localization, itself picking up on his reference to "Persia" in 9.278, of the site "Cuthah" mentioned in 2 Kgs 17:24.

[1089] Josephus anticipates this notice on the Assyrian re-population measures, corresponding to their deportation of the Israelites, from 2 Kgs 17:24, which lists a series of 4 sites, in addition to "Cuthah," from which the new populations are drawn. Of the 5 place names of 2 Kgs 17:24, Josephus singles out "Cuthah" alone for mention, given that this is the origin of the derogatory name for the Samaritans used by him (and Rabbinic tradition), i.e. "Couthaioi"; see on 9.290.

[1090] Josephus' expression here appears careless in that the 10 tribes in question were not inhabitants of "Judea," but rather of the Northern Kingdom, Israel.

[1091] My translation follows that of Marcus, who omits the words "it was 800 years" that follow the name "Iesous" in the codices (and the text printed by Niese) as a "scribal addition," lacking in ELat.

[1092] See *Ant.* 8.212-224.

[1093] This figure corresponds precisely to the datings

laws[1094] and disregarding the prophets who predicted this misfortune to them—unless they ceased their impieties.[1095] **282** The beginning of their calamities was the civil strife in which they rebelled[1096] against Roboam, the grandson of David, and appointed as their king his slave Hieroboam, who by offending the Deity, made him a enemy[1097] to them who imitated his lawlessness.[1098] But this was the judgment that he [Hieroboam] deservedly underwent.[1099]

(14.2) 283 Now[1100] the king of the Assyrians went up to make war on Syria and all Phoinike.[1101] The name of this king is recorded in the Tyrian archives,[1102] for he campaigned against Tyre when Eloulai[1103] was its king. Menander also attests to these matters (he made a chronicle-record and translated the Tyrian archives into the Greek language).[1104] He relates this:

284 "And Eloulai, who was surnamed Puas,[1105] reigned as king for thirty-six years. When the Kitieis[1106] revolted, he sailed there and made them subject again. In his time Selampsas,[1107] the king of the Assyrians, came up, making war on all

Menander's testimony or Shalmaneser's campaign against Tyre

---

given by Josephus for the reigns of the northern kings from Jeroboam I to Hoshea; see the chart in Marcus *ad loc*. With the above "chronological interlude," linking the fall of Israel with other key events of the nation's earlier history, Josephus highlights the importance of the former happening, just as he does Solomon's initiation of the building of the temple in *Ant.* 8.61-62.

[1094] See 2 Kgs 17:16a: "and they [the Israelites] forsook all the commandments of the Lord...." Josephus leaves aside the many particular cultic transgressions of the Israelites cited in illustration of this general charge in 17:7-12, 15, 16b-17.

[1095] See 2 Kgs 17:13-14, which speaks of Israel's refusal to heed the series of "prophets and seers" sent by the Lord to warn the people. The wording of Josephus' version here is reminiscent of his (added) reference (9.265) to the Israelites of Hezekiah's time despising the prophets who "predicted what they would experience if they did not shift to piety towards God." Those prophets' despised prediction has now proved true.

[1096] The underlying Greek here contains a cognate-accusative wordplay: ἡ στάσις ἥν ἐστασίασαν.

[1097] Greek: ἐχθρὸν ποιέω. Josephus' only other use of this phrase is in *Ant.* 4.190, where Moses warns the people of the consequences of their having antagonized God.

[1098] See 2 Kgs 17:21-22 on Jeroboam's accession, his apostasy, and the people's joining in this as further grounds for Israel's demise, beyond the cultic crimes adduced in 17:7-20. The reference to the people's participation in Jeroboam's offenses is reminiscent of Ahijah's charge in *Ant.* 8.271 that the Israelites "have followed the impieties" of Jeroboam.

[1099] In 2 Kgs 17:23 Israel as a whole is punished for its persistence in the sins of Jeroboam by being exiled to Assyria. In Josephus' presentation Jeroboam himself

undergoes his ultimate punishment in the overthrow of the kingdom that he inaugurated.

[1100] At this point Josephus interrupts his version of 2 Kings 17 in order to make use of the accounts given by his various extra-biblical sources concerning other military initiatives by Assyria, more or less contemporaneous with its campaign against Samaria. By means of the insertion, Josephus reminds gentile readers of the existence of extra-biblical evidence for the existence and military exploits of the Assyrian king Shalmaneser, the conqueror of Samaria according to the Bible.

[1101] The above formulation is Josephus' heading to the extra-biblical accounts he is about to relate.

[1102] Josephus mentioned the "Tyrian archives" in connection with his treatment of the correspondence between Solomon and Hiram of Tyre in *Ant.* 8.55-56, claiming that these confirm the biblical account of their exchanges.

[1103] Josephus draws the name of this Tyrian king (Greek: Ἐλουλαῖος) from the passage of Menander that he will cite in what follows.

[1104] Josephus earlier introduced Menander and mentioned his work as a translator of the "Tyrian records" in *Ant.* 8.144a, prior to citing that historian's testimony concerning the exchanges between Solomon and Hiram in 8.144b-146.

[1105] This phrase (Greek: θεμένων αὐτῷ Πύας), retained by Niese and Marcus, is missing in Lat and omitted by the *Ed. pr.* On the long-running discussion concerning the identity of "Puas," see Begg 2000: 376, n. 50.

[1106] This is the conjecture (Greek: Κιτιέων) of Niese, followed by Marcus and Schalit *s.v.*, for the reading of the codices, i.e. Κιτταῖων, which Niese prints in his text. The name designates the inhabitants of Cyprus.

[1107] This phrase translates the conjecture of Niese (Greek: ἐπὶ τούτου Σελάμψας [= Shalmaneser]), inspired

Phoinike;[1108] once he had concluded peace[1109] with all of them, he went back home. **285** Then Tyre, Sidon, and Arke,[1110] as well as old Tyre[1111] and many other cities that had handed themselves over to the king of the Assyrians revolted. Given the Tyrians' insubordination, the king returned against them again. The Phoenicians provided him with 60 ships and 800 rowers. **286** Sailing against them with twelve ships, the Tyrians scattered the ships of their adversaries and took 500 men captive.[1112] However, the prices of everything in Tyre went up on account of this.[1113] **287** But when the king of the Assyrians withdrew, he posted guards at the river and the aqueducts to prevent the Tyrians from drawing water. Although this went on for five years, they prevailed by drinking from the wells they had dug."

This then is what is written in the Tyrian archives concerning Salmanasses, the king of the Assyrians.[1114]

New settlers in Samaria

(14.3) 288 Now those who were settled in Samareia[1115] were the "Chouthaioi," for they are called by this name until today because they were brought in from the country called "Chouthas"; this is Persia, where there is a river that has this name.[1116] Each of the nations—there were five of them[1117]—brought its own god to Samareia. By adoring these, as was their ancestral [custom],[1118] they aroused the greatest

Plague averted

God[1119] to wrath and rage.[1120] **289** For he inflicted them with a plague, by which

---

by Lat's "*contra quos denuo salamanassis...*," which Marcus (*ad loc.*) follows "with hesitancy." By contrast, the codices MSPLauV and editors prior to Niese read ἐπὶ τούτους πέμψας ("against whom [the king of Assyria] having sent..."). See Begg 2000: 376-7, n. 55.

[1108] Josephus draws his own formulation at the opening of 9.283 from this portion of Menander's text.

[1109] The Greek phrase (σπεισάμενος εἰρήνην) used here translates literally as "libating peace"; see the related expression "libate friendship" in *Ant.* 5.51; 17.68.

[1110] The codices Lau and V read another place name here, i.e. "Acco," the later Ptolemais. Scholars are divided as to which reading is to be preferred; see Begg 2000: 377-8, n. 58.

[1111] "Old Tyre" was a mainland site, located opposite the island called "Tyre," from which the island Tyre drew its water supply.

[1112] On the problem of the marked numerical discrepancy between the Phoenician and the Tyrian contingents (60 vs. 12 ships) posed by the above reading, and on scholarly proposals for dealing with this (e.g., reading 16 rather than 60 for the number of Phoenician ships), see Rebuffat 1976 and Begg 2000: 378, n. 61.

[1113] The rendering of the Greek phrase (ἐπετάθη δὴ πάντων ἐν Τύρῳ τιμή διὰ ταῦτα) underlying the above translation has long been controverted. My translation follows a line of interpretation initiated by H. Grotius and adopted by Marcus. See Reinach 1924 and Begg 2000: 378, n. 63 for more details.

[1114] This formula picks up on Josephus' mention of the "Tyrian archives" (9.283), which Menander—whom he has been quoting in 9.284-287—is there said to have translated. Note that, contrary to Josephus' asser-

tion here in 9.287, the name "Salmanasses" (biblical Shalmaneser) does not actually appear in the Greek text of his quotation from Menander (in 9.284 "Selampsas" as the name for the Assyrian king is Niese's conjecture and the identification of that name with Salmanasses/ Shalmaneser a further conjecture; see note to "Selampsas" there).

[1115] At this juncture, Josephus resumes his account of the replacement population established by the Assyrians in the former territory of Israel, begun by him in 9.279 (// 2 Kgs 17:24) and interrupted by the extended intervening segment (9.280-287) dealing with the dating of the Israel's demise in relation to other significant biblical events (9.280-282) and the extra-biblical documentation concerning Samaria's conqueror, Shalmaneser (9.283-287).

[1116] Josephus supplies this non-biblical, collective name for the replacement population ("Couthaioi") and then connects this name with the population's place of origin as mentioned by him in 9.279.

[1117] With this figure Josephus alludes to the 5 cities/regions named in 2 Kgs 17:24 (Babylon, Cuthah, Avva, Hamath, and Sephar-vaim) from which Samaria was re-populated.

[1118] This is Josephus' version of the statement of 2 Kgs 17:25a, according to which the new immigrants to Samaria initially "did not fear the Lord"—an idiom Josephus regularly avoids.

[1119] In connection with the Samaritans this designation recurs in *Ant.* 9.289 and 12.257 (where their temple on Mt. Gerizim is said to be dedicated to this Deity). The designation replaces the phrase "the god of the land" of 2 Kgs 17:26-27, which might seem to suggest

they were afflicted.[1121] Ascertaining no cure for their calamities, they learned by way of an oracle that, if they worshiped the greatest God, this would be [a source of] safety to them.[1122] They therefore dispatched messengers to the king of the Assyrians and begged him to send them priests from those he had taken captive when he warred against the Israelites.[1123]

290 Upon his sending these and their being taught the ordinances and reverence for this God,[1124] they worshiped him lavishly and the plague immediately ceased.[1125] Even now the name "Chouthaioi" continues to be used for these nations in the Hebrew language,[1126] whereas in Greek they are called "Samareitai."[1127] **291** Whenever, by turns, they see things going well for the Judeans, they call themselves their relatives, in that they are descendants of Josep [Joseph] and have family ties with them in virtue of that origin. When, however, they see that things are going badly for them [the Judeans], they say that they owe nothing to them and that they have no claim to their loyalty or race. Instead, they make themselves out to be migrants[1128] of another nation. But about these matters we shall have to speak in a more suitable place.[1129]

The Samaritans ("Chouthaioi") and their stance towards the Jews

---

a geographical limitation to the Lord's power.

[1120] Josephus adds this reference to God's emotional response to the settlers' worship of other deities. The collocation "wrath and rage" (Greek: ὀργὴ καὶ χολός) occurs only once elsewhere in Josephus, i.e. in *Ant.* 6.16, where it is used of God's response to the lack of respect shown the ark by the people of Beth-shemesh.

[1121] Josephus generalizes the notice of 2 Kgs 17:25b, according to which God-sent "lions" killed the new settlers.

[1122] Josephus supplies this notice as a preparation for his modified rendering of the continuation of the biblical account of the settlers; the addition indicates that the solution to their plight was devised by God himself, not by the Assyrian king as in 2 Kgs 17:27.

[1123] Compare 2 Kgs 17:26, where the identity of those informing the Assyrian king of the settlers' plight is left unspecified and their condition is simply reported to him without any proposal being made as to how this might be alleviated, whereupon (17:27) the king, on his own, decides to send them a priest to teach them "the law of the God of the land." In line with his previous addition (see preceding note), Josephus has the settlers be the ones to report to the king and to make a request of him (i.e. that he send them priests), to which the king then accedes.

[1124] In 2 Kgs 17:28 the reference is to a single priest returnee, who settles at Bethel and teaches the inhabit-

ants "how they should fear the Lord." The phrase "reverence [Greek: ὁσία] for this God" recalls the expression "reverence [Greek: ὁσία] and honor towards God" in 9.261.

[1125] This double notice on the effect of the priest(s)' teaching has no explicit equivalent in 2 Kings 17. Josephus omits the long appendix of 2 Kgs 17:29-41 concerning the Samaritans' ongoing syncretism, even after their instruction by the priest (17:28).

[1126] This remark on the designation's ongoing use picks up on Josephus' earlier notice concerning the etymology of the name "Chouthaioi" (see 9.288).

[1127] In *Ant.* 10.184 Josephus gives a similarly worded notice on the 2 names for the Samaritans. There, however, the name "Samareitai" is not said to be the one used by the Greeks as here in 9.290, but rather to derive from the name of their place of residence, i.e. Samareia.

[1128] Greek: μετοικοί. Josephus' 1 other use of this word is in *Ant.* 14.115.

[1129] This concluding remark to his account of the origins of the Samaritans (9.279, 288-291) looks ahead to the continuation of Josephus' narrative, where he makes similar charges about the Samaritans' duplicitous vacillations regarding their (non-) kinship with the Jews; see *Ant.* 11.340; 12.257, 261. On Josephus' (ambivalent) stance towards the Samaritans overall, see Egger 1986; Coggins 1987; Feldman 1992; and Zangenberg 1994: 44-91.

BOOK TEN

(1.1) **1** Now Ezekias, the king of the two tribes, had already been exercising his leadership for fourteen years when the king of the Babylonians,[1] named Senacheirim,[2] campaigned against him with a large contingent; he took by storm all the cities of the tribes of Iouda and Benjamin.[3]

Sennacherib's invasion

2 When he was about to lead his army also against Hierosolyma,[4] Ezekias hastened to send messengers to him,[5] promising that he would be subject to him and pay whatever tribute he should impose.[6] When Senacheirim learned these things from the messengers, he decided not to make war; instead, he acceded to his request and agreed[7] that, once he had received 300 talents of silver and thirty of gold,[8] he would withdraw [as a] friend. He gave sworn pledges to the messengers that he would do him no wrong, but would thus turn back.[9]

Sennacherib accepts Hezekiah's appeal

3 Believing him,[10] Ezekias emptied his treasuries and sent the monies,[11] supposing that he would have relief from war and the struggle for his kingship.[12] **4** But once he received these things, the Assyrian thought nothing of his promises. Rather, while he himself campaigned against the Egyptians and the Ethiopians,[13] he left behind[14] his general Rapsakes[15] in great strength, as well as two other men of rank

Sennacherib reneges on pledges

Assyrian officers left to assault Jerusalem

---

[1] This is the reading of the codices RO, which Niese follows. The remaining MSS (and Marcus) have "(king) of the Assyrians," in accord with the title given "Sennacherib" in 2 Kgs 18:13// Isa 36:1. Historically, Sennacherib was king both of Assyria and Babylon.

[2] MT (2 Kgs 18:13// Isa 36:1) סנחריב (Eng.: "Sennacherib"); LXX B 2 Kgs 18:13 Σενναχερείμ; LXX L 2 Kgs 18:13 Σενναχερείβ; LXX Isa 36:1 Σενναχηριμ; Josephus Σεναχείριμος.

[3] See 2 Kgs 18:13// Isa 36:1. Josephus adds the reference to Sennacherib's "large contingent" and his capturing not only the cities of Judah, but also those of Benjamin. On Josephus' account of the delivery of Jerusalem from Sennacherib in 10.1-23 (// 2 Kgs 18:13-19:37// Isa 36:1-37:38; cf. 2 Chr 32:1-23), see Begg 2000: 387-417 and Höffken 1998: 37-48.

[4] Josephus adds this transitional phrase, motivating Hezekiah's following overture to Sennacherib as described in 2 Kgs 18:14-16 (no parallel in Isaiah 36).

[5] Josephus omits the specification of 2 Kgs 18:14aα concerning Sennacherib's current whereabouts, i.e. "at Lachish."

[6] From Hezekiah's statement to Sennacherib in 2 Kgs 18:14aβ, Josephus omits its opening confession "I have done wrong" (this alluding to the mention of Hezekiah's rebelling against and refusing to serve the king of Assyria in 18:7b) and the appended appeal "withdraw from me."

[7] These indications concerning Sennacherib's response expatiate on the notice regarding his financial demands of 2 Kgs 18:14b.

[8] Josephus' figures for the sums demanded by Sennacherib agree with those cited in 2 Kgs 18:14b (MT and LXX BL).

[9] The biblical account says nothing about any such promises on Sennacherib's part in return for the payment demanded by him in 2 Kgs 18:14b. Josephus' mention of these promises underscores the wrongfulness of the Assyrian's renewed attack on Hezekiah in what follows.

[10] This added allusion to Hezekiah's state of mind as he proceeds to fulfill Sennacherib's demand heightens the contrast between the good faith of the former and the perfidy of the latter.

[11] Josephus generalizes the notice of 2 Kgs 18:15-16 concerning the various "sources" (the temple and palace, as well as the gilding of the temple doors and doorposts) from which Hezekiah drew the required payment.

[12] Josephus appends this notice on the (deluded) expectations with which Hezekiah makes his payment to the Assyrian king.

[13] Josephus supplies this reference to Sennacherib's Egyptian/Ethiopian campaign here in order to prepare his subsequent citation of extra-biblical witnesses concerning that campaign; see 10.17-20. Cf. the notice on the Sennacherib's hearing of the advance of "Tirhakah king of Ethiopia" against him in 2 Kgs 19:9a// Isa 37:9a.

[14] In 2 Kgs 18:17// Isa 36:2 Sennacherib dispatches

(named Tharata[16] and Aracharis)[17] who were to ravage Hierosolyma.[18]

(1.2) 5 When they had come and encamped before the walls, they sent to Ezekias and requested that he come for negotiations.[19] He, however, out of cowardice, did not go out himself,[20] but sent out three of his closest friends to him [Rapsakes],[21] namely the steward of the kingdom[22] named Eliakias,[23] Soubanai,[24] and Joan[25] who was in charge of the records.[26] **6** These [men] came out then and took their stand opposite the leaders of the Assyrian army.[27]

Observing them, the general Rapsakes directed them to go off to Ezekias to say that Senacheirim, the great king, inquired of him on what he was relying and putting his confidence in that he was fleeing his master, not wishing either to listen to him nor receive his army into the city.[28] Or was he hoping that his army would be overcome by the Egyptians?[29] **7** If, however, he expected this, they should inform

---

his general(s) to Jerusalem "from Lachish." In Josephus he "leaves [them] behind" at an unspecified location within Hezekiah's territory, as he himself sets out against the Egyptians and Ethiopians.

[15] MT (2 Kgs 18:17// Isa 36:2) רב־שקה (Eng.: "Rabshakeh"); LXX BL 2 Kgs 18:17// LXX Isa 36:2 and Josephus Ῥαψάκης. Josephus takes the Assyrian title, meaning "chief steward," as the officer's proper name.

[16] MT (2 Kgs 18:17) תרתן (Eng.: "Tartan"); LXX BL Θανθάν; Josephus Θαρατά.

[17] MT (2 Kgs 18:17) רב־סרים (Eng.: "Rabsaris"; this title translates literally as "chief of the eunuchs"); LXX B Ῥαφείς; LXX L Ῥαψείς; Josephus Ἀράχαρις. In mentioning the 2 colleagues of the "Rabshakeh" Josephus goes together with 2 Kgs 18:17a against Isa 36:2a, which cites only the latter figure. On the other hand, Josephus, reverses the sequence of the 3 Assyrian titles in 18:17a, making "Rabshakeh" the 1st rather than the last of these, likely in consideration of the fact that this official will be the sole Assyrian speaker in what follows.

[18] Josephus appends this indication concerning the purpose of Sennacherib's dispatch of his officer(s) as mentioned in 2 Kgs 18:17a// Isa 36:2a.

[19] Josephus continues to follow the presentation of 2 Kgs 18:17b-18a (where the Assyrian officers summon Hezekiah upon their arrival) rather than Isa 36:2b-3 (where Hezekiah's officials simply go out to the Assyrians without a prior summons by them). He leaves aside the topographical indication, common to both biblical accounts, concerning the site where the Assyrians take their stand, i.e. "the conduit of the upper pool, which is on the highway to the Fuller's Field." Conversely, he appends the mention of the purpose (i.e. "negotiations") of the Assyrian summons to Hezekiah.

[20] Josephus supplies this unflattering explanation as to why Hezekiah did not go out in person to meet the Assyrians when summoned by them. On the addition, see Feldman 1998a: 367.

[21] Neither 2 Kgs 18:18b nor Isa 36:3 mentions this status of Hezekiah's 3 envoys as his intimate friends. Josephus' addition on the matter serves to explain why he chose these men in particular for the task at hand.

[22] In 2 Kgs 18:18// Isa 36:3 Eliakim's title is "the one over the house" (MT)/ "the steward" (LXX).

[23] MT (2 Kgs 18:18// Isa 36:3) אליקים (Eng.: "Eliakim"); LXX BL 2 Kgs 18:18 Ἐλιακείμ; LXX Isa 36:3 Ἐλιακιμ; Josephus Ἐλιακίας.

[24] MT (2 Kgs 18:18// Isa 36:3) שבנה (Eng.: "Shebneh"); LXX BL 2 Kgs 18:18// LXX Isa 36:3 Σόμνας; Josephus Σουβαναῖος. Josephus omits the biblical title of this official (RSV: "the secretary").

[25] MT (2 Kgs 18:18// Isa 36:3) יואה (Eng.: "Joah"); LXX B 2 Kgs 18:18 Ἰωσαφάτ; LXX L 2 Kgs 18:18 and LXX Isa 36:3 Ἰωάχ; Josephus Ἰώανος (this is the reading of R, which Niese follows; Marcus and Schalit *s.v.* read Ἰωάχος with MSP). Josephus omits the names of the fathers of both Eliakim and Joah, i.e. "Hilkiah" and "Asaph," respectively.

[26] Josephus' title corresponds to that given "Joah" in 2 Kgs 18:18// Isa 36:3, i.e. "the recorder" (RSV).

[27] Josephus supplies the notice on the position assumed by Hezekiah's envoys as the negotiations begin.

[28] In 2 Kgs 18:19-20// Isa 36:4-5 the Rabshakeh poses a series of 3 questions that the messengers are to convey to Hezekiah, all revolving around the grounds for the king's current "confidence." Josephus' version picks up on the 2nd of these questions ("on whom do you now rely that you have rebelled against me?"), likewise specifying the nature of Hezekiah's "rebellion" in terms of his refusal to listen to his overlord and admit his army.

[29] Josephus turns the Rabshakeh's statement of 2 Kgs 18:21a// Isa 36:6a about Hezekiah's "relying" on Egypt into this question by him about whether the king is expecting the Egyptians to defeat Sennacherib (whose current campaign against them Josephus has mentioned in 10.4).

him that he was being foolish and like a person who leans upon a shattered reed until this collapses and he, with his hand pierced, feels the pain.[30] "He [Ezekias] should know too that the Assyrian king was making his campaign against him by the will of God, who had enabled him to overthrow the kingship of the Israelites in order that he [Senacheirim] might, in the same way, now destroy those ruled by him [Ezekias]."[31]

8 Rapsakes said these things in Hebrew, a language with which he was familiar.[32] Eliakias, however, fearing that the crowd would fall into consternation on overhearing [his words],[33] requested him[34] to speak in Syrian.[35] The general, for his part, perceived his state of mind and the fright he felt.[36]

Judean envoys ask Rabshakeh to speak Aramaic (Syrian)

Employing a louder and more distinct tone of voice,[37] he answered that he would speak Hebrew[38] to him [Eliakias] in order that all might hear the orders of the king and, "choosing what was advantageous, hand themselves over to us.[39] **9** For it is clear that you and the king are persuading the people to hold out, deceiving them with vain hopes.[40] If, however, you are confident and think you can annihilate our

Refusing request, Rabshakeh resumes his threats in Hebrew

---

[30] Josephus expatiates on Rabshakeh's qualification of Egypt as "a broken reed of a staff, which will pierce the hand of any man who leans on it" of 2 Kgs 18:21a // Isa 36:6a, underscoring the delusiveness of such a hope. He leaves aside the Assyrian's allusion to another potential—but equally delusive—object of Hezekiah's confidence, i.e. the Lord himself, whose "high places and altars" outside Jerusalem the king has "removed" (2 Kgs 18:22// Isa 36:7). With regard to this latter element, Josephus may have found it implausible that a foreign general would have been thus informed about Hezekiah's cultic measures.

[31] See 2 Kgs 18:25// Isa 36:10, where the Rabshakeh concludes his speech to the envoys with the affirmation that the Lord as commissioned Sennacherib to destroy Hezekiah's land. Josephus amplifies this statement with a reminder of Assyria's recent destruction of Israel.

[32] Josephus supplies this remark about the Rabshakeh's knowledge of and use of Hebrew in speaking to the envoys in order to prepare the new turn the negotiations will now take.

[33] Josephus adds this remark on the motivation behind the Judean's request (2 Kgs 18:26// Isa 36:11) that the Rabshakeh switch languages in speaking to them. The reference to Eliakim's "fear" echoes Josephus' allusion to Hezekiah's own "cowardice" in 10.5. Both Josephan additions underscore the terror-engendering magnitude of the Assyrian threat (as well as the still greater power of God as displayed in his subsequent elimination of that threat).

[34] In 2 Kgs 18:26// Isa 36:11 all 3 Judean envoys make the request of the Rabshakeh. Josephus highlights the stature of Eliakim by having him alone address the Assyrian.

[35] Josephus uses the LXX's term (συριστί, "Syrian") for the language the Rabshakeh is being asked to

speak, whereas MT 2 Kgs 18:26a// Isa 36:11a call it אֲרָמִית (RSV: "in the Aramaic language"). Josephus omits the continuation of the envoys' request (18:26b // 36:11b), in which they first aver that they themselves understand "Aramaic" and then ask the Rabshakeh not to speak "the language of Judah" (i.e. Hebrew) in the presence of those on the wall.

[36] Josephus' added notice on the Rabshakeh's "perception" of what lies behind Eliakim's request picks up on his remark earlier in 10.8 about the "fear" that prompts the Judean's appeal.

[37] In 2 Kgs 18:28// Isa 36:13 the Rabshakeh uses "a loud voice" when he begins his address to the city's defenders (18:28-35// 36:13-20), following his separate, previous response to the 3 envoys in 18:27// 36:12. Josephus conflates the Assyrian's 2 distinct biblical discourses into a single one, this directed both to the envoys and to Jerusalem's defenders.

[38] Josephus substitutes this designation (Greek: ἑβραϊστί) for the language of the Rabshakeh's subsequent discourse for the biblical terms used in 2 Kgs 18:28// Isa 36:13, i.e. יְהוּדִית (MT; RSV: "in the language of Judah") /Ἰουδαιστί (LXX). The earliest extant attestation of the use of the word "Hebrew" to designate a language is in the Prologue to the Greek translation of the Book of Sirach, written sometime after 132 BCE by the author's grandson.

[39] This explanation as to why the Rabshakeh intends to use "Hebrew" in his subsequent discourse takes the place of the vulgar language used by him in his initial response to the envoys (alone) in 2 Kgs 18:27// Isa 36:12: "has my master sent me to speak these words to your master and to you, and not to the men on the wall, who are doomed with you to eat their own dung and drink their own urine?"

[40] This assertion—associating the envoys with Hezekiah himself—takes the place of the double

army, I am ready to award you 2,000 horses from my contingent. By giving them an equal number of riders, display your own force. But those [riders] that you do not have, you are unable to give.[41] **10** Why therefore do you hesitate to surrender yourselves to those who are better and who will take you even if you are unwilling?[42] And yet your security [lies] in voluntary surrender, whereas an involuntary one to those who are warring against you appears dangerous and the cause of misfortunes."[43]

Hezekiah appeals to God

(1.3) 11 When they heard the general of the Assyrians saying these things, the populace and the messengers reported it to Ezekias.[44] At this, he laid aside his royal garments[45] and, putting on sackcloth and donning humble dress[46], he, in accordance with the ancestral law, fell on his face and entreated God and implored him to help him, who had no other hope of safety.[47]

Hezekiah requests Isaiah's (Hesaias') intercession

12 He also sent some of his friends and the priests[48] to the prophet Hesaias[49] [Isaiah] and requested him to pray to God and, after making sacrifices on behalf of the common safety, to appeal to him [God] to take measures against the enemy's hopes and have mercy on his people.[50]

---

warning the Rabshakeh issues in 2 Kgs 18:29-30// Isa 36:14-15 about what the defenders should not "let" Hezekiah do, i.e. "deceive" them and make them "rely on the Lord." Josephus omits the general's opening call to attention ("hear the word(s) of the great king, the king of Assyria") of 18:28b// 36:13b.

[41] Josephus at this juncture incorporates into the Rabshakeh's address to the envoys and the defenders a portion of his previous speech to the former, earlier passed over by him, i.e. the general's "wager" about the 2,000 horses the Assyrian king will furnish to Hezekiah should he be able to provide riders for these (see 2 Kgs 18:23// Isa 36:8). In so doing, he has the Rabshakeh spell out both the intended "purpose" of the wager (the opportunity for the Judeans to "display their own force") and the fact of their inability to meet the challenge.

[42] With this question of the Rabshakeh to his hearers concerning their "hesitation," compare the appeal made by him in his master's name in 2 Kgs 18:31aβ// Isa 36:16aβ: "make your peace with me and come out to me." Josephus leaves aside the general's preceding negative admonition and attached messenger formula of 18:31aα// 36:16aα: "do not listen to Hezekiah; for thus says the king of Assyria...."

[43] This summarizing conclusion to the Rabshakeh's speech with its general allusion to the alternatives facing the hearers takes the place of the more specific items featured in the final portion of the general's biblical speech: promises for the hearers should they surrender (2 Kgs 18:31b-32a// Isa 36:16b-17) and warning not to listen to Hezekiah's assurances that the Lord will deliver Jerusalem (18:32b// 36:18a), given that "no god" has been able to defend his city/country against the Assyrian king hitherto (18:33-35// 36:18b-20).

[44] Josephus conflates the sequence of 2 Kgs 18:36-37// Isa 36:21-22, in which the reactions of the people and the envoys to Rabshakeh's address(es) are reported separately: the former remain silent as ordered by Hezekiah, while the latter go to the king with rent garments and make their report to him.

[45] In 2 Kgs 19:1aβ// Isa 37:1aβ Hezekiah "rends" his clothes.

[46] In 2 Kgs 19:1bα// Isa 37:1bα Hezekiah "covers himself with sackcloth."

[47] 2 Kgs 19:1bβ// Isa 37:1bβ simply state that Hezekiah went "into the house of the Lord." Josephus accentuates the king's piety with his mention of a prayer-appeal by him, carried out in "accordance with the ancestral law," i.e. traditional practice on such occasions.

[48] 2 Kgs 19:2// Isa 37:2 mention Eliakim and Shebna by name (and title) as members of the royal delegation. Josephus' general allusion to these figures via the term "friends" picks up on his earlier designation of Hezekiah's envoys as "3 of his closest *friends*" in 10.5. He omits the biblical detail about the delegation's being "clothed in sackcloth."

[49] Josephus made previous mention of "Isaiah" and Hezekiah's reliance on him in *Ant.* 9.276. Here he omits the name of the prophet's father (MT: Amoz) cited in 2 Kgs 19:2b// Isa 37:2b. On Josephus' overall treatment of Isaiah, see Feldman 1998a: 376-92.

[50] This is Josephus' rendering of the conclusion of Hezekiah's appeal to Isaiah as cited in 2 Kgs 19:4b// Isa 37:4b ("...lift up your prayer for the remnant that is left"). In his reworking of the king's biblical message to the prophet (19:3-4// Isa 37:3-4), Josephus has him add the reference to a prior sacrificing by Isaiah and makes more specific what it is that Hezekiah wants Isaiah to ask of God. He leaves aside the opening mess-

13 When the prophet had done these things, and God had spoken to him by way of an oracle, he encouraged the king himself and the friends around him.[51] He predicted that the enemy would be defeated without a fight and would withdraw in shame instead of their present confidence.[52] **14** For God would take care that they should be destroyed in this way.[53] He further predicted that Senacheirim himself, the king of the Assyrians, would fail utterly in the Egyptian affair;[54] he would return home and perish by the sword.[55]

Isaiah's assurance

(1.4) 15 It happened at this same time that the Assyrian [king] had written communications to Ezekias,[56] in which he said that he was foolish[57] to think that he would escape slavery under himself, who had subjugated many and great nations.[58] He threatened to utterly destroy him once he had taken him, if he did not open the gates on his own initiative and receive his army into Hierosolyma.[59]

Sennacherib's threatening letter

---

enger formula and attached figurative language about it being "a day of distress" of 19:3// 37:3, as well as the king's allusion (19:4a// 37:4a) to the possibility that, having heard the words of the Rabshakeh, the Lord will "rebuke" those words.

[51] This sequence, with its focus on Isaiah himself, replaces the mention of the delegation's approaching the prophet in 2 Kgs 19:5// Isa 37:5. The reference to God's speaking to Isaiah "by way of an oracle" (Greek: χρηματίσαντος) echoes the allusion to the pagan arrivals in Samaria "learning by an oracle" (Greek: χρησμῷ) about how they might appease God in *Ant.* 9.289. Josephus' mention of Isaiah's "encouraging" the king and his friends turns into a narrative notice the prophet's opening exhortation of 2 Kgs 19:6// Isa 37:6: "do not be afraid because of the words you have heard...."

[52] Compare Isaiah's initial announcement in 2 Kgs 19:7a// Isa 37:7a: "... I [God] will put a spirit in him [Sennacherib], so that he shall hear a rumor, and return to his own land." Josephus' reformulation might have in view the continuation of the biblical accounts (see 2 Kgs 19:35-36// Isa 37:36-37), where it is rather the angelic decimation of his army at Jerusalem that prompts Sennacherib's withdrawal. By means of the reformulation, Josephus, in line with his usual tendency, likewise avoids a biblical reference to the (divine) "spirit."

[53] Here Josephus has Isaiah make advance allusion to the destruction of the Assyrian army that he will relate in 10.21 on the basis of 2 Kgs 19:35// Isa 37:36.

[54] This element of Isaiah's prediction has no equivalent in those attributed to him in 2 Kgs 19:7// Isa 37:7. The addition recalls Josephus' (also added) reference to Sennacherib's "campaigning against the Egyptians and Ethiopians" in 10.4, and looks ahead to the account he will give of the outcome of the campaign in 10.17-20. With the addition, Josephus highlights the prophetic stature of Isaiah, who can predict also this event.

[55] This conclusion to Isaiah's prediction corresponds to the prophet's closing words as cited in 2 Kgs 19:7b// Isa 37:7b: "I [God] will cause him [Sennacherib] to return to his own land; and I will cause him to fall by the sword in his own land."

[56] In 2 Kgs 19:9b// Isa 37:9b Sennacherib "sends messengers" to Hezekiah; Josephus' reference to his "communications" is based on the subsequent biblical passages 2 Kgs 19:14a// Isa 37:14a, which refer to the king's "receiving the letter from the hand of the messengers." Josephus likewise generalizes the detailed background indications concerning the Assyrian's new initiative given in 19:8-9a// 37:8-9a: upon his return from Jerusalem the Rabshakeh finds that Sennacherib, having left Lachish (see 18:14// 36:2), is currently fighting against Libnah (19:8// 37:8). Sennacherib, for his part, sends to Hezekiah (19:9b// 37:9b) after hearing that Tirhakah of Ethiopia has set out to fight against him (19:9a// 37:9a).

[57] Greek: ἀνόητος; this is the same epithet that the Rabshakeh applies to Hezekiah in his words to the envoys in 10.7.

[58] Josephus compresses the concluding portion of Sennacherib's message, in which he asks rhetorically (2 Kgs 19:11b// Isa 37:11b [MT, > LXX]) "and shall you be delivered?," and then goes on to enumerate a whole series of nations and gods whom his ancestors have overthrown (19:12-13// 37:12-13). He likewise leaves aside the opening portion of the Assyrian's discourse with its commissioning formula for the messengers (19:10a// 37:10a), warning to Hezekiah not to let himself be deceived by the promises of his God (19:10b// 37:10b), and mention of the Judean's having heard of the destruction wrought by the earlier Assyrian kings (19:11a// 37:11a).

[59] This conclusion to Sennacherib's message is Josephus' own formulation, picking up on the Rabshakeh's earlier querying of why Hezekiah was

Hezekiah deposits letter and receives renewed assurances from Isaiah

16 When [Ezekias] read these things, he felt contempt on account of the confidence [he had received] from God.[60] Rolling up the communications, he deposited [them] inside the sanctuary.[61] When he again prayed to God concerning the city and the safety of all,[62] the prophet Hesaias said that God had heard him[63] and that, while at present they would not be besieged by the Assyrian,[64] in the future those under him [Ezekias], secure against everything, would farm in peace and take care of their possessions, fearing nothing.[65]

Failed Assyrian siege of Pelusion

17 When a short time had passed[66] and the king of the Assyrians had failed completely in his undertaking[67] against the Egyptians,[68] he returned home without achieving anything for the following reason: He had wasted much time at the siege of Pelusion.[69] When the earthworks, which he raised up to the level of the walls, were already high, and right as he was on the verge of assaulting them, he heard that Tharsikes,[70] the king of the Ethiopians, was coming at the head of a large army

---

"refusing to admit his [Sennacherib's] army" (10.6) and his further allusion to the advantage of "voluntary surrender" in 10.10. Josephus' compression and reworking of Sennacherib's 2nd warning discourse to Hezekiah (2 Kgs 19:10-13// Isa 37:10-13) reflects the fact that this discourse largely reiterates what has been said in the Assyrian king's initial discourse, as mediated by the Rabshakeh, in 2 Kgs 18:19-25, 28-35// Isa 36:4-10, 13-20.

[60] Josephus appends this allusion to Hezekiah's emotional reaction to Sennacherib's message to the notice (2 Kgs 19:14a// Isa 37:14a) on his reading the letter brought him by the messengers. Its reference to the "confidence" the king "had received from God" recalls the notice of 10.13 about Isaiah's "encouraging the king himself"; cf. also *Ant.* 9.276, where Josephus states that Hezekiah "gave no thought" to the earlier Assyrian threats, due to his being "encouraged by his piety towards the Deity and by the prophet Hesaias."

[61] Compare 2 Kgs 19:14b// Isa 37:14b, where Hezekiah goes in person to "the house of the Lord," and "spreads" Sennacherib's letter "before the Lord." On Sennacherib's (written) "communications" to Hezekiah, see 10.15.

[62] In line with his frequent tendency, Josephus reduces Hezekiah's prayer of 2 Kgs 19:15-19// Isa 37:15-20 to this brief allusion to its content. From the king's biblical prayer—which nowhere explicitly mentions "the city," i.e. Jerusalem—he omits Hezekiah's affirmation that the gods of the other nations destroyed by the Assyrians were in fact "no gods," but mere human productions (19:17-18// 37:18-19)—an affirmation gentile readers might well find offensive, just as they might Hezekiah's concluding appeal that the Lord act against Sennacherib in order "that all the kingdoms of the earth may know that thou, O Lord, art God alone" (19:19b; cf. 37:20b).

[63] See 2 Kgs 19:20b; the opening of Isaiah's res-

ponse in Isa 37:21 lacks an explicit statement concerning God's "hearing" of the king's prayer.

[64] This is the reading of MSP, which Marcus follows; Niese reads "the Syrian" with the remaining codices. With Isaiah's announcement here, compare his more expansive statement in 2 Kgs 19:32// Isa 37:33: "... he [the king of Assyria] shall not come into this city or shoot an arrow there, or come before it with a shield or cast up a siege mound against it."

[65] This portion of Isaiah's announcement is vaguely inspired by the figurative language of 2 Kgs 19:29-30 // Isa 37:30-31 concerning the promised agricultural revival of ravaged Judah. Overall, Josephus both rearranges and drastically shortens—in accord with his usual practice—the poetic, image-filled prophetic response to Hezekiah's appeal in 2 Kgs 19:21-34// Isa 37:22-35.

[66] At this point, Josephus interrupts his reproduction of the biblical accounts of Jerusalem's deliverance (2 Kings 18-19// Isaiah 36-37) in order to draw on various extra-biblical testimonies concerning related events that he will cite in 10.17-20.

[67] Greek: ἐπιβολή. This is the conjecture of G. Dindorf, which Niese and Marcus follow. The codices have ἐπιβουλή ("plot").

[68] This event represents the fulfillment of the Josephan Isaiah's prediction to Hezekiah in 10.14: "Senacheirim... would fail utterly in the Egyptian affair."

[69] The Bible itself makes no mention of this siege. Josephus is here drawing on the extra-biblical historians to whom he will allude in what follows. "Pelusion" was located on the Mediterranean, near Egypt's eastern frontier.

[70] MT (2 Kgs 19:9b// Isa 37:9b) תרהקה (Eng.: "Tirhakah"); LXX B 2 Kgs 19:9b Θαρά; LXX L 2 Kgs 19:9b Θαρθάκ; LXX Isa 37:9b Θαρακα; Josephus Θαρσίκης.

to the aid of his ally, the Egyptians, after having decided to make his way through the desert and fall suddenly on the Assyrian army.[71]

18 Thrown then into consternation by these things, King Senacheirim withdrew, as I said, without achieving anything, abandoning Pelusion. Herodotus also speaks concerning this King Senacheirim in the Second [Book] of his *Histories*;[72] he says that he came against the king of the Egyptians, who was priest of Hephaestus.[73] Having besieged Pelusion,[74] he [Senacheirim] raised the siege for this reason: when the king of the Egyptians prayed to God, God heard him[75] and inflicted a plague upon the Arab.[76] **19** (For he also errs in calling him [Senacheirim] the king, not of the Assyrians, but of the Arabs.)[77] For he says that in a single night a swarm of mice consumed the bows and other weapons of the Assyrians, and so, having no bows, the king withdrew his army from Pelusion.[78] **20** This is what Herodotus relates.[79] Berosus, the chronicler of Chaldean [affairs],[80] also mentions King Senacheirim and that he ruled over the Assyrians and campaigned against Asia [and Egypt].[81] He says the following....[82]

Herodotus' testimony on siege

(1.5) 21 Returning from the Egyptian war to Hierosolyma,[83] Senacheirim encoun-

Assyrian army devastated

---

[71] 2 Kgs 19:9b// Isa 37:9b simply state that Sennacherib heard that "Tirhakah" was marching against him. Josephus may have derived the additional details with which he elaborates this notice from the extra-biblical sources he utilizes in 10.17-20.

[72] The reference is to 2.141.

[73] The above translation reflects the reading of SPLauV, which Marcus adopts. Niese prints the rather different reading of ROM, which he views as a scribal attempt to fill a lacuna in the text of Josephus. In Herodotus (2.141) the figure of the king of Egypt and priest of Hephaestus, to whom Josephus alludes here, is called "Sethos." In Greek mythology Haphaestus was the smith-god; his Roman equivalent was Vulcan.

[74] According to Herodotus (2.141), once the Egyptian king Sethos had encamped at the frontier site Pelusion along with the rabble who followed him from Egypt, the Assyrian enemy headed towards the site as well.

[75] With the wording of Herodotus as cited by Josephus here, compare the latter's own notices on Hezekiah's "praying to God" and Isaiah's response that "(God) has heard him [the king]" in 10.16.

[76] In Herodotus (2.141) the Egyptian king's appeal to his god occurs prior to his going to Pelusion and facing the enemy attack there. In response to his appeal, the deity promises him that he would "suffer no ill by encountering *the host of Arabia*"—the (apparent) inspiration for Josephus' reference to the god-sent plague upon "the Arab," i.e. King Sennacherib. See next note.

[77] In Herodotus (2.141) Sennacherib is not explicitly called "king of the Arabs" or "the Arab," as Josephus avers (see preceding note). Also in this case then, as earlier in *Ant.* 8.253, 260-262, Josephus'

criticism of Herodotus' historical "mistakes" is itself open to criticism, given that he does not quote his predecessor with the requisite precision (this, of course, on the presumption that Josephus had the same text of Herodotus as we do today).

[78] Herodotus (2.141) depicts the outcome of the mice infestation of the Assyrian camp in more dramatic terms, i.e. on the following day the army fled unarmed, many of them being killed. Josephus omits Herodotus' appended etiological notice about the commemorative statue of the god standing in the temple of Hephaestus with a mouse in his hand and the accompanying inscription reading "look on me, and fear the gods."

[79] This formula rounds off Josephus' reproduction of the testimony of Herodotus on Sennacherib's Egyptian campaign and its disastrous outcome in 10.18-19.

[80] On Berosus (*ca.* 330-250 BCE) and Josephus' use of him, see Bloch 1879: 62-65; BJP 3 (Feldman) 34, n. 235. Josephus' other mentions of this figure are in *Ant.* 1.93, 107, 158; 10.34, 219; *Apion* 1.129, 130, 134, 143, 145. Berosus' own work on Babylonian history is no longer extant; Josephus himself quotes it, not directly, but from an abridgement of the work by Alexander Polyhistor dating to the 1st century BCE.

[81] This phrase, bracketed by Niese, is absent from RO. Marcus reads it without brackets.

[82] These words are absent from LauV. Niese and Marcus include them, following the other codices, and so posit that a quotation from Berosus has fallen out of the text of Josephus at this point.

[83] With this phrase Josephus resumes the thread of his main story line concerning the deliverance of Jerusalem, interrupted after 10.16 in order to make room for the extra-biblical interlude of 10.17-20.

tered there his force[84] under the general Rapsakes.[85] God inflicted a pestilent disease upon his army during the first night of the siege[86] that destroyed 185,000 [men] along with their leaders and military officers.[87]

Sennacherib's withdrawal and assassination

22 Reduced to fear and terrible agony[88] by this misfortune, and frightened for his entire army,[89] [Senacheirim] fled with his remaining force to his own kingdom, which was called Ninos.[90] **23** After residing there for a short time,[91] he ended his life, treacherously murdered by his elder[92] sons, Andromach[93] and Seleukar,[94] and was laid away in his own sanctuary, which was called "Araske."[95] They [the two sons], pursued by the citizens for the murder of their father, went off to Armenia,[96] while Asarachoddas,[97] who was contemptuous of those who came after them [the parricides] [in succession to] Senacheirim[98] received the kingship. This was how the campaign of the Assyrians against Hierosolyma turned out.[99]

---

[84] In the text printed by Marcus, itself based on Lat's reading, there follows the phrase διὰ λοιμοῦ κινδυνεύουσαν ("in danger from a plague"). This phrase has no equivalent in the Greek codices and is not included in Niese's text.

[85] This notice points back to 10.4, where Sennacherib "leaves behind" his 3 officers "in great strength" with the mission of "ravaging" Jerusalem, while he himself proceeds against the Egyptians and Ethiopians.

[86] 2 Kgs 19:35a// Isa 37:36a attribute the slaying of the Assyrians to "the angel of the Lord," as does Josephus himself in his address (*War* 5.362-419) to the defenders of Jerusalem in *War* 5.388; cf. Feldman 2001: 319.

[87] Josephus' figure for the Assyrian troops killed corresponds to that given in 2 Kgs 19:35a// Isa 37:36a (which, however, do not mention additional casualties among the army's leadership). Josephus omits the notice of 19:35b// 37:36b about the survivors' observing the dead bodies in the morning.

[88] Greek: ἀγωνία δεινή. Josephus uses this phrase of King Ahab's reaction to the Syrian threat in *Ant.* 8.373.

[89] Josephus adds this reference to Sennacherib's emotional state. The mention of the king's being "frightened" (Greek: δείσας) ironically echoes 10.8, where the Assyrian general perceives the "fright" (Greek: δέος) of Hezekiah's envoy, Eliakim. Now the tables have been turned.

[90] In 2 Kgs 19:36// Isa 37:37 Sennacherib simply "departs" for home and "dwells in Nineveh." Cf. *Ant.* 1.143, where "Assouras" founds the city of "Ninos" ("Nineveh" in Gen 10:11).

[91] Josephus adds this chronological indication on the span of time between Sennacherib's coming to Nineveh (2 Kgs 19:36// Isa 37:37) and his murder there (19:37// 37:38).

[92] 2 Kgs 19:37aα// Isa 37:38aα do not specify that the parricides were Sennacherib's "elder" sons.

[93] MT (2 Kgs 19:37aα// Isa 37:38aα) אדרמלך (Eng.: "Adrammelech"); LXX BL 2 Kgs 19:37aα// Isa 37:38aα Ἀδραμέλεχ; Josephus Ἀνδρόμαχος.

[94] MT (2 Kgs 19:37aα// Isa 37:38aα) שראצר (Eng.: "Sarezer"); LXX B 2 Kgs 19:37aα// LXX Isa 37:38aα Σαράσαρ; LXX L 2 Kgs 19:37aα Σαράσα; Josephus Σελεύκαρος.

[95] MT (2 Kgs 19:37aα// Isa 37:38aα) נסרך (Eng.: "Nisroch"); LXX B 2 Kgs 19:37aα Ἐσδράχ; LXX L 2 Kgs 19:37aα Ἀσράχ; LXX Isa 37:38aα Νασαραχ; Josephus Ἀράσκη. Whereas the sources identify "Nisroch" as Sennacherib's "god," Josephus understands the term as referring to a royal sanctuary in which Sennacherib is buried—a point not mentioned in the Bible.

[96] Josephus adds mention of a pursuit of the parricides to the notice on their "escape" in 2 Kgs 19:37bα // Isa 37:38bα. His designation for their place of refuge ("Armenia") corresponds to the reading of LXX Isa 37:38bα, whereas the MT of both biblical verses, as well as LXX BL 2 Kgs 19:37bα, call it "the land of Ararat."

[97] MT (2 Kgs 19:37bβ// Isa 37:38bβ) אסר־חדן (Eng.: "Esarhaddon"); LXX B 2 Kgs 19:37bβ and LXX Isa 37:38bβ Ἀσορδάν; LXX L 2 Kgs 19:37bβ Ἀχορδάν; Josephus Ἀσαραχόδδας.

[98] The Greek phrase qualifying "Esarhaddon" underlying the above translation is lacking in Lat and is called "undoubtedly corrupt" by Marcus. The Bible has no equivalent to this reference to still other sons of Sennacherib, intermediate in age (and right of succession) between the 2 parricides and Esarhaddon, who, nevertheless, secured the throne for himself. See Marcus' note *ad loc.*

[99] Josephus appends this closing notice to his account of Jerusalem's deliverance, 10.1-23 (// 2 Kgs 18:13-19:37// Isa 36:1-37:38).

213

(2.1) 24 King Ezekias, having been unexpectedly relieved of his fears, offered thanksgiving sacrifices to God along with all the people, since there was no other cause than their alliance with God for the destruction of some of the enemy and the withdrawal [of the remainder] from Hierosolyma, out of fear of a similar death.[100]

Hezekiah leads thanksgiving

25 After displaying all solicitude and generosity towards God,[101] Ezekias not long afterwards fell victim to a serious disease and was given up by the physicians; his friends too foresaw nothing good for him.[102] In addition to the disease itself, a terrible depression[103] [seized] the king when he considered his childlessness and that he was about to die, leaving his household and rule bereft of a legitimate successor.[104] **26** He was above all distressed by this thought; lamenting, he entreated God to give him a short additional period of life until he procreated children and not allow him to leave this life behind before he had become a father.[105]

Childless Hezekiah near death

27 God was merciful to him and accepted his request[106] since it was not because of his imminent deprivation of the good things of kingship that he was bewailing his supposed death and praying that a period of life might still be granted him. Rather, it was in order that he might have children who would inherit his leadership.[107] Sending the prophet Hesaias,[108] he [God] directed him to inform him that he

Good news for Hezekiah

---

[100] This account of Hezekiah's response to Jerusalem's deliverance (10.1-23) has no parallel in the biblical accounts. On the other hand, it does pull together elements of Josephus' own previous account, i.e. Hezekiah's "fear" here recalls the mention of his "cowardice" in 10.5; the allusion to the destruction of the enemy being solely due to the nation's "alliance with God" is reminiscent of the king's confession that he has "no other hope of safety" except in God (10.10), while the mention of the "fear" that prompts Sennacherib's withdrawal brings to mind the notice on the Assyrian's "fear and terrible anxiety" in 10.22. Josephus' addition concerning Hezekiah's "sacrifice," for its part, serves to underscore the king's piety; conceivably, it was inspired by Isaiah's announcement that the sick Hezekiah will be able to "go up to the house of the Lord" in 2 Kgs 20:5bβ. (*Songs Rab.* 4.8.3, noting the absence of any mention of Hezekiah's thanking God for the deliverance of Jerusalem in the biblical accounts, avers that this failure caused God to revoke his earlier decision to designate Hezekiah as the Messiah.)

[101] Greek: σπουδή καί φιλοτιμία; the wordpair occurs also in *Ant.* 6.292; 7.380; 12.83, 134; 14.154; 15.312. Josephus's added phrase here highlights the king's piety, even while it makes the transition to the subsequent, final events of Hezekiah's reign as told in 2 Kings 20// Isaiah 38-39 (cf. 2 Chr 32:23-33). On Josephus' account of the finale of Hezekiah's kingship in 10.24-36, see Begg 2000: 419-41.

[102] Josephus goes beyond 2 Kgs 20:1a// Isa 38:1a in highlighting the hopelessness of Hezekiah's condition as something to which even his doctors and friends are resigned.

[103] Greek: ἀθυμία δεινή. Josephus' 2 remaining uses of this phrase are in *War* 3.182 and *Ant.* 5.36. Compare the mention of Sennacherib's ἀγωνία δεινή ("terrible agony") in 10.22.

[104] This notice on Hezekiah's emotional reaction to his condition and the grounds for it has no biblical counterpart. Josephus' mention of the king's childlessness at this point in his reign is, however, paralleled in Rabbinic tradition (see *b. Ber.* 10a; *y. Sanh.* 10.28b; *S.Eli R.* 8, p. 46); in contrast to Josephus, these witnesses explicitly make Hezekiah's childlessness a matter of his own choice, inspired by the fear that any progeny he might have would turn out degenerate.

[105] This initial appeal by Hezekiah, picking up on Josephus' preceding addition concerning the king's distress at the prospect of his dying childless (see previous note), has no equivalent in 2 Kgs 20:1-11// Isa 38:1-22.

[106] Compare 2 Kgs 20:5// Isa 38:5, where Isaiah is sent back a 2nd time to announce to Hezekiah that God has "heard your prayer." Josephus turns this new, 2nd announcement by Isaiah, revoking his earlier prediction of death for the king (20:1b// 38:1b), into an (anticipated) editorial comment about the divine decision that precedes Isaiah's one-time approach to the king in what follows.

[107] Josephus' extended explanation as to why God gives a favorable response to Hezekiah's appeal, made even before Isaiah approaches the king—like that appeal itself as cited in 10.25-26—is without biblical parallel.

[108] 2 Kgs 20:1b-3a// Isa 38:1b-3 relate God's initial dispatch of Isaiah to Hezekiah with the announcement that he will not recover, whereupon the king makes a

would recover from his disease after three days,[109] would live fifteen years after this,[110] and would have children.[111]

Hezekiah requests and receives sign

28 When the prophet said these things in accordance with God's command,[112] Ezekias, due to the excessiveness of his disease and the unexpectedness of what was announced, was unbelieving.[113] He requested Hesaias to do some sign and portent,[114] so that he might believe in him who said these things as one coming from God.[115] For unlikely things and what is beyond hope are rendered believable by things of the same sort.[116]

29 When he [Hesaias] questioned him about what sign he wanted to occur,[117] he requested that the sun—since it, as it declined, had already made a shadow of ten paces in his house—might return to the same spot, causing it to cast [the shadow]

---

tearful appeal to God. Josephus markedly reworks this entire sequence. In his presentation, Hezekiah's appeal (and God's decision to honor this) precede Isaiah's (one and only) approach to him. In thus adapting the biblical account Josephus disposes of the problem posed by this, i.e. it seems to make Isaiah a "false" prophet whose initial announcement—for which he evokes divine authority (see the messenger formula, "thus says the Lord" in 20:1b// 38:1b)—is immediately abrogated by the instructions God gives Isaiah in 20:4-6// 38:4-6. See further 10.35.

[109] Compare Isaiah's (2nd) announcement to Hezekiah in 2 Kgs 20:5bβ (no parallel in Isaiah 38): "on the 3rd day you shall go up to the house of the Lord." Josephus leaves aside the biblical references to the healed king's going to the temple at this juncture; he will, however, make use of this element subsequently; see 10.29. He likewise omits the preceding, preliminary announcement (20:5bα// 38:5bα) that Isaiah is sent back to convey to the king in response to his appeal, i.e. that the Lord has heard his prayer (see, however, Josephus' anticipation of this at the opening of 10.27) and seen his tears.

[110] See 2 Kgs 20:6aα// Isa 38:5bβ: "I [God] will add 15 years to your [Hezekiah's] life."

[111] This final promise, responding to the Josephan Hezekiah's concern about dying without progeny (see 10.25-26), takes the place of the concluding divine announcement of 2 Kgs 20:6aβb// Isa 38:6b, i.e. that God will deliver and defend Jerusalem (and Hezekiah himself) against the king of Assyria. Josephus' non-use of this biblical announcement is understandable, given that it appears to come "too late" in the sequence of 2 Kings 18-20// Isaiah 36-39, where Jerusalem's deliverance has already been effected by the end of 2 Kings 19// Isaiah 37.

[112] Josephus adds this transitional phrase concerning Isaiah's fulfillment of his divine mandate. 2 Kgs 20:4-6// Isa 38:4-6 do not explicitly mention the prophet's delivering God's (2nd) message to Hezekiah. Conversely, Josephus omits Isaiah's directive (20:7//

Isa 38:21) that a "cake of figs" be applied to Hezekiah's "boil" in order that he might recover. He perhaps found such a presentation of the prophet too "magical" and/ or he may have noticed that the directive has no further function in/effect on the continuation of the biblical accounts.

[113] Josephus supplies this reference to Hezekiah's skepticism in response to Isaiah's announcement and the reasons for it.

[114] Greek: σημεῖον καὶ τεράστιον; this collocation is *hapax* in Josephus (prior to him it is used for the first time in Ezekiel the Tragedian, l. 90). His only other use of the word τεράστιον ("portent") is in 10.232, where it refers to the handwriting on the wall at Belshazzar's feast. In *War* 1.28 and *Ant.* 20.168 Josephus uses the more common collocation σημεῖα καὶ τέρατα.

[115] See 2 Kgs 20:8 (the parallel passage Isa 38:22 oddly has Hezekiah asking for a sign after this has already been given to him in 38:8b). Josephus supplies Hezekiah with a rationale (i.e. the accreditation of Isaiah's words as emanating from God) for making the request he does. He leaves aside the allusion to Isaiah's previous promise (see 2 Kgs 20:5bβ) that the king will go up to the house of the Lord on the 3rd day, which Hezekiah attaches to his request in 20:8 (and 38:22), given that in his rendering of Isaiah's predictions to Hezekiah in 10.27 he does not cite this promise (see note to "after three days" there).

[116] Josephus appends this editorial comment concerning Hezekiah's request for a sign. The terminology of "(un)belief" permeates Josephus' version of the king's request (see 2 Kgs 20:8// Isa 38:22) in 10.28.

[117] In Josephus Hezekiah gets to ask for whatever sign he wishes. In Isa 38:7-8a, by contrast, Isaiah simply informs him of the sign he will be given, while 2 Kgs 20:9-10 limits the king's choice to having the shadow advance or recede 10 paces. Josephus' version highlights the magnitude of the choice offered Hezekiah (and Isaiah's confidence that he can provide whatever the king may request).

again.[118] The prophet then appealed God to manifest this sign to the king.[119] When Ezekias saw what he wished,[120] and was immediately relieved of his disease,[121] he went up to the sacred precinct and after paying homage to God, made prayers.[122]

Healed Hezekiah prays

(2.2) 30 At this time it happened that the rule of the Assyrians was overturned by the Medes; I shall relate this elsewhere.[123] The king of the Babylonians, named Balad,[124] sent envoys to Ezekias to bring him gifts and to appeal to him to be his ally and friend.[125] 31 He, for his part, gladly received the envoys; he entertained them[126] and showed them his treasures, along with his supply of weapons and his other wealth, whatever he had in the way of stones and gold.[127] He then dismissed them to Balad, giving them gifts to bring to him.[128]

Hezekiah's reception of Babylonian envoys

32 When Hesaias the prophet came to him and inquired where the visitors were from,[129] [Ezekias] said that they came from Babylon, from God.[130] He had shown

Isaiah announces

---

[118] See 2 Kgs 20:10b. Josephus omits the king's opening biblical statement that it would be an "easy thing" to have the shadow advance 10 steps (20:10a). In its place he has Hezekiah refer, in line with the closing words of 2 Kgs 20:11b// Isa 38:8b with their mention of the "10 steps by which the sun had declined on the dial of Ahaz [38:8b lacks this mention of Hezekiah's father]," to the sun's previous "decline" and the result of this.

[119] See 2 Kgs 20:11a (no equivalent in Isaiah 38). Josephus spells out the content of Isaiah's "cry to the Lord" there.

[120] Cf. 2 Kgs 20:11b// Isa 38:8b, which state that the shadow did recede 10 steps.

[121] This notice on the fact of Hezekiah's cure, fulfilling the promise Isaiah makes him in 10.27, lacks a direct biblical counterpart. Cf., however, the allusion to the king's cure in the title of the "Psalm of Hezekiah" (Isa 38:10-20) in Isa 38:9: "a writing of Hezekiah after he had been sick and recovered from his sickness." (Like 2 Kings 20 and in line with his own practice of omitting or greatly reducing the content of such biblical prayer texts, Josephus has no equivalent to the lengthy "Psalm of Hezekiah" itself.)

[122] Josephus goes beyond the biblical accounts in making explicit mention of the cured Hezekiah's going to the temple, turning into a narrative notice on the matter Isaiah's promise of 2 Kgs 20:5bβ, omitted by him in his version of the prophet's announcement in 10.27 (see note to "after three days" there), that he would do this.

[123] Josephus supplies this notice by way of background to his following account of Hezekiah's dealings—not, as might be expected in light of what precedes—with an Assyrian, but rather a Babylonian king. His only subsequent allusion to the overthrow of the Assyrian empire—previously announced by Jonah (*Ant.* 9.208, 214) and Nahum (9.239)—comes in 10.74, where he attributes that event to the Babylonians as well as the Medes.

[124] MT (2 Kgs 20:12) בראדך בלאדן (RSV, following an emendation based on Isa 39:1, renders "Merodach-baladan")/ Isa 39:1 מרדך בלאדן (Eng.: "Merodach-baladan"); LXX B 2 Kgs 20:12 Μαρωδαχβαλδάν; LXX L 2 Kgs 20:12 Μαρωδαχ Βαλδάν; LXX Isa 39:1 Μαρωδαχ; Josephus Βαλάδας. Josephus omits the initial portion ("Merodach") of the king's biblical name as well as that of his father (MT: Baladan).

[125] 2 Kgs 20:12// Isa 39:1 mention "letters" brought by the envoys as well and attribute their visit to Merodach-baladan's having heard of Hezekiah's sickness and recovery. Josephus makes explicit the political purpose behind the Babylonian's initiative.

[126] With this added remark Josephus accentuates the welcome given the envoys by Hezekiah. *S. Eli.Rab.* (8)9, p. 47 mentions the king's dining with them in person.

[127] Josephus abbreviates the catalogue of objects shown the envoys by Hezekiah cited in 2 Kgs 20:13// Isa 39:2, which mention also silver, spices, and precious oil and end up with the hyperbolic assertion that there was "nothing" in his house or kingdom that the king did not show the messengers.

[128] Josephus adds this notice with its continuing accentuation of Hezekiah's hospitality: the king not only receives gifts from Merodach-baladan (so 2 Kgs 20:12// Isa 39:1), but himself sends back presents of his own to the latter.

[129] Compare 2 Kgs 20:14a// Isa 39:3a, whose initial question by Isaiah ("what did these men say?") Josephus omits—perhaps because it remains unanswered by Hezekiah in what follows.

[130] Greek: παρὰ τοῦ θεοῦ; this is the reading of ROM, which Niese follows. Marcus reads παρὰ τοῦ κυρίου αὐτῶν ("from their master," i.e. Merodach-baladan) with SPLauV. In 2 Kgs 20:14b// Isa 39:3b Hezekiah informs Isaiah that the envoys have come "from a far country, from Babylon." In the reading adopted by Niese Hezekiah offers an implicit justification for his dealings with the envoys, namely, the

them everything,[131] so that, seeing his wealth and power, they might get an idea
from this and have something to report to the king.[132] **33** But the prophet replied:
"You should know" he said, "[that] after no[133] little time, this wealth of yours will
be carried away to Babylon[134] and your descendants, having been made eunuchs[135]
and deprived of their manhood, will be slaves to the Babylonian king."[136] For this is
what God predicts.[137]

34 Ezekias, grieved by what was told him,[138] said that he did not wish these misfortunes to fall upon his nation,[139] but, since it was impossible to change what had
been determined by God, he prayed that there might be peace as long as he lived.[140]
(Berosus also mentions Balad, the king of the Babylonians).[141]

35 [Hesaias himself] was acknowledged as a divine prophet[142] and marvelous
with respect to truth, for he was confident that he never said what was false.[143]
Writing down in books everything he had prophesied, he left these to be recognized
as true from their fulfillment by people in the future.[144] And not only this prophet,
but also the others—twelve in number[145]—did the same, and whatever bad thing[146]

---

divine origin of their mission.

[131] In 2 Kgs 20:15// Isa 39:4 Hezekiah's statement about having shown the envoys everything comes in response to a further question by Isaiah, i.e. "what have they [the envoys] seen in your house?" Josephus depicts a more forthcoming king, who volunteers information without waiting to be asked for it.

[132] Josephus appends this motivation for Hezekiah's showing the envoys "everything," as he admits having done in 2 Kgs 20:15b// Isa 39:4b.

[133] Greek οὐ; this is the reading of ROLauVLat, which Niese follows; Marcus reads a different particle, namely ὡς ("that [after a little time]") with MSP.

[134] See 2 Kgs 20:17// Isa 39:6. Josephus omits Isaiah's opening summons to hear (20:16// 39:5) as well as the formula ("nothing shall be left"), with which the prophet sums up his announcement about the loss of Hezekiah's property in 20:17// 39:6. He holds over until the end of Isaiah's entire prediction his equivalent of the phrase "says the Lord" which stands between the 2 parts of the prophetic announcement in 20:17-18 // 39:6-7; see the end of 10.33.

[135] Greek: εὐνουχίζω; this verb is *hapax* in Josephus.

[136] See 2 Kgs 20:18// Isa 39:7. Josephus leaves aside the biblical references to the deportation of Hezekiah's descendants, while highlighting both the fact of their castration and the slavery that awaits them.

[137] Compare the phrase "says the Lord," with which Isaiah concludes the 1st part of his announcement (2 Kgs 20:17// Isa 39:6), before proceeding to the prediction about the fate of Hezekiah's descendants in 20:18// 39:7.

[138] Josephus supplies this reference to Hezekiah's emotional reaction to Isaiah's announcement.

[139] This expression of concern for his people has no

equivalent in the response of the biblical Hezekiah in 2 Kgs 20:19// Isa 39:8, where the king's whole focus is on what is (not) to happen to him personally. See next note.

[140] Josephus adds the reference to the immutability of God's decisions (see the similar affirmation attributed to the prophetess Huldah in 10.60). He likewise turns the king's self-assured, egotistical assertion in 2 Kgs 20:19// Isa 39:8 about there being "peace and security in his own days" into a humble prayer for such peace.

[141] On Berosus, see 10.20.

[142] With this phrase (Greek: προφήτης θεῖος), compare *Ant.* 18.64, where, as part of his "testimony" concerning Jesus, Josephus refers to "the divine prophets."

[143] Josephus' (added) emphasis on Isaiah's life-long veracity here helps explain his earlier omission of the biblical notice on Isaiah's initial approach to Hezekiah (2 Kgs 20:1b// Isa 38:1b) with a message that God subsequently countermands in response to Hezekiah's appeal; see note to "Hesaias" at 10.27.

[144] With this notice Josephus evidences his awareness of the existence of writings attributed to Isaiah and spells out the prophet's purpose in composing these.

[145] Josephus' figure for the "writing prophets" here is perplexing—one would expect rather 14 (as in the MT) or 15, i.e. the 12 "Minor Prophets," along with Jeremiah, Ezekiel, and Daniel (counting his book as part of the prophetic corpus with LXX). Marcus (*ad loc.*) links Josephus' figure with his statement in *Apion* 1.40 that the post-Mosaic prophets composed 13 books, of which Isaiah would be 1, with the rest of the prophetic corpus—however precisely Josephus may have counted this—amounting to 12 books. For more on the question of Josephus' biblical canon and rele-

that befalls us comes about according to their prophecy. But we shall tell about each of these later on.[147]

Hezekiah's death

(3.1) 36 Having lived therefore through the above-mentioned time[148] and spent the whole of it in peace,[149] King Ezekias died,[150] having filled out fifty-four years[151] of life and reigned as king for twenty-nine.[152]

Manasseh's (Manasses') transgressions

37 His son Manasses[153] inherited the kingship; his mother was named Echibas,[154] a native of the capital.[155] He broke away from the practices of his father and turned to the opposite,[156] manifesting every form of vileness in his manner and leaving no impiety aside.[157] He was rather an imitator of the lawlessness[158] of the Israelites, with which they offended against God and so perished.[159] He even dared to pollute the sanctuary of God,[160] as well as the city and the entire country.[161] **38** For in his con-

---

vant bibliography, see Mason 2002.

[146] Greek εἴ τι φαῦλον; this is the reading of R, which Niese follows. Marcus adopts the more expansive reading of MSPLauELat, i.e. εἴτε ἀγαθὸν εἴτε φαῦλον ("whether good or bad").

[147] In fact, Josephus nowhere mentions the 7 minor prophets Hosea, Joel, Amos, Obadiah, Habakkuk, Zephaniah, and Malachi.

[148] The reference is to the 15 extra years of life God promises Hezekiah in 10.27.

[149] With this addition Josephus indicates that Hezekiah's prayer for "peace" in his lifetime (see 10.34) was indeed fulfilled.

[150] See 2 Kgs 20:21a// 2 Chr 32:33aα, which speak of Hezekiah's "sleeping with his fathers." Like MT 2 Kgs 20:21, Josephus has no equivalent to the mention of Hezekiah's burial in 2 Chr 32:33aβ (and LXX BL 2 Kgs 20:21). In accord with his standard practice, he omits the source notices for the king of 20:20// 32:32.

[151] Josephus arrives at this figure for Hezekiah's life-span by combining those given in 2 Kgs 18:2a// 2 Chr 29:1a for the king's age at accession (25 years) and length of reign (29).

[152] This figure for the duration of Hezekiah's reign agrees with that given in 2 Kgs 18:2a// 2 Chr 29:1a.

[153] MT (2 Kgs 20:21b// 2 Chr 32:33bβ) מנשה (Eng.: "Manasseh"); LXX B 2 Kgs 20:21b// LXX B 2 Chr 32:33bβ Μανασσή; LXX L 2 Kgs 20:21b// LXX L 2 Chr 32:33bβ and Josephus Μανασσῆς. On Josephus' treatment of Manasseh in 10.37-46 (// 2 Kgs 21:1-18// 2 Chr 33:1-20), see Begg 2000: 441-52 and Feldman 1998a: 416-23.

[154] MT (2 Kgs 21:1b) חפצי־בה (Eng.: "Hephzibah"); LXX B Ὀψειβά; LXX L Ἐψιβά; Josephus Ἐχίβας. 2 Chronicles 33 does not mention the name of Manasseh's mother.

[155] Greek: πολῖτις; Josephus uses this feminine form of the royal mothers Ioade (*Ant.* 9.186) and Noosta (10.98) as well. 2 Kgs 21:1b does not mention the home

town of Manasseh's mother.

[156] Josephus generalizes the opening accusation of 2 Kgs 21:3aα// 2 Chr 33:3aα, according to which Manasseh rebuilt the high places Hezekiah had broken down.

[157] Josephus here intensifies the stereotyped charges of 2 Kgs 21:2a// 2 Chr 33:2a; 21:6b// 33:6b about Manasseh's "doing evil in the sight of the Lord."

[158] Greek: μιμούμενος... τὰς... παρανομίας. This construction is used in *Ant.* 9.282 of the Israelites who "imitate the lawlessness" of Jeroboam.

[159] In 2 Kgs 21:2b// 2 Chr 33:2b (see also 21:9// 33:9) Manasseh's evildoing is said to be in accordance with "the abominable practices of the nations whom the Lord drove out before the people of Israel." Josephus connects the king's transgressions rather with those of the Israelites themselves and their fate, perhaps under the influence of 2 Kgs 21:3bα, where Manasseh's making of an Asherah is associated with the same offense on the part of "Ahab, king of Israel." Cf. *Ant.* 9.243, where Josephus affirms that Ahaz "imitated the kings of the Israelites."

[160] Greek: μιαίνω τὸν ναόν; this construction occurs also in *Ant.* 11.297, 300; cf. 9.151 (object: τὸ ἱερὸν, "the sacred precinct"). With this formulation Josephus synthesizes the more expansive biblical notices about Manasseh's building altars for the host of heaven in the temple courts (2 Kgs 21:4-5// 2 Chr 33:4-5) and setting up an Asherah/idol in the temple (21:7a// 33:7a).

[161] Josephus concludes his enumeration of Manasseh's cultic abuses (10.37) by extending these to encompass Jerusalem and Judah as a whole. This generalization goes together with his drastic shortening of the catalogue of the king's illicit cultic initiatives given in 2 Kgs 21:2-9// 2 Chr 33:1-9, from which Josephus eliminates many details, e.g., Manasseh's burning his son(s) as an offering and involvement with divination (21:6a// 33:6a) and the extended quotation of the Lord's word to David and Solomon concerning

Prophetic warnings disregarded

Manasseh captured

tempt for God,[162] he hastened to kill all those who were just among the Hebrews;[163] he did not even have mercy on the prophets, but butchered some of them every day,[164] so that Hierosolyma ran with blood.[165]

39 God, therefore, becoming wrathful at these things,[166] sent prophets to the king and the crowd,[167] by whom he threatened them with the same misfortunes that had happened to their brothers, the Israelites, who had committed outrages against him.[168] They, however, did not believe their [the prophets'] words, by which they might have gained [the benefit] of not experiencing calamity.[169] They learned nonetheless by reality that what the prophets said was true.[170] **(3.2) 40** For when they persisted in these things,[171] [God] brought war upon them through the king of the Babylonians and Chaldeans,[172] who sent an army against Iouda, looted their country,[173] and by treachery captured King Manasses,[174] whom he brought to his coun-

---

his (conditional) presence in the temple (21:7b-8// 33:7b-8).

[162] Greek: εἰς τὸν θεὸν καταφρόνησις. Josephus supplies this characterization of Manasseh, employing a phrase used earlier by him for Nimrud (*Ant.* 1.113) and similar to the one employed of Saul in *Ant.* 6.264.

[163] For this item Josephus anticipates 2 Kgs 21:16aα (no parallel in 2 Chronicles 33), which charges Manasseh with "shedding very much innocent blood."

[164] Neither 2 Kings 21 nor 2 Chronicles 33 mentions Manasseh's killing the prophets in particular. Conceivably, Josephus' statement represents a generalization of the tradition, attested, e.g., by *Mart. Ascen. Isa.* 5.1 (cf. Heb 11:37) that Manasseh had the prophet Isaiah sawn in half. See Begg 2000: 444, n. 21.

[165] See 2 Kgs 21:16aβ: (Manasseh shed much innocent blood) "till he had filled Jerusalem from one end to the other."

[166] Josephus adds this reference to God's emotional response to Manasseh's crimes.

[167] Josephus here seems to combine the wording of 2 Kgs 21:10a ("the Lord said by his servants the prophets") and 2 Chr 33:10a ("the Lord spoke to Manasseh and to his people").

[168] Josephus compresses the prophets' elaborate judgment speech cited in 2 Kgs 21:11-15 (no parallel in 2 Chronicles 33), reducing this to an allusion to the crimes of king and people (compare 21:11, where Manasseh alone is charged with having acted more wickedly than the Amorites of old) and the announcement of a fate like that of the Israelites that awaits them (compare the figurative language of 21:13a: "I [God] will stretch over Jerusalem the measuring line of Samaria, and the plummet of the house of Ahab").

[169] This reference to the hearers' non-responsiveness elaborates on the statement that the people did "not listen" in 2 Kgs 21:9a// 2 Chr 33:10b.

Josephus' notice that the audience "did not believe" (Greek: οὐκ ἐπίστευον) is reminiscent of his remark in *Ant.* 9.265 that the Northerners were "not persuaded" (Greek: οὐκ ἐπείσθησαν) by Hezekiah's appeals.

[170] This added remark serves to prepare Josephus' following account of God's punishment of the recalcitrant king and people.

[171] This transitional phrase is a Josephan addition, highlighting the stubbornness of the hearers as further grounds for God's punishment of them.

[172] In 2 Chr 33:11 (no parallel in 2 Kings 21, which further lacks any equivalent to the whole sequence, 2 Chr 33:11-17, reproduced by Josephus in 10.40-45, concerning Manasseh's capture, release, and his initiatives once he returns to Jerusalem) Manasseh's nemesis is called "the king of Assyria." Josephus' designation reflects both his earlier statement about the overthrow of Assyria's power (10.30) and the problem posed by 2 Chr 33:11, where the "commanders of the king of Assyria" bring the captive Manasseh—not to the Assyrian capital Nineveh, as would be expected— but rather to Babylon. Finally, Josephus' double title (which recurs in 10.183 of Nebuchadnezzar) seems to distinguish the "Babylonians" and "Chaldeans" as 2 distinct peoples, rather than, in line with biblical usage, as equivalent names for the same people.

[173] In 2 Chr 33:11 the Assyrian measures affect only Manasseh personally. Josephus, who earlier insisted on the refusal of the entire people to heed the prophets' warnings, now has them also suffer punishment along with the king, in accordance with his statement (10.39) that "they learned nonetheless by reality that what the prophets said was true."

[174] Josephus' added reference to Manasseh's being captured by "treachery" helps explain how the enemy was able to get him in its power, given that 2 Chr 33:11 itself does not mention a battle, but simply a "binding" of the king.

try, holding him in subjugation for whatever punishment he should wish [to in-flict].[175]

41 But Manasses then perceived that he was in a state of calamity and, thinking himself to be the cause of all this,[176] he prayed God to make the enemy humane and merciful[177] to him.[178] Attending to his supplication, God granted this to him, and Manasses, having been released by the king of the Babylonians, was again restored to his own country.[179]

Manasseh released

42 When he came to Hierosolyma, he was solicitous, as far as it was possible for him, to cast even out of his soul his earlier offenses against God and the memory [of these], about which he hastened to change his mind[180] and to show him [God] all respect.[181] He also purified the sanctuary[182] and cleansed the city.[183] For the future, his only concern was to extend thanks to God for his safety and keep him benevolent for his entire life.[184] **43** He likewise taught the crowd to do the same, having learned how near he had been to misfortune on account of his opposite way of life.[185] Having repaired the altar, he offered the customary sacrifices, as Moyses had prescribed.[186]

Manasseh's new-found piety

44 When he had regulated matters pertaining to worship in the proper way,[187] he also took care of the security of Hierosolyma,[188] in that, after repairing the old walls

Manasseh's security measures

---

[175] Josephus elaborates on the reference to Manasseh's being brought "to Babylon" at the end of 2 Chr 33:11 with an allusion to his captor's intentions regarding him.

[176] Josephus supplies these indications on the captive Manasseh's state of mind.

[177] Greek: φιλάνθρωπος καὶ ἐλεήμων. Josephus' 1 other use of this collocation (and of its 2nd component term) is in *Ant.* 8.335, where Ben-hadad's servants characterize the kings of Israel with this phrase.

[178] Josephus spells out the content of Manasseh's "entreating the favor of the Lord" (2 Chr 33:12) and "praying to him" (33:13aα). The extra-biblical text known as the "Prayer of Manasseh" offers a still more elaborate version of the king's appeal.

[179] 2 Chr 33:13aβbα speaks of the Lord's "hearing" Manasseh's entreaty and "bringing him back again to Jerusalem into his kingdom." Josephus specifies how Manasseh's repatriation was accomplished, namely via his release by the Babylonian king in accord with Manasseh's prayer that God make him "humane and merciful."

[180] Greek: ὧν μεταβουλεύειν; this is the reading of the *Ed. pr.*, followed by Marcus. The codices have ὧν ἐπιβουλεύειν ("which [he hastened] to assault"), while Niese conjectures θεῷ δε δουλεύειν ("[he hastened] to be a slave to God") on the basis of Lat.

[181] Josephus elaborates on the summary notice of 2 Chr 33:13bβ: "Then Manasseh knew the Lord was God," highlighting the king's new-found piety. On the word "respect" (Greek: δεισιδαιμονία), see Spicq 1982: 113-6.

[182] Greek: τὸν ναὸν ἁγνίζω. This construction recurs in *Ant.* 12.318. Compare the negative parallel phrase "pollute the sanctuary of God" in 10.42.

[183] Josephus here anticipates and generalizes the notices of 2 Chr 33:15 about Manasseh's removing the "foreign gods" from the city and the "idol" from the temple, along with the "altars" he had built "on the mountain of the house of the Lord and in Jerusalem."

[184] Cf. the reference to Manasseh's "thank offerings" in 2 Chr 33:16aβ. The reference to Manasseh's concern to "keep God "benevolent (Greek: εὐμενής)" recalls Hezekiah's declaration in *Ant.* 9.262 that by restoring the ancient religious system "we shall make God benevolent (Greek: εὐμενής)."

[185] See 2 Chr 33:16b: "he [Manasseh] commanded Judah to serve the Lord the God of Israel." Josephus adds the reference to the motivation behind the king's instructing the people. Conversely, he omits 33:17, with its indication that the people only partially assimilated Manasseh's directives in that they "still sacrificed on the high places," albeit to the Lord alone.

[186] See 2 Chr 33:16a. Josephus adds the reference to Moses' prescription.

[187] Josephus adds this transitional phrase, summarizing the repentant Manasseh's cultic initiatives.

[188] In the Chronicler's presentation, Manasseh's military defense measures (2 Chr 33:14) are mentioned prior to his cultic initiatives (33:15-16). Josephus accentuates the repentant king's piety by reversing this sequence—Manasseh attends to divine matters in first place.

with great solicitude, he laid down another [wall] in addition to these.[189] He likewise erected very high towers and made the fortresses in front of the city more solid in different respects, namely [by gathering in][190] grains and[191] everything [else] that would be of use for them [the fortresses].[192]

Manasseh's end **45** Indeed, in these matters he exhibited such a change that, for as long as he continued to live, he was regarded as most blessed and enviable[193] from [the time] when he began to show piety towards God.[194] **46** Having lived then for sixty-seven years,[195] he ended his life,[196] after reigning as king for fifty-five years.[197] He was buried in his own gardens.[198]

Amon's (Ammon's) brief reign The kingship came to his son Ammon,[199] whose mother was named Emaselme,[200] of the city of Iazabate.[201] **(4.1) 47** He imitated those deeds of his father that he had ventured upon as a young man.[202] Plotted against by his own domestics, he died in his house,[203] after living twenty-four years[204] and reigning as king for two of these.[205]

48 The crowd[206] imposed punishment on his murderers and buried Amon with

---

[189] 2 Chr 33:14a speaks of Manasseh's building "an outer wall for the city of David." Josephus leaves aside the biblical details concerning the placement of this new wall, while adding mention of Manasseh's repair of the city's existing walls.

[190] Greek: συγκομιδῇ. This word is conjecturally supplied by Niese, whom Marcus follows.

[191] Greek: καί. This word is conjecturally supplied by Niese, whom Marcus follows.

[192] Josephus' mention of Manasseh's lofty "towers" seems to reflect the reference in 2 Chr 33:14aβ to the king's raising the outer wall "to a very great height." His notice on the building and stocking of the fortresses is a free modification of 33:14b, which has Manasseh placing "commanders in all the fortified cities of Judah."

[193] Greek: μακαριστὸς καὶ ζηλωτός. This collocation occurs only here in Josephus.

[194] With this summary notice concerning Manasseh's later reign, Josephus rounds off his account (10.40-45) of the king's capture, release, and new direction that he draws from 2 Chr 33:11-17 (no parallel in 2 Kings 21). The language of the notice is reminiscent of that employed of the repentant Manasseh in 10.42, even as it reverses the reference to the king's initial "contempt for God" of 10.38.

[195] Josephus obtains this figure for Manasseh's lifespan by combining the data for his age at accession (12 years) and length of reign (55) given in 2 Kgs 21:1a// 2 Chr 33:1.

[196] Compare 2 Kgs 21:18aα// 2 Chr 33:20aα, which use the figurative language of Manasseh's "sleeping with his fathers." Josephus omits the preceding source notices of 2 Kgs 21:17// 2 Chr 33:18-19.

[197] This figure for Manasseh's length of reign corresponds to that given in 2 Kgs 21:1aβ// 2 Chr 33: 1b.

[198] Josephus' burial notice for Manasseh stands closest to that of LXX BL 2 Chr 33:20aβ ("they buried him in the garden of his house"). Compare 2 Kgs 21:18aβ (MT and LXX BL): "he was buried in the garden of his house, in the garden of Uzza" and 2 Chr 33:20aβ (MT): "they buried him in his house."

[199] MT (2 Kgs 21:18b// 2 Chr 33:20b) אמון (Eng.: "Amon"); LXX B 2 Kgs 21:18b// LXX B 2 Chr 33:20b Ἀμώς; LXX L 2 Kgs 21:18b// LXX L 2 Chr 33:20b Ἀμών; Josephus Ἀμμών. On Josephus' treatment of Amon in 10.47-48, see Begg 2000: 452-4.

[200] MT (2 Kgs 21:19b) משלמת (Eng.: "Meshullemeth"); LXX B L Μεσσολλάμ; Josephus Ἐμασέλμη (2 Chronicles 33 does not mention Amon's mother). Josephus leaves aside the name of the woman's father (MT: Haruz).

[201] MT (2 Kgs 21:19b) יטבה (Eng.: "Jotbah"); LXX B Ἰεσεβάλ; LXX L Ἐτεβαθά; Josephus Ἰαζαβάτη (this is the reading of R, which Niese follows; Marcus reads Ἰαταβάτη with OLauV, while Schalit *s.v.* adopts the form Ἰατάβη of MSP).

[202] Josephus compresses the more expansive (negative) judgment notices concerning Amon of 2 Kgs 21:20-22// 2 Chr 33:21-22. His reference to Amon's imitating the young Manasseh presupposes his (and the Chronicler's) preceding account concerning the latter's repentance, whereas both 21:20 and 33:22 parallel Amon's evil-doing with that of his father without any such qualification.

[203] See 2 Kgs 21:23// 2 Chr 33:24.

[204] Josephus arrives at this figure for Amon's lifespan by combining the figures for his age at accession (22 years) and length of reign (2) given in 2 Kgs 21:19a// 2 Chr 33:21.

[205] This figure for Amon's length of reign corresponds to that given in 2 Kgs 21:19aβ// 2 Chr 33:21a.

[206] 2 Kgs 21:24a// 2 Chr 33:25a speak of "the

his father.[207] They handed over the kingship to his son Josiah,[208] who was eight years of age,[209] and whose mother, named Jedis,[210] was from the city of Bosketh.[211] **49** He had an excellent nature and was well-disposed to virtue,[212] an emulator[213] of King David, whose practices he adopted as the aim and standard[214] for his entire way of life.[215]

Josiah introduced

50 When he was twelve years old,[216] he manifested his piety and justice.[217] For he made his people prudent and urged them to turn away from their opinion about idols, [who were in fact] no gods, and to worship the ancestral God.[218] Reviewing the deeds of his ancestors, he perceptively rectified their offenses, as though he were a quite old man and perfectly capable of ascertaining what was needed. Whatever, however, he found well-ordered and in its [rightful] place, he preserved and imitated.[219] **51** He did these things employing his natural wisdom and insight[220] and

Josiah's piety and precocity at age 12

---

people of the land," an expression Josephus regularly avoids.

[207] See 2 Kgs 21:26a: "he [Amon] was buried in his tomb in the garden of Uzza" (2 Chronicles 33 does not mention Amon's burial). Like Chronicles, Josephus has no equivalent to the source notice for Amon of 2 Kgs 21:25.

[208] MT (2 Kgs 21:26b// 2 Chr 33:25b) יאשיהו (Eng.: "Josiah"); LXX BL 2 Kgs 21:26b// LXX B 2 Chr 33:25b Ἰωσείας; LXX L 2 Chr 33:25b and Josephus Ἰωσίας. On Josephus' portrayal of Josiah in 10.48b-80—in which he oscillates between the rather different presentations of 2 Kgs 22:1-23:30a and 2 Chr 34:1-35:27—, see Begg 2000: 457-97; Feldman 1998a: 424-36; Spilsbury 1998: 195-200; and Delamarter 2004: 43-48.

[209] See 2 Kgs 22:1aα// 2 Chr 34:1a.

[210] MT (2 Kgs 22:1b) ידידה (Eng.: "Jedidah"); LXX B Ἰεδεια; LXX L Ἰεδδεια; Josephus Ἰέδις. 2 Chronicles 34 does not mention the name of Josiah's mother, while Josephus omits the name of her father ("Adaiah" in MT 2 Kgs 22:1b).

[211] MT (2 Kgs 22:1b) בצקת (Eng.: "Bozkath"); LXX BL Βασουρωθ; Josephus Βοσκεθ.

[212] Greek: πρὸς ἀρετὴν εὖ γεγονώς. This construction is *hapax* in Josephus.

[213] Greek: ζηλωτής. This word is conjecturally supplied by Dindorf and Marcus. Niese holds that there is a lacuna in the text before the name "David." The word is often used in the *War* as a negative designation for the Jewish rebels; its only other occurrences in *Antiquities* are in 12.271; 20.47. In *Apion* 1.11 the term has the meaning "devotee"; see BJP 9 (Mason): 19, n. 81.

[214] Greek: σκοπὸς καὶ κανών. This collocation occurs only here in Josephus, who uses its 2nd component term a single time elsewhere, i.e. in *Apion* 2.174.

[215] Josephus varies the stereotyped wording of 2

Kgs 22:2// 2 Chr 34:2 concerning Josiah's "doing what was right in the eyes of the Lord" and "walking in the ways of his father David," without deviating "to the right or the left."

[216] Josephus here follows 2 Chronicles 34 against 2 Kings 22 in recounting an initial reform initiative by the boy Josiah (see 34:3-7) prior to that associated with the finding of the book in the temple in the king's 18th regnal year (and 26th year of life); see 2 Kgs 22:3// 2 Chr 34:8. Whereas, however, the Chronicler (see 34:3a) distinguishes between Josiah's initial turning to the Lord in his 8th regnal year (= his 16th year of life) and the practical effects of this "conversion" in his 12th regnal year (= his 20th year of life; see 34:3b), Josephus situates the entire process still earlier, i.e. when the king was a mere 12 years of age, thereby accentuating his precocious piety.

[217] Compare 2 Chr 34:3a: (in his 8th regnal year) "Josiah began to seek the God of David, his father."

[218] Such a teaching activity by the boy Josiah is not mentioned by either biblical account. That activity is, however, reminiscent of the instructional initiatives that Josephus, following the Chronicler, attributes to King Jehoshaphat in *Ant.* 8.395 (// 2 Chr 17:7) and 9.2 (// 2 Chr 19:4) and to Hezekiah in 9.264 (// 2 Chr 30:1-9); see Feldman 1998a: 428-9. Throughout his presentation of Josiah, Josephus, in this going beyond the Bible itself, depicts him as one who recapitulates the good deeds of his righteous predecessors.

[219] This notice on the youthful Josiah's comprehensive review of his predecessors' practices has no biblical counterpart. Its highlighting of the king's precocity does, however, recall Josephus' introduction of a like emphasis in his portrayals of the young Kings Solomon (*Ant.* 8.21) and Amaziah (*Ant.* 9.186).

[220] Josephus' only other use of this collocation (Greek: σοφία καὶ ἐπίνοια) is in *Ant.* 6.69, where he employs it of the stratagems of the brutal King Nahash.

relying on the counsel and tradition of the elders,[221] for by following the laws he was successful with regard to the order of the city[222] and piety towards God, because the lawlessness of the earlier [kings] was no more but had been exterminated.[223]

Box Josiah's cultic and judicial initiatives

52 For going round both the city and the entire country,[224] the king cut down the groves[225] dedicated to foreign gods and tore down their altars;[226] if there was any dedicatory offering that had been set up to these [gods] by his ancestors, he showed contempt for it[227] and demolished it.[228] **53** In this way he turned his people from their opinion[229] concerning these [gods] to the worship of God on whose altar he offered the customary sacrifices and whole offerings.[230] He also appointed certain judges and overseers, who by regulating the actions of each one were to make what was just [superior to] everything and to show no less consideration for this than for their own souls.[231]

---

[221] The translation follows the more expansive text read by Niese and Marcus; the codices ROLauV have no equivalent to the words "relying on the... of the elders." On the "Pharisaic" phrase "tradition of the elders" (Greek: τῇ τῶν πρεσβυτέρων... παραδόσει) here, see Feldman 1998a: 427-8 and S. Schwartz 1990: 181, n. 34. Cf. also its NT parallels in Mark 7:3// Matt 15:2.

[222] Greek: πόλεως; this is the reading of ROLauV, which Niese follows. Marcus reads πολιτείας ("of the constitution") with MSP.

[223] With this summary comment concerning the influences behind Josiah's initiatives and their efficacy, Josephus rounds off his extended elaboration of the notice of 2 Chr 34:3a regarding the 1st stirrings of the youthful Josiah's piety.

[224] With this phrase Josephus conflates into 1 Josiah's 2 separate reform initiatives, the 1st covering Judah and Jerusalem, the 2nd extending to the territory of the former Northern Kingdom as related in 2 Chr 34:3b-5 and 6-7, respectively.

[225] In his use of this term (Greek: ἄλση) Josephus follows LXX's rendition of the MT mention of the "Asherim" that Josiah eliminates first from Jerusalem and Judah (2 Chr 34:3b) and then from the former northern territory (34:7). See further the note to "trees" at *Ant.* 8.318.

[226] 2 Chr 34:4 (MT) speaks of Josiah's destruction of the "altars of the Baals" and the "incense altars" in Judah and Jerusalem, while 34:7 mentions the elimination of the "altars" and "incense altars" from the former northern territory.

[227] Greek: περιυβρίζω. In *Ant.* 9.103 this same verb is used in connection with the handling of the body of the reprobate King Joram of Judah by the populace.

[228] Josephus' mention of Josiah's destruction of the illicit royal votive offerings has no direct equivalent in the catalogue of the king's iconoclastic measures in 2 Chr 34:3b-7a. Conversely, Josephus omits from that catalogue a whole series of other items whose destruction/defilement by Josiah it records, e.g., the high places (34:3b), the graves of the idolaters and the molten images (34:4, 7), and the bones of the idolatrous priests (34:5). Such "abbreviation" is in line with Josephus' overall handling of the Bible's cultic particulars, especially illicit ones.

[229] Greek: δόξα. Josephus employed this same term in 10.50, where he refers to Josiah's urging the people to turn away from "their opinion about idols." The same term figures in Josephus' account of Elijah's efforts to induce the people to abandon their "opinions" about the existence of gods other than their own; see *Ant.* 8.337, 343. The terminological communality serves to associate the Josephan Josiah and Elijah as (successful) advocates of a sole deity.

[230] The account of Josiah's initial reform measures in 2 Chr 34:3-7 does not mention either the effect of these on the people or a sacrificial activity by Josiah at their conclusion, as Josephus does here. With the former addition Josephus notes the success of Josiah's instructional initiatives as mentioned in 10.50, while also introducing a reminiscence of his notice on the efficacy of Jehoshaphat's earlier teaching mission (see *Ant.* 8.395). As for the reference to the sacrifices that follow the king's cultic "cleanup," these have a parallel in *Ant.* 9.263, where, at the beginning of Hezekiah's reign, the priests, once they have removed the offending objects from the temple, proceed to offer the "customary sacrifices" on the altar.

[231] This notice on Josiah's judicial appointments early in his reign has no counterpart in either Kings or Chronicles. It does, however, serve to establish another parallel between him and a previous reform king, i.e. Jehoshaphat, who, like Josephus' Josiah, follows his instruction of the people (compare *Ant.* 9.2 and 10.50, 53a) with the appointment of judges over them (compare 9.3 and 10.53b).

54 Sending round to the entire country, he directed those who so wished to bring gold and silver—as each might have the intention or the capacity—for the repair of the sanctuary.[232] **55** When the monies were brought,[233] he entrusted responsibility for the sanctuary and its expenses[234] to Amasias,[235] who was over the city,[236] the scribe[237] Saphas,[238] Joates,[239] the keeper of the records,[240] and the high priest Eliakias.[241] **56** These men permitted no delay or postponement; having readied foremen and everything useful for the repair, they applied themselves to the work. The sanctuary that had been thus repaired made clear the king's piety.[242]

Temple repaired

(4.2) 57 When [Josiah] had already held the kingship for eighteen years,[243] he sent to the high priest Eliakias.[244] He directed him to melt down the leftover monies and to make bowls, libation vessels, and offering cups for the service. They were moreover to bring out whatever gold and silver was still in the treasuries and to spend this in similar fashion on bowls and vessels of that sort.[245]

Josiah's directive about use of leftover monies

---

[232] For this notice Josephus draws on, while also modifying, the reference to the monies that the Levites had collected from the "remnant of Israel, as well as Judah and Jerusalem" in 2 Chr 34:9. In his adaptation, the Levites' role in the collection is replaced by that of Josiah himself. This modification, in turn, serves to parallel Josiah with another of Judah's (initially) good kings, i.e. Joash, who initiated an (unsuccessful) attempt to collect a half-shekel from each person throughout the whole country for the temple's repair; see *Ant.* 9.161.

[233] This (added) transitional notice points up the success of Josiah's solicitation (10.54), while likewise serving to (favorably) contrast him with his predecessor Joash whose similar effort (see previous note) came to nothing, given the non-cooperation of the high priest Jehoiada; see *Ant.* 9.162.

[234] 2 Chr 34:8 (itself inspired by the chronological indication of 2 Kgs 22:3) dates Josiah's appointment of the commission charged with repair of the temple to the king's 18th regnal year.

[235] MT (2 Chr 34:8) מעשיהו (Eng.: "Maaseiah"); LXX B Μαασά; LXX L Μασσίαν; Josephus Ἀμασίας. In 2 Chr 34:8 this figure is mentioned in 2nd place, after "Shaphan."

[236] This title corresponds to that given "Maaseiah" in 2 Chr 34:8, i.e. "the governor of the city" (RSV).

[237] Josephus draws this title (RSV: "secretary") for Shaphan from 2 Kgs 22:8// 2 Chr 34:15, etc.

[238] MT (2 Chr 34:8) שפן (Eng.: "Shaphan"); LXX BL Σαφάν; Josephus Σαφᾶς. Josephus omits the name of his father (MT: Azaliah).

[239] MT (2 Chr 34:8) יואח (Eng.: "Joah"); LXX B Ἰουάχ; LXX L Ἰωάς; Josephus Ἰωάτης. Josephus omits the name of his father (MT: Joahaz).

[240] This title corresponds to that given "Joah" in 2 Chr 34:8, i.e. "the recorder" (RSV).

[241] MT (2 Chr 34:9, etc.) חלקיהו (Eng.: "Hilkiah"); LXX B Χελκείας; LXX L Χελκίας; Josephus Ἐλιακίας. In 2 Chr 34:8-9 "Hilkiah" is not mentioned as one of the 3-man commission set up by Josiah to oversee the repair of the temple; rather, the commission goes to him. Josephus makes Hilkiah himself a member of the commission, given his status as the temple's high priest.

[242] This notice on the alacrity with which the commission carries out its mandate to repair the temple and the resultant manifestation of Josiah's own piety are a compressed version of the more detailed account of the temple repair project and the many individuals and groups involved in this given in 2 Chr 34:10-13 (from which Josephus, characteristically, omits the segment, vv. 12-13, concerning the Levites' role as supervisors of the repair work).

[243] Josephus derives this dating indication for the incident of the finding of the book and its sequels from 2 Kgs 22:3. Cf. 2 Chr 34:8, where, in contrast to Josephus' presentation, the finding of the book (see 34:14) takes place during the course of the repair of the temple, rather than as a later, distinct moment.

[244] See 2 Kgs 22:3, which specifies that it was his "secretary" Shaphan whom Josiah sent to Hilkiah.

[245] The instructions Josiah gives Shaphan for Hilkiah in 2 Kgs 22:4-7 concern only a distribution of funds to those involved in the temple repair work. Josephus supplies a different content to the king's directives, given that in his presentation these are issued after the temple repair project has already been completed (see 10.56). That new content to Josiah's instructions, in turn, seems inspired by Josephus' account of an earlier king with whom he has already implicitly paralleled Josiah, i.e. Joash (see note to "the sanctuary" at 10.54), under whom, according to *Ant.* 9.165 (// 2 Chr 24:14), the monies remaining from the

Hilkiah finds books; these read to Josiah

58 When he was bringing forth the silver, the high priest Eliakias came upon the sacred books of Moyses that had been stored in the sanctuary;[246] bringing these out,[247] he gave them to the scribe Saphas.[248] After reading them,[249] he went to the king and reported that everything that he had directed had been completed.[250] He [Saphas] likewise read the books to him.[251]

Huldah (Oolda) consulted

59 When Josiah heard these [books] he tore his clothes.[252] He called the high priest Eliakias and sent him, along with the scribe himself and certain of his closest friends,[253] to the prophetess[254] Oolda,[255] the wife of Salloum,[256] a reputable man and distinguished on account of his noble birth.[257] He directed those whom he sent to her to tell her to propitiate God[258] and to try to make him benevolent.[259] For there

---

repair of the temple were used to make various sorts of cultic vessels—just as Josiah now commands be done with the leftover monies from his temple repair project.

[246] Josephus draws this notice from 2 Chr 34:14b, which recounts Hilkiah's finding "the book of the law of the Lord given through Moses" during the removal of the monies from the temple, but does not explicitly state where Hilkiah found the book. 2 Kings 22 lacks an equivalent narrative statement; in its v. 8 (// 2 Chr 34:15a) Hilkiah informs Shaphan of his having found "the book of the law in the house of the Lord." In contrast to both biblical accounts, Josephus has Hilkiah discover "book*s*."

[247] Josephus supplies this transitional phrase, alluding back to his likewise added reference to the books being found "stored in the sanctuary."

[248] In 2 Kgs 22:8// 2 Chr 34:15 Hilkiah's giving of the book to Shaphan is preceded by the former's announcement of his "find" to the latter.

[249] Josephus draws this reference to Shaphan's first reading the book(s) for himself from 2 Kgs 22:8bβ (no parallel in 2 Chronicles 34).

[250] Josephus' mention of Shaphan's going to the king corresponds to 2 Kgs 22:9a, whereas 2 Chr 34:16a refers to his "bringing" the book to Josiah. Josephus abbreviates Shaphan's more detailed initial report to the king with its mention of the pay given the temple workers—a matter not mentioned in the king's instructions to Hilkiah in his version (see note to "vessels of that sort" at 10.57)—as cited in 2 Kgs 22:9b// 2 Chr 34:16b-17.

[251] In 2 Kgs 22:10// 2 Chr 34:18 Shaphan's reading of the book to Josiah is preceded by the former's announcement that Hilkiah had given him "a book." Josephus' omission of this announcement parallels his non-use of Hilkiah's own statement about finding the book (22:8a// 34:15a); see note to "Saphas" at 10.58.

[252] See 2 Kgs 22:11// 2 Chr 34:19.

[253] This phrase replaces the names of the remaining members of the delegation cited in 2 Kgs 22:12// 2 Chr 34:20, i.e. Ahikam, Achbor/Abdon, and Asaiah. The same phrase is used of the 3 envoys dispatched by

Hezekiah to parley with the Assyrian general in 10.5.

[254] Greek: προφῆτις. Josephus uses this feminine noun twice elsewhere: *Ant.* 5.200 (Deborah) and 10.60 (Huldah).

[255] MT (2 Kgs 22:14// 2 Chr 34:22) חלדה (Eng.: "Huldah"); LXX Ὀλδα/῎Ολδα; Josephus Ὀολδά. In the presentation of both 2 Kings 22 and 2 Chronicles 34, Josiah does not specify through whom he intends the delegation to "inquire of the Lord" for him (22:13// 34:21), and thus the delegation approaches Huldah in particular (22:14// 34:22) on its own initiative. Josephus has the king himself designate the one to whom the delegation is to go.

[256] MT (2 Kgs 22:14// 2 Chr 34:22) שלם (Eng.: "Shallum"); LXX Σελλήμ; Josephus Σάλλουμος. LXX B 2 Kgs 22:14 calls Huldah the mother rather than the wife of Shallum.

[257] 2 Kgs 22:14// 2 Chr 34:22 mention the names of Shallum's father and grandfather, but do not comment on the family's social status. They likewise cite 2 further details not taken over by Josephus, i.e. Shallum's occupation as "keeper of the wardrobe," and Huldah's living in the "Second Quarter." Josephus' highlighting of Shallum's societal position would help account for Josiah's dispatching his delegation specifically to Huldah, i.e. she is the wife of a distinguished personage who shares in her husband's status.

[258] Greek: ἱλάσκεσθαι τὸν θεόν. Josephus uses this construction also in *Ant.* 6.124; 8.112 and in *Apion* 1.308 with "gods" as object.

[259] In 2 Kgs 22:13a// 2 Chr 34:21a Josiah's command to the delegation is that they "inquire of the Lord... concerning the words of this book that has been found." Josephus' Josiah gives the delegation a more definite charge, viz. to ask for Huldah's intercession with God. Also elsewhere, Josephus introduces references to the prophet's expected role as intercessor; see, e.g., *Ant.* 9.67, where King Joram is enraged against Elisha because of the latter's failure to appeal to God on behalf of famine-racked Samaria. The phrase "make benevolent" (Greek: ποιεῖν εὐμενῆ) used by Josiah here of what he hopes Huldah will effect with God recalls

were grounds for anxiety, given their ancestors' transgression of the laws of Moyses, that they were in danger of being driven from house and home, and after being banished to a foreign land and bereft of everything, of wretchedly ending their lives.[260]

60 When the prophetess heard from those who had been sent these things that the king had transmitted through them, she directed them to go back to the king to say[261] that the Deity had already taken his decision against them, which no one could nullify by entreaties.[262] This [decision] was to annihilate the people, expel them from their country, and deprive them of all the good things that were now present[263] because they had transgressed the laws and not thought better of this up until this time,[264] although the prophets had urged them to be prudent[265] in this regard and had predicted punishment for their impieties.[266] **61** This [punishment] he would surely bring about upon them in order that they might be convinced that he was God and had not lied in those things he had announced to them through the prophets.[267] Because, however, he [Josiah] was a just man,[268] he [God] would put off these misfortunes for a while. After his death he would, nevertheless, send down the decreed sufferings on the mob.[269]

Huldah's message for Josiah

Hezekiah's affirmation that the restoration of Judah's ancient cult will "make God benevolent" in *Ant.* 9.262.

[260] Josephus expatiates on the words with which Josiah motivates his dispatch of the delegation in 2 Kgs 22:13b// 2 Chr 34:21b: "for great is the wrath of the Lord that is poured out upon us, because our fathers have not kept the words of this book...." In particular, he portrays Josiah as foreseeing the exile that ultimately awaits his people.

[261] See 2 Kgs 22:14b// 2 Chr 34:22b-23.

[262] With this opening component of her response—unparalleled in the biblical accounts—Huldah implicitly rejects Josiah's appeal that she attempt to "propitiate God" (10.59) as pointless and underscores the irrevocability of God's decrees. For a comparable emphasis, see 10.34, where Hezekiah acknowledges that "it was impossible to change what God had determined."

[263] Josephus' Huldah makes more concrete and specific the announcement of doom pronounced by her biblical counterpart in 2 Kgs 22:16, 17b// 2 Chr 34:24a, 25b: "behold, I [God] will bring evil upon this place... my [God's] wrath will be kindled against this place, and it will not be quenched." At the same time, he leaves aside the biblical prophetess' identification (22:16β// 34:24b) of Judah's announced doom with the words/curses of the book that had been read to Josiah.

[264] Compare the more specific (cultic) accusations Huldah levels against the people in 2 Kgs 22:17a// 2 Chr 34:25a: "because they have forsaken me [God] and have burned incense to other gods, that they might provoke me to anger with all the works of their hands."

[265] Greek: σωφρονεῖν; Niese qualifies the word as "perhaps spurious." This is the same verb that is used in 10.50, where Josiah is said to "have made his people prudent."

[266] The biblical Huldah's speech does not refer to previous prophets and their admonitions. Josephus' added allusion to them recalls his references to the unheeded exhortations of the Israelite prophets in *Ant.* 9.265, 281.

[267] This indication concerning the purpose of the coming punishment, i.e. the demonstration of God's—and his prophets'—veracity, is a Josephan amplification of the biblical Huldah's judgment speech (2 Kgs 22:16-17// 2 Chr 34:24-25). Its language recalls Josephus' statement about Manasseh's people, who themselves had failed to believe the prophets' words, in 10.39: "They learned nonetheless by reality that what the prophets said was true."

[268] This phrase—with its reminiscence of Josephus' mention of Josiah's manifesting his "justice" at age 12 in 10.50—replaces Huldah's more expansive allusion (2 Kgs 22:18-19a// 2 Chr 34:26-27a) to Josiah's penitential gestures upon hearing the words of the book (see 2 Kgs 22:11// 2 Chr 34:19) that prompt God to exempt him personally from the coming catastrophe.

[269] Josephus' formulation of Huldah's announcement concerning Josiah's not living to see the calamity of his people avoids attributing to her the problematic statement of 2 Kgs 22:20aβ// 2 Chr 34:28aβ, namely, that the king would be "gathered to his grave in peace." That announcement could well seem an instance of false prophecy, given the fact that Josiah died a violent (and premature) death according to 2 Kgs 23:29// 2 Chr 35:23-24.

Josiah summens clergy

(4.3) 62 Once then the woman had prophesied, they [the delegation] came and announced [these things] to the king.[270] He, for his part, sending round everywhere, directed the priests and Levites to assemble in Hierosolyma, ordering those of all ages to be present.[271]

People's pledge and sacrifices

63 When they had gathered, he first read the sacred books to them.[272] Then, standing on the platform[273] in the middle of the crowd, he compelled them to take oaths and pledges that they would worship God and keep the laws of Moyses.[274] **64** They eagerly agreed and undertook to do what was urged by the king.[275] Immediately sacrificing and making pleasing offerings,[276] they kept entreating God to be

Josiah's cultic measures in Jerusalem

benevolent and gracious[277] to them.[278] **65** [Josiah] ordered the high priest that, if any vessel that had been put in place by his ancestors [in honor of] idols and foreign gods was still left over in the sanctuary, he should throw this out.[279] When many of these things had been gathered together, he burned them and scattered their ashes.[280] He likewise killed[281] the priests of the idols[282] who were not of the family of Aaron.[283]

---

[270] See 2 Kgs 22:20bβ// 2 Chr 34:28bβ.

[271] In 2 Kgs 23:1// 2 Chr 34:29 it is "the elders of Judah and Jerusalem" who assemble in response to Josiah's "sending." Josephus derives his indication concerning those convened from 2 Chr 34:30a, where "the priests and the Levites [2 Kgs 23:2: the priests and *the prophets*], all the people, both great and small" accompany the king to the temple for the covenant-making ceremony.

[272] In 2 Kgs 23:2b// 2 Chr 34:30b Josiah reads "the book of covenant" to the assembly. Compare 10.58, where Hilkiah discovers "the sacred books of Moyses."

[273] This is the same site from which the high priest and David issue their pronouncements in *Ant.* 4.209 and 7.370, respectively. According to 2 Kgs 23:3aα, Josiah stands "by the pillar" in concluding the covenant, while in 2 Chr 34:31aα he stands "in his place" (the Targums refer to his standing "upon the balcony").

[274] Josephus' wording concerning Josiah's initiative characteristically avoids the biblical reference (see 2 Kgs 23:3aβ// 2 Chr 34:31aβ) to the king's "making a covenant before the Lord." He likewise abbreviates the statement of the content of this covenant found in 23:3bα// 34:31b, eliminating, e.g., the reference to "the book" in which the terms of the covenant are set down.

[275] Josephus goes beyond 2 Kgs 23:3bβ// 2 Chr 34:32 in highlighting the people's willing acceptance of the king's directives.

[276] Greek: καλλιερέω. Marcus renders "while singing the sacred hymns," while noting the uncertainty surrounding the correct rendering of the verb (used previously in *Ant.* 9.268, 271, where he translates it with "sacrifice auspiciously") here. Neither biblical account mentions such cultic activities, whereby the people act on Josiah's demand that they "worship God" (10.63), at this juncture. The added mention of

sacrifices recalls Josephus'—also added—notice on Josiah's sacrificing following his initial reforms in 10.53.

[277] Greek: εὐμενής καὶ ἵλεως. Josephus uses this wordpair 1 other time, i.e. in *Ant.* 4.243, there too in reference to God.

[278] This reference to the people's entreating divine favor recalls Josiah's sending the delegation to ask Huldah to "propitiate God and try to make him benevolent" in 10.59. At the same time, the people's appeal at this point seems to reflect a certain self-delusion or willed ignorance, given Huldah's prior statement (see 10.60) that "no one could nullify God's decrees by entreaties."

[279] Compare 2 Kgs 23:4a, where Josiah addresses his directive, not only to Hilkiah himself, but also to 2 classes of subordinate cultic officials. Josephus generalizes the mention of "Baal, Asherah and the host of heaven" in 23:4bα, while adding the reference to Josiah's predecessors as the source of the illicit objects. His conditional (re-)wording of the king's command ("if any vessel... was left over....") reflects the fact that in his presentation—in contrast to that of 2 Kings 22-23—Josiah has already (see 10.52// 2 Chr 34:3-7) conducted a comprehensive cultic "cleanup."

[280] Josephus omits several details concerning Josiah's iconoclastic initiatives as cited in 2 Kgs 23:4bβγ, i.e. his burning the illicit objects "outside Jerusalem in the fields of Kidron" and carrying their ashes "to Bethel."

[281] In MT 2 Kgs 23:5aα Josiah "deposes" the idolatrous priests, while in BL LXX (and OL) he "burns" them.

[282] MT 2 Kgs 23:5aα designates the priests in question with the rare Hebrew term כמרים (RSV: "idolatrous priests"), which LXX B transliterates and LXX L translates neutrally as "the priests." 23:5aβb

(4.4) 66 Once [Josiah] had disposed of these matters in Hierosolyma,[284] he went
into the country. He exterminated everything that had been constructed in it by King
Hieroboam in honor of the foreign gods.[285] He burned the bones of the false prophets on the altar that Hieroboam was the first to construct.[286] **67** For this is what the
prophet,[287] who came down to Hieroboam when he was offering sacrifice, had announced in advance would happen in the hearing of the entire people, namely that
someone from the family of David, Josiah by name, would do the above-mentioned
things.[288] It happened that these things reached fulfillment after 360[289] years.[290]

(4.5) 68 After this[291] King Josiah went as well to the other Israelites who had
escaped from their captivity and slavery under the Assyrians.[292] He persuaded them

*Jeroboam's
altar desecrated*

*Josiah reforms
worship of*

---

goes on to qualify these priests as ones designated by
the kings of Judah to burn incense to an array of deities.

[283] Josephus appends this additional ground for
Josiah's execution of the idolatrous priests: not being
of the line of Aaron, they had no right to exercise
priestly functions of any sort. The phrase recalls
Jeroboam's claim that his people had no need of "the
sons of Aaron" in *Ant.* 8.228 and Uzziah's attempt to
offer the sacrifice that was reserved to the "family of
Aaron" in 9.224.

[284] This transitional phrase replaces the extended
list of further cultic initiatives undertaken by Josiah in
2 Kgs 23:4-14 (Josephus will return to this list
momentarily in 10.69 in order to cite an additional item
from it). In thus abbreviating Kings' list, Josephus
aligns himself with the Chronicler, who limits his account of Josiah's post book-finding cultic purification
measures to a single verse, 2 Chr 34:33. The reason for
such compression by the Chronicler and Josephus is
that both have already narrated a comprehensive reform
by Josiah prior to the finding of the book; see 2 Chr
34:3-7// 10.52.

[285] See 2 Kgs 23:19, where Josiah "removes all the
shrines of the high places that were in the cities of
Samaria, which the kings of Israel had made...."

[286] Josephus here combines elements of 2 Kgs
23:15a (Jeroboam's altar-building) and 23:16bα
(Josiah's burning of bones on the altar). The latter verse
does not specify whose bones were burnt. Josephus'
clarification on the point recalls the announcement he
attributes to the Judean prophet in *Ant.* 8.232, namely
Josiah will burn on the Bethel altar "the bones of these
misleaders of the people, these impostors and
unbelievers." From the sequence of 23:15-16abα,
Josephus leaves aside a variety of additional details:
the location of Jeroboam's altar at Bethel, Josiah's
pulverizing of this, his burning of the Asherah (v. 15),
as well as his seeing of tombs on the mount and his
removal of bones from these tombs (v. 16a).

[287] In *Ant.* 8.231 Josephus gives the name of
this prophet as "Jadon," whereas in 1 Kings 13 he remains nameless.

[288] With Josephus' cross-reference here to the
prediction he ascribes to the Judean prophet "Jadon" in
Ant. 8.232, compare 2 Kgs 23:16bβ, where Josiah
defiles the altar "according to the word of the Lord
which the man of God proclaimed, who had predicted
these things."

[289] This is the reading (Greek: ἐξηκονταέν) adopted
by Niese and Marcus. Curiously, however, the latter
translates "361" in accordance with the reading of Lau.

[290] Josephus' figure for the period between the Bethel confrontation under Jeroboam I and the reform of
Josiah in his 18th year is somewhat higher than that
calculated by modern historians, who would date the
former event to *ca.* 920 BCE and the latter to 622 BCE
for a total of just about *300* years; see Marcus *ad loc.* In
any event, this added chronological indication takes
the place of the sequence appended to the notice on
Josiah's defiling of the Bethel altar (2 Kgs 23:16) in
23:17-18, where the king asks about the tomb he sees
and it is told that is that of the Judean man of God
whose word he has just fulfilled (v. 17), whereupon
Josiah enjoins that the man's remains be left undis-
turbed, with the result that the bones of the prophet
who had misled him are also left in peace (v. 18)—just
as the latter had anticipated (see 1 Kgs 13:31-32).
Given Josephus' penchant for highlighting the fulfillment of prophetic announcements and given too that
he does reproduce the Bethel's prophet's expectation
from 1 Kgs 13:31-32 in *Ant.* 8.242, it appears surprising
that he does not make use of the content of 23:17-18,
which offers a dramatic instance of the realization of a
prophetic words centuries after its delivery. On the other
hand, however, Josephus explicitly qualifies the Bethel
prophet as a "false prophet" (see *Ant.* 8.236), and so
may not have wished to acknowledge that he did make
a true prediction, as he is represented as having done in
23:18.

[291] Josephus supplies this transition between
Josiah's initial iconoclastic measures outside Jerusalem
(10.67) and his subsequent such measures (10.68-69).

[292] The account of Josiah's measures outside of
Jerusalem in 2 Kgs 23:15-20 says nothing about such

*returned
Israelites*

to give up their impious practices and abandon their honors for alien gods and to show piety towards the ancestral and greatest God[293] and devote themselves to him.[294] **69** He further searched their houses, villages, and cities, suspecting that some might have something idolatrous inside.[295] Nor did he overlook the chariots for the royal officials that his ancestors had constructed,[296] just as he carried off anything else of this sort they were paying homage to as a god.[297]

*Chariots
eliminated*

*Josiah's
passover
(Pascha)*

70 Having thus cleansed the entire country,[298] he called the people together to Hierosolyma and there celebrated the feast of Unleavened Bread and that[299] called *Pascha*.[300] He donated to the people for *Pascha* 20,000[301] new-born kids and lambs, as well as 3,000 cattle for whole-sacrifices.[302] **71** Those who were first among the

---

Israelite escapees. Josephus' introduction of them here enables him to avoid having Josiah's (successful) teaching initiative that he will relate in what follows be directed to the reprobate "Chouthaioi"/ Samaritans, the inhabitants of the former Northern Kingdom since the time of Hezekiah.

[293] Greek: τὸν... θεὸν εὐσεβεῖν. This is the same phase used of the repentant Manasseh in 10.45.

[294] Josiah's (biblically unparalleled) success as a religious instructor of the repatriated Northerners here recalls the efficacy of his previous teaching of his Judean subjects concerning the senselessness of idolatry in 10.50, 53. The king's double success in this regard sets him in contrast to his predecessor Hezekiah, whose efforts to win over the Northerners were generally rebuffed by them; see *Ant.* 9.265.

[295] This notice represents an adaptation of the reference to Josiah's iconoclastic measures in the Samaritan cities of 2 Kgs 23:19-20a. The Josephan Josiah's efforts at eradicating all vestiges of idolatry from the former Northern Kingdom are far more thorough-going, extending even into private homes. Josephus' allusion to such a house-to-house search for idolatrous matter has a counterpart in *Midr. Rab. Lamentations* 1.53, where Josiah entrusts the search to 2 disciples of the Sages (whose efforts are, however, thwarted by the cunning of the householders).

[296] For this item, Josephus seems to make delayed (and modified) use of a portion of the earlier account of Josiah's measures regarding the illicit cult of Jerusalem and Judah in 2 Kgs 23:4-14, namely Kgs 23:11: "And he [Josiah] removed [MT; LXX BL: burned] the horses that the kings of Judah had dedicated to the sun, at the entrance of to the house of the Lord, by the chamber of Nathan-melech the chamberlain...; and he burned the chariots [MT; LXX BL: chariot] of the sun with fire." In Josephus' version the reference to the "royal officials" (Greek: βασιλευομένοις, literally: "those ruled over") might be inspired by the biblical mention of Nathan-melech the chamberlain. See further Marcus *ad loc.*

[297] With this formulation Josephus alludes to the

many additional cultic items whose elimination from Judah and Jerusalem by Josiah 2 Kgs 23:4-14 recounts. It takes the place of the closing notice on Josiah's return to Jerusalem (2 Kgs 23:20b), following his initiatives in the north (2 Kgs 23:15-20a).

[298] Josephus supplies this transitional phrase, rounding off his account of Josiah's cultic purification of both Judah/Jerusalem (10.65, 69b) and the former territory of Israel (10.66-69a), subsequent to the finding of the book. The phrase further serves to suggest the readiness of the entire land—north and south—to celebrate the pan-Israelite Passover Josephus will now describe.

[299] Greek: καὶ τήν. G. Dindorf conjectures τὴν καὶ, which yields the sense "Unleavened Bread also called *Pascha*," a reading involving the identification of the 2 feasts, rather than a distinction between them as in the above translation. See Marcus *ad loc.* and cf. next note.

[300] See 2 Kgs 23:21 (Josiah commands the people to observe the Passover)// 2 Chr 35:1 (Josiah keeps the Passover in Jerusalem). In 2 Chr 35:17 "Passover" and "Unleavened Bread" are also spoken of as 2 distinct feasts, although in reverse order to Josephus' mention of them here (see, however, previous note). Compare *Ant.* 9.271, where Josephus speaks of the *Phaska* being sacrificed following at the "festival of Unleavened Bread." Josephus' account of the Josianic Passover observance in 10.70-72 stands midway between the summary version of 2 Kgs 23:21-23 and the much more expansive ones in 2 Chr 35:1-19// 1 Esdras 1:1-20, from which he omits, e.g., most of the material featuring the activities of the Levites.

[301] This is the figure read by RO and followed by Niese. MSPLauVLat read rather 30,000, the figure cited in 2 Chr 35:7// 1 Esdras 1:7 and adopted by Marcus *ad loc.*

[302] Josephus' figure for Josiah's bovine donations corresponds to that given in 2 Chr 35:7// 1 Esdras 1:7. Like 1 Esdras, Josephus does not mention the contribution of victims made by the "princes" as cited in 2 Chr 35:8a.

priests likewise bestowed on the [other] priests 2,600 lambs for the *Pascha*;[303] to the Levites their chiefs gave 5,000 lambs, plus 500 cattle.[304] **72** The supply of victims being thus abundant, they offered the sacrifices according to the laws of Moyses, each of the priests directing and ministering to the mob.[305] No other feast had been thus celebrated by the Hebrews from the times of the prophet Samouel;[306] the reason was that everything was carried out according to the laws and the ancient observance of ancestral custom.[307]

73 After this Josiah lived in peace as well as wealth, and universal good repute.[308] He died, however, in the following way:[309]

(5.1) 74 Nechaus,[310] the king of the Egyptians, after raising an army,[311] marched towards the Euphrates river[312] to make war on the Medes and the Babylonians, who had overthrown the rule of the Assyrians.[313] For he desired to reign as king over Asia.[314]

Josiah's death in battle against Pharaoh Neco (Nechaus)

---

[303] This is the figure for the priests' contribution of sheep given in 2 Chr 35:8b// 1 Esdras 1:8 (where 3 of "the chief officers of the house of God" are mentioned by name and their contribution of "300 calves" is also mentioned).

[304] With these figures for the Levitical leaders' contributions compare those cited in 2 Chr 35:9 (5,000 lambs and kids, 500 bulls) and 1 Esdras 1:9 (5,000 sheep plus 700 calves). These 2 texts further mention 6 Levitical leaders by name.

[305] This notice on the priests' role replaces the more detailed description of the Passover observance given in 2 Chr 35:10-15// 1 Esdras 1:10-16, whose recurring references to the Levites' involvement in the proceedings Josephus leaves aside.

[306] In his specific mention of "the prophet Samouel" here Josephus agrees with 2 Chr 35:17// 1 Esdras 1:20 against 2 Kgs 23, which speaks more generally of the "days of the judges who judged Israel" as the last time such a Passover had been celebrated.

[307] With this added phrase Josephus spells out the distinctiveness of Josiah's Passover, viz. its full conformity to the requirements of law and custom.

[308] Conceivably, Josephus found inspiration for this summary statement concerning the characteristics of Josiah's reign in the reference to the king's "splendor" in 1 Esdras 1:31b (Eng. 1:33). Compare the concluding evaluation of Josiah in 2 Kgs 23:25, lauding him as unequaled in his adherence to the Lord and the Law. Like 2 Chronicles 35 and 1 Esdras 1 (although cf. v. 27), Josephus has no equivalent to the editorial remarks about the Lord's not relenting from his anger against Judah for the crimes of Manasseh of 2 Kgs 23:26-27, given that he, following the Chronicler, represents Manasseh as an ultimately repentant and forgiven king. He likewise dispenses with the source notices for Josiah of 2 Kgs 23:28// 2 Chr 35:26// 1 Esdras 1:31 (Eng. 1:33).

[309] Josephus introduces this heading to his account of Josiah's end (for which he follows the more expansive version of 2 Chr 35:20-25—itself (largely) paralleled in 1 Esdras 1:23-30 [Eng. 1:25-32]—rather than the summary narrative of 2 Kgs 23:29-30).

[310] MT (2 Kgs 23:29) נכה (Eng.: "Neco")/ 2 Chr 35:20 נכו (Eng.: "Neco"); LXX Νεχαώ; Josephus Νεχαῦς (this is the reading of O [and R subsequently], which Niese follows; Marcus reads Νεχαώ with SPLat). Josiah's Egyptian opponent is not named in 1 Esdras 1.

There is an odd reference in the context of Josephus' address to the defenders of Jerusalem (*War* 5.362-419) to "Neco" (Greek: Νεχαώς) as the Pharaoh, who, having invaded Palestine, threatened to take Sarah from Abram (*War* 5.379; compare Gen 12:10-10// *Ant.* 1.161-169); see Feldman 2001: 315.

[311] Josephus adds this preliminary detail.

[312] This indication concerning Neco's destination has a counterpart in 2 Kgs 23:29 and 2 Chr 35:20 (where MT—and 1 Esdras 1:23 [Eng. 1:25]—add the further specification "at Carchemish").

[313] According to 2 Kgs 23:29 (and LXX BL 2 Chr 35:20), Neco was marching to/against "the king of Assyria." Josephus' reformulation reflects the fact that in his presentation the power of Assyria has already been overthrown by the Medes during the reign of Hezekiah, with the resultant emergence of the Babylonian kingdom; see 10.30, 40. Josephus' indication concerning the Medes and Babylonians, rather than the Assyrians, as Neco's "target" is in accord with what is now known of the history of the time from extra-biblical sources, viz. Neco's objective was to prop up the remnant of the Assyrian empire against the rising power of Babylon.

[314] Josephus supplies this motivation for Neco's advance, which the biblical accounts leave without an explicit rationale.

75 Upon his coming to the city of Mende[315]—this was in Josiah's kingdom[316]—the latter met him with his force, seeing that he was marching against the Medes through his own country.[317] Nechaus, for his part, sent a herald[318] to him to say that he was not campaigning against him, but rather was hastening towards the Euphrates river.[319] He directed him not to provoke him so that he would make war on him [Josiah], who was preventing him from going where he had decided.[320] **76** Josiah, however, did not listen to these [words] of Nechaus. Rather, he acted as though he would not grant him permission to pass through his own country.[321] It was destiny,[322] I suppose, that incited him to this, so as to have a pretext against him.[323]

77 For after he had drawn up his force and was riding in his chariot from one wing to another,[324] a certain Egyptian shot him and ended his enthusiasm for battle.[325] For, being in great pain from his wound, he directed that the army be called back,[326]

---

[315] MT (2 Kgs 23:29) מגדו (Eng.: "Megiddo"); LXX B Μαγεδω; LXX L Μαγεδδω; Josephus Μένδη (Schalit *s. v.* reads Μαγιδδω in line with the biblical name for the site). On the problem of Josephus' site-name as read by Niese and himself, see Marcus *ad loc.* 2 Chr 35:20 and 1 Esdras 1:23 (Eng. 1:25; cf., however, 1:27 [Eng. 1:29]: in the plain of Megiddo) do not specify where the encounter took place.

[316] Josephus supplies this indication concerning the location of Megiddo/Mende.

[317] Josephus expatiates on the notices of 2 Kgs 23:29// 2 Chr 35:20b// 1 Esdras 1:23b (Eng. 1:25b), which have Josiah (alone) going to meet Neco, with no indication as to what lay behind his doing this. In supplying a motivation for Josiah's move, Josephus draws on—his likewise added—mention of Neco's projected campaign against the Medes (and Babylonians) in 10.74.

[318] 2 Chr 35:21 speaks of Neco's "messengers."

[319] Compare Neco's message as cited in 2 Chr 35:21a// 1 Esdras 1:24b-25a (Eng. 1:26b-27a; no parallel in 2 Kings 23): "What have we to do with each other, king of Judah? I am not coming against you this day, but against the house with which I am at war." Josephus' reference to the Euphrates as Neco's destination has a counterpart in the wording of the king's message in 1 Esdras 1:25a (Eng. 1:27a), where this replaces the Chronicler's above indication concerning the Egyptian's "target."

[320] Josephus' formulation of the warning with which Neco's message concludes eliminates the double invocation of "God" in 2 Chr 35:21b: "and God has commanded me to make haste. Cease opposing God who is with me, lest he destroy you." (no parallel in 2 Kings 23; in 1 Esdras 1:25b [Eng. 1:27b] Neco's closing warning is expanded and the Deity is designated as "the Lord"). Josephus may have thought it inappropriate (or implausible) that a pagan king should make such claims about his having the (true) Deity's backing.

[321] Josephus' notice on Josiah's initial response to Neco's warning seems to reflect the expanded version of the Chronicler's statement ("nevertheless Josiah would not turn back," 2 Chr 35:22a) found in 1 Esdras 1:26a (Eng. 1:28a): "but Josiah did not turn back to his chariot, but tried to fight with him [Neco]."

[322] Greek: τῆς πεπρωμένης. The codices add the word ἀλαζονείας to this nominalized participle of the verb πόρω, this yielding the reading—rejected by Niese, Marcus, etc.—"destined boastfulness."

[323] In attributing Josiah's ill-advised move to the influence of "destiny" here, Josephus diverges from both 2 Chr 35:22 (where Josiah's disastrous initiative is due to his failure to heed "the words of Neco from the mouth of God") and 1 Esdras 1:26b (Eng. 1:28b) (where his demise is ascribed to his not attending to "the words of the prophet Jeremiah from the mouth of the Lord"). On the other hand, Josephus' formulation is quite reminiscent of *Ant.* 8.409, where he associates Ahab's calamitous decision to put his trust in Zedekiah's promise of victory to the operation of "fate" (Greek: τὸ χρεών). By contrast, in *Ant.* 9.199 he represents God himself as inciting the Judean King Amaziah to foolishly provoke Joash of Israel.

[324] Josephus supplies these details concerning Josiah's preparations for battle. Like 1 Esdras 1:27 (Eng. 1:29), he lacks a parallel to the Chronicler's mention (see 2 Chr 35:22a) of Josiah's "disguising himself" prior to the battle—a move that might suggest cowardice on Josiah's part.

[325] Josephus' mention of Josiah's being "shot" during the battle corresponds to 2 Chr 35:23a ("the archers shot King Josiah"). Compare 2 Kgs 23:29b ("Pharaoh Neco slew him [Josiah] at Megiddo, when he saw him") and 1 Esdras 1:27b (Eng. 1:29b) ("and the commanders came against King Josiah"). Josephus appends the reference to the effect of the shooting upon Josiah's fighting spirit.

[326] Compare 2 Chr 35:23b// 1 Esdras 1:28a (Eng. 1:30a), where Josiah commands his servants to "take

while he returned to Hierosolyma.[327] There he died[328] from his wound and was magnificently interred in the graves of his ancestors.[329] He lived thirty-nine years[330] and reigned as king for thirty-one of these.[331] **78** Great mourning was made for him by all the people who bewailed and lamented him for many days.[332]

Likewise the prophet Hieremias[333] [Jeremiah] composed a funereal dirge[334] for him, which endures down to this day.[335] **79** This prophet[336] proclaimed in advance the terrible things that awaited the city; he also left behind writings[337] about its capture in our own time[338] and the destruction of Babylon.[339] Nor did he alone foretell these things to the mob; there was also the prophet Iezekiel,[340] who left behind two books[341] that he was the first[342] to write about these matters. **80** They were both

Mourning for Josiah

Prophets Jeremiah (Hieremias) and Ezekiel (Iezekiel) introduced

---

him away," on account of his being "badly wounded"/ "very weak." Josephus represents the suffering king as concerned not only, or in the first place, with his personal condition, but rather with the safety of his troops. In this, the Josephan Josiah recalls the historian's portrayal (*Ant.* 8.415) of Ahab, who, even though he is "in pain," stands in his chariot until sunset.

[327] Josephus leaves aside the various details of Josiah's "return" as given in one or other of the 3 source texts 2 Kgs 23:30aα// 2 Chr 35:24a// 1 Esdras 1:28b-29a (Eng. 1:30b-31a), i.e. his removal from the line of battle, transfer to a 2nd chariot, death in Megiddo, and his being brought by his servants to Jerusalem.

[328] In having Josiah die in Jerusalem itself, Josephus agrees with 2 Chr 35:24aβ// 1 Esdras 1:29bα (Eng. 1:31bα), against 2 Kgs 23:29bβ-30aα, where Josiah is killed at Megiddo, whence his corpse is brought to Jerusalem by his servants.

[329] 2 Chr 35:24aβ// 1 Esdras 1:29bβ (Eng. 1:31bβ) have Josiah buried "in the tombs of his fathers," 2 Kgs 23:30aβ rather "in his own tomb." Josephus adds the reference to the magnificence of Josiah's burial.

[330] Josephus obtains this figure for Josiah's life-span by combining the data of 2 Kgs 22:1a// 2 Chr 34:1, namely his accession at age 8 and 31 years of reign.

[331] This figure for Josiah's length of reign corresponds to that given in 2 Kgs 22:1a// 2 Chr 34:1b.

[332] 2 Chr 35:24bβ ascribes the mourning for Josiah to "all Judah and Jerusalem," 1 Esdras 1:30a (Eng. 1:32a) to "all Judea." 2 Kings 23 does not mention such mourning for the dead king.

[333] MT (2 Chr 35:25) ירמיהו (Eng.: "Jeremiah"); LXX BL 2 Chr 35:25// 1 Esdras 1:30 (Eng. 1:32) Ἰερεμίας; Josephus Ἰερεμίας. Josephus' use of the title "prophet" for Jeremiah here is paralleled in 1 Esdras 1:30.

[334] Greek: μέλος θρηνητικόν. The 2nd term of this phrase is bracketed by Niese, but not by Marcus.

[335] Josephus compresses the notices of 2 Chr 35:25aβb// 1 Esdras 1:30b (Eng. 1:32b) concerning the ongoing practice of lamentation for Josiah. Like the

latter text, he lacks an equivalent to the Chronicler's mention of the laments for Josiah being "written in the Laments" (the Book of Lamentations?).

[336] Josephus now takes the occasion offered him by the mention of Jeremiah in 2 Chr 35:25// 1 Esdras 1:30 (Eng. 1:32) to append a segment of his own composition (10.79-80), in which he supplies an initial characterization both of this prophet and his contemporary Ezekiel whose content he draws from their respective books.

[337] Josephus use of the plural "writings" here likely has in view the Book of Jeremiah and that of Lamentations (which LXX Lam 1:1 and *b. Bat.* 15a attribute to the prophet explicitly).

[338] With this phrase Josephus represents Jeremiah as having also announced the recent capture of Jerusalem by the Romans. On the phrase, see Marcus (*ad loc.*), who argues that it is original with Josephus himself.

[339] Josephus here refers to the predictions of the ultimate overthrow of Babylon itself found in Jeremiah 50-51 (MT).

[340] MT (Ezek 1:3) יחזקאל (Eng.: "Ezekiel"); LXX Ἰεζεκιηλ; Josephus Ἰεζεκίηλος.

[341] On this enigmatic reference to Ezekiel's "2 books," see Marcus (*ad loc.*) who suggests that it refers to the 2 distinct halves of the Book of Ezekiel, i.e. the words of judgment in chaps. 1-24 and the announcements of salvation in chaps. 25-48. In any case, Josephus' ascription of "2 books" to Ezekiel reinforces the parallelism between him and Jeremiah who is credited with leaving behind "writings" earlier in 10.79, and which he is concerned to accentuate throughout his presentation of the pair.

[342] This reference to Ezekiel's being the "first" to write the predictions about Jerusalem's fall is problematic in that it seems not to accord with the chronologies of the ministries of Jeremiah and Ezekiel as found in their respective books and in Josephus' own subsequent presentation; see further Begg 2000: 492, n. 254. In any case, Josephus will return to the topic of the 2 prophets' common message of doom in 10.106-107.

priests by birth.[343] Hieremias, however, lived in Hierosolyma from the thirteenth year of the reign of Josiah until the city and the sanctuary were demolished.[344] We shall, however, relate what happened to this prophet in its proper place.[345]

Jehoahaz succeeds

(5.2) 81 Upon Josiah's death, as we said before,[346] his son named Joaz,[347] aged already twenty-three,[348] succeeded to the kingship.[349] He ruled for three months in Hierosolyma;[350] his mother was Amitalc[351] of the city of Tomane.[352] He was of impious and disreputable[353] character.[354]

Jehoiakim (Joakeim) replaces Jehoahaz

82 Now the king of Egypt, returning from battle, summoned Joaz to himself at a city called Amatha[355] (it is in Syria). When he came, he bound him.[356] He handed over the kingship to his older[357] brother, who had the same mother as he[358] and

---

[343] On Jeremiah's priestly lineage, see Jer 1:2; on that of Ezekiel, see Ezek 1:3.

[344] Josephus derives this chronology for the duration of Jeremiah's ministry from Jer 1:3 (which, however, lacks the specification that Jeremiah was living in Jerusalem throughout this period). He adds the reference to the destruction also of the "sanctuary," just as he will supply allusions to that structure's coming fate throughout his account of Judah's last years.

[345] With this notice Josephus rounds off the "prophetic interlude" of 10.79-80 and looks ahead to his subsequent utilization of selected portions of the Book of Jeremiah in 10.89-180.

[346] This formula resumes the main story line from 10.77-78 after the "prophetic interlude" of 10.79-80.

[347] MT (2 Kgs 23:30b// 2 Chr 36:1) יהואחז (Eng.: "Jehoahaz"); LXX BL 2 Kgs 23:30b// 2 Chr 36:1 Ἰωαχάζ; 1 Esdras 1:32 (Eng. 1:34) Ἰεχονίας; Josephus Ἰώαζος (this is the reading of RO, which Niese and Schalit *s.v.* follow; Marcus *ad loc.* reads Ἰωάχαζος with LauVE).

[348] This figure for Jehoahaz' age at accession corresponds to that given in 2 Kgs 23:31aα// 2 Chr 36:2a// 1 Esdras 1:32 (Eng. 1:34).

[349] 2 Kgs 23:30b// 2 Chr 36:1 attribute Jehoahaz' accession to an initiative by "the people of the land" (1 Esdras 1:32 [Eng. 1:34]: the men of the nation).

[350] This figure for Jehoahaz' length of reign corresponds to that given in 2 Kgs 23:31aβ// 2 Chr 36:2b/ / 1 Esdras 1:33a (Eng. 1:35a).

[351] MT (2 Kgs 23:31b) חמוטל (Eng.: "Hamutal"); LXX B 2 Kgs 23:31b Ἀμειταί; LXX L 2 Kgs 23:31b / / LXX L 2 Chr 36:2a Ἀμιτάλ; LXX B 2 Chr 36:2α Ἀβειτάλ; Josephus Ἀμιτάλη (he leaves aside the name of her father, i.e. "Jeremiah," MT 2 Kgs 23:31b). Neither MT 2 Chronicles 36 nor 1 Esdras 1 mentions the name of Jehoahaz' mother.

[352] MT (2 Kgs 23:31b) לבנה (Eng. "Libnah"); LXX B 2 Kgs 23:31b Λημνά; LXX L 2 Kgs 23:31b// LXX L 2 Chr 36:2 Λοβεννά; LXX B 2 Chr 36:2 Λοβενά; Josephus Τομάνη (this is the reading of RO, which Niese follows; Marcus and Schalit *s.v.* adopt the

conjecture of J. Hudson, i.e. Λοβάνη).

[353] Greek: ἀσεβῆς καὶ μιαρός. Josephus' only other use of this collocation is in *Ant.* 13.316, where it appears in a confession by Aristobulus concerning his offenses.

[354] This characterization of Jehoahaz replaces the stereotyped phrase of 2 Kgs 23:32// LXX BL 2 Chr 36:2b: "he did what was evil in the sight of the Lord, according to all that his fathers had done." Neither MT 2 Chronicles 36 nor 1 Esdras 1 offers an assessment of the short-reigned Jehoahaz.

[355] In 2 Kgs 23:33a (and LXX BL 2 Chr 36:2c) "Hamath" is a region, within which is located the city of "Riblah," where Neco seizes Jehoahaz. Josephus makes "Amatha" itself a city (located in Syria), just as he did earlier in *Ant.* 9.206 (where the site is called "Amath").

[356] Josephus' account of Jehoahaz' deposition here follows the version given in 2 Kgs 23:33a// LXX BL 2 Chr 36:2c (Neco binds Jehoahaz "at Riblah in the land of Hamath," thereby ending his reign in Jerusalem) as opposed to MT 2 Chr 36:3a (the Egyptian king deposes Jehoahaz in Jerusalem) and 1 Esdras 1:33b (Eng. 1:35b) (the Egyptian king deposes Jehoahaz "from reigning in Jerusalem"). At the same time, Josephus also makes several additions to (Pharaoh's return from battle, i.e. against the Medes and Babylonians [see 10.74]) and his summoning of Jehoahaz) and modifications of (the confrontation occurs at the "city" of "Amatha" in Syria; see previous note) the Kings text.

[357] Josephus' derives his specification that Eliakim/ Jehoiakim was the "older" brother of his predecessor Jehoahaz from the notations given in 2 Kgs 23:31, etc. (Jehoahaz began his 3-month reign at age 23) and 23:36, etc. (Jehoiakim succeeded Jehoahaz when he [Jehoiakim] was 25 years old).

[358] In assigning the "same mother" to Eliakim/ Jehoiakim and Jehoahaz, i.e. "Amitale" (see 10.81), Josephus follows LXX L 2 Kgs 23:31, 36// LXX L 2 Chr 36:2, 5. (See, however, 10.83, where, contradicting his statement here in 10.82, Josephus assigns Jehoiakim a different mother than the one he mentions for

whose name was Eliakeim,[359] renaming him Joakeim.[360] He further imposed a tribute of 100 talents of silver and one of gold on the country.[361] **83** Joakeim paid this
sum of money.[362] [The Egyptian king], for his part, carried Joaz off to Egypt, where
he died,[363] after having reigned as king for three months and ten days.[364] The mother
of Joakeim was named Zabouda,[365] from the city of Abouma.[366] By nature he was
unjust and an evil-doer,[367] being neither reverent towards God nor gentle with humans.[368]

84 When he had already held the kingship for four years,[369] someone named   *Nebuchadnezzar*
Nabouchodonosor[370] assumed the rule of the Babylonians.[371] At this same time,[372]   *routs Egyptians*

Jehoahaz in 10.81.) By contrast, MT and B 2 Kgs
23:31, 36 (as well as B 2 Chr 36:2, 5) assign the 2 kings
different mothers, i.e. "Hamutal" (2 Kgs 23:31, MT) and
"Zebidah" (2 Kgs 23:36, MT), respectively. MT 2
Chronicles 36 and 1 Esdras 1 do not refer to Eliakim/
Jehoiakim's mother.

[359] MT (2 Kgs 23:34a// 2 Chr 36:4) אליקים (Eng.:
"Eliakim"); LXX BL Ἐλιακείμ; Josephus Ἐλιάκειμος. 1
Esdras 1 does not mention Jehoiakim's earlier name.

[360] MT (2 Kgs 23:34a// 2 Chr 36:4) יהויקים (Eng.
"Jehoiakim"); LXX BL 2 Kgs 23:34a// 2 Chr 36:4a
Ἰωακείμ; 1 Esdras 1:35 (Eng. 1:37) Ἰωακιμ; Josephus
Ἰωάκειμος.

[361] In 2 Kgs 23:33b// 2 Chr 36:3b// 1 Esdras 1:34
(Eng. 1:36). Pharaoh's imposition of tribute is men-
tioned prior to, rather than after, his appointment of
Eliakim/Jehoiakim.

[362] See 2 Kgs 23:35a; Josephus omits the further
biblical detail (23:35b) about Jehoiakim's taxing the
"people of the land" to obtain the required payment.
Neither MT 2 Chronicles 36 nor 1 Esdras 1 mentions
Jehoiakim's actual payment of the required tribute; the
latter text speaks rather (see 1:36 [Eng. 1:38]) of other
initiatives by the new king, i.e. his imprisoning the
"nobles" and bringing up his brother "Zarius" from
Egypt after "seizing" him.

[363] See 2 Kgs 23:34b// 2 Chr 36:4b (where MT—
but not LXX BL—lacks mention of Jehoahaz' dying in
Egypt). 1 Esdras 1 does not mention Jehoahaz' deportation to and death in Egypt.

[364] In 2 Kgs 23:31aβ// 2 Chr 36:2b// 1 Esdras 1:33a
(Eng. 1:35) Jehoahaz is assigned a 3-month reign, just
as he is earlier by Josephus himself (see 10.81). Marcus
(*ad loc.*) suggests that Josephus at this juncture confuses
Jehoahaz with his nephew Jehoiachin, who according
to 2 Chr 36:9, did reign for 3 months and 10 days.

[365] MT (2 Kgs 23:36b) זבידה (Eng.: "Zebidah");
LXX B 2 Kgs 23:36b Ἰελλά; LXX L 2 Kgs 23:36b// 2
Chr 36:5 Ἀμιτάλ; LXX B 2 Chr 36:5 Ζεχορά; Josephus
Ζαβουδᾶ (MT 2 Chronicles 36 and 1 Esdras 1 do not
mention Jehoiakim's mother). Josephus leaves aside the
name of her father, i.e. "Pedaiah," MT 2 Kgs 23:36b.
The indication Josephus gives here in 10.83 concerning

the identity of Jehoiakim's mother conflicts with his
previous statements on the matter, in which, after citing
the mother of Jehoahaz as "Amitale" (10.81), he goes
on to affirm (10.82) that Jehoahaz and Jehoiakim had
the same mothers; see the note to "as he" at 10.82.

[366] MT (2 Kgs 23:36b) רומה (Eng.: "Rumah"); LXX
B 2 Kgs 23:36b Κρουμά; LXX L 2 Kgs 23:36b// LXX 2
Chr 36:5 Λοβεννά; LXX B 2 Chr 36:5 Ῥαμά; Josephus
Ἀβουμᾶ.

[367] Greek: ἄδικος καὶ κακοῦργος. Josephus' only
other use of this collocation is in *Life* 290, where he
applies it to his opponent Ananias.

[368] Greek: μήτε πρὸς θεὸν ὅσιος μήτε πρὸς
ἀνθρώπους ἐπιεικής. This precise collocation occurs
only here in Josephus. It has, however, a positive
counterpart in Josephus' epithet for King Jotham of
Judah, whom he calls "pious towards God and just with
humans" in *Ant.* 9.236.

2 Kgs 23:37// 2 Chr 36:5b// 1 Esdras 1:37b (Eng.
1:39b) charge Jehoiakim with "doing what was evil in
the sight of the Lord" (2 Kgs 23:37 and LXX BL 2 Chr
36:5b add "according to all that his fathers had done").
On Josephus' treatment of Jehoiakim, see Begg 2000:
503-23; Delamarter 1998: 190-204.

[369] Josephus here introduces an interlude, unparalleled in the Bible's historical books, concerning Nebuchadnezzar's victory over Neco at Carchemish and its
immediate sequels (10.84-86), inspired by Jer 46:2
(MT; LXX 26:2), which dates that victory "in the 4th
year of Jehoiakim...."

[370] MT (2 Kgs 24:1// 2 Chr 36:6) נבוכדנאסר (Eng.:
"Nebuchadnezzar"); LXX BL 2 Kgs 24:1// 2 Chr 36:6
// 1 Esdras 1:38 (Eng. 1:40) Ναβουχοδονοσόρ; Josephus
Ναβουχοδονόσορος.

[371] Josephus adds this preliminary detail concerning
Nebuchadnezzar's accession to his subsequent mention,
drawn from Jer 46:2 (MT; LXX 26:2), of the Babylonian's advance against Neco.

[372] Historically, Nebuchadnezzar's succeeding his
father Nabopolassar as king of Babylon followed his
victory over the Egyptians at Carchemish; both events
occurred in the summer of 605 BCE.

he advanced with a large contingent to the city of Carchamissa[373] (this is on the Euphrates river), having decided to make war on the Egyptian Nechaus since all Syria was under him.[374] **85** Learning of the Babylonian's intention and his campaign against him, Nechaus, for his part, did not neglect this. Instead, with a large band, he hastened to resist Nabouchodonosor at the river Euphrates.[375] **86** Once battle was joined, he was defeated and lost many tens of thousands in the conflict.[376] Crossing the Euphrates, the Babylonian occupied Syria as far as Pelusion, with the exception of Iouda.[377]

Jehoiakim submits, then defeats

87 When King Nabouchodonosor had already been reigning for four years—this was the eighth year of Joakeim's rule over the Hebrews[378]—, the Babylonian campaigned with a great force against the Judeans, demanding tribute from Joakeim and threatening otherwise to make war [on him]. He, frightened by the threat and purchasing peace for money, brought him tribute that he paid for three years.[379] **(6.2) 88** But in the third [year], after hearing that the Egyptians were marching against the Babylonian and not having given his tribute,[380] he was disappointed in his hope, for the Egyptians lacked the courage to undertake the campaign.[381]

Jeremiah's warnings

89 The prophet Hieremias was announcing these things every day: they were placing their hopes in the Egyptians in vain, the city was bound to be desolated by

---

[373] MT (Jer 46:2) כרכמש (Eng.: "Carchemish"); LXX (Jer 26:2) Χαρχαμις; Josephus Καρχαμισσά. The city was situated in today's northern Syria.

[374] See Jer 46:2 (MT; LXX 26:2), from which Josephus draws the dating indication with which 10.84 opens. He appends the reference to Neco's being the master of "all Syria" at the moment Nebuchadnezzar moves against him.

[375] With these notices concerning Neco's response to Nebuchadnezzar's advance, Josephus elaborates on the allusion to the presence of the Egyptian army at Carchemish on the Euphrates in Jer 46:2 (MT; LXX 26:2).

[376] Josephus expatiates on the mention of Neco's "defeat" in Jer 46:2 (MT; LXX 26:2) in light of the poem describing the Egyptian rout in 46:3-12 (MT; LXX 26:3-12). In *Ant.* 10.220 Josephus quotes a passage from Berosus that apparently alludes to the battle of Carchemish as well. There, however, "Carchemish" is not mentioned by name and the opponent whom Nebuchadnezzar defeats is an anonymous "satrap" of Egypt, Coele-Syria and Phoenicia who had revolted against the Babylonians.

[377] Josephus adds this notice on the extent of the territory occupied by Nebuchadnezzar following his victory; the mention of Judah's exemption serves to prepare his subsequent account of the interaction between the Babylonian and Judah's king Jehoiakim. On "Pelusion," see 10.17-19.

[378] 2 Kgs 24:1a ["in his [Jehoiakim's days") provides only the vaguest of datings for Nebuchadnezzar's "coming up" and Jehoiakim's resultant submission to him. Josephus seems to have calculated his more

precise dating of these events on the basis of the chronological indications he found elsewhere in 2 Kings 23-24, i.e. Jehoiakim reigned a total of 11 years (2 Kgs 23:36a) and remained subservient to Nebuchadnezzar for 3 years, after which he revolted against him (24:1b). Assuming that the 3 years of Jehoiakim's subservience were the last of his 11-year reign, Josephus here dates the approach of Nebuchadnezzar, which resulted in Jehoiakim's initial submission to him, to the latter's 8th year, this in turn, being Nebuchadnezzar's own 4th regnal year, given Josephus' earlier statement (10.84) that the Babylonian began to rule (and launched his campaign against Neco) in Jehoiakim's 4th year of reign, i.e. 4 years before his advance against the Judean king (10.87).

[379] Josephus elaborates on the summary mention of Jehoiakim's 3-year submission to Nebuchadnezzar in 2 Kgs 24:1a, highlighting, e.g., the latter's overwhelming display of force and the fear this prompted in the former.

[380] Josephus expatiates on the notice concerning Jehoiakim's "rebelling against" Nebuchadnezzar after 3 years of subservience in 2 Kgs 24:1b with mention of the Judean's hearing of the Egyptian move and his non-payment of his earlier tribute.

[381] Josephus could have found inspiration for this notice that he appends to his preceding rendition of 2 Kgs 24:1 in the statement of 2 Kgs 24:7 that "the king of Egypt did not come again out of his land," this being due to Nebuchadnezzar's having despoiled all his possessions from "the Brook of Egypt to the river Euphrates."

the king of the Babylonians, and King Joakeim would be made subject by him.[382]

90 But he said these things unavailingly, [since] there was nobody who was due to be saved; for both the crowd and the rulers disregarded what they heard.[383] In their wrath at the things [he] said,[384] they accused Hieremias of being a prophet who used divination against the king,[385] and, bringing him to judgment, requested that he be sentenced to punishment.[386] **91** All the others cast their votes against him and thus went against [the view of] the elders.[387] The latter, however, in their wisdom of mind,[388] released the prophet from court and advised the others to do Hieremias no harm.[389] **92** "For," they said, "it was not he alone who predicted the things that were to happen to the city;[390] rather, also Michaias[391] before him[392] had announced these and many other things,[393] for which he did not suffer anything from the kings of

Jeremiah's trial and acquital

---

[382] The predictions that Josephus attributes to Jeremiah here pick up on his own foregoing description of Judah's situation following Jehoiakim's revolt in 10.88. They take the place of the announcements made by Jeremiah in the context of his "Temple Sermon" (Jeremiah 26, MT [LXX 33]) at the beginning of Jehoiakim's reign (v. 1), viz. "I [God] will make this house like Shiloh, and I will make this city a curse for all the nations of the earth." On Josephus' back-to-back reproduction of Jeremiah 26 (MT, LXX 33) and 36 (MT, LXX 43) in 10.89-95, see Begg 2000: 508-18; on his (sympathetic) treatment of Jeremiah as a scriptural precedent for his own stance during the siege of Jerusalem, see Wolff 1976: 10-15; Daube 1980; Johnson 1983. On Josephus' use of a MT-like, more expansive text of the Book of Jeremiah as opposed to the shorter form represented by LXX, see Piovanelli 1992: 11-36.

[383] Josephus supplies this heading to his account of the "trial" of Jeremiah that follows the prophet's "Temple Sermon" (Jer 26 [LXX 33]:1-6) in Jer 26 (LXX 33):7-24; the notice has in view the whole course of the interaction between Jeremiah and his audience, explaining this as something that was determined in advance, given that the whole people was already doomed to succumb to the dangers facing them, as Huldah announced in 10.60. Jer 26:7-8 identifies "the priests and the prophets and all the people" as those who take action against Jeremiah on this occasion.

[384] Josephus adds this reference to the emotional state of Jeremiah's accusers.

[385] In Jer 26:9 the accusation made against Jeremiah takes the form of a repetition of the prophet's own words concerning the temple and the city in 26:6, words reformulated by the Josephan Jeremiah in 10.89. Josephus' own version of the accusation picks up the announcement he there attributes to Jeremiah, i.e. that the rebellious Jehoiakim would be subjugated by Nebuchadnezzar, with the accusers' construing this prediction as a "using divination" (Greek: οἰωνίζομαι; the verb, *hapax* in Josephus, is employed of the augurer

Calchas in *Il*. 1.69; see Begg [2000: 511, n. 65]) against the king.

[386] Compare Jer 26:11, where the priests and the prophets demand the death penalty for Jeremiah from "the princes and all the people," given his previous words against the city. Josephus passes over the earlier statement "you shall die" addressed by the priests, prophets, and people to Jeremiah in 26:8, which seems to anticipate the verdict of the following trial.

[387] In making the "elders" the sole group to back Jeremiah, Josephus simplifies the account given in Jer 26:10-19, where it is "the princes" (introduced already in v. 10), who (joined at this point by the people, v. 16) first speak on Jeremiah's behalf, being thereafter seconded by "certain of the elders" (v. 17). Josephus' elimination of the princes' "pro-Jeremiah" role in the proceedings may have in view their subsequent hostility towards the prophet. In any case, their elimination also leads to Josephus' non-use of the speech of self-defense that Jeremiah addresses to princes and people in vv. 12-15.

[388] Josephus adds this positive characterization of the elders (and their subsequent intervention).

[389] These statements about the elders' authoritative disposition of Jeremiah's case go beyond the words attributed to them in Jer 26:18-19, which end up with them simply averring: "But we are about to bring great evil upon ourselves."

[390] Josephus introduces the elders' words, which in Jer 26:18 begin immediately with an invocation of Micah's prophecy, by having them make this explicit connection between the messages of the 2 prophets. The formulation here recalls Josephus' earlier comment in 10.80 that Jeremiah was not alone in predicting calamities for Jerusalem, but was seconded therein by Ezekiel.

[391] MT (Jer 26:18) מיכיה (Eng.: "Micah"); LXX (33:18) and Josephus Μιχαίας. This is Josephus' only mention of the classical prophet Micah. He leaves aside the Bible's qualification of him as "the Moreshite."

[392] In Jer 26:18 the elders date Micah's activity

that time,[394] but was held in honor as a prophet of God."[395]

Jeremiah reads book in temple

93 Having soothed the crowd by these words, they [the elders] delivered Hieremias from the punishment voted against him.[396] He, after compiling all his prophecies,[397] read his book while the populace was fasting and assembled in the sacred precinct[398] in the first month of the fifth year of the kingship of Joakeim.[399] In it he set down the things that were about to happen the city, the sanctuary, and the mob.[400]

94 When the leaders heard this, they took the book from him[401] and directed him

---

more specifically to "the days of Hezekiah, king of Judah."

[393] Josephus leaves aside the actual wording of Micah's announcement, which the elders in Jer 26:18 cite from Mic 3:12 ("Zion shall be plowed as a field; Jerusalem shall become a heap of ruins, and the mountain of the house a wooded height"), limiting himself to a very general allusion to its content.

[394] This statement replaces the elders' rhetorical question of Jer 26:19aα: "Did Hezekiah king of Judah and all Judah put him [Micah] to death?" As earlier in 10.92 (see note to "before him" there) Josephus omits the name Hezekiah—perhaps because in the biblical historical books, whose presentation of that king he previously followed, nothing is said of an interaction between Micah and Hezekiah.

[395] Once again (see previous note), Josephus transposes a biblical rhetorical question ("did he [Hezekiah] not fear the Lord and entreat the favor of the Lord?," Jer 26:19aβ) into a general, positive statement. He leaves aside the elders' additional rhetorical question of 26:19bα, i.e. "did not the Lord repent of the evil which he had pronounced against them?" This omission is likely prompted by the question's reference to a divine change of mind—something which Josephus elsewhere asserts to be impossible; see, e.g., 10, 34, 60. He omits as well the elders' (seemingly inconclusive) final statement of 26:19bβ: "but we are about to bring great evil upon ourselves," having previously mentioned their authoritative resolution of Jeremiah's case; see 10.91.

[396] This notice, with its explicit statement that Jeremiah was indeed acquitted, recalls Josephus' initial presentation of the elders and their initiative in 10.91. It takes the place of the complex of notices (26:20-24) appended to the account of Jeremiah's trial in Jeremiah 26 itself, i.e. the extradition and execution of Jeremiah's colleague Uriah (vv. 20-23) and the protection given Jeremiah by a certain Ahikam (v. 24).

[397] With this phrase, Josephus makes the transition to a 2nd episode drawn from the Book of Jeremiah, i.e. Jeremiah 36 (LXX 43), that he combines with that of chap. 26 (LXX 33) in 10.89-95. His reason for thus

combining these 2 passages, which in the Book of Jeremiah itself are separated by 10 chapters, is that both focus on the varying receptions accorded Jeremiah and his word by the hearers.

[398] In having Jeremiah, on his own initiative, both write down his words and read these to the assembled people, Josephus greatly simplifies the complicated scenario laid out in Jeremiah 36 (MT, LXX 43), where the Lord commands Jeremiah to write down his previous words (v. 2), whereupon the latter dictates these to Baruch (v. 4) and dispatches him to read these in the temple (vv. 5-7), as Baruch proceeds to do (vv. 8-10).

[399] In MT Jer 36:9 Baruch's reading occurs in the *9th* month of the 5th (LXX: 8th) year of Jehoiakim's reign on the occasion of a national "fast." Josephus disregards the chapter's initial, conflicting (?) dating indication, i.e. "in the 4th year of Jehoiakim" (36:1). His (inattentive) reproduction of the year-date of 36:9 involves him in a seeming chronological anomaly: in what precedes he has already recounted events of Jehoiakim's 8th year and of his revolt 3 years after this (10.87-8). Moreover, in 10.89, at the opening of his "Jeremiah segment" (10.89-95), Josephus has the prophet addressing that ill-advised revolt in what is implicitly Jehoiakim's 11th (and final) year, such that one is surprised here in 10.93 to hear of Jeremiah's activities at a much earlier point, i.e. Jehoiakim's *5th* year.

[400] Compare the indication concerning the content of the book that Jeremiah is divinely instructed to write down in Jer 36:2, i.e. "all the words that I [God] have spoken to you against Israel and Judah from the days of Josiah until today." Here, as in 10.80, Josephus singles out the temple and its fate as a particular focus of Jeremiah's message.

[401] Josephus continues to abridge the presentation of Jeremiah 36, where (vv. 11-18) there is an extended sequence in which various named princes command Baruch, following his public reading of Jeremiah's book, to bring this with him to the place where they are assembled; once he does this, they have him read it to them and ask him questions about it. In Josephus'

and the scribe Barouch[402] to hide themselves, so as not to be visible to anyone.[403] They themselves, bearing the book, gave it to the king.[404] He, with his friends present with him, directed his own scribe to take and read it.[405] **95** When the king heard what was in the book, he became wrathful,[406] tore it up and, throwing it into the fire, destroyed it[407]. He directed them to search for Hieremias and the scribe Barouch, [who] were to be brought to him for retribution.[408] They, however, escaped his wrath.[409]

Jehoiakim destroys Jeremiah's book; he and Baruch escape

(6.3) 96 When, not long afterwards,[410] the king of the Babylonians campaigned against him, Joakeim, in his fright at the things predicted by this prophet, admitted him. [He did this], thinking that he would suffer nothing terrible, seeing that he was neither shutting out nor making war on [the invader].[411] **97** But when he set out to

Jehoiakim surrenders to Babylonians

---

version, this Baruch-centered account disappears, given that he has previously depicted Jeremiah both writing and publicly reading his own book.

[402] MT (Jer 36:19) ברוך (Eng.: "Baruch"); LXX (43:19) Βαρουχ; Josephus Βαρούχος. Jer 36:19 itself does not use the scribe title for Baruch; Josephus anticipates the designation from Jer 36:26, 32 (MT, absent in LXX).

[403] In Jer 36:19 the princes tell Baruch that he and Jeremiah are to conceal themselves. Josephus has the order given directly also to Jeremiah, the protagonist in what precedes.

[404] In having the leaders as a group take the book directly to the king, Josephus once more simplifies the presentation of Jeremiah 36, where, leaving the book in the room of one of their number, they inform Jehoiakim of its contents (v. 20), whereupon the king sends one of his officials to fetch it (v. 21a).

[405] In Jer 36:21b a certain "Jehudi" reads the book to the king, beside whom "all the princes" are standing. Josephus omits the additional details of 36:22 about the time and place of the reading: in the 9th month (see 36:9) with the king in his winter house, where a fire is burning before him.

[406] Josephus supplies this reference to the king's emotional response—which recalls that of the audience to Jeremiah's speech in 10.90—to the reading of the book.

[407] See Jer 36:23. Josephus omits the additional biblical details about the king's using a pen-knife to successively dismember the book following the reading of 3 or 4 columns. As previously, he does not mention the "brazier" in which the fire is burning. He further passes over the notices of 36:24 and 25 concerning, respectively, the failure of the words of the book to affect the king and his servants in any way, and the unavailing efforts of 2 courtiers to keep the king from destroying the book.

[408] In Jer 36:26a, 2 named officials are commanded by Jehoiakim to arrest Jeremiah and Baruch (Josephus

agrees with MT in designating the latter as "the scribe," a designation absent in LXX). Josephus appends the notice on the intended purpose of the pair's arrest.

[409] Josephus' formulation of this notice stands closer to LXX Jer 43:26b ("and they [Jeremiah and Baruch] were hidden") than to MT Jer 36:26b ("but the Lord hid them"). The reference to Jehoiakim's "wrath" recalls the mention of the king's "becoming wrathful" upon his hearing the reading of the book at the start of 10.95. Josephus ends his version of Jeremiah 36 at this point, leaving aside the chapter's closing notices on the remaking of the destroyed book at the Lord's command (36:27-28, 32) together with the intervening divine word of doom for Jehoiakim (36:29-31—which, however, he will implicitly draw on in recounting the king's fate in 10.97).

[410] With this phrase Josephus makes the transition from his "Jeremiah interlude" (10.89-95), based on Jeremiah 26 and 36, to his account of Jehoiakim's end, drawn, with modifications, from the historical books.

[411] None of the biblical accounts that cite Nebuchadnezzar's move against Jehoiakim, i.e. 2 Chr 36:6a; 1 Esdras 1:38a (Eng. 1:40a); Dan 1:1 (in 2 Kgs 24:2-4 it is the Lord himself who dispatches raiding bands against Judah in punishment for the inexpiable sins of Manasseh) mentions such an initial voluntary surrender by Jehoiakim to the invader. That surrender is, however, paralleled in the initiative taken shortly afterwards by Jehoiakim's son Jehoiachin in the face of the ongoing Babylonian siege according to 2 Kgs 24:12; it likewise serves to account for Josephus' own subsequent presentation, in which Nebuchadnezzar will be in a position to have Jehoiakim executed (see 10.97)—something likewise not reported in the biblical narratives. Josephus further supplies several motivations for Jehoiakim's anticipation of his successor's move, i.e. the fear evoked by Jeremiah's predictions (see 10.89) and his (deluded) confidence that he will be left unpunished.

Babylonian measures against Jerusalem

him, the Babylonian did not keep his pledges.[412] Rather, he killed those of the Hierosolymites who were most fit and outstandingly handsome, along with King Joakeim,[413] whom he commanded to be tossed out unburied in front of the walls.[414] He designated his son Joakeim[415] king of the country and of the city.[416]

First deportation

98 Taking 3,000 men of rank as captives, he brought them to Babylon.[417] Among them was the prophet Iezekiel,[418] who was then a boy.[419] King Joakeim[420] ended in

---

[412] Nebuchadnezzar's disregard of his pledges here is reminiscent of Sennacherib's similar violation of his promises to Hezekiah in 10.4. In neither case is there a biblical basis for Josephus' charge against the foreign overlord.

[413] Compare BL 2 Chr 36:6b; 1 Esdras 1:38 (Eng. 1:40); and Dan 1:2, where Nebuchadnezzar transports the captive Jehoiakim to Babylon (in MT 2 Chr 36:6b he makes preparations to do this, while in 2 Kgs 24:6a Jehoiakim dies during the siege). None of these accounts mentions a killing of the city's inhabitants (Josephus' designation of these other victims as physically outstanding might be inspired by Dan 1:3, where Nebuchadnezzar commands that the best-looking among the exiled Israelite elite be prepared for service at his court) at this juncture. The reference to Jehoiakim's being killed at Nebuchadnezzar's command serves to prepare the additional order the Babylonian will give concerning the former's corpse, this fulfilling the prophecy cited in Jer 36:30.

[414] None of the biblical narratives recounts such a treatment of Jehoiakim's corpse (in LXX L 2 Kgs 24:6 and LXX BL 2 Chr 36:8 Jehoiakim is "buried with his fathers in the garden of Oza [LXX B 2 Chr 36:8 ἐν Γανοζα])." The notice does, however, represent a fulfillment of the prediction—not previously reproduced by Josephus (see note to "they, however, escaped his wrath" at 10.95)—of Jer 36:30b, concerning the king ("his dead body shall be cast out to the heat by day and the frost by night"), as also of the related announcement of Jer 22:19: "with the burial of an ass he [Jehoiakim] shall be buried, dragged and cast forth beyond the gates of Jerusalem."

[415] MT (2 Kgs 24:6b// 2 Chr 36:8b) יהויכין (Eng. "Jehoiachin"); LXX B 2 Kgs 24:6b Ἰωακείμ; LXX L 2 Kgs 24:6b Ἰωακείν; LXX BL 2 Chr 36:8b Ἰεχονίας; 1 Esdras 1:41 (Eng. 1:43) Ἰωακιμ; Josephus' Ἰωάκειμος (who thus gives the new king the same Greek name as his father). On Josephus' treatment of Jehoiachin, see Begg 2000: 523-31 and Feldman 1998a: 437-49, who notes that Josephus, in comparison with the biblical accounts, offers a more positive portrait of Judah's penultimate king, doubtless because he saw him—as he did Jeremiah—as a scriptural precedent for his own

advocacy of surrender to the overwhelming might of the Romans.

[416] In 2 Kgs 24:6b// 2 Chr 36:8b// 1 Esdras 1:41 (Eng. 1:43) Jehoiachin appears to assume the kingship prior to Nebuchadnezzar's gaining control of the city. In Josephus' presentation the Babylonian has secured such control already before Jehoiakim's death and so naturally appoints his successor—just as Neco did in the case of Jehoiakim (2 Kgs 23:34a// 2 Chr 36:4a// 10.82) and Nebuchadnezzar himself will do subsequently with Zedekiah (2 Kgs 24:17// 2 Chr 36:10b// 10.102).

[417] The biblical accounts do not record such a deportation at this point, i.e. prior to Jehoiachin's surrender of Jerusalem to the Babylonians, a development that Josephus will relate only later; see 10.100. (As to the figure for those deported at this point, i.e. 3,000, Josephus may have rounded this off from the number, i.e. 3,023, of those whom Nebuchadnezzar carried off in the initial deportation in his 7th year according to Jer 52:28 [MT; LXX lacks this reference]). Conversely, 2 Chr 36:7// 1 Esdras 1:39 (Eng. 1:41)// Dan 1:2b tell of the Babylonians' removal of certain temple vessels in connection with their deportation of Jehoiakim to Babylon.

[418] Josephus introduced this figure as an ideological fellow of Jeremiah in 10.79-80.

[419] The Bible does not relate the actual deportation of Ezekiel, nor his age when this occurred. In Ezek 1:2 Ezekiel receives his call among the exiles "in the 5th year of the exile of King Jehoiachin" (which itself took place following his reign of 3 months [and 10 days] according to the sequence of 2 Kings 24// 2 Chronicles 36// 1 Esdras 1, i.e. subsequent to the earlier deportation at the moment of Jehoiachin's accession posited by Josephus in 10.98). Ezek 1:1 further dates Ezekiel's call in "the 30th year"; this dating is often understood as a reference to the prophet's age at the time of his call. So understood, it could have inspired Josephus' allusion to his being "a boy" at the moment of his deportation several years prior to his call-experience.

[420] Josephus now returns momentarily to the figure of Jehoiakim (the elder "Joakeim" in his nomenclature) in order to conclude his account of him.

this way,[421] having lived thirty-six years[422] and reigned as king for eleven of these.[423] Joakeim, whose mother was Nooste,[424] a native of the capital,[425] succeeded to the kingship; he reigned as king for three months and ten days.[426]

Jehoiachin (Joakeim) succeeds

(7.1) 99 Once, however, the king of the Babylonians had given the kingship to Joakeim,[427] he immediately took fright. For he was frightened that [Joakeim], remembering against him the destruction of his father,[428] might cause his country to revolt.[429] He therefore sent a force and besieged Joakeim in Hierosolyma.[430] **100** He, being kind and just[431] by nature, did not think it right that the city should be permitted to be endangered for his sake.[432] Instead, abandoning his mother and relatives, he handed them over to the generals sent by the Babylonian,[433] after receiving their oaths that neither they nor the city would suffer anything.[434] **101** Their pledge, however, did not remain [operative] for even a year, for the king of the Babylonians did

Jehoiachin surrenders besieged city

second deportation

---

[421] See Josephus' account of his ignominious demise in 10.97.

[422] Josephus obtains this figure for the king's lifespan by combining the data for Jehoiakim's age at accession (25 years) and length of reign (11) given in 2 Kgs 23:36a// 2 Chr 36:5a; cf. 1 Esdras 1:37a (Eng. 1:39a), which only mentions his accession-age.

[423] This figure for Jehoiakim's length of reign corresponds to that given in 2 Kgs 23:36aβ// 2 Chr 36:5aβ.

[424] MT (2 Kgs 24:8b) נְחֻשְׁתָּא (Eng.: "Nehushta"); LXX B Νεσθά; LXX L Νεεσθάν; Josephus Νοόστη (2 Chronicles 36 and 1 Esdras 1 do not mention the name of Jehoiachin's mother). Josephus leaves aside the name of her father, i.e. "Elnathan" (MT 2 Kgs 24:8b).

[425] Josephus draws this datum about Nehushta from 2 Kgs 24:8b.

[426] This figure for Jehoiachin's length of reign corresponds to that given in 2 Chr 36:9a and 1 Esdras 1:42a (Eng. 1:44a). 2 Kgs 24:8a (MT; LXX BL), on the contrary, assigns him a round 3 months.

[427] This transitional phrase picks up on the reference to Nebuchadnezzar's appointment of Jehoiachin in 10.97.

[428] See 10.97.

[429] This whole sequence has no biblical parallel; its reference to Nebuchadnezzar's "fright" appears quite implausible in light of what precedes, where Jehoiakim opens Jerusalem to him out of a "fright" of his own (10.96) and where Jehoiachin himself is portrayed as Nebuchadnezzar's creature. The passage does, however, serve to make the necessary transition between Josephus' own earlier, "un-biblical," presentation (10.96-98), in which, at the start of Jehoiachin's reign, Nebuchadnezzar is already master of Jerusalem and the (biblically-based) continuation of his account which portrays Jerusalem as under siege throughout Jehoiachin's brief reign.

[430] See 2 Kgs 24:10, which attributes the siege to

Nebuchadnezzar's "servants." Josephus leaves aside the notice of 24:11 about Nebuchadnezzar himself arriving at Jerusalem during the course of the siege.

[431] Greek: χρηστὸς καὶ δίκαιος. This characterization of Jehoiachin—utilizing a collocation previously used of Jehoiada (*Ant.* 9.166) and Hezekiah (9.260)—differs sharply from the unanimous (and unqualified) judgment of 2 Kgs 24:9// 2 Chr 36:9b// 1 Esdras 1:42b [Eng. 1:44b]), according to which "he [Jehoiachin] did what was evil in the sight of the Lord." On this divergence see Feldman (2000a: 442-4), who attributes it to Josephus' sense of identification with a king who thought it better to surrender Jerusalem to an overwhelming enemy force than to see it destroyed. Feldman further points out that Josephus' "rehabilitation" of Jehoiachin has a certain parallel in Rabbinic tradition, according to which, during his long captivity, the once wicked Jehoiachin repented; it is likewise paralleled in Josephus' own earlier words to John of Gischala during the siege of Jerusalem in *War* 6.103-105, where he invokes King "Jeconiah" (= Jehoiachin) as a precedent for the course of action that he is calling John to adopt. See Begg 2000: 525, n. 134 and Feldman 2001: 321.

[432] Josephus supplies this explanation of Jehoiachin's motivation for his subsequent surrender of the city.

[433] In 2 Kgs 24:12 Jehoiachin surrenders himself, his mother, servants, princes and palace officials to Nebuchadnezzar (who according to 24:11 arrived in Jerusalem during the course of the siege) in person.

[434] The account in 2 Kgs 24:10-16, which Josephus is following here, says nothing about such oaths being given Jehoiachin in connection with his voluntary surrender. Compare, however, 10.2, where Josephus adds the reference to Sennacherib's swearing to Hezekiah's messengers "that he would not do him [Hezekiah] any wrong...."

not keep it.[435] On the contrary, he commanded his generals to take captive everyone in the city who was youthful in age, as well as the craftsmen, and to bring them
bound to himself.[436] All these amounted to 10,832,[437] along with Joakeim, his
mother, and his friends. **102** When they were brought to him, he held them in
prison.[438]

Zedekiah
(Sacchias)
made king

He [Nabouchodonosor] then appointed Joakeim's uncle[439] Sacchias[440] king, after
taking an oath from him that he would keep the country for him and would neither
do anything revolutionary[441] nor be loyal to the Egyptians.[442]

General
corruption

103 Sacchias was twenty-one years old when he assumed the rule;[443] he had the
same mother as his brother Joakeim.[444] He scorned what was just and requisite.[445]

---

[435] Like his preceding mention of the pledges given
Jehoiachin, this notice on the violation of those
pledges is without basis in Josephus' sources. It does,
however, recall other instances of the perfidy of foreign
kings introduced by Josephus into his retelling of
biblical history; see 10.4 (Sennacherib) and 10.97
(Nebuchadnezzar in his dealings with Jehoiakim). In
10.230 Josephus cites Nebuchadnezzar's deceitful
treatment of Jehoiachin as the motive behind the
former's son (the biblical Evil-merodach, 2 Kgs 25:27)
releasing the latter from prison on the occasion of his
own accession.

[436] For his listing of Nebuchadnezzar's captives
Josephus draws selectively on the various, repetitive
catalogues of such persons given in 2 Kgs 10:12-16;
see, vv. 14 and 16, where there is a double mention of
"the men of valor" and the "craftsmen." He makes no
mention of the removal of a portion of the temple (and
palace) fabric at this time as attested by 2 Kgs 24:13//
2 Chr 36:10a// 1 Esdras 1:43 (Eng. 1:45).

[437] Compare 2 Kgs 24:14, where the round number
of 10,000 deportees is given (24:16 speaks rather of
7,000). Josephus apparently derived the "extra" 832
persons of his total by adding the figure for Nebuchadnezzar's 2nd deportation, i.e. 832, given in Jer 52:29
(MT; LXX and OL lack the figure. On Josephus'
possible use of the figure, 3,023, cited by MT Jer 52:28
[MT] for Nebuchadnezzar's initial deportation in 10.98,
see note to "to Babylon" there).

[438] With this added notice on the imprisonment of
the Judean deportees Josephus prepares his later account of Jehoiachin's release; see 10.229-230 (// 2 Kgs
25:27-30).

[439] In designating Zedekiah as the "uncle" of
"Jehoiachin" (called by him "Joakeim," i.e. the same
name he uses for his father, the biblical "Jehoiakim"),
Josephus agrees with 2 Kgs 24:17 (MT and LXX L),
whereas in 2 Chr 36:10b he is called his "brother" and
in LXX B 2 Kgs 24:17 his "son." 1 Esdras 1:44 (Eng.
1:46) does not mention the familial relationship between the 2 men.

[440] MT (2 Kgs 24:17// 2 Chr 36:10b) צדקיהו (Eng.:

"Zedekiah"); LXX BL 2 Kgs 24:17// 2 Chr 36:10b (and
1 Esdras 1:44 [Eng. 1:46]) Ζεδεκίας; Josephus Σαχχίας.
Josephus omits the new king's earlier name, i.e.
"Mattaniah" (MT). On Josephus' (variable) treatment of
Zedekiah, see Begg 2000: 535-74 and Feldman 1998a:
450-62.

[441] Greek νεωτερίζω. Words of this stem are frequently applied by Josephus to the contemporary
Zealots. The Latin equivalent terminology (*novis rebus
studeo*; *rerum novarum studium*) is constantly used by
Roman authors writing on political-military developments; see, e.g., Cicero, *Cat* 1.1.3; Sallust, *Bel. Cat.* 37;
57. See also BJP 9 (Mason): 28, n. 122.

[442] Josephus expatiates on the biblical references
(see 2 Chr 36:13; 1 Esdras 1:46 [Eng. 1:48]; Ezek
17:13) to the "oath" Nebuchadnezzar imposed on
Zedekiah at the moment he made him king, spelling out
the content of that oath in light of future developments,
which will involve Zedekiah's doing the very things he
swears not to do here.

[443] This is the figure for Zedekiah's age at
accession given in 2 Kgs 24:18a// 2 Chr 36:11a// 1
Esdras 1:46b (Eng. 1:48b)// Jer 52:1a.

[444] Josephus' statement concerning the identity of
Zedekiah's mother differs from the notices of 2 Kgs
24:18b// Jer 52:1b, where her name is given as "Hamutal, the daughter of Jeremiah of Libnah" (neither 2
Chronicles 36 nor 1 Esdras 1 makes any reference to
this figure), and there is no mention of her being the
mother of Jehoiakim as well. In fact, according to the
indications of 2 Kings, the brother with whom Zedekiah
shared a common mother was Jehoahaz (see 2 Kgs
23:31b and 24:18b, where the mother of the 2 kings is
identified as "Hamutal, the daughter of Jeremiah of
Libnah"), rather than Jehoiakim (whose mother is called
"Zebidah" in MT LXX B 2 Kgs 23:36b). As Marcus (*ad
loc.*) suggests then, Josephus seems to have confused
Zedekiah's half brother Jehoiakim (son of "Zabouda"
[Bible: "Zebidah"] according to 10.83) with his full
brother Jehoahaz (son of "Amitale" [Bible: "Hamutal"]
according to 10.81) in his formulation concerning
Zedekiah's mother here. Compare the LXX L text in 2

For his contemporaries who were around him were impious, while the entire mob had authority to commit whatever outrages they pleased.[446]

104 Coming therefore to him, the prophet Hieremias kept witnessing continuously. He directed him to leave behind his other impieties and lawless ways and to care for what was just, and not pay attention to the leaders—among whom there were vile persons—or believe the false prophets who were misleading him [with their claim] that the Babylonian [king] would no longer make war on the city and that the Egyptians would campaign against him [Nabouchodonosor] and be victorious. For, he said, these things were not true, and it was impossible that they should come about.[447]

Jeremiah admonishes Zedekiah

105 Whenever Sacchias heard the prophet saying these things, he was convinced; he agreed that all of them were true and that it was to his advantage to believe them. But his friends corrupted him again, leading him away from the prophet's [words] wherever they wished.[448]

Zedekiah disregards messages of both Jeremiah and Ezekiel

106 Iezekiel in Babylon[449] likewise foretold the people's coming misfortunes;[450] writing these things, he sent [them] to Hierosolyma.[451] Sacchias, however, disbelieved their prophecies for the following cause:[452] It happened that these prophets were in agreement with each other in everything else they said, namely that the city

---

Kgs 23:31b, 36b; 24:18b, which assigns all 3 kings the same mother, i.e. "Amital, daughter of Jeremiah of Lobenna."

[445] This negative judgment on Zedekiah corresponds to the notice "he did what was evil in the sight of the Lord" of 2 Kgs 24:19// Jer 52:2 (both of which add "according to all that Jehoiakim had done") // 2 Chr 36:12a// 1 Esdras 1:45a (Eng. 1:47a).

[446] This notice on the depravity, not only of the king personally, but also of his associates and the people as a whole seems to reflect 2 Chr 36:14, which charges the "leading priests and the people" of Zedekiah's time with being "exceedingly unfaithful"; compare 1 Esdras 1:47 (Eng. 1:49), where similar charges are made against "the leaders of the people and of the priests."

[447] Josephus here expatiates on the summary allusion to "Jeremiah the prophet who spoke from the mouth of the Lord," which in 2 Chr 36:12b stands at the opening of the Chronicler's account of Zedekiah's reign; cf. the similar reference in 1 Esdras 1:47b (Eng. 1:49b) to "the words that were spoken by Jeremiah the prophet from the mouth of the Lord." Josephus' development of these allusions supplies a content for Jeremiah's initial message to the new king, this based on his admonitions to Zedekiah as found in various contexts of the Book of Jeremiah.

[448] Josephus nuances and differentiates the global statements of 2 Chr 36:12b (Zedekiah did not "humble himself before" Jeremiah) and 1 Esdras 1:47b (Eng. 1:49b) (Zedekiah did not "heed" Jeremiah's words) in

light of the presentation of the prophet-king relationship in the Book of Jeremiah, where Zedekiah is on occasion receptive to Jeremiah's words, but is also deterred from acting on them by those around him.

[449] This reference recalls 10.98, where Josephus mentions the boy Ezekiel's being brought to Babylon as part of a group of 3,000 deportees following the execution of Jehoiakim.

[450] This notice on the joint message of Ezekiel and Jeremiah recalls Josephus' mention of the former's seconding the latter's predictions in 10.79.

[451] The Book of Ezekiel itself does not mention such a written transmission of Ezekiel's message to Jerusalem; Josephus supplies the reference in light of his knowledge of writings ascribed to the prophet (see 10.79) and in order to account for Zedekiah's knowledge of the distant Ezekiel's message, as presupposed by the continuation of his account.

[452] The whole following sequence on Zedekiah's "disbelief" of the common message of the 2 prophets is Josephus' creation, based on his knowledge of a point of detail in their respective utterances, where they seemed to disagree. As will emerge, Josephus' point in this connection is that, even in this detail, the 2 prophets' announcements were ultimately compatible, with both reaching eventual fulfillment. As such, the example represents a notable instance of various general principles Josephus is concerned to inculcate, namely true prophets make accurate predictions even in the particulars of what they say and fully agree with one another in doing so.

would be stormed and that Sacchias himself would be captured.[453] In saying, however, that Sacchias would not see Babylon,[454] Iezekiel disagreed with Hieremias who told him [Sacchias] that the Babylonian king would lead him [there] bound.[455] **107** And because the two of them did not say the same thing, he despised and did not believe even those things in which they seemed to agree, as if they were not speaking the truth in these [matters]. And yet, everything occurred to him in accordance with their prophecies, as we shall relate in a more suitable place.[456]

Zedekiah's revolt; new Babylonian siege

108 After maintaining his alliance with the Babylonians for eight years,[457] he [Sacchias] abrogated his pledges to them[458] and went over to the Egyptians, hoping that he would overthrow the Babylonians if he were with them.[459] **109** Once he learned of this, the Babylonian king campaigned against him. Having devastated his country and taken its strongholds, he came to the city of the Hierosolymites itself and besieged it.[460]

Temporary Babylonian withdrawal

110 When the Egyptian [king] heard that his ally Sacchias was in this [state], he mustered a large force and came to Iouda to raise the siege.[461] Withdrawing from Hierosolyma, the Babylonian [king] went to meet the Egyptians. Once he joined battle with them, he defeated them, put them to flight, and pursued them through the whole of Syria.[462]

Claims of false prophets

111 When the Babylonian king retired from Hierosolyma,[463] the false prophets[464]

---

[453] See Jer 32:3-5 and Ezek 12:13a, both of which texts announce that the captured Zedekiah will be brought to Babylon.

[454] See Ezek 12:13b: "(I [the Lord] will bring him [Zedekiah] to Babylon...), yet he shall not see it," where Ezekiel seems to allude to the notice of 2 Kgs 25:7 on the blinding Zedekiah underwent prior to his transport to Babylon.

[455] See Jer 32:5, where Jeremiah states: "he [Nebuchadnezzar] shall take Zedekiah to Babylon...," an announcement that Josephus will cite in 10.141. It might be noted here that, Josephus to the contrary, the words of the 2 prophets are not necessarily discordant in that Jeremiah's announcement as quoted by Josephus does not exclude the captive Zedekiah's being taken to Babylon in a blinded state—just as Ezekiel predicted.

[456] See 10.141, where Josephus relates the fulfillment of both the seemingly "contradictory" prophecies of 10.106.

[457] This indication concerning the duration of Zedekiah's fidelity to Babylon has no explicit biblical basis. Josephus likely inferred the figure on the basis of 2 Kgs 25:1// Jer 39:1// Jer 52:4, which state that it was in Zedekiah's *9th* year that Nebuchadnezzar moved against the rebel king. Josephus will reproduce this biblical chronological indication in 10.116.

[458] See 2 Kgs 24:20b// 2 Chr 36:13a// Jer 52:3b// 1 Esdras 1:46 (Eng. 1:48). On Zedekiah's prior oath to Nebuchadnezzar, see 10.102. In Josephus' presentation, Zedekiah violates his "pledges" to Nebuchadnezzar,

just as the latter had transgressed his own pledges to Jehoiakim (10.97) and to Jehoiachin (10.101).

[459] Josephus appends this notice concerning the motivation behind Zedekiah's defection. The reference to the king's "hope" of support from the Egyptians picks up on Jeremiah's allusion to the claims of the false prophets that the Egyptians would move against Nebuchadnezzar in 10.104.

[460] Josephus holds over the precise dates for the beginning of the siege given in 2 Kgs 25:1// Jer 52:4// 39:1 to a later point; see 10.116. He adds the reference to Nebuchadnezzar's preliminary initiatives, prior to commencing the siege of Jerusalem itself.

[461] Josephus elaborates on the allusion to Pharaoh's army "coming out of Egypt" in Jer 37:5a (cf. 37:7 where the purpose of its advance is said to be "to help you [Zedekiah]"). Josephus' designation of Zedekiah as Pharaoh's "ally" alludes to the former's switch to the Egyptian side after "maintaining his alliance with the Babylonians for eight years" in 10.108.

[462] Josephus expatiates on the notice of Jer 37:5b (cf. 37:11) about the Chaldeans' "withdrawing from Jerusalem" once they hear of the advance of the Egyptian army (37:5a). In particular, he spells out what happened subsequent to that withdrawal, i.e. the Babylonians' crushing of the Egyptian attempt to relieve Jerusalem, contrary to Zedekiah's "hopes" (see 10.108).

[463] This added transitional phrase picks up on the reference to Nebuchadnezzar's "withdrawing from Jerusalem" in 10.110 (// Jer 37:5b), following Josephus' appended account of the resultant battle be-

led Sacchias astray, saying that the Babylonian would no longer war against him and that their compatriots, whom he had forcibly removed from their native land to Babylon,[465] would return, along with the vessels of the sanctuary the king had recently despoiled.[466]

112 Coming forward, Hieremias prophesied the truthful opposite of these things, namely that they [the false prophets] were acting wrongly and leading the king astray.[467] For there would be no profit to them from the Egyptians. Rather, having defeated them, the Babylonian [king] was about to campaign against Hierosolyma and would besiege it.[468] He would destroy the populace by famine and would lead the survivors away captive. He would plunder their possessions, and, after removing the wealth of the sanctuary, would then burn it down. He would demolish the city,[469] "and we shall be slaves to him and his descendants for seventy years.[470] **113** Then the Persians and the Medes will put an end to our slavery under them, by overthrowing the Babylonians.[471] Once we have been released by them, we shall rebuild the sanctuary and re-establish Hierosolyma."[472] **114** In saying this Hieremias

Jeremiah's word of doom

---

tween the Babylonians and Egyptians (see previous note). The transition serves to prepare Josephus' subsequent narrative of what happened in Jerusalem during the absence of the Babylonians.

[464] Mention of these figures and their deceptive announcement of the end of the Babylonian threat recalls 10.104, where Jeremiah alludes to their misleading Zedekiah with their claims about a coming Egyptian victory over the Babylonians.

[465] Cf. 10.96, 101 on Nebuchadnezzar's 2 earlier deportations of the Jerusalemites.

[466] For his "citation" of the false prophets' message on this occasion Josephus draws on—while also generalizing—the words attributed in Jer 28:2-4 (MT; LXX 35:2-4) to the prophet Hananiah, who announces the imminent breaking of the Babylonian yoke, the return of the temple vessels, as well as the repatriation of King Jeconiah (Jehoiachin) "and all the exiles from Judah who went to Babylon." (In contrast to the biblical accounts, Josephus himself has not mentioned a Babylonian removal of the temple vessels up to this point.)

[467] Jeremiah's assertion about his prophetic colleagues here recalls his earlier warning to Zedekiah (see 10.104) not "to believe the false prophets who were misleading him...." Cf. Jeremiah's warning (Jer 37:9) to the people subsequent to the temporary Babylonian withdrawal (Jer 37:5b): "Do not deceive yourselves, saying 'The Chaldeans will surely stay away from us....'"

[468] Josephus here adapts Jeremiah's announcement of Jer 37:7b-8a ("Pharaoh's army... is about to return to Egypt. And the Chaldeans shall come back and fight against this city" (cf. also 34:21-22) in light of his own earlier mention (see 10.110) of the Babylonian victory over the Egyptians.

[469] In attributing the above series of announcements to Jeremiah Josephus bases himself on the actual course of the siege of Jerusalem and its aftermath. In so doing, he elaborates on the prophet's terse prediction in Jer 37:8b: "they [the Babylonians] shall take it [Jerusalem] and burn it with fire" (see also 34:22), thereby highlighting Jeremiah's predictive powers (which the continuation of his speech in 10.112-113 will accentuate still further).

[470] For this prediction of the people's long-term future, the Josephan prophet draws on (cf. 29:10): "these nations shall serve the king of Babylon 70 years."

[471] Jer 25:12 speaks of God himself "punishing the king of Babylon and that nation, the land of the Chaldeans...." Josephus draws his mention of the earthly agents of Babylon's overthrow from another biblical context, i.e. Dan 5:28, where Daniel announces to King Belshazzar of Babylon that his kingdom has been "divided and given to the Medes and the Persians." As a further possible inspiration for Josephus' formulation here, Marcus (*ad loc.*) adduces 2 Chr 36:20 (the survivors of Jerusalem remain servants of the kings of Babylon "until the establishment of the kingdom of Persia [MT; LXX: of the Medes]").

[472] Cf. Jer 29:10, where, after promising to "visit" the exiles once Babylon's 70 years have been fulfilled (see 25:11-12 and 10.112), God goes on to announce "I will bring you [the people] back to this place." The Josephan Jeremiah's additional announcement of the eventual rebuilding of Jerusalem and its temple accentuates his long-term predictive capacities. The addition might be inspired by Ezra 1:1-4, where the "edict of Cyrus" (vv. 2-4) permitting the Judean deportees to return to Jerusalem and rebuild the temple there is attributed (v. 1) to God's prompting of Cyrus

was believed by the majority; the leaders and the impious, however, derided him, as though he were out of his mind.[473]

[Hieremias] decided to go to his ancestral town called Anathoth[474]—this was twenty *stadii* distant from Hierosolyma.[475] A certain one of the rulers, encountering him on the way, arrested and detained him, falsely charging him with being a deserter to the Babylonians.[476] **115** Hieremias, saying that it was a lying accusation he was making against him, stated that he was going to his ancestral town.[477] [The other man], however, was not convinced; he took him and brought him to the rulers for judgment.[478] Having undergone all [kinds of] ill-treatment and tortures[479] by them, he was kept under guard for punishment. And thus he lived on for some time, wrongfully suffering the above-mentioned things.[480]

(7.4) 116 In the ninth year of the kingship of Sacchias,[481] on the tenth day of the tenth month, the king of the Babylonians campaigned a second time against Hierosolyma.[482] Having positioned his army before it, he besieged it[483] with the ut-

---

"that the word of the Lord by the mouth of Jeremiah might be accomplished."

[473] Greek: ἐξεστηκός τῶν φρενῶν; this phrase occurs only here in Josephus. Jeremiah 37—Josephus' starting point for the series of predictions he attributes to the prophet in 10.112-113—does not mention a reaction on the part of the hearers to his words there. Josephus' depiction of the mixed response that Jeremiah's message receives on this occasion recalls his notices on the likewise varied reactions to the prophet's preaching at 2 earlier moments, i.e. his "Temple Speech" (see 10.90-92) and his reading of his collected words (see 10.94-95). That mixed reaction will characterize the "reception" of Jeremiah's message in what follows as well. For his mention of the leaders' deriding Jeremiah as though he were "out of his mind," Josephus may have found inspiration in Jer 29 (LXX 36):26, where Shemaiah (v. 24), writing to the priest Zephaniah (v. 25) in order to castigate him for his failure to rebuke Jeremiah, reminds him that the Lord has appointed him "to have charge in the house of the Lord over every *madman* who prophesies."

[474] In Jer 37:12 Jeremiah's destination is designated in more general terms as "the land of Benjamin." Josephus derives his mention of "Anathoth" as Jeremiah's home town and more specific destination by combining the related texts of Jer 32:8 (Jeremiah is urged to buy the field of his cousin Hanamel "at Anathoth in the land of Benjamin") and 1:1 (Jeremiah stems from "the priests who were at Anathoth in the land of Benjamin").

[475] Josephus supplies this indication concerning the distance (about 2.5 miles; see Marcus *ad loc.*) between the 2 sites. He leaves aside the source reference (Jer 37:12) to the motivation for Jeremiah's journey, i.e. "to receive his portion among the people" (cf. Jeremiah 32).

[476] Josephus omits several details concerning

Jeremiah's arrest given in Jer 37:13, i.e. the site (the Benjamin Gate), as well as the name and function of his captor (the sentry Irijah). Conversely, he goes beyond the Bible's neutral allusion to the fact of Jeremiah's being accused in his use of the verb συκοφαντέω ("to falsely charge") to refer to the accusation. This verb occurs only here in *Antiquities*; it recurs in *War* 1.11; *Life* 52; and *Apion* 2.42.

[477] Josephus supplements Jeremiah's denial of the charge made against him (Jer 37:14a) with a positive statement by the prophet, this recalling his own earlier narrative notice in 10.114 on Anathoth as Jeremiah's "ancestral town," about what he is actually doing.

[478] See Jer 37:14b. Josephus supplies the indication concerning the purpose of the arrestor's bringing Jeremiah before the rulers. The addition serves to associate this episode with Jeremiah's "Temple Sermon," which likewise results in the prophet's being "brought to judgment"; see 10.90.

[479] Greek: αἰκία καὶ βάσανοι. This phrase recurs (in reverse order) in *Ant.* 16.389; cf. *War* 3.321.

[480] See Jer 37:15-16. Josephus omits various details of the biblical account: the princes' rage against Jeremiah, their beating him, and his confinement in "the house of Jonathan the secretary," which had been converted into a prison. Conversely, he adds an explicit (negative) characterization of the treatment meted out to Jeremiah; cf. his use of the term "falsely charge" of the accusation made against Jeremiah in 10.114 as compared with the neutral wording of Jer 37:13.

[481] After the interlude concerning the activities of the false prophets and of Jeremiah himself during the temporary Babylonian withdrawal from Jerusalem (10.110-115), Josephus now resumes his account of the siege of the city, which he began in 10.109.

[482] Josephus now reproduces the biblical dating for

most intensity for eighteen months.[484] In addition to this, the besieged Hierosolymites were afflicted by two of the greatest sufferings, namely famine and plague,[485]
that overwhelmingly assaulted them.[486]

117 The prophet Hieremias, who was in prison,[487] did not keep quiet. Instead, he
cried out and sounded off, urging the crowd to admit the Babylonians by opening
the gates, for they along with their entire households would all be saved if they did
this,[488] but if not they would be destroyed. **118** He predicted that if anyone remained
in the city he would certainly perish, consumed either by plague or famine, or by
the sword of the enemy.[489] If, however, anyone fled to the enemy, he would elude
death.[490]

119 Even though they were in a terrible [state], the leaders did not believe when
they heard these things.[491] Rather, in their wrath, they went to the king and reported

*Jeremiah urges
surrender*

*Leaders
denounce*

---

the beginning of the siege (see 2 Kgs 25:1// Jer 52:4//
39:1 [MT; the month indication is lacking in certain
LXX MSS]) that he left aside when mentioning the start
of the siege in 10.109. The reference to Nebuchadnezzar's "2nd" campaign against Jerusalem alludes to
his breaking off his initial move against the city in order to counter the Egyptian advance; see 10.110.

[483] The collocation προσκαθίζω and πολιορκέω
("position before" and "besiege") used here is a
Josephan favorite (see *War* 1.61, 116; *Ant.* 10.116;
12.347). Before his time, the combination was used
most often by Thucydides (1.11.2, 61.3, 126.8, 134.3;
5.61), who always uses προσκαθίζω in the middle voice,
and by Polybius (1.12.4, 15.5; 5.61.8, 62.6; 8.7.6), who
favors the active voice. Cf. also Diodorus Siculus
(12.72.9, 76.4) and Dionysius of Halicarnassus (*Ant.
rom.* 3.3.74; 5.58.1). Josephus uses the active form of
the verb in *Antiquities*, the middle/passive in *War*. I
owe these remarks to Prof. Steve Mason.

[484] Josephus supplies a figure for the total duration
of the siege, calculating this on the basis of the dates
given in, e.g., Jer 52:4 (the siege began in the 10th
month of Zedekiah's 9th year) and 52:5-6 (the city's
bread supply ran out in the 4th month of Zedekiah's
11th year), i.e. some 18 months after the siege commenced. He goes beyond the biblical accounts in
underscoring the determination with which the siege
was conducted.

[485] Greek: λιμὸς καὶ φθορά. This collocation is
common in Josephus: *War* 1.377; 4.361; 6.421; *Ant.*
10.132. Before his time, it is attested in Hesiod (*Op.*
243), Thucydides (1.23.3; 2.54.3), and Herodotus
(7.171; 8.115), but most often in Dionysius of Halicarnassus (*Ant.rom.* 7.13.4; 10.58.8; *Dem.* 39; *Thuc.* 20)
and Philo (*Ebr.* 79; *Somn.* 2.125, 129; *Mos.* 1.110, 265;
2.16). I owe these remarks to Prof. Steve Mason.

[486] Josephus derives his reference to the "famine"

afflicting Jerusalem during the siege from the notice of
Jer 52:5-6, etc. that the city's bread supply ran out in
the 4th month of Zedekiah's 11th year; cf. also
Jeremiah's prediction of "famine" in 10.112. He adds
the allusion to the other calamity, i.e. "plague" under
the influence of the combination of the terms "famine"
and "pestilence" (along with "the sword") in the announcements concerning the fate of the city attributed
to Jeremiah in such texts as Jer 21:9; 32:24; 38:2.

[487] Cf. the reference to Jeremiah's being "kept
under guard for punishment" in 10.115. This reference,
in turn, is based on Jer 37:15, where the princes
"imprison Jeremiah in the house of Jonathan the secretary, for it had been made into a prison." Cf. Jer 37:21b
"so Jeremiah remained in the court of the guard."

[488] See Jer 38:2b, where the leaders overhear Jeremiah assuring the people that those who "go out to"
the Babylonians will preserve their lives by doing so;
cf. the similar promise Jeremiah makes to Zedekiah
personally should he surrender to the Babylonians in
38:17. See further note on "death" at 10.118b.

[489] See the words the leaders overhear Jeremiah telling the people in Jer 38:2a: "He who stays in this city
shall die by the sword, by famine, and by pestilence."
Cf. too Josephus' own reference to the "famine and
plague" that are assaulting Jerusalem in 10.116.

[490] Josephus here returns to the initial positive
alternative Jeremiah put before the people in 10.118,
now reproducing the prophet's words from Jer 38:2bα
("he who goes out to the Chaldeans shall live") more
closely. He leaves aside the prophet's concluding
promise of 38:2bβ: "he [the deserter] shall have his life
as a prize of war, and live."

[491] The leaders' disbelief here recalls Josephus'
earlier contrast between them and the majority of the
people who, as he states in 10.114, did believe Jeremiah's announcements.

Jeremiah to Zedekiah

[Hieremias];[492] speaking ill of him, they requested that he [Sacchias] kill the prophet as one who was like a madman.[493] He [they claimed] was likewise breaking down their souls in advance[494] and by his prediction of doom[495] was weakening the eagerness[496] of the crowd—for they were ready [to endanger][497] [themselves] on behalf of him [the king] and their country.[498] [Hieremias], on the other hand, was urging them to flee to the enemy, saying that the city would be captured and all would perish.[499]

Zedekiah hands Jeremiah over to leaders

(7.5) 120 The king himself, in virtue of his personal kindness and justice[500] was not enraged [at Hieremias]. In order however, not to incur the hostility of the leaders by opposing their intention at this time, he gave them permission to do as they wished with the prophet.[501]

121 When the king had given them this permission, they immediately entered the prison, took [Hieremias] out and let him down by a rope into a certain cistern that was full of mud, in order that he might suffocate and die on his own. He was in this [state], held fast up to the neck by the mire.[502]

Jeremiah rescued

122 A certain domestic of the king, however, who was held in honor by him and

---

[492] See Jer 38:4a. Josephus adds the reference to the leaders' wrath, this recalling the response he attributes to King Jehoiakim when Jeremiah's book is read to him in 10.95.

[493] Greek: μαίνομαι; this is the term twice used of Jehu's anointer in *Ant.* 9.110 and of King Amaziah of Judah in 9.244. The leaders' charge concerning Jeremiah's mental state here is not explicitly paralleled in those attributed to the princes in their denunciation of Jeremiah to the king in Jer 38:4. It does, however, recall the reference to the leaders and the impious' deriding Jeremiah as "being out of his mind" (Greek: ἐξεστηκός τῶν φρενῶν) in 10.114.

[494] Greek: προκατακλάω; this verb is *hapax* in Josephus.

[495] Greek: ἡ τῶν χειρόνων καταγγελία; this expression (like the noun καταγγελία) is *hapax* in Josephus.

[496] Greek: ἐκλύω τὸ πρόθυμον. This phrase recurs in *Ant.* 13.231.

[497] Greek: κινδυνεῦσαι; the word is missing in ROM, but is read by Niese (who offers the conjecture κινδυνεύσειν) and Marcus. Lat reads *pugnare* ("to fight").

[498] Compare the princes' charge in Jer 38:4: "he [Jeremiah] is weakening the hands of the soldiers... and the hands of all the people, by speaking such words to them." Josephus' leaders add the reminder that those whom Jeremiah is (purportedly) seeking to demoralize are (still) loyal supporters of king and country—a further reason for Zedekiah to act against him.

[499] This abbreviated "citation" of Jeremiah's own incriminating words as reported by Josephus in 10.117-118 takes the place of the princes' concluding assertion about him in Jer 38:4: "This man is not seeking the welfare of this people, but their harm."

[500] Greek: χρεστότης καὶ δικαιοσύνη; this noun combination is used of Ezra in *Ant.* 11.139. It recalls the adjectival collocation χρηστὸς καὶ δίκαιος ("kind and just") applied to Jehoiachin in 10.100. Josephus' positive characterization of Zedekiah here is without explicit biblical warrant and stands in contrast to his own earlier evaluation of the king as one "who scorned what was just [Greek: τῶν δικαίων] and requisite" in 10.103. It does, however, have a certain basis in the following episode, in which Zedekiah will show himself concerned for Jeremiah's welfare, just as it recalls Josephus' affirmation (*War* 5.391-392) in the context of his address to the defenders of Jerusalem in *War* 5.362-419, that, faced with the provocations of Jeremiah's words, Zedekiah proved himself "moderate" and (along with his people) refrained from putting the prophet to death—whereas Josephus' own contemporary audience is "assailing" him "with abuse and missiles," even as he tries to persuade them to save themselves and their city. See Feldman 2001: 320.

[501] Josephus prefaces his rendering of Zedekiah's response to the leaders as cited in Jer 38:5 ("behold, he [Jeremiah] is your power; for the king can do nothing against you") with this explanation as to why the king, notwithstanding his lack of personal animosity towards Jeremiah, nevertheless does give the leaders *carte blanche* to do as they wish with him.

[502] Greek: πηλοῦ; this is the generally accepted conjecture for the form πλήθους ("by the crowd") read by the codices and E. See Jer 38:6. Josephus omits the biblical specifications concerning Jeremiah's place of confinement, i.e. "the cistern of Malchiah, the king's son, which was in the court of the guard."

was an Ethiopian by race,[503] reported the prophet's suffering to the king.[504] He stated that his [the king's] friends and the leaders had not acted rightly in doing these things,[505] namely sinking the prophet in the mud and having devised against him something more painful than death in chains would be.[506] **123** When he heard this, the king, thinking better of his having handed the prophet over to the leaders,[507] directed the Ethiopian to take thirty[508] of the royal [attendants] with him, as well as ropes and whatever else he considered useful for rescuing the prophet, and pull Hieremias up in haste.[509] The Ethiopian, taking along what he had been commanded, drew the prophet up from the mud and let him go without a guard.[510]

(7.6) 124 When the king had secretly summoned him and asked him what he was able to indicate to him from God, and to produce a sign pertaining to the present,[511] he [Hieremias] kept saying that he had [something], but that when he said it he would not be believed and when he admonished he would not be followed.[512] "Rather," he said, "your friends have destroyed me as though I had performed something vile.[513] Where now are those who said that the Babylonian [king] would no longer campaign against us and misled you?[514] But now I am in fear of telling the truth, lest you condemn me to death."[515]

*Final king–
prophet
exchange*

---

[503] Jer 38:7a supplies the name ("Ebed-melech") and the status ("a eunuch," so MT; LXX [Jer 45:7a] lacks the term) of the king's informant as well. Josephus adds the reference to the royal favor he enjoyed.

[504] Jer 38:7b notes that the king "was sitting in the Benjamin Gate" when Ebed-melech approached him.

[505] Josephus adds this element of explicit (negative) evaluation to his version of Ebed-melech's report to the king, Jer 38:8-9.

[506] The Ethiopian's concluding allusion to the extreme painfulness of the death awaiting Jeremiah here takes the place of his closing words in Jer 38:9: "(Jeremiah will die there of hunger), for there is no bread left in the city."

[507] Josephus supplies the reference to Zedekiah's second thoughts; the addition gives a more positive depiction of the king in his dealings with Jeremiah, in line with Josephus' mention of his "personal kindness and justice" in 10.120.

[508] This figure agrees with that found in all but 1 of our extant Hebrew manuscripts of Jer 38:10 as well as in the corresponding LXX verse, Jer 45:10. The single Hebrew manuscript in question reads "3."

[509] Zedekiah's command to Ebed-melech in Jer 38:10 does not mention the "implements" he is to take with him. Josephus anticipates his mention of "ropes" from 38:11-13, where these are used in the actual rescue process.

[510] Josephus omits the various details of the "rescue process" as reported in Jer 38:11-13, e.g., the directives Ebed-melech gives Jeremiah about his (the prophet's) own part in the process in v. 12a.

[511] Cf. Jer 38:14. Josephus omits the biblical indication that the interview between king and prophet

took place "at the 3rd entrance of the temple of the Lord," as well as Zedekiah's concluding admonition to Jeremiah, i.e. "hide nothing from me."

[512] Cf. Jeremiah's direct address charge against Zedekiah in Jer 38:15 ("And if I give you counsel, you will not listen to me"), which Josephus turns into a generalized, impersonal formulation. He thereby attenuates Zedekiah's personal responsibility for Jeremiah's plight as well as the adversarial relationship between them.

[513] Josephus derives his reference to the royal friends from Jer 38:22b, where Jeremiah accuses Zedekiah's "trusted friends" of having "deceived" and "prevailed against" him (the king). The Josephan Jeremiah's affirmation that the friends have "destroyed" him (Jeremiah) recalls 10.121, where the "leaders" lower the prophet into the cistern "that he might die on his own." With Jeremiah's allusion to the "something vile" he has purportedly done here, compare the prophet's question to Zedekiah in Jer 37:18: "*what wrong have I done* to you or your servants or this people, that you have put [MT reads a plural verb here, while LXX 44:18 has the singular, making Zedekiah himself the subject] me in prison?"

[514] Josephus here seems to combine Jeremiah's words to Zedekiah from 2 different contexts, i.e. Jer 37:19 ("Where are your prophets who prophesied to you, saying 'The king of Babylon will not come against you and against this land?'") and 38:22b ("your trusted friends have deceived you...").

[515] Josephus turns Jeremiah's initial question to the king ("If I tell you, will you not be sure not to put me to death?") of Jer 38:15a into a statement by the prophet about his fear and the reason for this.

125 The king then gave him his oath that he would neither do away with him nor give him up to the leaders.[516] Encouraged by the pledge given him,[517] [Hieremias] advised him to hand the city over to the Babylonians. **126** For, he said, God was prophesying the following to him through him:[518] if he wished to be saved and escape the impending danger and not have the city fall to the ground nor the sanctuary burned down,....[519] for [if he disobeyed,][520] he would be the cause of all these calamities to the citizens and of misfortune for himself and his whole household.[521]

127 When he heard this, the king said that he wished to do what he was urging and said that this would be to his advantage.[522] He was frightened, however, of his compatriots who had deserted to the Babylonians, that, having been slandered by them to the king, he would be penalized.[523] **128** The prophet encouraged him and said that his supposition about punishment was groundless.[524] For if he surrendered to the Babylonians, neither he nor his children nor his wives would experience any calamity, just as the sanctuary would remain undamaged.[525] **129** Once Hieremias had said these things, the king released him, ordering him not to reveal what they had decided to any of the citizens, the leaders included.[526] If they [the leaders] should learn that he had been summoned by him[527] and inquire what he had said to him when called,[528] he should not tell [them] anything of this, but should allege to them

---

[516] See Jer 38:16. Josephus characteristically omits Zedekiah's oath formula: "as the Lord lives, who made our souls...."

[517] Josephus supplies this allusion to the positive effect of Zedekiah's oath upon Jeremiah.

[518] Compare the opening "messenger formula" of Jer 38:17: "Thus says the Lord of hosts, the God of Israel."

[519] Josephus adds the reference to the temple and its eventual fate (see 10.112) to the conditional promise Jeremiah makes to Zedekiah in Jer 38:17. There appears to be a lacuna in the text of Jeremiah after the phrase "or the sanctuary burned down"; compare Jeremiah's assurance in 38:17a: "if you [Zedekiah] surrender to the princes of the king of Babylon, then your life will be spared."

[520] This bracketed phrase (Greek: μὴ πεισθέντα) is a conjecture of J. Hudson, based on the Lat reading (*quod si non fieret*) that Marcus adopts.

[521] Jeremiah's words of conditional promise and warning here represent Josephus' adaptation of those addressed by the prophet to Zedekiah in Jer 38:17-18.

[522] This initial response by Zedekiah has no counterpart in the king's words as reported in Jer 38:19. It makes the king appear more insightful about the situation he is facing than is his biblical counterpart. The king's response to Jeremiah at this juncture recalls that which Josephus attributes to him at the start of his reign in 10.105: "Whenever Sacchias heard the prophet saying these things, he was convinced; he agreed that all of them were true and that was it to his advantage to believe them."

[523] See Jer 38:19. Josephus adds the king's allusion

to his being "slandered," this establishing an implicit connection between Zedekiah and himself, who was likewise slandered by his compatriots (see *Life* 425, 428-429). Zedekiah's confession of being "frightened" here recalls 10.124, where Jeremiah himself admits to being "in fear."

[524] Compare Jeremiah's opening response to Zedekiah in Jer 38:20: "you shall not be given to them [i.e. the Chaldeans, see 38:19]." Josephus accentuates the prophet's concern to allay the king's fears.

[525] The biblical Jeremiah highlights the negative consequences of Zedekiah's refusal to surrender to the Babylonians in his extended reply to the king in Jer 38:20-23, touching only briefly on the benefits of such surrender, i.e. "it will be well with you, and your life shall be spared" (v. 20b). Josephus, by contrast, has Jeremiah focus exclusively on the positive alternative facing Zedekiah. In so doing, he reapplies phrases used in a negative sense in 38:20-23 in positive terms (see the reference to Zedekiah's wives and children who are at risk of being handed over to the Babylonians according to 38:23a). He likewise adds yet another reference to the fate hanging over the temple—which is nowhere mentioned in 38:20-23 itself.

[526] Josephus expatiates on Zedekiah's initial response to Jeremiah in Jer 38:24: "Let no one know of these words and you shall not die." The biblical text does not mention the actual release of Jeremiah.

[527] See 10.124 on this summons of Jeremiah by Zedekiah.

[528] Josephus compresses the extended discourse that Zedekiah envisages the "princes" addressing to Jeremiah in Jer 38:25, leaving aside, e.g., their promise

that he had begged not to be [held] in chains and under guard.[529] **130** And this is how he spoke to them when they came to the prophet and inquired why he had gone to the king to make allegations against them.[530] Thus matters turned out.[531]

(8.1) 131 The Babylonian [king] prosecuted the siege of Hierosolyma most vigorously and eagerly.[532] For, building towers on top of great earthworks, he kept those positioned on the walls away from these; he also erected many siegeworks around the entire perimeter [of the city] that were equal in height to its walls.[533] **132** Nevertheless, those inside endured the siege bravely and eagerly.[534] For they did not tire, either in respect to the famine or to the wasting disease.[535] Even though they were tormented by these sufferings, they strengthened their souls against the enemy. Nor were they thrown into confusion by the devices and machines of their foes; instead, they invented counter-machines[536] against all those [used] by them.[537] **133** As a result, the entire contest between the Babylonians and the Hierosolymites was [one] of cleverness and sagacity[538]; the former supposed that the city could be more [easily] captured in this way, while the latter put [their hopes for its] safety in nothing else then their not growing weary or slackening in thinking up machines by means of which they might render those of the enemy ineffectual.[539] **134** Things continued in this way for eighteen months[540] until they [the Hierosolymites] were destroyed by famine[541] and by the projectiles that the enemy kept shooting against them from their towers.[542]

Course of siege

---

not to put him to death, if he tells them what he and the king had said to each other.

[529] In Jer 38:26 Jeremiah is instructed by the king to tell the princes that he had begged Zedekiah "not to send him back to the house of Jonathan to die there." Josephus, just as he did previously (see 10.115 and compare Jer 37:15) leaves aside the Bible's mention of Jonathan and the site associated with him.

[530] See Jer 38:27a. Josephus leaves aside the appended notice of 38:27b: "so they [the princes] left off speaking with him, for the conversation [i.e. that between Zedekiah and Jeremiah] had not been overheard."

[531] This closing formula rounds off the interlude of 10.117-130 focussed on the interactions among various inhabitants of Jerusalem during the course of the siege; in what follows Josephus returns to his account of the siege itself, initiated in 10.116. The formula takes the place of the notice of Jer 38:28: "and Jeremiah remained in the court of the guard until the day that Jerusalem was taken."

[532] Greek: ἐντεταμένως καὶ προθύμως. This collocation occurs only here in Josephus; he uses the adverb ἐντεταμένως twice elsewhere: *Ant.* 11.96; 18.262. Josephus' resumption of his account of the siege here picks up on the wording of 10.116: "Having positioned [his army] before it [Hierosolyma], he [the Babylonian king] besieged it with the utmost intensity for eighteen months." On Josephus' description of Jerusalem's fall in 10.131-154, see Begg 2000: 575-94.

[533] Josephus here expatiates on the summary notice

of 2 Kgs 25:1// Jer 52:4: "(the Babylonians) built siegeworks against it [Jerusalem] round about." His elaboration is doubtless inspired by his personal experience of the devices used by the Romans in their siege of Jerusalem.

[534] Greek: καρτερῶς καὶ προθύμως. This wordpair occurs only here in Josephus.

[535] On this double affliction of the besieged Jerusalem, see 10.116, 118 (which adds the sword as well).

[536] Greek: ἀντιμηχανήματα; this word is *hapax* in Josephus.

[537] Josephus' account here, which goes far beyond the summary references to the siege in 2 Kgs 25:1// Jer 52:4, seems to be describing the 1st great siege of Jerusalem in terms of the fanatical resistance with which Jews of his own time had faced the 2nd such siege.

[538] Greek: ὀχύτης καὶ σύνεσις. This wordpair occurs only here in Josephus.

[539] With these remarks Josephus sums up his portrayal of the Babylonian/Jerusalemite contest as a foreshadowing (or retrojection) of that between the Romans and Jerusalem's defenders in his own time; cf. the references to the stratagems devised by the Jews in countering the Roman siege measures in, e.g., *War* 5.109, 121; 6.152, 177.

[540] Josephus has already mentioned this duration of the siege in 10.116.

[541] Cf. the mention of the failure of the city's bread supply in 2 Kgs 25:3// Jer 52:6.

[542] On the Babylonians' siege-towers, see 10.131.

City falls to   **(8.2) 135** The city was captured in the eleventh year of the kingship of Sacchias,
Babylonians   in the fourth month, on the ninth day.[543] The Babylonian leaders to whom
Nabouchodonosor had entrusted the siege—for he was residing in the city of
Arablatha[544]—captured it. The names of these leaders who devastated and subdued
Hierosolyma, should anyone seek to know them, were as follows:[545] Regalsar,[546]
Aremant,[547] Semegar,[548] Nabosaris,[549] and Acarampsaris.[550]

Zedekiah's   **136** The city fell about midnight.[551] When King Sacchias found out that the en-
flight   emy leaders had entered the sacred precinct,[552] he took his wives and children, the
leaders, and his friends[553] and fled with them from the city by way of the secure
valley[554] and the desert.[555]

The mention of the use of "projectiles" against the
inhabitants is another detail based, not on the biblical
accounts, but rather on Josephus' own experience of
Roman tactics; cf. his description of the siege of
Jotapata in *War* 3.167-168, 240-248a, 285-287.

[543] Josephus draws this triple dating-indication for
the city's fall from Jer 39:2, where it refers to the
breaching of the city. In 2 Kgs 25:2-3// Jer 52:5-6 (MT;
LXX does not cite the month in question) the same 3-
fold dating-indication is used in connection with the
mention of the failure of the city's food supply, this
being followed by the breaching of the city in 25:4//
52:7.

[544] Josephus anticipates this reference to Nebuchadnezzar's headquarters during the siege from 2 Kgs 25:6
// Jer 52:9// Jer 39:5, which have the captured Zedekiah
being brought before his overlord "at Riblah, in the
land of Hamath." (The reading of the city's name as
"Arablatha" here follows the conjecture of Niese,
adopted also by Marcus and Schalit [*s.v.*], for the form
"Arabatha" in RMSLauV Lat 10.135.)

[545] Josephus uncharacteristically reproduces a list
of (minor) biblical names, perhaps aiming thereby to
enhance the credibility of his account of a key event of
his history, namely the fall of Jerusalem to the Babylonians. The only biblical account to cite the names in
question is Jer 39:3, where in MT these total 4, of
which the 1st and the 4th are the same ("Nergal-sharezer"), while the last 2 have titles attached to them. In
the LXX parallel text (Jer 46:3), 6 proper names are
listed, of which the last is the title ("the Rabmag") of
the 4th and final individual on the MT list. Like OL
(which has no equivalent to LXX's "Rabamag"),
Josephus cites a total of 5 names.

[546] This form (Greek: Ῥεγάλσαρος) appears to be
Josephus' equivalent for the 1st name in the listing of
Jer 39:3: MT נרגל שׂר־אצר (Eng.: "Nergal-sharezer");
LXX (46:3) Ναργαλασρασαρ (a close variant of this
name, i.e. Ναργαλασρασερ, appears in 5th position in the
LXX list).

[547] This form (Greek: Ἀρέμαντος) lacks a recog-
nizable equivalent in the names of either MT Jer 39:3

or LXX 46:3.

[548] This form (Greek: Σεμέγαρος) is an abbreviation
of the 2nd name on the MT list (סמגר־נבו, Eng.:
"Samgar-nebo") in Jer 39:3; compare Σαμαγωθ in LXX
46:3.

[549] This form (Greek: Ναβώσαρις) corresponds to
the 4th name in LXX Jer 46:3 (Ναβουσαρις), which
itself appears to conflate the concluding element of the
2nd name (Samgar-*nebo*) and part of the title of 3rd
figure (Sarsechem the Rab*saris*) in the list of MT Jer
39:3.

[550] This form (Greek: Ἀχάραμψαρις), apart from its
concluding element, i.e. *psaris*, corresponding to the
final portion of the title ("rab*saris*," MT רב־סריס) of the
3rd name ("Sarsechem," MT שׂר־סכים) in the list of MT
Jer 39:3, lacks a discernible equivalent among the
names of either MT or LXX. Josephus lacks an equivalent to the concluding reference to "all the rest of the
officers of the king of Babylon" common to MT LXX
and OL.

[551] 2 Kgs 25:4// Jer 52:7// 39:4 (MT; LXX and OL
have no equivalent to MT's Jer 39:4-13) all speak in
more general terms of the flight of the soldiery taking
place "by night."

[552] Josephus adapts the presentation of MT Jer 39:3-
4, where Zedekiah and his men "see" (v. 4) the
Babylonian commanders, who have themselves taken
their seat "in the Middle Gate" (v. 3).

[553] 2 Kgs 25:4// Jer 52:7// Jer 39:4 (MT) speak only
of the "men of war" accompanying Zedekiah in his
flight. Josephus' added reference to other groups of
fugitives, i.e. the king's "wives and children," the "leaders," and the royal "friends," recalls the mention of
these groups in 10.128 and 10.124, respectively. His
mention of Zedekiah's taking these persons along on
his flight introduces another positive element into
Josephus' portrait of the king in comparison with the
biblical accounts, which say nothing of such a concern
by the fugitive Zedekiah for the safety of those close to
him.

[554] Greek: καρτερὰ φάραγξ. Marcus (*ad loc.*) proposes as an alternative translation "steep valley."

137 Some of the deserters, however, reported this to the Babylonians[556] who at daybreak[557] hastened to pursue him; overtaking him not far from Jericho, they surrounded him.[558] When the leaders and his friends who had fled along with Sacchias saw the enemy nearby, they abandoned him and scattered in different directions, each one having decided to save himself.[559]

Zedekiah captured

138 The enemy seized him with just a few men left around him[560] along with his children and wives,[561] and brought him to the king.[562] When he arrived, Nabouchodonosor began to call him an impious and treacherous[563] man, who was unmindful of the words he had spoken earlier, promising to preserve the country for him [Nabouchodonosor].[564] **139** He also reproached him for his ingratitude [towards himself], from whom he had received the kingship (for he had taken this away from Joakeim, whose it was, to give it to him),[565] using his power against him who had conferred it.[566] "But," he said, "the great God, hating[567] your behavior, has made you subject to us."[568]

Zedekiah denounced

140 Having used these words with Sacchias, he directed that his sons and friends be done away with immediately, as Sacchias and the other prisoners watched.[569]

Zedekiah's punishment

---

[555] Josephus simplifies the topographical indications concerning the flight route given in 2 Kgs 25:4, etc.: "by way of the gate between the two walls, by the king's garden... they went in the direction of the Arabah." He likewise leaves aside the parenthetical biblical notices about the Chaldeans' being "around the city" from which Zedekiah is attempting to escape.

[556] The fear expressed by Zedekiah to Jeremiah in 10.127 now comes upon him, as "deserters" report his flight to the Babylonians. The biblical accounts lack a corresponding indication as to how the Babylonians came to learn of Zedekiah's flight.

[557] This chronological indication (cf. the phrase "about midnight" in 10.136) lacks a counterpart in the biblical notices (2 Kgs 25:5// Jer 52:8// Jer 39:5 [MT]) on the Babylonian pursuit.

[558] 2 Kgs 25:5a// Jer 52:8a// Jer 39:5a (MT) specify "in the plains of Jericho."

[559] In 2 Kgs 25:5b// Jer 52:8b (Jeremiah 39 [MT] lacks a corresponding indication) it is Zedekiah's army —his sole entourage according to 2 Kgs 25:4// Jer 52:7 // Jer 39:4 (MT)—who are "scattered from" him. Josephus focusses rather on the behavior of another group whose accompanying of Zedekiah he mentioned in 10.136, i.e. the royal "friends." In so doing, he highlights the deliberateness with which the king's so-called "friends" abandon him in search of their personal safety. He thereby reinforces his unrelievedly negative portrayal of these figures, which began with his reference to their "corrupting" Zedekiah once again in 10.105.

[560] In 2 Kgs 25:6a// Jer 52:9a (cf. Jer 39:5a, MT) Zedekiah appears to be alone at the moment of his capture, his army having been "scattered from him" in 25:5b// 52:8b. The "men" to whom Josephus alludes here are presumably (some of) the "leaders" who, along

with the "friends" are said to accompany Zedekiah on his flight in 10.136. Since the latter group has now abandoned the king (10.137), it is only the former group that could furnish those men who still remain with him.

[561] On these persons as part of the Josephan Zedekiah's entourage in his flight, see 10.136.

[562] 2 Kgs 25:6// Jer 52:9// Jer 39:5b identify the site as "Riblah in the land of Hamath." Josephus has already drawn on this indication concerning Nebuchadnezzar's current whereabouts in 10.135.

[563] Greek: παράσπονδος. This adjective occurs only here in Josephus.

[564] This denunciation of Zedekiah by Nebuchadnezzar prior to his punishment of him lacks a biblical basis. It does, however, recall 10.102, where Nebuchadnezzar makes Zedekiah swear "to preserve the country for him."

[565] On this event, see 10.102.

[566] This additional charge by Nebuchadnezzar concerning Zedekiah's "ingratitude" is another Josephan invention.

[567] On God as the subject of the verb "hate" (Greek: μισέω) in Josephus, see note to "God so hated" at *Ant.* 6.138.

[568] Josephus' placing of this invocation of (the one) God on the lips of a pagan king is noteworthy since, e.g., he leaves aside the biblical references to a similar invocation on the part of Pharaoh Neco; see on 10.75. His doing so in this instance is indicative of his own negative feelings about Zedekiah's rebellious dealings with his overlord—which, of course, foreshadowed those adopted by the contemporary Zealots towards their Roman rulers.

[569] See 2 Kgs 25:7aα// Jer 52:10// Jer 39:6 (MT). In contrast to 2 Kings, but like the 2 Jeremiah passages,

*Words of
Jeremiah and
Ezekiel fulfilled*

Then, after gouging out Sacchias' eyes, he bound him and brought him to Babylon.[570] **141** So those things happened to him that both Hieremias and Iezekiel had prophesied to him,[571] in that, after being arrested, he was brought to the Babylonian [king] and spoke to him face to face and looked into his eyes with his own.[572] This is what Hieremias had said. Having been blinded and brought to Babylon, however, he did not *see* it, just as Iezekiel had predicted.[573] **(8.3) 142** These things that we have stated can suitably manifest to those who do not know the nature of God[574] that it is varied, manifold, and timely[575] at any hour. [Our account also manifests] that what he [God] predicts has to happen, as well as the ignorance and unbelief[576] of humans, which does not allow them to foresee what is to be. Caught off guard, they are handed over to misfortunes, so that it is impossible for them to escape experiencing these.[577]

*Duration of
Davidic dynasty*

(8.4) 143 Those of the family of David who ruled as kings thus terminated their lives; there were twenty-one[578] of them down through the last king. In all, they ruled as kings for 514 years, six months and ten days. For twenty years of this time, the first of them, King Saoul, exercised the rule,[579] though he was not of the same tribe.[580]

Nebuzaradan's

144 The Babylonian [king] sent his general Nabouzardan[581] to Hierosolyma to

----

Josephus mentions the execution not only of Zedekiah's sons, but also of other persons. Whereas, however, Jer 39:6b designates the latter group as "all the nobles of Judah," and Jer 52:10b calls them "all the princes of Judah," he equates these additional victims with Zedekiah's "friends" (whose accompanying of the fugitive king and their subsequent desertion of him he cites in 10.136 and 137, respectively). Josephus goes beyond all the biblical accounts in noting that prisoners other than Zedekiah himself (his wives? the leaders?) witnessed the executions as well. Compare *War* 5.391, where, in the context of his address to the defenders of Jerusalem (*War* 5.362-419), Josephus alludes to the captive Zedekiah's "seeing," not the execution of his sons as here in 10.140, but rather "the town [Jerusalem] and the temple leveled to the ground." See Feldman 2001: 321.

[570] See 2 Kgs 25:7aαb// Jer 39:7 (MT). Jer 52:11 adds that, having brought Zedekiah to Babylon, Nebuchadnezzar imprisoned him there "till the day of his death"; Josephus will make use of this additional item in 10.154.

[571] Josephus supplies this allusion to his earlier discussion of the apparent discrepancy between Jeremiah's and Ezekiel's announcements concerning Zedekiah's fate (10.106-107), a discussion that concludes with the promise that he will return to the matter, as he does here in 10.141.

[572] Josephus at this point draws on the wording of the relevant Jeremian passage, i.e. Jer 32:4b (Zedekiah is to speak face to face with Nebuchadnezzar and see him eye to eye), whereas previously in 10.106, he simply had Jeremiah announce that Zedekiah will be

taken to Babylon "in chains."

[573] See 10.106= Ezek 12:13.

[574] Greek: φύσις τοῦ θεοῦ. On this expression, see note to "the nature of God" at *Ant.* 8.338.

[575] Greek: τεταγμένος. This word is *hapax* in Josephus.

[576] Greek: ἄγνοια καὶ ἀπιστία. This collocation occurs only here in Josephus.

[577] This appended moral about the theological lessons to be learned from Zedekiah's calamity recall the remarks with which Josephus concludes his account of the death of Ahab in *Ant.* 8.418-420. In both passages, e.g., he points out that, even with the benefit of divine predictions, people still do pursue the course that leads to their own destruction.

[578] As Marcus (*ad loc.*) points out, this figure for the succession of kings from David to Zedekiah excludes the non-Davidic Athaliah, who usurped the Judean throne.

[579] Several chronological problems arise with the above figures. First, according to *Ant.* 6.378 Saul reigned, not 20, but *40* years. In addition, if one adds the 20 years ascribed to Saul here to the lengths of reign given by Josephus for the 20 Davidic kings in what precedes, one comes up with a figure of *534* rather than 514 years for the monarchical period. See further Marcus *ad loc.*

[580] With this notice Josephus reminds readers that Saul was from the tribe of Benjamin, in contrast to David and his successors who were of the tribe of Judah.

[581] MT (2 Kgs 25:8// Jer 52:12) נבוזראדן (Eng.: "Nebuzaradan"); LXX BL 2 Kgs 25:8// LXX Jer 52:12

pillage the sanctuary,[582] likewise ordering him to burn it down, along with the pal- *measures in* ace, to raze the city to the ground, and to deport the people to Babylon.[583] *Jerusalem*

145 Having arrived in Hierosolyma in the eleventh year of the kingship of Sacchias,[584] he pillaged the sanctuary.[585] He likewise carried out the gold and silver vessels of God[586] and the great laver that Solomon had erected,[587] together with the bronze columns and their capitals[588] and the golden tables and the lampstands.[589] **146** Having carried off these [items],[590] he set fire to the sanctuary[591] in the fifth month, at the new moon, in the eleventh year of Sacchias' kingship[592] and the eighteenth of that of Nabouchodonosor.[593] He also burned down the palace[594] and leveled the city.[595]

Ναβουζαρδάν; Josephus Ναβουζαρδάνης.

[582] Greek: συλλάω τὸν ναόν. This phrase is characteristic of Josephus (*War* 1.32; *Ant.* 10.144, 145, 233, 275; 11.10, 58, 91, 102; 12.357), though not attested in earlier or contemporary authors. I owe this remark to Prof. Steve Mason.

[583] In 2 Kgs 25:8// Jer 52:12 (no equivalent in Jeremiah 39) Nebuzaradan simply "comes" to Jerusalem, without being sent or receiving orders from Nebuchadnezzar about what he is to do. Josephus fills this lacuna, thereby making clear that what the former does in Jerusalem is not done on his own initiative. The orders he attributes to Nebuchadnezzar here recall (elements of) the predictions made by Jeremiah in 10.112.

[584] Nebuzaradan's coming to Jerusalem is dated to Nebuchadnezzar's 19th year in 2 Kgs 25:8// Jer 52:12 (MT; LXX and OL lack an equivalent). Josephus' dating of the event by reference rather to Zedekiah's 11th year picks up on his mention of the city's capture in that same year in 10.135. He leaves aside—for the moment, but see 10.146—the month and day references given in the biblical accounts.

[585] In the sequence of 2 Kings 25// Jeremiah 52 (cf. also 2 Chr 36:19), the temple's despoliation (25:13-16 // 52:17-23) is cited after the "burning" of the structure itself (25:9// 52:13) (Jeremiah 39 [MT] mentions neither of these events in its account of the Babylonian measures in the fallen Jerusalem, vv. 8-14.) Josephus rearranges this sequence so as to have the Babylonians follow a more logical order in their operations—first they remove the temple valuables and only then demolish the edifice.

[586] With this phrase, Josephus abridges the detailed catalogue of confiscated temple vessels given in 2 Kgs 25:14-15// Jer 52:18-19 (no parallel in Jeremiah 39).

[587] See 2 Kgs 25:13b// Jer 52:17b. Josephus appends the reference to Solomon's placement of this object as recounted by him in *Ant.* 8.79-80.

[588] Josephus here combines (and notably abbreviates) the indications concerning the pillars and their accoutrements found in 2 Kgs 25:13a, 17// Jer 52:17a,

21-23. On the fabrication of these objects, see *Ant.* 8.77-78.

[589] These 2 objects are not mentioned in the catalogue of items plundered by the Babylonians in 2 Kgs 25:13-17// Jer 52:17-23. Conversely, Josephus passes over several items found in one or both of the biblical lists, e.g., the "stands" (25:13// 52:17) and the "12 bronze oxen" (52:20).

[590] See 2 Kgs 25:15b// Jer 52:19b: "what was of gold the captain of the guard [Nebuzaradan] took away as gold, what was of silver, as silver."

[591] See 2 Kgs 25:9a// Jer 52:13a (and 2 Chr 36:19a). Jeremiah 39 does not mention the burning of the temple. Nebuzaradan's initiative fulfills Jeremiah's announcement in 10.112 that, "after removing the wealth of the sanctuary, [the Babylonian king] would then burn it down."

[592] Compare 2 Kgs 25:8, where Nebuzaradan's coming to Jerusalem and his initiatives there are dated to the 7th (so MT LXX B; LXX L reads 9th) day of the 5th month (Jer 52:12 [MT; LXX reads the 10th day of the 5th month; OL has the 5th year, rather than the 5th month]) of Nebuchadnezzar's 19th year (see note to "Sacchias" at 10.145). Josephus' reference to the 11th year of Zedekiah's reign picks up on the same dating indication in 10.135, 145.

[593] 2 Kgs 25:8// Jer 52:12 (MT; LXX and OL lacks the indication) date Nebuzaradan's arrival in Jerusalem and his activities there to the *19th* year of Nebuchadnezzar's reign; see note to "Sacchias" at 10.145.

[594] 2 Kgs 25:9b// Jer 52:13b// 39:8a (MT), as well as 2 Chr 36:19b, mention the burning of other houses (mansions) in Jerusalem as well.

[595] 2 Kgs 25:10// Jer 52:14// Jer 39:8b (MT) speak of the pulling down of the city's walls. Josephus' notice provides a fulfillment of Jeremiah's prediction in 10.112 that Nebuchadnezzar will "demolish the city." Compare *War* 5.391, where, in the context of his address to the defenders of Jerusalem (*War* 5.362-419), Josephus alludes to the captive Zedekiah's seeing "the town and the temple levelled to the ground."

*Dating
indications*

147 The sanctuary was burned down 470 years, 6 months and 10 days after it had been constructed.[596] From the Egyptian sojourn of the people it was 1,062 years, 6 months, and 10 days.[597] From the Deluge to the demolition of the sanctuary the whole length of time was 1,957 years, 6 months, and 10 days.[598] **148** From the generation of Adam until what happened to the sanctuary it was 4,513[599] years, 6 months, and 10 days.[600] This then is the total of these years; we have related the things that happened, each in order.[601]

*Jerusalem's
leaders
executed*

149 Now the general of the Babylonian king, after leveling Hierosolyma and deporting the people,[602] took captive the high priest Sebai,[603] and Sephenias,[604] the priest who [came] after him,[605] and the leaders who guarded the sacred precinct —there were three of them[606]—as well as the eunuch[607] who was in charge of the troops, seven friends of Sacchias[608] and his scribe,[609] together with sixty other lead-

---

[596] In *Ant.* 20.232 the figure given by Josephus for the duration of the high priesthood from the time of Solomon down to the temple's destruction by Nebuchadnezzar is 466 years, 6 months, and 10 days, i.e. 4 years less than the total cited in 10.147. Feldman (*ad loc.*) attributes the discrepancy to Josephus' failure to incorporate Solomon's first 4 years prior to his building of the temple into the figure given in 20.232. He further points out that according to *b. Yoma* 9a Solomon's temple lasted *410* years.

[597] Josephus arrives at this figure by combining those given by him for the interval between the Exodus and the building of the temple in *Ant.* 8.61 (i.e. 592 years) and for the period from the latter event to the temple's destruction cited just previously in 10.147, i.e. 470 years, 6 months, and 10 days. In *Ant.* 20.230 and *Apion* 2.19, on the other hand, he gives a much lower figure for the period in question, i.e. *612* years.

[598] On the basis of this figure, there would have been an interval of 1,487 years from the Flood to the building of the temple, whereas in *Ant.* 8.61 the figure given for that period is 1,440 years.

[599] This is the reading adopted by Niese and Marcus. RO read 4,510; LauVEZonLat have 3,513.

[600] A notably lower figure, i.e. 3,572+ years, for the number of years from Adam to the burning of the temple results if one tallies the totals given for the time between Adam and the building of the temple in *Ant.* 8.62 (3,102 years) and the 470+ years for the interval between the temple's construction and its destruction cited in 10.147.

[601] The above notice serves to round off Josephus' chronological notices for the period from Adam to the temple's destruction. His added chronological interlude of 10.147-148 highlights the significance of the demolition of the temple as an event on a par with the other key biblical events cited in this segment.

[602] Josephus here resumes the thread of his narrative after the chronological interlude of 10.147-148; the resumption picks up on the language of Nebuchad-

nezzar's orders to Nebuzaradan in 10.143, these including the razing of Jerusalem and the deportation of the inhabitants. For the latter event—not previously mentioned by him—see 2 Kgs 25:11// Jer 52:15// Jer 39:9 (MT), which mention various categories of persons deported by Nebuzaradan, e.g., the remaining inhabitants of the city and the deserters. Josephus will return to the topic of Nebuzaradan's dealings with the Judean survivors in 10.155.

[603] MT (2 Kgs 25:18// Jer 52:24) שריה (Eng.: "Seraiah"); LXX BL Σαραίας (LXX and OL Jer 52:24 do not name the high priest); Josephus Σεβαῖος (this is the reading of RO adopted by Niese; Marcus and Schalit *s.v.* follow LauV's Σαραίας; see further on 10.150).

[604] MT (2 Kgs 25:18 צפניהו (Eng.: "Zephaniah")/ Jer 52:24 צפניה (Eng.: "Zephaniah"); LXX B 2 Kgs 25:18 Σοφονίας; LXX L 2 Kgs 25:18 Σαφανίας (LXX and OL Jer 52:24 do not name the "2nd priest"); Josephus Σεφενίας.

[605] 2 Kgs 25:18// Jer 52:24 speak of "the second priest."

[606] In 2 Kgs 25:18// Jer 52:24 the 3 figures in question are designated as "keepers of the threshold" (LXX and OL Jer 52:24: "of the way").

[607] Josephus uses the same term (Greek: εὐνοῦχος) as does the LXX for this figure; the corresponding Hebrew word סרים (MT 2 Kgs 25:19// Jer 52:25) may have a broader meaning (RSV: officer).

[608] In 2 Kgs 25:19// Jer 52:25 the reference is to "men of the king's council who were found in the city"; Josephus' substitution reflects his highlighting of the (negative) role played by the royal "friends" throughout Zedekiah's reign. His figure for this group corresponds to that given in Jer 52:25, whereas 2 Kgs 25:19 reads 5.

[609] Josephus simplifies the complicated designation used of this figure in 2 Kgs 25:19// Jer 52:25, i.e. "the secretary (scribe) of the commander of the army who mustered the people of the land."

ers.[610] He brought all these, along with the vessels he had pillaged,[611] to the king at Arablatha,[612] a city of Syria.[613] **150** The king directed that the heads of the high priest and leaders be cut off there.[614] He himself led all the captives to Babylon, along with the bound King Sacchias[615] and Josadak,[616] the high priest, who was the son of Saraias[617] the high priest whom the Babylonian had killed in Arablatha a city of Syria, as we related earlier.[618]

Survivors deported

151 Since we have told about the family of the kings and related who they were and their times,[619] we also thought it necessary to mention the names of the high priests and who they were who exercised[620] the high priesthood under the kings.[621] **152** Now then the first high priest of the temple that Solomon built was Sadok.[622] After him his son Achimas[623] succeeded to the honor, and after Achimas, Azarias,[624] then Joram[625] his son, then Jos, the son of Joram, then his son Axioram, **153** then Phideas the son of Axioram, then Soudai the son of Phideas, then, Jouel the son of Soudai, then his son Jotham, then Ourias, the son of Jotham, then Nerias, the son of Ourias, then Odaias, the son of Nerias, then Saloum,[626] the son of Odaias, then

High priestly succession

---

[610] Compare 2 Kgs 25:19// Jer 52:25 (MT LXX) "60 men of the people of the land, who were found in the city." OL Jer 52:25 does not mention this last group of captives.

[611] 2 Kgs 25:20// Jer 52:26 speak only of Nebuzaradan's bringing of the prisoners cited in 25:18-19// 52:24-25, not also the temple vessels, to Nebuchadnezzar at Riblah. On Nebuzaradan's removal of the vessels from the temple, see 10.145.

[612] MT (2 Kgs 25:20// Jer 52:26) רבלה (Eng.: "Riblah"); LXX Δεβλάθα; Josephus᾽ Αραβλαθα (this is the conjecture of Niese, which Marcus and Schalit *s.v.* adopt; RO read Σαλάβαθα). Niese, followed by Marcus and Schalit, conjectures the same form also in 10.135, 150.

[613] 2 Kgs 25:21// Jer 52:27 locate "Riblah" in "the land of Hamath."

[614] 2 Kgs 25:21a// Jer 52:27 have Nebuchadnezzar executing all the prisoners listed in 25:18-19// 52:24-25// 10.149.

[615] Nebuchadnezzar's transport of the bound Zedekiah to Babylon has already been reported by Josephus in 10.140.

[616] Josephus derives his mention of this figure and his deportation from another biblical context, i.e. 1 Chr 5:40-41 (MT; Eng. 6:14-15) where MT calls him יהוצדק (Eng.: "Jehozadak"); LXX B Ἰωσαδάκ; LXX Ἰωσεδέκ. Josephus' form is Ἰωσάδακος.

[617] Greek: Σαραίας. In 10.149 the name is given by RO (followed by Niese) as Σεβαῖος, whereas Marcus reads Σαραίας there too.

[618] See the opening of 10.150, where, in contrast to 2 Kgs 25:21// Jer 52:27, Josephus makes explicit mention of the execution of the "high priest," i.e. the biblical Seraiah. Josephus' notice on Nebuchadnezzar's deportation of the king and the high priest's son here

replaces the more general notice of 2 Kgs 25:21b// Jer 52:27b (MT, > LXX OL) concerning Judah's being removed from its land.

[619] See 10.143, with its summary allusion to the succession of Israel's kings beginning with Saul.

[620] The codices (and Niese) read κακαδείξαντες ("founded"). On the basis of Lat's *habuerunt* ("they held"), Marcus, following J. Cocceius, proposes the reading κατάχοντες, which I adopt.

[621] The "priestly interlude" that follows in 10.152-153 has a counterpart in the listings of the successive priests in *Ant.* 6.361-362 and 8.12. It is (very loosely) based on the list of high priests in 1 Chr 5:34-41 [Eng. 6:7-14] from Zadok to the exiled Jehozadak.

[622] Compare 1 Chr 5:36 (Eng. 6:10), which states that it was Zadok's great-great grandson Azariah who officiated in the temple Solomon built.

[623] MT (1 Chr 5:35) אחימעץ (Eng. [1 Chr 6:8]: "Ahimaaz"); LXX᾽ Αχιμάας; Josephus᾽ Αχιμᾶς.

[624] MT (1 Chr 5:35) עזריה (Eng. [1 Chr 6:9]: "Azariah"); LXX and Josephus᾽ Αζαρίας.

[625] With this great-grandson of Zadok Josephus' list begins to diverge markedly from that of 1 Chr 5:34-41 [Eng. 6:1-15], only rejoining that list for its name "Shallum" of 5:38-39 [Eng. 6:12-13]. In the MT listing the 5 names between Azariah (I) and Shallum are as follows: Johanan, Azariah, Amariah, Ahitub, and Zadok, Compare the 10 names covering the same interlude as cited by Josephus: Joram, Jos, Axioram, Phideas, Soudaias, Jouel, Jotham, Ourias, Nerias, and Odaias.

[626] MT (1 Chr 5:38-39) שלום (Eng. [1 Chr 6:12-13]: "Shallum"). With this name Josephus rejoins the biblical listing, from which he deviated after the figure of Azariah (I); see previous note.

Elkias,[627] the son of Saloum, then Azar,[628] the son of Elkias, then his son Josadak who was taken as a captive to Babylon.[629] All these succeeded to the high priesthood, son from father.

Events in Babylon

(8.7) 154 Once he arrived in Babylon, the king [Nabouchodonosor] held Sacchias in prison until he died in prison.[630] He then buried him royally,[631] and dedicated the vessels pillaged from the sanctuary of Hierosolyma to his own gods.[632] He settled the people in the Babylonian country,[633] but released the high priest from his bonds.[634]

Gedaliah (Gadalias) appointed governor

(9.1) 155 After taking the people of the Hebrews captive,[635] the general Nabouzardan left behind there the poor and the deserters[636] and appointed as their leader one named Gadalias,[637] the son of Aïkam.[638] (Of good birth, [Gadalias] was gentle and just.)[639] He [Nabouzardan] commanded them [those left behind], by cultivating the soil, to pay their fixed tribute to the king.[640]

---

[627] MT (1 Chr 5:39) חלקיה (Eng. [1 Chr 6:13]: "Hilkiah"); LXX Χελκίας; Josephus Ἐλκία. In 10.55-58 this figure is called Ἐλιακίας.

[628] MT (1 Chr 5:39-40) עזריה (Eng. [1 Chr 6:13-14]: "Azariah"); LXX Ἀζαρίας; Josephus Ἄζαρος (this is the reading adopted by Niese and Marcus). In making this figure the father, rather than the grandfather of "Jehozadak" here, Josephus differs not only from 1 Chr 5:40 (MT; Eng. 6:14), but also from his own 10.150, where he gives the name of Jehozadak's father as "Saraias," corresponding to the biblical "Seraiah." Accordingly, Niese posits a lacuna in the text of Josephus after the name "Azar" in 10.153.

[629] See 10.150.

[630] This notice corresponds to the plus of Jer 52:11bβ (no parallel in 2 Kgs 25:7), mentioning Nebuchadnezzar's keeping Zedekiah in prison "till the day of his death." The word used for Zedekiah's place of confinement here in 10.154 (Greek: εἱρκτή) is the same used for Jeremiah's "prison" in 10.117, 121.

[631] The biblical narrative accounts do not mention the fact of Zedekiah's burial. Josephus' notice on the matter does, however, represent an implicit fulfillment of the prediction made to the king by Jeremiah in Jer 34:5 "... as spices were burned for your fathers. so men shall burn spices for you and lament for you, saying 'Alas, lord'." Rabbinic tradition as well (see *b. Mo'ed Qat.* 28b; *S. 'Olam Rab.* 28.3) goes beyond the Bible itself in affirming that Zedekiah did receive the burial due a deceased king; see Begg 2000: 594, n. 132.

[632] See Dan 1:2 (cf. 5:2; Ezra 1:7) where—at a much earlier point, i.e. the 3rd year of the reign of Jehoiakim (see 1:1)—Nebuchadnezzar brings some of the temple vessels "to the land of Shinar, to the house of his god, and placed the vessels in the house of his god." Josephus' mention of Nebuchadnezzar's disposition of the vessels at this point picks up on his (also added) mention of Nebuzaradan's bringing these to him at "Arablatha" (biblical Riblah) in 10.149.

[633] Cf. 2 Chr 36:20: "He [Nebuchadnezzar] took into exile in Babylon those who had escaped from the sword, and they became servants to him...."

[634] This notice on Jehozadak's release has no biblical counterpart; it picks on the mention of his being taken to Babylon by Nebuchadnezzar in 10.150 // 1 Chr 5:41 (Eng. 6:15).

[635] This transitional phrase picks up on the reference to Nebuzaradan's deportation of the people in 10.149.

[636] See 2 Kgs 25:12// Jer 52:16// Jer 39:10 (MT), which mention "some of the poorest of the land" being left behind by Nebuzaradan for agricultural purposes, while 25:11// 52:15// 39:9 (MT) have Nebuzaradan taking the "deserters" (along with some [others] of the poorest of the land and those "left in the city") into exile in Babylon. Josephus thus modifies the biblical notices on the fate meted out to the deserters; they—who had reported Zedekiah's flight to the Babylonians (see 10.137)—are "rewarded" by being allowed to remain behind in the land.

[637] MT (2 Kgs 25:22; cf. Jer 40:5) גדליהו (Eng.: "Gedaliah"); LXX BL Γοδολίας; Josephus Γαδαλίας.

[638] MT (2 Kgs 25:22) אחיקם (Eng.: "Ahikam"); LXX BL Ἀχεικάμ; Josephus Ἀϊκαμος. Josephus omits the name of Gedaliah's grandfather (MT: Shaphan).

[639] These positive characterizations of Gedaliah have no counterpart in the notice on his appointment in 2 Kgs 25:22 (cf. Jer 40:5). Significantly, Josephus' only other use of the collocation "gentle and just" (Greek: ἐπιεικὴς καὶ δίκαιος) is in reference to David in *Ant.* 7.391. For his account of Gedaliah, his short-lived governorship, and its sequels Josephus bases himself on the extended account given in Jeremiah (39:11-14) 40-44 as opposed to the much shorter version of 2 Kgs 25:22-26 (Jeremiah 52 does not mention Gedaliah). On the Josephan Gedaliah, see Begg 2000: 599-622 and Feldman 1998a: 463-72.

[640] The biblical accounts do not report such a

156 Taking the prophet Hieremias out of prison,[641] [Nabouzardan] [tried to] persuade him to go with him to Babylon, for he had been directed by the king to provide everything for him.[642] But if he did not wish [to do] this, he should disclose to him where he had decided to stay, in order that this [reply] might be dispatched to the king.[643] **157** The prophet, however, was not willing to follow him, nor to stay anywhere else, but was content to spend his life among the ruins of his native land and its pitiable[644] remains.[645] Once the general knew that this was his intention, he ordered Gadalias, whom he had left behind, immediately to take every care of him [Hieremias] and supply him with whatever he needed.[646] Having gifted him with costly gifts, he released him.[647]

158 Hieremias then settled down[648] in a city of the country, called Mosphotha,[649] after having appealed to Nabouzardan to release for him also his disciple Barouch,[650]

Nebuzaradan's solicitude for Jeremiah

---

command being issued by Nebuzaradan himself. In Jer 40:9-10 it is Gedaliah who gives analogous instructions to the assembled Judeans: "dwell in the land and serve the king of Babylon... gather wine and summer fruits and oil, and store them in your vessels...."

[641] See Jer 39:13-14, where Nebuzaradan, along with the other Babylonian commanders, removes Jeremiah "from the court of the guard." For his presentation in 10.156-157 Josephus conflates the double account of an interaction involving Nebuzaradan and Jeremiah that eventuates in the latter's joining Gedaliah found in Jer 39:11-14 and 40:1-6. He makes no use of the word of assurance that God instructs the still-imprisoned Jeremiah to convey to his rescuer Ebed-melech (cf. 10.122-123) cited in Jer 39:15-18.

[642] Josephus derives this 1st alternative that Nebuzaradan offers to Jeremiah from Jer 40:4aβ: "if it seems good to you to come with me to Babylon, come, and I will look after you well." He draws the appended reference to Nebuchadnezzar's command concerning the prophet from Jer 39:12, where the king directs Nebuzaradan to "look after him [Jeremiah] well." He leaves aside Nebuzaradan's opening words (vv. 2-3) to Jeremiah, in which the commander speaks of what has happened as a divine punishment for what "you" (plural) had done. The words which Josephus earlier attributes to Nebuchadnezzar in his denunciation of Zedekiah (10.138-139) might, however, be viewed as an anticipation/adaptation of their content.

[643] Cf. Nebuzaradan's exhortation to Jeremiah in Jer 40:4b: "but if it seems wrong to you to come with me to Babylon, do not come. See, the whole land is before you; go wherever you think it good and right to go." Josephus adds the reference to Nebuzaradan's intention of reporting Jeremiah's decision to the king.

[644] Greek: ταλαίπωρος. Josephus uses this term in reference to the divine punishment of King Uzziah for his arrogation of priestly prerogatives in *Ant.* 9.226.

[645] Jeremiah 40 does not report a response by

Jeremiah to Nebuzaradan's extended discourse (vv. 2-5a// 10.156) to him, offering him a double option; rather, the latter simply lets the prophet go, following his words to him (v. 5b). The reply Josephus attributes to Jeremiah highlights the prophet's sense of solidarity with his surviving compatriots and their wretched state.

[646] This sequence lacks an equivalent in Jeremiah 40, where Nebuzaradan simply mentions the possibility of Jeremiah's joining Gedaliah (v. 5a) and Jeremiah ends up doing this (v. 6). It corresponds rather to the alternative presentation in Jer 39:13-14, where Nebuzaradan and other Babylonian officers entrust Jeremiah to Gedaliah so that he "might take him home." Josephus' added reference to the command given by Nebuzaradan to the governor concerning Jeremiah's care highlights the general's solicitude for the prophet's welfare.

[647] See Jer 40:5b. Josephus' mentions of "gift*s*" corresponds to the LXX reading in 47:5b, whereas the MT parallel 40:5 speaks of a single "gift." Josephus accentuates the favor shown Jeremiah by Nebuzaradan still more by specifying that the general's gifts were "costly" ones. The "costly gifts" the Babylonian general gives the captive Jeremiah here have a counterpart in *War* 3.408, where the Roman commander Vespasian awards the captured Josephus "precious gifts."

[648] At this point there follows in the codices the words εἰς Δάναν ["to Dana"] which have no equivalent in Lat; the words are bracketed by Niese and omitted by Marcus. They may reflect the LXX reading "from Dama" of LXX Jer 47:1 (MT 40:1 has "from Ramah"); see Marcus *ad loc*.

[649] MT (Jer 40:6) המצפתה (Eng.: "Mizpah"); LXX (47:6) Μασσηφα; Josephus Μοσαφθά (this is the reading of RSP, which Niese follows; Marcus reads Μασαφαθά, the reading adopted by Niese for the subsequent mention of the site in 10.159, with O).

[650] In his earlier mentions of "Baruch" in 10.94, 95,

Leaders approach Gedaliah

the son of Ner,[651] who was of a very distinguished family and thoroughly educated in his native language.[652]

(9.2) 159 Once he had arranged these matters, Nabouzardan hastened to Babylon.[653] Now those who fled when Hierosolyma was being besieged were dispersed throughout the country.[654] Then when they heard that the Babylonians had withdrawn and left behind a certain remnant in the region of the Hierosolymites and[655] some who were to cultivate this,[656] they assembled from all sides and came to Gadalias at Masphatha.[657] **160** Among their leaders were Joad,[658] the son of Kari,[659] Sereas,[660] Ioazanias,[661] and others in addition to these;[662] there was also a certain Ismael[663] of the royal family.[664] He was a vile and very crafty man,[665] who, during the siege of Hierosolyma, fled to Baaleim,[666] the king of the Ammanites, and lived with him during that time.[667]

Josephus designates him as the prophet's "scribe."

[651] MT (Jer 43:3) נריה (Eng.: "Neriah"); LXX (50:3) Νηρία; Josephus Νῆρος.

[652] Neither Jeremiah's request on behalf of Baruch nor the appended characterization of the latter has a biblical counterpart. Josephus' added notices on these points serve to prepare for Baruch's presence in the subsequent course of the story (see 10.178-179// Jer 43:3, 6) while the characterization of him as an important personage helps account for Jeremiah's asking for his release in particular and the Babylonian general's willingness to grant this. The addition likewise sets up a parallelism between the prophet's initiative and that of Josephus himself, who, following the destruction of Jerusalem, requests Titus to free some of his compatriots; see *Life* 418.

[653] This notice, unparalleled in Jeremiah 40, rounds off Josephus' account of the activities of Nebuzaradan, whom he first introduced in 10.144.

[654] This added notice prepares Josephus' subsequent account, based on Jer 40:7-8, of the gathering of the dispersed survivors to Gedaliah.

[655] Greek: καί. Niese brackets this word; if it is eliminated, Josephus would be speaking of a single group of those left behind by the Babylonians, rather than of 2 different groups as in the above translation.

[656] Cf. 10.155, which cites Nebuzaradan's directing the survivors to "cultivate the soil" and thereby meet their obligations to the king.

[657] See Jer 40:7 (MT), where "the captains of the forces in the open country and their men" hear that Gedaliah has been appointed governor and entrusted with the "men, the women, and children, those of the poorest of the land," who had not been taken to Babylon. On Josephus' name for the site ("Masphatha") where the survivors convene to Gedaliah, see note to "Mosphotha" at 10.158.

[658] The 1st leader cited (after the miscreant Ishmael) in Jer 40:8// 2 Kgs 25:23 is called "Johanan" (MT יוחנן; LXX [Jer 47:8] Ἰωανάν), whereas Josephus here names

him Ἰωάδης (subsequently, see 10.164, etc., however, he uses the more biblical form "Joannes") .

[659] MT (Jer 40:8// 2 Kgs 25:23) קרח (Eng.: "Kareah"); LXX (Jer 47:8) Καρῆε; Josephus Κάριος.

[660] MT (Jer 40:8// 2 Kgs 25:23) שריה (Eng.: "Seraiah"); LXX (Jer 47:8) Σαραιά; Josephus Σερέας. Josephus omits the name of Seraiah's father, i.e. "Tanhumeth" (MT).

[661] MT (Jer 40:8// 2 Kgs 25:23) יזניהו (Eng: "Jezaniah"); LXX (Jer 47:8) Ἰεζονίας; Josephus Ἰωαζανίας. Josephus omits the biblical qualification of "Jezaniah" as "the son of the Maacathite" (MT).

[662] With this phrase Josephus encompasses the mention of the "the sons of Ephai the Netophathite," and of the "men" accompanying each of the leaders named in Jer 40:8.

[663] MT (Jer 40:8// 2 Kgs 25:23) ישמעאל (Eng.: "Ishmael"); LXX (Jer 47:8) Ἰσμαήλ; Josephus Ἰσμάηλος. In Jer 40:8 this figure appears 1st in the list of those who come to Gedaliah. Josephus omits the name of his father, i.e. "Nethaniah" (MT).

[664] Josephus anticipates this indication concerning Ishmael's royal status from a later point in the biblical accounts; see Jer 41:1// 2 Kgs 25:25.

[665] Josephus adds this characterization of Ishmael, thereby already imparting a sense of foreboding to his version of the Gedaliah story. The characterization serves to set Ishmael in sharp opposition to Josephus' Gedaliah himself, whom in 10.155 he has qualified as "gentle and just." It further associates Ishmael with Josephus' own arch-rival, John of Gischala, to whom he applies both of the above terms, i.e. "vile" (Greek: πονηρός; see *War* 2.585; 4.213, 389; 5.441; *Life* 102) and "very crafty" (Greek δολιώτατος; see *War* 2.585; 4.208), as is pointed out by Feldman 1998a: 466-7.

[666] MT (Jer 40:14) בעלים (Eng.: "Baalis"); LXX (Jer 47:14) Βεελιας; Josephus Βααλείμ; in 10.164 Josephus calls this king "Baalim."

[667] This "flight" by Ishmael is not mentioned in the biblical accounts. Josephus infers its occurrence from

161 Once they came to him, Gadalias persuaded them to stay for now and not be frightened of the Babylonians.[668] For if they farmed the ground, they would suffer nothing terrible.[669] He assured them of this by oath,[670] saying that they had a protector in him, such that if anyone were in trouble, he would find him [Gadalias] eager [to help].[671] **162** He further advised each of them to settle in whichever ruined city he wished and to send [others] along with his own men, to restore[672] the foundations and to settle there.[673] He predicted that they would procure, while there was yet time, grain and oil and olives so that they might have something to eat during the winter.[674] When he had spoken these things to them, he dismissed them, each to the place in the country that he wished.[675]

Gedaliah addresses leaders

(9.3) 163 When the report spread to the nations[676] around Judea that Gadalias had humanely received those who came to him from their flight and had allowed them to farm the soil and settle,[677] provided that they paid tribute to the Babylonian [king],[678] they[679] rushed together to Gadalias and settled the country.[680]

Jewish refugees join Gedaliah

---

the reference to Ishmael's having been dispatched by the Ammonite king to kill Gedaliah in Jer 40:14—if Ishmael is now being sent by the king, he must have joined him earlier, and the siege of Jerusalem would have provided a suitable occasion for his doing this.

[668] See Gedaliah's opening words to the survivors as cited in Jer 40:9a: "do not be afraid to serve the Chaldeans."

[669] Gedaliah's urging the survivors to "farm the ground" here reflects Nebuzaradan's similar directive in 10.155 (cf. 10.159). Compare the continuation of the governor's exhortation to his visitors in Jer 40:9b: "dwell in the land, and serve the king of Babylon, and it shall be well with you."

[670] This is Josephus' delayed use of the reference to Gedaliah's "swearing to" the assembly with which Jer 40:9 begins.

[671] Josephus expatiates on the promise made by Gedaliah in Jer 40:10a: "As for me, I will dwell at Mizpah, to stand for you before the Chaldeans who will come to us." There is a note of irony to Gedaliah's promise to be a "protector" to the assembled Judeans here, in that subsequently he will be unable to protect even himself against Ishmael's assault.

[672] Greek: ἀνακτίζω. This verb is characteristic of Josephus (*War* 1.155, 160, 166, 200, 416; 3.414; *Ant.* 10.162; 11.9, 12, 84; 14.92; 15.421; *Life* 45), but is extremely rare before his time: in literature it occurs only in Strabo (9.2.5, 32; 13.1.42). I owe this remark to Prof. Steve Mason.

[673] Compare Jer 40:10bβ, where Gedaliah concludes his discourse with the words: "dwell in your cities that you have taken." Here, as in 10.157, Josephus highlights the devastated state of the country.

[674] Compare Gedaliah's words to the assembly in Jer 40:10bα: "but as for you, gather wine and summer fruits and oil, and store them in your vessels." Josephus

supplies a motivation (getting through the winter) for the initiative advocated by Gedaliah.

[675] This "dismissal" of the assembly by Gedaliah at the end of his words to them is not mentioned in Jeremiah 40. The addition serves to explain how it happened, as reported in 40:11, that further Judean survivors came to hear of Gedaliah's appointment, i.e. they did so via the governor's initial hearers, whom he had sent off to settle wherever they see fit.

[676] Jer 40:11a specifies that those who now hear of Gedaliah were the Jews in Moab, among the Ammonites, in Edom and in other lands.

[677] The "report" cited in Jer 40:11b has a more general and less "inviting" character than it does in Josephus' rendering, i.e. merely that Nebuchadnezzar had left a remnant in Judah and appointed Gedaliah governor. Josephus' wording of the report draws on his previous account of Gedaliah's dealings with the first group of survivors in 10.161-162.

[678] The combination of the expressions "farming the soil" and "paying tribute to the Babylonian [king]" here recalls the directive issued by Nebuzaradan in 10.155.

[679] As Marcus (*ad loc.*) points out, Josephus' formulation here evidences carelessness on his part since the referent of its "they" can only be "the nations around Judea," whereas according to Jer 40:11-12a it was not the nations themselves who came to Gedaliah, but rather the Jews who had been living among these nations.

[680] Josephus omits the notice of Jer 40:12b according to which the resettled survivors "gathered wine and summer fruits in great abundance," perhaps on the consideration that the rapid (and violent) course of subsequent events would not have allowed time for this.

Gedaliah
warned about
Ishmael

164 When they had gotten a sense both for the country and the kindness and humanity[681] of Gadalias, Joannes[682] and the leaders with him felt great affection[683] for him.[684] They kept saying that Baalim,[685] the king of the Ammanites, had sent Ismael to kill him deceitfully and secretly,[686] so that he [Ismael] might [assume] rule of the Israelites, for he was of the royal family.[687] **165** They[688] kept saying as well that they would deliver him from the plot if he would give them permission to kill Ismael without anyone knowing [of this].[689] For they stated that they were frightened that his [Gadalias'] murder by him [Ismael] would entail the total annihilation of the surviving Israelites' strength.[690]

Gedaliah
rebuffs warning

166 He, however, declared that he did not believe them in their reporting such a plot on the part of a man who had been well-treated.[691] For it was unlikely that one, who in [a situation of] such great poverty had not lacked for anything of what he needed, would be found to be thus vile and unholy[692] towards him who had benefitted him that he would not only not save him from the wrong plotted against him by others, but would himself be solicitous to seek his [life] with his own hand.[693] **167** But even if these things had to be thought true, it would, he said, be better for him to die by that one's [hand] than to himself destroy a man who had fled to him for refuge and who had entrusted and committed his own safety to him.[694]

---

[681] Greek: χρηστότης καὶ φιλανθρωπία. This combination of nouns applied to Gedaliah recalls Josephus' initial characterization of him as "gentle and just" (Greek: ἐπιεικὴς καὶ δίκαιος) in 10.155, as well as the mention of the governor's "humanely" (φιλανθρώπως) receiving the fugitives in 10.163. Cf. also *Ant.* 8.214, where an equivalent phrase, employing nominalized adjectives (τὸ χρηστὸν καὶ φιλάνθρωπον), is used to refer to what the people (vainly) seek from Rehoboam.

[682] See the note to "Joad" at 10.160.

[683] Greek: ὑπεραγαπάω. Josephus uses this verb of one character's intense love for another also in *Ant.* 1.222 (Abraham for Isaac) and 12.295 (Hyrcanus for his son Joseph); it appears elsewhere in *Ant.* 2.224; 11.132.

[684] Jeremiah 40 does not mention the leaders' sentiments towards Gedaliah. Josephus' added reference to their feelings helps explain their subsequent exertions in warning him about Ishmael and their volunteering to act on his behalf against Ishmael.

[685] Compare 10.160, where the form of the king's name read by Niese is "Baaleim."

[686] Greek κρυφίως. Josephus uses an equivalent form (κρυφαίως) 1 other time, i.e. in *Ant.* 2.219.

[687] Josephus elaborates on the leaders' reference to Ishmael's dispatch by Baalis to kill Gedaliah in Jer 40:13, supplying a motive for this initiative that itself incorporates mention of Ishmael's royal status, a point already cited by him in 10.160, where he anticipates it from Jer 41:1 (// 2 Kgs 25:25).

[688] In Jer 40:15 Johanan alone volunteers to kill Ishmael, doing so after the narrator has noted (40:14b) that Gedaliah did not "believe" the leaders' claims about Ishmael (40:14a). Josephus has the whole group

of leaders offer to do the deed—a more realistic scenario.

[689] Compare Johanan's appeal to Gedaliah in Jer 40:15aβ: "let me go and slay Ishmael..., and no one will know it."

[690] Josephus turns into an affirmation by the leaders Johanan's rhetorical question in Jer 40:15b: "Why should he [Ishmael] take your [Gedaliah's] life, so that all the Jews... would be scattered, and the remnant of Judah would perish?"

[691] Josephus combines the narrative notice of Jer 40:14b ("but Gedaliah. would not believe them") and Gedaliah's word to Johanan in 40:16bβ ("you are speaking falsely of Ishmael") into a statement by the governor in which he adduces a reason for his "disbelief," i.e. the fact that Ishmael had been "well-treated" by himself. Mention of this fact, in turn, serves to heighten the wrongfulness of Ishmael's eventual murder of Gedaliah.

[692] Greek: πονηρὸς καὶ ἀνόσιος. This collocation has a counterpart in *Ant.* 2.22, where Reuben calls the brothers' plan to kill Joseph "vile and unholy to God and humans."

[693] Josephus supplies these further—unfortunately altogether unfounded—considerations that motivate Gedaliah's refusal to "believe" (see Jer 40:14b, 16bβ) the leaders' charges against Ishmael.

[694] This concluding statement by Gedaliah, in which he declines to act on the leaders' proposal even should their charges be true, takes the place of the governor's final response to Johanan in Jer 40:16b: "you shall not do this thing, for you are speaking falsely of Ishmael." Josephus' version highlights the

(9.4) 168 Unable to convince Gadalias, Joannes and the leaders who were with him went away.[695] Following a period of thirty days,[696] Ismael, along with ten men, came to Gadalias at the city of Masphatha.[697] He set a splendid table for them and welcomed them as guests, falling into drunkenness in his lavish [treatment] of Ismael and those with him.[698] **169** Observing him in this state and fallen into insensibility[699] and sleep due to drunkenness,[700] Ismael jumped up along with his ten friends and massacred Gadalias and those reclining with him at the banquet.[701] Following their elimination, they went out by night and murdered all the Judeans in the city and those of the troops who had been left behind in it by the Babylonians.[702]

170 The next day eighty men from the country came to Gadalias with their gifts, who knew nothing of the matters involving him.[703] When he saw them, Ismael called them inside, as if to Gadalias.[704] Once they entered, he closed the main door,[705] murdered them, and cast their bodies down a certain deep cistern, in order that they might be unseen.[706] **171** Some,[707] however, of the eighty men were preserved; these appealed not to be done away before they handed over to him [Ismael] the things

Ismael murders Gedaliah

Fate of Gedaliah's 80 visitors

---

highmindedness of Gedaliah, but also his fatal mis-assessment of the character of Ishmael. On Ishmael's earlier coming to Gedaliah, see 10.160.

[695] This departure of the leaders is not narrated in Jeremiah 40-41, where one is left wondering whether the leaders were on hand for Ishmael's appearance, and if so, why they did not act to protect to Gedaliah, and where it is only after the governor's murder that it emerges that the leaders in fact had not been on the scene (see 41:11, where they "hear" about what has happened).

[696] Compare the chronological indication of Jer 40:1// 2 Kgs 25:25: "in the 7th month."

[697] See Jer 41:1a// 2 Kgs 25:25a.

[698] Josephus elaborates on the summary reference to the 2 parties' "eating bread together" in Jer 41:1b. The expansion accentuates Gedaliah's hospitality, but also his criminal irresponsibility in failing to stay vigilant—also for the sake of all those committed to his care (see 10.155)—in the presence of one about whose murderous intentions he has just been warned. At the same time, the added reference to Gedaliah's "drunkenness" serves to explain how Ishmael and his small band were able so easily to overpower the governor and those around him—Gedaliah was in no state to organize resistance to the assailants.

[699] Greek: ἀναισθησία. Josephus uses this term twice elsewhere, i.e. *Ant.* 2.150 and 4.47.

[700] This added transitional phrase underscores the unscrupulous ruthlessness of Ishmael, who thinks nothing of attacking his helpless host, thereby proving himself to be indeed the "vile and very crafty man" Josephus calls him in 10.160.

[701] This group of persons is not mentioned in the list of those killed by Ishmael in Jer 41:2-3.

[702] See Jer 41:3. Josephus adds the specification that the killings took place "by night," the time when

Ishmael's small band would have more of an advantage in assaulting the (sleeping) Babylonian soldiers. The Josephan detail likewise underlines Ishmael's readiness, here too, to take advantage of his opponents' diminished capacity for self-defense. Ishmael may be "very crafty" (10.160), but he is not at all a hero concerned to fight fairly.

[703] See Jer 41:4-5a, which specifies (v. 5a) that the arrivals came from "Shechem, Shiloh, and Samaria." Josephus leaves aside the description of the 80 as having—for reasons left unexplained—"their beards shaved, and their clothes torn, and their bodies gashed," as well as the biblical indication that they were "bringing cereal offerings and incense to present at the temple of the Lord." His omission of this last item likely has in view the fact that it not does seem to make sense for the travelers to be bringing offerings for a temple that had just been totally destroyed.

[704] See Jer 41:6, from which Josephus omits the allusion to Ishmael's "weeping" as he comes forth to meet the visitors. The Bible does not explain why Ishmael does this, and in any case such weeping might well have alarmed the visitors and thus interfered with Ishmael's plans to get them in his power so that he can murder them too.

[705] Greek: αὔλειον; this is the reading printed by Niese; Marcus reads αὐλήν ("court[yard]") with the codices and Lat.

[706] See Jer 41:7. Josephus represents Ishmael acting alone, whereas in the source he is assisted by his men. He adds the references to the closing of the "door" (or court[yard]; see previous note) and the purpose of Ishmael's casting the corpses down the cistern. He omits the Bible's subsequent, parenthetical allusion (Jer 41:9) to the well in question being one built by King Asa.

[707] Jer 41:8 specifies that the survivors amounted to 10 men.

hidden in the fields, namely implements, clothing, and grain. When he heard this, Ismael spared these men.[708]

Ishmael's captives liberated

172 He took the people in Masphatha captive, along with their wives and infants, among whom were also daughters of King Sacchias, whom Nabouzardan, the Babylonian general, had left behind with Gadalias.[709] Once he had arranged these matters, [Ismael] went to the king of the Ammanites.[710]

173 When Joannes and the leaders with him heard of the things done in Masphatha[711] by Ismael and of the death of Gadalias, they became indignant.[712] Each man taking along his own troops, they hastened to make war upon Ismael, whom they overtook at the well in Ibron.[713] **174** When those who had been taken prisoner by Ismael saw Joannes and the leaders, they were joyful, supposing that he had come to their aid.[714] Abandoning their captor, they went over to Joannes.[715] Ismael therefore fled with eight men to the king of the Ammanites.[716]

Survivors plan to flee to Egypt

175 Joannes, for his part, taking those whom he had rescued from the hands of Ismael along with the eunuchs, the women, and the infants,[717] came to certain place called Mandra.[718] Having stayed there that day,[719] they decided to leave there and set out to go to Egypt,[720] fearing that the remaining Babylonians in the country would kill them in their wrath over the murder of Gadalias, who had been appointed leader by them.[721]

Jeremiah consulted about plan

(9.6) 176 With this in mind, Joannes, the son of Kari, and the leaders who were with him[722] approached the prophet Hieremias. They appealed to him to pray God to show them—who were at a loss concerning this—what they ought to do;[723] they swore as well that they would do whatever Hieremias should say to them.[724]

---

[708] Josephus expands the catalogue of hidden foodstuffs given in Jer 41:8 (wheat, barley, oil, and honey) to encompass other kinds of items.

[709] To the list of those carried off by Ishmael in Jer 41:10a Josephus adds the "wives and infants" of those living at the time in Mizpah.

[710] See Jer 41:10b.

[711] Greek: τὰ ἐν τῇ Μασφαθῇ. This phrase is absent in ROE and bracketed by Niese. Marcus reads it without brackets.

[712] See Jer 41:11. Josephus adds the reference to the emotional effect of the news upon the leaders; compare his likewise added mention of their "feeling great affection" for Gedaliah in 10.164.

[713] MT (Jer 41:12) גבעון (Eng.: "Gibeon"); LXX (Jer 49:12) Γαβαών; Josephus Ἰβρών (this is the reading adopted by Niese and Marcus; Schalit *s.v.* reads the LXX form of the city's name). Josephus omits the biblical reference to the "great pool" at the site.

[714] See Jer 41:13. Josephus supplies the motivation for the captives' joy.

[715] See Jer 41:14.

[716] See Jer 41:15. Neither the Bible nor Josephus explains how Ishmael's original retinue of *10* men (see 41:1// 10.168) has now been reduced to *8*.

[717] From the list of those rescued by the leaders cited in Jer 41:16 Josephus omits "the soldiers," given the reference in 10.169 (// Jer 41:3) to Ishmael's having

killed "the troops who had been left behind by the Babylonians" in Mizpah. The presence of "eunuchs" among Ishmael's captives has not been mentioned previously either by the Bible or Josephus.

[718] MT (Jer 41:17) גרות כמוהם (Eng.: "Geruth Chimham"); LXX (Jer 49:17) Γαβηρωθ Χαμααμ; Josephus Μάνδρα (on the various scholarly proposals concerning this form and its origin, see Begg 2000: 613, n. 50). Josephus omits the biblical indication that the site in question was "near Bethlehem."

[719] Josephus supplies this chronological indication.

[720] See Jer 41:17b.

[721] See Jer 41:18. Josephus supplies the specification concerning the identity of the Babylonians (namely, those who had survived Ishmael's massacre; see 10.169) whom the Judeans fear as well as the reference to the former's presumed "wrath" over Gedaliah's murder.

[722] Jer 42:1 mentions 2 other leaders by name as well as "all the people from the least to the greatest." Josephus keeps attention focussed on the one leader he does name, i.e. "Joannes."

[723] See Jer 42:2-3. Josephus omits the assembly's allusion to their "remnant" status and their opening appeal that their "supplication come before" Jeremiah of 42:2a.

[724] In Jeremiah 42, the assembly's oath of v. 5—whose actual wording Josephus leaves aside—follows

177 The prophet promised that he would minister with God for them;[725] it happened, ten days later, that God appeared to him,[726] to tell him to disclose to Joannes and the other leaders as well as the entire people that, if they stayed in that country, he would stand by them, care for them, and preserve them unharmed by the Babylonians, of whom they were frightened.[727] If, on the contrary, they went to Egypt, he would abandon them and, in his wrath, would inflict on them those same things, "which, as you know, their brothers had previously suffered."[728] **178** When the prophet told these things to Joannes and the people, which God had predicted,[729] they did not believe that it was in accordance with God's command that he was directing them to stay in the country.[730] [They asserted] rather that it was to please Barouch, his own disciple, that he was telling lies in God's [name],[731] by trying to convince them to stay there so that they might be destroyed by the Babylonians.[732] **179** Thus disregarding the counsel[733] of God, which he urged upon them through the prophet,[734] the people and Joannes departed for Egypt, leading both Hieremias and Barouch.[735]

(9.7) **180** Upon their arrival there,[736] the Deity indicated to the prophet that the king of the Babylonians was about to campaign against the Egyptians.[737] He further directed him to announce the capture of Egypt to the people; he [Nabouchodonosor]

Jeremiah's response

Rejecting Jeremiah's word, people go to Egypt

God informs Jeremiah of coming Babylonian

Jeremiah's initial reply to them in v. 4.

[725] Josephus compresses the wording of Jeremiah's positive response to the people in Jer 42:4, omitting in particular his (presumptuous) statement "whatever the Lord answers you I will tell you...," which seems to presuppose that God is bound to provide Jeremiah with an answer.

[726] Compare Jer 42:7, where, after 10 days, it is simply "the word of the Lord" that comes to Jeremiah. On Josephus' penchant for adding divine appearances to biblical accounts of God's speaking, see Begg 1993: 53-54, n. 300; Begg 2000: 32, n. 16.

[727] Josephus abbreviates the extended, positive alternative the Lord sets out for the people in Jer 42:9b-12. Characteristically, he omits God's affirmation about his "repenting of the evil which I did to you" of 42:10b, just as elsewhere he leaves aside biblical references to divine changes of mind.

[728] Josephus compresses the lengthy, highly repetitious divine word concerning the 2nd, negative possibility facing the hearers presented in Jer 42:13-22, where (see v. 21) the people's disregard of God's warning is spoken of as having already occurred. The phrase "those things which... their brothers had already suffered" synthesizes the biblical Jeremiah's repeated references to "the sword, famine, and pestilence" (see vv. 16, 17, 22).

[729] With this notice Josephus conflates the double biblical reference to Jeremiah's conveying the divine message of Jer 42:8-9a (Jeremiah summons Johanan, the commanders, and all the people and says to them) and 43:1 ("when Jeremiah finished speaking to all the

people all the words of the Lord...").

[730] Josephus supplies this editorial notice on the audience's disbelief with their subsequent reply (see 43:2-3) to the prophet in view. The assembly's refusal to believe Jeremiah recalls Gedaliah's disbelief of the leaders' claims about Ishmael in 10.166. In both instances, their disbelief has disastrous consequences for those who adopt such a posture.

[731] Greek: καταψεύδεσθαι τοῦ θεοῦ. Josephus uses this construction of the Jewish false prophets in *War* 6.228 and in formulating Micaiah's affirmation about his being unable to "tell lies in God's name" in *Ant.* 8.404.

[732] See Jer 43:2-3, where Baruch is charged (v. 3) with inciting Jeremiah against the audience with the intention of handing them over to the Chaldeans.

[733] Greek: συμβουλίας; this is the reading adopted by Niese and Marcus; SP read συμμαχίας ("alliance").

[734] Compare Jer 43:4: "so Johanan... and all the commanders of the forces and all the people did not obey the voice of the Lord..."

[735] See Jer 43:5-6, whose wording Josephus compresses.

[736] Jer 43:7b-8a identifies the Egyptian site where the refugees arrive and where God communicates to Jeremiah as "Tahpanhes."

[737] In having God's discourse begin immediately with this announcement (// Jer 43:11a), Josephus passes over the obscure divine directives about the stones that Jeremiah is to conceal and on which Nebuchadnezzar will spread his "canopy" of 43:9-10.

would kill some of them, while others he would lead to Babylon as captives.[738]

181 And this is what happened.[739] For in the fifth year after the demolition of Hierosolyma—this was the twenty-third year of Nabouchodonosor's kingship[740]—Nabouchodonosor campaigned against Coele-Syria;[741] after occupying it, he made war on the Moabites and the Ammanites.[742] **182** Once he had made these nations subject, he invaded Egypt in order to subjugate it.[743] He killed the king of the time, designated another one,[744] and, once again capturing the Judeans who were in it [Egypt], led them to Babylon.[745]

183 And so, we have received [the tradition that] the race of the Hebrews came to such an outcome, having twice gone beyond the Euphrates. For the people of the ten tribes were expelled from Samareia by the Assyrians when Osees ruled as king over them.[746] Then [it was the turn] of [the people] of the two tribes who survived the capture of Hierosolyma under Nabouchodonosor, the king of the Babylonians and Chaldeans.[747] **184** Once Salmanasses had then deported the Israelites, he settled in their place the nation of the Chouthaites, who previously were in the interior of Persia and Media.[748] Thereafter, however, they were called the Samareians, getting this name from the country in which they were settled.[749] The king of the Babylonians, by contrast, once he had led away the two tribes, did not settle any nation

---

[738] Compare Jer 43:11, where God's announcement is that Nebuchadnezzar will "smite" Egypt, handing over some to pestilence, others to captivity, and still others to the sword, and where it is unclear whether it is the fate of the Egyptians or that of the Judean fugitives that is being described. Josephus clarifies that it is the latter group which is in view, likewise adding mention of the place to which the captives will be taken. He leaves aside the extended sequence of additional divine words of doom for both the Egyptians and the Judean refugees of Jer 43:12-44:30.

[739] In this appendix to his presentation of Gedaliah's governorship and its aftermath (10.155-180// 2 Kgs 25:22-26// Jeremiah 40-44) Josephus goes beyond the Bible's narrative accounts in relating (10.181-182) later campaigns of Nebuchadnezzar, whereby he fulfills various biblical prophecies against a variety of nations.

[740] Josephus calculates this figure by combining the dates given in 10.146 (Jerusalem fell in Nebuchadnezzar's 18th year) and 10.181 (the king's later campaigns took place 5 years later).

[741] Cf. *Apion* 1.143, where Josephus avers: "statements like those of Berosus are found in the Phoenician archives, which relate how the king of Babylon subdued *Syria* and the whole of Phoenicia." On the various uses of the designation "Coele-Syria" over time, see Smith (1896: 538) who states: "For Josephus Coele-Syria is all Eastern Palestine, and the only town west of the Jordan which belonged to it was the capital of the Decapolis, Beth-Shan."

[742] For the association between "Coele-Syria" and

the above 2 nations, see *Ant.* 1.206, where Josephus states that the Moabites and Ammanites are both "peoples of Coele-Syria." Josephus may have found inspiration for his notice on Nebuchadnezzar's assault upon the Moabites and the Ammonites in the oracles announcing doom for them of Jeremiah 48 and 49:1-6, respectively.

[743] Josephus now comes to relate the fulfillment of the divine announcement concerning the fate of Egypt cited in 10.180.

[744] This notice is an implicit realization of Jer 44:30, where God announces his intention of giving Pharaoh Hophra "... into the hand of Nebuchadnezzar... who was his enemy and sought his life."

[745] This development fulfills the announcement of 10.180 that Nebuchadnezzar will lead some of the Judeans who had fled to Egypt "to Babylon as captives."

[746] See *Ant.* 9.277-278 (and 10.184) which mention King "Salmanasses" as the one responsible for this deportation.

[747] On this double title, see 10.40, where it is used of the nameless monarch who brings God's punishment upon Manasseh.

[748] See *Ant.* 9.279, 283 for Shalmaneser's initiatives and the (original) name of the people resettled by him in the former territory of Israel.

[749] Compare *Ant.* 9.290, where Josephus states: "(they) are called 'Chouthaioi' in the Hebrew language, whereas in Greek they are called 'Samareitai'."

in their country. As a result, all Judea and Hierosolyma and the sanctuary[750] remained desolate for seventy years.[751]

185 The entire time that elapsed from the captivity of the Israelites until the deportation of the two tribes was 130 years, 6 months, and 10 days.[752]

*Interval
between
deportations*

*Excursus: Josephus on Daniel (*Judean Antiquities *10.186–281)*

Daniel was a figure with immense popular appeal in Jewish circles in Josephus' time
(Collins 1993: 72–89; Mason 1994: 165–167; Neuman 1952–1953), and Josephus
gives more attention to him than to any other "prophet" in the Bible. There is good
reason to believe that Josephus' historical outlook had been significantly shaped by
the Book of Daniel long before he set about writing the *Antiquities* (Bruce 1965;
Mason 1994), and that the Book supplied Josephus with at least one of the central
themes of his entire literary output (*Ant.*10.277–281). More than that, Josephus
seems to have based his own sense of identity and mission on this biblical figure
(Daube 1980; for specific indications of this, see note to "noblest" at 10.186 and
the other passages cross-referenced there). The richness and complexity of the
Daniel traditions in antiquity raises the question of which version or versions of the
story Josephus had access to, and which ones exerted the most formative influence
on his own presentation of this biblical figure.

Of particular interest is the biblical text Josephus may have used. The Book of
Daniel is extant in three major ancient forms: the Masoretic Text (MT) in Hebrew
and Aramaic, the Old Greek or Septuagint (LXX), and the translation of Theodotion
(Θ), also in Greek (a third Greek translation, by Symmachus, is extant only in frag-
mentary form). On the Greek versions of the Hebrew Bible, see Jobes and Silva
2000: 29–44; Swete 1989: 29–58. The relationship of the two main Greek versions
to the MT is highly complex, with first one then the other seeming to adhere more
closely to the MT. In some cases (most obviously in the deuterocanonical additions
to the Book of Daniel: the Prayer of Azariah and the Song of the Three Young Men
inserted after 3:23; Susanna, before chapter 1 in Θ but after chapter 12 in LXX, Bel
and the Dragon after chapter 12) both Greek versions diverge from the MT. For an
excellent discussion of these ancient texts, see Collins 1993: 2–11. In the present
commentary extensive use has been made of Koch and Rösel 2000, which lays out
the ancient versions of the Book of Daniel in synoptic columns.

As to what kind of biblical text Josephus may have used for his own reading of
the Book of Daniel, the evidence is complex (cf. Bruce 1965: 148–51, 160 n. 3;

---

[750] Greek: ναός. This is the reading of LauVELat,
which Niese and Marcus adopt. ROMSP read λαός
("people").

[751] Earlier (see 10.112), Josephus, basing himself on
the concluding element of Jeremiah's announcement in
Jer 25:11, has the prophet predict a 70-year period of
enslavement to the Babylonians for the Jews. Here,
drawing on the allusion to the Jeremiah text in 2 Chr
36:21, he notes the fulfillment of the prophetic word,
at the same time adding a reference to the temple and
its fate. He gives the same figure for the duration of the
Judean exile in *Apion* 1.132, whereas in *Apion* 1.152-
159 he reduces the figure for the period in question to

about 50 years, so as to bring it into line with the data
of other records alluded to by him.

[752] Marcus (*ad loc.*) points out that this figure for
the period between the 2 deportations diverges slightly
from the dates for the regnal years between Hezekiah's
7th year (in which the Israelite deportation took place;
see *Ant.* 9.278) and the 11th year of Zedekiah (in which
the Judean deportation occurred; see 10.135), which
come to a total of *132* years, 6 months, and *20* days.
The figure likewise differs somewhat from that based
on modern computations for the dates of the 2
deportations (722/721 and 587/586, BCE respectively),
i.e. *ca. 135* years.

Feldman 1998: 630 n. 3; Madden 2001: 9–15, 29–76; Vermes 1991: 151–53; on Josephus' biblical text generally, Thackeray 1929: 80–93). Thackeray concludes that Josephus "employed at least two texts, one in a Semitic language, the other in Greek. Sometimes one was used almost to the exclusion of the other: sometimes both were consulted and amalgamated" (81). On the Book of Daniel in particular he states, though without any detailed discussion, "He appears to have used a Greek Daniel combining the peculiarities of the two known versions" (89). Bruce notes that Josephus "shows no knowledge of the deuterocanonical additions found in the Septuagint" (148). Vermes adds that these apocryphal supplements to the story of Daniel—Susanna, the Song of the Three Young Men, and Bel and the Dragon— "are without trace in the Hebrew-Aramaic textual tradition" (Vermes 1991: 150). This could lead us to conclude that Josephus was at least familiar with the main differences between the Hebrew-Aramaic text of Daniel and those found in either of the main Greek versions of the Book of Daniel that have come down to us, and further, that he opted to relate only stories supported by the original Hebrew-Aramaic version. However, it is also possible that Josephus worked from a Greek text (now lost) that contained none of the additional material. Indeed, it seems unlikely that he worked directly from the Hebrew-Aramaic text (though see note to "smaller" at 10.271), as there are a number of affinities between his paraphrase of Daniel and the Greek of both LXX and Θ. In relation to these two ancient Greek versions of Daniel, Bruce asserts that Josephus' narrative has closer affinities with LXX than with Θ, though occasionally he seems to favor Θ over LXX. Vermes supports this conclusion, pointing first to a number of instances in which Josephus follows LXX rather than the text preserved in Θ; e.g. ὄσπρια in *Ant.* 10.190/Dan 1:12; ἔτεσιν in *Ant.* 10.216/Dan 4:16; ἀπὸ τῆς δύσεως in *Ant.* 10.209/Dan 8:5; and πρῶτος τῶν φίλων in *Ant.* 10.263/Dan 3:91, 94; 5:3; 6:14. Numerous other instances where Josephus seems to agree with LXX rather than Θ could be added to this list; see notes at *Ant.* 10.186, 190, 213, 215, 216, 236, 259, 269, and 270. Vermes also notes instances where Josephus seems to agree with the text of Θ rather than LXX: ἅπασαν...τὴν γῆν...πεπληρῶσθαι in *Ant.* 10.207/Dan 2:35; and μάνη, θεκέλ, and φαρές in *Ant.* 10.243–244/Dan 5:26–28 (though on these words in LXX see the notes at 10.243 and 244). Another striking instance where Josephus seems to agree with Θ rather than LXX is *Ant.* 10.239/Dan 5:11, on which see note to "spirit" at 10.239. For other such instances, see also notes at 10.212, 232, 239, 241, 248, and 270. Vermes concludes that "Josephus' Greek Daniel appears to have been a mixture of LXX and Theodotion," (152; see also Thackeray 1929: 89) and further that "[Josephus'] immediate source was a Greek Bible and when the LXX differs from 'Theodotion', [*Ant.*] is more often dependent on the former than on the latter" (161). Vermes (152) notes that Justin Martyr also seems to have used a Greek text that shared characteristics of both LXX and Θ in his *Dialogue with Trypho*. He observes (152) one instance, however, in which Josephus' text (*Ant.* 10.206–214) differs from both LXX and Θ in favor of a reading (ἀνδριάς instead of εἰκῶν) found in Symmachus' version of Dan 2:31.

Josephus may also have had access to traditions about Daniel that are not represented in any of the ancient texts that have come down to us. This may explain his reference to more than one book written by Daniel in *Ant.* 10.267. Outside the biblical book named after him, a "Daniel" appears in Ezek 14:14, 20; 28:3 (though the variant spelling דנאל, "Danel," may indicate a person other than our prophet); *Jub.* 4.20 and the Aqhat legend (*dnil*; see Mason 1994:162, n. 1). The name "Daniel" also appears in Ezra 8:2 and Neh 10:6 but it is unlikely that these are intended to refer to the prophet since they are both in priestly lists. On Daniel's genealogy see note to "Sacchias" at 10.188. For rabbinic legends that Daniel did indeed return from exile to Judea see note to "memorial" at 10.266.

(10. 1) 186[753] When Nabouchodonosor[754] the king of the Babylonians had taken[755] the noblest[756] of the Judean youths, including the relatives of their king[757] Sacchias,[758] who were admirable both for their bodily strength and for their beauti-   *Daniel and his friends are educated in the king's court.*

---

[753] Josephus opens his narrative of Daniel by emphasizing the youths' aristocratic lineage and bearing. Daniel is among those relatives of the Judean king who are outstanding both physically and intellectually. In addition to natural qualities that Daniel possesses, he also receives the best possible education, continues to grow in wisdom, and enjoys the Babylonian king's honor and favor. Josephus' account essentially omits the first two verses of the Book of Daniel, which problematically date the opening scenes of the book to the third year of the reign of King Jehoiakim of Judah, i.e. 605 B.C.E. Josephus, by contrast, connects the story of Daniel to the immediate aftermath of the destruction of the temple in 586 B.C.E. Perhaps the biggest surprise in this section is the insinuation that Daniel may have been among those in the king's court who were castrated.

[754] Ναβουχοδονόσορος with variant spellings: Ναβουχοδονόσαρος (e.g. *Ant.* 10.222), Ναβουχαδανάσσαρος (e.g. *Ant.* 10.220, P; –άσαρος, S), Ναβουχοδονόσωρ (e.g. *Ant.* 10.195, Exc.). MT נבוכדנאצר (Dan 1:1), נבכדנצר (Dan 1:18), נבוכדנצר (Dan 3:1), נבוכדראצר (e.g. Jer 21:2); Θ and LXX have Ναβουχοδονοσορ; Nebuchadnezzar II (var. Nebuchadrezzar; ruled 605–562 B.C.E.), the second king of the Neo-Babylonian empire founded by his father Nabopolassar (Sack 1992d, 4: 1058–59). For notes on Josephus' portrait of Nebuchadnezzar, see Feldman 1993: 52–54.

[755] Josephus implies that the deportation of Daniel and his friends coincided with the end of Zedekiah's reign in 586 B.C.E. (Bruce 1965: 148; Collins 1993: 132 n. 29; Braverman 1978: 64 n. 54). This may have been motivated by a desire to maintain chronological continuity from the end of the previous section of the *Antiquities* to the beginning of the Daniel story. However, the change also enabled Josephus to side-step the chronological difficulty in Dan 1:1, which dates the opening events of the Book of Daniel to "the third year of the reign of King Jehoiakim of Judah" (i.e. 605 B.C.E.). Josephus elsewhere correctly dates the destruction of Jerusalem to the eleventh year of the reign of Zedekiah and the eighteenth year of the reign of Nebuchadnezzar (*Ant* 10.146; cf. Jer 52:29). For a survey of the difficulties associated with Daniel's opening chronology see Collins 1993: 130–33. Madden,

who accepts the chronology of Daniel, suggests that Josephus understood Daniel's deportation to have taken place in 605 B.C.E. in the aftermath of the battle of Carchemish, but has difficulty explaining why Josephus associated the Judean youths with Zedekiah who would not become king until eight years later (Madden 2001: 37). For a summary of the complicated chronology of this period see Cogan 1992, 1: 1008. Josephus makes a similar chronological modification in *Ant* 10.195 (see note to "Egypt" at 10.195)

[756] Josephus' emphasis on the nobility of Daniel and his lineage (see also *Ant* 10.188) parallels the way he describes himself in *Life* 2 and *War* 5.419. Indeed, there are numerous instances throughout his recounting of the story of Daniel where Josephus seems to draw connections between the biblical hero and the way he describes himself in other places. In *Ant.* 10.187 his depiction of the youths' intellectual abilities is reminiscent of the way he describes himself in *Life* 8–9. In 10.190 he uses an expression he will later use of himself as well to describe Daniel's determination to "discipline himself" (cf. *Life* 11). Daniel's aptitude for dream interpretation is akin to Josephus' own in *War* 3.352. In *Ant.* 10.204 Daniel defends the integrity of men described as "noble and good," while in *Life* 13 Josephus claims also to have defended individuals of this description. Finally, Josephus may also have seen a parallel between himself and Daniel in the foretelling of imperial succession (cf. *Ant.* 10.205–210, 270–275 // *War* 3.401; 4.623, 626). For further possible parallels between Josephus and Daniel, see also notes at 10.194, 237, 250, 253 and 268. On this subject see also Daube 1980; Begg 1993; Gnuse 1996: 29–32; Gray 1993: 70–78.

[757] On the genealogy of Daniel and his companions see note to "Sacchias" at 10.188.

[758] Σαχχίας. VE σεδεκίας (In *War* 5. 391 Josephus uses the form Σεδεκίας). Hebrew צדקיהו; LXX Σεδεκιας; Zedekiah (ruled ca. 597–586 B.C.E.). On the derivation of the form Σαχχίας from זכאי, an Aramaic form of צדקיהו, see Schalit 1968 s.v. The king's given name was Mattaniah but it was changed by Nebuchadnezzar, who made him king in place of his nephew Jehoiachin (2 Kgs 24:17), who ruled Judah for only three months (2 Kgs 24:8). He was a brother to Jehoiachim who ruled

ful appearance,[759] he handed*[760] them over to the care of the tutors[761]—after having some of them castrated.[762] **187** And, treating them the same way he did others whom

---

Judah from 609/8–597 B.C.E. (Althann 1992, 6: 1068–71). It is striking that Josephus chooses to associate Daniel and his friends with Zedekiah even though the biblical account passes negative judgements on him (2 Kgs 24:19; 2 Chron 36:12). Josephus himself echoes this perspective in *Ant* 10.103 when he states that Zedekiah "scorned what was just and requisite" (Begg, BJP) and turned a blind eye to outrages committed by the mob. However, in *Ant* 10.120 Josephus refers to Zedekiah's "kindness and personal justice" (Begg, BJP) in his treatment of the prophet Jeremiah. Schalit (1968 s.v.) cites rabbinic tradition (*b. Šabb.* 149b; *b. Moʾed Qaṭ.* 28b and *b. ʿArak.* 17a) that treats Zedekiah as a righteous (צדיק) king. See also Ginzberg 1909–38, 4: 294.

[759] While the biblical text also emphasizes the youths' physical qualities, calling them "young men without physical defect and handsome," (Dan 1:4) Josephus seems to go further in his praise of their physical perfection. As Feldman (1998: 91–93) has shown, this is a common feature of Josephus' portrayal of his biblical heroes; cf. *Ant.* 1.200; 2.9, 41, 98, 224, 230, 231, 232; 5.277; 6.45, 130, 137, 164; 7.189. For similar themes in other ancient literature, see Homer, *Il.* 22.370; Plato *Resp.* 7.535 A11–12; *Phaedr.* 279; Isocrates *Evagoras* 22–23; Dionysius of Halicarnassus *Ant. rom* 1.79.10; Philo *Mos.* 2.14.70.

[760] Josephus omits the role of Ashpenaz (אשפנז; Θ Ασφανεζ; LXX Αβιεσδρι), the chief eunuch, in selecting the Judean youths (Dan 1:3; Vermes 1991: 153), but see note to "Aschanes" at *Ant* 10.190. Vermes suggests that this enhances the status of Daniel and his friends. See also next footnote and note to "renamed" at 10.188.

[761] In Hellenizing fashion, Josephus has the youths' education entrusted to tutors (παιδαγωγοί) rather than to the "palace master" (NRSV) or "chief eunuch" of the biblical narrative (Dan 1:3). In this he may have taken his lead from LXX Dan 1:5, which uses the verb ἐκπαιδεῦσαι, "to educate," for the Hebrew גדל. Θ has θρέψαι, "to nourish." Josephus has ἐπαίδευε in *Ant.* 10.187. On Greek and Roman ideals and practices of education, see Thomas 2003 and Muir 2003. Again, Josephus omits the role of Ashpenaz as the individual in charge of the youths' education at this stage (Vermes 1991: 153, 164), though he does introduce him as the one entrusted with their care at a slightly later point in the story (*Ant* 10.190). See also previous footnote.

[762] Greek ποιήσας τινὰς αὐτῶν ἐκτομίας. Josephus, or the tradition on which he drew, apparently derived this assertion, which is not found in the Book of Dan-

iel, from 2 Kgs 20:18/Isa 39:7—"Some of your own sons who are born to you shall be taken away; they shall be eunuchs (סריסים, LXX σπάνδοντας) in the palace of the king of Babylon." (Bruce 1965: 148; Vermes 1991: 153). In *Ant.* 10.33 Josephus renders this passage: "…after no little time, this wealth of yours will be carried away to Babylon and your descendants, having been made eunuchs (εὐνουχισθησομένους) and deprived of their manhood (ἀπολέσαντας τὸ ἄνδρας εἶναι), will be slaves to the Babylonian king" (Begg, BJP). Commenting on Dan 1:3 Jerome states: "From this passage the Hebrews think that Daniel, Hananiah, Mishael and Azariah were eunuchs, thus fulfilling that prophecy which is spoken by the prophet Isaiah to Hezekiah…." (Jerome, *Expl. Dan.* on Dan 1:3; cited by Braverman 1978: 53). In another place (*Jov.* 1.25) Jerome states: "…the Hebrews, up to the present day, declare that both [Daniel] and the three boys were eunuchs, drawing proof from that sentence of God which Isaiah speaks to Hezekiah….And they argue that if Daniel and the three boys were chosen from the royal seed…and if Scripture predicted that there would be eunuchs from the royal seed…these men were those who were made eunuchs" (cited by Braverman 1978: 63). Jerome's claim concerning Jewish views on this subject is well supported in the rabbinic literature, e.g. *b. Sanh.* 93b; *Pirke R. El.* 52; *Tg. Esth. I,* 4:5 (cited by Braverman 1978: 54–56). A similar tradition is found in Origen, *Comm. Matt.* 15:5 *Fr. Ezech.* 14:16 and *Hom. Ezech.* 14:14 (cited by Braverman 1978: 57). In *Midrash Meg.* 176 Daniel and his friends castrate themselves in order to prove their innocence in the face of accusations of immorality. In *y. Šabb.* 6, 8d the virility of the castrated Daniel and his three companions is miraculously restored in the fiery furnace (Braverman 1978: 54, n. 8; Ginzberg 1909–38, 6: 415 n. 78; Vermes 1991: 153). Feldman (1998: 632) suggests that this tradition would have constituted a delicate problem for Josephus, as it did for the rabbis, because the biblical text states that the youths were "without blemish" (Dan 1:4). Be that as it may, it is difficult to understand why Josephus included the reference at all since it is not found in the book of Daniel itself, nor is it a necessary implication of anything in the biblical text.

Still, Josephus does not explicitly include Daniel and his companions among those who were castrated, though he does not rule out the possibility either. Vermes (1991: 153) notes that in the *Lives of the Prophets* 4.1 Daniel was only *thought* to be a eunuch because of his chastity. In Josephus' summary of the laws of Moses

he had taken in the prime of life from whatever other nations he had subdued,[763] he began to supply them with food from his own table[764] as a regimen[765] and to teach them the local ways[766] and to instruct them in Chaldean[767] literature. And so they began to be adept[768] in the wisdom[769] he directed them to study.[770] **188** And among these there were four of the line of Sacchias,[771] who were by nature[772] both noble

---

he includes the biblical narrative's negative assessment of eunuchs (cf. Deut 23:1): "Turn away from eunuchs (γάλλους) and flee companionship with those who have deprived themselves of their manhood and its fruit.... Banish them just as [you would deal] with a murderer of children" (*Ant.* 4.290; Feldman, BJP). Josephus does not address the issue of whether Daniel and his friends would have been unfit for participation in the temple cult. On attitudes to eunuchs in Greek and Roman society, see Hunt 2003. Hunt cites Herodotus, *Hist.* 3.92 as evidence that Darius I exacted boys for castration as tribute from some subject peoples; see also *Hist.* 8.105; Collins 1993: 134; Madden 2001: 136. See further note to "eunuch" at 10.190.

[763] This line is Josephus' addition. Perhaps he wanted to emphasize the point that deportation was not an ignominy experienced by the Jews alone. In LXX Dan 1:10 Daniel is compared to youths of other nations (νεανίας τῶν ἀλλογενῶν). Josephus has τοὺς ἄλλων ἐθνῶν. For Josephus' views on foreign ethnicities, see Rajak 2001: 137–145.

[764] Josephus reflects LXX and Θ here, both of which have τραπέζης for פַּת־בַּג, "portion,"a Persian loan word that made its way into Greek as ποτίβαζις, which is attested in Athenaeus, *Deipn.* 11.503 (Collins 1993: 127, 139–40 and n. 109).

[765] Greek δίαιτα. On Josephus' use of this term in the present narrative and elsewhere, see note to "regimen" at 10.190.

[766] Greek τὰ ἐπιχώρια, which Josephus distinguishes from τὰ τῶν Χαλδαίων γράμματα. The Hebrew text refers to סֵפֶר וּלְשׁוֹן כַּשְׂדִּים, "the literature and language of the Chaldeans" (Dan 1:4). Θ reads, γράμματα καὶ γλῶσσαν Χαλδαίων, while LXX reads, γράμματα καὶ διάλεκτον Χαλδαϊκήν. In *Ant.* 10.194 Josephus states that the youths mastered all the learning of the Hebrews and the Chaldeans.

[767] Roman readers of this section of Josephus' narrative would presumably have understood the term "Chaldean" to have some connection to ancient Babylonian traditions of astrology, though they may also have thought of the term as having specific ethnic connotations as well. In *Apion* 1.129 Josephus seems to convey both aspects when he describes Berosus as a native Chaldean (ἀνὴρ Χαλδαῖος...τὸ γένος) famous for his writings on astronomy and philosophy. The term could also denote, as it often does in the Daniel stories,

a special profession. In Roman circles opinion was divided between suspicion (e.g. Cicero, *Div.* Book 2; Juvenal *Sat.* 6.554–564), sometimes leading to harsh treatment (Valerius Maximus 1.3.3), and begrudging respect (Diodorus 2.29–31; Tacitus, *Hist.* 2.22); see further Barclay, BJP on *Apion* 1.128, Collins 1993: 137–38 and note to "seers" at 10.195.

[768] The portrayal of Daniel's outstanding intellectual abilities is just one of the ways in which Josephus uses the biblical figure as a type of himself (cf. *Life* 8–9). For other such parallels, see note to "noblest" at 10.186.

[769] Daniel's wisdom is a major motif of Josephus' presentation of the biblical figure (e.g. *Ant.* 10.200, 204, 239, 240). In the present instance, though, σοφία refers more to a body of knowledge mastered by Daniel than to an attribute of Daniel (see also *Ant.* 10.189, 194). Josephus also uses the adjective σοφός for Daniel in *Ant.* 10.237 and classes him among the "wise men" (σόφοι) of Babylon. On this last point, see note to "seers" at 10.195. As in the biblical narrative, Daniel's wisdom in Josephus' paraphrase is "not the gnomic wisdom of Ben Sira, but rather an occult insight into the meaning of dreams and visions" (Mason 1994: 163; see also Collins 1993: 144; Gray 1993: 67–69). Gray notes that "as in the case everywhere in Jewish tradition, this kind of esoteric wisdom is regarded by Josephus partly as an acquired skill and partly as a gift from God" (68). In rabbinic tradition Daniel's wisdom was said to outweigh the combined wisdom of all others (*b. Yoma* 77a; cited by Feldman 1998: 633 n. 10).

[770] The biblical text implies that the Israelite youths were already "versed in every branch of wisdom, endowed with knowledge and insight, and competent to serve in the king's palace" before they were taught "the literature and language of the Chaldeans" (Dan 1:4). It also goes on to say that the youths' education would last three years (Dan 1:5). Josephus omits this reference to the duration of the studies (Vermes 1991: 153), perhaps because of the chronological difficulties it caused; see note to "Egypt" at 10.195.

[771] The Hebrew text, followed by both Θ and LXX, states only that Daniel and his three companions were of the tribe of Judah (Dan 1:6), though the possibility that they belonged to Zedekiah's line is presumably derived from Dan 1:3, where the youths are char-

and good,[773] of whom one was called Daniel,[774] another Ananias,[775] another Misael[776] and the fourth Azarias.[777] These the Babylonian king renamed[778] and ordered that they be called by different names. **189** So they called Daniel Baltasar,[779] Ananias Sedrach,[780] Misael Misach,[781] and Azarias Abdenago.[782] These, making progress because of their exceptional natural qualities[783] and their enthusiasm for their studies and for wisdom,[784] the king held in honor[785] and continued favoring.[786]

---

acterized as coming from "the royal family and of the nobility." In addition to this, 2 Kgs 20:18/Isa 39:7, which Josephus clearly applied to the beginning of the Book of Daniel (see note to "castrated" at 10.186), is addressed to king Hezekiah, and refers to "some of your own sons who are born to you." Josephus explicitly places Daniel and his companions in the royal lineage, and implies later (*Ant.* 10.201) that they were all, in fact, brothers. In Dan 2:17 the three youths are said only to be Daniel's "companions" (חברוהי, Θ: φίλοις; LXX: συνεταίροις). Feldman (1998: 631) following Braverman (1978: 66–68) cites the tradition that while Daniel was from the tribe of Judah, the three companions came from other tribes (*b. Sanh.* 93b; cf. *Pirqe R. El.* 53; Jerome on Isa 39:7). Josephus connects the youths with Zedekiah rather than with Jehoiakim, with whose reign the Book of Daniel begins, in order to side-step the chronological difficulty raised by the reference in Dan 1:1. On this, see further note to "taken" at 10.186.

[772] Greek τὰς φύσεις. On Josephus' treatment of the youths' "natural qualities" see note to "qualities" at 10.189.

[773] Greek καλοί τε καὶ ἀγαθοί. In *Ant.* 10.204 Josephus uses the contracted form καλοὺς κἀγαθούς, on which see note to "noble and good" at 10.204. Marcus (LCL) omits this phrase from his translation even though it is in the Loeb Greek text.

[774] Δανίηλος. Hebrew דניאל; Θ and LXX Δανιηλ. The transcription of names in Josephus' text is a complex matter. In the present translation an editorial decision has been made to omit the standard Greek endings from Josephus' declined forms (-ος, -ης, etc) in cases where such an ending alone would distinguish the form from that familiar in English. Thus, we have "Daniel" in our translation, rather than "Danielos," and "Misael" instead of "Misaelos," and so on. It should be noted, though, that in contrast to the practice of the LXX translators, Josephus deliberately attempted to make the biblical names sound more familiar to Greek readers. In *Ant.* 1.129 Josephus explains his practice concerning names, stating, "For the names have been hellenized for the sake of the beauty of the narrative with a view toward the pleasure of those who come upon it" (Feldman, BJP). One of the effects of this alteration would undoubtedly have been to give the

impression that the biblical figures were themselves hellenized in some way.

[775] Ανανίας. Hebrew חנניה; Θ and LXX Ανανιας; Hananiah.

[776] Μισάηλος. Hebrew מישאל; Θ and LXX Μισαηλ; Mishael.

[777] Αζαρίας. Hebrew עזריה; Θ and LXX Αζαριας; Azariah.

[778] Josephus implies that it was the king himself who renamed Daniel and his companions, while the biblical text attributes this action to Ashpenaz the palace master (Dan 1:3, 7; Vermes 1991: 153). Josephus' version of the story undoubtedly enhances the status of Daniel and his companions (Feldman 1998: 631; Vermes 1991: 164). On similar omissions of the role of Ashpenaz, see notes 760 and 761 above.

[779] Βαλτάσαρος. Hebrew בלטשאצר; Θ and LXX Βαλτασαρ; Belteshazzar. Neither Θ nor LXX distinguishes between the name given to Daniel and the name of the king in Dan 5. Josephus, however, calls the king Βαλτασάρης (*Ant.*10.231). Josephus repeats the changing of Daniel's name in *Ant.*10.212.

[780] Σεδράχης. Hebrew שדרך; Θ and LXX Σεδραχ; Shadrach.

[781] Μισάχης. Hebrew מישך; Θ and LXX Μισαχ; Meshach.

[782] Αβδεναγώ. Hebrew עבד נגו; Θ and LXX Αβδεναγω; Abednego.

[783] Greek εὐφυΐας, natural goodness of shape, shapeliness; also, good natural parts, cleverness, genius, goodness of disposition (LSJ s.v.); natural ability, talents (Rengstorf 1973–1983, s.v.). Feldman (1998: 641) points out that in *Apion* 2.148 Josephus cites Apollonius Molon deriding the Jews for being "the most untalented (ἀφυεστάτους) of all the barbarians." In contrast to such calumnies, Josephus has already claimed that the Judean youths were "by nature" both noble and good (*Ant.* 10.188), and will later represent Nebuchadnezzar marveling at Daniel's nature (*Ant.* 10.211).

[784] See note to "wisdom" at 10.187.

[785] The honor Daniel enjoyed is an important theme in this part of the *Antiquities*, on which see further note to "public" at 10.266.

[786] This statement is an addition to the biblical narrative (Vermes 1991: 153), but see Dan 1: 18–19. In

(2) 190[787] But Daniel, along with his relatives,[788] determined to discipline himself[789] and to abstain[790] from the food[791] from the royal table and from all living things[792]

LXX Dan 1:20 it states that the king appointed them rulers (ἄρχοντας).

[787] In this section Josephus builds on the theme of the youths' superior personal qualities and education by presenting them as individuals dedicated to the kind of disciplined regimen worthy of the most sophisticated philosophers. It also becomes clear in this section that Daniel, far more than being merely intelligent in a conventional way, has a wisdom extending to unusual insight into things of the divine realm. One of the features of this story that perhaps attracted Josephus the most was the experimental nature of the youths' diet and the proof that it seemed to provide of the validity of the Judean way of life.

[788] See note to "brothers" at 10.201.

[789] Greek σκληραγωγεῖν ἑαυτόν. Marcus (LCL) translated the term "to live austerely." S. Mason translates the expression "to live ascetically" (Mason 1994: 169) in the present context, but uses the expression "to toughen himself" in his translation of *Life* 11, which is the only other place where Josephus uses the expression (Mason 2001: 17). In that context Thackeray rendered it with the phrase "to submit to hard training" (Thackeray, LCL; see also Feldman 1998: 642). Significantly, the context of the term's use in *Life* is Josephus' own experience with various philosophical schools, on which see Mason 2001: 18 n. 76. C.T. Begg (1993: 541) finds significance in the fact that Josephus uses the same language to describe Daniel's and his own experience. For other such parallels between Daniel and Josephus himself, see note to "noblest" at 10.186. In Philo's writings (*Spec.* 4.17.102; *Contempl.* 69) the noun form σκληραγωγία is used with reference to the austerity of the Spartans (cited by Satran 1980: 45 n. 12). Mason points out that it was the goal of philosophical training to make a person insensitive to hardships, weakness and desire. It is significant in the present context that Josephus points out that the youths' diet kept their bodies from becoming soft (*Ant.* 10.194). It is also significant to note that Josephus avoids the biblical assertion that Daniel and his friends rejected the king's food and wine for fear of defilement, whether ritual or moral: "But Daniel resolved that he would not defile (גאל; ἀλισγηθῇ) himself with the royal rations of food and wine; so he asked the palace master to allow him not to defile himself" (Dan 1:8; see further Collins 1993: 141–43; Satran 1980: 34). The closest Josephus comes to the theme is in *Ant.* 10.194, on which see note to "uncorrupted" at 10.194. Instead, as we have noted, Josephus provides philosophical reasons for Daniel's

abstention; see further note to "dates" at 10.190 and to "cause" at 10.194. This is particularly striking when seen in contrast to the widespread concern among Judeans in the Second Temple period to avoid dietary defilement; e.g. *Jub.* 22:16; Jdt 10:5; 12:1–2; Tob 1:10–11; 1 Macc 1:61–62; 2 Macc 5:27; Satran 1980:34, 44 n. 4. Josephus' reasons for avoiding the defilement motif may have included a desire to avoid the kind of pagan ridicule of Jewish food scruples reflected in Plutarch's *Quaest. conv.* 4.4.4 (cited by Feldman 1998: 642). Josephus may also have wanted to avoid the explicit condemnation of idolatry sometimes associated with Jewish aversion to gentile food; e.g. Add. Esth C 14:17. At one point in the Book of Daniel (Dan 10:12), in the context of Daniel's mourning and fasting, he is said to have "humbled himself" (התענות; LXX ταπεινωθῆναι; Θ κακωθῆναι) and so to have been heard by God.

Josephus' concept of self-discipline has different connotations. On the connection between self-affliction and visionary experiences in Second Temple literature, see Satran 1980: 36. On the importance of the related concept of ἄσκησις, asceticism, in the Greek philosophical tradition and the later Christian adaptations of it, see Rousseau 2003. In *Apion* 2.171–174 Josephus claims that the Law of Moses uniquely combines rational education (λόγῳ διδασκαλικός) with the training of character (διὰ τῆς ἀσκήσεως τῶν ἠθῶν). The training of morals, moreover, is closely tied to instructions about which kinds of food are appropriate and which are not. See also *Ant.* 1.6. In *Ant.* 20.265 Josephus speaks of the "discipline" (ἄσκησις) of attaining exact knowledge of sacred writings. In *War* 2.150 and *Ant.* 6.296 Josephus speaks of the ἄσκησις, "training," of the Essenes and the Cynics respectively.

[790] Greek ἀπέχεσθαι. The term has significant philosophical connotations, on which see further note to "living things" in this paragraph.

[791] Greek ἐδεσμάτων, meats, food. Josephus does not seem to share the biblical text's concern to specifically include the king's wine in that which was to be avoided (Dan 1:8, 10, 12, 16).

[792] Greek πάντων τῶν ἐμψύχων. The expression is the opposite of τῶν ἀψύχων used later in the same paragraph (see note to "vegetarian" below). In *War* 6.267 Josephus uses the term ἔμψυχοι to refer generally to all living things. The biblical text does not specifically state that Daniel wished to avoid the flesh of living things, though it is perhaps implied by Daniel's request for vegetables and water (Dan 1:12). Later in the Book of Daniel (Dan 10:3) the prophet relates how

in general. Approaching Aschanes[793] the eunuch[794] who had been entrusted with their care, he appealed to him when receiving the food provided for them from the king to consume it himself,[795] and to supply them instead with lentils[796] and dates[797]

---

during a time of mourning he abstained from meat and wine. More significantly, abstention from animal food was part of a well established theme in a philosophical tradition running at least from Plato in the fourth century B.C.E. till Porphyry in the third century C.E. (Satran 1980: 36–37). In his *Laws* Plato provides a description of the Orphic way of life which is characterized by abstention (ἀπεχόμενοι) from animal (ἐμψύχων) food in favor of non-animal (ἀψύχων) food *Leg.* 782 C-D. Porphyry, for his part, wrote an entire treatise originally entitled Περὶ Ἀποχῆς Ἐμψύχων (*On Abstinence from Animal Food*). Apollonius of Tyana, a contemporary of Josephus, whose *Life* was written by Flavius Philostratus in the third century, epitomized the Pythagorean virtues of abstention from animal food (*Vit. Apoll.* 6.11; 8.5). These were, of course, not the only voices on the subject of animals in the ancient world. A significant debate centered on whether or not animals possessed a rational soul, and thus whether or not they should be accorded justice. Aristotle denied reason to animals, as did the Stoics and the Epicureans, while others, especially the Neopythagoreans, argued otherwise. On these issues see further Sorabji 2003. Josephus refers to animals as "irrational" (ἄλογος) in *War* 4.170; 6.197; *Ant.* 10.262; *Apion* 1.224; 2.213; 271. The last two of these references are particularly significant because they speak of the Jews' kind treatment of animals (on which see also *Ant.* 4.275). *Ant.* 10.262 is of interest because it speaks of irrational animals having insight into the morality of humans. In contrast to the philosophical concern about eating that which is ἔμψυχος, Philo speaks of the Therapeutae's concern for eating that which was ἔναιμος (*Contempl.* 73), "containing blood," which is a reflection of the Hebrew Bible's prohibition against eating blood (e.g. Gen 9:4; Lev 3:17; 7:26–27; 17:10–14; 19:26; Deut 12:16, 23–25; 15:23; Beckwith 1988: 408–9). Josephus reflects these concerns in *Ant.* 1.102 ("For I have made you lords of all creatures...but without blood...for the soul is in it" [Feldman, BJP]), and 3.260 ("He prohibited the use of all blood for food...considering it to be the soul and the spirit" [Feldman, BJP]). Note in particular the connection between blood (αἷμα) and soul (ψυχή) in these passages.

[793] Ἀσχάνης. The biblical text distinguishes between the palace master (רב סריסים, Dan 1:3, שר הסריסים, Dan 1:7, 9; LXX ἀρχιευνοῦχος), called Ashpenaz (אשפנז; Θ Ασφανεζ; LXX Αβιεσδρι, Dan 1:3), who refuses Daniel's request for a special diet despite the fact that God had allowed Daniel to receive favor

and compassion from this individual (Dan 1:9), and "the guard" (המלצר) appointed to care for Daniel and his companions (Dan 1:11), who complies with the request on a trial basis. Θ treats the latter term as a proper noun (Αμελσαδ, with variants Αμελσαρ, Αμερσαρ, Αμελλασαρ, Αμεσαδ, Αμελσαλ, Αμελασαδ, αμαλεσαδ, Αμελδαδ, etc.), while LXX and Josephus treat the two palace officials as the same person (Vermes 1991: 154).

[794] Josephus uses the term εὐνοῦχος for the Hebrew סרים, "eunuch" (cf. the various terms in the previous footnote), but which often refers to high military and political officials without the necessary implication of emasculation. In Jer 39:3 it applies to the officials of the king of Babylon, and in Gen 39:1 the term is used of Potiphar even though he is married (Collins 1993: 134–135; Schneider 1964, 2: 766). On the etymology of the term and its various uses, see also Madden 2001: 40–41. On the possibility that Daniel and his companions were castrated, see note to "castrated" at 10.186.

[795] This statement is an addition to the biblical narrative.

[796] Greek ὄσπρια. The term may refer to any kind of pulse or legumes including fava beans, lentils, and chickpeas. Satran (1980: 38–39, 46 n. 16) points out that Josephus' retention of this item in the youths' diet does not fit well with his otherwise complete transformation of Daniel into a Greco-Roman sage, since beans generally were not considered an appropriate part of a philosopher's diet because of their tendency to cause flatulence. Cf. Empedocles in Diels 1934: 1.368; ch. 31 (21) no. 141; Tertullian *De anima* 48.3. For ancient medical and philosophical attitudes to the consumption of beans, see Arbesmann 1949–1951: 25 nn. 89–91. Feldman (1998: 642 n. 30) notes that Josephus may have felt constrained by the Greek biblical text to include ὄσπρια, and reflects further that readers in antiquity might not have identified pulse with beans, for which a different word (κύαμος) is used.

[797] The MT has זרעים at Dan 1:12 and זרענים at Dan 1:16, both of which are hapax legomena (Satran 1980: 34). According to Goldingay 1987: 6 the terms, which derive from "seeds," (*BDB* 281–283) could refer to vegetables, grain and non-meat products generally. Θ has σπέρματα "seeds," while LXX has ὄσπρια (see previous footnote). The Vulgate renders the terms *legumina*. Josephus has ὄσπρια καὶ φοίνικας, "lentils and dates." In the context of Levitical dietary legislation it is the characteristic dryness of this food that renders it clean even under adverse conditions (cf. Lev 11:37–38; Satran 1980: 34). Josephus' inclusion of

for sustenance and whatever other vegetarian[798] food he might wish. For they were drawn to[799] this regimen[800] but disdained others.[801] **191** And Aschanes said he was prepared to comply with their proposal,[802] but suspected that when it was discovered by the king from the leanness of their bodies and the change in their appearance, which would be especially clear in comparison with the flourishing of the other youths—for their bodies and complexions would certainly change along with their regimen[803]—, they would be to blame for the danger and punishment he faced.[804] **192** Therefore, since Aschanes was responding cautiously about this, they persuaded* him to supply them with these foods for ten days[805] as an experiment; if the condition of their bodies had not changed he should keep doing the same, since

---

dates in the youths' diet would seem to be in keeping with a certain philosophizing tendency, because dates were a well-known favorite food of Pythagorean philosophers (Mason 1994: 169; Satran 1980: 38); cf. Flavius Philostratus, *Vit. Apoll.* 1.21; 2.26. For other philosophizing aspects of Josephus' portrait of Daniel, see notes at 10.194.

[798] Greek τῶν ἀψύχων, non-animal; see also note to "living things" above. Vegetarianism was also a defining characteristic of the Therapeutae according to Philo (*Contempl.* 37, 73), and Judith's diet consisted of roasted grain, dried fig cakes and bread (Jdt 10:5). In *Life* 14 Josephus highlights the piety of certain priests whose commitment in adverse circumstances included subsisting on a diet of figs and nuts. On this incident see further Mason 2001: 23 n. 103. On motivations for vegetarianism in antiquity, see Beckwith 1988: 407–10.

[799] Greek κεκινῆσθαι, to be stirred up, aroused, urged on, LSJ s.v.

[800] Josephus uses the term δίαιτα here and throughout this episode (*Ant.* 10.187, 191, 192) to refer to the youths' choice of food, or diet, but as Satran as aptly noted, "the choice of food is not only a matter of taste or nourishment but a question of outlook and values" (Satran 1980: 45 n. 13; also Feldman 1998: 634, 644). Thus, while it is clearly the specifics of food that are in the forefront of the present episode, the broader implications of the story relate to Daniel's way of life in general (see also *Ant.* 15.371 where δίαιτα is used of the Essenes' "way of life," which is similar to that taught by Pythagoras; also *War* 2.137, 138, 151, 160). At other points in the biblical narrative, Josephus uses the term with a wide range of meaning, e.g. "abode/dwelling/residence" (*Ant.* 1.336, 345; 8.225; 9.5, 18), "fare/rations/food/eating" (*Ant.* 2.39, 61; 3.57, 78; 6.34; 7.114; 8.134; 11.178), "customs" (*Ant.* 2.257), "arbitration" (*Ant.* 3.69), "household items" (*Ant.* 2.297). In the sense of "way of life" Josephus uses the term at *Ant.* 3.278; 5.306, 344; 10.216 and 242. In an instructive comparison to Daniel, Josephus comments

on the young Samson's "frugality of regimen" (περὶ τὴν δίαιταν σωφροσύνης *Ant.* 5.285; cf. *Apion* 1.182), which was one of the early indications that the youth was destined to become a prophet. Later in the same context it was precisely Samson's abandonment of his own rule of life (τὴν οἰκείαν δίαιταν) in favor of foreign customs (ξενικῶν...ἐθισμῶν) that proved to be the beginning of his decline (*Ant.* 5.306). In *Apion* 2.174 Josephus claims that Moses' laws cover both the food eaten in infancy and "the private life of the home" (κατὰ τὸν οἶκον...διαίτης).

[801] In *Ant.* 4.137, where he relates the story of Midianite (bibl. Moabite) women who seduced Hebrew youths to follow strange gods (cf. Num 25), Josephus puts in the mouth of these women the charge that the Hebrews "follow customs and a way of life that is most contrary to everyone else, even as your food is of a peculiar type and your drink is not common to others" (Feldman, 2000; see also 4.139). Strikingly, Josephus accepts this characterization as true, though without accepting the libelous insinuation that Jewish food scruples imply misanthropy of any kind. On this incident see further Spilsbury 1998: 127–29; van Unnik 1974. In *Ant.* 3.259–260 Josephus gives a much abbreviated list of laws concerning unclean foods.

[802] Josephus omits the biblical statement that "God allowed Daniel to receive favor and compassion from the palace master" (Dan 1:9).

[803] Greek δίαιτα. See note to "regimen" at 10.190.

[804] Greek αἴτιοι κινδύνου καὶ τιμωρίας αὐτῷ καταστῶσιν, literally "they would become the causes of danger and punishment for him." LXX has κινδυνεύσω τῷ ἰδίῳ τραχήῳ, "I will endanger my own neck."

[805] Collins (1993: 144) notes that the setting of a specific time limit is in continuity with the visions of the second half of the Book of Daniel, which set specific times for their predictions. In *Ant.* 10.267 Josephus highlights the specificity of Daniel's prophecies as indicative of his superiority over other prophets.

no further harm would be done to it. But if he should observe that they had grown thinner and were faring worse than the others, he could put them back on their former regimen.[806] **193** And since not only did nothing harm them when supplied with that food, but their bodies were better fed and starting to get bigger than the others, it came about that those to whom the royal food was provided seemed to lack more, while those with Daniel seemed to be living in abundance and complete luxury.[807] After that Aschanes began fearlessly to take for himself[808] the food that the king habitually sent every day from his table to the youths, and continued to provide them with the food described above. **194** And so they readily mastered all the learning[809] among the Hebrews[810] and the Chaldeans,[811] their souls[812] having become pure and uncorrupted[813] for learning because of this [regimen],[814] and their

---

[806] Greek δίαιτα. See note to "regimen" at 10.190.

[807] Josephus embellishes the biblical narrative which states simply that "they appeared better and fatter than all the young men who had been eating the royal rations" (Dan 1:15).

[808] The biblical narrative states only that the guard "continued to withdraw" the unwanted food and drink (Dan 1:16; Vermes 1991: 154). Nevertheless, a similar theme appears in the *Testament of Joseph* (3.4) where after a seven-year period of fasting Joseph "seemed to the Egyptian as if living in luxury, for those who fast for the sake of God receive grace of countenance" (cited by Satran 1980: 42).

[809] The biblical text reads: "To these four young men God gave knowledge (מדע; Θ: σύνεσιν; LXX: ἐπιστήμην) and skill (השכל; Θ: φρόνησιν; LXX: σύνεσιν) in every aspect of literature (ספר; Θ: γραμματική; LXX: γραμματικῇ τέκνῃ) and wisdom (חכמה; Θ: σοφία)" (Dan 1:17).

[810] The variant reading in LauELat reads βαρβάροις instead of Ἑβραίοις. *Ant.* 10.187 refers to the youths learning both "the local ways" and "Chaldean literature."

[811] C.T. Begg (1993: 541) suggests that Daniel's mastery of both Hebrew and foreign learning constitutes a similarity been Josephus' portrayal of Daniel and his own self-presentation (cf. *Ant.* 20.263). For other such parallels, see note to "noblest" at 10.186.

[812] In this passage Josephus reflects a bipartite view of the human person made up of body (σῶμα) and soul (ψυχή). See also *War* 1.84; 2.31, 60, 136, 357, 476, 580; *Ant.* 13.317; 15.251; 17.238; 18.333; 19.325; etc. Josephus expresses a similar view in his speech against suicide at Jotapata: "All of us...have mortal bodies (σώματα θνητά), composed of perishable matter (φθαρτῆς ὕλης), but the soul lives forever, immortal: it is a portion of the Deity housed in our bodies" (*War* 3.372; Thackeray, LCL; cf. *Ant* 6.3). In *War* 7.341–348, however, Josephus has Eleazar use a similar understanding of the soul in relation to the body to argue *in favor* of suicide. Josephus ascribes a similar view of

soul and body to the Essenes in *War* 2.154: "For it is a fixed belief of theirs that the body is corruptible and its constituent matter impermanent, but that the soul is immortal and imperishable" (Thackeray, LCL). On these passages see further Mason 1991: 158–70; Smith 1987: 238–9. On Josephus' views on the afterlife, see Sievers 1998. In *Ant.* 4.153 Josephus comments on Phinehas' courage of both soul and body (τόλμη δὲ καὶ ψυχῆς καὶ σώματος ἀνδρείᾳ; cf. *Ant.* 4.298; 6.375; 15.158; *War* 1.429–430; 2.476, 580), while in *Ant.* 6.160 God distinguishes between "comeliness of body" (σωμάτων εὐμορφίας) and "virtue of soul" (ψυχῶν ἀρετῆς). A different, tripartite, perception is reflected in *Ant.* 1.34 where Josephus nuances the biblical account of creation by saying that "God fashioned humanity, taking dust from the earth, and he injected breath [or "spirit," πνεῦμα] and soul into him" (Feldman, BJP). Similarly, in *Ant.* 3.260 in his description of the biblical prohibition against eating blood (Lev 17:11; Deut 12:23), Josephus states that Moses "prohibited the use of all blood for food...considering it to be the soul and the spirit" (Feldman, BJP). On this understanding even animals would have to be considered body, soul, and spirit. Wis 15:11 also uses the three-fold division as does 1 Thess 5:23. This understanding has roots in the classical tradition (e.g. Plato *Resp.* 4.439 D-E; *Phaedo*; see Jacob 1974, 9: 608–17). The tripartite composition of humanity can also be found in *Lev. Rabbah* 32.2 and *Eccl. Rabbah* 10.20 (cited by Feldman 2000: 13 n. 59). In *Ant.* 11.240 "spirit" and "soul/life" are virtually equivalent, while in *Ant.* 15.190 Josephus uses a tripartite designation of "soul and body and substance" (ψυχῆς καὶ σώματος καὶ περιουσίας).

[813] The expression καθαρῶν...καὶ...ἀκραιφνῶν is the closest Josephus comes to the theme of purity and defilement that characterizes this story in the biblical narrative (cf. Dan 1:8; see further note to "discipline himself" at 10.190), though even here cultic or ritual defilement is not in view. Elsewhere in Josephus' biblical paraphrase (*Ant.* 1.23) he uses the term

bodies having become more vigorous for hard work,[815] for neither were the former dragged down and made heavy[816] by a variety of foods, nor were the latter made softer[817] by the same cause.[818] And Daniel especially, already being sufficiently adept in wisdom,[819] had applied himself zealously to the interpretation[820] of dreams,[821] and the deity[822] was becoming known[823] to him.

ἀκραιφνής to speak of the "purity" of God's virtue (ἀρετή; cf. *Ant.* 18.288), while in *Ant.* 17.238 he uses the same term to describe Herod's "unimpaired" reason. In *Ant.*18.366 the term is used of soldiers who are "fresh," or "well rested" for battle.

[814] Dan 1:17 attributes the youths' progress in learning directly to God (see note to "learning" at 10.194).

[815] Josephus' description of the youths here is reminiscent of Moses' description of the Israelites as those "who scorn labors and who have trained [their] souls in virtue" (*Ant.* 4.460 Feldman, BJP).

[816] Apollonius of Tyana expounds the virtue of a lighter diet in Philostratus' *Vit. Apoll.* 8.5. Significantly, this diet is cited as the cause of the philosopher's ability to predict the future.

[817] The toughening of the youths' bodies is a result of their decision to discipline or toughen themselves (cf. *Ant.* 10.190). In *Ant.* 10.215, where Josephus relates the story of the youths being thrown into the fiery furnace, he states that God made their bodies too strong to be consumed by the fire.

[818] Here Josephus provides the philosophical rationale for the youths' choice of diet—a rationale that enables Josephus to avoid the issue of defilement explicit in the biblical text (Dan 1:8). Satran refers to Josephus' argument here as "a classic description of that balance of physical and mental training which becomes synonymous with the philosophic existence" (1980: 37). He cites Plato, *Resp.* 9.571D–72B; *Leg.* 6.782C–D and Philostratus, *Vit. Apoll.* 1.21; 2.26 as examples. See also Cicero, *Div.* 1.53.121 (cited by Feldman 1998: 643 n. 31). Seth Schwartz speculates that Josephus has Daniel use the same kind of rationale that Jews in similar situations in Josephus' day (including Josephus himself) actually did use (Schwartz 1990: 182 n. 35). The rabbis based Daniel's actions on considerations of piety rather than those of health (*b. 'Abod. Zar.* 36a; cited by Feldman 1998: 644).

[819] See note to "wisdom" at 10.187.

[820] Dan 1:17 states, "Daniel also had insight into all visions (חזון) and dreams (חלמות)." LXX refers to Daniel's understanding of ὁράματι καὶ ἐνυπνίοις, while Θ has πάσῃ ὁράσει καὶ ἐνυπνίοις. The ability to interpret dreams was an important aspect of Josephus' presentation of his own identity in the *Judean War* (3.352). On other such parallels between Josephus himself and Daniel, see note to "noblest" at 10.186.

Besides Daniel and himself, only Josephus' biblical namesake, Joseph (*Ant.* 2.9–17, 63–90) and the Essenes (*War* 2.158; *Ant.* 13.311–312; 15.373, 379; 18:20) are presented as interpreters of dreams (Mason 1994: 177). On parallels between Josephus' presentation of himself and various biblical figures, especially Joseph, Jeremiah, and Daniel, see further Daube 1980; Begg 1993; Gnuse 1996: 29–32; Gray 1993: 70–78.

[821] Josephus seems to have been particularly drawn to dreams and their interpretation. Gnuse (1996: 181) has noted that in contrast to his extensive treatments of the dreams in the first half of the Book of Daniel, Josephus pays little attention to the visions of the latter half of the book. In the present context Josephus uses the term ὄνειρος for "dream," instead of ἐνύπνιον, which is used by both LXX and Θ throughout the Book of Daniel. Josephus does use ἐνύπνιον five times in his Daniel narrative (*Ant.* 10.196, 198 [twice], 202, 217), but favors the term ὄναρ, which he uses a total of eleven times (*Ant.* 10.195 [three times], 196, 200, 203 [twice], 205, 208, 211, 216) in the story of Daniel. ὄνειρος, which is used in the present context, is used again in *Ant.* 10.234. Gnuse (1996: 17–18) treats ὄναρ and ὄνειρος as synonyms, stating that "the two terms function together as one word in common usage, not only in Josephus but in Greek literature in general" (18; see also Oepke 1967, 5: 221; Gray 1993: 59–60). Elsewhere in the biblical paraphrase Josephus uses ἐνύπνιον only in the story of Pharaoh's dream (*Ant.* 2.75), while in *Apion* it is used of dubious dreams at 1.207, 211, 294, 298 and 312. Mason, following Oepke 1967, 5: 221, suggests that Josephus "already seems sensitive to Artemidorus' distinction [see *Onir.* 1.1b] of ἐνύπνιον from ὄνειρος on the criterion that the former refers to an insignificant dream, whereas the latter signifies an event susceptible of interpretation" (Mason 1994: 170; see also Gray 1993: 60–64). In *Ant.* 10.199 and 216 Josephus uses ὄψις ("vision") as a synonym for "dream," while in *Ant.* 10.234 and 272 the "vision" is not associated with sleep. On Josephus' use of the language of dreams and the historical context, see further Gnuse 1996: 17–20; Gray 1993: 58–79; Oepke 1967, 5: 220–238; Price 2003.

[822] Greek τὸ θεῖον. Josephus uses this term for God six times in his retelling of the story of Daniel (*Ant.* 10.194, 242, 250, 258, 260, 262), and many times throughout his writings. More often throughout he uses θεός. Versnel (2003) notes that τὸ θεῖον became an equi-

Nebuchadnezzar **(3) 195**[824] After the second year from the sack of Egypt,[825] when King Nabou-
forgets his
dream

valent for θεός, which from Herodotus onwards could be used to account for occurrences that could not be explained by natural causes (see also Kleinknecht 1965, 3: 122). In *Ant.* 10.241 Daniel refers to his prophetic gift as that which is "wise and divine" (τὸ...σοφὸν καὶ θεῖον). Earlier in the same context Belshazzar had acknowledged the "divine spirit" (τὸ θεῖον...πνεῦμα) which attended Daniel (*Ant.* 10.239). See further Smith 1987.

[823] Greek φανερὸν, "visible, manifest, known." This statement is an addition to Scripture. Josephus, however, omits the biblical assertion that the king found the four Judean youths to be "ten times better than all the magicians and enchanters in his whole kingdom" (Dan 1:20). It is possible that Josephus found the statement too inflated, or perhaps he wanted to avoid any implication that the youths dabbled in magic. The overall impact of Josephus' portrait of Daniel is that it presents him as an illustrious Jewish philosopher (Mason 1994: 169). As Satran points out, "the disciplined pursuit of purification has brought Daniel to the supreme achievement of the Greco-Roman sage—the movement from human to divine wisdom" (Satran 1980: 38). It is possible that Josephus was prodded in this direction by a Greek text similar to the one in LXX Dan 1:20, which states that Daniel became ten times wiser than all the "sages and philosophers" (τοὺς σοφιστὰς καὶ τοὺς φιλοσόφους) in the kingdom. In the narrative that follows Josephus often implies that Daniel had achieved a level of existence, or access to the divine, not normally associated with mere mortals; e.g. *Ant.* 10.196, 204, 215, 237, 239, 264, 267. On similar themes in the Greco-Roman world at large, see Bieler 1935–1936; Hengel 1974: 210–18.

[824] Except for the chronological adjustment at the very beginning of this episode (see next footnote), Josephus adheres fairly closely to the biblical narrative in this section. Josephus apparently was drawn to the story's palpable demonstration of Daniel's skills as an interpreter of dreams, and he makes sure to take the opportunity to heighten the dramatic elements within the story.

[825] The notice in Dan 2:1 that places Nebuchadnezzar's dream of the great statue in the second year of the king's reign has long caused biblical commentators difficulties. These difficulties are connected to the fact that Dan 1:5 and 18 imply that Daniel has already been in the king's court for three years by this point in the narrative. Numerous attempts have been made to explain or rectify the discrepancy including, for example, the variant reading in Chester Beatty Papyrus 967 of LXX that reads "twelfth" instead of "second"

(cited by Vermes 1991: 154). Collins 1993: 154–5 surveys various proposed solutions to the problem. *S. 'Olam Rab.* 28.124 dates the dream to two years after the destruction of the Temple. For other rabbinic and patristic solutions, see further Braverman 1978: 72–76. Josephus was clearly also aware of the difficulty, perhaps because of the reason stated above, but also because in his own reconstruction of the chronology of events he has already implicitly synchronized the deportation of the Judean youths with the end of Zedekiah's reign (*Ant.* 10.186 and note to "taken" there). By this reckoning Daniel could not have come into Nebuchadnezzar's custody until the eighteenth year of his reign. Thus, Josephus tries to avoid the chronological difficulty by dating the events "after the second year from the sack of Egypt." Just which event Josephus is referring to here is not clear, but there is reason to believe that Josephus saw the events of the Book of Daniel as following immediately after the fall of Jerusalem and the destruction of the temple in 586 B.C.E. What is more, he linked these events to Nebuchadnezzar's defeat of the Egyptian army described by Berosus (see *Ant.* 10.220–222; *Apion* 1.135–137; on which see note to "satrap" at 10.220). In doing this Josephus was in error because the Berosus passage actually deals with events surrounding the Battle of Carchemish between Nebuchadnezzar and Necho II of Egypt in 605 B.C.E. However, it seems clear from references to the destruction of the temple in *Apion* 1.132 and 145, both before and after his citation of Berosus' account of the Battle of Carchemish, that Josephus read it as applying directly to the events of 586 B.C.E. If this is indeed the case, then Josephus' reference in the present instance to "the sack of Egypt" is most likely connected to the statement in Berosus about Nebuchadnezzar "settling the affairs of Egypt" (*Apion* 1.137//*Ant.* 10.222). It should be noted, too, that on this reading Josephus would have taken the Judean captives in the Berosus passage (*Ant.* 10.222; *Apion* 1.137) to be a reference to the group that included Daniel and his companions. When we look at Josephus' account of the events leading up to the final fall of Jerusalem we find an extra-biblical account of a battle between Nebuchadnezzar and the Egyptians who were attempting to rescue Zedekiah's Jerusalem from the Babylonians' siege (*Ant.* 10.110). This event, though not attested in the Hebrew Bible (but see Jer 37:7, cited by Marcus 1937: 218 n. a), roughly corresponds to the end of Zedekiah's reign and the destruction of Jerusalem, and may be the same event that Josephus refers to in our present passage as "the sack of Egypt." It is perhaps relevant in this regard to remember that

chodonosor had an amazing[826] dream whose interpretation God himself made clear to him[827] in his sleep, he forgot* it[828] when he got out of bed. So, after summoning the Chaldeans and the magi and the seers,[829] and telling them that he had seen a certain dream and that he happened to have forgotten what he had seen, he directed them to tell him both what the dream was and its meaning.[830] **196** But when they

---

some rabbinic exegetes, who also discerned the chronological difficulty in the biblical passage, assigned the events in this story to the second year after the destruction of the temple. Madden (2001: 47) argues that the "sack of Egypt" in *Ant.* 10.195 refers to the Battle of Askelon (603 B.C.E) since this city was under Egyptian rule at the time. The main difficulty with this suggestion is that it falls foul of the fact that Josephus coordinates Daniel's deportation with the end of Zedekiah's reign (586 B.C.E.); see *Ant.* 10.186.

[826] Greek θαυμαστός. The biblical narrative indicates that the dreams (plural) troubled the king's spirit and deprived him of sleep (Dan 2:1). The same is said of Pharaoh in Gen 41:8.

[827] The claim that God revealed the interpretation of the dream to Nebuchadnezzar in the dream is an addition to the biblical narrative motivated, perhaps, by the need to explain how the king would have recognized the correct interpretation when he heard it. Similarly, in his paraphrase of the story of Pharaoh's dream in the time of Joseph (*Ant.* 2.75/Gen 41:1–8), Josephus states that the king had been given the explanation of his dream in his sleep along with the dream itself, but that he forgot the explanation.

[828] "It" refers to the dream (the demonstrative adjective is masculine/neuter, whereas the word for "interpretation" is feminine). The biblical narrative does not say that the king *forgot* the dream (or its interpretation). The king states, rather, "I have had such a dream that my spirit is troubled by the desire to understand it." The implication of the biblical story seems to be that the king withheld the dream from the wise men as a test to see if they really did have insight into such things; see especially Dan 2:9. Feldman (1993: 52; 1998: 645–6) suggests that Josephus' version of the story presents a more favorable, less capricious, picture of the king.

[829] Josephus uses the terms Χαλδαῖοι, μάγοι, and μάντεις for those the king expected to be able to interpret the dream. The biblical terms are "magicians (חרטמים; Θ and LXX: ἐπαοιδούς), enchanters (אשפים; Θ and LXX: μάγους), sorcerers (מכשפים; Θ and LXX: φαρμακούς), and the Chaldeans (כשדים; Θ: Χαλδαίους; LXX has the expression φαρμακούς τῶν Χαλδαίων)" (Dan 2:2). Later in the story (*Ant.* 10.197) Josephus refers to these people collectively as "wise men" (οἱ σόφοι; cf. Dan 2:12) and a little later as σόφοι, Χαλδαῖοι,

and μάγοι (*Ant.* 10.198). Twice in *Ant.* 10.198–199 he uses μάγοι as a collective term for the whole group, and once he uses μάγοι and Χαλδαῖοι. In *Ant.* 10.203 Josephus apparently includes Daniel among the Χαλδαῖοι and μάγοι. In *Ant.* 10.234 the magi and Chaldeans are referred to as "all of those among the Babylonians who were able to interpret signs and dreams." The term μάντεις occurs nowhere else in Book 10 of the *Antiquities*. Elsewhere in the *Antiquities* the term is used of Balaam (*Ant.* 4.104, 112) and the diviners expelled from the land by King Saul (*Ant.* 6.327, 331). In this context they are classed alongside ventriloquists (ἐγγαστριμύθοι), but distinguished from the prophets (οἱ προφῆται). In *War* 1.79–80 and *Ant.* 13.311–313 μάντις is used of Judas the Essene who correctly predicted the murder of Antigonus, while in *War* 2.112 and *Ant.* 17.345 it is used of certain individuals skilled in interpreting dreams. When the related terms μαντεία and μαντικός are considered, the references include the Egyptian seers (*Ant.* 2.241; *Apion* 1.236, 256–258, 267, 306), the witch of Endor (*Ant.* 6.330–331, 338), a seer in Alexander's army (*Apion* 1.203–204), the emperor Tiberius (*Ant* 18.217, 222), the Delphic oracle (*Apion* 2.162), and soothsayers in general (*War* 2.112; *Ant* 17.345; Gnuse 1996: 32). In *War* 4.625 Vespasian refers to Josephus' own μαντεί-αι, i.e. "predictions," and Josephus uses the related term προμαντεύσαιτο for himself in *War* 3.405. On Josephus' use of this terminology, see Blenkinsopp 1974: 246–7; Gray 1993: 107–10. On another note, S. Mason (1994: 182–3) has observed that the only other context in Josephus' writing in which the terms μάντεις and Χαλδαῖοι appear along side each other is *War* 2.111–113 in which the story is told of Archelaus' dream of nine ears of corn being eaten by oxen. In addition to the story's obvious echo of the Joseph story in Gen 41:2–4, Mason argues that it provides evidence that Josephus already had the Book of Daniel in mind as he wrote the *Jewish War*. The significance of this point is discussed at length by Bruce (1965: 153–60) and Mason (1994: 178–90). See also note to "wise men" at 10.197.

[830] Collins (1993: 155) points out that the assembly of interpreters is a familiar scene in dream reports of Persian kings; see Herodotus, *Hist.* 1.106; 7.19; Cicero, *Div.* 1.23.46.

said[831] that it was impossible for humans to discover this,[832] and that if he would describe the details of the dream to them they would promise to explain its meaning, he threatened them with death[833] unless they would tell the dream. And when they admitted that they were unable to do what was directed, he ordered all of them to be executed.[834] **197** But when Daniel heard that the king had ordered all the wise men[835] to be killed, and that along with them he and his relatives[836] were also in danger,[837] he approached* Arioch,[838] who was entrusted with the command of the king's bodyguards.[839] **198** And when he asked to learn from him the reason why the king had ordered all the wise men and Chaldeans and seers[840] to be executed, Daniel learned the matter about the dream, which, although he had forgotten, they had been ordered by the king to explain to him, and that when they had said that they were not able to do it they had enraged him.[841] So Daniel appealed to Arioch[842] to go in[843] to the king and to ask for one night[844] for the magi[845] and to delay the

---

[831] Josephus omits the biblical statement that the Chaldeans spoke to the king in Aramaic (Dan 2:4), nor does he indicate that this marks the beginning of the section of the MT (Dan 2:4–7:28) that is in Aramaic. On the presence of Hebrew and Aramaic in the earliest layers of the textual tradition of the Book of Daniel, see Vermes 1991: 149.

[832] Here Josephus condenses the words of the biblical Chaldeans: "There is no one on earth who can reveal what the king demands! In fact, no king, however great and powerful, has ever asked such a thing . . . . The thing that the king is asking is too difficult, and no one can reveal it to the king except the gods (LXX τι ἄγγελος; Θ θεοί), whose dwelling is not with mortals" (Dan 2:11). In *Ant.* 10.204 Josephus has Daniel himself affirm that what the king demanded was not within human abilities to perform. In *Ant.* 10.237 and 239 Daniel is described as privy to knowledge not normally accessible to mortals.

[833] Josephus greatly condenses the biblical king's threats and promises of reward (Dan 2:5).

[834] Josephus omits the direct discourse between the king and the Chaldeans in this section (Dan 2:5–11)

[835] Greek τοὺς σοφούς. On Josephus' use of this term, see note to "seers" at 10.195. Mason (1994: 185) has drawn a connection between this reference, along with the description in *Ant.* 10.267 where Daniel is described as the prophet who specified not just what would happen in the future but also the time (καιρόν) at which it would happen, with *War* 6.313. This last refers to an "ambiguous oracle" found in the sacred scriptures "to the effect that at that time (κατὰ τὸν καιρὸν ἐκεῖνον) one from their country would become ruler of the world," but which many of their wise men (τῶν σοφῶν) misinterpreted. Mason adduces this as further evidence that Josephus' presentation of the Judean war was deeply influenced by his reading of the Book of Daniel.

[836] See note to "brothers" at 10.201.

[837] Jerome reports the concern of Jewish commentators to explain why, if Daniel and his friends had not been initially a part of the group who had been unable to explain the king's dream, they should share their punishment (*Expl. Dan.* on Dan 2:12–13, cited by Braverman 1978: 77). Jerome's answer to the question is that Daniel and his friends were too modest to put themselves forward or to grasp at the rewards offered by the king. Nevertheless, the Chaldeans, because of their envy, were only too happy to have the Judean youths share in their peril. Josephus comments similarly on Daniel's aversion to rewards (*Ant.* 10.241, 251) and the envy of his enemies (*Ant.* 10.212, 250, 256).

[838] Ἀριόχης. MT אריוך; Θ: Αριωχ; LXX: Ἀριώχης.

[839] Dan 2:14 uses the term רב־טבחיא; Θ and LXX: ἀρχιμάγειρος, chief of the royal guard. The NRSV renders the term "chief executioner." In the next verse Arioch is referred to as שליטא די־מלכא, "royal offical" (Θ: ἄρχων τοῦ βασιλέως).

[840] On Josephus' use of these terms, see note to "seers" at 10.195.

[841] Josephus characteristically, and somewhat tediously, repeats the main elements of the story he has just told, rather than follow the example of his biblical precursor which states simply, "Arioch then explained the matter to Daniel" (Dan 2:15).

[842] In the biblical narrative Daniel makes the request directly to the king (Dan 2:16). Feldman (1998: 648) suggests that Josephus wanted to avoid the impression of brazenness on the part of Daniel.

[843] In the biblical narrative Daniel himself "goes in" to make his request of the king. Daube (1980: 28–29) has suggested that Josephus' adaptation of the narrative so as to include an intermediary between Daniel and the king reflects Josephus' own use of an intermediary in order to get his "prophecy" heard by Vespasian (*War* 3.399). The suggestion is not entirely compelling.

[844] The biblical Daniel requested that the king "give him time" to interpret the dream (Dan 2:16). Josephus

execution for this long, for he hoped in that time to discover the dream by asking God.[846] **199** Arioch reported to the king what Daniel was requesting. And he directed* [him] to delay the execution of the magi[847] until he knew [the outcome of] Daniel's undertaking.[848]

Then, after retiring to his own house, the young man together with his relatives[849] begged* God all through the night[850] to reveal[851] the dream and to rescue from the king's anger the magi and the Chaldeans,[852] along with whom they too would of necessity be destroyed, by displaying to him and making clear the vision that the king had seen in his sleep the previous night but had forgotten. **200** Then God, having mercy[853] on those in danger and at the same time honoring[854] Daniel for his wisdom,[855] made known[856] to him both the dream and its interpretation, so that the king too might learn from him what it meant.[857] **201** And when Daniel came to know

Daniel prays for insight

---

heightens the drama of the episode by implying that Daniel had but a single night to come up with the interpretation.

[845] On Josephus' use of this term, see note to "seers" at 10.195.

[846] Josephus supplies the motivation only implicit in the biblical narrative (Dan 2:16).

[847] On Josephus' use of this term, see note to "seers" at 10.195.

[848] This sentence is Josephus' own expansion of the biblical narrative.

[849] See note to "brothers" at 10.201.

[850] This is an addition to the biblical narrative.

[851] Greek γνωρίσαι, "to reveal [the dream]." A variant reading in MSPExc has σῶσαι, "to save," while E reads ἐλεῆσαι, "to have mercy."

[852] Josephus' Daniel is more concerned for the welfare of the magi and Chaldeans than the biblical counterpart; cf. Dan 2:18 (Feldman 1998: 645). On Josephus' use of the terms "magi" and "Chaldeans," see note to "seers" at 10.195.

[853] In Dan 2:18 Daniel instructs his companions "to seek mercy from the God of heaven concerning this mystery."

[854] The Greek term ἀγασάμενος is the aor. part. mid. masc. nom. sg. of either ἄγαμαι ("to admire") or ἀγάζω ("to honor"). Rengstorf (1973–1983, s.v.) does not list the latter possibility, and Marcus (LCL) clearly opted for ἄγαμαι. Nevertheless, the idea that God honored Daniel's wisdom is perhaps to be preferred over the notion that God admired him. For this usage see also Pindar, *Nem.* 11.6. I am grateful to Steve Mason for this suggestion.

[855] This statement is typical of Josephus' tendency to aggrandize the major biblical characters in general (see Feldman 1998: 74–131), and of his tendency to emphasize the wisdom of Daniel and his companions in particular (see further note to "wisdom" at 10.187).

In Dan 2:20 Daniel praises God "for wisdom and power are his." In 2:21 he states that God "gives wisdom to the wise and knowledge to those who have understanding. He reveals deep and hidden things; he knows what is in darkness, and light dwells with him." Daniel concludes his praise with the acknowledgement: "for you have given me wisdom and power" (Dan 2:22). Josephus picks up on this aspect of the story in *Ant.* 10.203, where he has Daniel humbly insist that he is not in fact wiser than the Chaldeans and magi, but rather the recipient of God's mercy.

[856] It is at this point (Dan 2:19) that Θ first uses the verb ἀποκαλύπτω, "to reveal," for the Aramaic גלה, גלא. Θ uses the same word again at 2:22, 28, 29, 30, 47 and 10:1 (the usage in 11:35 is a mistranslation). In none of these instances, or anywhere in Daniel, does LXX use ἀποκαλύπτω, but rather ἀνακαλύπτω (2:22, 28, 29), δείχνυμι (10:1), δηλόω (2:47), or ἐκφαίνω (2:19, 30, 47). Josephus, too, never uses ἀποκαλύπτω in his Daniel narrative or, indeed, in his paraphrase of the Bible. When he does use the term it is only in a non-theological sense (*War* 1.297; 5.350; [6.209]; *Ant.* 12.90; 14.406). The terms he prefers in the Daniel narrative include γνωρίζω (*Ant.* 10.199), δείκνυμι (*Ant.* 10.205, 270, 277), δηλόω (*Ant.* 10.195, 198, 201, 202, 205, 208, 210, 218, 234, 235, 243, 244 [twice], 245, 254, 272, 273, 274), ἐπιδείκνυμι (*Ant.* 10.271), μηνύω (*Ant.* 10.195, 239, 241), and σημαίνω (*Ant.* 10.200, 208, 213, 214, 216, 238, 239, 241, 243, 244, 245, 259, 270, 272 [twice]). Bilde 1998 has shown that these terms indicate that Josephus was indeed very much interested in themes and concerns associated with "apocalypticism" despite his avoidance of the technical term ἀποκαλύπτω. On Θ's use of ἀποκαλύπτω in Daniel see Collins 1993: 159.

[857] Cf. Dan 2:30 "… in order that the interpretation may be known to the king and that you may understand the thoughts of your mind."

these things from God he arose* joyfully and, telling it to his brothers,[858] who had already despaired of life and whose thoughts were set on dying, he aroused them to cheerfulness and hope of life.[859] **202** And after giving thanks[860] with them[861] to God for taking pity on their age,[862] he went to Arioch at daybreak[863] and asked him to take him to the king, for he wanted to explain to him the dream that, he related, he had seen two nights previously.[864]

Daniel interprets the king's dream

(4) 203[865] When he entered the king's presence, Daniel first begged the king's leave that he should not esteem him wiser than the other Chaldeans and magi[866] because none of them had been able to discover the dream whereas he himself was* about to declare it.[867] For this happened* neither on the basis of skill nor because he had worked out the meaning better than they, "but because God had mercy on us[868] who were in danger of dying after I pleaded concerning my own life and that of my fellow-nationals,[869] and he made clear both the dream and its interpretation. **204** For no less than my distress that we ourselves had been condemned by you not to live was my concern about your own reputation, since you had thus unjustly condemned men to die,[870] and these noble and good,[871] of whom you ordered things not acces-

---

[858] The idea that the four young men were brothers (ἀδελφοί) is Josephus' embellishment of the story. He has already implied that they all belonged to the royal lineage of King Zedekiah (*Ant.* 10.186, 188), and in *Ant.* 10.190, 197, 199, 212 and 214 he calls them "relatives" (συγγενεῖς). In Dan 2:17 the three youths are said to be Daniel's "companions" (חברוהי, Θ: φίλοις; LXX: συνεταίροις).

[859] Daniel's joy and the despair of his friends, along with Daniel's words of encouragement to them are additions to the biblical narrative. Josephus heightens the psychological dimensions of the story and seeks to increase the sense of tension and drama. Feldman (1998: 635) has pointed out further that this scene is reminiscent of Aeneas' attempts to raise the flagging spirits of his men in Virgil's *Aeneid* 1.198–207.

[860] Thus Josephus summarizes the content of the biblical Daniel's hymn of praise to God (Dan 2:20–23).

[861] The participation of the friends is an addition to the biblical narrative.

[862] The biblical narrative does not highlight the youthfulness of Daniel and his friends at this point. Josephus alludes to their youthfulness to increase readers' sympathy with the protagonists.

[863] "Daybreak" is not explicit in the biblical narrative.

[864] Literally, "before the preceding night."

[865] Of all the accounts of dreams and visions in the Book of Daniel only this one gets anything like a full treatment by Josephus. While this may well have something to do with Josephus' not wanting to repeat dreams and visions that he may have taken to be referring to the same things, it would still probably be fair to say that Nebuchadnezzar's dream of the statue

was of enormous personal importance for Josephus. Among other things, it seems to have exerted a formative influence on his understanding of the ebb and flow of world history.

[866] Josephus implies that Daniel is to be understood as belonging to the same group as the Chaldeans and the magi. On these terms see further note to "seers" at 10.195.

[867] The biblical Daniel's modesty takes a slightly different form from Josephus'. In Dan 2:27 Daniel says to the king: "No wise men, enchanters, magicians or diviners can show to the king the mystery that the king is asking, but there is a God in heaven who reveals mysteries …." The biblical Daniel does go on to affirm that his knowledge of the dream and its interpretation are in no way to be attributed to his own wisdom (Dan 2:30), but Josephus' Daniel emphasizes God's mercy in responding to his prayer. On the importance of the virtue of modesty throughout Josephus' biblical narrative, see Feldman 1998: 112–3.

[868] Josephus switches from third person to first person part way through the sentence necessitating the introduction of quotation marks.

[869] The reference to God's mercy on Daniel and his friends is an addition to the biblical narrative at this point, but it echoes the biblical Daniel's instructions to his friends that they should "seek mercy from the God of heaven…so that Daniel and his companions with the rest of the wise men of Babylon might not perish" (Dan 2:18).

[870] The concern for the king's honor (δόξα, "the opinion which others have of one, estimation, reputation, credit, honor, glory," LSJ s.v.) and the implied criticism of his petulance is an addition to the biblical

sible to human wisdom—for you were demanding from them that which was from God.[872] **205** In any case, while you were worrying about who will rule the world after you,[873] you fell asleep, and because God desired to reveal to you all who will rule[874] he showed you a dream like this: **206** you imagined seeing standing a huge[875] image of a man,[876] of which the head happened to be of gold,[877] the shoulders and arms[878] of silver, the belly and thighs of bronze, and the legs and feet of iron.[879] **207** Then a stone that had been broken off from a mountain[880] fell upon the statue[881] and

---

narrative; but see Θ Dan 2:15 where Daniel asks Arioch why the king's decree is so "shameless" (ἀναιδής). Feldman (1998: 646) sees this as part of a pattern of presenting the king in a more favorable light than does the biblical narrative. Tomasino (1995: 235) sees this as an example of Josephus' presentation of Daniel as "the ideal collaborator," someone whom the monarch may trust implicitly to look out for his interests. Similarly, Madden 2001: 49. Tomasino argues further that in presenting Daniel in this way Josephus was seeking to justify his own association with the Romans.

[871] Greek καλοὺς κἀγαθούς. Marcus (LCL) has "fine and excellent men." Feldman (1998: 646) suggests the translation "perfect gentlemen." Mason uses "gentlemen" throughout his translation of *Life* (BJP *Life* 13, 29, 256). In his discussion of the expression Mason (2001: 22 n. 97) points out that it was already a proverbial way of referring to those who were simply honest and decent (e.g. Aristophanes, *Eq.* 184, 227, 735; *Lys.* 1060; Herodotus *Hist.* 1.30; 2.144; Isocrates, *Soph.* 13.6; *Antid.* 15.316; Lucian *Patr. Enc.* 3) on the one hand and, more specifically, to those of aristocratic class (Diogenes Laertius 3.88), on the other. In philosophical discourse the expression took on the weightier connotation of moral perfection (e.g. Aristotle *Mag. Mor.* 1207b.2.9.2–5). See further LSJ s.v. καλοκἀγαθος. In the present context Josephus applies the expression to "the Chaldeans and magi" generally, though one may discern a certain emphasis on Daniel and his friends within that group. In *Ant.* 10.188 Josephus uses the uncontracted form καλοί τε καὶ ἀγαθοί of Daniel and his companions. Begg (1993: 542) has noted a similarity between Josephus' Daniel and Josephus' self-presentation in that he too claims to have defended individuals described as καλοὺς κἀγαθούς (*Life* 13). For other such parallels between Daniel and Josephus, see note to "noblest" at 10.186.

[872] Josephus follows the biblical narrative in emphasizing the point that insight into dreams is a divine prerogative; e.g. Dan 2:10–11, 21–23, 27–28, 47. Josephus several times emphasizes the point that, unlike the wise men of Babylon, Daniel is indeed privy to divine knowledge (*Ant* 10.194, 196, 237, 239).

[873] Josephus supplies the psychological detail which explains the subject matter of the king's dream.

For Josephus the king's thoughts and the dream are apparently of a purely political nature. In the book of Daniel the king is troubled by the dream itself (Dan 2:1), though we are not told why it came to him. Later we are told that the king had been given thoughts of "what would be hereafter" (Dan 2:29) and that God had revealed to the king what will happen "at the end of days (באחרית יומיא; Θ and LXX: ἐπ' ἐσχάτων τῶν ἡμερῶν)" (Dan 2:28). Josephus does not convey the eschatological flavor of this expression.

[874] God's desire is an explanation supplied by Josephus.

[875] Josephus does not follow the biblical narrative's emphasis upon the fearsomeness of the image: "This statue was huge, its brilliance extraordinary; it was standing before you, and its appearance was frightening" (Dan 2:31).

[876] Josephus uses the term ἀνδριάς throughout this section (*Ant.* 10.206–214) rather than εἰκών used by both LXX and Θ for the Aramaic צלמא. Vermes (1991: 152) points out that Symmachus' version of Dan 2:31 twice uses the same term as Josephus. On Josephus' use of a Greek text of the Book of Daniel see the *Excursus* at the beginning of this section (*Ant.* 10.186).

[877] Dan 2:32: "fine gold."

[878] Dan 2:32: "chest and arms;" Θ: αἱ χεῖρες καὶ τὸ στῆθος καὶ οἱ βραχίονες ("the hands and the chest and the arms"); LXX: τὸ στῆθος καὶ οἱ βραχίονες ("the chest and the arms")

[879] Dan 2:33 states that while the statue's legs were of iron, its feet were partly of iron and partly of clay. See further notes to "kings" and "bronze" in 10.208 and 209 respectively.

[880] In MT the stone is not at first (Dan 2:34) described as coming from a mountain, but is described that way in the interpretation in Dan 2:45. In LXX and Θ the stone comes from a mountain in both passages. The Book of Daniel also states that after destroying the statue, the rock became a great mountain that filled the whole earth (Dan 2:35). In *4 Ezra* 13, which is dependent on the Book of Daniel, the mountain stands for Zion. Josephus omits the significant phrase in Dan 2:34 to the effect that the stone "was cut out, not by human hands." The image of a mountain was an important motif in the prophetic literature of the Hebrew Bible,

after knocking it down crushed it, leaving no part of it unbroken, so that the gold and the silver and the bronze and the iron became finer than flour;[882] and when the wind blew more violently they were carried off by its force and scattered.[883] But the stone grew so large that the whole earth seemed to have been filled by it.[884] **208** So that is the dream that you saw, and its interpretation is in this vein:[885] The golden head was indicating both you and the Babylonian kings who were before you.[886] But the hands[887] and the shoulders signify that your sovereignty is to be destroyed by two kings.[888] **209** But a different one from the west[889] wearing bronze will put down their rule,[890] and yet another like iron will bring its power to an end,[891] and

---

e.g. Isa 2:2; Mic 4:1. The same is true the ancient Mesopotamia generally; cf. Collins 1993: 165, n. 128.

[881] The biblical narrative specifies that the stone struck the statue on its feet (Dan 2.34).

[882] Greek ἀλεύρων λεπτότερον. LXX states that the crushed statue became λεπτότερον ἀχύρου "finer than chaff," while Θ has ὡσεὶ κονιορτὸς "like dust." MT states that the crushed pieces became "like the chaff (כעור) of the summer threshing floors" (Dan 2:35). Josephus reverses the order of metals given in Dan 2:35, which starts from the bottom of the statue.

[883] The biblical image of the chaff of the summer threshing floors being blown away (Dan 2:35) would seem to be more coherent than the picture Josephus suggests of the flour being blown away. Josephus apparently intended to emphasize the violence of the scene.

[884] Josephus' phrase (ἄπασαν...τὴν γῆν ὑπ' αὐτοῦ πεπληρῶσθαι) is closer to Θ (ἐπλήρωσεν πᾶσαν τὴν γῆν, "filled the whole earth"), than to LXX (ἐπάταξε πᾶσαν τὴν γῆν, "struck the whole earth"), here. The picture of the world-filling stone is reminiscent of the prophecies of Balaam who in Josephus' account predicted the world-wide dispersion of the Jewish people so that "all land and sea will be filled with the glory surrounding them, and there will be enough of you for the world to supply every land with inhabitants from your race" (*Ant.* 4.115, Feldman, BJP). On this passage as the key to interpreting Josephus' understanding of the stone in Nebuchadnezzar's vision, see Spilsbury 2003: 17–20; also Bilde 1998: 52–55.

[885] Josephus' account of the interpretation follows the pattern common from the first century C.E. onward; so Bruce (1965: 148). For a summary of the history of ancient interpretation, see Rowley 1964: 70–137.

[886] Dan 2:37–38 states that the head of gold represents Nebuchadnezzar alone, while Josephus has it that the head symbolizes all the Babylonian kings down to Nebuchadnezzar (Vermes 1991: 155). Josephus omits the biblical Daniel's fulsome praise of the king: "You, O king, the king of kings—to whom the God of heaven has given the kingdom, the power, the might and the glory, into whose hand he has given human

beings, wherever they live, the wild animals of the field, and the birds of the air, and whom he has established as ruler over them all—you are the head of gold" (Dan 2:37–38).

[887] A textual variant in SPLauVELatZon has "two hands." Only Θ specifically mentions the statue's hands (Dan 2:32). Cf. note to "arms" at 10.206.

[888] The biblical text attaches no significance to the fact that the statue has two hands and shoulders. Josephus' rendition makes it clear that the second kingdom is to be understood as the 'partnership' of Cyrus the king of Persia and Darius the Mede (*Ant.* 10.232). Josephus omits the biblical statement (Dan 2:39) that the second kingdom will be inferior to the first. Josephus may have wanted to avoid the implication that the kingdoms grew successively weaker, since in his view the fourth kingdom was Rome. Josephus also omits the biblical reference to the statue's feet being made of iron mixed with clay; see further notes at 10.206 and 209.

[889] Greek ἀπὸ τῆς δύσεως. The biblical text contains no reference to the third kingdom being from the west. Josephus apparently borrowed this detail from the vision of the male goat in Dan 8:5 which comes "from the west" (מן־המערב, ἀπὸ δυσμῶν in LXX, but ἀπὸ λιβὸς ["from the southwest wind"] in Θ). Josephus presumably identified the third kingdom of the statue with the third beast that came up from the sea in Dan 7:6. Hippolytus made the connection in *Comm. Dan.* 1–3 (cited by Madden 2001: 53). This beast had four wings of a bird and four heads. These details in turn may have suggested a connection with the male goat in chapter 8 since it moved "without touching the ground," (8:5) and later grew "four prominent horns" (Dan 8:8; Goldingay 1987: 209; Madden 2001: 53). In any case, Josephus clearly implies that the third kingdom of the statue is to be understood as Alexander's (Bruce 1965: 149; Mason 1994: 171; Vermes 1991: 155). See further note to "from there" at 10.270.

[890] Josephus will relate later in his narrative how Alexander the Great himself read the prediction in Scripture that "one of the Greeks would destroy the

this one will dominate everything[892] because of the nature of iron—for it is stronger than gold and silver and bronze."[893] **210** And Daniel also explained to the king about the stone,[894] yet it seemed to me proper not to recount this, being obligated to record past events and things that have happened[895] but not what is about to happen.[896] But

---

empire of the Persians" (*Ant.* 11.337).

[891] In Josephus' reading the iron kingdom is Rome. In *Ant.* 10.276 Josephus states explicitly that Daniel "wrote about the empire of the Romans." In the rabbinic tradition, *Exod. Rab.* 35.5 also identifies the fourth kingdom with Rome (cited by Vermes 1991: 155 and Feldman 1998: 649 n. 38). In *Ant.* 15.385–387 Josephus makes explicit the sequence of the four empires: Babylon, Persia, Macedonia, Rome. On the four-kingdom schema in the Book of Daniel and other literature in the Hellenistic and Roman periods, see Collins 1993: 166–170; Flusser 1972.

[892] Greek κρατήσει δὲ εἰς ἅπαντα. The present translation is to be preferred over that of Marcus (LCL) "will have dominion forever." See also Fischer 1987: 179; Mason 1994: 172 and Lindner 1972: 44 ("und sie wird herrschen über alles"). Josephus clearly did not believe in the perpetual rule of the iron kingdom: it is destroyed by the stone along with the rest of the statue; see further Spilsbury 2003: 15–16. In the biblical vision the phrase "which shall rule over the whole earth" (די תשלט בכל־ארעא; Θ and LXX: ἣ κυριεύσει πάσης τῆς γῆς) is applied to the third (bronze) kingdom (Dan 2:39). Josephus used the phrase εἰς ἅπαντα in *Ant.* 4.114 to speak of God's word-wide alliance with the Hebrew people, though both Thackeray, LCL ("perpetual"), and Feldman, BJP ("for eternity"), translate the phrase in a temporal sense.

[893] Josephus takes over from the biblical text the reference to the destructive power of the fourth kingdom: "just as iron crushes and shatters everything, it shall crush and shatter all these" (Dan 2:40). LXX adds καὶ σεισθήσεται πᾶσα ἡ γῆ, "and the whole earth will be shaken." However, Josephus omits the biblical detail that the fourth kingdom would be a divided kingdom (Dan 2:41), a mixture of iron and clay (Dan 2:33, 41), which Daniel interpreted to mean that this kingdom "shall be partly strong and partly brittle" (Dan 2:42). Josephus also makes no reference to the biblical implication (Dan 2:43) that the fourth kingdom's weakness was due to mixing in marriage. Such marriages are mentioned again in Dan 11:6, 17 where they apparently refer to inter-dynastic marriages between the Ptolemies and Seleucids. On this issue see Collins 1993: 170–1 and the literature cited there. Josephus' primary concern seems to have been to avoid any implication of weakness in the fourth kingdom, Rome (Bruce 1965: 149). Mason (1994: 185) suggests that

Josephus may have derived the wholly iron kingdom by conflation of the vision in Dan 2 with the vision of the fourth beast in Dan 7:7, which is described as "terrifying and dreadful and exceedingly strong. It had great iron teeth and was devouring, breaking in pieces, and stamping what was left with its feet." If this is correct, it provides us with evidence that Josephus had in fact reflected on Dan 7, even though there is no other evidence of this chapter in Josephus' biblical paraphrase. On Josephus' reasons for omitting chapter 7, see note at beginning of 10.263. See also note to "about" at 10.267. On rabbinic interpretations of the fourth beast of chapter 7 as Rome, see Braverman 1978: 90–94.

[894] Dan 2:44–45: "And in the days of those kings the God of heaven will set up a kingdom that shall never be destroyed, nor shall this kingdom be left to another people. It shall crush all these kingdoms and bring them to an end, and it shall stand forever; just as you saw that a stone was cut from the mountain not by hands, and that it crushed the iron, the bronze, the clay, the silver, and the gold." Jerome noted that "the Jews and the impious Porphyry" believed the stone to be the Jewish people (Collins 1993: 171). *4 Ezra* 13:6 and 36 seem to fit Porphyry's observaton (cf. Fischer 1978: 180 and n. 68). Ginzberg (1909–38, 6: 415 n. 80), cites rabbinic interpretations of the stone as the Messiah: *Tanh.* [Buber] 2.91–92; *Tanh.* Terumah 7. See also *Num. Rab.* 13 (cited by Fischer). A Christian messianic appropriation of the stone in Dan 2 is found in Luke 20:18, "Everyone who falls on that stone will be broken to pieces; and it will crush anyone on whom it falls;" cf. Mark 12:10–11; Matt 21:42; Luke 20:17; 1 Pet 2:6–8; Rom 9:33. When read in conjunction with Josephus' commentary on Num 24 in *Ant.* 4.115–116, it becomes clear that he understood the stone to be "the Jewish nation dispersed abroad throughout the world" (Spilsbury 2003: 19–20). See also note to "it" at 10.207 and to "them" at 10.276.

[895] Josephus uses balanced and synonymous expressions to summarize his historical duty: He is to relate τὰ παρελθόντα and τὰ γεγενημένα. His claim to be focusing only on the historical material of the Scriptures is, by and large, sustainable. He excludes from his biblical paraphrase, for example, all the wisdom literature, the psalms and most of the prophets. From the Book of Jeremiah he excerpts only the historical material and he summarizes the visionary

if anyone, anxious for precision, will not be deterred from being curious to the extent of even wishing to learn about the unexplained—what is to happen[897]—let him make the effort to read the book of Daniel.[898] He will find this among the sacred writings.[899]

Daniel's friends are saved from the furnace

(5) 211[900] And when King Nabouchodonosor heard these things and recognized the dream, he was amazed at Daniel's nature[901] and, falling on his face, began to ad-

---

material in Dan 7–12 with a single composite vision based mainly on Dan 8 and pertaining to events already (for Josephus) in the past (Mason 1994: 173). His summaries of legal material from the Pentateuch (e.g. *Ant.* 3.90–286 and 4.196–301) could also be justified as aspects of the historical experience of the Hebrews. Nevertheless, it is interesting to note that Thucydides saw the historical task as shedding light on what is likely to happen in the future (1.22.4; cited by Feldman 1998: 650). Feldman points out, further, that Josephus did in fact see a kinship between the prophet and the historian: e.g. *Apion* 1.37, 41. See also Gnuse 1996: 22–23: "Josephus never calls himself a prophet…. But he is a successor to the prophets, especially in his function as a historian" (23). Robert Hall has shown, further, that Josephus distinguished between the "inspired prophetic histories" of the canonical prophets and the "interpretive prophetic histories" of later historians such as himself (Hall 1971: 22–30).

[896] Josephus' reticence to comment on the meaning of the stone is, presumably, due to his belief that the iron kingdom destroyed by it is Rome; e.g. Blenkinsopp 1974: 245; Braverman 1978: 109–11; Delling 1974: 117–8; Feldman 1998: 649; Flusser 1972: 158–9; Gray 1993: 40. It should be noted, though, that Josephus could have omitted the account of the stone altogether, but chose not to (though he did omit Dan 7:18). This might suggest that Josephus was not willing to bypass the opportunity to express his view about the future demise of Rome. On this subject, see further Spilsbury 2003: 15–20; Mason 1994: 172–3: Josephus' references to the end of Rome lack apocalyptic urgency and "seem…to fall into the category of harmless philosophical reflection, not revolutionary aspiration" (173). Be that as it may, Josephus seems to have cherished discrete hopes about the future overthrow of the Roman Empire. So also Davies 1991: 174.

[897] *Ant.* 4.125 contains a similar reference to prophetic insights that might be gained by a reading of the Jewish scriptures. Both there and here the passages in question relate, in Josephus' mind, to the future destiny of the Jewish people; on this passage see further Spilsbury 2003: 17–20; Bilde 1998: 52–55.

[898] Mason (1994: 173) has observed that since the Book of Daniel does not materially clarify the meaning

of the stone beyond what Josephus has already said, Josephus must not have expected his readers actually to consult the biblical book. Similar invitations to read further are found in *Ant.* 16.398 (on the Jewish 'philosophies') and *Life* 6 (on Josephus' genealogical records). Mason concludes that Josephus "wants to leave the impression that the Jewish scriptures contain all sorts of oriental mysteries beyond what he as a historian can presently discuss." This is almost certainly true, but we should not conclude from this that Josephus did not have a genuine exegetical basis for his claim here. On this matter, see further Spilsbury 2003: 17–19.

[899] Josephus gives an account of the twenty-two books of Hebrew Scriptures in *Apion* 1.37–41. He breaks these down into five books of Moses, thirteen books of prophets who wrote the history of their own times in the period from the death of Moses to Artaxerxes, and four books of psalms and wisdom. Thackeray (1926: 179 n. b) suggests that Josephus places the Book of Daniel within the thirteen books of the prophets; however it should be noted that the Book of Daniel was not widely considered to fall with the prophetic section of the Hebrew Bible. On the state of the Hebrew canon in Josephus' day, see further Mason 2002; Leiman 1989; Meyer 1974; Rajak 2001: 16–17; Thackeray 1929: 79. On Daniel as a prophet, see note to "prophets" at 10.267.

[900] The first two paragraphs of this section cover the last paragraph of Dan 2 (vv. 46–49), while the next three paragraphs (213–215) summarize the entire narrative of Dan 3. Josephus makes no use at all of the Prayer of Azariah or the Song of the Three Young Men found in the Greek versions, but possibly not in the Greek text he was using. He also makes no mention of the notice in both LXX and Θ (but not in MT) that this event took place in the eighteenth year of Nebuchadnezzar. The section is characterized by the theme of the honor paid to both Daniel and his companions by the king, despite their refusal to follow Gentile religious practices. It also reflects Josephus' tendency to provide rationalistic explanations for miraculous events.

[901] Greek φύσις, the nature, natural qualities, powers, constitution, condition, of a person or thing (LSJ s.v.). Josephus makes much of Daniel's natural

dress Daniel in the manner in which they worship God; ⁹⁰² **212** he also ordered sacrifices as to a god.⁹⁰³ Moreover, having given him the name of his own god,⁹⁰⁴ he
made him administrator⁹⁰⁵ of his whole kingdom along with his relatives,⁹⁰⁶ who
because of jealousy and malice⁹⁰⁷ happened to fall into danger when they offended
the king for the following reason. **213** After the king constructed a golden statue⁹⁰⁸
sixty cubits high and six wide and erected it in the great plain of Babylon⁹⁰⁹ and
was about to consecrate it, he called together the leading citizens⁹¹⁰ from the whole
land that he ruled.⁹¹¹ First of all he ordered them, when they heard the signaling of
the trumpet,⁹¹² to fall down at that time and to worship the statue; those who did not

---

abilities and his exemplary character. He also
emphasizes his relation to God and possession of the
divine Spirit. See further notes at 10.196 and 237.

⁹⁰² The biblical king also falls on his face before
Daniel, but does not address him as a god. Later in his
narrative Josephus will have Alexander the Great
perform a similar act of obeisance before the Jewish
high priest, *Ant.* 11.331. B.A. Mastin (1973: 85) argues
with reference to the biblical book of Daniel that
"Nebuchadnezzar is simply expressing in an extrava-
gant way his gratitude for the very considerable service
which Daniel has done him by interpreting his dream."
Further, he notes that Josephus' readers would likely
have understood the king's action within the framework
of the benefactor cult in Rome (88).

⁹⁰³ Josephus adheres closely to Dan 2:46–47 here,
but changes the emphasis from praise of Daniel's God
to praise of Daniel himself. The picture of Daniel being
honored as a god is repeated later in Josephus' narrative
where he makes the comment that Daniel had a
reputation for divinity (*Ant.* 10.268; cf. 10.25). On this
theme, see further notes at 10.250 and 268.

⁹⁰⁴ Josephus gleaned this detail from Dan 4:8 where
Nebuchadnezzar refers to Daniel, "who was named
Belteshazzar after the name of my god." The text of
LXX is quite different at this point and omits this
reference, while Θ retains it. Josephus has already
related Daniel's name change in *Ant.* 10.189. Collins
(1993: 141, 222) notes that the etymology of the name
implied by the Book of Daniel, and followed by
Josephus, is incorrect. Josephus omits the biblical statement in Dan 4:8 (also in vv. 9 and 18) that Daniel is
"endowed with a spirit of the holy gods." On this point
see further note to "spirit" at 10.239.

⁹⁰⁵ Greek ἐπίτροπος. This was the standard equivalent to the familiar Latin term *procurator*—used of an
official ranging from a minor steward to an imperial
financial agent to a praesidial governor. See note at
War 2.16 in BJP 1. Josephus implies that all four of the
youths were rewarded with the same rank (Vermes 1991:
156). See further next footnote.

⁹⁰⁶ In the biblical narrative (Dan 2:48–49) Daniel is
given many gifts and is promoted to ruler (השלטה; LXX

κατέστησεν ἐπὶ τῶν πραγμάτων τῆς Βαβυλωνίας; Θ
κατέστησεν αὐτὸν ἐπὶ πάσης χώρας βαβυλῶνος) over
the whole province of Babylon and chief prefect
(רב-סגנין; LXX ἄρχοντα καὶ ἡγούμενον; Θ ἄρχοντα
σατραπῶν) over all the wise men of Babylon. At his
request his three friends are given positions of authority
over the affairs of the province of Babylon. In Dan 4:9
the king refers to Daniel as "chief of the magicians"
(רב חרטמיא; Θ ὁ ἄρχων τῶν ἐπαοιδῶν; LXX [= Dan
4:18] τὸν ἄρχοντα τῶν σοφιστῶν καὶ τὸν ἡγούμενον).
Josephus refers to the three youths as Daniel's
"relatives" (συγγενεῖς) here, as also in *Ant.* 10.190, 197,
199 and 214. In *Ant.* 10.201 he calls them brothers; see
also *Ant.* 10.186, 188.

⁹⁰⁷ Josephus often attributes his protagonists' woes
to the jealousy and malice of others (e.g. *Ant.* 10.250,
256; 13.288, 310; *War* 1.67, 208, 634; *Life* 80, 122,
204, 423; Daube 1980: 29; Feldman 1998: 644). The
theme is common in Hellenistic moral philosophy; e.g.
Plato, *Ep.* 316E; Isocrates, *Demon.*7.26; etc. (Mason
2001: 66 n. 435).

⁹⁰⁸ Note the connection with the statue of Nebuchadnezzar's dream in which the golden head
represented the Babylonian kings (*Ant.* 10.208).

⁹⁰⁹ Dan 3:1 reads "the great plain of Dura in the
province of Babylon." Θ calls the plain Δεῖρα. LXX
translates the word דורא with the noun περίβολος,
which means "enclosure;" hence, "the plain of the
enclosure." On the possible meanings of this phrase, see
Collins 1993: 182. Josephus introduces a plain into the
narrative in *Ant.* 10.269

⁹¹⁰ Greek οἱ πρῶτοι. Dan 3:2–3 identifies these
people as "the satraps, the prefects, and the governors,
the counselors, the treasurers, the justices, the
magistrates, and all the officials of the provinces." Later (Dan 2:4) they are addressed as "peoples, nations,
and languages" (cf. verse 7).

⁹¹¹ LXX specifies that Nebuchadnezzar ruled the
entire region from India to Ethiopia (Dan 3:1).

⁹¹² Dan 3:5 and 7 specify the playing of "the horn,
pipe, lyre, trigon, harp, drum, and entire musical ensem-
ble;" however, LXX Dan 5:7, 10 and 15 summarize the
list with "the trumpet and every musical sound."

do this he threatened with being thrown into the furnace of fire. **214** So when everyone, upon hearing the signaling of the trumpet, worshiped the statue, Daniel's relatives,[913] [to explain] not doing this, declared that they did not want to transgress the ancestral laws.[914] They were convicted[915] and immediately were thrown into the fire, but were* saved by divine providence[916] and, incredibly,[917] escaped* death.[918] **215** The fire did not touch[919] them and was too weak to burn the youths when it had them in it, I think,[920] because they were thrown into it when they had done no wrong[921] and because God had prepared their bodies to be stronger[922] so as not to

---

[913] See note to "brothers" at 10.201.

[914] Greek οἱ πάτριοι νόμοι. The Judeans' loyalty to their ancestral laws is one of their key identity markers for Josephus (cf. *Ant.* 4.71, 130; 5.108; 7.130, 131, 374; 8.361; 9.243; 10.11; 11.109, 140, 231, 338 etc.). Similar expressions used by Josephus include τὰ πάτρια ἔθη (*Ant.* 5.90, 101; 8.192, 340; 9.95, 137, 339 etc.), οἱ πάτριοι ἐθισμοί (*Ant.* 1.72; 8.190), τὰ πάτρια νόμιμα (*Ant.* 1.310; 8.129; 9.99 etc.), and τὰ πάτρια (*Ant.* 4.139; 8.281 etc.). On this subject see further Mason 1991: 96-106, Schröder 1996, and Spilsbury 1998: 111–13. In the biblical narrative the Judeans (יהודיא, Ἰουδαῖοι) are denounced to the king by "certain Chaldeans" and accused of paying no heed to the king and not serving his gods (Dan 3:8–12).

[915] Josephus makes no reference to the king's furious rage, nor to the king's offer of a second chance for the youths to comply (cf. Dan 3:13–15).

[916] Josephus inserts the notion of divine providence (θεία προνοία) in place of the biblical reference to the angel who rescued the youths from the furnace. For another instance of this strategy, see *Ant.* 10.259–260. For the significance of πρόνοια in Josephus, see note to "providence" at 10.278.

[917] See note to "unexpected" at 10.266.

[918] Josephus' highly condensed and rationalized account of the youths' survival is a far cry from the biblical narrative at this point. Josephus omits the king's challenge to the youths which makes it clear that a showdown of divinities and religious loyalties is in view: "Who is the god that will deliver you out of my hands?" (Dan 3:15). To which the youths respond, "If our God whom we serve is able to deliver us from the furnace of blazing fire and out of your hand, O king, let him deliver us. But if not, be it known to you, O king, that we will not serve your gods and we will not worship the golden statue that you have set up" (Dan 3:17–18). Josephus also omits the biblical narrative's dramatic references to the furnace being heated up seven times more than was customary (Dan 3:19) and that the flames killed the men who threw the youths into the fire (Dan 3:22). He also omits the colorful description of the youths' "tunics, their trousers, their hats and their other garments" (Dan 3:21), which are

not harmed by the fire or even by the smoke (Dan 3:27). Finally, Josephus omits the biblical reference to a fourth personage in the fire called by Nebuchadnezzar first a son of the gods and then an angel of the Most High God (Dan 3:24–28). The rabbinic tradition, cited by Feldman (1998: 640 n. 28) and Ginzberg (1909–38, 6: 418–9 n. 90), is sharply critical of Nebuchadnezzar's reference to the figure as a son of God: see *y. Sabb.* 6 (end), *Exod. Rab.* 20.20, *Song Rab.* 7.9, *Midr. Sam.* 5.60, *'Ag. Ber.* 27.55. Josephus also omits the biblical reference to the angel who rescued Daniel in the lions' den (Dan 6:22; *Ant.* 10.259), where once again he gives a rationalizing explanation; see further notes at 10.216, 259, 271, and 272. It should also be noted that Josephus shows no knowledge of the Prayer of Azariah and the Song of the Three Young Men that are found in both ancient Greek versions at this point.

[919] LXX uses the same phrase (οὐκ ἥψατο) at Dan 3:27 [= LXX 3:94].

[920] Josephus often adds moralizing editorials to the narrative; e.g. *Ant.* 1.46–51, 65–66, 72, 194–195; 4.45–53, 154–155, 312–314; 5.107–109; 6.3–7, 147–151; 8.190–198, 265, 284, 313–314; 9.103–104; 10.37–39; 17.168–171; 19.201–211.

[921] Josephus very typically reflects on the matter of rewards and punishments, and God's protection of the upright. Indeed, he states at the very beginning of the *Antiquities* that the main lesson to be learned from the work is that "those who comply with the will of God and do not venture to transgress laws that have been well enacted succeed in all things beyond belief and that happiness (εὐδαιμονία) lies before them as a reward from God" (*Ant.* 1.14, Feldman, BJP). A similar point is made in *Ant.* 1.20 when he writes, "God...grants a happy life (εὐδαίμονα βίον) to those who follow Him and surrounds with great misfortunes (μεγάλαις... συμφοραῖς) those who transgress virtue" (Feldman, BJP). See also *Ant.* 1.23, 72; 6.307; 7.93; 17.60; 19.16 (cited by Sterling 1992: 296 n. 321).

[922] In the story about the youths' choice of diet (*Ant.* 10.190–194), Josephus had argued that their regimen had toughened their bodies; see notes at 10.190 and 194. It is not clear whether Josephus intends his readers to understand that the youths' diet played a part

be consumed by the fire.⁹²³ This commended them to the king as just⁹²⁴ and dear to God,⁹²⁵ for which reason afterwards they continued being deemed worthy by him of all honor.⁹²⁶

(6) 216⁹²⁷ And a little while later the king saw in his sleep another vision, to the effect that after falling from power he would make his life⁹²⁸ with wild beasts and,

Daniel interprets the king's second dream

---

in their survival of the furnace.

⁹²³ The biblical narrative states that all saw that "the fire had not had any power over the bodies of those men" (Dan 3:27). A more elaborate explanation is offered in the narrative interlude between the deuterocanonical Prayer of Azariah and Song of the Three Young Men, where the author writes, "But the angel of the Lord came down into the furnace, and made the inside of the furnace as though a moist wind were whistling through it. The fire did not touch them at all and caused them no pain or distress" (Add. Dan 1:26–27).

⁹²⁴ Greek δικαίους. On the importance of this virtue for Josephus, see note to "just man" at 10.246.

⁹²⁵ Greek θεοφιλεῖς. Josephus uses the same term for Daniel in *Ant.* 10.264. Three times in the Book of Daniel (Dan 9:23; 10:11, 19) the prophet is addressed by an angelic figure as "greatly beloved" (חמודות; Θ ἀνὴρ ἐπιθυμιῶν, LXX ἄνθρωπος ἐλεεινός). Goldingay (1987: 256) states that the term חמד "suggests both a feeling and an attitude that expresses itself in being drawn toward the object of love and committing oneself to it," and further, "Daniel is one to whom God is committed." A closely related theme is the honor in which Daniel and his friends were held by both the king and God. See further note to "public" at 10.266. *Ant.* 14.22 is of particular interest in the present context because it describes a certain Onias whose prayers for rain in a time of drought were heard by God because he was "a righteous man and dear to God" (δίκαιος ἀνὴρ καὶ θεοφιλής), which is very similar to the expression used of Daniel's three companions. *War* 1.331 and *Ant.* 14.455 are parallel accounts of Herod's amazing escape from a collapsing building that led all to conclude that he must be a "favorite of heaven." In *War* 5.381 Josephus refers to Abraham and those with him, who were unexpectedly enriched by Pharaoh, as "beloved of God." In his biblical paraphrase Josephus applies the term to the patriarchs (*Ant.* 1.106), Isaac (*Ant.* 1.346), David (*Ant.* 6.280), Solomon (*Ant.* 8.49, 190), and Elisha (*Ant.* 9.182).

⁹²⁶ On the honor in which Daniel and his companions were held, see previous footnote. The biblical narrative is both more detailed and more effusive. Nebuchadnezzar blesses the God of the three youths and

praises them for disobeying his own command and yielding up their bodies "rather than serve and worship any god except their own God" (Dan 3:28). Additionally, the biblical king issues a decree to the effect that anyone who utters blasphemy against the God of Shadrach, Meshach and Abednego "shall be torn limb from limb, and their houses laid in ruins; for there is no other god who is able to deliver in this way" (Dan 3:29; on the omission of this passage, see Feldman 1993: 53). The three young men are also promoted in the province of Babylon (Dan 3:30). The biblical Daniel refers back to this incident again in his address to the later king, Belshazzar (Dan 5:18–21).

⁹²⁷ In this section Josephus summarizes the content of Dan 4 with just two paragraphs followed up by a rather defensive notice (*Ant.* 10.218) about why he included the story at all. He omits the Book of Daniel's description of the dream itself, in which an enormous tree is ordered to be felled by a "holy watcher," and its stump bound with an iron and bronze band (Dan 4:13–17). He omits the biblical Nebuchadnezzar's first-person praise of God (Dan 4:2–3, 34–35, 37), his acknowledgement of Daniel as endowed with a divine spirit (Dan 4:8, 18), his description of the dream itself (Dan 4:10–17), Daniel's detailed interpretation of the dream and counsel to the king (Dan 4:19–27), and the fulfillment of the dream just as Daniel had predicted it (Dan 4:28–33). The overall impact of Josephus' summary is to present a slightly more sanitized picture of the king's humiliation (cf. Feldman 1993: 53). It is noteworthy that Josephus often omits biblical references to heavenly or angelic beings in his narrative; cf. notes at 10.214, 259, 271 and 272. The biblical tradition at this point is complicated by significant differences between MT/Θ and LXX. The chapter also has a very complex tradition history in which sources originally referring to Nabonidus, rather than Nebuchadnezzar, have likely been woven into the story. On this issue see Collins 1993: 216–21. Josephus' summary of the story is too short for us to determine whether his biblical text was closer to MT/Θ or LXX; but see notes to "desert" and "years" in this paragraph.

⁹²⁸ Greek δίαιτα. On Josephus' use of this term, see note to "regimen" at 10.190. Josephus uses a similar expression in *Ant.* 10.242.

after surviving thus in the desert[929] for seven years[930] he would take power back again. After gazing at this dream he again summoned the magi and questioned them closely about it[931] and demanded that they say what it might signify. **217** But none of the others was able to discover the import of the dream or to make it known to the king except for Daniel alone. He interpreted the dream, and just as he himself predicted to him so it happened. For having spent the aforementioned period in the desert, when no one dared to take over the government for the period of seven years,[932] when he asked God permission to take the kingdom again he was* restored to it.[933] **218** Now let no one bring a charge against me[934] for thus reporting each of these episodes throughout my book just as I find them[935] in the ancient books;[936] for right from the beginning of my history[937] I safeguarded myself against those who would criticize the content or would find fault, committing only to translate[938] the

---

[929] Josephus uses the phrase ἐπὶ τῆς ἐρημίας, "in the desert" (also in the next paragraph), which is reminiscent of LXX Dan 4:25 εἰς τόπον ἔρημον, "a desolate place."

[930] So also LXX. MT and Θ have "times" (עדנין, καιροί).

[931] Josephus omits the reference to the king's fear in relation to the dream (Dan 4:5). Feldman (1993: 53) suggests that this is part of an overall tendency on Josephus' part to present a somewhat more positive picture of the king than the biblical narrative.

[932] Josephus apparently felt the need to comment on the state of the government during Nebuchadnezzar's absence, in keeping with *Antiquities'* ongoing interest in constitutions (1.5-6, 10), not only in Judea (see bks 18-19). The biblical Nebuchadnezzar states only that, "My counselors and my lords sought me out, I was reestablished over my kingdom, and still more greatness was added to me" (Dan 4:36). Josephus must have assumed that the king's counselors and lords had been in charge of the kingdom during this period. In the passage which Josephus quotes from Berosus there is a reference to a Chaldean nobleman who oversees the affairs of state immediately before Nebuchadnezzar's accession (*Ant.* 10.223).

[933] The biblical Nebuchadnezzar does not ask for the kingdom back again, but acknowledges God's sovereignty over all the earth. Then reason returns to him (Dan 4:34–36).

[934] Josephus' seems somewhat embarrassed by the historical implausibility of this story, but no doubt retained it in his narrative because it served his overarching purpose of emphasizing God's sovereignty over the kingdoms and rulers of the world: To the king's boast ("Is this not magnificent Babylon, which I have built as a royal capital by my mighty power and for my glorious majesty?" Dan 4:30) the divine response is, "You shall be made to eat grass like oxen...until you have learned that the Most High has sovereignty over the kingdoms of mortals, and gives it

to whom he will" (Dan 4:25).

[935] At the end of *Ant.* Book 10, Josephus again insists that he has reported what he has found in his reading (*Ant.* 10.281). For other passages where Josephus makes similar claims, see note at 10.281.

[936] Greek ἐν τοῖς ἀρχαίοις...βιβλίοις. Josephus is probably referring to the Scriptures in general here, despite the fact that in one place he refers to the books of Daniel in the plural (*Ant.* 10.267).

[937] Josephus reminds his readers of the claim made at the very beginning of the *Antiquities* that this would be a work of translation following the precedent set by the translators of the Septuagint (*Ant.* 1.10–17; also 1.5). Mason (1994: 170) points out that this reference to the book's introductory material indicates that Josephus maintained a sense of unity throughout the *Antiquities* despite its unwieldy nature.

[938] Josephus distinguishes between translating or paraphrasing (μεταφράζειν) the Scriptures and explaining (δηλώσειν) them. In the course of his biblical narrative Josephus uses a number of different terms to refer to translating, paraphrasing, or interpreting the Hebrew Bible. In *Ant.* 1.5 he states that his work is going to cover the Jews' history and constitution "translated (μεθηρμηνευμένην) from the Hebrew writings" (see also *Apion* 1.228 of Manetho). Later in the same context he implies that this involves setting down the "precise details" (τὰ ἀκριβῆ) of the Scriptures without omission or addition (*Ant.* 1.17). In his account of the translation of the Septuagint, Josephus uses μεθερμηνεῦσαι as distinct from μεταγράψαι, "to transcribe" (*Ant.* 12.20; see also *Ant.* 12.48), though he uses the term μεταβαλεῖν of the same event in *Ant.* 1.10. In *Ant.* 1.52 and 8.142 Josephus uses μεθερμηνευόμενον to refer to the translation or interpretation of individual terms (see also *War* 4.11; 5.151; *Apion* 1.167). In *Apion* 1.54 he refers back to his translation of the Scriptures in the *Antiquities* with the verb μεθηρμήνευκα, though it is perhaps instructive to note that at the end of the *Antiquities* itself, Josephus had characterized his work

Hebrew books into the Greek tongue and promising to explain[939] them, neither adding to the content anything of my own nor taking anything away.[940]

(xi.1) 219[941] After being king for forty-three years,[942] King Nabouchodonosor completed* his life, an audacious man[943] and more fortunate than the kings before him. Berosus[944] has also mentioned his deeds in the third book of his *Chaldean History*,[945] writing as follows: [946]

Berosus
describes
Nebuchadnezzar's
rule

---

as an accurate cataloguing of the line of the high priest and the succession, conduct, achievements and policies of the kings and the judges. This, he states, is what he had promised to do at the beginning of his history (*Ant.* 20.261). A fascinating parallel to this, which is nevertheless in contrast to Josephus' claims, is 2 Macc 2:19–32 where the author explains his intention to "condense" (ἐπιτεμεῖν) five books of Jason of Cyrene into a single book. This author writes of "abbreviating" (ἐπιτομῆς) the original text (2:26), and of focusing on the "outlines of the condensation" (ὑπογραμμοῖς τῆς ἐπιτομῆς) while avoiding the "exact details" (διακριβοῦν). Like a painter or decorator who leaves the construction of a building to the master builder, so he sees his task as recasting the narrative while striving for brevity of expression and not exhaustive treatment. One wonders whether Josephus would not have been better served by an analogous characterization of his work. See further Feldman 1998: 37–46.

[939] The promise "to explain" (δηλώσειν) the Scriptures here would appear to be more than Josephus promised at the beginning of the *Antiquities* (1.17)—where Josephus undertook to set down only the precise details of the Scriptural records—but gives a more accurate picture of how Josephus envisaged his task as a "translator." For various views on how to understand Josephus' claim to be offering a literal translation of the Hebrew Bible, see Feldman 1998: 37–46 and 2000: 7–8 n. 22.

[940] Greek μήτε προστιθεὶς τοῖς πράγμασιν αὐτὸς ἰδίᾳ μήτ' ἀφαιρῶν. This statement is an echo of *Ant.* 1.17 where Josephus similarly promises to render the Hebrew Scriptures into Greek "neither adding nor omitting anything" (οὐδὲν προσθεὶς οὐδ' αὖ παραλιπών). Josephus' pledge, which calls to mind the biblical requirements of Deut 4:2 and 12:32, is also reminiscent of the resolve of the translators of the Septuagint to ensure that no alterations be admitted to their to work (*Let. Aris.* 311; cf. *Ant.* 12.109). In *Apion* 1.42 Josephus refers to Jewish reverence for Scripture, claiming that "no one has ventured either to add, or to remove, or to alter a syllable" (οὔτε προσθεῖναί τις οὐδὲν οὔτε ἀφελεῖν αὐτῶν οὔτε μεταθεῖναι τετόλμηκεν). Feldman (2000: 7–8 n. 22) has pointed out that similar formulae appear in Dionysius of Halicarnassus (*Thuc.* 5 and 8) and Lucian (*Quomodo Historia Conscribenda Sit* 47), as well as in

a number of other ancient sources.

[941] In this section Josephus departs from the biblical narrative in order to cite a number of non-Jewish historians on Nebuchadnezzar, and thus presumably by a process of association to place Jewish history on the world stage (Mason 1994: 170). It is striking that Josephus inserts this extra-biblical information immediately following the statements in the previous paragraph (itself an abbreviation of the biblical account) about his commitment "to translate the Hebrew books into the Greek tongue" and his promise "to explain them, neither adding to the content anything of my own nor taking anything away" (*Ant.* 10.218). Josephus apparently did not see the addition of this kind of non-biblical corroborative material as a contradiction of his promise.

[942] 605–562 B.C.E. This is an extra-biblical detail that Josephus apparently derived from the third book of Berosus' *Chaldean History* (see *Apion* 1.146). Nebuchadnezzar's 43-year reign is also mentioned in the Uruk king list (Barclay, BJP).

[943] Greek ἀνὴρ δραστήριος. Feldman (1993: 52–54) has shown that Josephus' criticism of Nebuchadnezzar is far less severe than that offered by the Book of Daniel.

[944] Βηρωσός, a Babylonian historian (Josephus calls him a "native Chaldean" in *Apion* 1.129; cf. *Ant.* 1.93; c. 330-250 B.C.E.), who was a priest of Bel (Tatian, *Oratio ad Graecos* 36), and known in some circles for his publication in Greek of works on Babylonian astronomy and philosophy (*Apion* 1.129). Barclay (BJP *ad loc.*) cites Seneca, *Nat.* 3.29.1; Pliny, *Nat.* 7.123 and Athenaeus, *Deipn.* 14.14 as examples of Berosus' modest reputation among later authors.

[945] Χαλδαϊκά. Berosus' history (also referred to as Βαβυλωνιακά) consisted of three books presented to Antiochus I and preserved now only in fragments (cf. *FGH* 680). Book 1 described the country and creation; book 2 continued down to Nabonassar (747-734 B.C.E.); and book 3 contained political history to Alexander the Great (Kuhrt, 2003). In *Apion* 1.130–131 Josephus provides his own synopsis of the contents of Berosus' work. Josephus cites Berosus on six other occasions besides the present instance (*Ant.* 1.93, 107, 158; 10.20, 34; *Apion* 1.129–153). Within the last of these passages, *Apion* 1.135–141 is an almost verbatim

Nebuchadnezzar campaigns on behalf of his father

220 "But when his father Nabouchodonosor[947] heard that the man who had been appointed satrap[948] in Egypt and over the regions of Coele-Syria[949] and Phoenicia

---

repeat of the quotation in *Ant.* 10.220–226 (notwithstanding some forty textual variants). The commentary that follows is dependant upon Barclay's comments (BJP 10) on the *Apion* passage at numerous points. On whether Josephus knew Berosus directly or, as is more likely, indirectly through an intermediary source such as Alexander Polyhistor or Nicolaus of Damascus, see Feldman 2000: 34, n. 235.

[946] The passage that follows is Berosus' account of the events surrounding the Battle of Carchemish (605 B.C.E.) between Nebuchadnezzar and Pharaoh Necho II (ruled 609–595 B.C.E.), though Josephus suppresses the connection with Carchemish for reasons that I will suggest below. The historical events reflected in the Berosus citation are known to us from Babylonian records, which read as follows: "In the twenty-first year the king of Akkad [Nabopolassar] stayed in his own land, Nebuchadnezzar, the crown prince, mustered (the Babylonian army) and took command of his troops; he marched to Carchemish which is on the banks of the Euphrates, and crossed the river (to go) against the Egyptian army which lay in Carchemish,...fought with each other and the Egyptian army withdrew before him. He accomplished their defeat and to nonexistence [beat?] them. As for the rest of the Egyptian army which had escaped from the defeat (so quickly that) no weapon had reached them, in the district of Hamath the Babylonian troops overtook and defeated them so that not a single man [escaped] to his own country. At that time Nebuchadnezzar conquered the whole area of the Hatti-country (Palestine). For twenty-one years Nabopolassar had been king of Babylon. On the 8th of the month of Ab he died (lit. 'the fates'); in the month of Elul Nebuchadnezzar returned to Babylon and on the first day of the month of Elul he sat on the royal throne in Babylon. In the 'accession year' Nebuchadnezzar went back again to the Hatti-land; in the month of Sebat he took the heavy tribute of the Hatti-territory to Babylon" (D.J. Wiseman 1956: 68–69). Josephus, who knows about these events, supplies his own account in *Ant* 10.84–86 without any reference to the passage from Berosus (biblical references to the battle may be found in 2 Chron 35:20 and Jer 46:2–12). Most significantly, Josephus does not explicitly link the quotation from Berosus with the events surrounding the battle of Carchemish. His intention seems to be, rather, to present the Berosus passage as if it supplies a summary of Nebuchadnezzar's conquest of Judea and subsequent deportation of the inhabitants of Jerusalem to Babylon. In other words, he presents the passage as if it applied directly to the story of Daniel. See further note to

"satrap" at 10.220..

[947] The text as it stands implies that Nebuchadnezzar had a father by the same name (the textual variants are simply variant spellings of the name Nebuchadnezzar), which is incorrect. Nebuchadnezzar's father was Nabopolassar (ruled 626–605 B.C.E.; Sack 1992d, 4: 977–8), founder of the neo-Babylonian empire. The mistake would seem to be due to a copying error on Josephus' own part since he quotes the same passage from Berosus in *Apion* 1.135–141 in which the father's name is correctly identified.

[948] The text refers to the rebellion of a satrap, i.e. a subordinate Babylonian official in control of a region of the Babylonian empire, against Nabopolassar's rule. This is a distortion of the account given in the Babylonian Chronicle, which identifies the antagonists as "the Egyptian army which lay in Carchemish" (cited in previous footnote). The question that this raises is whether the distortion is due to Josephus, or to Berosus, or to an abbreviator of Berosus (such as Alexander Polyhistor) from whom Josephus may have obtained this passage. Unfortunately there is no way to decide this issue on currently available evidence. However, we may note a number of features of Josephus' use of the passage which have some bearing on the subject.

First of all, we should note that Josephus clearly was knowledgeable of the Battle of Carchemish and the combatants involved in that event. In his own description of these events (*Ant.* 10.84, following Jer 46:2 = LXX 26:2; cf. 2 Kgs 24:1) he identifies "the Egyptian king Necho, to whom all Syria was subject" as the object of Nebuchadnezzar's aggression at Carchemish. Earlier in his narrative Josephus had described Necho and his army marching towards the Euphrates "to make war on the Medes and the Babylonians who had overthrown the Assyrian empire" (*Ant.* 10.74//2 Kgs 23:29; 2 Chron 35.20; 1 Esd 1:25). Thus, Josephus was fully aware of this important historical event, and more, he knew that it had nothing to do with the final fall of Jerusalem and destruction of the temple. However, Josephus does not cite the passage from Berosus in connection with Carchemish at all. Rather, he manipulates the citation in such a way as to make it apply to events surrounding the fall of Jerusalem and the destruction of the temple. This is seen especially clearly in *Apion* 1.132 where he states that Nebuchadnezzar led his army "against Egypt and against our land, when he learned that they had rebelled" (Barclay, BJP 10). In that context, Josephus implies that this military action led immediately to the destruction of the temple and the deportation of the

had rebelled against him, since he was not himself able to undertake campaign hardships himself, he assigned the task to his son Nabouchodonosor, who was in the
prime of life, and sent him out against him with part of his force. **221** And when
Nabouchodonosor engaged the rebel and drew up in battle order against him he
defeated[950] him and made his territory[951] part of his own kingdom. And it so happened about the same time that his father Nabouchodonosor[952] fell ill in the city of
the Babylonians and quit his life, having reigned twenty-one years.[953] **222** And having learned not a long time later of the death of his father, and having settled the
affairs of Egypt and the rest of the region, [954] Nabouchodonosor assigned to some
of his friends[955] the task of carrying up to Babylon the prisoners of war from the
Judean,[956] Phoenician, Syrian, and Egyptian peoples[957] with the heaviest force and
the rest of the plunder, while he himself hastened through the desert with a few men
and arrived* in Babylon. **223** And after taking over the affairs that had been managed by Chaldeans—the kingdom having been maintained by the best man among
them[958]—and after becoming master of his father's whole empire, he arranged for

Nebuchadnezzar returns to Babylon

population of Jerusalem to Babylon (see also *Apion*
1.145)

Returning to the question of the unnamed satrap at
the beginning of the excerpt from Berosus, we may
perhaps be justified to suspect that Josephus would
have been happy to keep the identity of this individual
as vague as possible in order to facilitate his use of this
passage for a context unrelated to its original setting.
Barclay observes that the quotation from Berosus
strangely omits the names of all key people and battle-
sites. It may well be that it was Josephus himself who
omitted the names in order to dislodge the passage from
any explicit historical connection to the Battle of
Carchemish in 605 B.C.E., and thus to render the passage more amenable to the different uses he had in mind
for it.

[949] The term Coele-Syria was applied to various
portions of Syria and Palestine by authors of different
periods. Hellenistic authors used the term to include
much of the Eastern Mediterranean seaboard extending
as far as the Euphrates river, but excluding Phoenicia.
For a summary of the complex variations in the usage
of the term, see Smith 1992.

[950] Greek ἐκράτησε; see also *Apion* 1.133. The parallel passage in *Apion* 1.136 has ἐκυρίευσε, "over-
powered."

[951] Greek τὴν χώραν ἐκ ταύτης τῆς ἀρχῆς, literally
"the territory from that empire/rule." The parallel passage in *Apion* has ἐξ ἀρχῆς, "again," which may be taken to reflect the assumption that the territory was
originally Babylonian (Barclay, BJP 10).

[952] See note at 10.220.

[953] That this number is historically accurate is
confirmed by a fragment of a Babylonian chronicle
(British Museum 21946, cited by Wiseman 1956: 67–
75), which gives the date of his death as the 8th of the

month of Ab = 15/16th August, 605 B.C.E.

[954] It is not entirely clear what Berosus may have
meant by "settling the affairs of Egypt and the rest of
the region." According to a fragment from the Babylonian Chronicles (cited in note at 10.219), Nebuchadnezzar returned to Babylon fairly soon after his victory
at Carchemish and the subsequent military operations
in the region. He certainly did not invade Egypt or gain
control of its territory. It is possible, however, that
Josephus mistakenly understood Berosus to be
speaking about an actual sacking of Egypt—an event
he possibly refers to in *Ant.* 10.195.

[955] On "friends" as court officials, see note at
10.263.

[956] It is apparently this reference to Judean captives
that forms the basis of Josephus' insinuation in *Apion*
1.132 and 145 that the events described here formed
part of the sequence that led to destruction of the
temple and the deportation of the people of Jerusalem.
In *Ant.* 10.238 Josephus uses the same term that is used
here for the "prisoners of war" (αἰχμάλωτος) to refer to
Daniel. In fact, Berosus is most likely referring to
Judean mercenaries captured during the Battle of
Carchemish and subsequent skirmishes (Collins 1993:
132).

[957] The parallel text in *Apion* 1.137 omits the final
καί, "and," before "Egyptian peoples" (τῶν κατ᾽
Αἴγυπτον ἐθνῶν), giving the impression that this last
designation should be read in apposition to all the
others. Barclay (BJP 10), translates the final phrase as
"peoples bordering Egypt."

[958] The term τοῦ βελτίστου αὐτῶν, "their best man"
might also be rendered "their noblest man" (so Barclay
in BJP 10) or "their ablest man" (so Marcus *Ant.*, LCL).
Thackeray (*Apion*, LCL) has "their chief nobleman." As
with the "satrap" at the beginning of this excerpt from

settlements to be assigned to the prisoners of war, on their arrival, in the most suitable places in Babylonia. **224** Then he himself lavishly adorned both the temple of Bel[959] and the rest of the temples[960] out of the spoils of war,[961] and he also refurbished the original city and fortified it with another one.

Nebuchadnezzar's building projects

In order that those besieging the city might no longer be able to divert the course of the river[962] and redirect it against the city,[963] he surrounded the inner city by three enclosures and the outer city with three of baked bricks.[964] **225** And after remarkably walling the city and adorning the gates[965] in a way befitting a sacred place, he built among his father's palaces another palace adjoining them, of whose height and other extravagance it may perhaps be superfluous to speak,[966] except to say that despite its greatness and splendor it was completed in fifteen days.[967] **226** And among these palaces he built stone retaining walls, giving them an appearance similar to mountains—he accomplished this by planting trees of every kind—and he built the so-called hanging garden[968] because his wife,[969] who was brought up in the regions of Media, longed for the way things were at her home."[970]

Megasthenes, Diocles, and Philostratus on Nebuchadnezzar

227 And also Megasthenes[971] mentions these things in the fourth book of the *Indica*,

---

Berosus, this individual is not named. It is possible that Josephus left out the names from his source in order to make it fit into his historical scheme; see note to "satrap" at 10.220.

[959] The temple of Bel, or Marduk, called "Esagila" was one of Babylon's most famous buildings. It adjoined the great ziggurat called "Etemenanki." On these structures see further Wiseman 1985: 64–73 and Unger 1970: 165–87.

[960] Archaeologists have identified temples dedicated to Ninmah, Gula, Ninurta, Ishtar of Agade and Nabu (Margueron 1992). Later in his narrative (*Ant.* 10.233) Josephus refers to a shrine (ναός) of Nebuchadnezzar himself.

[961] Josephus undoubtedly intended for his readers to think that these "spoils of war" included items taken from the temple in Jerusalem (on this point see note to "satrap" at 10.220). In his account of the downfall of Belshazzar (following the biblical narrative of Dan 5:2) he refers to the king's sacrilegious act of using the sacred vessels (τὰ τοῦ θεοῦ σκεύη) plundered by Nebuchadnezzar from the Jerusalem temple (*Ant.* 10.233).

[962] Herodotus (*Hist.* 1.191) tells of Cyrus' tactic of diverting the river upstream to enable his men to enter the city along the river's bed. The tactic envisioned in the present passage seems to be quite different from that. Abydenus, cited by Eusebius, writes that Nebuchadnezzar "changed the course of the river Armacales, which is a branch of the Euphrates" (Eusebius *Praep. ev.* 9.41.7; *FGH* 685, frag. 6). See also Xenophon, *Cyr.* 5.9.19 cited by Barclay, BJP 10.

[963] There are numerous textual corruptions in this sentence (from "... he also refurbished"); I have followed the emendations of Marcus (LCL), but see

also Barclay (BJP 10).

[964] The Greek text is very complex at this point and appears to be corrupt. Marcus emends the text, following *Apion* 1.139, to read: "[the walls] of the inner city being of burnt brick and bitumen, while those of the outer city were of brick alone" (Marcus, LCL). Babylon's walls were particularly famous in antiquity; cf. Herodotus, *Hist.* 1.178–179; Strabo, *Geogr.* 16.1.5; Diodorus 2.7; Curtius Rufus 5.1.16. Abydenus (cited in Eusebius, *Praep. ev.* 9.41.7; *FGH* 685, frag. 6b) also refers to "a triple circuit of walls."

[965] Herodotus, *Hist.* 1.179 mentions bronze gateways. See also Abydenus in Eusebius, *Praep. ev.* 9.41.5 (*FGH* 685, frag. 1, cited by Barclay, BJP 10).

[966] The parallel text in *Apion* 1.140 reads "it would perhaps take too long to describe" (Barclay, BJP 10), for what is here "it may perhaps be superfluous to speak."

[967] Unger (1970: 22) cites an inscription that similarly claims that the structure was completed in fifteen days. Abydenus refers to the walls of Babylon being completed in fifteen days (cited by Eusebius, *Praep. ev.* 9.41.7; *FGH* 685, frag. 6b).

[968] The hanging garden of Babylon was considered one of the seven wonders of the world (Strabo, *Geogr.* 16.1.5; Diodorus 2.10).

[969] Amytis, daughter of the Median king Astyages (cf. Berosus, *FGH* 680, frag. 7d).

[970] Diodorus 2.10 and Curtius Rufus 5.1.35 (cited by Barclay, BJP 10) claim that the garden was planted by a Syrian king for his Persian concubine.

[971] Megasthenes (c. 350–290 B.C.E.) was a diplomat who served under Sibyrtius, whom Alexander the Great appointed satrap of Arachosia and Gedrosia. The *Indika*

in which he tries to show that this king surpassed Heracles in courage and in greatness of deeds; for, he said, he subdued much of Libya and Iberia.[972] **228** And Diocles[973] in the second book of the *Persica* mentions this king, and Philostratus[974] in the *Indian* and *Phoenician Histories* states that this king besieged Tyre for thirteen years at the time Ithobal[975] was ruling Tyre.[976] Such were the things recorded by all the historians concerning this king.[977]

(2) 229[978] But after the death of Nabouchodonosor, his son Abilmathadach[979] took over*[980] the kingship. He immediately[981] released Iechonias[982] the king of Jerusalem from chains and held him as the most indispensable of his friends,[983] giving him many gifts and setting him above the kings in Babylonia.[984] **230** For his father had not kept faith[985] with Iechonias when he voluntarily surrendered himself along with

The royal succession from Nebuchadnezzar to Belshazzar

---

embodied Megasthenes' firsthand experience of India, covering geography, the system of government, classifications of citizens and religious customs, archaeology, history and legends (Barber and Sacks 2003). Barclay (BJP 10) considers it unlikely that Josephus knew this author firsthand, but that Josephus gleaned this reference from the work of Alexander Polyhistor.

[972] Abydenus (cited by Eusebius, *Praep. ev.* 9.41.1; *FGH* frag. 6) quotes Megasthenes saying that "Nebuchadnezzar was braver than Hercules, and made an expedition against Libya and Iberia, and, having subdued them, settled a part of their inhabitants on the right shore of the Pontus." Barclay (BJP 10) cites Strabo, *Geogr.* 15.1.6 to the effect that Nebuchadnezzar had a greater reputation among the Chaldeans than even Heracles, and led an expedition to the Pillars.

[973] There were several ancient historians by this name (cf. *Oxford Classical Dictionary* [3d rev. ed.] 470–71), though we do not know of one who wrote a history of Persia.

[974] We know nothing of this historian beyond what Josephus says of him here. He does mention him again in *Apion* 1.144 as agreeing with "Phoenician archives" on the siege of Tyre. The 13-year siege is referenced again in *Apion* 1.156 but here the information is said to come from "the Phoenician records." It is possible that Josephus was using Philostratus at this point as well, but Barclay (BJP 10) thinks it more likely that his source at this point was Menander of Ephesus, whose work on Phoenicia Josephus quoted in *Apion* 1.116–127.

[975] Ethbaal III (ruled *c.*591–573 B.C.E.)

[976] The siege of Tyre, which lasted from 585 to 573 B.C.E. and exhausted the city of all of its strength, is mentioned in Ezek 29:17–18. See further Katzenstein 1992.

[977] In the parallel passage in *Apion* Josephus' citation of Berosus continues to Cyrus' defeat of Nabonidus (*Apion* 1.146–153).

[978] In this section Josephus again goes beyond the biblical narrative by providing details concerning the royal succession from Nebuchadnezzar to Belshazzar. His sources for this information include the Babylonian historian Berosus along with historical narratives in 2 Kings, 2 Chronicles, and Jeremiah. When it comes to the narrative of Dan 5, it is noteworthy that once again there are significant differences between MT/Θ and LXX, with LXX much the shorter this time. Another difference is that LXX prefaces the chapter with a summary of the story's main points (on which, see Collins 1993: 241), including the 3 mysterious words, which are lacking in the narrative of LXX. At one point (see note to "still more" at 10.236) Josephus seems to follow the narrative of LXX rather than MT/Θ.

[979] Ἀβιλμαθαδάχος with textual variants ἀβιαμαθα-δάχος O (R), ἀβελμάρθαχος P, ἀβελμάθαχος S, ἀβιλα-μαρώδαχος LauV, ἀβιλαραμάταχος E, amilmathapacus (amilmatharacus cod. Neapol.) qui et abimathadocus Lat; Εὐειλμαράδουχος *Apion*; Hebrew אויל מרדך; LXX Ευιλμαρωδαχ, Ουλαιμαραδαχ; Evil-merodach (ruled 562–560 B.C.E.). In Akkadian his name was *Amel-Marduk*, "Man of Marduk" (Sack 1992b, 2: 679).

[980] This is historically accurate (a fact gleaned from Berosus; cf. *Apion* 1.146), though not mentioned in the biblical narrative; see further Sack 1992b, 2: 679.

[981] 2 Kings 25:27/Jer 52:31 "in the year that he began to reign."

[982] Ἰεχονίας. In *Ant.* 10.97–102 Josephus refers to this king (the biblical Jehoiachin) as Ἰωάχιμος. Hebrew יהויכין; LXX Ιωακιμ.

[983] 2 Kings 25:27–30/Jer 52:31–34. On the use of the term "friend" to designate a court official, see note at 10.263.

[984] 2 Kings 25:28/Jer 52:32 "He spoke kindly to him, and gave him a seat above the other seats of the kings who were with him in Babylon."

[985] Greek τὴν πίστιν οὐκ ἐφύλαξεν. In *Ant.* 10.97 Josephus uses the similar expression: οὐκ ἐφύλαξε τὰς πίστεις, "did not keep his promises." Josephus implies

his wives and children and all of his relatives for the benefit of his native city, that it might not be razed after being taken by siege, as we related before.[986] **231** And when Abilmathadach died after eighteen years[987] of kingship, Eglisar[988] his son[989] inherited the rule; after ruling for forty years[990] he came to the end of his life. And after him the royal succession passed to his son Labosordach,[991] and when he died[992] — the kingdom having rested with him for nine months in all[993]—it passed* on to Baltasar[994] who was called Naboandel[995] by the Babylonians.[996]

Belshazzar offends God

232 Against him Cyrus[997] the king of Persia and Darius[998] the Mede[999] went* to war.

---

that Evil-merodach was making amends for his father's treachery. In *Apion* 1.147, though, Josephus quotes Berosus who characterizes Evil-merodach's rule as "lawless and debauched" (Barclay, BJP 10).

[986] *Ant.* 10.97; cf. 2 Kings 24:12; 2 Chron 36:10; Jer 22:24–27.

[987] This appears to be incorrect. *Apion* 1.147, quoting from Berosus, gives Evil-merodach only 2 years. It is not clear why Josephus has 18 years for this king here, though it may have something to do with Josephus' calculations in connection with the 70 years of exile prophesied by Jeremiah (Jer 25:11). In *Ant.* 11.2 (cf. Ezra 1:1) Josephus cites Jeremiah's prediction that "after they had served Nebuchadnezzar and his descendants and survived this servitude for seventy years he would restore them to their ancestral land" (Spilsbury, BJP 6). Since the temple fell in the eighteenth year of Nebuchadnezzar's 43-year reign (*Ant.* 10.146 and 219), the first 25 years of exile were under Nebuchadnezzar. 18 years were endured under Evil-merodach, 4 years under Nergal-sharezer (following the variant reading in *Apion* 1.148), 9 months under Labasi-Marduk, and 17 years under Balshazzar (*Ant.* 10.247), for a total of 64 years and 9 months under Nebuchadnezzar and his "descendants" (cf. *Ant.* 10.248). The missing 5 years and 3 months were perhaps ascribed to "Darius the Mede."

[988] Ἡλίσαρος, with textual variants ἰγλίσαρος SP, νιγλίσαρος LauVE; *helesarus* Lat; Νηριγλίσαρος *Apion*. In Jer 39:3, 13 he appears as נרגל שר־אצר; LXX Ναργαλασαρ; Nergal-sharezer (ruled 560–556 B.C.E.). In *Ant.* 10.135 the name appears as Νηρεγάλασαρος with variants. His Babylonian name was *Nergal-śar-uṣur* (Marcus 1937: 286 n. b), which means "Nergal [i.e. the Babylonian sun god] protect the king;" Bracke 1992.

[989] This king was not, in fact, Evil-merodach's son. According to Berosus (quoted in *Apion* 1.147) he was Evil-merodach's brother-in-law, who plotted against him and murdered him.

[990] Berosus (quoted in *Apion* 1.148) ascribes to this ruler only four years, which is closer to historical fact.

[991] Λαβοσόρδαχος, with textual variant λαβροσό-δαχος SP; Λαβοροσοάρδοχος *Apion*; Labasi-Marduk (ruled 556 B.C.E.).

[992] According to *Apion* 1.149 he was an evil person and was assassinated by his friends. Barclay (BJP 10) cites the Nabonidus stele (*ANET*, 309), which states that his accession to power was against the will of the Gods. See also Abydenus (*apud* Eusebius, *Praep. ev.* 9.41.4).

[993] According to Thompson (*CAH* 3: 218, cited by Marcus 1937: 286, n. d) his reign lasted from March to the end of summer, 556 B.C.E.

[994] Βαλτασάρης with textual variants Βαλτασάρις O, Βαλτάσαρις SP, Βαλτάσαρος LauV; Aramaic בלשאצר; Θ and LXX Βαλτασαρ; Belshazzar. He ruled as co-regent for at least 3 years between 556 and 539 B.C.E. during his father Nabonidus' reign (Sack 1992a, 1: 661).

[995] Ναβοάνδηλος with textual variants ναβοὰν δῆλος O, ἀβοάνδηλος E, *naboan* Lat; Ναβόννηδος *Apion*; Nabonidus (ruled 556–539 B.C.E.). Sack 1992c, 4: 973–6. Herodotus referred to him as Labynetus (*Hist.* 1.188).

[996] Josephus treats Belshazzar and Nabonidus as the same person, though Belshazzar was in fact Nabonidus' son, who shared his father's rule for at least three years during the latter's absence in Arabia (see the *Nabonidus Chronicle* and the *Verse Account of Nabonidus* 2.20, *ANET.* 313, cited by Collins 1993: 32). Marcus suggests that Josephus has conflated the Book of Daniel's account of the last Babylonian king (Belshazzar) with the accounts of Herodotus and Berosus in which Nabonidus and Labynetos respectively are identified as the last Babylonian king (Marcus 1937: 287, note f). Dan 5:11, 18, and 22 refer to Belshazzar as Nebuchadnezzar's son. See further note to "grandmother" at 10.237.

[997] Κῦρος. Hebrew כורש and כרש; Θ and LXX Κῦρος; Cyrus (590–530 B.C.E.).

[998] Δαρεῖος. Hebrew דריוש; Θ and LXX Δαρεῖος.

[999] Josephus retains the biblical reference to Darius the Mede who is otherwise unknown to history. 2 Chron 36:20 summarizes the succession from Nebuchadnezzar to Cyrus thus: "He [i.e. Nebuchadnezzar] carried into exile to Babylon the remnant...and they became servants to him and his sons until the kingdom of Persia came to power." This passage, along with the numerous other references to Cyrus in the Hebrew Bible, implies that he was the successor of the Baby-

And to those besieged[1000] in Babylon there occurred a strange and prodigious spectacle.[1001] Baltasar was reclining, eating and drinking with his concubines and friends[1002] in a great hall designed for royal banquets.[1003] **233** And because it seemed good to him, he directed* that the vessels of God[1004] be brought from his own shrine, which Nabouchodonosor, although he plundered them from Jerusalem, had not used but had placed in his own shrine.[1005] But Baltasar, driven by such audacity[1006] as to use them, between drinking and defaming God[1007] saw* a hand[1008] coming out of the city wall and engraving certain syllables on the wall of the banquet hall.[1009]

---

lonian empire (e.g. Ezra 1:1-2, 7-8). For a summary of difficulties and discussions surrounding Darius the Mede in history and tradition-history, see Collins 1993: 30–31; Koch 1992. Jer 51:11 contains the idea that the Medes will destroy Babylon. Since Josephus clearly subscribed to the view that the four kingdoms of Nebuchadnezzar's statue were Babylon, Persia, Macedonia, and Rome (see note to "end" at 10.209), it was necessary for him to subsume the reign of Darius the Mede under that of Cyrus. In *Ant.* 10.248 Cyrus and Darius the Mede are said to be relatives.

[1000] The biblical narrative makes no reference to a siege but does state that Darius the Mede took over the kingdom on the very night of the fateful banquet (Dan 5:30). Josephus states that Darius took the city "not long afterwards" (*Ant.* 10.247). Josephus' scenario of a banquet in the middle of a siege greatly increases the drama of the episode. Herodotus (*Hist.* 1.191) and Xenophon (*Cyr.* 7.5.15) state that the Babylonians were celebrating a festival at the time of the city's capture. Collins (1993: 243–4) cites the *Nabonidus Chronicle* on the *akitu* festival, which is known to have been celebrated in Babylon in the year the city fell.

[1001] In LXX Dan 5:9 the writing on the wall is referred to as a sign (τοῦ σημείου) that is great (μέγα).

[1002] Dan 5:1 "a thousand of his lords;" Dan 5:3 "his lords, his wives and his concubines." LXX lacks the reference to the women in the scene, while Θ includes them. On the significance of the term "friends," see note at 10.263. The preface to LXX Dan 5 states that two thousand powerful nobles had been invited to the celebration.

[1003] The biblical narrative (Dan 5:1) does not specify where the banquet took place, though the preface to chapter 5 in LXX states that it occurred "on the day of the inauguration of his palace" (translation by Collins 1993: 237).

[1004] Greek τὰ τοῦ θεοῦ σκεύη. Dan 5:3 refers to the "vessels of gold and silver that had been taken out of the temple, the house of God in Jerusalem." Dan 5:23 refers to them as "the vessels of his temple." In *Ant.* 10.145 Josephus describes the despoiling of the temple thus: "He…carried out the gold and silver vessels of God (τὰ σκεύη τοῦ θεοῦ) and [or, "in particular"—καὶ δὴ

καὶ] the great laver that Solomon had erected, together with the bronze columns and their capitals and the golden tables and the lampstands" (Begg in this volume). See also *Ant.* 9.263; 10.242; 11.10, 31; 12.250. Jewish tradition was very interested in the fate of the temple vessels: e.g., *2 Baruch* 6:7–9; *4 Baruch* 3:8–11, 17–20. In 1 Macc 1:21–23 and 2 Macc 5:16 robbery of the temple vessels features prominently among the crimes of Antiochus Epiphanes (Collins 1993: 133).

[1005] The biblical narrative does not mention personal shrines for Nebuchadnezzar and Belshazzar. Dan 1:2 states that Nebuchadnezzar took some of the vessels of the house of God and placed them in the "treasury of his gods." Nevertheless, the structure of the biblical narrative does indeed imply that Belshazzar had exceeded Nebuchadnezzar's arrogance.

[1006] Greek θράσους, "daring, rashness, audacity, impudence, recklessness;" see also *Ant.* 1.66; 7.313; 10.13. The biblical narrative attributes the king's decision to the influence of wine (Dan 5:2), as well as to arrogance (Dan 5:22). The preface to LXX Dan 5 states that the king was "puffed up" (ἀνυψούμενος) from the wine (cf. LXX Dan 5:2). Arrogance features prominently in the description of Antiochus Epiphanes' robbery of the temple vessels in 1 Macc 1:21–22. Josephus shows no awareness of the rabbinic tradition referred to by Jerome to the effect that Belshazzar was gloating over the fact that Jeremiah's prophecy of 70 years had not been fulfilled (Jerome, *Expl. Dan.* 5:2; cf. *b. Meg.* 11b–12a; cited by Braverman 1978: 79–80).

[1007] The book of Daniel states that they drank wine from the sacred vessels and "praised the gods of gold and silver, bronze, iron, wood, and stone" (Dan 5:4). Later Daniel himself repeats the accusation that they have praised these gods "which do not see or hear or know" but have neglected to honor the God to whom they owe their very existence (Dan 5:23). See further *Ant.* 10.242.

[1008] Dan 5:5 specifies the "fingers of a man's hand."

[1009] Josephus apparently differentiates between the city wall (τεῖχος) and the wall of the banquet hall (τοῖχος), but omits the biblical reference to the writing being on the wall "next to the lampstand" (Dan 5:5). Both LXX and Θ use only the term τοῖχος. Bruce 1965:

234 Troubled[1010] by the vision, he summoned the magi and the Chaldeans[1011]—all of this group among the Babylonians who were able to interpret signs and dreams[1012]—so that they might explain to him what had been written. **235** But when none of the magi were able to discover its meaning and said that they did not understand it, the king,[1013] being in agonies of mind and great pain because of the paradox,[1014] made a proclamation throughout the whole country promising to give to the person making plain the letters and the meaning indicated by them a golden chain necklace and a purple robe to wear just like the Chaldean kings,[1015] and the third part[1016] of his own kingdom. **236** When this announcement was made, even though still more[1017] magi assembled, ambitious to discover the meaning of the writing, no one was any less puzzled. **237** But the king's grandmother,[1018] observing the king disheartened by this began to encourage him and to say that there was* a certain prisoner of war[1019] from Judea, a native from there called Daniel, who had been brought

---

149–150 finds Josephus' differentiation between τεῖχος and τοῖχος to be "odd" and suggests that it might best be explained as an attempt to introduce a stylistic variation of vocabulary. Josephus does something similar at *War* 5.57 (cf. Polybius 8.4.2; 21.28.8 and Diodorus Siculus 1.48.1. I am grateful to S. Mason for these references). Marcus (1937: 288–9 n. b) suggests that Josephus may have followed the text of Θ, which, he claims, reads "on the plaster of the wall *and* of the king's palace" (italics Marcus'). It should be noted, though, that Θ does not have καί at this point.

[1010] The biblical narrative emphasizes the king's terror caused by the hand (Dan 5:6,9,10).

[1011] Dan 5:7 refers to "the enchanters, the Chaldeans, and the diviners," and to all of them collectively as "the wise men of Babylon." On Josephus' use of these and similar terms see further note to "seers" at 10.195.

[1012] Greek τά τε σημεῖα καὶ τὰ ὀνείρατα. Josephus seems to have regarded the ability to interpret dreams as relevant in the present case even though the spectacle of the writing on the wall was not a dream. We have seen already that he regarded the terms ὄνειρος, ὄναρ, and ὄψις as broadly synonymous; see note to "dreams" at 10.194.

[1013] Josephus follows the biblical narrative (throughout Dan 5) in referring to Belshazzar as "king," though in fact he was never technically king of Babylon. Rather, he served as coregent with his father Nabonidus during the latter's sojourn in Arabia. On this complex issue see further Collins 1993: 32–33 and the literature cited there.

[1014] See note at 10.266.

[1015] The comparison with the Chaldean kings is Josephus' addition, derived perhaps from texts such as 1 Esd 3:6; Esth 8:15; 1 Macc 10:20; 62, 64; 14:43; Xenophon, *Anab.* 1.5.8; 8.29; *Cyr.* 1.3.2; 2.4.6; Herodotus, *Hist.* 3.20; etc. See also Gen 41:42.

[1016] Dan 5:7 "...and rank third in the kingdom." On the (unlikely) suggestion that the biblical text alludes here to the historical situation in which Belshazzar as co-ruler with his father Nabonidus offers the rank of third in the kingdom to one who is able to decipher the writing, see Collins 1993: 247.

[1017] The second wave of wise men follows the narration of events in LXX Dan 5:7. Josephus amplifies the story, though, by stating that the offer of a reward increased the number of people trying to decipher the riddle.

[1018] Dan 5:10 identifies this person as "the queen." Josephus apparently understood her to be the queen mother, i.e. Nebuchadnezzar's wife and Belshazzar's grandmother (μάμμη). This would take account of the longer passage of time in his own account between the reigns of Nebuchadnezzar and Belshazzar, though it does not account for the fact that, according to his own record of the succession of the various kings, Belshazzar was not related to Nebuchadnezzar. Josephus thus failed fully to integrate his historical sources with the biblical account, which presents Belshazzar as Nebuchadnezzar' son (Dan 5:11, 18 and 22; also Bar 1:11, 12); cf. note to "Babylonians" at 10.231. Bruce (1965: 150) suggests that Josephus may have wanted to identify the queen in this story with Nitocris in Herodotus' *Hist.* 1.185–187. On the importance of the queen mother in the ancient Near East, see Collins 1993: 248. Josephus follows MT and Θ at Dan 5:10 in having the queen take the initiative in addressing the king, whereas LXX has the king seeking out the queen's advice (LXX Dan 5:9; cf. Esth 4:11).

[1019] Josephus apparently found the term αἰχμάλωτος, "prisoner of war, captive," to be a point of contact between Daniel and the prisoners from Judea mentioned by Berosus in *Ant* 10.222. Begg (1993: 453 n. 20) has also pointed out that Josephus uses the term αἰχμάλωτος for himself in *War* 3.400; 6.107 and 626.

by Nabouchodonosor after he destroyed Jerusalem, a wise man[1020] skilled at discovering inexplicable things known only to God.[1021] When no one had been able to advise the king about the things he wanted to know, Daniel brought to light the things being sought.[1022] **238** And so she asked the king to summon him and to enquire of him about the writing and so to condemn the ignorance of those who had not deciphered it, even though the prospect being signified by God might be gloomy.[1023]

(3) 239[1024] When he heard these things Baltasar summoned* Daniel, and after explaining how he had learned of him and his wisdom[1025]—that a divine spirit[1026] was

Daniel is summoned by the king

For other possible parallels between Josephus' self-presentation and his portrayal of Daniel, see note to "noblest" at 10.186.

[1020] Greek σοφὸς ἀνήρ. On Josephus' presentation of the wisdom of Daniel, see note at 10.187.

[1021] Josephus emphasizes several times that Daniel had access to knowledge not normally granted to human beings (*Ant.* 10.194, 196, 204, 239). In the present context the biblical queen refers to Daniel as someone "endowed with the spirit of the holy gods" and as someone found to possess "enlightenment, understanding, and wisdom like the wisdom of the gods" (Dan 5:11). She then adds that "an excellent spirit, knowledge and understanding to interpret dreams, explain riddles, and solve problems" were found in him (Dan 5:12; cf. 5:14). These statements are similar to those of Nebuchadnezzar in Dan 4:8–9, 18 (in MT and Θ, but not in LXX). On the attribution of a divine spirit to Daniel see note to "spirit" at 10.239.

[1022] Cf. *Ant.* 10.195–210/Dan 2:1–45; *Ant.* 10.216–217/Dan 4:4–27.

[1023] The motivation to condemn the ignorance of the Babylonian wise men and the foreshadowing of a gloomy (σκυθρωπόν) prospect are amplifications of the biblical narrative. Like the biblical author, Josephus does not comment on the anomaly that someone as prominent as Daniel seems to be completely unknown to the king.

[1024] In this section of Dan 5 (vv. 13–28) Josephus follows the narrative of MT/Θ rather than LXX, which is significantly shorter, lacking much of vv. 13–16, 18–22, and 24. LXX also lacks the mysterious words themselves, though they are supplied in the preface to chapter 5 in a different order (μανη, φαρες, θεκελ). In LXX 5:26–28 there are 5, rather than 3, explanatory phrases for the meaning of the writing on the wall, on which see Collins 1993: 243. Josephus' concern in this section and the next is to emphasize Daniel's wisdom and the honor he enjoyed from both the king and God.

[1025] On the importance of Daniel's wisdom throughout Josephus' narrative see note at 10.187. In the present context Josephus makes explicit what, for him, was the primary nature of Daniel's wisdom, namely a

divinely imbued ability "to discover things that do not enter into the thinking of others." See also *Ant.* 10.237 where Belshazzar refers to Daniel as a man "skilled at discovering inexplicable things known only to God."

[1026] The *editio maior* reads θεῖον πνεῦμα, without the article, following RO. The LCL text, following SPLauV, reads τὸ θεῖον πνεῦμα, "the divine spirit." Josephus' term is reminiscent of the biblical narrative's attribution of a divine spirit (רוח אלהין קדישין, "a spirit of the holy gods;" Θ: πνεῦμα θεοῦ, "a spirit of God") to Daniel by the queen in Dan 5:11, and the king in Dan 5:14 (אלהין רוח, "a spirit of the gods;" Θ πνεῦμα θεοῦ). Both of these references are closely connected to Nebuchadnezzar's thrice-repeated affirmation in chapter 4 (vv. 8, 9, 18) that Daniel is endowed with "a spirit of the holy gods" (רוח אלהין קדישין; Θ: πνεῦμα θεοῦ ἅγιον, "a holy spirit of God); cf. Gen 41:38 of Joseph. Significantly, LXX does not have any of these references to a divine spirit, either from chapter 4 or from chapter 5. The only partial exception is when the queen in Dan 5:12 refers to the "excellent spirit" (רוח יתירה; Θ πνεῦμα περισσόν) in Daniel. For this statement LXX has πνεῦμα ἅγιον, "a holy spirit." These observations suggest that Josephus' biblical text may have been more like Θ than LXX at this point (cf. Levison 1996: 250, n.72). Later in his narrative (*Ant.* 10.250) Josephus paraphrases part of Dan 6:3 by stating that Daniel was believed to have the divinity (τὸ θεῖον) in himself, which is akin to his statement in the present context. In Dan 6:3 the LXX again has πνεῦμα ἅγιον, "a holy spirit," for MT's רוח יתירא; and Θ's πνεῦμα περισσόν. Earlier in his paraphrase of the Bible we find the same association between the divine spirit and the gift of prophecy: Josephus states that the deity (τὸ θεῖον) abandoned Saul and that "the divine spirit" (τοῦ θείου πνεύματος) passed to David, enabling him to prophesy (*Ant.* 6.166). Later in the story of Saul and David armed soldiers are overcome by "the divine spirit" (τοῦ θείου πνεύματος) and they begin to prophesy (*Ant.* 6.222). In *Ant.* 8.408 the "true prophet" is characterized as the man who has "the power of the divine spirit" (τοῦ θείου πνεύματος ἔχει τὴν δύναμιν). On Josephus' understanding of

present with him[1027] and that he alone was sufficiently skilled to discover things that do not enter into the thinking of others[1028]—he began to ask him to declare to him the writing and to reveal what it meant; **240** for to the one who did this he would give purple to wear and a golden collar around his neck and a third of his kingdom as an honor and reward for his wisdom, so that by them he might become most distinguished to those who saw and asked the reason for which he obtained them.[1029] **241** But Daniel implored him to keep the gifts for himself; for that which is wise and divine[1030] is incorruptible[1031] and a gift given to help those who ask;[1032] but he would reveal to him the writing, which indicated a catastrophic end of his life because he had not learned to live piously or to avoid improvising matters beyond human nature,[1033] even from the punishments his ancestor suffered on account of his acts of insolence toward God.[1034] **242** Yet even though Nabouchodonosor was shown mercy to return to a human manner of living[1035] and to his kingdom after many supplications and prayers, after his mode of life[1036] had been transformed to that of the beasts because he was impious[1037]—and because of these things he

---

the divine spirit in general, see Levison 1996, 1997; Best 1959. On the related matter of Josephus' use of the the notion of "divine inspiration" (ἔνθεος γενόμενος), see *Ant.* 6.56, 76; 8.346; 9.35; *War* 3.353; Gray 1993: 28–30.

[1027] The biblical narrative states three times (Dan 5:11, 12, 14) that the divine spirit was "in" Daniel. However, Josephus states that the spirit was "present with" (συμπάρεστι) him; cf. *Ant.* 10.250 and footnote there. Levison (1996: 250–51; 1997: 169–170) argues that Josephus deliberately distances himself from the biblical view in which God's spirit resides within Daniel, partly because such a view was vulnerable to easy caricature, as in Plutarch's *Cessation of Oracles* (*Mor.* 414e), where divine inspiration is seen as something akin to mechanical manipulation. Alternatively, Levison suggests Josephus may have been aware of (and keen to avoid) understandings of divine inspiration as sexual penetration (cf. Lucan, *Bell. civ.* 5.163–167, cited by Levison 1996: 251). While it is possible that concerns such as these may have played a part, it is important to note that the verb συμπάρειμι is used 6 times in Josephus' paraphrase of the Bible (*Ant.* 1.260; 2.268, 340; 3.316; 8.108; 10.239. Cf. *War* 5.380), and in each case it refers to God's presence with the people involved. This suggests that Josephus is more concerned to show the continuity of God's presence with significant individuals at significant times in biblical history than he is to distance Daniel from pagan notions of divine presence.

[1028] The biblical king states in Dan 5:14, "I have heard of you that a spirit of the gods is in you, and that enlightenment, understanding and excellent wisdom are found in you." Josephus frequently emphasizes Daniel's access to knowledge not normally available to

human beings (e.g. *Ant.* 10.194, 196, 204, 237).

[1029] The reason for the gifts is Josephus' addition.

[1030] Greek θεῖον. For related uses of this term, see note at 10.194.

[1031] Greek ἀδωροδόκητος. On the importance of being free from corruption, see note at 10.251.

[1032] Josephus softens the retort of the biblical Daniel: "Let your gifts be for yourself, or give your rewards to someone else!" (Dan 5:17). Feldman (1998: 634) sees in this statement a retort to the likes of Juvenal (*Sat.* 14.103–104) who claimed that the Jews never offered any kind of help to non-Jews.

[1033] Greek ὑπὲρ τὴν ἀνθρωπίνην φύσιν. In contrast to the king's hubris, Josephus several times describes Daniel as one who functions with divine enabling at a level beyond that normally allowed to humans; see notes at 10.194 and 215.

[1034] Josephus follows the narrative of MT and Θ, in which Daniel recalls the humiliation of Nebuchadnezzar because of his impiety. LXX, however, lacks Dan 5:18–22. Dan 5:20, "But when his heart was lifted up and his spirit was hardened so that he acted proudly, he was deposed from his kingly throne, and his glory was stripped from him." Josephus does not emphasize Nebuchadnezzar's insolence toward God as much as the biblical narrative, though he does refer to him as an audacious man in *Ant.* 10.219.

[1035] Greek βίος, "manner of living," is used in this context as a synonym of δίαιτα in the same passage.

[1036] Greek δίαιτα, "mode of life," is used in this context as a synonym of βίος in the same passage. On the use of this term elsewhere in Josephus, see note to "regimen" at 10.190.

[1037] *Ant.* 10.216–217/Dan 4:4–37.

praised God right up until the day he died as the one who possesses all power and who provides for humanity[1038]—Baltasar forgot these things and defamed[1039] the deity[1040] greatly when he was served with the vessels along with his concubines.[1041] **243** When God saw these things he was provoked with him and was making known beforehand, through the writing, to what end he himself would be subjected. And the words meant this.[1042] *Mane*:[1043] "This," he said, "may signify 'number' (in the Greek language),[1044] just as if God had numbered the time of your life[1045] and your rule, and the time still left to you is short.[1046] **244** *Thekel*:[1047] this means

Daniel deciphers the writing on the wall

[1038] Dan 5:21 ". . . until he learned that the Most High God has sovereignty over the kingdom of mortals, and sets over it whomever he will."

[1039] On Josephus' scruples against defaming the gods of others, see *Ant.* 4.207 and *Apion* 2.237. Philo expresses similar scruples in *QE* 2.5; *Spec.* 1.9.53; *Mos.* 2.37.203–38.208. Cf. Exod 22:27 (28). See further Feldman 2000: 403 n. 623.

[1040] Greek τὸ θεῖον. For other uses of this term, see note at 10.194.

[1041] Daniel's condemnation of the king is reminiscent of Josephus' own condemnation of the Judean revolutionaries who had defiled the temple during the siege of Jerusalem in his day (*War* 5.401–402). One cannot escape the suspicion that the criticism also has a bearing on Josephus' attitude to the Roman desecration of the temple and the removal of its sacred objects to Rome.

[1042] The riddle of the words on the wall continues to be a matter of scholarly debate and speculation. Part of the difficulty lies in the fact that there is some discrepancy in the original story between the form of the words on the wall (Dan 5:25) and the form of the words as they are given in Daniel's interpretation (Dan 5:26–28); e.g., the first word, *mene* is repeated on the wall but not in Daniel's interpretation; and the third word *parsin* is the plural of the word *peres*, which Daniel interprets. Also, the original words appear to be noun forms, while the interpretations of Daniel take them to be passive participles. This has led many scholars to conclude that the words originally had different meanings from those ascribed to them by Daniel (Collins 1993: 250–51). Josephus treats the words as nouns. On another note, it has often been suggested that the mysterious words originally referred to weights or monetary units listed in order of descending value. מנא, *mene*, stood for the *mina*, פרס, *peres*, stood for the half-*mina*, and תקל, *tekel*, stood for the *shekel*. On this understanding the declining values would be analogous to the declining value of the metals in Nebuchadnezzar's dream of the statue made of different metals. As the narrative presently reads in the Book of Daniel, though, the order has been disrupted, with פרס standing last rather than תקל, perhaps in order to make a pun on

"Persia." The preface to chapter 5 in LXX preserves the likely original order (Collins 1993: 251). Josephus follows the order of MT and does not seem to have appreciated the possible monetary or weight connotations of the terms.

[1043] Greek μάνη with textual variants μανῆ P and μανή LauE. Aramaic מנא אא; Θ Μανη; LXX omits the divine words at Dan 5:25 and 26, but the preface to chapter 5 renders it Μανη. Collins (1993: 252) notes a word-play with מני, the word used for "fate" in Isa 65:11. The term could also be used for the monetary unit or weight of a *mina* (see previous note).

[1044] Greek ἀριθμός. This is an editorial aside for the reader. Josephus is not implying that the king spoke Greek. The MT does not provide a single-word translation of the divine word (see note to "short" in this paragraph), though LXX, in the preface to chapter 5, renders this divine word ἠρίθμηται, "it has been numbered" (Vermes 1991: 152, n. 9; Collins 1993: 237).

[1045] In the biblical text (Dan 5:26) it is the king's rule alone that has been numbered (Vermes 1991: 157).

[1046] MT Dan 5:26 reads מנה־אלהא מלכותך והשלמה: "God has numbered the days of your kingdom and brought it to an end." LXX follows this reading closely with ἠρίθμηται ὁ χρόνος σου τῆς βασιλείας, ἀπολήγει ἡ βασιλεία σου, "the time of your kingdom is numbered, your kingdom is coming to an end" (translation by Collins 1993: 239). Θ renders this verse ἐμέτρησεν ὁ θεὸς τὴν βασιλείαν σου καὶ ἐπλήρωσεν αὐτήν, "God has measured your kingdom and completed it." The Latin, apparently rendering a text that combines aspects of LXX and Θ, reads *Numeravit Deus regnum tuum et conplevit illud.*

[1047] Greek θεκελ with textual variant θεκέλ SPLauE. Aramaic תקל; Θ θεκελ; LXX omits the divine words at Dan 5:25 and 27, but the preface to chapter 5 renders it θεκελ. Collins (1993: 252) notes that תקל can also be read as the imperfect of קלל (be light), hence Rashi's rendering: "You have been weighed before him and have been found light in every way." This is reminiscent of the biblical text's "you have been weighed on the scales and found wanting" (Dan 5:27). Collins points out further that the motif of weighing

'weight,'[1048] for God, having weighed the time[1049] of your kingdom, shows that it is already declining," he said*.[1050] "*Phares*:[1051] this means 'a fragment'[1052] (according to the Greek language); accordingly he will break up your kingdom and divide it between the Medes and the Persians."[1053]

Belshazzar rewards Daniel

(4) 245[1054] When Daniel had shown to the king that the writing on the wall meant these things, grief and misery—such as is reasonable for those to whom things hard to bear have been shown—seized Baltasar.[1055] **246** However, he did* not withhold the gifts he had promised to give, as from a prophet[1056] of evil tidings[1057] to himself, but gave them all, reasoning[1058] on the one hand that the things for which these tidings should be given were peculiar to himself and his fate, and not of the one who prophesied them, and deciding on the other hand that the rewards agreed upon were for a good and just man,[1059] even if the things about to happen should be gloomy.[1060]

---

the actions of people is common in eschatological contexts, e.g. *1 En.* 41:1; *2 En.* 52:15; *T. Ab.* 13:10; *4 Ezra* 3:34. The term *thekel* could also be used for the monetary unit of a *shekel*.

[1048] Greek τὸν σταθμόν. The MT does not provide a single-word translation for the divine word (see note to "he said" in this paragraph), though LXX, in the preface to chapter 5, renders this divine word ἕσταται, which is the perf. ind. mid/pass. 3rd sing. of ἵστημι. Collins (1993: 237) renders "it is established," which is possible (cf. LXX Gen 6:18; 12:8), though it could also have the specific sense of being set *in a balance or scale* (cf. Xenophon, *Cyr.* 8.2.21, where the verb is paralleled with ἀριθμέω as here); thus "it has been weighed" (so Vermes 1991: 152, n. 9), which seems better in context (cf. LXX 2 Sam 14:26).

[1049] The rather strange image of God weighing time, τὸν χρόνον, may arise from an imperfect recollection of the image in LXX Dan 5:26, which refers to μανη rather than to θεκελ; see note to "short" in previous paragraph.

[1050] MT Dan 5:27 reads תקילתה במאזניא והשתכחת חסיר "You have been weighed on the scales and found wanting." LXX differs from this widely with the statement, συντέτμηται καὶ συντετέλεσται ἡ βασιλεία σου, "Your kingdom is cut off and finished" (Collins 1993: 239). Θ follows the biblical text more closely with ἐστάθη ἐν ζυγῷ καὶ εὑρέθη ὑστεροῦσα, "[Your kingdom] has been weighed in the balance and found lacking." The Latin follows MT and Θ with, *adpensum est in statera et inventus es minus habens*.

[1051] Greek φαρές. MT פרסין (Dan 5:25), פרס (Dan 5:28); Θ φαρες; LXX omits the divine words at Dan 5:25 and 28, but the preface to chapter 5 renders it φαρες. The word may refer to the monetary unit of a half-*mina*, but it also contains a play on "divide" and "Persia" (Collins 1993: 252).

[1052] Greek κλάσμα. This is a hapax legomenon in Josephus. The MT does not provide a single word

translation for the divine word (see next footnote) though LXX, in the preface to chapter 5, renders this divine word ἐξῆρται, which is the perf. ind. mid/pass. 3rd sing. of ἐξαίρω, "to be carried or taken away" (thus Collins 1993: 237; cf. LXX 3 Kgdms 8:25). Vermes (1991: 152 n. 9) renders "it has been divided" with unclear justification.

[1053] MT Dan 5:28 reads פריסת מלכותך ויהיבת למדי ופרס "Your kingdom is divided and given to the Medes and Persians." Θ follows the biblical text closely with διήρηται ἡ βασιλεία σου καὶ ἐδόθη Μήδοις καὶ Πέρσαις, "Your kingdom has been divided and given to the Medes and Persians." LXX omits the first part of the sentence and has only τοῖς Μήδοις καὶ τοῖς Πέρσαις δίδοται, "it has been given to the Medes and Persians." The Latin follows MT and Θ with *divisum est regnum tuum et datum est Medis et Persis*.

[1054] In this section Josephus expands on the last 2 verses of Dan 5 and the first 2 verses of chapter 6. In the process he heightens the drama of the story, and once again places it in the context of wider history (though not without some deft maneuvering to accomplish this). As in previous episodes Daniel emerges as a man held in high esteem by kings.

[1055] Belshazzar's emotional response is Josephus' addition.

[1056] On Daniel as a prophet, see note to "prophets" at 10.267.

[1057] In *Ant.* 10.268 Josephus claims that Daniel was distinguished from other prophets in that he was a prophet of good news. For other instances where Daniel in fact predicted bad news, see note there.

[1058] Belshazzar's thought processes are Josephus' own addition to the narrative. Collins (1993: 253) argues that the reward of the successful interpreter is a traditional motif in such tales.

[1059] Greek ἀνδρὸς ἀγαθοῦ καὶ δικαίου. Josephus consistently emphasizes the exemplary character of

Such was his ruling. **247** And not long afterwards[1061] both he and the city were captured by Cyrus the king of Persia who marched against him;[1062] for it was in the time of Baltasar that the capture of Babylon took place, when Baltasar had reigned for seventeen[1063] years. **248** And so, such was the end of the line of King Nabouchodonosor as we have received it.[1064] And Darius, who crushed the Babylonian hegemony with his relative[1065] Cyrus, was sixty-two years old when he took Babylon.[1066] He was a son of Astyages,[1067] but was called another name among the Greeks.[1068] **249** And he took Daniel the prophet[1069] and brought him to Media to himself and shared all honor with him[1070] and kept him with him; for he was one of three satraps whom he appointed over 360 satrapies; for Darius appointed this many rulers for each.[1071]

Daniel (see Feldman 1998: 631–5). On the virtue of justice throughout Josephus' writings see also *War* 5.27; 5.34; *Ant.* 1.158; 3.66, 67; 4.46; 217, 223; 6.36, 160, 212, 290, 294, 305; 7.110, 391; 8.21; 10.50, 155; 11.121, 139, 183; 13.294; 16.176, 177; *Apion* 2.293; Feldman 1998: 113–6.

[1060] Dan 5:29 states only that Belshazzar gave to Daniel the things that had been promised.

[1061] Dan 5:30 states that Belshazzar was killed "that very night." Collins (1993: 252–253) cites Xenophon, *Cyr.* 7.5.17–29 to the effect that Babylon fell to a nighttime attack. See also Herodotus, *Hist.* 1.191; *Nabonidus Chronicle* col. 3.15.

[1062] The biblical narrative makes no mention of Cyrus at this point. In *Apion* 1.150–153 (on which, see Barclay, BJP 10) Josephus quotes Berosus' account of the end of the neo-Babylonian empire, which makes it clear that it was Cyrus of Persia who defeated the last Babylonian king, Nabonidus. Cf. Herodotus, *Hist.* 1.188–191; Xenophon, *Cyr.* 7.5.15. In the present context, though, Josephus' task is complicated by the Book of Daniel's introduction of Darius the Mede, and by the handwriting's prediction that the Babylonian kingdom would be divided between the Medes and the Persians.

[1063] Josephus gleaned this information from Berosus (cf. *Apion* 1.150). Nabonidus, with whom Josephus identifies Belshazzar (*Ant.* 10.231), reigned from 556–539 B.C.E. According to rabbinic tradition, Belshazzar reigned only 2 years (Ginzberg 1909–38, 6: 430).

[1064] Belshazzar was not in fact of the line of Nebuchadnezzar, despite the biblical representation of him as Nebuchadnezzar's son (Dan 5:11, 18 and 22); cf. notes at 10.231. Josephus' claim to be passing on what he knows of the succession of these kings is belied by his own work in *Apion*, in which he quotes Berosus' more accurate account.

[1065] Josephus makes Darius the Mede a relative (τοῦ συγγενοῦς) of Cyrus. According to *Ant.* 10.232 they were comrades in arms. This association would seem to be Josephus' own innovation motivated in part by his interpretation of the fourth kingdom of Nebuchad-

nezzar's statue as Rome. See further note to "the Mede" at 10.232.

[1066] This accords with MT Dan 6:1 [= English 5:31], which is followed by Θ. LXX states that Darius was "full of days and illustrious in old age." Unlike MT and Θ, LXX states that the kingdom was given to Ἀρταξέρξης ὁ τῶν Μήδων, "Artaxerxes of the Medes." A variant reading in Pap. 967 reads "Xerxes, king of the Medes."

[1067] Astyages (ruled 585–550 B.C.E) was the last king of the Medians whose daughter, Mandane, was the mother of Cyrus; Yamauchi 1992. Dan 9:1 states that Darius the Mede was the son of Ahasuerus (on which see Collins 1993: 348).

[1068] Josephus' vague comment about another name for Darius the Mede betrays the difficulty created by the fact that Josephus' non-biblical sources contained no reference to Darius the Mede, whose identity has long been a puzzle to historians. Bruce (1965: 150) suggests that Josephus may have had in mind Cyaxares II of Xenophon's *Cyropaedia* 1.5.2 etc.

[1069] On Daniel as a prophet, see note to "prophets" at 10.267.

[1070] Josephus anticipates Dan 6:28 (Vermes 1991: 158). The honor Daniel enjoyed is an important theme in this part of the *Antiquities*, on which see further note to "public" at 10.266.

[1071] Dan 6:1–2 refers to three "presidents" (סרכין; Θ τακτικούς "officers" [Marcus 1937: 296, n. a], "ministers" [Collins 1993: 256, n. 11]; LXX ἡγουμένους "governors") in authority over 120 satraps (אחשדרפניא; Θ and LXX σατράπας). LXX has 127 satraps. Josephus apparently read the passage to mean each of the three presidents was in charge of one hundred and twenty satrapies, for a total of three hundred and sixty satrapies. Herodotus (*Hist.* 3.89) ascribes to Darius I of Persia the organization of his realm into twenty satrapies. In Esther we read that Xerxes had 127 provinces administered by "satraps" and "governors" and "officials" (1:1; 8:9). Similarly, 1 Esd 3:2 speaks of the 127 satrapies of Darius I under "satraps and generals and governors."

Daniel is the victim of a plot

(5) 250[1072] Accordingly Daniel, being held in such honor[1073] and brilliant regard by Darius that he alone was consulted by him in all things,[1074] because he was believed[1075] to have the divinity[1076] in himself, was envied; for those who see others held in greater honor than themselves by their kings resort to slander.[1077] **251** But although those who were vexed with him were seeking an occasion for slander and accusation against him because he was held in esteem by Darius, he provided them not even a single cause; for being both above money and disdaining all unjust gain,[1078] he thought it shameful to take even what was given legitimately,[1079] and so

---

[1072] In this section and the next Josephus covers the biblical narrative of Dan 6 for which LXX differs from MT/Θ in many small ways (Collins 1993: 262–264), though no clear pattern emerges regarding Josephus' use of either. Josephus' primary concern in this part of his narrative seems to be to show how Daniel's success, and in particular the honor in which he was held by the king, led to envy and malice on the part of others.

[1073] The honor Daniel enjoyed is an important theme in this part of the *Antiquities*, on which see further note to "public" at 10.266.

[1074] Dan 6:3 states that Darius planned to appoint Daniel over the whole kingdom. Josephus claims something more modest for Daniel. Feldman (1998: 653–4) argues that Josephus was careful to avoid any suggestion that Jews exercise undue power.

[1075] Feldman (1998: 638) and Levison (1996: 251; 1997: 170) argue that Josephus' use of πεπιστευμένος in connection with Daniel's possession of the divine spirit betrays reticence on Josephus' part to affirm that God was actually "in" Daniel rather than simply "with" him; cf. *Ant.* 10.239 and note to "with him" there. It should be noted, however, that Josephus several times hints that Daniel was blessed with an intimacy with God not normally associated with mere mortals (e.g. *Ant.* 10.194, 196, 200, 204, 211–212, 215, 237, 239, 264, 267, 268, 277). By stating in the present context that Daniel "was believed" to possess the divine spirit Josephus can appear to be modest while at the same time greatly enhancing Daniel's profile in a Roman setting. In other words, the present statement is closely akin to Josephus' claim in *Ant.* 10.268 that Daniel had "a reputation for divinity (θειότητος) with the public." The ascription of the view to the public (τοῖς ὄχλοις) lends an air of authority to the statement without implying that Josephus was uncomfortable with it. Indeed, in the paragraph immediately preceding this one (*Ant.* 10.267), Josephus states that on the basis of the books Daniel wrote, "*we* believe (πεπιστεύκαμεν) …that Daniel kept company with God" (emphasis added). A similar strategy may be detected in Josephus' presentation of Moses (cf. *Ant.* 3.75, 96–97, 99, 180, 318, 320; *Apion* 1.279). I have argued in another context (Spilsbury 1998: 106–9) that Josephus was not

averse to his Roman audience forming opinions of his biblical characters that were akin to their own views of divine figures (Tiede 1972: 207–40). On a related note, Josephus states in *Ant.* 6.263 that humble people are persuaded (πεπιστεύκασιν) that the deity is present (πάρεστι) in all that happens in life. Here again Josephus clearly does not intend to distance himself from the affirmation of God's presence.

[1076] Greek τὸ θεῖον. Josephus makes a similar statement about Daniel in *Ant.* 10.268. For other uses of this term, see note to "deity" at 10.194. For other references to Daniel's possession of the divine Spirit, see note to "spirit" at 10.239. Dan 6:3 states that an "excellent spirit" (רוח יתירא; Θ πνεῦμα περισσόν, LXX πνεῦμα ἅ-γιον) was in him.

[1077] Josephus makes explicit and emphasizes what is implicit in the biblical narrative, namely that the presidents and satraps conspired against Daniel because they were jealous of his high position (Dan 6:3–4). In MT the number of those envious of Daniel includes 120 satraps and the two presidents who served alongside Daniel. Θ calls these latter individuals οἱ τακτικοί, "the ministers" (Collins 1993: 164). Josephus does not follow LXX at Dan 6:4, which specifies that it was the two young men (νεανίσκοι), his fellow presidents, who were Daniel's chief opponents in the story (Collins 1993: 262–263). Josephus often attributes his protagonists' woes to the jealousy and malice of others (e.g. *Ant.* 10.212, 256; Daube 1980: 29; Feldman 1998: 644). In the present instance one might well detect a rueful reflection on Josephus' own experience of the jealousy and slander of others (e.g. *Life* 80, 84, 122, 189, 204, 416, 424, 425, 428). On other such parallels between Josephus and Daniel see note to "noblest" at 10.186.

[1078] Josephus has already demonstrated this virtue of Daniel in *Ant.* 10.241. Dan 6:4 states that "they could find no grounds for complaint or any corruption, because he was faithful and no negligence or corruption could be found in him." Earlier in his biblical narrative (*Ant.* 4.46) Josephus describes Moses as having never accepted a gift so as to corrupt justice. See also Thucydides 2.60.5 (cited by Feldman 1998: 115). Further, it should also be noted that the only

did not provide to those who were jealous of him the chance to discover any charges. **252** But because they had nothing of which they might accuse him before the king, and so damage him in his esteem by disgrace and false accusation, they began to seek another method by which they might do away with him. [1080] And so, when they saw Daniel praying to God three times a day they realized they had found a pretext by which they might destroy him. [1081] **253** They went to Darius and reported to him that his satraps and governors had decided to give the public leave for thirty days, during which none of them might make a request or pray, either to himself or to the gods,[1082] and, further, that anyone who transgressed this decree of theirs they resolved to throw into the pit[1083] of lions to be killed.

(6) 254[1084] And the king, neither recognizing their malice nor suspecting that these resolutions had been trumped up against Daniel, [1085] said he was pleased with the things they decreed, and promising to ratify their resolution, he circulated a proclamation making clear to the public what had been resolved by the satraps. **255** And while all the others kept quiet, taking care not to transgress the orders, Daniel took no thought of them[1086] but, as was his custom,[1087] prayed to God standing[1088] in the

Daniel defies the king's edict

---

other time Josephus uses the phrase παντὸς λήμματος is with reference to himself in *Life* 79. On other such parallels between Josephus himself and Daniel, see cross- references in previous footnote.

[1079] Josephus embellishes the biblical narrative in characteristic fashion, matching his claims about his own probity (*Life* 80).

[1080] According to the biblical narrative the conspirators initially tried to find a way to impeach Daniel in connection with the affairs of state (literally, 'from the side of the kingdom," Dan 6:4), but quickly concluded, "We shall not find any ground for complaint against this Daniel unless we find it in connection with the law of his God" (Dan 6:5). Josephus does not specifically raise the matter of the law here, but focuses on Daniel's practice of daily prayers. Braverman (1978: 81) notes Jerome's claim that Jewish interpreters took the phrase "from the side of the kingdom" to be a reference to the queen or the king's concubines. In other words, the conspirators tried to catch Daniel in some sexual impropriety, but were unable to do so because he was a eunuch. Jerome himself did not hold to this interpretation. While there is no extant evidence of such an interpretive tradition in rabbinic literature, Braverman cites *Midrash Meg.* 176, in which Daniel and his companions subjected themselves to castration in order to remove suspicions of immorality. On the tradition that Daniel and his companions were eunuchs, see further note to "castrated" at 10.186.

[1081] Josephus brings this detail forward from its slightly later position in the biblical narrative (Dan 6:10; Vermes 1991: 158). In the biblical narrative the

conspirators are already aware of Daniel's religious practice.

[1082] The prohibition against prayer is not extended to prayers to the king in the biblical narrative. Dan 6:7 states "whoever prays to anyone, divine or human, for thirty days, *except to you*, O king, shall be thrown into a den of lions" (emphasis added). The biblical narrative would seem to be more coherent than Josephus' in that it suggests that the king's vanity was the cause for his blindness to the evil intent of the plot. Josephus' version excludes this motivation, thus making the story that much less plausible. It is possible that Josephus was influenced by a desire not to appear to be criticizing the imperial cult in Rome.

[1083] Throughout this episode Josephus, following both LXX and Θ, uses the term λάκκος for the "pit" of lions (*Ant.* 10.253, 257, 258, 259, 261). Significantly, the term functions as a point of comparison between Daniel, Jeremiah, Joseph and Josephus himself, all of whom had experiences in a pit at one time or another (*Ant.* 2.31–35; 10.121; *War* 3.341). For Josephus' sense of personal identification with these biblical figures, see further Daube: 1980, Gnuse 1996: 27–32, and note to "noblest" at 10.186.

[1084] In this section Josephus highlights Daniel's piety and his innocence in the face of the accusations brought against him by his enemies. Josephus' account of Daniel in the lions' den is embellished in terms of drama, and glossed with rationalization.

[1085] These insights into the king's state of mind are Josephus' own contribution.

[1086] The biblical narrative makes no reference to the actions of others at this point. Josephus' portrayal of

sight of all.[1089] **256** But when the occasion against Daniel that they were eager to receive presented itself to them, the satraps immediately came to the king and began to make the accusation that Daniel alone[1090] was transgressing his orders. For none of the others dared to pray to the gods, and this not because of impiety but because of watching and preserving . . .[1091] by jealousy;[1092] **257** for supposing that Darius might do this from greater favor than they were expecting, and would even be ready to grant indulgence to one who had despised his orders, and begrudging Daniel this very thing, they would not change to a milder course but were demanding that he throw him into the pit of lions in accordance with the law.[1093] **258** But Darius, hoping[1094] that the deity[1095] would rescue Daniel and that he might not suffer any danger from the wild beasts, exhorted him to bear the events cheerfully.[1096] After Daniel had been thrown into the pit, and the stone lying against the door of the opening was sealed, he went to bed but spent the whole night fasting and sleepless, agonizing about Daniel; **259** and at dawn he arose and went to the pit and, finding the seal that he had left to mark the stone intact, he opened it and shouted, calling Daniel and enquiring if he was* safe.[1097] And when Daniel heard the king

Daniel survives the pit of lions

Daniel emphasizes his courage (Feldman 1998: 633). Collins (1993: 268) notes that the biblical Daniel is less confrontational than Josephus' Daniel at this point.

[1087] The biblical narrative states that Daniel continued to go to his house to pray, "just as he had done previously" (Dan 6:10). *b. Ber.* 31a (cited by Collins 1993: 269) states that Daniel's practice in the present story already had the force of custom. See also *b. Ber.* 26b.

[1088] Dan 6:10 states that Daniel got down on his knees three times a day to pray. Θ follows MT, but LXX depicts Daniel prostrating himself (ἔπιπτεν ἐπὶ πρόσωπον αὐτοῦ). Josephus depicts Daniel *standing* to pray, and omits the reference to the thrice daily repetition. The Gospel of Mark assumes standing as a common posture in prayer: "Whenever you stand praying..." (Mark 11:25; see also Matt 6:5; Luke 18:11, 13). The Mishnah takes standing to be the normal posture for prayer; *m. Ber.* 5.1 (cited by Collins 1993: 269; see also Bockmuehl 1990). In *Ant.* 4.212 Josephus reports Moses as requiring that prayers of thanksgiving be offered to God twice daily. Feldman (2000: 406 n. 639) takes this as a reference to recitation of the *Shema* (Deut 6:7) rather than the three daily prayers that were instituted to replace the daily sacrifices (*b. Ber.* 26b). Biblical support for three times of daily prayer includes Ps 55:17, but see also Ps 119:164 which speaks of praying seven times a day. *Did.* 8 and *2 En.* 51:4 also make mention of thrice daily prayers. On the complex practice in Qumran, see Collins 1993: 269.

[1089] The biblical account tells of Daniel going in his own house to the upper room which had windows open toward Jerusalem (Dan 6:10). Josephus makes no mention of the upper room, or of praying toward

Jerusalem, on which see 1 Kgs 8:35; 1 Esd 4:58; *m. Ber.* 4.5. In *War* 2.128 the Essenes are said to pray toward the sun; but see Ezek 8:16.

[1090] The emphasis on Daniel as the only one to disobey the king's edict is an addition to the biblical narrative.

[1091] There appears to be text missing at this point. Feldman (1998: 653 n. 47) states: "the import appears to be that those who observed the edict not to pray did so not because of impiety but because they realized how important it was to maintain respect for law and order."

[1092] Josephus often attributes his protagonists' woes to the jealousy and malice of others (e.g. *Ant.* 10.212, 250; Daube 1980: 29; Feldman 1998: 644).

[1093] Josephus' narrative implies that the king might well have been tempted to overlook the law or even to change it in favor of Daniel. The biblical narrative, though, speaks of the unchangeable law of the Medes and Persians, which bound the king to fulfill its requirements despite his desire to rescue Daniel (Dan 9:8, 12, 15).

[1094] Josephus supplies the element of Darius' hope in God.

[1095] Greek τὸ θεῖον. For other uses of this term, see note to "deity" at 10.194.

[1096] The biblical Darius gives no such exhortation to cheerfulness, but utters the prayer, "May your God, whom you faithfully serve, deliver you!" (Dan 6:16).

[1097] Josephus abridges the biblical king's words in which he asks whether Daniel's God has been able to deliver him (Dan 6:20). Feldman (1998: 638) notes a tendency on Josephus' part to deemphasize the role of God at certain points in his narrative.

and said he had suffered no harm,[1098] Darius ordered him to be drawn up out of the pit of lions. **260** But when his enemies saw that Daniel had suffered nothing terrible, they did not think that he had been saved because of the deity[1099] and his providential care[1100] of Daniel, but supposed it was because the lions had been filled up with food[1101] that they had not touched Daniel or even approached him; and they were saying this to the king.[1102] **261** But hating their wickedness he commanded* that many pieces of meat be thrown to the lions, and when they were sated he ordered the enemies of Daniel to be thrown into the pit, so that he might learn whether it was because of surfeit that the lions had not come near.[1103] **262** But it became plain to Darius when the satraps were thrown to the beasts that the deity[1104] had rescued Daniel; for the lions did not spare even one of them,[1105] but tore them all to pieces as if they were extremely hungry and in need of food.[1106] I do not think hunger aroused them to anger, since they had been filled a little while before by plentiful meat; but it was for the punishment of the men's evil,[1107] for this was conspicuous even to irrational animals[1108]—a punishment purposed beforehand by God.[1109]

[1098] Josephus omits the biblical Daniel's reference to an angel sent from God to shut the lions' mouths (Dan 6:22). He made a similar omission in the story of the three youths in the furnace (Dan 3:24–28; *Ant.* 10.214–215); cf. notes at 10.216, 271 and 272. LXX similarly omits the reference to the angel found both in MT and in Θ. Instead, LXX Dan 6:19 has the statement ὁ θεὸς τοῦ Δανιηλ πρόνοιαν ποιούμενος αὐτοῦ ἀπέκλεισε τὰ στόματα τῶν λεόντων, "the God of Daniel took providential care of him and shut the mouths of the lions" (Collins 1993: 259). This is the only instance in either of the Greek versions of the Book of Daniel in which the term πρόνοια occurs (πρόνοια is used elsewhere in LXX at 2 Macc 4:6; 3 Macc 4:21; 5:30; 4 Macc 9:24; 13:19; 17:22; Wis 14:3; 17:2). The term is highly significant for Josephus' conception of God's involvement in human affairs (on which see note to "providence" at 10.278). In the present context it is noteworthy that Josephus uses πρόνοια in the very next sentence. This may indicate that Josephus was using a biblical text similar to LXX at this point. It is also significant to note that in another of the stories where Josephus omits a biblical reference to divine aid mediated through an angelic figure, namely the story of the three youths in the furnace, Josephus once again used the notion of divine providence (θεία προνοία) as a substitute (*Ant.* 10.214).

[1099] Greek τὸ θεῖον. For other uses of this term, see note to "deity" at 10.194. In the present instance the expression used by Josephus, τὸ θεῖον καὶ τὴν τούτου πρόνοιαν, is reminiscent of the expression θεία προνοία in *Ant.*10.214; cf. previous footnote.

[1100] Josephus uses the highly significant term πρόνοια here to speak of God's providential care of Daniel. On Josephus' use of this term throughout his works, see

note to "providence" at 10.278.

[1101] Feldman (1998: 639) cites a rabbinic parallel to this motif from the Midrash on Ps 64:1.

[1102] The biblical narrative makes no such reference to the views of Daniel's enemies.

[1103] This test of the lions' hunger is an addition to the biblical narrative.

[1104] Greek τὸ θεῖον. For other uses of this term, see note to "deity" at 10.194.

[1105] Josephus omits the biblical detail that the wives and children of Daniel's enemies were thrown to the lions as well (Dan 6:24). He also does not follow LXX Dan 6:25 in specifying that it was just two men who along with their families were thrown to the lions. On these individuals, see note to "slander" at 10.250. Josephus' vagueness of this matter enabled him to sidestep the rather difficult implication of the biblical narrative that 122 men along with their wives and children were all thrown to the lions.

[1106] Vermes (1991: 158 n. 15) cites a similar haggadic account in the *Midr. Ps.* on Psalm 64:1 (ed. S. Buber, 311).

[1107] Josephus makes a similar editorial comment about the demise of Haman in *Ant* 11.268.

[1108] The rationality, or otherwise, of animals was a matter of significant debate in the ancient world; see Sorabji 2003. Josephus calls the lions ἄλογος, "without λόγος, lacking reason", yet ascribes to them insight into the morality of humans. See also *War* 4.170; 6.197; *Apion* 1.224; 2.213, 271. In *Ant.* 4.108 Balaam's donkey is said to discern (συνεῖσα) the divine spirit.

[1109] This rationalizing explanation is Josephus' addition. The biblical Daniel expresses the view that God sent an angel to save him because he was blameless before God and the king, and no harm came

Daniel, honored by King Darius, builds a fortress

(7) 263[1110] And so after those who plotted against Daniel had been destroyed in this manner, King Darius sent into the whole country[1111] praising the God whom Daniel worshipped*, saying that he alone was true and the possessor of all power;[1112] and he also held Daniel in exceeding honor by appointing him first of his friends.[1113]

---

to him because he trusted in God (Dan 5:22–23).

[1110] In this section, which runs from here all the way to the end of Book 10, Josephus composes an elaborate conclusion to his recitation of the story of Daniel. This conclusion can be divided into three distinct parts. In Part 1 (*Ant.* 10.263–265) Josephus covers the closing verses of Dan 6 (vv. 25–28), emphasizing once again the honor Daniel enjoyed with both the king and God, and then going beyond the Bible in portraying Daniel as a man of action not unlike Nebuchadnezzar himself, whose famous building projects are described in *Ant.* 10.224–226. In Part 2 (*Ant.* 10.266–275) Josephus praises Daniel's prophetic abilities and provides in the process first a summary and then an interpretation of Dan 8, as an example of the precision and reliability of his predictions. In Part 3 (*Ant.* 10.276–281) Josephus brings his conclusion to a climax by arguing that Daniel's prophecies prove beyond all doubt that God excercises providential oversight over human affairs, and that those who, like the Epicureans, deny this are sorely mistaken.

Part 1 of this conclusion to the story of Daniel functions for Josephus as a bridge between the story of lions' den and the vision of Dan 8. As such, it stands in the narrative in the place of the Dan 7, which Josephus omits altogether. We may only speculate at to why Josephus chose to omit this chapter. He might have defended his actions with a rationale similar to the one he used in *Ant.* 10.210, namely that it was his duty as a historian to record the past and not predictions about the future. More important than that, though, is the fact that Josephus would very likely have perceived significant thematic continuities between the Nebuchadnezzar's vision of the statue in Dan 2 and Daniel's own vision of the four beasts and the "one like a human being" in Dan 7. His reasons for omitting chapter 7 would thus likely have been the same as for his reticence to speak of the meaning of the stone in chapter 2. In both visions a 4-staged procession of Gentile kingdoms is succeeded by an eternal kingdom that is in some sense not simply a continuation of the human empires. Of the stone in Dan 2 we read: "And in the days of those kings the God of heaven will set up a kingdom that shall never be destroyed, nor shall this kingdom be left to another people. It shall crush all these kingdoms and bring them to an end, and it shall stand forever" (Dan 2:44). In a similar vein in Dan 7:14

we read of the kingdom given to the one like a human being: "To him was given dominion and glory and kingship, that all peoples, nations and languages should serve him. His dominion is an everlasting dominion that shall not pass away, and his kingship is one that shall never be destroyed." A few verses later: "But the holy ones of the Most High shall receive the kingdom and possess the kingdom forever—forever and ever" (Dan 7:18; see also v. 27). Josephus may have felt that his oblique comments on Nebuchadnezzar's stone vision were already bold enough, and that to repeat chapter 7 for a Roman audience would be pushing their patience a little too far. Josephus may also have felt more comfortable reporting such predictions when they came from the mouths of a Gentile (like a Nebuchadnezzar or a Balaam; cf. *Ant.* 4.114–117, 125) than when they came from a Judean like Daniel. Of course, we should observe that Josephus also omits Daniel's visions in chapters 9–12. P.R. Davies has suggested that this might be due to the fact that while in the first half of the book empires are granted to various peoples according to the divine will, in the latter visions "they emerge as the outcome of angelic warfare…as if to deny the direct working of divine providence in the imperial sequence" (1991: 166). Be that as it may, Josephus may simply have felt that his summary of chapter 8 already said as much as he wanted to, and that he had by this time already given Daniel more than his fair share of space in the *Antiquities*. As is made clear in the notes below, there are indications that Josephus occasionally modified his account of Dan 8 with narrative details gleaned from the final chapters of the Book of Daniel. On Daniel's omission of chapters 7 and 9–12, see also Fischer 1978: 175–7.

[1111] The biblical narrative has it that Darius wrote to "all peoples and nations of every language throughout the whole world" (Dan 6:25).

[1112] Dan 6:26–27 is more effusive: "I make a decree, that in all my royal dominion people should tremble and fear before the God of Daniel: For he is the living God, enduring forever. His kingdom shall never be destroyed, and his dominion has no end. He delivers and rescues, he works signs and wonders in heaven and on earth; for he has saved Daniel from the power of the lions." In LXX the king requires all his subjects to worship Daniel's God and he renounces idol worship.

[1113] The honor Daniel enjoyed is an important theme in this part of the *Antiquities*, on which see

264 And being thus eminent and famous because of his reputation as someone be-loved of God,[1114] Daniel built in Ecbatana[1115] of Media a fortress:[1116] a most beauti-ful structure and wonderfully made, which still exists and is preserved, and to those who see it it seems to have been built recently and to have come into being upon that very day on which each person examines it; so new and in full bloom is its beauty, and not aged by so much time; **265** for even buildings suffer the same as humans and grow old, and their strength is weakened by the years, and their beauty wastes away. They still bury the kings of Media and Persia and Parthia in the for-tress, and the person entrusted with this is a Judean priest—and this still happens right up to this very day.[1117]

266 Now in the case of this man [Daniel] it is worth relating even what someone who has heard [it] would really marvel at, for everything prospered for him in an unexpected[1118] way, [1119] as for one of the greatest:[1120] even in the course of his life-time he had* honor and fame from kings and the public,[1121] and since his death an

Daniel's enduring legacy

---

further note to "public" at 10.266. The title πρῶτος τῶν φίλων, "first of friends," was characteristic of Helle-nistic courts; cf. Stählin 1974, 9: 147–8; Bickerman 1938: 40–42; Millar 1977: 110–22. . Dan 6:28 states simply that "Daniel prospered during the reign of Darius and the reign of Cyrus the Persian;" though LXX Pap. 967 states: "Daniel was appointed over all the kingdom of Darius" (cited by Collins 1993: 259, n. 27). Vermes (1991: 151) notes that Josephus' phrase echoes LXX's use of φίλος as a court official in Dan 3:91, 94; 5:23 and 6:14. In the last of these references Daniel is explicitly referred to as the king's friend (τὸν φίλον σου). In the present context, Josephus also states that Daniel was a friend of God (see next footnote). See also *Ant* 11.32, 121.

[1114] Greek θεοφιλής. On Josephus' use of this term, see note at 10.215. In the present context Josephus draws a clear connection between the fact that Daniel was "friend" (φίλος) of the king and a "friend of God" (θεοφιλής)

[1115] Bruce (1965: 150) suggests that Josephus may have confused Ecbatana, where according to Ezra 6:2 there was a fortress (בירתא; LXX βάρις), with Susa.

[1116] It is not at all clear where Josephus got the idea that Daniel built a fortress in Ecbatana, or anywhere else. It may be relevant to note, that the term used for fortress here, βάρις, does occur in Θ Dan 8:2. MT states that Daniel was in the fortified city (הבירה) of Susa (for this translation of הבירה see Collins 1993: 329), which Θ renders ἐν Σούσοις τῇ βάρει, "in the fortress of Susa." LXX has ἐν Σούσοις τῇ πόλει ("in the city of Susa"). This slight evidence, however, does not relate to Ecbatana; nor does it say anything about Daniel actually building the fortress. Feldman suggests that Josephus added the claim motivated by a desire to pre-sent Daniel as the ideal man of action (Feldman 1998: 635–636), not unlike Nebuchadnezzar.

[1117] For various rabbinic traditons related to this point, see note to "memorial" in next paragraph.

[1118] Greek παραδόξως, "contrary to expectation, incredible" (LSJ, s.v.). Josephus uses the term two other times in his paraphrase of the Book of Daniel (*Ant.* 10.214, 235), and a total of 29 times in his biblical paraphrase as a whole (*Ant.* 2.91, 216, 223, 267, 285, 295, 345, 347; 3.1, 14, 30, 38; 5.28, 37, 125; 6.171, 290; 7.239; 8.130, 317; 9.14, 58, 60, 182; 10.24, 28). It often refers to the divine or miraculous element in the narrative. On Josephus' ambivalent attitude to miracles, see Betz 1974, 1987; MacRae 1965.

[1119] I have followed the emendation of Marcus (LCL, following SPLauV) for this clause: ἅπαντα γὰρ αὐτῷ παραδόξως...εὐτυχήθη. The *editio maior* reads ἀπαντᾷ γὰρ αὐτῷ παραδόξως, "for it happened* unexpectedly for him."

[1120] A textual variant (SPLauV and followed by Marcus, LCL) has "as for one of the greatest prophets." The present reading is supported by RO, and it seems to be the (preferred) "more difficult reading" in light of the Christian copyists' tendency to include Daniel among the prophets. On Josephus' presentation of Dan-iel as a prophet, see note at 10.267.

[1121] The honor in which Daniel was held by all is an important theme of this section of the *Antiquities*; cf. *Ant.* 10.189, 215, 240, 249, 250, 252, 263. A closely related theme is the honor Daniel received from God. In *Ant.* 10.263–264, after speaking of the exceptionally high honor in which Daniel was held by King Darius, Josephus refers to Daniel's reputation as a man dear to God (θεοφιλής). A similar pattern pertains in *Ant.* 10.215 with respect to Daniel's three friends who are also honored by the king and referred to as θεοφιλεῖς. In *Ant.* 10.277 Josephus remarks on how readers of Daniel's prophecies marvel at the honor he received from God.

eternal memorial.[1122] **267** For the books[1123] that he wrote and has left behind are read by us even now, and we believe from them that Daniel kept company with God;[1124] for not only did he keep prophesying the future, [1125] like the other prophets,[1126] but he also determined the time when these things would come about;[1127] **268** and while

---

[1122] Josephus does not describe the place or time of Daniel's death. Various rabbinic and Christian traditions on this matter (R. Benjamin of Tudela 74–76; R. Pethahiah 7b; *Chronicon Paschale* 92.396) are cited by Ginzberg (1909–38, 4: 350; 6: 437 n.20), who deems them to be dependent upon Josephus. *The Lives of the Prophets* 4:18 states that Daniel died in Babylon and was buried in the royal tomb. Other sources cited by Ginzberg were of the opinion that Daniel returned to Judea in later life and died there (*Song Rab.* 5.5; *b. Sanh.* 93 b). The mausoleum of Danial-e-Nabi is today a prominent and revered site, known since at least the 12th century, in the excavated city of Shoosh (Susa), in Iran's Khuzestan province. Samarkand in Uzbekistan also hosts a tomb of Daniel, however, on the claim that his remains were transported there from his place of death.

[1123] The biblical canon contains only one book ascribed to Daniel. Either Josephus is simply using language carelessly or a more extensive Daniel literature is no longer extant. Collins (1993: 38 n. 335) suggests that this is probably a reference to the different visions in Dan 7–12, "as there is nothing to indicate that Josephus knew other Danielic literature." Begg (1993: 543 and n. 19) has suggested that this is yet another way in which Josephus shapes the Daniel narrative to parallel his own self-presentation (cf. *War* 7.454–455; *Ant.* 20.258–260; *Life* 361–367, 430). In *Ant.* 10.210 and 11.337 Josephus refers to a single book of Daniel.

[1124] Greek ὡμίλει τῷ θεῷ. This claim is in keeping with a theme running throughout Josephus' portrayal of Daniel; cf. note to "believed" at 10.250 and the references cited there.

[1125] Josephus viewed prophecy as primarily predictive. On this subject, see further van Unnik 1978: 52–54; Blenkinsopp 1974: 244–45; Feldman 1990: 394–97; Mason 1994: 171. Mason points out that "Josephus is characteristically ambiguous about the possibility of avoiding what is determined." In *Ant.* 8.418–419 (cited by Mason) Josephus asserts that "nothing is more beneficial than prophecy and the foreknowledge (πρόγνωσις) which it gives, for in this way God enables us to know what to guard against;" but also, that "it behoves us to reflect on the power of Fate (τὴν τοῦ χρεὼν ἰσχύν), and to see that even with foreknowledge (προγινωσκόμενον) is it impossible to escape it..." (Thackeray and Marcus, LCL). In *Ant.*

10.35 Josephus asserts that "whatever happens to us whether for good or ill comes about in accordance with their [i.e. the prophets'] prophecies" (Marcus, LCL).

[1126] Josephus considered Daniel to be a prophet (cf. *Ant.* 10.246, 249, 268) despite the fact that he is not called a prophet in the book of Daniel itself. In Dan 9:2–24 Daniel refers to "the prophets" (including Jeremiah) as a distinct group not including himself. It is also noteworthy that the book of Daniel did not appear in the prophetic section of the Hebrew Bible. Daniel was not considered a prophet by some of the later Talmudic tradition: *b. Meg.* 3a; *b. Sanh.* 93b–94a (Vermes 1991: 158, n. 14). Ancient sources that did view Daniel as a prophet include the *Lives of the Prophets*, 4QFlor II, 3, Matt 24:15, *Mek.* 1b, *Pesiq. Rab Kah.* 4.36b, *Pesiq. Rab.* 14.61, and *S. 'Olam Rab.* 20 (Feldman 1998: 636 n. 17, Ginzberg 1909–38, 6: 413 n. 76). On the place of the Book of Daniel in Josephus' canon, see note to "writings" at 10.210. On the importance of prophecy to Josephus generally, see Aune 1982; Blenkinsopp 1974; Delling 1974; Feldman 1990: 387–94; Gnuse 1996: 21–33; Gray 1993: 23–26; Paul 1975.

[1127] Josephus is perhaps referring here to passages in the Book of Daniel where specific periods of time and numbers of years or days are given: e.g. Dan 7:25; 12:7 ("a time, two times, and half a time"); 8:14 (2,300 evenings and mornings); 9:24–27 (70 weeks divided into 7 weeks, 62 weeks, and 1 week divided into 2 halves); 12:11 (1,290 days); 12:12 (1,335 days). There are also numerous more vague time indicators in Dan 11, for example (Dan 11:6, 7, 8, etc.). It is noteworthy, however, that Josephus omits most of these passages from his paraphrase. The only exception is his paraphrase of chapter 8 in which he renders the 2,300 evenings and mornings (rather confusingly) as 1,296 days in *Ant.* 10.271, but as 3 years in *Ant.* 10.275. Despite Josephus' omission of both chapter 7 and chapter 9 from his biblical paraphrase, scholars have long speculated, with varying results, about whether these chapters influenced his presentation of history, especially as it unfolded in his own time (e.g. Bruce 1965; Mason 1994). F.F. Bruce argued that the Book of Daniel's references to the "abomination that desolates" (Dan 9:27) influenced Josephus' description of events during the Jewish war (e.g. *War* 4.150, 157, 201; 5.16–17). Bruce also suggests that the oracle mentioned by Josephus (*War* 6.311) to the effect that the city and

the other prophets predicted bad news and because of this were intolerable to the kings and the public, Daniel was a prophet of good news to them,[1128] so that from the auspiciousness of his predictions he draw favor from all, and obtained from their outcomes credit for truth and at the same time a reputation for divinity[1129] with the public.

269 And he wrote and left behind [works][1130] in which he made clear to us the precise and unchangeable truth of his prophecies.[1131] For he says that when he was in

Daniel has a vision of the future

---

sanctuary would fall when the temple became a square may have been drawn from Dan 9:25: "and for sixty-two weeks it shall be built again with streets (רחוב, Θ: πλατεῖα) and moat, but in a troubled time." Further, Bruce suggests that oracles of "ancient prophets" circulating in the city during the siege that the city would fall if the Jews fought against each other or defiled the temple (*War* 4.388; 6.109) may recall Dan 11:30–32 and 12:7. Finally, he suggests that the "ambiguous oracle" to which Josephus refers in *War* 6.312, to the effect that "*at that time* one from their country would become ruler of the world" (Thackeray, LCL; emphasis added) was an allusion to the "prince who is to come" of Dan 9:26, because of its reference to a specific date. In that context Josephus notes that, contrary to the rebels' expectation, the oracle in fact predicted the rise of Vespasian (*War* 6.313). In contrast to Bruce, Mason argues that it was in Dan 7 (perhaps read in conjunction with Num 24:17) that Josephus found predictions of his own time. In particular it was in the fourth beast of Daniel's vision that Josephus would have discerned a clear prediction of the rise of Rome, and in that beast's tenth horn he would have found a clear reference to Vespasian, the 10th ruler from Julius Caesar (Mason 1994: 185–6). Blenkinsopp (1974: 245) argues that the "ambiguous oracle" was not drawn from the Book of Daniel at all, but from Gen 49:10–12 and/or Num 24:17. On how the vision of the fourth beast may have influenced Josephus' description of the iron kingdom in Nebuchadnezzar's dream, see note to "bronze" at 10.209.

[1128] Josephus' narrative does not bear this out. Both Nebuchadnezzar (*Ant.* 10.217) and Belshazzar (*Ant.* 10.243–244) received bad news from Daniel. Daniel also predicted the sufferings under Antiochus Epiphanes (*Ant.* 10.275–276) and the destruction of Jerusalem by the Romans (*Ant.* 10.276) according to Josephus, so it is not entirely clear what he means by good news here. According to the biblical narrative Daniel's favor with the kings was due to his ability to interpret dreams and visions related to the rise and fall of political powers. Feldman (1998: 652) has suggested that Josephus was cryptically addressing his Jewish readership here and alluding to passages like Dan 9:24–27 (omitted by Josephus) that refer to future

Jewish greatness. Josephus' statement in the present context, however, would seem to relate to Daniel's message to the various kings he served, and not to the Jews. Daube (1980: 28) has suggested, on the contrary, that it was Josephus' sense of personal identification with Daniel that influenced his statement here, since he saw himself as one who had predicted good tidings for the Flavian house. See also Fischer 1978: 175–7. For other parallels between Josephus' Daniel and his own self-presentation, see note to "noblest" at 10.186.

[1129] Greek θειότης, "divine nature, divinity" (LSJ s.v.). The word is a hapax legomenon in Josephus. It is used of the "divine" law in Wis 18:9, and of God's "divine nature" in Rom 1:20. The term was also used as a title of Roman emperors. The reputation that Josephus here ascribes to "the public" (τοῖς ὄχλοις) is one which he has been hinting at throughout his narrative; cf. *Ant.* 10.194, 196, 200, 204, 211–212, 215, 237, 239, 250, 264, 267, 277). Josephus makes similar claims about other biblical figures in his paraphrase of the Bible, e.g. Moses (*Ant.* 3.180 [on which see Feldman 2000: 279 n. 473]; *Apion* 1.279), and Isaiah (*Ant.* 10.35). See further Smith 1987: 239 and notes at 10.239 and 250 above.

[1130] "Works" is not in the Greek text, which reads κατέλιπε δὲ γράψας. Josephus uses a similar expression in *Ant.* 10.267 where he writes τὰ...βιβλία, ὅσα δὴ συγγράψαμεος καταλέλοιπεν, literally, "the books which, having written, he has left behind." It is unclear in the present context whether Josephus would have us think of "works" in the plural, or simply a singular book since, while in *Ant.* 10.267 he refers to "the books" (τὰ βιβλία) left behind by Daniel, in *Ant.* 10.210 and 11.337 he refers to but a single book of Daniel. See further note to "books" at 10.267.

[1131] Josephus' display of confidence in the accuracy of Daniel's prophecies was, apparently, more than rhetorical flourish, as is seen by his reluctance to relate the meaning of the stone in *Ant.* 10.210. Josephus' account of the vision that follows is taken mainly from Dan 8, with some of the introductory material drawn from Dan 10 (see notes at 10.269). It should be noted that Josephus has omitted the vision of the 4 beasts, the little horn, "the ancient of days" and the "one like a human being" in Dan 7, on which see note at 10.263.

Susa[1132] the metropolis of Persia,[1133] as he went out into the plain[1134] with his companions,[1135] there happened suddenly a shaking and turmoil of the earth[1136] and he was left alone after his friends ran away,[1137] and being troubled he fell with his face in his hands,[1138] and someone touched him[1139] and at the same time ordered him to rise up[1140] and to see what was about to happen to his fellow citizens after many generations.[1141] **270** And when he stood up, he says, a great ram[1142] was shown to him, which had grown many horns,[1143] but the last of them was the loftiest.[1144]

[1132] Commentators on Dan 8:2 debate whether Daniel was claiming to have actually visited Susa, or whether he only saw himself in Susa in a vision, though the latter seems to be what is indicated. Josephus, however, historicizes the incident by situating him bodily in Susa. Having said this, though, it should also be noted that Josephus does not specify *when* Daniel was in Susa despite the notice in Dan 8:1 that these events took place "in the third year of the reign of King Belshazzar." The effect of this omission is to avoid some of the complex chronology of the Book of Daniel in which chapters 7 and 8 return to the time of King Belshazzar after chapter 6, which is set in the time of Darius the Mede. Chapters 9 and 11 are set in the time of Darius, while chapter 10 is set in the third year of Cyrus the Great.

[1133] Josephus correctly identifies Susa as the capital of the Persian kings. Collins (1993: 329) notes that Susa was one of three royal residences of the Achaemenid Empire. The others were Babylon and Ecbatana (cf. Xenophon, *Cyr.* 8.6.22). Josephus' use of the term "metropolis" (μητροπόλει) may indicate his use of a Greek text similar to LXX at this point, since it reads ἐν Σούσοις τῇ πόλει. Θ, on the other hand, reads ἐν Σούσοις τῇ βάρει, "in Sousa the fortress," which closely follows MT בשושן הבירה.

[1134] The biblical narrative does not refer to a plain, but states rather that Daniel was standing by the river Ulai (Dan 8:2). The reference to a plain is reminiscent of Nebuchadnezzar's golden statue erected, according to Josephus, in the great plain of Babylon (*Ant.* 10.213; Dan 3:1)

[1135] Greek ἑταῖροι. Josephus uses this term as a synonym for φίλοι (on which see further note to "friends" at 10.263), which he uses later in the sentence. On the ἑταῖροι as official "companions" of early Macedonian kings, see Errington 2003.

[1136] The earthquake is apparently Josephus' own introduction to the narrative, perhaps for dramatic effect.

[1137] The account in Dan 8 does not refer to Daniel's companions. Josephus has apparently borrowed these details from Dan 10, where Daniel states, "the people who were with me did not see the vision, though a great trembling fell upon them, and they fled and hid

themselves" (Dan 10:7).

[1138] Literally, "on his face on his two hands." The biblical narrative states in a number of places that Daniel fell on this face (Dan 8:17, 18; 10:9).

[1139] Daniel's fearful state and the personage who touches him (called Gabriel in Dan 8:16) are only mentioned after the vision in Dan 8:15–18. It is possible that once again Josephus actually borrowed these narrative details from chapter 10 (Dan 10:8–10).

[1140] The order to stand up is apparently borrowed from Dan 10:11.

[1141] This statement seems to have been borrowed from Dan 10, where the angelic personage says that he has come "to help you understand what is to happen to your people at the end of days" (Dan 10:14). However, there is also the statement of Gabriel in chapter 8 which says, "The vision is for the time of the end" (Dan 8:17), and, "I will tell you what will take place later in the period of wrath; for it refers to the appointed time of the end" (Dan 8:19).

[1142] Josephus' "great ram," rather than the "one ram" of MT and Θ Dan 8:3, is found also in LXX. 4QDan a, b and the text of Aquila also have a "great" ram (Vermes 1991: 159 n. 17). In MT/Θ the ram becomes great in Dan 8:4.

[1143] Dan 8:3 has "two horns." The Hebrew form is dual (קרנים), while both Θ and LXX simply have κέρατα, "horns." However, in both of these texts the next line implies that there were in fact only two horns: τὸ ἓν ὑψηλότερον τοῦ ἑτέρου. The same is true of the subsequent narrative in MT; e.g., in verse 3 it states that the second (שני) horn was longer than the first. This reading is further borne out by the interpretation given later in the chapter, in which the horns represent the kings of Media and Persia (Dan 8:20). Josephus took the ram itself to represent the combined kingdoms of the Medes and the Persians, and the horns to represent their many kings (*Ant.* 10.272).

[1144] Josephus' term ὑψηλότερον, "highest, loftiest, most proud or arrogant," is used by both LXX and Θ in Dan 8:3. Josephus' picture of one arrogant horn among many is reminiscent of the "little horn" in Dan 7:8, 11 and 20. Josephus omits the biblical details that the ram came from the east (implied by the statement that it charged "westward and northward and southward" [Dan

Thereupon he looked up into the west and gazed upon a male goat flying[1145] through the air from there,[1146] and when it clashed with the ram and twice[1147] shattered it with its horns, it hurled it down to the ground and trampled it.[1148] **271** Next, he saw that out of the male goat's forehead had grown a great horn,[1149] and when it was broken off[1150] there grew up again four horns directed toward each of the winds.[1151] And from them,[1152] he wrote, came up also another smaller[1153] horn, which God,[1154] who was showing these things, told him would grow large[1155] and make war on his nation and take the city by force,[1156] and frustrate the affairs of the temple and prevent the sacrifices from being offered[1157] for 1,296 days.[1158]

8:4]), and that "all beasts were powerless to withstand it, and no one could rescue from its power; it did as it pleased and became strong" (Dan 8:4). LXX, however, includes "eastward" (ἀνατολὰς) in its description of the directions of the ram's aggression.

[1145] Dan 8:5 states that Daniel saw the male goat "coming across the face of the whole earth without touching the ground." Josephus' expression, δι' ἀέρος φερόμενον, means literally, "being carried through the air." The present translation is suggested by Vermes 1991: 159.

[1146] Josephus states that Daniel looked into the west (εἰς τὴν δύσιν) to see the male goat. This corresponds with Dan 8:5 in both MT and LXX which both refer to the goat coming from the west (מִן־הַמַּעֲרָב, ἀπὸ δυσμῶν), while Θ has ἀπὸ λιβὸς, "from the southwest wind." Josephus transfers this description to the third kingdom of Nebuchadnezzar's vision of the great statue, *Ant.* 10.209.

[1147] The reference to two attacks is additional to scripture, though Josephus may have derived it from the statement in Dan 8:7 that the male goat broke the ram's two horns. Josephus later interprets these attacks as two battles in which the Greek king would defeat the Persian (*Ant.* 10.273).

[1148] Josephus uses the term πατῆσαι for "trampled," which is close to Θ's συνεπάτησεν. LXX has συνέτριψεν, "to shatter, to crush" (LSJ s.v.).

[1149] Dan 8:5 has a "conspicuous" (חזות) horn between its eyes. Hence, Θ's κέρας θεωρητόν. LXX has ἓν, "one" horn, presumably reading אחת for חזות (Collins 1993: 325 n. 19). In the biblical account this horn is described before the encounter with the ram (Dan 8:5). Josephus' account is less coherent, since it introduces the great horn almost as an afterthought and only after the male goat's military victories. A great horn appears on a ram in *1 En.* 90:9.

[1150] Dan 8:8 states that after the overthrow of the ram the male goat "grew exceedingly great," but that "at the height of its power" the great horn was broken.

[1151] Josephus omits the biblical characterization (Dan 8:8) of the four winds as being "of heaven" (השמים; LXX and Θ τοῦ οὐρανοῦ).

[1152] Dan 8:9 states that the small horn grew up "out of one of them." See also *Ant.* 10.275.

[1153] Greek μικρότερον. The Hebrew text has a "little" (מצעירה) horn, while both Θ and LXX have a "strong" (ἰσχυρόν) horn. Feldman (1998: 630 n. 3) argues that this constitutes evidence that Josephus worked directly with a Hebrew-Aramaic text of the Book of Daniel. This is possible, but it is just as possible (and perhaps more likely) that Josephus used a Greek text which closely reflected the Hebrew original at this point. On the Josephus' biblical text, see further the *Excursus* before 10.186.

[1154] Josephus ignores the biblical reference to Gabriel as the interpreter of the vision (Dan 8:16). This is in keeping with Josephus' tendency to reduce the role of angels in his narrative; see notes at 10.214, 216, 259, and 272.

[1155] Dan 8:10 "It grew as high as the host of heaven...."

[1156] The Book of Daniel does not explicitly mention an attack on his nation or city, though it does state that the little horn "grew exceedingly great toward the east and toward the beautiful land" (Dan 8:9). Josephus omits the statements of Dan 8:10–11 to the effect that the little horn would throw down some of the stars and trample on them, and that it would act arrogantly against "the prince of the host."

[1157] The Book of Daniel states that the little horn took the regular burnt offering away from the prince of the host and "overthrew the place of his sanctuary" (Dan 8:11). Further, "Because of wickedness, the host was given over to it together with the regular burnt offering; it cast truth to the ground and kept prospering in what it did" (Dan 8:12).

[1158] It is not clear why Josephus uses this number, as it does not correspond to any of the numbers given in the Book of Daniel. Dan 8:14 has 2,300 evenings and mornings, which is a reference to the evening and morning sacrifices in the temple, not, as in the Greek versions, a reference to 2,300 days. This number of sacrifices would take 1,150 days to complete (Collins 1993: 336; Marcus 1937: 309 n. d). Collins notes that this period is shorter than the three and a half years of

God interprets
Daniel's vision

272 These things Daniel wrote that he saw in the plain in Susa, and God himself[1159] interpreted to him the appearance of the phantom he had shown thus: he said the ram signified the kingdoms of the Medes and the Persians, and the horns were those who were about to reign,[1160] and the last horn signified the last king; for this one would surpass all in wealth and glory.[1161] **273** And the male goat showed how a certain one of the Greeks[1162] would rule who, having engaged the Persian king twice[1163] in battle, would prevail and take over the whole empire. **274** And the thing indicated by the great horn in the forehead of the male goat was the first king[1164] and, when that one had fallen out, what was manifested by the sprouting up of the four horns facing the four regions of the earth, was each of the Successors[1165] after the death of the first king and the division of the kingdom between them; and these, though neither his children nor his relatives,[1166] would rule the world for many years.[1167] **275** And there would come into being from them[1168] a certain king who

---

Dan 7:25 because chapter 8 was written somewhat later and some of the predetermined time was assumed to have already passed (Collins 1993: 336). Another significant time period appears in Dan 12:11 where we read, "From the time that the regular burnt offering is taken away and the abomination that desolates is set up, there shall be 1,290 days." This is followed in the next verse by the statement: "Happy are those who persevere and attain the 1,335 days." The specific significance of all these figures and their relationship to each other is a matter of ongoing debate. However, it would seem to be clear that they all bear some relation to the period of three and a half years of Dan 7:25; 9:27 and 12:7 (Collins 1993: 400). It has been suggested by Bruce (1965: 161 n. 7) that Josephus intended to use the figure of 1,290 from Dan 12:11 in the present context, but that he inadvertently conflated it with the figure of 1,260—a number that in some circles in Josephus' time was taken to be the meaning of the expression "a time, times, and half a time" (cf. Rev 11:3; 12:14). The result of the conflation was the confusing 1,296 days of the present text. It is also possible that this number represents Josephus' own reinterpretation of Daniel's schema. However, when Josephus relates the interpretation of the present vision in *Ant.*10.275 he indicates that this period will last for three years, a figure that derives from 1 Macc, on which see further note to "years" at 10.275.

[1159] Josephus ignores the biblical reference to Gabriel as the interpreter of the vision (Dan 8:16). See also *Ant.* 10.271. This is in keeping with Josephus' tendency to reduce the role of angels in his narrative; see notes at 10.214, 216, 259, and 271.

[1160] Dan 8:20 "As for the ram that you saw with the two horns, these are the kings of Media and Persia."

[1161] The biblical narrative does not comment on the meaning of this horn, which Josephus apparently took to refer to Darius III of Persia (reigned 336–330 B.C.E.),

though the implication of the Book of Daniel seems to be that that it stands for the Persians as a whole, who were stronger than the Medes (Dan 8:3, 20).

[1162] In *Ant.* 11.337 Josephus asserts that Alexander the Great, when reading the Book of Daniel, recognized himself as the king in question. Cyrus, too, read of his own actions towards the Jews in advance of their occurrence in the Book of Isaiah (*Ant.* 11.4–5).

[1163] This is an addition to the biblical narrative. Josephus is presumably referring to the battles of Issus (333 B.C.E.) and Gaugamela (331 B.C.E.).

[1164] So Dan 8:21. The reference is to Alexander the Great (356–323 B.C.E.). Josephus seems to make both the male goat and the great horn refer to Alexander.

[1165] The "Successors" or "Diadochi" (διάδοχοι) is the term applied to the more important of Alexander's officers who ultimately partitioned his empire: Antigonus I (*c.*382–301 BCE), Antipater (*c.*397–319 BCE), Cassander (?–297 BCE), Lysimachus (*c.*355–281 BCE), Ptolemy I (*c.*367–282 BCE), and Seleucus I (*c.*358–281 BCE). See Hornblower 2003. The notion that there were four Successors is a simplification of the complex reality.

[1166] Josephus inserts this detail from Dan 11:4, though the form of his expression, οὔτε δὲ παῖδας αὐτοῦ...οὔτε συγγενεῖς, suggests that he was aware that one child (παῖδας) and one relative (συγγενεῖς) were in fact involved in minor ways in the wars of the Diadochi. Philip Arrhidaeus (*c.* 357–317 B.C.E.), Alexander the Great's mentally impaired brother, was joint ruler with Alexander's infant son, Alexander IV. Neither exerted any real influence on affairs and both were eventually murdered, Philip in 317 B.C.E. and Alexander in 310/11.

[1167] Dan 8:22 states only that four successor kingdoms would arise, "but not with his [i.e. Alexander's] power." A much more detailed account of these kingdoms is given in Dan 11, a part of the book which Josephus largely omits.

would make war against his nation and their laws and would take away the way of life[1169] based on them and would plunder[1170] the temple and would prevent the sacrifices from being offered[1171] for three years.[1172]

276 And our nation did indeed suffer these things[1173] under Antiochus Epiphanes[1174] just as Daniel saw and wrote they would happen many years beforehand.[1175] And in the same way Daniel also wrote about the empire of the Romans[1176] and that it would

Subsequent events confirm Daniel's vision and confound the Epicureans

---

[1168] Dan 8:23 has, "At the end of their rule…." Cf. *Ant.* 10.271.

[1169] Josephus uses the term πολιτεία to refer to the Jews' way of life. On Josephus' use of this important term, see further Rajak 2001: 195–217; Schwartz 1983–1984, Amir 1994, Colautti 2002: 224–229; Mason 1998: 80–87; Troiani 1994.

[1170] Dan 11:31 speaks of Antiochus "profaning" (חללו) the temple (Θ: βεβηλώσουσιν; LXX: μιανοῦσι). Josephus' term, συλήσοντα, strikes a different note, emphasizing the theft of holy objects rather than the desecration of the temple. Josephus uses the same term for actions taken against the temple by Nebuchadnezzar in *Ant.* 10.111. 144, 145, 149, 154, 233; 11.10, 14, 58, 91, 100. The word is also used of Antiochus' actions against the temple in *Ant.* 12.249, 357; *War* 1.32; 7.44

[1171] Josephus is drawing this characterization of events from chapters 9 (v. 27) and 11 (vv. 30–31), rather than chapter 8.

[1172] 1 Maccabees, on which Josephus draws in *Ant.* 12.320, also states that the desolation of the temple lasted three years. 1 Macc 1:54 dates the beginning of the desolation to the 15th of Chislev in the 145th year of the Seleucid era (i.e. 167 B.C.E. by our reckoning), and 4:52 dates the rededication to 25th of Chislev in the 148th year (164 B.C.E.). The ten-day differential between the days of Chislev is overlooked by 1 Macc 4:54, which says the two events happened on the very same day of the month (so too 2 Macc 10:5, though the duration of the desolation is set at only two years in verse 3). Josephus places both events on 25th Chislev in *Antiquities* (*Ant.* 12.248, 319–321), but in *War*, clearly under the influence of the Book of Daniel rather than 1 Maccabees, he states that the desolation of the temple lasted for three years and six months (*War* 1.32; 5.394). In the present context Josephus has already indicated that this period lasted for 1,296 days, i.e. roughly three and a half years (*Ant.* 10.271). Josephus does not seem to have resolved the discrepancy between the Book of Daniel and 1 Maccabees.

[1173] Josephus' statement corresponds to the affirmation in Dan 8:26, which states, "The vision of the evenings and the mornings that has been told is true."

[1174] Antiochus (IV) Epiphanes, *c.*215–164 BCE; Sherwin-White 2003. Josephus relates the narrative of

these events in *Ant.* 12.248–256 and, briefly, in *War* 1.32–35, 5.394.

[1175] Josephus omits the statement in Dan 8:27 that Daniel "was dismayed by the vision and did not understand it" (Feldman 1998: 633). In *Ant.* 12.322, in his description of the events of Antiochus' time, Josephus writes: "Now the desolation of the temple came about in accordance with the prophecy of Daniel, which had been made 408 years before; for he had revealed that he Macedonians would destroy it" (Marcus, LCL). By this reckoning Daniel's prophecy was given in the year 575 B.C.E.

[1176] Since it is clear that Josephus interpreted Dan 8 with help from Dan 11 (see notes at 10.274 and 275), it is significant to note that LXX Dan 11:30 has "Romans" (Ῥωμαῖοι) for the "ships of Kittim" (ציים כתים) of MT (Θ: Κίτιοι; Lat: *trieres et Romani*, "triremes and Romans"). If Josephus' text of the Book of Daniel was like LXX at this point he would undoubtedly have taken this reference as justification for his claim that Daniel also prophesied about the Romans, even though earlier in *Ant.* he associated the term "Kittim" (Χεθίμ) with Cyprus and hence with all island and most maritime countries (*Ant.* 1.128). "Kittim," either as a designation of the descendants of Javan (Gen 10:4; 1 Chr 1:7), or as a place, occurs in numerous places throughout the Hebrew Bible, and often with a maritime connection (Num 24:24; Isa 23:1, 12; Jer 2:10; Ezek 27:6). While the author of 1 Maccabees took the term to refer to Macedonia (the birth place of Alexander the Great, 1 Macc 1:1; 8:5), other Jewish sources treat the term as a reference to the Romans (e.g. *Tg. Onq.* on Num 24:24; *Tg. Ps.-J.* on Num 24:24; *Frg. Tg.* on Num 24:24; *Pesher Habakkuk* cols. 2–6 [on Hab 1]; *Gen. Rab.* 37:1 see also *Jub.* 24:28–29). In Jerome's commentary on Daniel 11:31 he writes: "The Jews…would have us understand that this [i.e. the coming of the Kittim in Dan 11:30] is referring not to Antiochus Epiphanes or the Antichrist but to the [coming of the] Romans [in 63 B.C.E.]" (Braverman 1978: 115). Jerome then goes on to comment on v. 31 by asserting that the Jewish tradition he knows states that, "a king, Vespasian, shall emerge from the Romans themselves….It is his arms and descendants who will rise up, namely his son Titus, who with his army will defile the

be laid waste by them.[1177] **277** That man wrote and left behind all these things, which God had shown to him; so that those who read and look at the things that have happened marvel at the honor Daniel had from God[1178] and discover from them[1179] that the Epicureans[1180] have been deceived. [1181] **278** They cast aside providence[1182]

---

sanctuary and remove the continual sacrifice and hand over the Temple to permanent desolation" (Braverman 1978: 115). On Dan 11:33 Jerome comments: "The Hebrews interpret these things [as taking place] at the final destruction of the Temple, which took place under Vespasian and Titus; that there were many of their nation who knew their God and were slain for keeping his Law" (Braverman 1978: 119). There is no extant rabbinic tradition to corroborate Jerome's claims on these points, though Braverman cites a number of medieval Jewish commentaries on the theme (116 n. 6). On a related matter, it is quite possible that Josephus understood the Kittim of Num 24:24 to be the Romans, in which case the prophecies of Balaam would appear to have a direct bearing on Josephus' understanding of the Book of Daniel; on this issue, see further Spilsbury 2003: 17–20. Josephus also believed that Jeremiah and Ezekiel had predicted the Roman destruction of Jerusalem (*Ant.* 10.79). It may be relevant to observe in this connection that both of these prophets also made mention of the Kittim (see references above). Josephus' statement in the present context also confirms our suspicion that for him the 4th kingdom of Nebuchadnezzar's statue vision represented Rome; cf. *Ant.* 10.209. On the Kittim, see further Baker 1992.

[1177] Josephus' statement is highly ambiguous and open to a number of different interpretations. The text of the *editio maior* reads τὸν αὐτὸν δὲ τρόπον ὁ Δανίηλος καὶ περὶ τῆς Ῥωμαίων ἡγεμονίας ἀνέγραψε, καὶ ὅτι ὑπ᾽ αὐτῶν ἐρημωθήσεται. The final clause of this sentence, "and that it would be laid waste by them," leaves both the "it" and the "them" ambiguous. The most straightforward reading would be to take "the empire of the Romans" to be the subject of the passive verb, hence, it is "the empire of the Romans" that would be laid waste. If this reading were adopted, the "them" of the sentence would presumably be "our nation" from the previous sentence. Those who lean toward such a reading (e.g. Braverman 1978: 109) suggest that Josephus is alluding to a passage like Dan 9:26, which reads, "…and the troops of the prince who is to come shall destroy the city and the sanctuary [and his] end shall come with a flood.…" If this is indeed what Josephus intended, then this statement would correspond to the meaning of the stone in Nebuchadnezzar's dream, since both would be about the demise of the Roman Empire at the hands of the Jewish nation (see note to "stone" at 10.210). However, it would be very surprising for Josephus to make such a bold state-

ment here given his refusal to explain the meaning of the stone earlier. A second way to read the statement—perhaps the better of the two readings—is to take the "them" to refer to the Romans, and "it" to be "our nation." Support for this sense of the statement is provided by an alternative reading of the ambiguous final clause in Chrysostom's *Adv. Jud.* 5.8 and followed by Marcus in LCL. The text reads αἱρεθήσεται τὰ Ἱεροσόλυμα καὶ ὁ ναὸς ἐρημωθήσεται, "Jerusalem would be taken by them [i.e. the Romans] and the sanctuary laid waste." The fragment most likely represents Chrysostom's attempt to clarify his understanding of Josephus' meaning. Braverman argues, however, that Josephus intended his Roman and Jewish audiences to read his ambiguous statement in quite different ways. To Romans it would seem obvious that Josephus was talking about the Roman destruction of Jerusalem and the Temple, while to Jewish readers there would be a palpable allusion to the prophesied destruction of the superpower by the Jews (Braverman 1978: 109–111).

It has also been noted (e.g. Begg 1993: 541) that in foretelling matters of imperial succession in general (*Ant.* 10.205–210, 270–275 // *War* 3.401; 4.623, 626), and in predicting the rise of Rome in particular (*War* 3.351, 354), Josephus saw himself as parallel to Daniel. For other such parallels between Josephus himself and Daniel, see note to "noblest" at 10.186.

[1178] The honor Daniel received from God is an important theme in this section of the *Antiquities*, on which see further note to "public" at 10.266.

[1179] In *Ant.* 10.142 Josephus reflects similarly on the lessons to be learned from fulfilled prophecy and the folly of those who deny God's providence.

[1180] The followers of the philosophical school of Epicurus (341–270 BCE). For a summary of his life and teaching see Furley 2003. The only other place where Josephus names the Epicureans is in *Ant.* 19.32 where they are characterized as advocating a quiet, i.e. non-political, life (ἀπραγμονος…βίου). On this aspect of Epicurean philosophy, see De Witt 1954: 187; also O'Connor 1993 and Inwood, Gerson, and Hutchinson 1994. In *Apion* 2.180 Josephus refers to the Epicureans without explicitly naming them, and characterizes them, as he does in the present passage, as philosophers who deprive God of his providential care of humanity (τὴν ὑπὲρ ἀνθρώπων αὐτὸν πρόνοιαν ἀφαιρουμένων). The Jewish religion, by contrast, affirms that God "sees all things."

[1181] Rivalry among philosophical schools was a

from life and do not think that God administers[1183] its affairs, and hold that it is not steered by the blessed and incorruptible Being[1184] towards perseverance of the whole; but they say that the world is borne along automatically[1185] without a

---

common feature of philosophical discourse in antiquity, yet this is the only place in Josephus' writings where he takes sides against a Greek philosophical school in such a direct way (van Unnik 1973: 343). Nevertheless, one may observe veiled criticism of the Epicureans in those places where he describes the three so-called philosophical schools (αἱρέσεις) within Judaism (*War* 2.119–166; *Ant.* 13.171–173; 18.11–20; see also *Ant.* 13.297–298). The Pharisees he compares with the Stoics (*Life* 12) and the Essenes with the Pythagoreans (*Ant.* 15.371). Although he never says so explicitly, it is likely that he would have his readers compare the Sadducees with the Epicureans since they deny life after death and the role of fate in human affairs (Mason 2001: 16–17, n. 72). Van Unnik (344) points out that in the context of conflict between various philosophical schools, Josephus' decision to defer to the Stoic-like school of the Pharisees in public life (*Life* 12) meant by implication the rejection of Epicurean teachings. On Josephus' personal connection with the Pharisees, which is a matter of some debate, see Mason 1991: 325–56; Feldman 1998: 367. Gnuse (1996: 6) regards Josephus' claim to have studied with each of the three sects within Judaism (*Life* 10–11) as artificial. Rajak (1983: 34–36), who recognizes the traditional patterning of Josephus' claim, is nevertheless not so dismissive of its veracity.

Josephus was by no means the only Jewish writer to criticize the Epicureans. Both Philo (*Conf.* 23.114; cf. Wolfson 1948, 1: 108–9 and 2: 511–2) and the rabbis (e.g. *m.* '*Abot* 2.14; *m. Sanh.* 10.1) rejected their teachings. In the latter, the term '*apikoros* (אפיקורוס) came to signify an atheist or unbeliever; see further Krauss 1898–99, 2: 107–108. Feldman (1998: 640 n. 26) cites Maimonides defining the '*apikoras* as one who denies prophecy, divine revelation, or divine knowledge of human actions (*Mishneh Torah, Teshu-vah* 3.8). Finally, Josephus' attack on the Epicureans makes him a conversation partner with contemporary writers such as Plutarch (*Pyth. orac.* [*Mor.*] 8; Mason 1994: 169).

[1182] Greek τὴν...πρόνοιαν ἐκβάλλουσι; cf. *Apion* 2.180, cited in note to "Epicureans" in previous paragraph. Josephus' outburst against the Epicureans might seem strange were it not for the fact that he, along with others in antiquity (e.g. Cicero *Nat. d.* 2.73–75; Irenaeus *Haer.* 3.38.2 [3.24.2]; Origen *Cels.* 1.8, 13; 2.13; cf. van Unnik 1973: 344, 353 n. 11), epitomized them as philosophers who rejected divine providence (πρόνοια)—one of the most important themes in the

Antiquities. The term πρόνοια occurs some 120 times in the *Antiquities*, with 78 of those occurrences falling within the biblical paraphrase (*Ant.* 1.1–11.296). The term sometimes refers generally to human "provision" or "forethought" (e.g. *Ant.* 2.39, 104, 236 Mason 2001: 24 n. 107), but often refers specifically to God's protection, provision, or providence (e.g. *Ant.* 1.46; 225; 2.24, 60, 219, 286, 330 etc.). The concept of God's providence also occurs in passages where the term itself is not used, e.g. *Ant.* 1.14, 20. On the Josephus' use of the term in his biblical paraphrase, especially in connection with God's punishing of evil and rewarding of good, see Attridge 1976: 71–108, 145–51; also Spilsbury 2003: 7–12; van Unnik 1973: 349–51.

[1183] Josephus uses the verb ἐπιτροπεύειν [τῶν πραγμάτων] to refer to God's role as the "guardian" of the world's affairs. He uses the same verb of God's role in *Ant.* 4.2. In *Ant.* 10.212 he used the noun ἐπίτροπος for the role of administrator or governor of the kingdom of Babylon awarded to Daniel and three friends by Nebuchadnezzar.

[1184] Greek τῆς μακαρίας καὶ ἀφθάρτου...οὐσίας. This phrase echoes the teaching of Epicurus as reflected in the *Kyriai doxai* 1 (cited by van Unnik 1973: 344): τὸ μακάριον καὶ ἄφθαρτον οὔτε αὐτὸ πράγματα ἔχει οὔτε ἄλλῳ παρέχει: "The blessed and incorruptible Being has no trouble himself and brings no trouble upon any other..." Josephus is using Epicurus' phrase for God, but in the opposite sense, in that while Epicurus held that God did not involve himself with human affairs, Josephus held that he did.

[1185] Greek αὐτομάτως. The term refers to things that happen of themselves or spontaneously, without apparent cause, accidentally, or "naturally." Josephus makes a similar point in *Ant.* 4.47 where Moses implores God, addressed as "Master of everything" (δέσποτα τῶν ὅλων), to prove that "all things are governed by your providence (προνοίᾳ) and that nothing happens by itself (αὐτομάτως) and that they come to their goal (τέλος) through your directed will (βούλησιν βραβευόμενον)" (Feldman 2000; on this passage see ibid. 344 n. 115). While Josephus is opposed to the Epicurean notion that the entire natural order simply operates by natural (i.e. non-providential) processes, he is not opposed to the notion that some things within the natural order seem to operate by their own internal laws or principles (a similar distinction is found in Plato, *Pol.* 270A). In his retelling of the biblical story of the first humans, Josephus used αὐτομάτως and the

driver[1186] and without a care.[1187] **279** If it was without a protector[1188] in this way, then when the world was crushed by an unforeseen misfortune it would have been destroyed and ruined, in just the same way that we also see ships without helmsmen being sunk by winds or chariots being turned around when they have no one holding the reins.[1189] **280** Therefore, on the basis of the things predicted by Daniel, it seems to me that they go very much astray from the true opinion who hold the view that God exercises no providence at all over human affairs; for we would not be seeing all things coming about according to his prophecy if the world went along by some automatic process.[1190]

---

related form αὐτόματος in a positive sense to describe how plants in the garden of Eden would spring up spontaneously, without anyone having to cultivate them—a benefit that was taken away after the first humans' disobedience (*Ant.* 1.46, 49). In the story of Cain and Abel (*Ant.* 1.54), Abel's offering is said to have pleased God because he offered something that arose "spontaneously and according to nature" (τοῖς αὐτομάτοις καὶ κατὰ φύσιν γεγονόσι), i.e. milk and the firstlings of his flocks, rather than something forced from the earth by human artifice. A similar usage occurs in *Life* 11 where Josephus refers to Bannus who lived in the wilderness eating only such things as grew by themselves (αὐτομάτως [On this passage see Mason 2001: 19 n. 83]; see also *Ant.* 3.281; 12.317). Feldman (2000: 18 n. 102, 20 n. 116) points out that spontaneous growth was often associated with the Golden Age in antiquity; e.g. Plato, *Pol.* 272A; Hesiod, *Op.* 109 ff.; Ovid, *Metam.* 1.101 ff. In *Ant.* 2.347 Josephus allows that the amazing passage of the Israelites through the Red Sea may have been either "by the will of God or maybe by accident" (εἴτε κατὰ βούλησιν θεοῦ εἴτε κατὰ ταὐτόματον, Thackeray LCL), while in *Ant.* 3.207 αὐτόματον is used of the fire that sprang up spontaneously to consume the first offering on the altar, and unexpectedly (παρὰ δόξαν, *Ant.* 3.210) caused the deaths of two of Aaron's sons. Again in *Ant.* 4.55 Josephus compares the divine fire that killed Korah and his party to a forest fire that bursts spontaneously from the woods. It is clear that in this case, as in the one cited previously, "spontaneously" does not mean the same thing as "accidentally." The same point can be made about the use of the term in *War* 6.293 and 295 where the gates of the temple are said to have opened "of their own accord" as an evil omen of things to come. Interestingly Josephus can also use our term negatively to say essentially the same thing. Thus the change of wind direction that spelled the doom of the besieged in Masada *did not* happen of its own accord, or by mere accident (οὐκ αὐτομάτως, *War* 7.332). In other instances the term does refer to things that happen by chance or accident (e.g. *War* 1.373, 378; 3.100, 101, 386, 433; 5.292; *Ant.* 1.262; 7.284; 19.236; *Apion* 2.24,

186). *Ant.* 18.249 refers to "naturally occurring" hot springs. Feldman (1998: 640 n. 24) notes that the term ἀbtomtos occurs in *Midr. Ps.* 1.5 in reference to heretics, presumably the Epicureans.

[1186] Greek ἡνίοχος, "driver, charioteer, guide" (LSJ s.v.).

[1187] God's care of the universe is one of the main themes of the *Antiquities* as a whole (see, e.g., *Ant.* 1.20). Josephus thus uses Daniel to prove his thesis that God exercises a careful providence over human affairs (Mason 1994: 168). It is worth noting, however, that Josephus does not criticize the Epicureans for their rejection of divination, despite the prevalence of this theme among their other critics (e.g. Cicero, *Nat. d.* 2.162; *Div.* 1.5; Plutarch, *Adv. Col.* 27). His reason for this may have been the biblical prohibition of such practices (e.g. Deut 18.10–11; van Unnik 1973: 348–9).

[1188] Greek ἀπροστάτητος, a rare term that signifies lack of a προστάτης, in the sense of "one who stands before and protects, guardian, champion" (LSJ s.v.). It may also have the sense of "patron," a concept that Josephus uses in other places to characterize God's relation to Israel; see Spilsbury 1998. The term ἀπροστάτητος occurs again in *Ant.* 13.5 (where Marcus [LCL] translates it "without a defender") and 20.180 (where Feldman [LCL] renders it "no one in charge").

[1189] Van Unnik (1973: 346) has observed that his is an argument *per viam negativam*: without "providence" there would be complete chaos, but since this is not the situation, there must be "providence." Philo uses similar analogies of helmsmen and charioteers to argue for providential care of the world (*Conf.* 23.114–115; see also Plato, *Resp.* 6.488A7–489A2).

[1190] Greek αὐτοματισμῷ. "Something that happens of itself, chance," LSJ s.v. The expression is a hapax legomenon in Josephus, though the related terms αὐτομάτως and αὐτόματος occur more frequently. Josephus' argument in favour of "providence" differs from that in Cicero, Philo, and others in that he argues from the fulfillment of prophecy in history rather than from nature (van Unnik 1973: 347).

281 Now concerning these things: as I found and read, so have I written;[1191] but if anyone should want to think differently concerning them, let him hold his difference of opinion without reproach.[1192]

[1191] Josephus frequently reminds his readers of his claim to be relating what he finds in the Hebrew Scriptures; e.g. *Ant.* 1.17 (the introduction to Josephus' biblical history); 2.347 (crossing the Sed Sea); 3.81 (Moses on Mount Sinai); 9.214 (the story of Jonah); 10.218 (Nebuchadnezzar's insanity).

[1192] Josephus frequently extends to his readers the option of holding a different opinion on the matters he relates, especially when they involve the actions of God; e.g. *Ant.* 1.108; 2.348; 3.81, 268, 322; 4.158; 8.262; 17.354; 19.108; *War* 5.257. Similar formulae appear in Herodotus (*Hist.* 2.123; 3.122.1), Thucydides (6.2.1), Dionysius of Halicarnassus (*Ant. rom.* 1.48.1, 4; 2.40.3; 2.74.5; 3.36.5), Lucian (*Quomodo Historia Conscribenda Sit* 60), and Pliny (*Nat.* 9.18). See Feldman 2000: 39 n.271; Thackeray 1929: 56–58; MacRae 1965: 140–42. MacRae, following Delling 1958: 300 and 306, argues that the statement does not indicate scepticism on Josephus' part. "Instead, it must be regarded as a ... gesture of courtesy to the pagan readers who cannot accept the interpretation of the author, an expression of the tolerance of Diaspora Judaism for the religious or philosophical convictions of others" (141; see also van Unnik 1973: 350–51).

BIBLIOGRAPHY

Alexander, P. H. et al., eds. 1999. *The* SBL *Handbook of Style for Ancient Near Eastern, Biblical, and Early Christian Studies*. Peabody, Mass.: Hendrickson.

Althann, R. 1992. Zedekiah. *ABD* 6: 1068-71.

Amir, Y. 1994. Josephus on the Mosaic 'Constitution.' Pp. 13-27 in H.G. Reventlow et al. eds. *Theopolitics in the Bible and Postbiblical Literature*. JSOT Sup 171. Sheffield: JSOT Press.

Arbesmann, R. 1949–1951. Fasting and Prophecy in Pagan and Christian Anitquity. *Traditio* 7:1–71.

Attridge, H. W. 1976. *The Interpretation of Biblical History in the* Antiquitates Judaicae *of Flavius Josephus*. Missoula, Mont.: Scholars.

Aune, David E. 1982. The Use of προφήτης in Josephus. *JBL* 101: 419-21.

Baker, D.W. 1992. Kittim. *ABD* 4: 93.

Barber, G.L. and K.S. Sacks. 2003. Megasthenes. OCD³: 952.

Barclay, J.M.G. Forthcoming. *Flavius Josephus: Translation and Commentary*, ed. S. Mason. Vol 10: *Against Apion*. Leiden: Brill (= BJP 10).

Beckwith, R.T. 1988. The Vegetarianism of the Therapeutae, and the Motives of Vegetarianism in Early Jewish and Christian Circles. *RQ* 13:407–410.

Begg, C. T. 1988. The "Classical Prophets" in Josephus' *Antiquities*. *LS* 13: 341-57.

———. 1991. Josephus' Portrayal of the Disappearances of Enoch, Elijah and Moses: Some Observations. *JBL* 109: 691-3.

———. 1993. *Josephus' Account of the Early Divided Monarchy (AJ 8,212-420): Rewriting the Bible*. Leuven: Leuven University Press.

———. 1993. Daniel and Josephus: Tracing Connections. Pp. 539–545 in *The Book of Daniel in the Light of New Findings*, ed. A.S. van der Woude. BETL 106; Leuven: University Press/Peters.

———. 1996. Solomon's Two "Satans" according to Josephus. *BN* 85: 44-55.

———. 1996a. Solomon's Two Dreams according to Josephus. *Anton* 71: 687-704.

———. 1996-7. The Jeroboam-Ahijah Encounter according to Josephus. *AbrN* 34: 1-17.

———. 1997. Solomon's Apostasy (1 KGS. 11,1-13) according to Josephus. *JSJ* 28: 294-313.

———. 2000. *Josephus' Story of the Later Monarchy (AJ 9,1-10,185)*. Leuven: Leuven University Press.

Best, E. 1959. The Use and Non-Use of Pneuma by Josephus. *NovT* 3: 218-25.

Betz, O. 1987. Miracles in the Writings of Flavius Josephus. Pp. 212-35 in *Jesus, Judaism and Christianity*, ed. L.H. Feldman and G. Hata. Detroit: Wayne State University.

Bieler, L. 1935–1936. *Theios Aner*. 2 vols. Vienna: Osker Höfel.

Bickerman, E. 1938. *Institutions des Séleucides*. Bibliothèque historique 26. Paris: Geuthner.

Bilde, P. 1988. *Flavius Josephus Between Jerusalem and Rome: His Life, his Works and their Importance*. Sheffield: JSOT.

Blenkinsopp, J. 1974. Prophecy and Priesthood in Josephus. *JJS* 25: 239-62.

Bloch, H. 1879. *Die Quellen des Josephus in seiner Archäologie*. Leipzig: Teubner.

Bockmuehl, M. 1990. Should We Kneel to Pray? *Crux* 26:14–17.

Bogaert, P.-M. 2003. La *vetus latina* de Jérémie: texte très court, témoin de la plus ancienne Septante et d'une forme plus ancienne de l'hébreu (Jer 39 et 52). Pp. 51-82 in *The Earliest Text of the Hebrew Bible: The Relationship between the Masoretic Text and the Hebrew Base of the Septuagint Reconsidered*, ed. Adrian Schenker. Atlanta: Society of Biblical Literature.

Bowley, J. E. 1994. Josephus's Use of Greek Sources for Biblical History. Pp. 202-15 in *Pursuing the Text: Studies in Honor of Ben Zion Wacholder on the Occasion of his Seventieth Birthday*, ed. John C. Reeves and John Kampen. Sheffield: JSOT.

Bracke, J.M. 1992. Nergal-Sharezer. *ABD* 4: 1074-75.

Braude, W. G. and I. J. Kapstein, tr. 1981. *Tanna děbe Eliyyahu: The Lore of the School of Elijah*. Philadelphia: Jewish Publication Society of America.

Braverman, J. 1978. *Jerome's* Commentary on Daniel. *A Study of Comparative Jewish and Christian Interpretations of the Hebrew Bible*. CBQMS 7; Washington: Catholic Biblical Association of America.

Brooke, A. E. and N. McLean. 1930. *The Old Testament in Greek*, vol. 2, pt. 2: *I and II Kings*. Cambridge: Cambridge University Press.

————. 1932. *The Old Testament in Greek*, vol. 2, pt. 3: *I and II Chronicles*. Cambridge: Cambridge University Press.

Bruce, F.F. 1965. Josephus and Daniel. *ASTI* 4:148–162.

Brüne, B. 1913. *Flavius Josephus und seine Schriften in ihrem Verhältnis zum Judentume, zur griechisch-römischen Welt und zum Christentume*. Gütersloh: Bertelsmann.

Burstein, S.M. 1978. *The Babyloniaca of Berossus*. Sources and Monographs: Sources from the Ancient Near East, vol. 1, fascicle 5. Malibu: Undena Publications.

Charlesworth, M.P. 1935. Some Observations on the Ruler-Cult especially in Rome. *HTR* 28:5–44.

Cogan, M. 1992. Chronology, Hebrew Bible. *ABD* 1: 1002-11.

Coggins, R.J. 1987. The Samaritans in Josephus. Pp. 257-73 in *Josephus, Judaism and Christianity*, ed. L.H. Feldman and G. Hata. Detroit: Wayne State University.

Cohen, S. J. D. 1979. *Josephus in Galilee and Jerusalem: His Vita and Development as a Historian*. Leiden: Brill.

Colautti, F. 2002. *Passover in the Works of Josephus*. Leiden: Brill.

Collins, J.J. 1993. *Daniel. A Commentary on the Book of Daniel*. Hermeneia. Minneapolis: Fortress.

Collins, J.N. 1990. *Diakonia: Reinterpreting the Ancient Sources*. Oxford/New York: Oxford University Press.

Daube, D. 1980. Typology in Josephus. *JJS* 31: 18-36.

Davies, P.R. 1991. Daniel in the Lion's Den. Pp. 160–178 in L. Alexander ed. *Images of Empire*. JSOTSup 122; Sheffield: JSOT Press.

De Jonge, M. 1974. Josephus und die Zukunftserwartungen seines Volkes. Pp. 205–219 in O. Betz, K. Haacker and M. Hengel eds. *Josephus-Studien. Untersuchungen zu Josephus, dem antiken Judentum und dem Neuen Testament. Otto Michel zum 70. Geburtstag gewidmet*. Göttingen: Vandenhoeck & Ruprecht.

Deines, R. 2003. Josephus, Salomo und die von Gott verliehene τέχνη gegen die Dämonen. Pp. 365-94 in *Die Dämonen: Die Dämonologie der israelitischen-jüdischen und frühchristlichen Literatur im Kontext ihrer Umwelt*, ed. Armin Lange, Hermann Lichtenberger and K.F. Diethard Römheld. Tübingen: Mohr Siebeck.

Delamarter, S. 1998. The Vilification of Jehoiakim (A.K.A. Eliakim and Joiakim) in Early Judaism. Pp. 190-204 in *The Function of Scripture in Early Judaism and Christian Tradition*, ed. C.A. Evans and J.A. Sanders. Sheffield: Sheffield Academic Press.

————. 2004. The Death of Josiah in Scripture and Tradition: Wrestling with the Problem of Evil? *VT* 54: 29-60.

Delling, G. 1958. Josephus und das Wunderbare. *NovT* 2: 291-308.

————. 1974. Die biblische Prophetie bei Josephus. Pp. 109–121 in O. Betz, K. Haacker and M. Hengel eds. *Josephus-Studien. Untersuchungen zu Josephus, dem antiken Judentum und dem Neuen Testament. Otto Michel zum 70. Geburtstag gewidmet*. Göttingen: Vandenhoeck & Ruprecht.

De Witt, N.W. 1954. *Epicurus and his Philosophy*. Minneapolis: University of Minnesota Press.

Diels, H. 1934. *Die Fragmente der Vorsokratiker*. Edited by W. Kranz. Berlin: Weidmann.

Dietrich, E.K. 1936. *Die Umkehr (Bekehrung und Busse) im Alten Testament und im Judentum*. Stuttgart: Kohlhammer.

Dindorf, G. 1845-7. *Flavii Josephi Opera*. Paris: Didot.

Droge, A. G. 1996. Josephus between Greeks and Barbarians. Pp. 115-42 in *Josephus' Contra Apionem: Studies in its Character and Context with a Latin Concordance to the Missing Portion in Greek*, ed. L. H. Feldman and J.R. Levison. Leiden: Brill.

Egger, R. 1986. *Josephus Flavius und die Samaritaner*. Freiburg: Universitätsverlag; Göttingen: Vandenhoeck & Ruprecht.

Endres, J. C., W. R. Millar, and J. B. Burns. 1998. *Chronicles and its Synoptic Parallels in Samuel, Kings, and Related Biblical Texts*. Collegeville: The Liturgical Press.

Epstein, I., ed. 1935-48. *The Babylonian Talmud*. London: Soncino.

Errington, R.M. 2003. hetairoi. *OCD*[3]: 702.

F. Fallon, tr. 1985. Eupolemus. Pp. 861-72 in OTP 2. Garden City, New York: Doubleday and Co.

Feldman, L. H. 1981. *Josephus*. vol. 7. *Jewish Antiquities*. Book XX. Loeb Classical Library. Cambridge, Mass.: Harvard University Press.

————. 1990. Prophets and Prophecy in Josephus. *JTS* 41: 386-422.

————. 1992. Josephus' Attitude towards the Samaritans: A Study in Ambivalence. Pp. 23-45 in *Jewish Sects, Religious Movements, and Political Parties*, ed. M. Mor. Omaha: Creighton University Press.

————. 1992. Josephus' Portrait of Daniel. *Henoch* 14: 37–96.

————. 1993. Josephus' Portraits of the Pharaohs. *Syllecta Classica* 4: 49–63.

————. 1998. *Josephus' Interpretation of the Bible*. Berkeley: University of California Press.

————. 1998a. *Studies in Josephus' Rewritten Bible*. Leiden: Brill.

————. 2000. *Flavius Josephus: Translation and Commentary*, ed. S. Mason. Vol. 3: *Judean Antiquities 1-4*. Leiden: Brill (= BJP 3).

————. 2001. Josephus' Liberties in Interpreting the Bible in the *Jewish War* and in the *Antiquities*. *JSQ* 8: 309-25.

Fernández Marcos, N. and Busto Saiz, J. Ramón, eds. 1992. *El texto antioqueno de la Biblia griega*, vol. 2: *1-2 Reyes*. Madrid: Instituto de Filología del C.S.I.C.

————. 1996. *El texto antioqueno de la Biblia griega*, vol. 3: *1-2 Crónicas*. Madrid: Instituto de Filología del C.S.I.C.

Fischer, U. 1978. *Eschatologie und Jenseitserwartung im hellenistischen Diasporajudentem.* BZNW 44; Berlin: Walter de Gruyter.

Flusser, D. 1972. The Four Empires in the Fourth Sybil and in the Book of Daniel. *IOS* 2:148–175.

Freedman, H. and M. Simon, eds. 1983. *Midrash Rabbah*. 7 vols. London: Soncino.

Furley, D.J. 2003. Epicurus. Pages 532–534 in *The Oxford Classical Dictionary*. 3d rev. ed. Edited by S. Hornblower and A. Spawforth. Oxford: Oxford University Press.

Garbini, G. 1980. Gli "Annali di Tiro" e la Storiographia Fenica. Pp. 114-27 in *Oriental Studies: Festschrift B.S.J. Isserlin*, ed. R.Y. Ebied and M.J.L. Young. Leiden: Brill.

Gibbs, J. G. and L. H. Feldman. 1985-6. Josephus' Vocabulary for Slavery. *JQR* 76: 281-310.

Ginzberg, L. 1909-38. *The Legends of the Jews*. 7 vols. Philadelphia: Jewish Publication Society.

Girón Blanc, L.-F., tr. 1996. *Seder 'Olam Rabbah El Gran Orden del Universo: Una cronologia judia*. Estella (Navarra): Verbo Divino.

Glessmer, U. 1994. Leviten in spät-nachexilischen Zeit. Darstellungsinteressen in den Chronikbüchern und bei Josephus. Pp. 127-51 in *Gottes Ehre erzählen. Festschrift für Hans Seidel zum 65. Geburtstag*, ed. M. Albani and T. Arndt. Leipzig: Thomas Verlag.

Gnuse, R. K. 1996. *Dreams and Dream Reports in the Writings of Josephus: A Traditio-Historical Analysis*. Leiden: Brill.

Goldingay, J.E. 1987. *Daniel*. Word Biblical Commentary 30. Dallas: Word.

Goodblatt, D. 1994. *The Monarchic Principle: Studies in Jewish Self-Government in Antiquity*. Tübingen: Mohr Siebeck.

Gray, R. 1993. *Prophetic Figures in Late Second Temple Jewish Palestine: The Evidence from Josephus*. New York: Oxford University Press.

Hall, R. 1971. *Revealed Histories: Techniques for Ancient Jewish and Christian Historiography*. JSPSup 6; Sheffield: JSOT Press.

Halpern-Amaru, B. 1980-81. Land Theology in Josephus' *Jewish Antiquities*. *JQR* 71: 201-29.

————. 1994. *Rewriting the Bible: Land and Covenant in Post-Biblical Jewish Literature*. Valley Forge: Trinity International Press.

Harding, M. 1994. Making Old Things New: Prayer Texts in Josephus' *Antiquities* 1-11: A Study in the Transmission of Tradition. Pp. 54-72 in *The Lord's Prayer and Other Prayer Texts from the Greco-Roman Era*, ed. J.H. Charlesworth et al. Valley Forge: Trinity Press International.

Harrington, D J. and A. J. Saldarini, tr. 1987. *Targum Jonathan of the Former Prophets*. Collegeville: The Liturgical Press.

Harvey, G. 1996. *The True Israel: Uses of the Names Jew, Hebrew, and Israel in Ancient Jewish and Early Christian Literature*. Leiden: Brill.

Hengel, M. 1974. *Judaism and Hellenism*. Tr. J. Bowden. London: SCM.

Höffken, P. 1998. Hiskija und Jesaja bei Josephus. *JSJ* 29: 37-48.

————. 1999. Weltreiche und Prophetie bei Flavius Josephus. *TZ* 55: 47-55.

————. 2001. Bekehrung von Nichtjuden als (Nicht-) Thema bei Josephus Flavius. *TZ* 57: 391-401.

Hogan, L.P. 1992. *Healing in the Second Temple Period*. Freiburg: Universitätsverlag; Göttingen: Vandenhoeck & Ruprecht.

Hornblower, S. 2003. Diadochi. OCD[3]: 460–461.

Hunt, E.D. 2003. Eunuchs. OCD[3]: 569.

Inwood, B., L.P. Gerson and D.S. Hutchinson, eds. 1994. *The Epicurus Reader*. Toronto: Hackett.

Jacob, E. 1974. ψυχή κτλ. *TDNT* 9: 608–631.

Jacoby, F. 1958. *Die Fragmente der Griechischen Historiker*. Leiden: Brill.

Jaubert, A. 1963. *La notion d'alliance dans le Judaïsme aux abords de l'ère chrétienne*. Paris: Seuil.

Jobes, K.H. and M. Silva. 2000. *Invitation to the Septuagint*. Grand Rapids: Baker.

Johnson, G.L. 1983. Josephus—Heir Apparent to the Prophetic Tradition? Pp. 337-46 in *SBL Seminar Papers 22*. Chico, Calif.: Scholars.

Katzenstein, H.J. 1992. Tyre. *ABD* 6: 686-90.

Kleinknecht, H. 1965. θεῖος. *TDNT* 3: 122–23.

Koch, K. 1992. Darius the Mede. *ABD* 2: 38-9.

Koch, K. and M. Rösel. 2000. *Polyglottensynopse zum Buch Daniel*. Neukirchen-Vluyn: Neukirchener.

Krauss, S. 1898–99. Griechische und lateinische Lehnwörter in Talmud, Midrasch und Targum. 2 vols. Berlin: Calvary.

Krenkel, M. 1894. *Josephus und Lukas*. Leipzig: Haessel.

Krieger, K.S. 1994. *Geschichtsschreibung als Apologetik bei Flavius Josephus*. Tübingen: Franke.

Kuhrt, A.T.L. 2003. Beros(s)us. *OCD*[3]: 239–240.

Leiman, S.Z. 1989. Josephus and the Canon of the Bible. Pages 50–58 in L.H. Feldman and G. Hata (eds.) *Josephus, the Bible, and History*. Leiden: Brill.

Levine, D. B. 1993. *Hubris* in Josephus' *Jewish Antiquities*. *HUCA* 64: 51-87.

Levison, J. R. 1994. The Debut of the Divine Spirit in Josephus' *Antiquities*. *HTR* 87: 123-38.

———. 1996. Josephus' Interpretation of the Divine Spirit. *JJS* 47: 234-55.

———. 1997. *The Spirit in First Century Judaism*. AGJU 29; Leiden: Brill.

Liddell, H. G., Scott, Robert, Jones, Henry S. 1940. *A Greek-English Lexicon*. Oxford: Clarendon.

Lindner, H. 1972. *Die Geschichtsauffassung des Flavius Josephus im Bellum Judaicum. Gleichzeitig ein Beitrag zur Quellenfrage*. AGJU 12; Leiden: Brill.

Lindsay, D. R. 1996. *Josephus and Faith:* Πίστις *and* Πιστεύω *as Faith Terminology in the Writings of Flavius Josephus and in the New Testament*. Leiden: Brill.

Lohfink, G. 1971. *Die Himmelfahrt Jesu*. Munich: Kösel.

Lührmann, D. 1971. Epiphaneia. Zur Bedeutungsgeschichte eines griechischen Wortes. Pp. 185-99 in *Tradition und Glaube: Festschrift K.G. Kuhn*, ed. G. Jeremias et al. Göttingen: Vandenhoeck & Ruprecht.

Mach, M. 1992. *Entwicklungsstadien des jüdischen Engelsglaubens in vorrabinischer Zeit*. Tübingen: Mohr Siebeck.

McIvor, J. S.. tr. 1994. *The Targum of Chronicles*. Collegeville: The Liturgical Press.

MacRae, G. W. 1965. Miracle in the *Antiquities* of Josephus. Pp. 127-47 in *Miracles: Cambridge Studies in Their Philosophy and History*, ed. Charles F.D. Moule. London: Mowbray.

Madden, S.C. 2001. Josephus's Use of the Book of Daniel: A Study of Hellenistic-Jewish Historiography. Ph.D. diss., The University of Texas at Arlington.

Maier, J. 1994. Amalek in the Writings of Josephus. Pp. 109-26 in *Josephus and the History of the Greco-Roman Period: Essays in Memory of Morton Smith*, ed. Fausto Parente and Joseph Sievers. Leiden: Brill.

Marcus, R. 1933. *Josephus*, vol. 7: *Jewish Antiquities*. Books XII-XIV. Loeb Classical Library. Cambridge, Mass.: Harvard University Press.

———. 1934. *Josephus*, vol. 5: *Jewish Antiquities*. Books V-VIII. Loeb Classical Library. Cambridge, Mass.: Harvard University Press.

———. 1937. *Josephus*, vol. 6: *Jewish Antiquities*. Books IX-XI. Loeb Classical Library. Cambridge, Mass.: Harvard University Press.

Margueron, J.-C. 1992. Babylon. *ABD* 1: 563-65.

Marmorstein, A. 1968. *The Doctrine of Merits in Old Rabbinic Literature*. New York: Ktav.

Mason, S. 1991. *Flavius Josephus on the Pharisees: A Composition-Critical Study*. Leiden: Brill.

———. 2000. Introduction. Pp. xiii-xxxvi in *Flavius Josephus: Translation and Commentary*, vol. 3: *Judean Antiquities 1-4*, tr. L. H. Feldman. Leiden: Brill.

———. 2001. *Flavius Josephus: Translation and Commentary*, vol. 9: *Life of Josephus*. Leiden: Brill (= BJP 9).

———. 2002. Josephus and his Twenty-Two Book Canon. Pp. 110-27 in *The Canon Debate*, ed. L.M. McDonald and J.A. Sanders. Peabody, Mass.: Hendrickson.

———. 2003. Flavius Josephus in Flavian Rome: Reading on and Between the Lines. Pp. 559-90 in *Flavian Rome: Culture, Image, Text*, ed. A.J. Boyle and W.J. Dominik. Leiden: Brill.

———. *Josephus and the New Testament*. 2003a. 2nd ed. Peabody, Mass.: Hendrickson.

Mastin, B.A. 1973. Daniel 2:46 and the Hellenistic World. *ZAW* 85:80–93.

Mayer, R. and C. Möller. 1974. Josephus—Politiker und Prophet. Pp. 271–184 in O. Betz, K. Haacker and M. Hengel eds. *Josephus-Studien: Untersuchungen zu Josephus, dem antiken Judentum und dem Neuen Testament. Otto Michel zum 70. Geburtstag gewidmet*. Göttingen: Vandenhoeck & Ruprecht.

Mayer-Schärtel, B. 1995. *Das Frauenbild des Josephus: Eine sozialgeschichtliche und kulturanthropologische Untersuchung.* Stuttgart: Kohlhammer.

Metzler, K. 1991. *Der griechische Begriff des Verzeihens. Untersucht am Wortstamm* συγγνώμη *von den ersten Belegen bis zum vierten Jahrhundert n. Christus.* Tübingen: Mohr Siebeck.

Meyer, R. 1974. Bemerkungen zum literargeschichtlichen Hintergrund der Kanontheorie des Josephus. Pp. 285–299 in O. Betz, K. Haacker and M. Hengel eds. *Josephus-Studien: Untersuchungen zu Josephus, dem antiken Judentum und dem Neuen Testament. Otto Michel zum 70. Geburtstag gewidmet.* Göttingen: Vandenhoeck & Ruprecht.

Millar, F. 1977. *The Emperor in the Roman World (31 BC–AD 337).* London: Duckworth.

Mitchell, H. 1952. *Sparta.* Cambridge: Cambridge University Press.

Moehring, H. R. 1957. Novellistic Elements in the Writings of Flavius Josephus. Diss, Ph.D., University of Chicago.

———. 1973. Rationalization of Miracles in the Writings of Flavius Josephus. *TU* 112: 376-83.

Montgomery, J. A. 1920-21. The Religion of Flavius Josephus. *JQR* 11: 277-305.

Moore, E. 1974-5. ΒΙΑΖΩ, ΄ΑΡΠΑΖΩ and Cognates in Josephus. *NTS* 21: 519-43.

Muir, J.M. 2003. Education, Roman. *OCD*[3]: 509–510.

Mulzer, M. 1992. *Jehu schlägt Joram. Text-literar-und strukturkritische Untersuchung zu 2 Kön 8,25-10,36.* St. Ottilien: EOS.

Mulzer, M. and K.S. Krieger. 1996. Die Jehuererzählung bei Josephus (*Ant. Jud.* IX, 105-109,159f.). *BN* 83: 54-82.

Mutius, H.G. von. 1980. Hoshea, der letzte König des Nordreiches bei Josephus und im Talmud. *Henoch* 2: 31-36.

Naber, S.A. 1888-96. *Flavii Josephi Opera omnia.* 6 vols. Leipzig: Teubner.

Neuman, A.A. 1952–53. Josippon and the Apocrypha. *JQR* 43:1–26.

Niese, B. 1885-95. *Flavii Josephi Opera.* 7 vols. Berlin: Weidmann.

O'Connor, E.M. ed. 1993. *The Essential Epicurus: letters, principal doctrines, Vatican sayings, and fragments.* Buffalo: Prometheus Books.

Oepke, A. 1967. ὄναρ. *TDNT* 5: 220–238.

Paul, A. 1975. Le Concept de prophétie biblique. Flavius Josèphe et Daniel. *RSR* 63:367–384.

Pax, E. 1955. ΕΠΙΦΑΝΕΙΑ: *Ein religionsgeschichtlicher Beitrag zur biblischen Theologie.* Munich: Zink.

Pérez Fernández, M., tr. 1984. *Los capítulos de Rabbí Eliezer.* Valencia: Institución San Jerónimo.

Piovanelli, P. 1992. Le texte de Jérémie utilisé par Flavius Josephus dans le Xᵉ Livre des *Antiquités Judaïques.* *Henoch* 14: 11-36.

Powell, M. A. 1992. Weights and Measures. *ABD* 6: 897-908.

Price, J. J. 1992. *Jerusalem under Siege: The Collapse of the Jewish State 66-70 C.E.* Leiden: Brill.

Price, S.R.F. 2003. Dreams. *OCD*[3]: 496–497.

Rahlfs, A. 1911. *Septuaginta-Studien III: Lucians Rezension der Königsbücher.* Göttingen: Vandenhoeck & Ruprecht.

Rajak, T. 2001. *The Jewish Dialogue with Greece and Rome. Studies in Cultural and Social Interaction.* AGJU 48; Leiden: Brill.

———. 1983. *Josephus: The Historian and his Society.* Philadelphia: Fortress.

Rappaport, S. 1930. *Agada und Exegese bei Flavius Josephus.* Vienna: Alexander Kohut Memorial Foundation.

Rebuffat, R. 1976. Une bataille navale au VIIIᵉ siècle (Josèphe, *Antiquités Judaïques* IX,14). *Semitica* 26: 71-79.

Reiling, J. 1971. The Use of ψευδοπρφήτης in the Septuaginta, Philo and Josephus. *NovT* 13: 147-56.

Reinach, T. 1924. Un passage incompris de Josèphe ou la vie chère à Tyr au temps de Sennachérib. *REG* 37: 257-60.

Remus, H. 1982. Does Terminology Distinguish Early Christian from Pagan Miracles? *JBL* 101: 531-5.

Rengstorf, K. H. 1973-83. *A Complete Concordance to Flavius Josephus.* 4 Vols. Leiden: Brill.

Rousseau, P. 2003. Asceticism. *OCD*[3]: 186–187.

Rowley, H.H. 1964. *Darius the Mede and the Four World Empires in the Book of Daniel.* Cardiff: University of Wales Press.

Sack, R.H. 1992a. Belshazzar. *ABD* 1: 661.

———. 1992b. Evil-Merodach. *ABD* 2: 679.

———. 1992c. Nabonidus. *ABD* 4: 973-76.

———. 1992d. Nabopolassar. *ABD* 4: 977-78.

———. 1992e. Nebuchadnezzar. *ABD* 4: 1058-59.

Satran, D. 1980. Daniel, Seer, Philosopher, Holy Man. Pp. 33–48 in J.J. Collins and G.W.E. Nickelsburg eds. *Ideal Figures in Ancient Judaism: Profiles and Paradigms.* SBLSCS 12; Chico: Scholars Press.

Schalit, A., ed. 1944-63. *Josephus. Antiquities of the Jews* [Hebrew]. 3 vols. Jerusalem: Mosad Bialik.

———. 1968. *Namenwörterbuch zu Flavius Josephus* (A Complete Concordance to Flavius Josephus, ed. Karl H. Rengstorf, Supplement 1). Leiden: Brill.

Schenkel, J.D. 1968. *Chronology and Recensional Development in the Greek Text of Kings*. Cambridge, Mass.: Harvard University Press.

Schenker, A. 2004. *Älteste Textgeschichte der Königsbücher. Die hebräische Vorlage der ursprünglichen Septuaginta als älteste Textform der Königsbücher*. Fribourg: Academic Press; Göttingen: Vandenhoeck & Ruprecht.

Schlatter, A. 1910. *Wie Sprach Josephus von Gott?* Gütersloh: Bertelsmann.

———. 1913. *Die hebräischen Namen bei Josephus*. Gütersloh: Bertelsmann.

———. 1932. *Die Theologie des Judentums nach dem Bericht des Josephus*. Gütersloh: Bertelsmann.

Schneider, J. 1964. εὐνοῦχος, εὐνουχίζω. Pages 765–768 in vol. 2 of *Theological Dictionary of the New Testament*. Edited by G. Kittel and G. Friedrich. Translated by G. Bromiley. 10 vols. Grand Rapids: Eerdmans.

Schröder, B. 1996. *Die 'väterlichen Gesetze': Flavius Josephus als Vermittler von Halachah an Griechen und Römer*. Tübingen: Mohr Siebeck.

Schwartz, D. R. 1983-4. Josephus on Jewish Constitutions and Community. *SCI* 7: 30-52.

Schwartz, S. 1990. *Josephus and Judaean Politics*. CSCT 18; Leiden: Brill.

Sherwin-White, S. 2003. Antiochus (4) IV. OCD³: 108-109.

Shutt, R. J. H. 1961. *Studies in Josephus*. London: SPCK.

———. 1980. The Concept of God in the Works of Flavius Josephus. *JJS* 31: 171-89.

Sievers, J. 1998. Josephus and the Afterlife. Pp. 20–34 in S. Mason ed. *Understanding Josephus: Seven Perspectives*. JSPSupp 32; Sheffield: Sheffield Academic Press.

———. 1999. Michea Figlio di Imla e la profezia in Flavio Giuseppe. *RStB* 11: 97-105.

Smit, E.J. 1976. Josephus and the Final History of the Kingdom of Judah. Pp. 53-6 in *Studies in the Chronicler*, Ou-Testamientiese Werkgemeenskap in Suider-Afrika 19, ed. W.C. van Wyk.

Smith, G.A. 1896. *The Historical Geography of the Holy Land*. London: Hodder & Stoughton.

Smith, M. 1987. The Occult in Josephus. Pages 236–256 in L.H. Feldman and G. Hata, eds. *Josephus, Judaism and Christianity*. Leiden: Brill.

Smith, R.W. 1992. Coele-Syria. *ABD* 1: 1075-76.

Sorabji, R.R.K. 2003. Animals, attitudes to. OCD³: 90.

Spicq, C. 1958. La philanthropie hellénistique, vertu divine et royale. *ST* 12: 161-91.

———. 1978. *Notes de lexiocographie néo-testamentaire*. Vol. I. Fribourg: Editions universitaires; Göttingen: Vandenhoeck & Ruprecht.

———. 1978. *Notes de lexiocographie néo-testamentaire*. Vol. II. Fribourg: Editions universitaires; Göttingen: Vandenhoeck & Ruprecht.

———. 1982. *Notes de lexiocographie néo-testamentaire*. Supplément. Fribourg: Editions universitaires; Göttingen: Vandenhoeck & Ruprecht.

Spilsbury, P. 1998. *The Image of the Jew in Flavius Josephus' Paraphrase of the Bible*. Tübingen: Mohr Siebeck.

———. 2003. Flavius Josephus on the Rise and Fall of the Roman Empire. *JTS* 54:1–24.

Spilsbury, P. and J. Sievers. Forthcoming. *Flavius Josephus: Translation and Commentary*, ed. S. Mason. Vol. 6: Judean Antiquities 11-13. Leiden: Brill (= BJP 6).

Spottorno, V. 1987. Some Remarks on Josephus' Biblical Text for 1-2 Kings. Pp. 277-85 in *VI Congress of the International Organization for Septuagint and Cognate Studies*, ed. C. Cox. Atlanta: Scholars.

———. 1997. The Book of Chronicles in Josephus' *Jewish Antiquities*. Pp. 381-90 in *IX Congress of the International Organization for Septuagint and Cognate Studies, Cambridge, 1995*, ed. B.A. Taylor. Atlanta: Scholars.

Stählin, G. 1974. Das Schicksal im NT und bei Josephus. Pp. 319-43 in *Josephus-Studien: Festschrift Otto Michel*, ed. Otto Betz et al. Göttingen: Vandenhoeck & Ruprecht.

———. 1974. φιλέω κτλ. *TDNT* 9: 113–71.

Sterling, G. E. 1992. *Historiography and Self-Definition: Josephos, Luke-Acts and Apologetic Historiography*. Leiden: Brill.

Swete, H.B. 1989. *An Introduction to the Old Testament in Greek*. Revised by R.R. Ottley. Cambridge: Cambridge University Press, 1914. Repr. Peabody, Mass.: Hendrickson.

Tabor, J. D. 1989. "Returning to the Divinity": Josephus' Portrayal of the Disappearances of Enoch, Elijah, and Moses. *JBL* 108: 225-38.

Thackeray, H. St. John. 1926. *Josephus*, vol. 1: *The Life / Against Apion*. Loeb Classical Library. Cambridge, Mass.: Harvard University Press.

———. 1929. *Josephus the Man and the Historian*. New York: Jewish Institute of Religion.

Thomas, R. 2003. Education, Greek. OCD³: 506–509.

Tiede, D.L. 1972. *The Charismatic Figure as Miracle Worker*. SBLDS 1; Missoula: Scholars Press.

Tomasino, A.J. 1995. Daniel and the Revolutionaries. The Use of the Daniel Tradition by Jewish Resistance Movements of Late Second-Temple Palestine. 2 vols. PhD. Dissertation; University of Chicago.

Torijano, P. A. 2002. *Solomon the Esoteric King: From King to Magus: The Development of a Tradition*. Leiden: Brill.

Troiani, L. 1994. The ΠΟΛΙΤΕΙΑ of Israel in the Graeco-Roman Age. Pp. 11-22 in *Josephus and the History of the Greco-Roman Period*, ed. F. Parente and J. Sievers. Leiden: Brill.

Unger, E. 1970. *Babylon. Die heilige Stadt nach der Beschreibung der Babylonier*. 2d ed. Berlin: de Gruyter.

van Unnik, W.C. 1973. An Attack on the Epicuraeans by Flavius Josephus. Pp. 341–355 in W. den Boer et al. eds. *Romanitas et Christianitas: Studia Iano Henrico Waszink A.D. VI Kal. Nov. A. MCMLXXIII lustri compleni oblata*. Amsterdam: North Holland Publishing Company.

———. 1974. Josephus' Account of the Story of Israel's Sin with Alien Women in the Country of Midian (Num 25:1 ff). Pp. 241–61 in M.S.H.G. Heerma van Voss et al. eds. *Travels in the World of the Old Testament. Studies Presented to Prof. M.A. Beek on the Occasion of his 65th Birthday*. Studia Semitica Neerlandica 16; Assen: Van Gorcum.

———. 1976. *Het Godspredikaat "Het Begin en Het Einde" bij Flavius Josephus en in de Openbaring van Johannes*. Amsterdam: Noord-Hollandsche Uitgeversmaatschappij.

———. 1978. *Flavius Josephus als historischer Schriftsteller*. Heidelberg: Verlag Lambert Schneider.

Vermes, G. 1991. Josephus' Treatment of the Book of *Daniel*. JJS 42:149–166.

Versnel, H.S. 2003. *Theos*. OCD³: 1506.

Villaba i Varneda, P. 1986. *The Historical Method of Flavius Josephus*. Leiden: Brill.

Wacholder, B. Z. 1962. *Nicolaus of Damascus*. Berkeley: University of California Press.

———. 1989. Josephus and Nicolaus of Damascus. Pp. 147-72 in *Josephus, the Bible and History*, ed. Louis H. Feldman and G. Hata. Detroit: Wayne State University Press.

Weill, J. et al., trs. 1900-1932. *Oeuvres complètes de Flavius Josèphe*, ed. Thédore Reinach. Paris: Leroux.

Weill, J. 1923. Nahoum II, 9-12 et Josèphe (*Ant.* IX, XI, ## 239-241). REJ 76: 96-98.

Weiss, H.F. 1979. Pharisäismus und Hellenismus. Zur Darstellung des Judentums im Geschichtswerk des jüdischen Historikers Flavius Josephus. OLZ 74: 421-33.

Wilkens, M.J. 1988. *The Concept of Disciple in Matthew's Gospel*. Leiden: Brill.

Wiseman, D.J. 1956. *Chronicles of the Chaldaean Kings (625–556 B.C.) in the British Museum*. London: British Museum Publications.

———. 1985. *Nebuchadrezzar and Babylon*. Oxford: Oxford University Press.

Wolff, C. 1976. *Jeremia im Frühjudentum und Urchristentum*. Berlin: Akademie-Verlag.

Wolfson, H.A. 1947. *Philo. Foundations of Religious Philosophy in Judaism, Christianity and Islam*. 2 vols. Cambridge, Mass.: Harvard University Press.

Wright, D. P. and R. N. Jones. 1992. Leprosy. ABD 4: 277-82.

Yamauchi, E.M. 1992. Astyages. ABD 1: 507-8.

Zangenberg, J. 1994. ΣΑΜΑΡΕΙΑ: *Antike Quellen zur Geschichte und Kultur der Samaritaner in deutscher Übersetzung*. Tübingen/Basel: Franke.

INDEX OF MODERN SCHOLARS

INDEX OF ANCIENT AUTHORS

334

10.275-276 10n1128
10.276 10n891
10.276-281 10n1110
10.277 10n856, 10n1075, 10n1121, 10n1129
10.277-280 9n14
10.277-281 p265, 8n1156
10.281 10n935
11.2 10n987
11.3 9n732
11.4-5 10n1162
11.9 10n672
11.10 10n582, 10n1004, 10n1170
11.12 10n672
11.14 10n1170
11.31 10n1004
11.32 10n1113
11.58 10n582, 10n1170
11.82 8n905
11.84 10n672
11.91 10n582, 10n1170
11.96 10n532
11.100 10n1170
11.102 10n582
11.109 10n914
11.115 8n1423
11.121 10n1059, 10n1113
11.132 10n683
11.139 10n500, 10n1059
11.140 10n914
11.141 9n50
11.169 8n992
11.175 9n50
11.178 10n800
11.183 10n1059
11.213 8n1130
11.231 10n914
11.240 10n812
11.257 8n1092
11.265 8n1092
11.268 10n1107
11.297 10n160
11.299 8n1015
11.300 9n717, 10n160
11.331 10n902
11.332 9n833
11.337 10n1123, 10n1130, 10n1162, 10n890
11.338 10n914
11.340 9n1129
12.4 9n503
12.12 8n609
12.20 10n938
12.40 9n986
12.48 10n938
12.59 8n609
12.83 10n101
12.90 10n856
12.109 10n940
12.133 8n1423
12.134 10n101
12.248 10n1172
12.248-256 10n1174
12.249 10n1170
12.250 10n1004
12.252 8n831, 9n4
12.257 9n1119, 9n1129

12.261 9n1129
12.271 10n213
12.277 9n105
12.280 9n1020
12.281 8n907, 8n1443
12.291 8n1443
12.295 10n683
12.301 9n1020
12.307 8n1443
12.317 10n1185
12.318 10n182
12.319-321 10n1172
12.322 10n1175
12.347 10n483
12.357 10n582
12.384 8n905
12.385 8n831, 9n4
12.394 8n1562
13.5 10n1188
13.34 8n831, 9n4
13.171-173 10n1181
13.231 10n496
13.288 10n907
13.294 10n1059
13.297-298 10n1181
13.310 10n907
13.311-312 10n820
13.311-313 10n829
13.316 10n353
13.317 10n812
14.22 10n925
14.54 8n574
14.92 10n672
14.115 9n1128
14.116 8n1166
14.154 8n1166, 10n101
14.309 8n890
14.406 10n856
14.455 10n925
14.458 8n1019
15.25 8n1443
15.68 8n633
15.96 8n574
15.138 8n843, 9n155
15.158 10n812
15.190 10n812
15.194 9n245
15.201 8n185
15.234 9n392
15.251 10n812
15.299 8n374
15.312 10n101
15.345 9n919
15.371 10n800, 10n1181
15.373 8n796, 10n820
15.379 10n820
15.385-387 10n891
15.413-416 8n328
15.414 8n327, 8n455
15.417 8n324
15.417-420 8n325
15.418-419 8n326
15.421 10n672
16.21 8n633
16.22 9n919

CLASSICAL GREEK AUTHORS

CLASSICAL LATIN AUTHORS

(POST-BIBLICAL) CHRISTIAN AUTHORS

OTHER ANCIENT SOURCES

BIBLICAL PASSAGES

16:24	8n1142, 8n1143, 8n1146, 8n1147, 8n1148	18:17	8n1263
		18:18	8n1264, 8n1265
16:25	8n1149	18:19	8n1182, 8n1267, 8n1268
16:26	8n1149	18:20	8n1270
16:27	8n1149	18:21	8n1271, 8n1272, 8n1275, 8n1276, 8n1277
16:28	8n1151, 8n1152, 9n63		
16:28f (LXX)	9n135	18:22-25	8n1278
16:29-34	8n1164	18:22	8n1279
16:29	8n1164	18:23	8n1280, 8n1282, 8n1283
16:30-34	8n1182	18:24	8n1284, 8n1285, 8n1286
16:30	8n1165	18:25	8n1287
16:31	8n1167, 8n1170, 8n1171, 8n1172, 8n1173, 8n1199, 8n1217	18:26	8n1288, 8n1289, 8n1292, 8n1293
		18:27	8n1290, 8n1291
16:32-33	8n1169	18:28	8n1293
16:32	8n1180, 9n508	18:29	8n1294
16:33	8n1181, 8n1184	18:30	8n1295, 8n1297
16:34	8n1184	18:31	8n1296
17:1	8n1185, 8n1187, 8n1188, 8n1189, 8n1190, 8n1217	18:32	8n1295, 8n1297, 8n1298
		18:33-35	8n1301
17:2-7	8n1196	18:33	8n1299, 8n1300
17:2-5	8n1191, 8n1192, 8n1197	18:36-37	8n1304
17:2-4	8n1191	18:36	8n1303
17:2	8n1191	18:37	8n1304
17:3	8n1193	18:38	8n1306, 8n1308
17:5	8n1193	18:39	8n1309, 8n1311, 8n1313
17:6	8n1194, 8n1195	18:40	8n1314
17:8	8n1197, 8n1198	18:41	8n1315, 8n1316, 8n1317
17:9	8n1191, 8n1200	18:42	8n1317, 8n1318
17:10	8n1201, 8n1203	18:43	8n1319, 8n1320
17:11	8n1204	18:44	8n1321, 8n1322, 8n1323, 8n1327
17:12	8n1205, 8n1206, 8n1207		
17:13-14	8n1213	18:45	8n1324, 8n1325
17:13	8n1208, 8n1209	18:46	8n1326, 8n1327
17:14	8n1210, 8n1211	19	8n1328, 8n1378, 8n1379
17:15	8n1212	19:1	8n1328
17:16	8n1213	19:2	8n1329, 8n1349
17:17-24	8n1218, 8n1220	19:3	8n1192, 8n1330, 8n1331, 8n1332, 8n1333
17:17	8n1220		
17:18	8n1223	19:4	8n1334, 8n1335
17:19	8n1124, 8n1225	19:5	8n1334, 8n1336, 8n1337, 8n1338
17:20	8n1226		
17:21	8n1227	19:6-8	8n1340
17:22	8n1229	19:6	8n1340
17:23	8n1229	19:8	8n1340, 8n1342
17:24	8n1230, 8n1231	19:9	8n1343, 8n1344, 8n1345
18	8n1232	19:10	8n1346, 8n1347, 8n1348, 8n1349
18:1	8n1232, 8n1233, 8n1234		
18:2	8n1234, 8n1236, 8n1246	19:11	8n1350, 8n1351, 8n1352, 8n1353
18:3	8n1237, 8n1239		
18:4	8n1239, 8n1244, 8n1245, 8n1246, 9n192, 9n193	19:12	8n1354, 8n1355
		19:13-14	8n1356
18:5	8n1236, 8n1242, 8n1251	19:13	8n1355
18:6	8n1243	19:14	8n1356
18:7-8	8n1248	19:15-18	8n1356, 8n1357
18:7	8n1247	19:15	8n1356, 8n1358, 8n1362, 8n1363, 9n336
18:8	8n1249, 8n1252		
18:9	8n1250	19:16-17	9n401
18:10	8n1241, 8n1251, 8n1252	19:16	8n1359, 8n1360, 8n1361, 8n1364, 8n1365, 8n1366
18:11	8n1252, 8n1258		
18:12	8n1254, 8n1255, 9n191	19:17	8n1367, 8n1368
18:13	8n1258, 9n192, 9n193	19:18	8n1368
18:14	8n1258	19:19-21	8n1366
18:15	8n1260	19:19	8n1369, 8n1370, 8n1371, 8n1372
18:16	8n1261		

Passage	Reference	Passage	Reference
10:36	9n593, 9n595	13:16-17	9n671
11	9n533, 9n545, 9n563, 9n576	13:16	9n670
11:1-20	9n526, 9n527	13:17	9n671, 9n672, 9n673
11:1	9n526, 9n528, 9n529, 9n530	13:18	9n672
11:2-3	9n531, 9n536	13:19	9n673, 9n674
11:2	9n532, 9n533, 9n534, 9n535	13:20-21	9n679, 9n682
11:4	9n533, 9n537, 9n540, 9n541, 9n543	13:20	9n675. 9n678
		13:21	9n680
11:5-6	9n546	13:22-23	9n682
11:6	9n546	13:25	9n663, 9n673, 9n683, 9n685, 9n686
11:7-8	9n549		
11:9	9n550	14	9n693, 9n709, 9n710, 9n738, 9n753
11:10	9n552, 9n553		
11:11	9n555	14:1-22	9n687
11:12	9n556, 9n557, 9n558	14:1	9n687
11:13	9n559, 9n561	14:2	9n688, 9n690, 9n743, 9n749, 9n750
11:14	9n562, 9n563, 9n564		
11:15	9n565, 9n566, 9n567	14:3-4	9n690
11:16	9n568	14:5-6	9n692
11:17	9n571, 9n572	14:5	9n691
11:18	9n573, 9n574, 9n575	14:7	9n695, 9n704, 9n705, 9n706
11:19-20	9n579	14:8	9n722, 9n724
11:19	9n578	14:9	9n725, 9n727, 9n728
11:20	9n580	14:10	9n729, 9n731, 9n733
12:1-22	9n581, 9n619, 9n644	14:11-12	9n735
12:1-2	9n648	14:13-14	9n740
12:1	9n581	14:13	9n736, 9n738, 9n739
12:2	9n581, 9n582	14:14-16	9n743
12:3	9n584	14:14	9n742
12:4	9n584	14:15-16	9n742
12:5-6	9n597	14:18	9n752
12:7	9n600, 9n601	14:19	9n744, 9n745, 9n746
12:8	9n602, 9n603, 9n604	14:20	9n747
12:9	9n604	14:21	9n752
12:10	9n606, 9n607, 9n609	14:22	9n816, 9n943
12:11	9n611, 9n612	14:23-29	9n766
12:12-13	9n614	14:23	9n753, 9n754, 9n755, 9n802
12:12	9n614	14:24	9n758
12:13	9n614	14:25	9n760, 9n761, 9n762, 9n763, 9n765, 9n766
12:14	9n616		
12:17	9n617	14:28	9n803
12:18	9n639, 9n640	14:29	9n803, 9n804
12:19	9n642, 9n643	15	9n811
12:20	9n649	15:1-7	9n805
12:22	9n645, 9n646, 9n649	15:1	9n806
13	9n650, 9n653	15:2	9n807, 9n859, 9n860
13:1	9n651	15:3	9n810
13:2	9n652, 9n663	15:4	9n810
13:3-7	9n682	15:5	9n847, 9n854, 9n855, 9n856, 9n861
13:4-6	9n653		
13:4	9n653, 9n656, 9n657	15:6	9n858
13:5	9n658, 9n659	15:7	9n858, 9n861
13:6	9n659	15:8-31	9n862, 9n867
13:7	9n653	15:8	9n862
13:8	9n661	15:9	9n863
13:9	9n660, 9n661	15:10	9n865, 9n866, 9n867
13:10	9n662	15:11-12	9n867
13:11	9n663	15:12	9n867
13:12-13	9n663, 9n686, 9n742	15:14	9n868, 9n869, 9n870
13:12	9n686	15:15	9n870
13:13	9n686, 9n687	15:16	9n871, 9n872, 9n873, 9n875
13:14-25	9n663	15:17	9n877
13:14	9n664, 9n666, 9n667, 9n669	15:18	9n877
13:15-16	9n670	15:19	9n878, 9n880, 9n892
13:15	9n670	15:20	9n880, 9n881

2:31	10n873, 10n876, p266	5:5	10n1008, 10n1009
2:32	10n877, 10n878, 10n887	5:6	10n1010
2:33	10n879, 10n893	5:7	10n912, 10n1011, 10n1016, 10n1017
2:34	10n880, 10n881		
2:35	10n880, 10n882, 10n883	5:9-11	10n1018
2:35	p266	5:9	10n1001, 10n1010
2:37-38	10n886	5:10	10n912, 10n1010
2:39	10n888, 10n892	5:11	10n996, 10n1021, 10n1026, 10n1027, 10n1064, p266
2:40	10n893		
2:41	10n893	5:12	10n1021, 10n1026, 10n1027
2:42	10n893	5:13-28	10n1024
2:43	10n893	5:14	10n1021, 10n1026, 10n1027, 10n1028
2:44	10n1110		
2:44-45	10n894	5:15	10n912
2:45	10n880	5:17	10n1032
2:46-47	10n903	5:18	10n996, 10n1018, 10n1064
2:46-49	10n900	5:18-21	10n926
2:47	10n856	5:18-22	10n1034
2:48-49	10n906	5:20	10n1034
3	10n900	5:21	10n1038
3:1	10n754, 10n909, 10n911, 10n1134	5:22	10n996, 10n1006, 10n1018, 10n1064
3:2-3	10n910	5:22-23	10n1109
3:5	10n912	5:23	10n1004, 10n1007, 10n1113, 10n1042, 10n1047, 10n1051
3:7	10n912	5:25	
3:8-12	10n914	5:25-26	10n1043
3:13-15	10n915	5:26	10n1045, 10n1046, 10n1049
3:15	10n918	5:26-28	10n1024, 10n1042, p266
3:17-18	10n918	5:27	10n1047, 10n1050
3:19	10n918	5:28	9n1085, 10n471, 10n1051, 10n1053
3:21	10n918		
3:22	10n918	5:29	10n1060
3:23	p265	5:30	10n1000, 10n1061
3:24-28	10n918, 10n1098	6	10n1072, 10n1132
3:27	10n918, 10n919, 10n923	6:1	10n1066
3:28	10n926	6:1-2	10n1071
3:29	10n926	6:3	10n1026, 10n1076
3:30	10n926	6:3-4	10n1077
3:91	10n1113, p266	6:4	10n1077, 10n1078, 10n1080
3:94	10n1113, p266	6:5	10n1080
4	10n927	6:7	10n1082
4:2-3	10n927	6:8	9n1085
4:4-27	10n1022	6:10	10n1081, 10n1087, 10n1088, 10n1089
4:4-37	10n1037		
4:5	10n931	6:14	10n1113, p266
4:8	10n904, 10n927, 10n1026	6:16	10n1096
4:8-9	10n1021	6:19	10n1098
4:9	10n904, 10n906, 10n1026	6:20	10n1097
4:10-17	10n927	6:22	10n918, 10n1098
4:16	p266	6:24	10n1105
4:18	10n904, 10n927, 10n1021, 10n1026	6:25	10n1105, 10n1111
		6:25-28	10n1110
4:19-27	10n927	6:26-27	10n1112
4:25	10n929, 10n934	6:28	10n1070, 10n1113
4:28-33	10n927	7	10n1110, 10n1127, 10n1131, 10n1132, 10n893
4:30	10n934		
4:34-35	10n927	7:6	10n889
4:34-36	10n933	7:7	10n893
4:36	10n932	7:8	10n1144
4:37	10n927	7:11	10n1144
5	10n779, 10n978, 10n1013	7:14	10n1110
5:1	10n1002, 10n1003	7:18	10n896, 10n1110
5:2	10n632, 10n961, 10n1006	7:20	10n1144
5:3	10n1002, 10n1004, p266	7:25	10n1127, 10n1158
5:4	10n1007	7:27	10n1110

INDEX OF GEOGRAPHICAL NAMES

8n1363, 8n1431, 8n1513, 9.88, 9.89, 9.93, 9.245, 9.253, 9.254, 9n336, 9n354, 9n984, 9n985, 9n992, 9n994

Damascus, wilderness of, 8n1358, 8n1363

Dan, 8.226, 8.228, 8.305, 8n763, 8n764, 8n774

David, City of, the, 8n61, 8n681, 8n701, 8n703, 8n936, 8n1022, 9n393, 9n453, 9n646, 9n747, 9n861, 9n925, 10n189

Dead Sea: *see* Asphaltitis, Lake

Decapolis, 10n741

Dor (Naphath-dor), 8.35, 8n112

Dothaein (Dothan), 9.54, 9n215

Dothan: *see* Dothaein

Ecbatana, 10.264, 10n1115

Egypt, 10n825

Egypt, 8.61, 8.155, 8.157, 8.159, 8.165, 8.202, 8.210, 8.212, 8n144, 8n183, 8n529, 8n614, 8n660, 8n668, 8n669, 8n699, 8n701, 8n898, 8n899, 9.217, 9.280, 9n301, 10.20, 10.82, 10.175, 10.179, 10.180, 10.182, 10.195, 10.220, 10.222, 10n30, 10n69, 10n73, 10n74, 10n362, 10n363, 10n376, 10n381, 10n461, 10n468, 10n745, 10n825

Egypt, Brook of, the, 10n381

Egypt, Gulf of, the (Aqaba, Gulf of, the), 8.163, 8n537

Eipa (Hippam), 8.246, 8n856

Elath: *see* Ilan

Elom (Aijalon), 8.246, 8n863

Eloth: *see* Ilan

Endor, 8n1201

Engade (En-gedi), 9.7, 9.11, 9n26, 9n28

En-gedi: *see* Engade

En-rogel: *see* Eroge

Ephesus, 8n208, 8n492

Ephraim, hill country of, 8n107, 9n9

Ephraim, Mount, 8n701, 8n710

Ephron/Ephrain, 8n1019

Eroge (En-rogel/ gy' hry), 9.225, 9n848

Etam: *see* Etame

Etame (Etam) 8.246, 8n606, 8n851

Etan, 8.186, 8n606

Ethiopia, 8.159, 8.165, 8.175, 8.192, 9n385, 10n13, 10n56

Euphrates, River, 8.39, 8.189, 8.271, 8.363, 10.74, 10.75, 10.84, 10.85, 10.86, 10n319, 10n375, 10n381

Euxine, Sea, the (Black Sea, the), 9.213, 9n793

Exoche (Ziz), 9.10, 9n39

Ezion-geber: *see* Gasion-Gabel

Fullers' Field, the, 9n19

Gabaa (Geba), 8.305, 8n1115

Gabathon (Gibbethon), 8.288, 8.308, 8.310, 8n1032, 8n1129

Galaad: *see* Galaditis

Galaditis (Galadene/ Gildead/ Galaad), 8.36, 8.37, 8.157, 8n129, 8n1188, 9.235, 9n589, 9n893

Galilee, 8.36, 8.141, 8n487, 9.235, 9n893

Garis, 8.331

Gasion-gebel (Ezion-geber), 8.163, 9n65

Gath: *see* Gitta

Gath-heper, 9n760

Gaulanitis, 8.36

Gazara (Gaza), 8.151, 8n506, 8n507, 8n525, 9.275, 9n1072

Gebal, 8n200, 9n695

Gedor: *see* Gerar

Gerar, 8.294, 8n1058, 8n1059

Gerizim, Mount, 9n1119

Geruth-chimham: *see* Mandra

Geth: *see* Gitta

Gibbethon: *see* Gabathon

Gibeah, 8n877

Gibeon: *see* Gibron

Gibron (Ibron/ Gibeon), 8.22, 8n64, 8n65, 8n427, 10.173, 10n713

Gilead: *see* Galaditis

Gischala, 8n1174, 10n431, 10n665

Gitta (Gath/ Geth), 8.18, 8n52, 8n856, 9.170, 9.217, 9.275, 9n640, 9n812

Gold, land of, the: *see* Sopheir

Gozan, 9n1085

Great Plain, the (Megiddo, Valley of/ Jezreel, Plain of), 8.36, 8n113, 10n315

Greece: *see* Thrace

Gur, Ascent of, 9n450

Gurbal, 9n815

gy' hry: *see* Eroge

Habor, the, 9n1085

Halah, 9n1085

Halicarnassus, 8n721, 8n1015

Hallow of Blessing, 9.15

Hamath: *see* Amathe

Hamath, entrance of, the, 9.762

Hamath, land of, the, 10n356, 10n544, 10n562, 10n613

Hazazon-tamar: *see* Engade

Hazor: *see* Asor

Hebron: *see* Chebron

Hierosolyma (Jerusalem), 8.17, 8.18, 8.21, 8.25, 8.41, 8.54, 8.99, 8.100, 8.145, 8.147, 8.150, 8.116, 8.186, 8.187, 8.188, 8.198, 8.205, 8.206, 8.211, 8.221, 8.225, 8.227, 8.230, 8.231, 8.236, 8.241, 8.248, 8.255, 8.264, 8.285, 8.290, 8.295, 8.303, 8.314, 8.393, 8.399, 8.411, 8.412, 8n55, 8n61, 8n71, 8n78, 8n181, 8n332, 8n341, 8n417, 8n435, 8n436, 8n501, 8n504, 8n612, 8n681, 8n760, 8n767, 8n777, 8n781, 8n823, 8n872, 8n894, 8n909, 8n911, 8n913, 8n932, 8n966, 8n1101, 8n1577, 9.1, 9.4, 9.5, 9.7, 9.8, 9.11, 9.16, 9.17, 9.19, 9.31, 9.44, 9.95, 9.100, 9.104, 9.112, 9.117, 9.121, 9.142, 9.144, 9.161, 9.166, 9.170, 9.171, 9.177, 9.186, 9.194, 9.201, 9.202, 9.203, 9.216, 9.218, 9.236, 9.243, 9.254, 9.260, 9.264, 9.267, 9n15, 9n16, 9n20, 9n136, 9n139, 9n189, 9n453, 9n599, 9n603, 9n625, 9n640, 9n644, 9n738, 9n740, 9n743, 9n819, 9n820, 9n821, 9n901, 9n965, 9n994, 9n1016, 9n1042, 9n1043, 9n1061, 9n1062, 9n1084, 10.2, 10.4, 10.15, 10.21, 10.23, 10.24, 10.42, 10.44, 10.62, 10.66, 10.70, 10.77, 10.80, 10.81, 10.99, 10.106, 10.110, 10.111, 10.114, 10.116, 10.131, 10.135, 10.144, 10.145, 10.149, 10.154, 10.159, 10.160, 10.181, 10.183, 10.184, 10n3, 10n14, 10n30, 10n52, 10n56, 10n62, 10n66, 10n83, 10n85, 10n86, 10n99, 10n100, 10n111, 10n161, 10n165, 10n168, 10n172, 10n183, 10n224, 10n225, 10n226, 10n232, 10n271, 10n291, 10n292, 10n296, 10n297, 10n298, 10n300, 10n310, 10n327, 10n328, 10n332, 10n338, 10n342, 10n344, 10n356, 10n390, 10n393, 10n414, 10n417, 10n429, 10n431, 10n433, 10n460, 10n462, 10n463, 10n469, 10n472, 10n481, 10n482, 10n489, 10n500, 10n531, 10n532, 10n533, 10n539, 10n545, 10n569, 10n583, 10n585, 10n595, 10n602, 10n652, 10n667, 10n740

Himmon, son of, Valley of, the, 9n931

Hippam: *see* Eipa

Horeb, Mount: *see* Sinai, Mount

INDEX OF MONTH NAMES

INDEX OF PERSONAL NAMES

INDEX OF GREEK, LATIN, HEBREW AND ARAMAIC WORDS AND PHRASES

GREEK WORDS AND PHRASES

ἀγάζω, 10n851
εἴτε ἀγαθὸν εἴτε φαῦλον, 10n146
ἀγαθὸς καὶ δίκαιος, 9n808
ἡ τῶν ἀγαθῶν ὄνησις, 8n393
ἄγαμαι, 8n1443, 10n851
ἀγαπᾶν τὴν δουλείαν, 8n715
ἀγαπάω, 8n650
ἀγασάμενος, 10n854
τι ἄγγελος, 10n832
τὸ ἅγιον ἔλαιον, 9n406
ἁγνίζω, 10n182, 10n182
ἄγνοια καὶ ἀπιστία, 10n576
ἀγριότης, 9n874
ἀγρογείτων, 8n1381
ἀγωνία δεινή, 10n88, 10n103, 8n1461
ἀδελφοί, 10n858
ἀδικία, 8n1155
ἄδικος καὶ κακοῦργος, 10n367
ἀδωροδόκητος, 10n1031
δι ἀέρος φερόμενον, 10n1145
ἀηδούς, 8n1449
ἀθάνατος ἰσχύς, 9n836
ἀθλητῆς κακίας, 8n1097
ὁ ἀθλητῆς τῶν καλῶν, 8n1097
ἀθυμία, 9n857
ἀθυμία δεινή, 10n103
τῶν κατ Αἴγυπτον ἐθνῶν, 10n957
τὸ αἰδοῖον, 8n729
αἰδοῦς, 8n1449
αἰκία καὶ βάσανοι, 10n479
αἰλάμ, 8n463
αἷμα, 10n792
αἱρεθήσεται τὰ Ἱεροσόλυμα καὶ ὁ
   ναὸς ἐρημωθήσεται, 10n1177
αἱρέσεις, 8n1181
τῆς αἰσχύνης, 8n1268
αἴτιοι κινδύνου καὶ τιμωρίας αὐτῷ
   καταστῶσιν, 10n804
αἰχμάλωτος, 10n956, 10n1019
ἀκαταφρόνητος, 9n904
ἀκραιφνής, 10n813
τὰ ἀκριβή, 10n938
ἀλαζονείας, 10n322
ἀλαζών, 8n933
ἀλεύρων λεπτότερον, 10n882
ἀληθής, 8n1073, 9n90
ἀληθής καὶ μόνος, 8n1274, 8n1311
ἀληθῆς μόνος, 8n1311
ἀληθὴς προφήτης, 8n1073
ἀληθῶς, 8n1311, 9n990
ἀλήτης, 8n1076
ἀλισγηθῇ, 10n789
ἀλλοτριόχωρος, 8n627
ἀλλόφυλοι, 9n385
τὸν ἀλλόφυλον, 9n682

τοὺς ἄλλων ἐθνῶν, 10n763
ἀλόγιστος, 8n629, 8n635
ἄλογος, 10n792, 10n1108
ἄλση, 10n225
ἄλσος, 8n1181
ἀμαυρόω, 9n225, 9n235
ἀμαύρωσις, 9n235
ἀμελέω, 9n717
ἀμηχανία, 9n237
ἀνάγκη, 9n179
ἀνάγκη καὶ δέος, 9n737
ἀναιδής, 10n870
ἀναισθησία, 10n699
ἀνακαλύπτω, 10n856
ἀνακτίζω, 10n672
ἀνατολάς, 10n1144
ἀνδριάς, p266, 10n876
ἀνδρὸς ἀγαθοῦ καὶ δικαίου, 10n1059
ἀνελθόντα, 8n1266
ἀνὴρ δραστήριος, 10n943
ἀνὴρ ἐπιθυμιῶν, 10n925
ἀνὴρ Χαλδαῖος...τὸ γένος, 10n767
ἀνθρώπινον καὶ ἐλεεινόν, 9n181
ὑπὲρ τὴν ἀνθρωπίνην φύσιν, 10n1033
ἄνθρωπος ἐλεεινός, 10n925
μήτε πρὸς ἀνθρώπους ἐπιεικής,
   10n368
τὴν ὑπὲρ ἀνθρώπων αὐτὸν πρόνοιαν ἀφαιρουμένων, 10n1180
ἀνόητος, 8n834, 8n934, 8n1312,
   10n57
ἀνόητος καὶ ἀσυλλόγιστος, 9n986
ἄνοια καὶ πονηρία, 8n1183
ἀνομημάτα, 8n890, 8n1040
ἀνόσιος, 10n692
ἀντιμηχανήματα, 10n536
ἀνυπόστατοι, 9n827
ἀνυψούμενος, 10n1006
ἀξιομαχος, 9n946
ἀπάνθωποι, 8n391
εἰς ἄπαντα, 10n892
ἀπαντᾶ γὰρ αὐτῷ παραδόξως,
   10n1119
ἄπαντα γὰρ αὐτῷ παραδόξως ...
   εὐτυχήθη, 10n1119
τῶν ἀπάντων, 8n1005
ἄπασαν...τὴν γῆν...πεπληρῶσθαι,
   p266
ἄπασαν...τὴν γῆν ὑπ...αὐτοῦ πεπληρῶσθαι, 10n884
ἀπάτη καὶ δόλος, 9n503
ἀπελθόντα, 8n1266
ἀπέχεσθαι, 10n790
ἀπεχόμενοι, 10n792
ἀπιστία, 10n576

ἀποδιδράσκει τὸν θεόν, 9n771
ἀποκαλύπτω, 10n856
ἀπολέσαντας τὸ ἄνδρας εἶναι,
   10n762
ἀπραγμονος...βίου, 10n1180
ἀπροδεής, 8n371
ἀπροστάτητος, 10n1188
ἄρδην, 9n1083
ἀρετῆ, 10n813
ἀρετὴ καὶ σοφία, 8n595
ἀρετὴ καὶ φρόνησις, 8n548, 8n595
πρὸς ἀρετὴν εὖ γεγονώς, 10n212
τῆς ἀρετῆς, 8n639
ἀριθμέω, 10n1048
ἀριθμός, 10n1044
ἄριστος, 8n836
καὶ ἀρτήρας, 9n831
ἄρτων, 8n1235
ἐν τοῖς ἀρχαίοις...βιβλίοις, 10n936
ἀρχαῖος καὶ πάτριος, 9n1020
ἀρχῆ καὶ τέλος τῶν ἁπάντων,
   8n1005
ἐξ ἀρχῆς, 10n951
ἀρχιευνοῦχος, 10n793
ἀρχιμάγειρος, 10n839
ἄρχοντα καὶ ἡγούμενον, 10n906
ἄρχοντας, 10n786
ἄρχοντα σατραπῶν, 10n906
τὸν ἄρχοντα τῶν σοφιστῶν καὶ τὸν
   ἡγούμενον, 10n906
ἄρχων, 8n1605-6
ἄρχων τοῦ βασιλέως, 10n839
ὁ ἄρχων τῶν ἐπαοιδῶν, 10n906
ἀσέβεια, 8n1040, 9n116
τῆς ἀσεβείας, 8n996
ἀσεβεῖς πράξεις, 8n888
ἀσεβής, 8n831, 8n1085
ἀσεβὴς καὶ μιαρός, 10n353
ἀσεβὴς καὶ παράνομος, 9n891
ἀσεβὴς καὶ πονηρός, 9n4
ἀσέλγεια, 8n1177-78
διὰ τῆς ἀσκήσεως τῶν ἠθῶν
ἄσκησις, 10n789
ἀστεῖος, 9n105
ἀσυλλόγιστος, 9n986
ἀταξία καὶ θόρυβος, 9n304
αὔλειον, 10n705
αὐλήν, 10n705
αὐτοκράτωρ, 8n521
αὐτοματισμῷ, 10n1190
τοῖς αὐτομάτοις καὶ κατὰ φύσιν
   γεγονόσι, 10n1186
αὐτόματον, 10n1186
αὐτόματος, 10n1185, 10n1190
αὐτομάτως, 10n1185, 10n1190

LATIN WORDS AND PHRASES

HEBREW WORDS AND PHRASES

בני־קדם, 8n143
ברית, 9n538

גאל, 10n789
גבול, 8n487
גדלם, 10n761

דביר, 8n232

היכל, 8n234
הסלע: see סלע
התענות, 10n789

זרעים, 10n797
זרענים, 10n797

חזון, 10n820
חזות, 10n1149
חכמה, 10n809
חללו, 10n1170
חלמות, 10n820
חמד, 10n925
חמודות, 10n925
חרטמים, 10n829

יהודית, 10n38

כבול, 8n487-88

כף, 8n1322
כשדים, 10n829

לא, 9n342
לו, 9n342

מדע, 10n809
מכבר, 9n352
מכנות, 8n288
מכשפים, 10n829
המלצר, 10n793
מנה, 5n588
מן־המערב, 10n889, 10n1146
מנחה, 6n338
מני, 10n1043
מצעירה, 10n1153
מחשבי, 8n1187

נצב, 9n135

סאה, 9n286
הסלע, 9n706
ספר, 10n809
ספר ולשון כשדים, 10n766
סריס, 8n1575, 9n607, 10n794
סריסים, 10n762

עגל, 8n479
עשרנים, 8n310

פארור, 9n916
פת־בג, 10n764

צדיק, 10n758
ציים כתים, 10n1176
צפנה, 8n1052

קדם, 8n143
קדש־הקדשים, 8n232
קלל, 10n1047
קרנים, 10n1143

ראש־עגל, 8n479
רב סריסיו, 10n793
רוח יתירא, 10n1076
רחוב, 10n1127

בשושן הבירה, 10n1133
שטן, 8n654
השכל, 10n809
השמים, 10n1151
שני, 10n1143
שר הסריסים, 10n793

ARAMAIC WORDS AND PHRASES

אחשדרפניא, 10n1071

באחרית יומיא, 10n873
בירחא, 10n1115
בניח, 9n437

גלא, 10n856
גלה, 10n856

דורא, 10n909
די תשלט בכל־ארעא, 10n892

זכאי, 10n758

חברוהי, 10n858

יהודיא, 10n914

כעור, 10n882

מנא, 10n1042
מנא מנא, 10n1043
מנה־אלהא מלכותך והשלמה, 10n1046
מתלמידי נבייא, 9n405

נביאי שקרא, 8n805

סרכין, 10n1071

עדנין, 10n930

פרס, 10n1042, 10n1051
פרסין, 10n1051
פריסת מלכותך ויהיבת למדי ופרס, 10n1053

צלמא, 10n876

רב חרטמיא, 10n906
רב־טבחיא, 10n839
רב־סגנין, 10n906
רוח אלהין, 10n1026
רוח אלהין קדשין, 10n1026
רוח יתירא, 10n1026
רוח יתירה, 10n1026

שליטא די־מלכא, 10n839
השלטה, 10n906

תקילתה במאזניא והשתכחת חסיר, 10n1050
תקל, 10n1042, 10n1047

LATIN WORDS AND PHRASES

HEBREW WORDS AND PHRASES

ARAMAIC WORDS AND PHRASES

Flavius Josephus
Translation and Commentary
edited by Steve Mason